THE
BOOK *of*
TRUTH

THE BOOK *of* TRUTH

A Channeled Text

PAUL SELIG

THE MASTERY TRILOGY: BOOK II

A TARCHERPERIGEE BOOK

tarcherperigee

An imprint of Penguin Random House LLC
375 Hudson Street
New York, New York 10014

Tarcher and Perigee are registered trademarks, and the colophon is a trademark
of Penguin Random House LLC.

Most TarcherPerigee books are available at special quantity discounts for bulk
purchase for sales promotions, premiums, fund-raising, and educational needs.
Special books or book excerpts also can be created to fit specific needs. For
details, write: SpecialMarkets@penguinrandomhouse.com.

LIBRARY OF CONGRESS CATALOGING-IN-PUBLICATION DATA
Names: Selig, Paul, author.
Title: The book of truth : a channeled text / Paul Selig.
Description: New York : TarcherPerigee, 2017.
Series: The mastery trilogy ; book 2
Identifiers: LCCN 2016058085 | ISBN 9780399175718 (pbk.)
Subjects: LCSH: Spirit writings. | Truth—Miscellanea.
Classification: LCC BF1301 .S35 2017
DDC 133.9/3—dc23 LC record available at https://lccn.loc.gov/2016058085

Printed in the United States of America
3   5   7   9   10   8   6   4   2

CONTENTS

The following are transcripts of channeling sessions conducted between February 24, 2016, and April 6, 2016. Paul Selig served as the channel. Sessions were recorded in New York City with Victoria Nelson present via telephone from Berkeley, California, and before students in online seminars, in workshops in Annapolis, Maryland, and at the Esalen Institute in Big Sur, California. Selected student questions have been included.

INTRODUCTION

Day One

We have a few things to say about what will come over the next several weeks. We have two books to be writing, one after the other, and the current book—we call it *The Book of Truth*—will be known by you as a vibratory oracle, and we use the word *oracle* intentionally. This is a text to support people, the reader, if you wish, in moving, aligning to their knowing, at the highest level that they have attained thus far.

When you operate as truth, which is the mission of this text, the alignment as truth calls knowing in octaves that will be known and agreed to as the resonance of the field that the reader holds. Now what we are doing with you each through this passage is aligning you above and beyond what you've known thus far. And in order to do this, we need to call the reader forward and outside of agreements made in prior history.

The alignment each of you hold, every one of you here, is attained by you through expression and experience. You've been expressed in many ways over many lifetimes and the life you are living now in all ways is the agreement to be in the incarnation you hold and agree to move beyond what you've known.

The issue you all have, and we will say all of you, is that you replicate your history. You see something before you, you know it through what it was, you claim it by the name it was given, and you attend to it as you've known it. The landscape you exist in is full of things that have been named by others that you are in agreement with. "Because my father called it this, it will be that. I will know it as that."

Now a name, we will say, is a codification of an idea that is an energetic structure, and as you move beyond what you have agreed to, what may be created by you will be living or agreeing to you at a higher level of knowing.

Now everything you see before you was created for a reason—the chair you sit in, the floor you walk upon, the structure you call a home. These were originally ideas that were imprinted in matter, made manifest, built or created to realize the need. Everything you see before you, high and low and in between, is of the same idea. It had a reason. It was made so.

What mankind has done is replicate history in several ways. Some of you idealize things, you call the new into being, you have an idea of what can be made, and you manifest it by intention, by industry. It matters not. Many of you, though, see a landscape that was made by others.

You align to what was and you go into agreement with names that are historically based, and not only the names but the intentions for everything you see have been impressed by others who came before you.

If you can imagine for a moment that the life that you are living is actually taking place in a field, and the field is made of things that were constructed historically to fulfill the needs of those who came before you, you will understand that the world that you see is made of relics, some of them wonderful relics, perhaps, but everything that was made was made by those who came before you. The ideas you see manifested in form were created prior to your incarnation or perhaps during it through the intentions of others. What we will do in this text as we align through Paul and work with you directly—you the reader, yes—is support you each in a replication of a landscape that has not been known yet on the manifested plane.

"Replicate?" he* asks. "That means it exists somewhere."

And, in fact, it does. The manifestation of the Kingdom or the Divine in all things already exists, but the claiming of it and calling it into form as truth will be the issuance of this work. And how we do this with you, individually and collectively, will be the operation, and a significant one, that we will work with you on.

---

* Paul.

Now the first thing we wish to attend to in this instruction is a belief that things will not change. If you all attend to yourselves for a moment, the lives that you are living currently, and see what areas of your life you have decided—underline the word *decided*—will not change, you will see where you are holding energy in abeyance to historical structure. And the alignment you have in this very moment is what is claiming this thing as static. It will not change.

What we would like you to do now, the reader, yes, is decide for a moment that one of the things you see in your life that you agree will not change will be changed—underline *will*—and not through force of will, but because it can. The moment you decide that it can change, you have shifted the frequency of the thing that has been static. The moment that thing is shifted, it can be lifted in higher resonance to be manifested as changed.

The alignment that you hold in your own being is what is claiming your life into being, and the agreements you've made thus far about who and what you are, what it means to be a man or woman, a success or failure, even happy or sad, yes, is what claims you in all ways. The decree we give you by our authority is that this thing will be changed, this thing you've decided will be changed by your agreement to be in change. And already you are deciding to move beyond the known, or the codification of what was, to a new landscape where change will be possible. We are saying "will" intentionally, not *may* be possible, which would support you in wavering on the fence. "Perhaps this is so, perhaps this is not." But it *will* change, which aligns you in your intention to claim the higher and to call it into being.

Now when you live in a world that has shared constructs, things you've all agreed to, you must understand that the same method applies. When humanity decides that they can change and move beyond what they've known, the landscape must effect the change that is claimed. So much of what you attend to, what you see before you, what you agree is there before you, are constructs that were made in collective use over the millennia. "We have always had this, so it will always be there."

As mankind collectively gives in to her inner authority, his inner authority, which is the Divine Self in truth, mankind realizes itself outside of the landscape that was claimed in lower nature. As mankind lifts to a new potential, what must happen is that those things that were called into being by mankind in fear, in a need to control others, in defiance of the light that they truly are, will be attended to as the things that will change.

Now hear these words. This is not only an instruction, but it is a manual for ascension of the being that you are as truth. And we call it *The Book of Truth* because the truth of knowing who and what you are is actually what transforms you.

Most of you like to do things. "Today I will go fix this or that. I will make this or that a little better." But we will say this to each of you. While you may attend to your days that way, you will never transform to the True Self by changing your dress or fixing your hair or opening another bank account or buying a bigger house. What you would attend to as a manifestation of change without the truth in alignment is simply an expression of choice. As the True Self—underline the word *true*—comes forth and claims victory, her purview is all she sees before her.

Now the consequence of that—and we will use very simple language here—is that the one who sees truth calls truth into being. When you have a lie, or something that was constructed as a lie, when you claim it as truth and you align that thing to truth, the lie is gone because it will not exist in the truth, in the octave of truth, as the vibration of truth.

If you can imagine for a moment that the being that you are is holding a vibration, and the vibration it holds is informing all it sees, you can begin to comprehend that the alignment to the vibration as truth, the truth of what you are, will then inform all you encounter. When a lie is encountered by truth, the lie no longer exists.

Now he is interrupting. What are you interrupting? Why are you saying this? Here is what he wishes to know. When one knows herself in truth and one aligns to what she sees before her, what one is actually doing is bypassing an agreement that was made in lower nature, that was holding something in form, in a lie, and the transmutation of this, the shifting to truth, must be the effect of the witnessing of truth on the witness and what she sees.

Here we go, everybody:

"On this day I choose to embark on this new journey where I may know all things in truth. And as I agree to be on this journey, I claim that the identity I hold is in alignment as truth, in truth, with truth, to truth, and truth may be in my being as its expression. As I agree to express as truth, I agree to allow the release of all beliefs I have held that would align me to a lie, any belief in unworthiness, any belief in collective fear, any agreement to be as separate from my light or the light of others. As I say yes to what I embark on now, I give permission to the landscape that I exist in to be in alignment with truth. And as I say yes, I will go forth as a lantern, as a bright light to illumine the truth in all I witness and all I see. I know who I am in truth. I know what I am in truth. I know how I serve in truth. I am here. I am here. I am here."

The journey has begun. As we work with you each in this endeavor, we must assure you that you will be cared for. When you release what was known or believed to be true, when you attend to the new that would seek its place, its agreement to your life, when you withstand the transformations that come, please agree to be supported in all ways. Where we are taking you is to a very new place. It exists already. It has always existed. The Kingdom, we say, or the witnessing of the Divine in all manifestation, is here now as the one you are aligns to it. The Kingdom may be claimed, will be known, as you say, "Yes, in my truth, I am here."

Paul is asking, "What comes of us now as a result of this journey?" We will attempt to answer that as we may. Any structure that you've claimed and gone into agreement with that is supported in lies will be seen for what it is. And in truth, as you are the authority of and as truth by way of your alignment, you can re-create the thing you see to exist at the higher octave that truth aligns as. Every aspect of the life that you have lived that was made in history, if you can imagine, has the thumbprints, the fingerprints, of all who have come before you informing the nature of the thing you see. As something is lifted to the light, and you can say that the truth is light, what has tarnished the thing, what has been made in fear or believed to be fearful and compounded by thousands of years of agreement, will be made new.

The issuance of this teaching, as we are who we are, is to

benefit humanity in agreeing to what it always has been. Your own Divine natures were suppressed in your own agreements to be in fear. But the light that you are and have always been has never been extinguished, and we will say will never be. The truth of who you are, eternal beings all, is being returned to you in truth. And *The Book of Truth*, the treatise of truth, the agreement to be as truth in our alignment with you, will be what will support you in this beneficence.

We are with you now as we are. We are with you now as we be. And with these words we say the new text has begun. We are Word. Thank you and good night. Stop now, please. Period. Period. Period.

Chapter One

UNDERSTANDING TRUTH

Day One (Cont.)[*]

We ask you this, each and every one of you on this night: Are you willing to know yourselves outside of what you claimed or decided upon in prior times? If the answer is yes, we have much to do, much to claim, much to say yes to, and we will do this in joy.

The time has come for the resonance of truth to be what you are. The freedom of being as truth as what you are, and the claiming of truth as who and what you truly are, claims a new inheritance that the vibration you hold in truth aligns to all things and claims them in like accord.

The freedom you each have at this juncture in time is to say yes to what is true, what can only be true. And in the claim of truth—"I am here, I am here, I am here in truth"— you align to all things that are of equal accord.

---

[*] Recorded during an online seminar.

The world that you exist in, that has been claimed by you each, decided upon by you each in coresonance, seeks to be reborn in a higher awareness of what is true. And the alignment as truth, what you truly are, will be the benediction that calls everything forward, everything you may see, to the new octave.

A new octave, we say, is a new chord that may be played, that may be sung, that may be in resonance as. And the benediction of truth—"I am truth in all I see"—will begin to call a world into manifestation that goes into agreement only with truth.

Now the world that you live in is prepared for this, believe it or not. The disassembling of structures is well under way. And what we mean by this is all those things you deem to be permanent, believe could never change, are beginning to rock. And in the movement of them, the potential of the new may be known and claimed. But the world as you've known it, the entire heritage you've claimed as a species, is ready to be reckoned with. And a reckoning is, as we have taught, a facing of oneself and what one has claimed.

What you have claimed as a species may be witnessed by you by looking out the window, by looking across the world. It is the same thing. And the landscape that you know, that you have chosen to exist in, is prepared now for a rising to the climate of truth. In truth all will be seen, all will be known, and the things you've used to obscure the truth of what you are, the masks you have created, the identities you've used to separate one man from the next, will be moved.

Now the movement is not subtle. You like a subtle movement. "I feel a little different today." The movement we foresee is a grand movement, a grand gesture, an awakening of man to the Source of what he and she is. And the vibration of being in all things may be known anew.

Now a reckoning, we say, a facing of the self, implies a realization, and the realization that you may be attending to, one and all, is that you are frightened at your very core of what you are. And the moment you realize that you are frightened at what you are at your very core, the field will release.

"Well, what are we," he asks, "at our very core that we could be so frightened of?"

We have a simple answer for you. You are God in form. Each and every one of you is of the Source that manifested you. You are not the only God and you must not run away with an emblemization of this instruction. "He said I was God. I will go move a mountain. I will do as I wish."

When we say you are God, we say everything is. Everything is of its source. And finally, we say, the belief that you are separate from your Source shields you from truth, because if you accept this truth, you cannot be what you are not. You cannot be afraid. You cannot be frightened. You can only be as you can only be. And the light that you are, in its full bloom and resonance, will claim all it sees, all it witnesses, in an agreement to be as the same.

Now as mankind awakens to what she truly is, there is a disassemblance of structure and form. And we must describe what this means. When you build a house of clay, you expect it to stand. But when the firmament is not there, it will not stand. When the ground begins to shift, all that will be left standing is that which is in alignment to the foundation in its knowing of its being, its true being, not how it's been codified or built or named.

Now when a structure fails, most of you get frightened— "Oh, there go the banks." "Oh, there goes the castle"—when, in fact, when something falls, it is time for it to fall. And what is time to fall and be reckoned with are the structures of fear that you have been ruled by and been in agreement to. The reckoning with these structures takes you very far away from the history you've known and believed would always be there, and for the best of reasons. That which is not in truth will not stand the changes.

Now you are the house that we described, and the house that you are is inhabited by the truth, the truth of what you are. And in its expression, the structure around it must finally go into agreement with truth and what it truly is. We underline the words *truth* and *what*. The vibration of you as it aligns to truth claims all aspects of your life into a new alignment, and those things that were held, that were conceived of in fearful ways, the things you believed to be you that cannot be you, will be dust.

Now we will say this for each of you. This is great cause of celebration. We are not talking about ruination. We are talking about a rebuilding of each of you as what you truly are. And as you are rebuilt, everything you see around you will be transformed as well, by your consciousness, yes, but by the collective that is no longer willing to agree to lies. All things that have been born in lies, all kingdoms and countries, all rules and laws, all things decided upon by man in fear to agree to stay fearful, will be rising to be met. And in the witnessing of them, in the seeing of them as truth, the lie disappears and what is left, finally, finally, finally, is the light of God.

"Well, what does this mean practically?" he asks. "This doesn't sound like fun. I don't want to look in the mirror and see my failings anymore. I am very good at that. What has it gotten me?"

We will tell you what the process is. Stop thinking of yourselves. Each and every one of you is so small in your investments that are so small, you forget the magnitude of who and what you are. As the Divine Self awakens and experiences himself, herself in truth, the small self with her prescriptions of how things should look and be, the small behaviors she would like to attend to, the small self who seeks to be perceived as improving, will not be the face in the mirror. What you will witness and can only see will be the truth of what you are, and what is not in alignment as truth will no longer be seen because you cannot be in resonance with it.

Now your heritage, mankind's heritage, has always been the Kingdom, and the Kingdom as we have taught, the awareness of the Creator in all manifestation, which is always here, will be met by you in this alignment to truth. But what will not be seen is what was agreed to in past structure.

We will describe this. The attitudes you hold to the world you see is to agree or disagree to what this one says or that one says, to these rules or that rule. Your opinions are your own. We don't take them from you. You do what you wish with them. But you attend to these things and you try to reorder them, make them better. "We will fix this this year and two years from now perhaps we will attend to that." And the collective agreement to move the bomb around the world—"Oh, now we have it; well, they have it too"—is a game that will not be placated any longer.

What is happening here, finally, finally, finally, is the realization of the truth of man and what he has wrought, what he has claimed, what he would do with it if the small self continues to embellish the importance of his fears.

Now here we go:

"On this night I choose to claim myself in full liberation of the structures of man that were claimed in fear. And as I say yes to this, I lift myself above the walls that have been perpetuated by others, agreed to by my small self. And as I lift, I claim a new world into manifestation. The light that I am, uninhibited by these structures, will be in broadcast, and my world and all I see will be claimed in alignment to the truth of what I am. I know who I am in truth. I know what I am in truth. I know how I serve in truth. I am here. I am here. I am here."

The song has been sung, my friends. We have sung it with you, and the claim that you have just made will be your broadcast and will be attended to in the higher culture that is operating now. As we teach you, we seek to share what we are, what we claim, how we know ourselves, with all of you. The being that we are, the collective energy that we are operating as, is a magnitude of vibration that you may be attending to as you echo the sound of the claim of truth. And in coresonance with us, we lift a world to its true nature.

Now Paul is concerned. "You talk about earthquakes and structures falling. I know these people, the readers of the text. They will be alarmed."

Didn't we say it was a celebration? The leaving of the old and the claiming of the new is a grand gift, my friends, and all you are frightened of is the clinging of the old to what you've known, what you've encountered and held so dear. The life that you've lived is ending now, a new page turned, a new journey begun, and we are here to share it with you as you wish to be attended to by all of us.

And we utilize the word *all* intentionally. The singularity of the voice you hear in broadcast with Paul is intended to serve in instruction and resonance. But the fullness of our being is of a magnitude that cannot be contained yet by his field or any one field upon this plane. So we operate as each of you, the light of the Christ that we finally are in resonance with you.

The key of being, "I am here, I am here, I am here," sung as you, calls you into agreement with a great service. Mankind has said yes to what she truly is. It has been done, it has been claimed, and because it has been claimed, the freedom of being will finally be known.

"Freedom of being," he asks, "are we not free now?" You are far more free than you can conceive of. But you build yourselves shelters, you wall yourselves into dark rooms, you live in caves outside of the light that is ever present.

All mankind is being called outside to witness the new light that is here, that is here, that is here. And in the new light, freedom is known, not as a potential, but only truth. The mask you wear that has shielded you from the truth of what you are is being disassembled. The egoic structure that you have relied upon to sanctify your names—"I am this or that according to the dictates of the time or what would merit me as a public being"—these issues are being dismantled because the time has come to be as you can only be.

Now here we are together, the students of the text and the man who stands before us in echo, in service of the teaching. As one group, as one collective, we have an announcement to make. The time has come to sing and the song of your broadcast will be heard. The claim "I am here," the song of the Divine Self announcing itself in purview, will not be silenced. So when you will, when you will, when you will, agree, agree, agree to lift your song to the grand chorus that is singing already. We sing your song for you so you may learn the words, but the echo of the song on this plane will bear resonance and claim a new world into being, and at the cost of the old.

Now the cost of the old—we will attend to this for a moment. You all have investments in the landscapes you've created, the money in the banks, the bills you pay, what you've known yourself as important through or desire to be important with. The beliefs that you've held that you will be saved by anything outside of the self is coming to pass, coming to be recognized as a false teaching. Finally you will not be saved by anything outside the True Self, because the True Self in its resonance is the savior of all men.

Now he doesn't like talk of saviors. "That sounds religious."

The teaching is true. The Divine Self as you, the Christed Self, if you prefer, the Divine Creator operating as and through you, if you wish, or the Infinite Self, if you like, the truth of manifestation, will be what sings your song and calls your life forward, not a reliance upon the old because the old is always passing. And the new that seeks to be born in the higher field—"I am here, I am here, I am here"—is magnificent in its being, so there is no loss, you see.

You clutch at shadows, believing them to be permanent, when what is always permanent is truth. And truth, we say, eternal truth, that mankind is of God, that all is of God or what you would name as God because it may go by many names, the truth of all these things will still be here when what you have clung to has turned to dust.

We will embark on this journey with you through the creation of the new text, *The Book of Truth*, and we will intend this work in inclusion when we tell him it will be so. But the manifestation of each of you as the truth of what you are is what is being sung tonight. You will say this after us, if you wish:

"I know who I am in truth. I know what I am in truth. I know how I serve in truth. I am here. I am here. I am here."

Now align to truth and allow truth to be as you, and as this is done, release all the aspects of the self that would stand in the way of its expression. This is the journey you are undertaking now.

Paul is asking, "I am feeling cold. Is this a release of the old?" It is a release of the lie, that which was never true and will not be known in truth. Prepare yourselves, friends, for a wonderful adventure. We are excited and pleased to be your escort, your instructor if you would have us, and we say these words to you in love.

As we stand before you, we cannot conceive of you outside of truth because that is what you are and, finally, what all mankind is in alignment with its Source.

We thank you each for your presence. We will return with your questions shortly. Period. Period. Period. Stop now, please.

Q: I can't think of an institution that's not created in fear, and I'm wondering if, at this higher level of vibration, those just all cease to exist—insurance and health care and all the things that we . . .

A: Those are not all in fear, but the application of them has been to keep you fearful. The dentist tells you to brush your teeth. If you don't brush your teeth, he makes more money. He goes to fix your teeth. He is not frightening you by saying, "Go brush your teeth or your teeth will fall out."

A bank in principle need not be a dark thing, but how you've attended to banks and how banks have attended to all of you may be out of alignment with truth. So when something goes into alignment with truth, it is disassembled. It may not be destroyed, but it may be realigned or moved to a higher purpose. There are many ways to attend to a civilization. Those of you who are willing to be taught to care for your partners, the ones beside you, the ones who may not have food and shelter, will benefit more easily from the changes that come. And those of you who would leave them in the dark because you are in denial of who and what they are will be surprised at how you awaken. One man is no higher than the next. There is not one of you here, including the man speaking, who is higher than the one beside you.

How you treat your fellows as a culture is the first indication of the consciousness and agreement to be. So as all cultures have to realign and awaken to their creations, the individual as well as the collective, how things transform will be very dependent on how you all attend to the changes that you are claiming. You all understand that you may wake up with a gentle nudge and a loving whisper, but somebody else has to get moved out of the bed by a kick in the rump because they prefer to stay asleep. The awakening that is occurring now in all humankind is requiring a wake-up call, and how this comes and is claimed by individuals and group souls or collective agreements will be dependent on the requirements of the ones waking up. Thank you for the very good question. We will continue. Period. Period. Period.

Q: How can we finally take the mask off and truly allow ourselves just to be in the light?

A: Aligning to truth, which is the mission here. If you can all understand that the vibration of truth, which is available to you each, will not hold a lie, you can actually see that the claiming of truth as who and what you are by its very intention will disassemble the mask. What no longer works is pulling at it, investing in it as something that has to go, but aligning to the Divine Truth, which lives at an octave where the mask itself does not exist. Do you understand this?

Now the best news here is that it actually responds to you as the one claiming truth and supports the action of truth in releasing you from the lie, or the invention, if you prefer, that is the structure that you might call the false self. Now we don't divest you of personality. There is nothing wrong with a personality. But you are not your personality any more than the teeth in your head. Do you understand this? It's an aspect of what you are. It's one of the ways you may be expressed as in uniqueness, but it is not the truth of who you are. Period. Period. Period.

Q: *Can you explain to me what truth is in my everyday life?*

A: Ah, very good question. But there are two levels of truth that we teach. Eternal truth, that which is always true, and we will say this for all of you: When something is true, it is always true. But the convenience of a daily truth—on this day, "That market has the fresh produce," and on that day, "You'd better stay away from the fish"—do you understand that may be an opinion or an experience of truth, but it is not an eternal truth? As we teach truth, the Divine Self or the causal being that you are *is* truth, and as it is truth, it aligns to all things true.

Now in your daily life, aligning to truth simply means that the claim has been made to operate as truth. Now, truth is not a little book you carry and you check and see if it's true. It's actually an energetic form that you can align as. And as you become truth, what you claim must be in truth. And the knowing that you hold, because knowing is always truth, will be what directs you in your days. Period. Period. Period.

Q: I have trouble trusting my life as it unfolds and I want to stay in my truth, but I'm afraid I'm off from it so far. It scares me.

A: Tell this young lady the magic of who she is, is actually much stronger than anything she could believe about herself to the contrary. The freedom that you actually have is to say yes to the path you are choosing, and we say choose it in faith. The truth of who you are seeks to be revealed as you and every day affords you a new opportunity to be expressed as the truth of who you are. The fear that you experience in some ways is the reckoning we speak to: "Who am I if I am not what I was told? What am I if I am not doing what they say? How do I live if the rules no longer apply that I was taught to agree to?" While you stand in this place where the unknown is there and the known no longer serves you, you are gifted with opportunity to be as you are in this moment. In this moment you may be claimed anew.

We will say these words in parting. The lecture tonight, when transcribed, will be decided upon by us if it will be included in the text. So, Paul, you have no worries here. The investment he has in the text is born in personality. He is not the author, so it's a lovely waste of time. We are in agreement to be here with you and with all of you as long as you wish to be with us. We thank you each for the uniqueness that is you. And we will say these words. You are here. You are here. You are here. Thank you. Good night.

Day Two

We are asking you this: If you are willing, will you leave behind the past, will you relinquish what you have thought to be true in realization of an infinite truth?

The beings that you are, are stepping forward to be re-claimed in your heritage, your birthright, your right to be, and the acclimation to this requires each and every one of you to stand forth as truth. Underline the word *as*. When you operate *as* truth, you are not in alliance with fear.

Understand this, friends. The action of fear, as we have said many times, is to claim more fear, and a world made of fear is a world made of lies. As you align to truth as who and what you are, the being that you are imprints it-self in the highest frequency that it may align to, and the acclimation to the imprinting is a resolute self as truth. And as truth, the one that you are steps forward to liberate a world.

Now, if you can understand this principle, the remain-der of this text will fall into place for you with rapidity. What is in truth cannot be in agreement to a lie. What is in truth will not be in agreement and could never be in agreement to a lie.

So the system that you are in, this imprinting—and by "imprinting" we mean encoding the field you have as what you truly are as an aspect of the Creator in form in agreement to be as truth—all things you witness must cohere to this vibration.

What actually happens to each man and woman who makes this agreement is that they are appropriated by the True Self. And as the True Self, they actually witness a new world that they claim into being through their perception in truth. When what is in truth witnesses what we would call a lie, the action of fear that would seek to invest itself in all you do, cannot be. And by "cannot be" we mean you have lifted above it to a level where there is no coresonance.

We've discussed this prior and we will continue to do it here. There is nothing that you can see, nothing in your landscape, nothing in the world before you that you are not in agreement to. Now this is not a convenient truth. "I didn't create the war. I didn't cause the famine." You are all so busy looking at your lives and the out-picturing of the small self that you cannot see where you are contributing to the action of the whole. And we will tell you this: If you are in witness to it, you are in collective agreement to it. All mankind is in witness to a world and all mankind imprints its consciousness upon what it sees. As mankind witnesses anything, he claims form, he has names for things, and the names he has given things are standing before you as you witness them.

Now when we speak of coresonance, we very simply mean that the requirement of being as a resonant self is that you call things to you that you are agreeing to. Everything you see before you, high and low and in between, can only be present in your world through conscious agreement, or perhaps, as Paul says, unconscious, because we are not intending.

Now we will explain this. When you see something on the other side of the ocean, you are investing it with your consciousness. You know what it is, what to call it. You can make up a name if you wish. But the thing on the other side of the ocean is in accord with you simply by nature of the fact that you perceive it. The perceiver and the object, whatever the object is, or thing is, and wherever it may be, is always in coresonance with the one that perceives it.

As a collective group witnesses anything, decides what it is or means, the collective group invests that very thing with the properties it assumes it should have. And as you have done this in many ways, you are acclimating your own vibration to the object in the way that you've decided it is. When you witness something as the small self, what you witness is invested with the historical data that you perceive with. "My mother told me this was that. I saw this or that in a book, so it must be this or that." And the replication of history in all you see before you is what is going to be attended to in this text.

Until human beings realize that they are creators and not living in historical data that must be remade every day as it has been, they will not realize that what can be claimed in new ways will be of greater benefit.

Now as you are operating as truth, what you witness must move into accord with that agreement. The one who says, "I know who I am in truth," is aligning as truth, and how he witnesses, how she perceives, will be in truth. However, we will say you will not be as truth as long as you continue to act as appropriations of history, emblemizing everything you see as you have been taught that they are, even if what you were taught is incorrect.

As we teach you in this text, we will work with a dismantling of structures that were created by man in order to lift man to the potential that she may hold as the creator of a new world. Now hear these words: Because you perceive something, because you witness it before you, you are in agreement to its being. When something is in agreement with you, it is in coresonance with you, or accord, a-c-c-o-r-d or a c-h-o-r-d as on a piano. The instrument you are plays the note that corresponds in vibration to what she sees. And in coresonance you are in relation to the landscape you exist in.

If you will understand this concept, that you are not distinct from the landscape you inhabit but are actually the perceiver and cocreator with all you see, you will understand the magnitude of this teaching. How all of you decide to be in relation to a world has claimed the world you have. But as you've been operating in fear, in a belief in your separation not only from your fellows but from the world you exist in, as you have been independent beings seeking to get your needs met as a small self who does not know her Source, you have agreed to a world in fear.

Now understand this, friends. As the one who knows herself as truth, one becomes a light that illumines the darkness. And if you wish to say the light as truth and darkness as the lie, you would be accurate.

Imagine, if you would, that you walk into a room that was invested in yesterday's history. You don't deny the truth of yesterday. It happened as it was. Things were created in form to meet yesterday's needs. But as the one in truth, your very being and ability to witness actually transforms the material realm.

"How can this be so?" he asks. We will answer. By nature of your being. As a coresonant being you cannot be in agreement with a lie. And as you can't be in agreement with a lie, the lie itself, the thing created in fear, must be recognized for what it is and known in a higher way.

When something is known in a higher way—underline

the word *known*—that very thing is lifted to its true nature. If you can imagine that the shell of a pea, the structure that holds the peas in a pod, is disassembled, what is inside the pod may be seen for what it is. And there was nothing that was created in fear, not anything that you can imagine, that wasn't created in an identity born in lower nature.

The construct of war is not holy. It's a man-made idea. And as you perceive holiness, which we would call truth, in *anything*, that thing that was made in fear will be lifted and made new.

Now Paul is asking, "But is this real? Do we look at a war and create peace?" That is not what you are doing. You are witnessing the world before you with new eyes in alignment with the frequency of truth. And by your being, the consciousness you hold cannot agree to what is in fear. And the one who sees the truth in anything calls the light to it. And it is the light that lifts it to its true nature.

Stop thinking that your hands do the work here, that it is an act of will that will transform this plane from war to peace. The only thing that will transform this plane from war to peace is a level of consciousness that cannot adhere to war.

There is no way that mankind, through effort and force of will, will change its small nature and investments in fear. The small self or personality structure does not fix itself. It is the Divine Self, as and through you, appropriating its world to its true nature that calls the Kingdom into manifestation. And the Kingdom again, the awareness of the Creator in all things, already exists but is only perceived by one who knows who she truly is.

Now the masquerade you are all engaging in here, the belief that you are small, that you will not be met on this journey by us, by the light that you truly are and is in all things, the belief that you have that alchemy and transformation are not true, actually limit you to a level of coherence in manifestation that operates in consort with fear. And we will explain why.

Imagine for a moment that you were taught that there was another continent, another world on the other side of the ocean, but you cannot imagine it because the plane you see before you has edges. You walk in any direction and there is only the sea. You cannot imagine that there is another way of being beyond the ocean that stretches out forever.

Now if you could understand that the belief that there could be nothing else there would keep you tethered to the land mass you are on and not aligning to what could be beyond it, you would never discover a new world.

Well, the new world we teach is the Kingdom, and the Kingdom of heaven is here as you claim it. And as all of you claim it, "I am here, I am here, I am here," the True

Self that I am in the claim "I am here," who manifests the Kingdom, knows itself in a new world and that new world is born in consciousness.

Now here we go, friends. If you would like to say this with us, you may, but our intention here is that each of you who read this text will be imprinting yourselves in the alignment to truth as your days go on. What you must understand, that truth is a vibration, and aligning as it—which means you are as and with it, informed and being as it—is the work that we do with each of you. Here are the words we will speak on your behalf:

> "The ones we see before us, in awareness or unawareness of what they truly are, the Divine Beings that they truly are, are stepping forward to be claimed in resonance with truth. And as they agree to this, they are called forth to align to the higher nature of all things made manifest. As they lift their world, their world is healed. As their world is healed, the celebration echoes throughout the atmosphere to all nature, to all things, into infinity. We know who you are in truth. We know what you are in truth. We know how you serve in truth."

Now the nature of your beings, habituated natures we should say, is what has been. You know yourself through yesterday's clothing, what you saw on the television, where you went to market. You know yourself through your creations, those things that you have made in form. So what we will do next is actually an exercise in re-creation.

Imagine that everything you see before you, everything in the room you stand in that was named by someone else—that lamp, that chair, the rug beneath my feet—imagine everything you see had no name, and with no name it simply is.

Now imagine that thing that has no name holds no history. The usage of these things has not been described to you because you need nothing from the landscape except to be.

Now as you agree to this, you are actually deconstructing the history of the world that you see before you in your room. You are not denying what is there. You are simply leaving behind the names that have been claimed for them, for those things you see, so that you may claim yourself outside of history. By claiming oneself outside of history, one is actually claiming the True Self because the True Self exists outside of time.

"Now if it exists outside of time," Paul asks, "how can we be this? We exist in time."

You exist in an agreement to know your reality in a sequence you call time. But the true nature of your being, while it informs your present self in linear time, also exists beyond it. So what is true is always true regardless of the time you stand in. It is always true on this day that you are reading this page in the text. A million years from now it will still be true that at this moment in time you are hearing these words, seeing these words on the page, and knowing what you think of them.

But the true nature of your being, the Infinite Self as we claim it, knows itself beyond structure. And aligning to that energy, the manifested self as you in form now is the Creator serving in perfect ways as you in the life that you are living.

So back to the room. Everything was claimed by you with a name, then with no name. Now imagine, if you would, that everything in the room is in vibration. Everything is moving, and as it moves the shapes it's held may become transformed. The wood on the table may be claimed as a tree. The bricks on the wall may be made back to earth. Everything that is in form now was once another form. Do you comprehend this? And because it was once another form, it can be claimed anew and transformed again. Underline this, please. *Everything that has been created can be re-created.* Everything that's been created can be re-created in its true nature.

Now know this to be so. Everything you see before you that is of God cannot be outside of God. And what you put outside of God claims you outside of the light you truly are. As we have said many times, God is all things, so there is nothing that can be outside of God but your belief in separation. Your own separation, the separation from you and your fellows, supports the agreement in separation that you perceive yourself as holding. So when you know who you are—"I am a Divine Being"—you claim a world in agreement to that. And when you know what you are— underline the word *what*—the manifested self, the Divine Self in form, the world that you see before you may also be known in congruence.

If you've excluded God from the physical realm and placed it upon a cloud somewhere unreachable, you have affirmed separation. But when God is the tree, and the rug beneath your feet, and the man you see across the way, and in all those people over there that don't do what you want, you will begin to understand truth.

And that will be the name of this chapter: "Understanding Truth." And we will say this for Paul, who has been questioning. We are including last night's lecture as this chapter begins.

Now as we continue this teaching, we have several mandates for the dictation. We would prefer to operate in lengthier sessions than you have agreed to thus far. The teachings will come quickly and the regimentation of daily teachings, as they can occur, will support the man in the chair in being a clear receiver for the ongoing message.

We will also be pleased to complete this text so that we may be moving forward to the next as we can. And because we issue this, we will also give a promise to the reader and the man in the chair that this teaching will be concise and structured in the perfect way to acclimate the vibration of truth in a way that you may know in your experience.

Each of you here, each of you encountering these words, encountering this teaching, is being known by us as truth. And as we say these words, "You are here, you are here, you are here," we speak to the truth of what you are. We bear witness to your truth, not the lies you hold, not what you believe yourselves to be, not what your mother called you or your father did.

The "what" that you are, the Divine Self in manifestation, is here as you. *You are here. You are here. You are here.* And as we claim this for you, you are in coresonance with us, your teachers. We hold you each in a field of vibration in truth so that the lives that you know may acclimate to truth, and that which is not in truth will be seen for the lie that it is.

Each of you here, each of you joining us, will become a blazing light. And the light of truth, we say, when it meets the darkness, will inform all things in truth.

We will stop in a few moments, for the dictation today is almost done. But we would like to say a few more things about what you should not expect from this text. This is not the text that will fix your personal lives. We could care less at this moment about the nature of the personality structure seeking to fix itself, and for one reason only. It does not happen in truth.

When we teach transformation, or alchemy, we are actually teaching the deepest level of manifestation and re-knowing that you may come into contact with. So the idea of fixing the small self—"I would like to be a little better at this, fix that a little bit"—will not be met by us for the simple reason that in truth, in actual truth, you are already perfect, and known by us as so.

Can you imagine, friends, that as a result of being on this journey, the face you see in the mirror will be the face of the light because you know yourself as such and not what you were taught?

The last thing we will say about what this is not is blasphemy, and you must understand this, friends. When we say you are God, you are of God as all manifestation is. So we are not anointing you as special. We are claiming you as what you are. But you cannot be this thing if it is not true for all mankind. You cannot be truth and be in agreement to a lie. And any belief that any one of you is higher than the one beside you is a lie, no matter what you think of them or what you would claim them as in lower nature.

Until you understand that what you are and can only be is the manifestation of the Divine in this expression, you will be playing the game of the small self—attaining spirituality. Spirituality is not attained. It is simply your true nature. You are Spirit knowing itself in form. You have simply put the cart before the horse.

Now Paul is saying, "*Blasphemy*—why did you use that word?"

To condemn any man is to condemn the God within him, and to condemn God or the true nature of all things is to deny the light. And the denial of light is the action of fear. And fear, we would say, and the action of fear is to deny God, and you can call that blasphemy, if you like.

As we use language, we come with history and we inform the history that language has been endowed with, with truth so that you may comprehend the true nature of a teaching that has been misaligned through institutional misuse. When we say we know who you are as an aspect of the Divine, we mean all mankind, and we are pleased for your presence as we say these words to you now:

Thank you each for your presence. Stop now, please. Period. Period. Period.

Chapter Two

WHAT YOU ARE

Day Three

We'd like to say a few things about where we stand in this dictation. The triumph of this text is less for the individual than the collective, who is beginning to wake up to what they truly are.

Now when we speak to the individual, we actually have a promise for you, that the lives that you are living now will claim a whole new broadcast, and a wonderful one, so you have great benefits coming to you through your requirements of learning and expressing the True Self in all aspects of your life. We would not be teaching you if we did not know—and underline *know*—that the result of this text would be a new way of being. And the being that you are now, individually in the acquisition and expression of this teaching, will be participatory in the expression of a whole new world.

Now each one of you here, with your small selves in tow,

is preparing for a great journey as you realign the life you live. And the life you live is actually expressed in agreement with the lives of everyone you meet because you are sharing a plane, a way of being expressed, a way of knowing the self in a common landscape. So the agreement you are making here, by its very nature, assumes you as one who will claim a landscape in truth for the benefit of all.

Now Paul in the background is saying, "Well, people want to feel better. That's why they buy a book."

People *will* feel better, and not because they bought a damned book, but because they will know who they are. And the celebration of this, we will promise you, will transform everything that the small self could have known.

We will ask you this: The journey that you are undergoing will have several issues that do attend to the personality self that must be agreed to as something that may be on the table to be lifted. And when we say these things, we are simply asking for the agreement to pursue the whole love as you that is what you are as its true expression. And when we say this, "whole love," we mean *you* as expressed as fully in consort with love as you may align to.

As each man lives his life in his own way, there are aspects of the life he lives that may be very out of alignment with the True Self. And the agreement here, for each and every one of you, is that nothing will be left on the table that is unexpressed by the True Self. And as the True Self expresses itself fully, the lifting that occurs will actually relegate the symptoms of your past expression—the fears you've had, the disdain for others, perhaps, the perplexing habits that seem to have no solution—all of these things, the symptoms of your misalignment, will be released and lifted to the truth.

Now the vibration of truth that we speak as knows what it is. The truth of who you are in every cell of your being, expressed by you in consort with the teaching that will support you in realigning your life, will be what calls you forward. The vehicle you have, the expressed being you are in her knowing of herself in truth, must call forth a life that is in agreement to truth. By knowing this is so, and by accepting the potential that every aspect of you, even the corn on your foot, must be aligned as truthful, you are saying "yes" to the passage we have prepared.

"What is the passage?" he asks.

Well, if you lived on a continent where lies were spoken and lies were known to be true so you have accepted the lie because you had nothing other, and the conversations you have with your fellows are all peppered in lies pretending to be truth, you would understand the landscape that you exist in. The continent you live in has an expression: "We will not tell the truth because if we tell the truth we will be fearful. We will be seen for what we are or we will be exposed, and hunted, or burned, or at least ignored, because who wants to hear the truth anyway?"

So in this agreement, this collective agreement that you've all had to barter in lies—and we don't mean just the individual, but the institutions that you all interact with, which are also in lies as the collective in its engagement with a language in lies—serves itself. It actually leaves you all in a very dark place.

Now the journey we speak to is from one continent to the next, and Paul is saying, "Well, what is 'continent' a metaphor for? You had us climb a mountain in the last text.* What are we doing now?"

Here is what the metaphor is: A landscape in fear, or a landscape where lies are agreed to, to be truth, is one continent. The passage to another across a sea to a new land, where only the truth is spoken and is known, is simply another way of saying that in the higher dimension or the higher landscape where the lies are not commerce, where there is no agreement to be in fear to protect the self from the belief that truth is harmful, at that level that you abide in as the True Self is the language and the being that you express as.

The passage from one continent to the other is a metaphor here, yes. But it's also a way for you to comprehend that what a journey is, is moving from one landscape to a higher one where what has been tolerated and agreed to, what has been uttered in fear and heard as truth, will be dismantled and lifted.

---

* *The Book of Mastery.*

Now the individual herself must begin this journey by recognizing that she, too, is in consort with lies. Everything you say about yourself on a cosmetic level is only one fraction of the truth of who you are. "I have blond hair, I live in a house, I have a job that I go to" are all ways of knowing the self. But if you've understood our teachings thus far, you already understand that you are not those things. So transitional truths—you may not always have blond hair, or live in a house, or have a job you go to—is not what we teach. The Eternal Self, though, who lives in truth, is what dismantles the lies that you attend to yourselves in.

"Well, what are these lies?" he asks. "How do I do this myself? Help me understand what I do so that I may know where I am out of alignment."

Every time you claim yourself as inferior to another, you are lying. Every time you condemn yourself for what you have done or could do, or believe what you think is wrong about you, you are lying.

"Now how is this so?" he asks. "If I did something that I regret, I have the right to blame myself."

You have the right to do anything you like, but if you want to be in truth, you actually must understand that anything that was done or expressed by you at any time was simply how you knew yourself and the expression of you as an active being in consort with your needs—or perhaps your fears, yes—at the time. But they were just what they were, things done.

They were not who you are. You may have expressed as who
you were at that moment in time, but who you were at that
level of expression more than likely was acting out of alignment. To blame the self for acting out of alignment condemns
the self, which actually reinforces the misalignment, strength-
ens its hold upon you, and supports fear. "I am to be frightened of" would be the claim of the one who condemns himself.

Now in response to what Paul is thinking, yes, you do
learn from error, but not from blaming the self. If you
touch a hot pan, you scald your finger, you know not to do
it again. You don't berate yourself for the rest of your life
for having had a sting upon the finger.

Now the aspects of you that are in alignment are also being
expressed by you, and it becomes imperative, for this teaching
to be understood, to know that you are not wrong. When
something is disassembled and, perhaps, put back together
again, the aspects of the self that are operating well are simply
placed forward. They keep. They have the right to be as they
are because they are serving their purpose. And we say this
only because some of you are intending to use a teaching like
this to denounce the self or assume that you all must be wrong.

"Well, what is right?" he asks. "What aspects of me are
operating well, are in alignment with truth?"

Every time you look at a human being—and we say this
to you, Paul—and you recognize their worth, their inherent right to be, you are in alignment. Every time you lift

your frequency by claiming truth—"I know who I am as an aspect of the Creator, what I am in manifestation, and how I serve"—you are elevating your broadcast to support others in their awakening.

What you also don't realize is that just by being—by Paul as he is, *being*—people are lifted because the vibration you hold is operating in resonance as the Divine Self. And the aspect of you that knows this to be so is what is calling you forward in the work you do with us.

Now the truth of every man, every woman, every being *is* the Divine Self. And as the activated aspect of you—the "I Am" presence, if you wish, announcing itself in purview, "I am here, I am here, I am here," which is the claim of the Divine as you in full broadcast—you claim this for all that you encounter. The idea that you become spiritual, which we have already mentioned, is never so, is not what does this. The claim of your true nature expressed by you—"I am here"—is what transforms the world.

Now some of you believe that your own evolution or comprehension of the self as spiritual is the purpose of this text. In fact, it is not. It's the being of it as truth. But please comprehend this: By *being* truth, you light the world. So this is not done just for you, but for all mankind.

To believe yourself to be inferior is to deny the truth of who you are. To believe another man as unworthy is to deny the truth of who he is. To stand in your knowing as truth, when lies are thrown, is an act of truth. And the truth will hold and the claim of freedom—"I know who I am, what I am, how I serve, I am here, I am here, I am here"—will witness for you a transformed plane.

The eyes with which you see have been claimed by you in truth in a new octave. And the witnessing as truth—"I am witnessing *as* truth"—claims all things in truth, so you cannot be in witness to a lie of any kind without seeing it transformed.

"Now, what is the practical application of this?" he asks.

We would like you to know that the metaphors we use—"I see things transformed"—are far more than metaphor. They are actually the interaction of consciousness in a material form.

Now we will explain this. You exist in material form, and your expression in this plane as a man or a woman with feet and toes, a way to walk and speak, are ways you know yourself here. But the vibration you hold, which informs all these things that you express as in the material plane, has the opportunity to remanifest things that were created in lower vibration. We are teaching alchemy now, and what we mean by this is that what the perceiver sees is transformed through this perception. And we mean this as truth.

Now the fears you all have of your true nature were given to you historically through calamities past, through agreements made in fear, through teachings that were unsavory or distorted. And we come today to reclaim these things in truth.

The historical being that in fact you are, through race memory has acquired many things—and assumptions, perhaps—about the nature of reality that have been attended to for so long that they have become codified in form. In knowing what you are, "I am a manifestation of God in material form"—underline the word *material*—you begin to claim something beyond what has been aligned to prior to this time.

When mankind realizes what it is—again, underline *what*—which is the manifestation in form of the Divine, you actually create a relationship with the physical plane that you exist in that allows for its transformation. The idealization of spirit as above form has created a dichotomy that most of you attend to. "God is in the clouds, man is in the mud, and here we stay."

Now we will use this metaphor for you. Imagine that the sky you see above you is permeating all things. It's only your belief that you are sitting indoors. The sky that seems so blue out the window is actually indoors as well, but you believe yourself to be separate from it.

Now we will go even farther. The sky that you see above you is actually in your skin as well, and in your flesh and bones and blood—marrow, if you like. Every aspect of you is still being permeated by the same sky. But because you have a layer of skin that protects you from the elements, you don't understand that the sky is in all things.

Now we will take it even farther. What if the sky is all that's real, all that's real or eternally real? And the body and the house that you sit in will one day be dust, but the sky that was informing you will still be there, and you were part of it once, so cannot be separate or other from it, you will understand the nature of God or Spirit permeating as all. Circle or underline the word *all*. It cannot be separate from its Source. The being that you are cannot be separate from its Source, even though she imagines herself to be.

Now the what that you are, the manifested being who knows she is made of God, that God—or the sky, if you prefer—permeates every aspect of her, now begins to comprehend that she is no different from the wall, the sky beyond it, the ones who live in the shared plane she exists in. Because she is reidentifying herself in matter as the Divine Self, she is able to transform the plane that she expresses in because she has not diminished herself as in the mud, with God somewhere else. The only one who can make alchemy expressed as what they are is the one who knows herself as what she truly is, as an aspect of the Creator in truth.

Now manifestation, as we have taught you prior, is simply something claimed and made into being. You are already manifested: you have a body, you are already here, so the reidentification of who you are, which has been the basis of all our teachings, is what supports this understanding. "I know who I am as an aspect of the Divine" is who you are, but the what expressed by you operates as the Creator in manifestation, which simply means you are not separate from your Source.

Now the realization of what it means to be this is actually somewhat cataclysmic to the small self, who depends upon the belief in separation to support her requirements through the lies that this continent you are in pretends to teach through to be truthful. When the small self is seen for what she is, which in many ways is a reflection of what she was taught, she does what she can to protect herself from the sky that we might call truth.

"I will build a bigger house with thicker walls. I will do something or other to forget my true nature, to deny the light that I am. I must run to the cave where I may know myself as safe."

Well, the small self ultimately exists under the same sky, is permeated with truth, is not extinguished, but is reborn in her true nature.

Imagine, if you would, that you are a child that has been taught to be fearful of the sky. "Your skin will burn in the sun, you will freeze in the cold, come stay in this safe place I have erected where you will be known in the ways we say." And you agree to this. You live a life that is operating at cost of the expression of truth that you truly are.

But here we go again. The sky is still there in that cave and that dark house, and the moment you recognize that it is, that even your cells in your body cannot be separate from the sky, you realize that the lie that you are separate can only be a lie, and anything that supports the lie, any teaching of separation, is seeking to affirm itself at the cost of truth.

"What is the cost of truth?" he asks.

Well, look at your lives for a moment and ask yourself this: "If I knew myself as a Divine Being, if I really knew this, what would be different? What could I no longer claim as what I am?" Do you hear these words? If you truly know yourself as a Divine Being—"I am what I am, I am the manifestation of the Divine in all expression"—then what is no longer true?

Here is a little list for you, if you like: "I am the one that hates people. I am the one who is afraid. I am the one who is debased, or a victim, or enraged. I am the one that perpetuates frustration, the one that is ugly, the one that cannot be loved, the one that will always have this problem, the one who can never get it right, the one who is failed, the one who will never be known as worthy, the one that God forgot."

You cannot be these things because these things are not true. And in truth, a lie will not be held. The vanquishing of the lie of what you are is the attendance to you by the vibration of truth. And the text you hold in your hands, the words you hear, are in truth, and they echo through every cell of your being and your auric field as what it is. Truth has come to be known as you.

> "In truth I am. I am in truth. In truth I know. I know in truth. In truth I have my being. I have my being in truth. I am here. I am here. I am here."

Now the teachings you receive today will be part of what we call the second chapter. And the title of the second chapter, "What You Are," will be continuing for the next four sessions. The teaching of what you are, or the manifested self, is key to where you go next—not just you, the reader, but the species that you stand with. Each one of you here is claiming victory, not only for yourselves, but for all men. And the gift you get for undergoing this passage, and we include you, Paul, as well, is a life in truth. And in truth there is no fear, because fear is a lie.

We will stop this transmission shortly. We will continue with a few more things.

You acquire things in your lives. You buy things. You go to the store and you get what you need. We would like you to try something different today. Decide, if you wish, that the alignment to truth, the actual alignment to the frequency of truth, is now informing these decisions. You are not getting what you think you need. You are purchasing what you do need. You are operating as the one who knows.

When you walk down the street, we would like you to realize one thing: that nobody that you're passing knows who they are on a superficial level, but the truth of who they all are as an aspect of God is fully present in them. Underline the word *fully*. It is *fully* present in them. God is fully present in all men, even when they don't know it. And as you acknowledge this, say these words to yourselves as you meet their faces: "I know who you are in truth. I know what you are in truth. I know how you serve in truth." And you will be met by the frequency of the God within them. You will feel the vibration, the acknowledgment, because God within is always recognized by the one who knows truth and will reply, "I am here."

The last thing we will say is for Paul, and it is actually in gratitude for how far you have come, even in spite of yourself, on this journey with us. We are finding the dictation very easy, uninterrupted actually, and we are grateful for the opportunity to know you as you bloom as well. We thank you each for your presence. Good night. Stop now, please. Period. Period. Period.

Day Four

So we are ready to teach, and as we speak, we know, and as we know, we conquer those aspects of the self that are invested in lies.

You all have investments in lies, you see. Like it or not, most of your lies were born in agreement with what you were taught to be. And what you were taught to be was in agreement with historical data of what it meant to be a man or a woman or a citizen or a spiritual person.

Each and every one of you, like it or not, is ascribing to history. Every day you walk out onto the street. What you see before you is in fact the codification of thought, the things made in form by those who came before you. And you announce yourself, "Here I am," in acquiescence to what you were taught to be.

Now when you know what you are—underline the word *what*—the Divine as self, the True Being that you are, what begins to happen in the lifting of the vibration that you hold is that your perception begins to move beyond what was agreed to through the personality system, agreements made in form, "I will be this kind of man or that kind of woman." Become aware in a new way of truth, and the truth of who you are actually releases you from the masks you have claimed in lower nature.

Now the what that you are, the manifestation of the Divine in form, already knows what she is. She doesn't require convincing. The true nature of every being, like it or not, is as the Divine Self. The Divine Self is, in fact, what you are. And the being that you know yourself as is the manifestation of this, and not excluding the form that you hold.

Now let's understand this, please. "Excluding the form that you hold" means that most of you adhere to a belief that the physical self is not in union with your true nature, but perhaps it's the car you drive around in, the tank you sit in with all of your protections. In fact, that is not so, and the disassociation of heaven and earth, or the physical self and the spirit that expresses through it, is what we must understand and claim if we are to be in union with the Source of our being.

Now there is no one born who is unworthy of this awareness. And as we teach you, you the reader, you the student of the work, we must comprehend the requirements of the individual to know who and what they are in a way that they may maintain.

Now when we use the word *maintain*, we use it intentionally. When you maintain anything, you go into agreement with it as you are. You maintain yourself in an ongoing way. Now to hold an idea—"I am a Divine Being in form"—is all well and good. But claiming that as truth that may be expressed by and through you is what we must attend to as your teacher. How do we support you each in a realization of what you are, the manifestation of the Divine, that you can operate as in your knowing and in your vibratory expression? When you use the words "I know who I am in truth, I know what I am in truth, I know how I serve in truth," you are actually aligning as the Divine Self.

If you are new to our teachings, you must understand that the language we serve you through is actually encoded to support the field you hold in acclimating to the higher music that is already playing. And in the claim of truth—"I know who I am in truth, what I am in truth, how I serve in truth"—the Divine as you announces herself as her true being, and the field that you hold is transitioned to support the new claim.

Now as you live your lives, you are assaulted by things you see. "I got bad news today, I am in low vibration, those people aren't doing what I think they should, I will be in my outrage." And you go up and down in accord with how you are met in circumstance.

Once you understand who and what you are, the Divine Self as you, you are not swayed by external action because you realize everyone and everything as an aspect of the Divine expressing itself as it may best.

Now what you don't do is go into an alignment with negative behavior, or what you would ascribe as negative. "They are fighting over there, what a wonderful thing." You don't give agreement to the action. You give agreement to the truth that is in each participant, because each participant is expressing themself as an aspect of the Divine, but perhaps in ignorance of their true Source.

When you understand that the perceiver and the thing perceived are in relation, and that the higher vision will always lift in field what she sees before her to its true nature, you actually understand the power of claiming truth in all you see.

When one is in denial of their True Self, one is making decisions, calling things into being, if you like, in accord with their belief in separation. The self that believes himself to be separate from its Source codifies its expression in ways she thinks will serve her safety. "I will not talk to that man over there, I will conquer these men over there, I will be right because if I am not right I will not know myself as safe."

Now the Divine as you does not operate in this way. Because she knows herself in union, she has no need to protect, no great investment in seeing the self or anyone else as separate from herself or the Source of your being, the being that you share in the higher octave that is being expressed in individuated ways through the selves you know.

Now the Divine Self in her purview knows the truth of all things. And this is a key to understanding this text: The Divine Self knows. The small self assumes. She thinks she knows, but she does not know.

When the Divine Self, expressed as you in truth, claims purview, she claims the truth in all she sees because she operates as truth and truth is her expression. She announces herself in the vibration of truth and that vibration itself lifts all she sees before her.

In some ways, what we are saying is that the creations

made by the small self—"I will have it my way or not, I will get what I want or I will be in trouble," whatever the small self believes herself as needing—is simply amplifying the belief in separation that she exists as and through.

Now when you align to the Divine as you and you claim purview—the claim "I am here, I am here, I am here," which is the Divine as you in its expression claiming the Kingdom in all she sees before her—you lay claim to your true identity. And the gift of your being, the shared gift of your very being, is what you call forth in grace.

Now we will say these words for Paul, who gets concerned about the dictation. We have to lay the foundation now for where we intend to take you all, and there are things that must be understood about how we operate and the text you hold. The text you hold is actually an imprinting of consciousness. Any book you ever read is imprinted with the consciousness of its author, and the vibration they held at the time the book was written is actually present for the reader to be in exchange with.

But the Divine Self that we are, operating as one entity to support the manifestation of this text, imprints our consciousness upon the text. So when you are in exchange with the text, you are in exchange with us and we operate outside of time. So as we witness you, the reader, we also witness the man in the chair taking the dictation as we see him, and we see the text in your hands. We understand the requirements of the reader to regard herself as in consort with the teaching that she may comprehend. So as we operate with Paul, we imprint the vibration of us in the language we use, and the encoded language in the form of energetic attunements is what actually assumes you to move into vibratory accord with us.

What we would like to say is that, as we teach, we not only anticipate the needs of the reader, we regard the reader as realized. So as we hold you in our vision—we know who you are, we know what you are, we know how you serve— we are in fact disassembling the structure of the personality self that would resist the transformation that she is claiming to embark upon.

If you can understand this, friends, we witness you as you truly are, not as you think you are or were taught to be. And as we realize you in truth, we actually support the lifting of the field you hold to be in congruence with your Divine nature that is the truth of who you are.

"What does it mean that you move outside of time?" he asks.

We will respond as we can. You know yourself through the constructs of time, yes, agreed upon structures, the calendars you hold, the timepieces you wear on your wrists. You have many agreements to time and you build a world, and constructs within the world, that are in consort with a belief in time that actually separates you from the action of the Divine.

Now we will explain this. When something is true, it is always true. And your Divine nature is true now, will be true a million years from now, and was true at the beginning of time. The aspect of you that is in consort and relation with your Source—the eternal self, if you wish, the Christed Self, if you prefer, the Divine Self, if you like— exists outside of time, but agrees to know you in the small agreements that you have confined yourself with here.

So if you say it's Tuesday, the Infinite Self as you is there on Tuesday, but she can only be there because she is always present. She exists beyond the construct, but you may know her within it.

As we work, we actually perceive you each outside of the linear structure that you have all been attending to, and not just you, the reader, but the beings that you are on this plane who finally, we say, are beginning to address their true natures.

"Why is this happening now?" he asks. For one reason only. Because you've claimed a trajectory in fear that must be realized—must, underline *must*—by the Divine Self in order to know what you are and reclaim the plane of existence that you share on a higher level.

If you look around you, you look anywhere, you will see the evidence of fear manifested before you. And when you know who and what you are, the Divine Self as you impressing herself in the field you see actually re-creates the field and all that was made in it to be operating in higher accord.

Time is not an illusion as much as an agreement, and collective agreements—what mankind has believed, made, and claimed in manifestation—will be understood in this text because the individual, or what you know as an individual, is always in consort with the whole. When one man realizes himself as what he truly is, he gives permission to a thousand more to lift their fields, and not by speaking, but by the very nature of their being. The vibratory field he holds is in consort with all he meets, and the recognition of the Divine that he brings to all he sees claims it into being, and there your world is lifted.

A collective agreement may be operating in a very high way, but most of the agreements you've claimed that we wish to attend to here are the collective agreements to war, to starve your fellows, to claim victory over the landscape you live in at the cost of your well-being and the well-being of others. The belief in poverty and scarcity, the belief in idiotic rule by those who would govern, and the acquiescence to structures of power that are not born in truth must all be addressed now, for humanity is waiting to tip the scales toward her benefit, toward her freedom, and toward the claim of who and what she is.

When we address you individually, please understand, friends, that while we are happy for your progress and we are very pleased that the teachings we give you are supporting you in claiming a new life outside of what you've known yourself as in fear, we do this for the good of all. You are all beacons of light, and as you illumine your world and you bring the light to all you see by the knowing of who and what you are, you claim the Kingdom.

Now the Kingdom we will describe again. As we have taught, the Kingdom is the awareness of the Divine in all manifestation. It is not something that is sought. You cannot seek the Kingdom in traditional ways, but the understanding that you must seek the Kingdom is keeping you all looking outside of yourselves. In fact, what the Kingdom is, the realization of the Divine in all manifestation, is something that is aligned to because it exists here, but in the higher landscape or other continent we have previously described. The alignment to the Kingdom may happen in a number of ways, and we have been teaching you sequentially the ways that you may each address your lives in consort with this reality.

The teaching of truth, we say, is our most ambitious and most effective way to support you each in this alignment, because as you align to the truth of what you are, you claim it. And as truth cannot hold a lie, the true nature of all things, the inherit Divinity in all manifestation, may be witnessed by you. And the claiming of the Kingdom is done in consort with truth and perhaps at the cost of what you've believed to be truth that is in fact a lie.

As we stand before you, as we claim you in freedom, as we say, "Yes, here you are," we know what you are, and the support of the self as the manifested truth will be where we go next. The encouragement we offer you each, now, is to claim yourselves. And as you say these words with us, we would encourage you to know them as true.

"On this day I claim that all I may know may be in truth, that all I may see may be in truth, and all I may experience will be in truth. And as I agree to this, I claim truth in all I see, in all I know, and in every word I speak. I know who I am in truth. I know what I am in truth. I know how I serve in truth. I am here. I am here. I am here."

We will continue with this teaching tomorrow. We thank you all for your presence. Good night. Stop now, please. Period. Period. Period.

Day Five

We will ask a few questions today about what you require. If you need to be taught, do you require to be taught in a certain manner? Must you understand every word to comprehend the larger gesture, the true teaching that is implicit here?

We say this for two reasons. The teaching you are receiving now, while encoded in language in vibration, may adhere to teachings that may not be understood by the small self. And if the small self stumbles in her regard to the teachings and tosses the book across the room, she will actually meet with her own resistance in form.

Now the requirement for the student here who is being addressed by us is simply to align to the teachings as they occur. "By alignment" means agreement energetically, not in the personality self who is always welcome to decide for herself what she experiences, how she responds, or what she chooses to accept as truth. The value here in moving forward in spite of resistance is that the field that you hold will still be met in the new octaves and aligned so that your comprehension will not only improve, but the Mastery we offer you will become apparent as what you are.

Now the Master as what you are is the concept we wish to offer you now. The small self in her way, in her dictates, has failed miserably at her alignment to the Divine Self. Now there are many ways one small self may do this. You may take a million classes, read a million more texts, but without alignment, which is not done as the small self, you will be chasing your tail. You may have higher comprehension of ideas and ways of being in the world that may be nicely informed by teaching. However, until your alignment is present, you are still playing the game of self-help.

We must understand, as we teach you, that your comprehension of what may be known will always be informed by history. But our intention here, to bypass history, to render it as what it was, a thing that was created that is not the truth of who you are, we intend to establish you in an alignment that can contain the frequency and the expression of it, the Master embodied as you.

The small self, you see, likes to think of things in increments. "I will be a little happier today, lose another pound or two. I will be very happy when I have the right home or the right partner or the right employment." While we don't discount these things, the teaching you are encountering is operating at a completely different level.

If you can imagine yourself standing in a great wind, a great and wonderful wind, and the wind has the purview to transform, reshape, render obsolete the aspects of the self that are not in truth, you will comprehend the level that we are beginning to teach you at.

"Beginning to teach us at?" Paul asks. "What does that mean?"

Well, there are several things happening here. The foundation has been laid in vibration from the expressions you have undertaken with this work thus far and must continue to contend with as the creations that you've known yourselves through are being lifted to a higher realm. What we say to you is that the man or the woman that you are has been prepared for the teaching you are receiving now and is prepared—underline the word *is*—to comprehend the teachings on an energetic level even when the small self seeks to toss the book away.

Now the small self engages with us and we enjoy the small self and her engagement, but we are operating in tandem with truth. And the True Self that you are is actually being met in vibration through your encounter with us and the words we impress through Paul into the volume you are with now.

As one teacher would like to say, "We are here with open arms for our students." And another teacher might add, "not only to embrace them, but to lift them to truth." And a third teacher might say, "And in this agreement to be in truth, we send them back to the world to see their world anew." And a fourth teacher would say, "We are here with them each as we comprehend their requirements for learning." The ones we are, in consort with you, are claiming you in Mastery as the manifested self.

Now what Mastery is not is doing things a little better. What it is, is an actual reclamation of one's identity outside of what's been claimed thus far. And the frequency of each man and woman that is being addressed by us now is being addressed in consort with the individual's requirements for change.

Imagine this, if you like. There are aspects of the self that are troubling to you, that keep you awake at night. They may be calling you forward, or they may be stopping you from a transition that you require to know yourselves through. However you stand, you will be met, and we promise you, met in truth. So the dissemination of the vibration through language that we offer you is intended to greet you where you stand, wherever you stand and align as.

Now as we spoke of alignment earlier, we would like to recommend that every day you set an intention: "I am in alignment to my own knowing." Now your knowing, if you can understand this, is truth. Whenever you know, you are in alignment to truth. But in the claim of knowing—"I know this to be so, I must do this in my knowing"—you are actually claiming that the being that you are has access to what you are, which is the True Self.

And hear these words, friends, because it is only the True Self that may know. The small self, as we have said, thinks. The Divine Self knows. And the creations made in fear that you have believed to be so important will be seen once and for all as nothing more than a lie that may be countered and aligned in truth.

"Now what is this teaching today?" Paul is asking. "Where are we going today?"

We are actually deciding that the ones we see before us

are in comprehension of their requirements for learning. And the ones in requirements for learning are being taught in vibration, sound, and information.

"How are we teaching in sound?" Paul asks.

By resonance. When the mind operates in union with its knowing, its comprehension to the attunement of the vibration of the language we operate with happens immediately, and the cells in the body are actually moving into agreement with the tone or the octave or the sound that we emit in vibration to assume you each.

Paul is asking, "Are you the great wind that reforms us?"

No, we are not. But we are as of the great wind in truth as you are in truth. The big difference is that as we know who we are, we have bypassed, overridden the requirements of fear, and are unfettered in our expression, which supports us in our alignment with the whole. We do not fix you. We do not fix anyone. But we are witness to transformation as we know who and what we are. And we promise you this, friends. You will do the same. The wind we speak of is the Divine in action, the Word, if you like.

When we began our teaching several years ago, we offered you a very simple claim in the form of an attunement: "I am Word through my body. Word I am Word. I am Word through my vibration. Word I am Word. I am Word through my knowing of myself as Word. Word I am Word." And the acclimation of the physical self, the field you hold, and the identity to the truth of who and what you are, "I am Word," was imprinted with you as what you are.

Now the alignment henceforth has been in increments. Once you understood that the Word, the energy of the Creator in action, was the truth of what you are, we had an intention to support you each in your realization of it as the incarnated beings that you are. "I know who I am, I know what I am, I know how I serve" was the claim we made for you. "I know who I am as the Divine Self, what I am as the manifested self, the True Self, the Christed Self, the one who knows who she is," and "I know how I serve as the Divine in its perfect expression."

Then we continued with the Divine Self in its purview: "I am here, I am here, I am here," the Divine as you claiming herself in all her life, in all she sees.

Now in the addition we make here—"I am in truth"— you are in complete alignment with the vibration of truth as your broadcast, which dismantles all aspects, beliefs, and creations that operate outside of the alignment to truth.

Now a creation, as we have said, is a thing made. The body that you stand in is a creation. The eyes in your head perceive the creations of others in a shared landscape you collectively inhabit in truth, the vibration that you are. Imagine this is re-created in a higher octave, and the realization of the being that you are, the true Master Self, may be reborn.

Now we are teaching you this today because a new reader may be struggling, and an old reader may be comprehending things, perhaps, in a new way. But where we intend to bring you, which is to a new world, the higher plane, the better continent, if you wish, cannot be achieved by renunciation of the old, but by an agreement to truth that renders the old as gone. "Behold. I make all things new."

Here is the teaching, friends. The night before you wake up, you realize yourself through the changes you have undergone. The day you wake up, you witness your world either as you saw it yesterday or as you now know it to be. If you can understand that we are really saying that what you become is the Divine in manifestation in a way that is realized and not conjecture, you will comprehend the enormity of the teaching.

"But how is this done?" Paul asks.

The preparation has been made, as we have suggested, in the prior teachings, but the alchemy of transformation is done by truth. Now if you understand that truth and God are one and the same, truth and love are one and the same as aspects of the Divine, and that the freedom that you have is to be in this alignment, you can comprehend that the union you are moving toward is a reclamation of what is always true, has always been true, and must always be so when you know what you are.

The vessel that you are, the body that you stand in, has

been acclimated to this change. And the issuance of vibration may well be known to you now as you claim these words:

"I align to truth. I know myself in the vibration of truth. And I permit the vibration of truth to heal me of all lies."

If you feel the vibration as you claim this intention, a current through the body, a feeling around the skin, an expansion in the field, you will know it to be so. If you do not feel the vibration, we suggest that you will as it works with you in tone and vibration because the wind, you see, the wind of the truth, the wind of the Creator, the great wind that reshapes all things, does not need your agreement to be. It requires your agreement to be reknown as what you truly are.

Now Paul has an interesting question. We will attempt to respond to it. He is actually asking if all the changes we see before us are the winds of change, are the winds of the Divine reshaping our landscape.

Some of them may be, but the result of the changes born in love and born in truth will always be wonderful to the eyes. When you see a society on the brink of collapse, you may be seeing a house of cards collapse beneath the wind that has come, and what will grow in its place will be in truth. The collapse itself is frightening to you because you have invested in the structures, the physical structures, perhaps, that you expect to keep you safe, to keep your reality intact. But as we have suggested already, when an earthquake comes, the ground shakes and that which has a foundation in truth will be held, and that which was created in fear will be met with violence.

Now we say "violence," not to frighten you, but if you can imagine that there is an entrenched belief that has dug itself in and refuses to move, resists the winds of change, you will see that old thing rock violently as it is dislodged in order to be made anew. We are not destroyers, we are re-creators as we claim these words, "I see all things before me with the eyes of truth."

Now "the eyes of Christ" has been a teaching we have used, and it is a perfect teaching. When you witness with the eyes of the Christ, you see all things as they truly are, and that is the Divine. When you operate with the vibration of truth, you are not discounting the Christ vibration, but you are implicitly stating that what is a lie will be met in truth, and through the seeing of it, by your very witness, the thing you witness is transformed. Herein lies the truth of a new world.

"So if our world is changing," Paul says, "how do we attend to this? We have families and jobs. We have things we need to protect."

In fact, you don't have what you think. You think you

have these things, they are ways of knowing the self, but they are not the truth of what you are. And if these things that you have claimed—your job, your family—are in resonance with the truth of who you are, they will stand with you if it is for your highest development, but you cannot attach yourself to any of your creations.

Imagine this, my friends. You have a boat, the boat is sinking. You have a vault on the boat. It is too heavy, it would sink the lifeboat that would save you. So you go down with the ship, hugging the vault that has the money, those things you have valued most, at the cost of the journey without it. Do not be so attached to what you have made in form, or agreed to be, that you miss the boat.

Now Paul is concerned here. "But we were told we could never miss the boat. Another boat will come."

There is always an opportunity for growth. The one who goes down with the ship will be taught again. And perhaps in his next incarnation he will realize that things do not save a man, the Divine Self does, the truth will. Transformation always requires a releasing of the old for the new to be in form. The Christ Self, which is the Divine as you, and the Christ as we teach it, the aspect of the Creator that may be realized in form as you, is always present— underline *always*—because God must be with you whether or not you agree to it, because you cannot be away from it.

It is simply an impossibility that you can be without your Source.

But by clinging to the vault, you deny the savior, the life-boat we suggested, the truth of who you are, which will carry you to safety, because you believe the old will call you where you need to go, and it never will.

Now Paul has a correction to make. "You said the word *savior*. Was that your intention?"

We were using the metaphor of a life raft that would carry one to safety. And the life raft that we describe is Spirit, the Divine Self, which you may call the Christ. The idea of the Christ as savior is not a wrong teaching, but it is also not a religious one. There is confusion here for many of you, and we must take the moment to address it now.

The Christ exists in all mankind. It may be realized in fullness, which is the work we bring to you, but in its realization it becomes itself. It assumes the being that it is in. You become the Christ as you know who you truly are, and not the only one. The teaching of Jesus is in fact a very high teaching. We do not discount it, and his teachings are present here because a teaching that is true is always true, as Jesus was the Christ, one who moved toward realization, embodiment, and complete expression of his Divinity. In other words, he knew what he was, he knew how he served. His claim was made for all mankind. It may be realized in truth.

The confusion you all have is that the embodiment of God, while it is God, is also in all men. So seeking to worship another is never a true teaching. Aligning to the truth, and to be in vibratory accord with the Divine Self, is to be in Christ. If Jesus is the way shower that you require, he is a beautiful one. But the religion that has been claimed in his name has been distorted, is fraught with fear, and the politics of all religions seek to obscure the beauty that is inherent in all of them. When you know the truth of the teaching, the truth will set you free. And the biases you may have about the language of religion will fall away as well.

At their essence, all religions are teaching the same thing. The Divine is present in all manifestation. And the only one who may know it is the one who knows who he is in consort with the True Self in Divinity expressed in all ways.

Now can you be the Christ, you may be asking? Well, in fact, you already are, but at a level that is unrealized by you.

"Is this a sacrilege?" he asks. "Will people be burning this book?"

If they are frightened of truth, perhaps. But as we have taught many times, the action of fear is to claim more fear. And burning a book because you are frightened of its contents actually empowers the very book that you are frightened of. So there is no need here.

Now you are not the only Christ, as Jesus was not. But Jesus in full realization, the ascension of consciousness as a way shower, is a pivotal vibration that you may attend to and be served with in love. When you know what you are, you are not Jesus, you are who you are, the Christ as Judy, the Christ as John, the Christ as Kamir or Josephine, the Christ as you. The Christ has come to express as what you are, and we will say these words: Not at the exclusion of the form that you hold.

The teaching of the water turning to wine is a teaching of alchemy, and the realization of one who knows what he is will be able to transform his plane, not because she wants things different, thinks things should improve, be fixed this way or that, but transformed because truth will always transform a landscape.

"So does that mean that the reader gets to work miracles?" Paul asks.

In fact, it does, but not as the egoic structure would perceive it. The aspect of you that would like to throw the book away is also the aspect of you that says, "Oh, nice. Now I get to work miracles. This will be fun. Everybody will see me working a miracle." That is the false self, and always the false self, seeking to be announced as the Divine Self.

Hear these words: Because the Divine Self knows who he is, he needs no glory from man. The Divine as you knows who he is, knows what he is, has no vanity and no need to be the one who is elevated in the sight of his fellows.

So if you attempt to use this teaching to describe yourself as the Christ without comprehension of what it means and pretend to be something you are not, you will be giving yourself an extremely challenging lesson in humility because you will be met, as everyone must be, in truth.

Now the Divine Self, the Christed Self, the True Self, does not seek fame, does not seek to be known. As she knows who she is, she seeks to be in full expression, and to be in full expression means "I know how I serve."

The service that you each provide at this level of manifestation is in being. Underline the word *being*. What you do informed by being at this level will be in truth because you have aligned to it. And in this alignment, you are always called forward in service.

What *service* means in our language is true expression. You are expressed in truth. And whatever abilities you have been gifted with, whatever you see before you that must be done because it is being presented to you to do, will be known by you, the Divine Self, as part of your expression.

The other aspect of this, and we will continue with this later in the text, is that the expression of being itself aligns those you witness to the higher octave; because you be, you serve, and not because you do. You are the radio, you see, as Paul is a radio in broadcast. And the song you play brings everyone to it in a higher dimensional reality. You are singing the music of the heavens and lifting people to it by your very being. The amplification of the vibration in union with its Source will transform everything you see.

You imagine yourself picking up a heavy rock and carrying it up the mountain. "Oh, so much work to do. I have to get rid of my boulders. All my old creations must be lifted by hand. I will never be happy. I will always be working upon myself."

Here is the truth: When the wind of truth is blowing, when you are aligning as it, even the biggest boulder you can imagine will be carried away. None of your creations, nothing you have known or sown or created and made in form or identity, are more powerful than the action of God. And if you believe any of these things to be so, you are in idolatry. You have made an idol out of your problems, the boulders you would carry up the hill.

"So we just drop the boulder? We don't work on ourselves?"

Being in alignment requires intention and agreement to be here. The work of alignment is brought to you each day as you encounter yourself through your creations. How one creation may be attended to may be quite different than the next, but the freedom you have now in this agreement—"I know who I am in truth, I know what I am in truth, I know how I serve in truth"—will do the heavy lifting.

The wind of truth, blowing through every cell of your

body, will be your liberator with the Christ that is the truth of who you are.

We will continue this dictation when we speak next. This has been a productive morning. We thank you each for your presence. We will continue soon. Good night. Period. Period. Period. Period. Stop now, please.

Day Six*

Now the thing you don't know about being is that it doesn't require work. It doesn't require work to be as you are. It requires allowance and alignment. Allowance and alignment will support you all far more than any work you could possibly do. As each one of you here stands forth and is witnessed by us as you truly are, the claim that is made—"I am here, I am here, I am here"—will be who you are, the expression of what you are.

Now the manifested self, as she incarnates or expresses as, the one you know yourself as, has work to do. But the being of the self at this level requires no effort. We are saying this for one reason. So many of you here are seekers and you position yourselves as the one who must know, who must discover, who must find out, and your hobbies, we say, are discovering.

---

* Recorded in a workshop in Annapolis, Maryland.

Now there is nothing wrong with this, but a teaching of being and aligning is counter to the path you have led. "What will I do next? How must I find? Where do I look? What will be given to me so I may be different?"

Why do you need to be different? You need to be.

Now once you are in an agreement to the higher alignment, which is the Christed Self, the miracle is that the Christed Self does what she requires to reclaim you as her. So the work is actually done as the Divine Self, not by the small self.

Now this is contradictory to how you've lived your lives thus far. The reclamation of the self—"I am here"—sings a new song for you, yes, but the being of this and aligning as truth will claim you outside of the shame and fear and doctrine that you've believed yourself to be or in abidance to.

Now the claim we make now, "I am in truth," is quite a different claim than "I am here." The Divine Self in its presence knows all, in consort with truth, yes, but the structures that have been made in fear must be attended to. Now the Divine Self as she is, is in agreement to truth, so they are not separate. But it is a different action to claim the truth in what you see before you as the Divine Self.

Now here is the conundrum: The Divine Self is the one who has the ability to claim as truth. Do you understand this? So when we claim you in truth—"I know who you are

in truth, what you are in truth, how you serve in truth"—
we claim as the Divine that we know ourselves to be.

Now as we operate as the Christ—and we will say we
do, as we instruct at this level, because the being that we are
is not obscured by a mask, a false identity—the being that
we are as we express is truth. So as we know ourselves as
truth, we can claim you in it as well.

Now the difference between you and us is only one
thing. We have left this plane, we may attend to it from a
different octave, and we no longer believe ourselves to be
what we were taught in lower nature. Because we are not
playing by the rules of history as you are, we have been
liberated from attendance to fear as anything other than
what it is—a lie.

Understand this, friends. As you operate as truth, you do
not lie because you cannot. There has never been a lie told
that was not told in fear. And as you do not lie, you are not
in consort with lies, and by that we mean in vibratory
accord.

The relinquishing of the need to be as a lie is extremely
important. The need to be as a lie is the need to defend the
self. Understand this, dears. To defend the self is to present
yourself to opposition as the one who believes herself to require defense. The Christed Self has no need to be in defense because she couldn't be in obstacle to anything else.
And we will explain why.

As the Christ is known as you, the creations you have made in fear, in consort with fear, will be recognized by you, one and all. But the small self has had a deep investment in hiding in the cave. She does not seek the light, as the Divine Self knows herself, and she believes that as she is brought to the light she is extinguished. This is not quite true. What is extinguished, or realigned, perhaps, is the aspect of the self that was never true. And that is the aspect that is always in defense.

So you seek yourselves in this teaching, but you believe that the self that you are seeking is an improved small self, the one that doesn't have the issue, the attachment, the fear. This is not quite true. The one you become is the one who has never had it. Do you understand the difference here?

The aspect of you that self-identifies through history—"I am the one who was a drug addict," "I am the one that left his family," "I am the one that chose the wrong path," "was hurt so badly"—is not who you are. It's how you've known yourselves. So you improve yourselves: "I've made up with my family," " I no longer take the drugs." While this is all wonderful, what we are teaching you is that the Divine as you is not in consort with the creations of the small self as a means of identifying. However, the attachment you have to what you think you are is at opposition with the truth of your being.

Now we attend to this in several ways, not only in the

teaching we attend to you with, but in the frequency that we hold you in as we instruct. So those of you who have a deep investment in a false self—and, perhaps, we would say, are in denial of it—are going to be met without your denial. And those of you who believe that the path that you are embarking on should resemble a certain thing, have a certain attitude or way of expressing, will be surprised that this is not that.

What this is, is manifestation as the Divine Self. Clear these issues, not by doing, but by being, and by being at this octave of expression: "I am in truth." The claim is made to relinquish or reform all aspects of the self that are not in consort to truth.

Now Paul has a question. We will attend to it. "So if you say, 'I don't love my husband, but I pretend to,' that means you will leave your husband. Is that the teaching here?"

Absolutely not. What it means is that the small self who doesn't love her husband realizes who he is outside of what she's claimed for him. If she chooses to leave, she is led by the Divine Self, not by the authority of the small self who finally realizes that she did not love. The small self, dears, is not the one who loves anyway. Do you understand that? The Divine as you is what loves, what expresses as love, and knows the world in a higher way. The testament of your lives, the manifestation that you see before you, will always be the agreement you have made to be. And as you are being in this very moment, you are witnessing your creations.

Now the field that Paul holds has been attuned to claim you as we work through him. And the gesture he gives you by standing before you and claiming your true name—"You are here, you are here, you are here"—is not so much a benediction, but a restructuring of what you are as the Divine Self.

Now as we teach, the octave we teach at is present to you in his field as we as him know you as us. Do you understand that? When we know you, we know you without the claims of the small self and her small inheritance. We know who you are in spite of yourselves, because of yourselves, and because what you can only be in truth is how we can witness you as we align as truth.

The distinction you must make, as the one being witnessed, is that the agreement you have to be seen as you truly are actually requires you to release what you thought you were supposed to be and the creations of the small self that seek to be affirmed as what she thinks she is at the cost of what she truly is.

Now the Creator as you needs no instruction. But because you have been living on a plane that has been so invested in lies, the small self cannot always tell the difference. She has done the best she could. "I thought I was doing the right thing, I did what I knew how to do." And, yes, you did. We do not make you wrong. We do not make you anything. We know you beyond the claims, beyond the issuance, beyond the fabrications that the small self has known and believed to be herself. Once the small self is encompassed by the Divine Self, the alchemy of being and the transition that you make is apparent to you in new ways.

He has a question. We will attend to it. "But how?" he asks. "How do we know that this is so?"

The manifested being that you know yourself as, once assumed as truth, is reframed, reclaimed, reknown. And what is not in truth will be known and gone, or transformed and lifted to what you truly are and can only be. The acquiescence to this is being. You don't pull away the shingles on the old house to reveal the woodwork that was beneath them. The wind of truth will come and remove them. They will become so uncomfortable they will fall away. You may touch them and realize they are not even really there. But because you have seen them for so long and believed them to be what they were, you were re-creating them all day long. The being as truth is a reclamation to what you are, and the Divine nature that you may hold as the True Self expressing itself is what does the work.

"Is this a passive teaching?" he asks.

Not in the least. It's not at all passive. A hurricane is not passive, but to be in the hurricane simply is being. The vibration of truth, as it claims itself, is the wind that moves the shingles off of the house and perhaps even what is not in truth in the foundation of the very structure you have known.

"Well, that's not very encouraging," he says. "I know what a hurricane looks like. If I am the house, do I still stand?"

The wind may be very loving. The wind may be a caress. But the amplitude of the wind will be in agreement to your investment in lies.

Now he has a question. "But the world we see and all the change—is this the wind as well?"

Oh, my friends, it is. You are not so special that the wind would blow on you alone. It is blowing upon all mankind, not just those of you who are deciding to be in agreement to a teaching by us. The difference, though, is that you are aligning through intention to the vibration of truth. And because you are doing this, wherever you stand, you are in agreement to it. What you are is exposed by the self in agreement to be in the wind. Do you understand, yes?

Imagine, if you wish, that you are adorned with jewels. Your face is a masquerade in cosmetics. You wear the clothing of thousands of years of ritual, and the wind comes, and what is taken is what never was, could never be, will never be in truth.

Now the agreement we make with you today, you our

students and the readers of the text, is that any dismantling of form and structure is done in attendance with your Divine worth. Hear these words: You are not being punished by the relinquishing of what you thought you were. You are being gifted by truth as what you are as truth. But the dismantling, in its way, may appear as a renovation that was unasked for.

But if you look at your world and what you have all claimed and what you see around you, you will also see that fear would like to be known as your accompaniment to the song you will be singing. Do not let it sing. Do not dance to fear. Do not sing along with it. Do not pretend it is your ally.

When you are invited to fear, "Thank you so much and I don't need it" is always a beneficial answer. The fear seeks to reclaim you as what you thought you were, because if you still think you are small and damaged and in need of love, you will seek it in a fearful way.

We guarantee you, dears, that what you are, the manifested self, will survive the storm, and we say why: Because the Divine is in truth and will always be. The bodies you know yourselves through will not be yours one day. The houses you abide in will be dust. The comforts you've known through physical form have served you here, but they are not what you are. They are what they have been and must be for you as they are required, but they are not what you are.

The diminishment of the Divine Self in favor of comfort must now be attended to. "I want this path, but I want to sit on my duff and I want to be as I was yesterday. And if there is a storm, I will watch it on the television and keep my windows shut. I have a spiritual book in my lap and that is all I need."

Get ready, dears, for a reckoning. And a reckoning, as we say again, is a facing of the self and all of her creations. We have no need to frighten you with this because we actually perceive it as an opportunity. But the requirements of comfort—"I should have what I want when I want it, and if I have all my needs met in the material realm, I have no need for anything else"—will be what you see dismantled because the Divine Self in its purview, "I am here, I know what I am, I am in truth," will claim the life for you that you require to express as.

The claim "I am here," as we have instructed, is the Divine Self, the Master Self, in her purview. And the claim "I am here, I am here, I am here" will always align you as the Divine Self you truly are. But the creation as the self in truth actually brings you forth in visibility as the one who perceives it.

Now what we would like to do with you, each of you,

each one reading this text and those before us in form, is to realize you as you are, and not what you think. And if you will allow us to hold the vision for you, we will do this now in all the octaves we may sing in.

The name we call you—"You are here in truth"—will be known by us. And the benefit to you will be the reclamation of what you are in your agreement. "I know what I am in truth. I am here in truth. I am here. I am here. I am here."

We will say these words for all of you, now, and our witness of you, as you stand before us, is the claim of freedom. The Christ within you is aligning you now to what you may only be. We will say this for you. The Christ that you are, in its purview, is aligning you to what you can only be, all of you, all of you, all of you, in this claim of truth. "I am here. I am here. I am here."

Be received by us as you are, wherever you are. We hold you now and we say the words for you:

"You are as you are, as you can only be, in the field of truth that we hold you in. You are here. You are here. You are here."

We thank you each for your presence. We will stop now and let the man take a pause. Yes, this is in the text. We thank you each for your presence. Stop now, please.

Day Seven

The book that we are writing is operating on multiple levels. The mind that you have is incorporating the information into his daily life, and the field that you hold is acquiescing, aligning, receiving the vibration in intonation that is encoded in the language we use. So the whole being is being addressed.

Now the physical body is being assumed as what you are through the engagement with these words. The what that you are—the Divine in manifestation, in alignment—is the expression of the Creator as you in form. Understand these words, friends. We are not talking about an idea. We are talking about fact. And as you can only be the Creator when you know what you are, you do not exclude the form that you stand in.

Now once you understand this as what you are, your relationship to the world that you exist in is altered permanently. You've experienced yourself as separate from the fields and the flowers and the sky, and while you will still have a way of understanding what other things are that are not you, you will begin to operate in alignment with truth. And what this means is the landscape that you perceive yourself in is not excluded from the Divine, and consequently the radius of your perception, and consequently the impact of the field that you hold, is upon all things that it encounters. If you can imagine this, God meets God in all God sees because God is not separate from its creations.

Now the value of your engagement with the missive we write is that you create an accord in energy that supports this. And the incarnation and expression of the Divine as you in material form is what comes of your claim "I am here in truth."

Now some of you may believe that a claim of truth is a convenient way of expressing the self to announce a truth that is casual. "I am in a man's body," says the man who knows he's in a man's body. And he can shrug that off as so.

When you can get to the level of agreement when you know in your being what you truly are—"I am a Divine Being in manifestation, and what I am is this in consort with all I see before me"—the level of agreement may be, "Yes, I know this." But the creation of the new self who is seeing and experiencing will be anything but a casual shrug.

Now we must explain this. The triumph of this teaching, when it is realized, is that the manifestation of God as what you are is expressed *in the physical self*—underline those words—and the causal field that embarks on a triumph of witness. The being that you are, in its incarnate form, claims the landscape in accord with what she is, and the level of separation that you've believed would always be there is no longer, because in truth it never was.

Now Paul is interrupting. "But can this be so? Can our

brains hold this? Are our systems built to have this level of experience?"

We will answer this question, and for one reason. The system that you hold in form and vibration must be altered to align, agree, and acquiesce. Now when we say "altered," we do not mean wrongfully. We speak of restoration. The being that you are is always in union at a higher octave, but the dismantling of the small self's needs to perpetuate itself as separate is what is being restored and realigned so that it no longer holds itself as other from its Source.

"Now how did this happen?" you may ask. "How did mankind come so far from the truth of her being?"

We would like to answer this very simply, although it could be a book in itself. When mankind decided she was separate from her Source—and we will use the word *decided* intentionally—she claimed a structure in her field that aligned her to a lower octave, one in separation from what was always so. If you can imagine a permeable membrane that believes itself to be permanent and impermeable, you will have your understanding here. But as the Source cannot be separate from its creation, even the illusion of separation may be announced as untrue.

Now, as we have taught you, when something is true, it is always true. And the claims you make now with our assistance are to operate with you throughout time.

Paul is asking, "When we do this work now, are we

working through all time? This lifetime that we know ourselves in, or all time?"

We will say the latter. You are working outside of time, and consequently the idea of time becomes an idea that you would need to invest in to create form with. If you can imagine that the claim "I am here," a timeless claim because the Divine Self is always present, the octave that she sings that note at may be broadcast through all manifestations that the small self may have known and claimed throughout time. So the realization of what you are as you stand before us today in form is actually in broadcast through all time because the claim is always true.

Now when we teach you, we actually support you in acclimating to the vibration, but we require your permission at a certain level to support the life you live in moving into this agreement. "The life you live" means how you see, what you know, how you invest, what you decide. The "you" that aligns as the True Self does not require permission. She is activated in the claim "I am here in truth." But the small self that we are attending to now, who is about to see her world move up a whole level to a higher awareness, must be prepared for the transformations that seek to be known.

"Why?" he asks.

We will tell you once and for all. We cannot and will not override free will, and if you are tempted to hoard your fears because you are frightened of being without them, they will be your fears, no matter what we claim on your behalf. As we claim "you are here, you are here, you are here," we announce to the entire field you hold the truth of your being, and the echo of our claim does reform you, but if you key into the lock of your history and seek to hide behind its door, you will find a dark corner and shield yourself from the light that is yours in truth.

We would recommend, before we continue this text, that you take a few moments and consider the implications here. What we are telling you is that the life you live must transform to be in agreement to your truth, and unless you are willing to go to the new continent, the higher field—"Behold. I make all things new"—you will cling to the old.

If you can imagine clinging to a phone pole in the midst of a hurricane that seeks to carry you to a much higher place, you will find yourself sad and confused at what you have claimed when the storm you see carries everything with it but you.

We recommend that you let go and be lifted by truth, and by the wind of truth that will caress and lift more than it will sear and compel. We will claim these words for you, if you like, but we will reassure you that if you consider the claim you make to undergo this journey, you will not be meeting it alone. The claim we make now, as you decide your path and your purview, is as follows:

"In my knowing, I align to my truth, and I lift my hands to be taken so that I may be lifted to the higher octave that is present now by my agreement. And as I allow myself to be lifted, I give my consent to support my world as it undergoes change. And as I accept this, I have faith in my being that the truth of who and what I am will keep me steady and knowing of my worth as a Divine Being in spite of all appearances, all claims, all fears that may be lifted to be witnessed as they are transformed. In my agreement, I say my name, 'I know who I am in truth, I know what I am in truth, I know how I serve in truth, I am here, I am here, I am here.' And as I say this, the song of my being claims me as the one who has said 'yes' to the journey she says 'yes' to in truth."

We will stop this chapter in a few moments, but Paul has had a question about where this text goes.

This is not a primer. This text is very different than the ones that have preceded it. In fact, what this teaching is, and the volume you hold is, is an anchoring of truth through the reader that will shift her world and the world she sees for the highest good of all. While there is instruction here, and there will continue to be, and we will attend to your needs as practically as we can, our interests are no longer the comfort of the known but the triumph of the truth that is indwelling as you and finally, finally, finally seeks its reclamation as, through, and with you and all you see.

"How do we fill up a book?" he asks.

This is the easiest dictation you have received thus far and for the very reason that you are already acclimating to the teaching in your field. So you do not resist the concepts and you agree to the vibration. The reader will undergo a similar passage.

We will say this to all of you right now. If you decided with us to be on this journey, we sing with you now:

"We are here. We are here. We are here. And as we go forth, we will take you to a new world."

This is the end of the chapter. We will reconvene tomorrow. Thank you for your presence. Good night. Stop now, please. Period. Period. Period.

Chapter Three

ALCHEMY AND TRANSFORMATION

Day Eight

We teach as we will, and congratulations are in order for each one of you who has decided to join us on this next phase of our journey together. The requirements have been met, the requirement to be willing, to release the self from what the self has known itself through. And the landscape that you've existed in is about to reflect this.

On this new day we would encourage you to decide that the world that you've lived in perhaps is not the world that is true—underline *true* please—and in the true world, the higher world that exists in coherence with your vibration and consciousness in the higher octave, the world is a reflection only of truth.

Now when we say these words to you, we understand that the comprehension of their intent is still being filtered by a mind that holds itself in agreement to history. And so we say these words for you so that you may begin to decide that the what that you are, the manifested self, can be in agreement with a total change of awareness of a landscape. The words we speak are imprinted with meaning, intent, and light, and the light that we bring to you is to illumine the etchings, the scratchings, the small things that the small self has made known and believed to be permanent. As we give you these words, we claim them with you and for you in our dominion.

"On this day I claim that I give agreement to perceive a new world, and that the investments I have made in what things were is being released for me by the Divine Self I know myself as and all the support that is present for me as an initiate on this wondrous journey. The claim that I make now is being imprinted in my field for the purpose of remembrance. As I remember who I am in totality, I give every aspect of my life permission to reflect the Divine truth that I know is in all. I say these words of my own free will, and as I say them, I say 'yes' to all that may meet me, all I may know, and all I will witness in Divine truth. I am Word through this intention. Word I am Word."

Now the sacrilege of history has only been one thing, an investment in separation of man from its Source. And everything that was built to mandate that is being reflected back to you as a lie. The next two years of your life may be a journey in sanctifying what you see, and by this we mean the reflection of the one who knows who she is must be met in grace. So when you witness something that is not in alignment as the True Self, the True Self can only hold it in its highest vibration.

Now we will explain this for you. One of the questions we recently received from a student implied that we should be deciding, we the Guides, what is good and what is not. And that is not for us to do. In fact we do not make those decisions because we exist outside of the reference that you would imprint upon what you see. What we do decide is that all is holy and all may be operating at one level of alignment or outside of it.

When something is operating outside of alignment to truth, it establishes itself and seeks to lay claim to what it encounters. An example would be a structure, perhaps war, that is not in alignment, but seeks to confirm its existence by applying to other's fears or the need for war to be the victor at the cost of someone else being the one who loses.

Now when a structure is made, any structure you can imagine, there is an intent. And when the intent is understood, it may be moved, but for the most part you perceive the structure as fact, and not the intent that was born in manifestation as the thing you see.

Here is an example. When one goes to war, is one seeking to dominate another, to reclaim territory that was perhaps lost? Is one seeking rule or to oppress those on the other side of the border? Or is there something else? "We are claiming what is truly ours. We have been robbed. We must take back what was ours once upon a time." Or even better still, "The only way to save ourselves is to kill the ones who exist over there."

Once you understand that each and every impulse here is in dominance, the intent to dominate and rule or protect, which is to defend, which is a response to fear, you can also understand that when the intent itself is seen for what it was intended to do, and the result of it manifested in form is how you call a war a war, you can begin to move to truth.

"How is this done?" he asks.

By application of one principle, and one principle only: The alignment as the Divine Self, which is where we are bringing you now, gives you purview as the witness of any act to be in renunciation of what is in fear, because fear is a lie and what was claimed in fear, however massive the structure seems, was not born in truth.

So as the one who holds the vibration of truth—"I know who I am in truth, I know what I am in truth, I know how I serve in truth"—the witness that you hold of what you see will claim it as it truly is. And when you see something in truth, you collect it and lift it to its true essence.

So he has a question. "Do you mean we bypass what we see and lift it to a higher level of understanding?"

Not at all. Your comprehension of what you see as a small self will be filtered by what you have been taught to know. The good guys wear white, the villains wear black, and good must triumph. You have been emblemized in your understanding of what good and evil is and entrenched to believe that the ones you think are good are the ones who need to triumph.

What you do by this thinking is create polarity and release truth that is not convenient to your understanding. Here is the truth. All men are of God. All beings are of God. And as they express, they learn, and they choose their paths of learning in the ways that are for their highest benefit.

When you witness a war as an object, as a thing, as an act, at the cost of realizing those participating on either side, and you don't realize their true divinity, what you end up doing is reinforcing the very structure that you say you do not want. When you go to truth—"I know who you are in truth, I know what you are in truth, I know how you serve in truth"—you claim the ones who may be operating out of alignment in the higher accord.

Imagine, if you would, that a battle is ensuing. There are two sides, perhaps, or perhaps many who have an investment in rule and in a final outcome. If you play the chord of truth for all involved and you reclaim them as they truly are through your own awareness of what they are, you emblazon them in the field of truth where the lie can no longer exist.

"What is the lie in this case?" he asks.

The belief in rule, one above another, is in fact a lie. The belief in good and bad as they have been ascribed to you is a lie. The belief that one should be the victor at the cost of someone's losing is a lie. The entrenchment of these beliefs throughout this land must be remedied, but they cannot be picked apart. You have no time to sit back and assume that the conversations that you might have to bring about peace will do the job when what you have created are the mechanisms for global destruction.

Now when we say these words, we are not intending to frighten you at all. We like conversation and we encourage it. So we are not saying don't go into theoretical discussions about what will transform this plane. You will and you can.

But when you know what you are, the Divine in action—and remember that our definition of the Word, the energy of the Creator in action, is the foundation of all of these teachings—you will comprehend that your very presence on this plane is what calls it into reformation.

Now the transition that an individual makes as the one who perceives truth is a very interesting one. Paul is seeing layers of skin peeling away. They don't look very attractive as they go away, but the intent of the movement is to reveal the pure skin or the truth that lies beneath the layers of artifice that may have accrued through mistaken beliefs and false teachings throughout time.

Now Paul cannot comprehend the utilization of the teaching we are bringing through because it is so true. And we will explain what this means.

You have all become so invested in looking at yourselves, deciding why you are the way you are and what you must do to correct what you perceive to be a problem, that you invest in all of the data from history that would support a kind of self-reflection that is ultimately a reinforcement of the personality and egoic structure. "I will fix myself by looking at myself, making decisions about what I should be or could be by this or that regard, and then I will presume to go about my business as a new woman or man." All you have done is correct something on a superficial level when you attend to things in that regard.

The teaching of truth as a vibration that is so powerful that it can topple a kingdom is what we are giving you now. And not only this, we are claiming you in it because it is the truth of what you are.

Now when something is built in lies, it usually looks very attractive. It has wonderful ways of preparing you to engage with it as something that should be. And the small self, unable to comprehend the intent of something in its creation, why it was made and the truth of it, will always be confused when one bears witness to a creation emblazoned in fear.

When we teach, we teach quite differently the small self, who may not be able to comprehend the infrastructure of what she sees and the intent that was made and claimed into form. The Divine Self sees only one thing—"I see you in truth; I know what you are in truth"—and as the perceiver of truth, the one who cannot go into a lie because she cannot claim what is unlike her, will be the catalyst for the reforming of the thing she witnesses.

Now we have discussed this prior and we will again. This is a teaching of witness, and to be in witness means to be the perceiver. Everything that you can perceive, everything at all you have a relationship to energetically, your consciousness creates form, sees what she sees, gives it names, usually the names it has been given prior, and negotiates how she is to attend to it. As the perceiver, you bear witness to your entire world in relationship to you, which quite simply means, if you are not in relationship to it, it does not exist without your permission.

Now this is the experience of the self, and we are not implying that if there is an unread book on a desk in Paris you are in relationship to it and made it there. But in fact, by nature of its being and your relationship to your world, our very pronouncement of the desk and the book has put you into relationship to them and now they are within your purview.

What we are teaching you is that the manifested world is claimed in consciousness in relation to you and to all men, to all women. You share the landscape that you inhabit. But you are all informing it with meaning. You decide what is good and what is bad. You create the war or the peace. You decide yourselves how you imprint anything with meaning.

Now when we say these words to you, the world that you have known must be disassembled in order for you to comprehend a world in truth. We don't mean a leveling of this plane. What we do mean is an uninvestment in meaning, an uninvestment in what things have been named and called, an uninvestment in what your relationship to things has been, in order for the new to be present.

The image we give Paul again and again is of a plate of food from yesterday's dinner still sitting on the table at today's meal. Your intention may not be to dine on yesterday's leftovers, but in fact you are, every day you claim yesterday into today.

Now while this is a metaphor, it simply speaks to your investment in re-creating the known at the cost of what is in truth.

Now Paul is getting concerned. "This is a rather heavy teaching. We don't like this. We want to feel better. What about our problems? If we are still unhappy, what does it matter if we are living in a new world?"

We will tell you this, once and for all. The unhappiness you speak to is a result of misalignment and not knowing who you are, and are always, in truth. And the projections of your world, the things you see around you, are the result of that misalignment, individually and collectively.

Our first order of business is you and your alignment, because once your alignment is clear and you stop reinvesting in what you claimed once upon a time in fear, you will perceive a new world that is already present. You can imagine that you wear glasses that limit your vision—you all do, in fact. You perceive the world in its most obvious form. You do not see thought forms riding across the sky at the speed of light, you do not witness the Divine in fire, in the heart of every man and woman who awakens to herself. But these things are present in the higher octave.

Now the challenge here for Paul, we would say, as the one who must speak these words aloud, is he cannot imagine an uninvestment in what he has created and known to attend to the level of vibration and commensurate experience that we describe here. And he is right to question this, as are you, the reader. You must understand, dears, that the work we do is outside of the frames of reference that you have attended to.

The sequence of teachings you've received through us

have been catalyzing you to this level of agreement. And for this work to commence, the Divine Self, who is what you are, exists outside of time, and her knowing of what is true in realization will be what calls this world into being, not your going for another class, reading yet another book, or thinking about your childhood and who did what to you when.

As long as you keep attending to the symptoms of your misalignment and trying to correct them externally, you will miss the opportunity that we are offering you here. And aligning to truth as what you are claims victory over the landscape that you have inherited.

"So what do we do with history?" Paul asks. "We have great works of art. We have wonderful culture. Are we to make these things null and void?"

We don't discount your history and the achievements of man. In fact, the greatest achievements of men have been divinely inspired, and any work of art of any merit will be the proof of this. When the Divine operates as the artist, the artist creates. He doesn't know how he does it, but he is moved to create something of beauty that is a reflection of something that exists outside of form or is being presented and rendered in a whole new way.

It's a wonderful example of one who knows who he is. When the creator is creating, he is a vessel for the expression of the Divine, and the manifestation is the art he makes. And the vibration of that art, and the imprinting of the consciousness of the artist at the time the art was born, will be implicit in the creation while it is still here in form.

What becomes of the art when it is no longer present is that the intent and the being of it is imprinted still in the field that you hold and may still be known in a higher octave, if you can comprehend that, at one level of realization, everything that was ever made exists, because once something is made it is there to be re-created in form. The energy that it was born of is still present in whatever form it may take.

The consequence of living in your history at the cost of the present moment is a very different thing. When you see a relic in a museum, you comprehend it as what it is. "This is what they baked with five hundred years ago, and this is how they mixed their paints, or buried their dead." The exhibit is giving you information and an opportunity to be in consort with a culture or a mind or an artist from another day.

But what you don't understand is that when you walk out of your house, you are also in a museum that you are interacting with, the creations of those who came before you, those who painted the houses, designed, and built them, those who paved the roads, and those who hundreds of years ago, perhaps, decided that the way they walked to work would one day become a road.

The imprinting of history is ever-present and we cannot lie to you by telling you it will not be there. But as the perceiver of your world, the one who knows who she is, the lifting of the landscape actually aligns you outside of what's been created, to its true essence. Once again we use the words, "Behold. I make all things new." The existence in history, un-assuming your truth, is quite different than knowing your truth and being in witness to what was created by others.

As the manifestation of the Divine, imprinting herself in the environment she exists in, her true nature is what lifts the landscape. There is no heavy lifting here at all. There is only perception.

Now the eyes of the Christ, as we have taught you, are the eyes that see the Divine in all manifestation. And the eyes of the Christ do not judge and do not see in fear. And the claim "I am in my truth as the Divine Being or the Christed Self" actually invests you in an alignment— underline the word *alignment*—to truth that will clear you of your creations, your own needs that were made in fear, and reclaim you as what you are so that you can be the perceiver of a brand-new world.

Now Paul is asking the obvious question. "So what does this world look like? Are you speaking of our world in a different manner, or some other world with thought forms flying around the globe?"

Well, we will tell you this. Thought forms *are* flying around the globe, and the etheric body holds information that may be witnessed by sight or feeling to one who knows who she is. But what we are saying is that the world that you live in is perceived in truth, and those creations which are not aligned to truth will be realigned, and your presence, as the response to what you see is known, will be the one who claims the Kingdom into manifestation.

Now there's some confusion here for Paul. He has understood that witnessing the Kingdom or the Divine in all he sees is a wonderful, peaceful way of expressing, and he is not wrong in the least. Because the Divine Self is in alignment, what the Divine Self sees is in accord with God or the Source of your being. But the belief that the landscape does not invest in other things would be false.

"What does that mean?" he asks.

Well, when you see things change—"Oh, look at that store, it just closed, those poor people, they lost their business"—you are assuming for those poor people what you intend. In fact, those poor people have lots of money and retired someplace nice and are very thrilled never to walk in that door again.

Now the assumptions you make about how things should be, your idea of a peaceful world, doesn't operate in truth as much as what you've been taught. You expect little birds flying, singing happy songs as you walk under the rainbow.

That is not the Kingdom. The Kingdom is a profound awareness of the Divine in all. It is rapturous, yes. It is glorious, yes. But you will still see death and decay, but you will comprehend these things with the eyes who know the truth.

We are not prettying up your world, dears. This isn't a new paint job. This is true reclamation to what you are as the one who may receive, be, and know what she is.

Now when we continue this teaching, we intend to take you on a journey to a higher octave, to a way of being outside of what you've known, so that you may anchor the creation, the potential, the being at this level, into your system. As we have taught, nothing may be claimed until you first realize it as possible. And while we are teaching you in abstracts, in some cases things you cannot know until they are known, having an experience of what it is like to be at this level of vibration will be in support of you knowing it—underline the word *know*—when you have aligned to it.

As we are your teachers, we will support you each in your comprehension of the teaching. The one today, and in all days, are instructions happening on multiple levels. So if you ask for comprehension, you will be met in support of your request.

We will end this session by saying these words: The landscape that you live in, that you see and express through, is not what you think. There is a whole other world here as well, operating in higher vibration. If you would, close your eyes for a moment, and when you open them again, say these words, "Behold. I make all things new."

We bless you each for your presence. Good night. Stop now, please. Period. Period. Period.

Day Nine

The teachings you will receive today are about authority and what you have authority over. If you can understand that, as the one who sees anything, you have a relationship to what you see, you can understand that how you see anything implies the kind of relationship you hold. And in that there is authority.

You are always choosing how you perceive—now in ignorance, perhaps, because you have been misinformed about the meaning of things—but the effort we bring you with which to see anew is the key to the Kingdom. Now the Kingdom is a teaching we have given you before. "I see all things with the eyes of the Christ" aligns you in perception to the Christed manifestation that you truly are, as the one who may perceive. And the Divine Self in her purview can see all things at this level of agreement.

The teaching you receive today in authority is about what is yours to transform, and by "transform" we mean see anew. And in the seeing anew, in your participation to what is seen, you actually transform the object to its true nature.

Now this doesn't sit very well with Paul. "Well, if I see a rock, it's a rock."

And as we have said, the rock may build a wall, the rock may be thrown in anger or in play. The rock may be lifted to reflect the sun, or buried in the earth to be the foundation for a house. How you operate with the rock is always in agreement to your intention. And how you see anything is born in agreement, not only with what you are, but what you see in your authority.

Now the small self has great authority. She chooses her clothes, she goes to work, she does the job she's been given, and her authority is to maintain a world that she has inherited. The Divine Self's purview exceeds well beyond this to the alchemy of transformation, and that will be the title of this chapter, "Alchemy and Transformation," because this is where we wish to take you.

The Divine Self in her purview holds a grand vision. Now by "grand" we don't mean splendorous or how you would imagine this to be. By "grand" we mean invested in great truth as the one in authority.

When a child is held by her mother, the mother knows the child as her, as what has come through her, and at the same time independent. The mother cherishes the child, but also sends the child forth into a new world where she may claim for herself.

When you perceive your world in consort with others, you have collective creations, many children, perhaps, that you all have different relationships with. But for one reason or another you've come to a common understanding of what things are in order to share one reality that is congruent enough with all of your needs.

The shared construct of reality that we attend to in this text is simply what was chosen by humanity at a stage of its development, brought into form, claimed as such, and then utilized in different manner for the purpose of responding to your needs.

Now the key to the teaching we give you is that you must realign—that is the key word here—as the perceiver in order to be the alchemist. The small self has the investment in what things have been. She was taught by her parents, she is taught by the books she inherits, she is taught by the religion she has held, and in consummate agreement with all these things, she reclaims history as the landscape she stands in.

The authority we say that she holds is to decide that these were creations, things made once upon a time that don't require her adherence once she realizes that the Divine Self that she truly is exists in a higher landscape—

underline the word *higher*, if you wish, because it's the easiest way for you to begin to comprehend this.

The old images of heaven as a city on a cloud were there to depict a higher alignment and a manifested reality that exists beyond the known world. It was an evocation of something true. Now there is no heaven upon a cloud. That is not where heaven is. But heaven is here in the room you sit in, in the sky outside, and even in the basement and its darkest corner—heaven is there, as well. But the perceiving of heaven is not done by the small self, who is moored in the lower landscape or lower vibration.

The depiction of heaven as elsewhere has confused humanity for far too long. And the truth of the teaching "The Kingdom of heaven is at hand" is that it is here, has always been, and can only be. It is a higher octave, a higher level of vibration—dimensional reality, if you prefer—that may be known through you, but only as you attend to it as the one who may perceive it.

In our prior texts, we assumed you as responsible for what you see. We sent you to the streets with the instruction to witness the Divine or the God within or the true spiritual nature of each one you pass, and in doing so you lift your consciousness and your vibration to a higher level. The claim "I am here, I am here, I am here," which we have instructed you in, the claim of the Divine in and as purview, was the announcement that is made by the True Self to call into agreement all she witnesses in the Divine truth that must exist in the higher nature.

The claim we give you now, "I am in truth," actually blazes a trail, a bright trail, perhaps a fiery trail, to illumine your life so that your consent, your agreement, and the authority you hold is in agreement and alignment to Divine truth.

The key to the Kingdom, you see, has always been you. But the True Self, the Divine Self, is the one who enters the Kingdom, and not by rule and not by commanding or deciding she should be there, but by alignment to the level of vibration that the Kingdom exists as. The teaching of heaven on earth, which we will bring you eventually, has been misconstrued by you because your ideas of what heaven should be—all of your needs are met in the most splendid ways you can imagine—is still informed by the egoic self who believes that her heaven should resemble a catalog of riches where she is in luxury and attended to by angels. That is not the truth.

The Kingdom of heaven is a level of consciousness that the knower embarks into by realization. Knowing and realization are identical in meaning. When you know something in truth, you realize it. If you understand the word realization, it means to realize, to be made known. The key here is to know what is, not what should be, not what you have acquiesced to or agreed to be, but what is and can only be in truth.

Now the field that you hold thus far has been imprinted with many things, the lesions from the past incarnations, the desires filled and unfulfilled. And the form that you have taken in embodiment here, the form that you are required to embark on in, will be met by us in a new way.

And we will say this for Paul. The form that you stand in must be re-created to affirm its truth, not to be in agreement with what the form thinks it should be. If you've been shaming your body, or damning this or that in form, you have aligned to that level of vibration. And that is a lie because the truth of any being in manifestation is the brilliance of the Divine, and nothing else is true.

When we began this text, we spoke to you about the exclusion of the physical form as being a problem. "Heaven is up there and we are in the mud." If the Kingdom is in all things, the Kingdom is in the mud with you. And if you are in the mud, you are in the Kingdom in the body you hold, and the body that you hold is also the Kingdom because nothing is excluded from God. Finally, finally, finally, nothing can be or will ever be except that which you decide is outside of the light, and even that is in God as well, just not in your experience of it.

The creations you hold, you see, in form made by you are testament to your beliefs. This includes the form you stand in. And the vibratory field you hold in many ways is encyclopedic in its information that is informing your being now.

Now the cleansing of the vibratory field, which we will embark on next, is a patterning, a repatterning, of what you are outside of prior agreement. In many of our teachings, we have instructed you to be reclaimed in truth, in the truth of what you are, which by its very intention mandates that the needs of prior incarnation that are out of alignment with truth will be reclaimed in alignment to it. But the cause of the issuance in the field has not yet been fully addressed, so the requirement for the patterning that may be holding you back must also be disassembled and reclaimed in a higher way.

Paul wishes an example. We will attend to it. You have a tree, but the fruit is poor. You can cut the fruit off from the branches, but the branches will always produce poor fruit. That is the nature of the tree. Until what has invested the tree in its poor fruit is addressed and reknown, the tree cannot produce other. And what we are saying, that if you are the tree, what you are producing in your field that is claiming your reality into being that has not been addressed, that is not yet in alignment to truth, must be known by you and realized again in a higher way.

The repatterning that we speak of here is done in stages. We have worked with you in prior texts to surmount many issues through the realization of the True Self. But Paul and many of you are still rebounding from the walls that you find yourself bumping against again and again. So we will attend to this in a true way in *The Book of Truth*, because the seed that the tree grew from has also been corrupted in manifestation and must be cleansed so that its expression, meaning the life that you live, is in complete alignment with its true nature.

Now Paul asks a question. "'Its true nature'—if it was producing poor fruit, perhaps that *is* its true nature. There are plants that produce poison fruit. That is their nature."

If you wish to use the metaphor that way, you have the right to, but this would also state that there are bad people, and that the intrinsic truth or the seed of God, which exists in all men, is not powerful enough to transform them to a realization of their true nature. And we call this blasphemy. If you can understand that the seed of God that is in you— and in fact in every cell of your being, because like equals like—may be known, revitalized, expressed in fullness, and that the expression that you are will produce like in vibration, you will understand that the resurrected self, the man who has been reborn in truth, will be known by a world in equal vibration. Here we go:

"On this day I claim that the truth of my being in every cell of my body or my field will be reborn and reknown

and realized in Divine truth so that the expression of
my being may be the field of truth, and that the field of
truth will claim me in agreement with a world of equal
vibration. I set this intention of my own free will and in
alignment to the truth of all mankind and its ability to
reclaim its own Divine nature. I know who I am in truth.
I know what I am in truth. I know how I serve in truth.
I am here. I am here. I am here."

Here we go, everybody. The fields that you stand in are
being shifted to bring you to an alignment of the causal
field, the true field, the aspect of the self that already knows
and expresses at this level of creation. And as you lift to be
encompassed by the Creator, the truth of what you are, the
field that you hold begins to disassemble the investment it
has had in knowing itself as other or different or apart
from its Source. The claim "I am free" will support you in
this because the bondage of humanity is and always has
been its perceived separation from the Source of its being.
But we say "perceived" intentionally. When a lie is realized
in truth, the lie no longer exists.

Now the claim you made in truth operates on multiple
levels. The mind hears the words you speak, but the words
you speak are intoned and impressed into your field to support you in the agreement made. We said earlier that the
work happens in stages, and for one good reason. You must

align to what you are in form, the Divine in form as you, to be the alchemist you are. Your belief that you are separate from the physical realm because the physical realm is not of God is the lie that is being addressed. If the form is of God, then all you see is of God as well. And as of the same vibration, the material realm may be known and met in higher accord.

When we claim you as what you are, we are actually imprinting you and the field you hold with the vision of truth that may sustain you as you agree to it. But you must agree or you will witness the world with one eye on the light and one eye in the shadow, and you will confuse yourselves to no end. You are better off, we would say, with two eyes downcast or both eyes to the light because at least you will see where you are going.

The lifting we give you now as a collective group is a gift for those who can attend to it. And by "can" we mean those of you who have done the work thus far that we have instructed you in, which supports you in the realignment of the vibratory field that may be lifted.

When we ended the last section, we will say that what we said was that you would be lifted to a realization of what exists in the higher octave. And we intend to do this for you now.

If you can imagine for a moment that wherever you sit, wherever you lie, wherever you stand, is one place, but that there are other ways of describing this place than you have been taught. "Well," you may say, "I am in my room with my things about me." But you may say it in other words. And we would like you to describe the room that you are in, or the place you stand in, in a new way, outside of language and description that has been invested in history.

If you call it a bedroom, you expect the bed. If you simply say, "I am in a space with things that were purchased to provide comfort to the body and familiarity to the small self. I am in a space that is shared by others, but on this day there is no one else present. On this day, I look at the walls and I realize they are simply obstructions that keep the elements from me or align privacy for my need to be alone. As I witness the world beyond the windows, I no longer see towns and countries, but I see people and places they have erected to shield them from the elements, and the names of countries and towns were simply creations by one who came before me."

If you can do this in the space you sit in, you will begin to deconstruct your relation to a reality that was made by others and inherited by you. This is the first step. The claims we are making for you now are there to support you in lifting the vibration of your world, but your world may only be lifted in its vibratory state and in witness of the vibratory truth, which is the Divine that invests in all. So by taking the names away and realigning the relationship to these things, what you actually do is take away the reinforcement of consciousness that solidifies them.

Now the next thing we would ask you to do is look around this space you sit in, or stand or lie in, and align to the possibility that everything here that was created by someone else was once some other thing. Do you understand this?

The floor was once a tree, perhaps, and the blanket that holds you warm in your bed perhaps was once a field of cotton. If you can imagine that everything you see was once named something else, known as something else in another form, you can begin to understand the transient nature of physical reality.

Now, we would say, what was once this or that at one time was not. Once the tree was just a seed. Once the field was bare of cotton. But the seeds were planted and grew into form. So before there was the tree, there was the seed. And if you can imagine that before there was a seed, there was frequency, you can begin to distribute this consciousness to all that you witness.

Imagine, if you would, that the place that you sit, stand, or lie is a field of vibration. And everything in it is alive in its awareness of the Source with which it came from. Everything is in vibration, as you are as well. And as you in vibration—in the place you sit, stand, or lie—collectively agree to this, we will lift you in our intention, in our purview and authority, to the true nature of what you are.

If you can imagine that the field that you are in is lifting in stages, and you are lifting within it, you can feel this within the field that you hold. Now the interesting thing here is we are not just lifting you, we are lifting all we see that you are in consort with because you are of the same stuff as the floor, and the window, and the sky, and what is outside and beyond what has been known by you thus far in form. And as we lift you, we will say these words: Each one here is being granted a glimpse of their eternal self in agreement to a vibratory field that knows no distinction, no name and form. And as each one is known by us at this level of agreement, the imprinting in their field of what it means to be in heaven, the dimensional octave described as heaven, will be known by them so it may be realized, known, and claimed by them in their true authority as the Divine Being they are.

The name we give you now is yours forever because it is your true name. You are here, you are here, you are here as what you are in truth, in alignment to truth, and in consort to the vibratory Kingdom of heaven.

We bless you as you are and we say these words to you: Come with us now because where we wish to take you next will be outside of the known, for in the known you find what was, but in the unknown, the as yet to be known, you may claim the freedom of the one who knows who she is in truth.

We will stop the dictation in a moment, but we have to say this. Paul has been asking a question. "Are you just going to leave us here in this vibratory space?"

Absolutely yes. Why would you want to return? The awareness of the Divine Self in consort with her landscape is an incredible gift. And as you begin to attend to it, your experience begins to align it to its truth, its impermeable truth, the eternal truth that nothing is outside of God.

We thank you for your presence. Stop now, please. Period. Period. Period.

Chapter Four

PRESCRIPTIONS*

Day Ten

To justify yourselves to anyone is to give your authority away. To decide for yourself that you have the right to be as you are is the claim of freedom. And the claim of freedom that we bring to you now—"I am here in my knowing as what I am"—will claim you in freedom in all aspects of your life. It brings to bear the teachings you've received thus far in a perfect way that will meet you wherever you stand.

Now the claim we have just made for you will support you in each situation you could ever meet that will support the awareness of the purview of the Divine Self. When you are witnessed by another as they want you to be—underline the word *want*, please, because that means they are holding an intention for you and expect you to meet them where

---

* Recorded in workshops at the Esalen Institute.

they stand at the cost of what you are—you will be claimed by the speaking of the words we intone for you.

Now the frequency you hold is an embellishment of the Creator manifested through and as you in each situation you meet. We will ask you this: Can you decide on this morning that you are free from the desires of others' intention for you, who they want you to be, need you to be, in order to support the identity that they have claimed?

Now what you know from your experience with us thus far—that who you are is what you say you are, and what you are is the manifestation of the Divine in form—what you are must be known by you in all circumstance. When somebody decides for you—"He is the man I want him to be"—in fact, what they are doing is deciding for you who you should be in their vibration, in collusion or agreement with an intention that may not be in alignment to truth. "I want that man to be my lover; I want that woman to give me the job" is deciding for someone else who they must be to you to meet the requirements that the small self has designed.

Now, you live in a world, yes, where these interactions are everyday occurrences. But what you don't realize is that by moving beyond them to what you are, you are no longer in alignment to the small self's requirement to respond as it has been instructed thus far.

So we say, now, the claim we make—"I am in my

freedom"—is an announcement of the purview of the Divine Self that breaks all promises that were made in fear, cancels all agreements that were made in lower form. Now, this is not a legal action. It is an unrequiring of the self to debase herself or misalign herself to require the benefit to another.

When you decide that what you are—the man you are, the woman you are, the being you are—is truly sovereign in her freedom, you can agree at this level to be in any engagement with anyone you meet, and you do not override them or their free will by claiming truth. In fact, when you honor yourself at this level, you are honoring them as well. You are all free men. The designs you hold—who another should be to you, about what they should be to you—will be reconnected to a higher knowing of what they truly are.

Now, does this mean you don't need others? In fact, it means that the Divine Self is aware of the Divine in all you encounter, and that becomes the requirement of the interaction.

Now Paul has a question. "But we have all these interactions. People are attracted to one another. They need employment. There is a kind of conversation happening silently all the time that is based in expectation. We expect people to do what we ask when we have that agreement with them. Are you saying that these things are null and void now?"

In a way, we are. Not that they don't exist, but you are not empowering them through the command of the lower self to have someone do your bidding, meet your need. And please understand that most of these agreements are not of benefit to you.

Some of you believe that you will not be loved, so you encounter others with the design, "Do not love me, I will not be loved." And that is the expectation you hold for them in spite of what they would give you.

Now, the claim we make about freedom is inclusive of free will. When someone has a design on you—"I would like to hire her for the job," which is, in fact, a design—you may agree to it if you wish. You are always sovereign in your choice.

What we are actually saying is that the agreements that are made with others in intention to deny the Divine within them, or to circumvent their will, will not hold in the vibration we claim with you, "I am free."

Now, if you can understand that the teaching you are receiving is not just an instruction, but a statement of fact, of what happens to one at the level of vibration of truth that we call forth as you, you will understand that what commences now is a new agreement, and that the relationships you hold that are not in alignment to truth will be re-created or re-leased as needed under the purview of the Divine Self.

Understand, friends, that when you enter into an agreement, "You will be who I want you to be or I will not love you," it is an agreement made in fear. "You will do what I say, or you will not be who I want you to be, and if you are not who I want you to be, I will not know you" is manipulation and debasement of the free will of the one you know.

Now, you enter into contracts all day long. "I am supposed to work seven hours in a day. If I don't meet the seven hours, I will not be remunerated for my time." And you go into the agreement of your own free will, to live in accordance with a rule that was made by another. This is your choice.

If the same authority says, "You will now work twelve hours for the same money," you may decide that you are worth more and discontinue the agreement. You are still in authority and you are not being manipulated. Somebody is changing the rules, you don't wish to play by them, and you leave the agreement that was made prior.

The disinvestment of what people want from you, or expect you to be because it's what you have been, is what is being discussed now. And the triumph of this teaching is that it is already done in alignment to truth. What you don't realize is that by the attunements that you have received thus far to the vibration of the Word, to the freedom of knowing what you are, to the claim of the purview of the

Divine Self who announces, "I am here in all I see before me," you have already negated the lies that you have perpetuated and agreed to. It has been done already.

But the manifestation of it through the three-dimensional world you live in may not be known by you yet until you decide that you are safe as the man you are who knows himself as free. "Here I stand today amidst my creations, the things that I have made in form, the agreements signed, the things that I have used to claim an identity. They surround me, my creations, and I have two choices—to comprehend each of these things as what were required by me at a stage of evolution and allow them, each and every thing, to be vibrating with me in accord to truth, even if it means they are released from me because they have been invested by lies, or to decide to unpack your old belongings that were ready to be moved to a higher realm and stay where you are."

If you can imagine that you have lived in a house that served you well, but you now realize that the land that the house sits upon is not true, is not good ground, you have a choice—to stay in the house, or move to a new house on a ground that is in alignment to truth. If you choose to stay in the old, you will be met by your creations, all of them, you see, they invest in all things, what has been made by you at another time.

We will say this: This is a teaching we will use in text. We are being very careful with language to support Paul in the transmission. If there is interruption, he will panic, and we will have to resume at another time.

To continue with the metaphor: If the house is built on old ground, and the ground no longer supports you and you choose to stay there, you will be surrounded by your creations—what has been made in fear, perhaps what has been made in love. But you will know yourself again as what you were at the cost of what you are. The what you are, the Divine Self in its amplitude, re-creates the landscape that she exists in by nature of her purview, her jurisdiction, if you prefer.

Once again, if you can see it, if you can perceive it, if it is in your witness, you are in vibration and accord to it. And the Divine Self must claim all things in accordance to truth.

Now when you move beyond the known, there is a requirement for you, which is trust, which is faith. And you may move to your knowing or your realization to give you this. But it is a requirement.

Imagine that the house that you were living in, which is the life you have known yourself through, is being pulled apart, the old boxes being carted away, the stones of the chimney being reduced to the rocks in the garden that they once were. You have two choices here—to try to hold the structure up, maintain what was, or trust, or trust, or trust that where you are being taken next is to a higher level, a better place, a place where what will be there will be in accordance with truth and your true needs.

The evolution of a soul requires that the soul have experiences. Some you may perceive as joyful; some may be very hard. But all of these things that you encounter in your world are there to support you, finally, we say, in knowing who and what you are. The truth of what you are, the Divine Self, or the Christ principle operating as you, is unchangeable. It is a fire that burns within your heart, and that fire, in its truth, will envelop you and transform all the matter that you encounter by your touching it in your perception.

When you understand what a miracle is, which is a re-seeing and a re-creation, a reknowing of what was made once and is made new in a higher way, you will have the understanding of what is being instructed here.

The teaching of the soul who aligns to her True Self and manifests it is legendary on this plane, and you know the stories of the ones who have achieved. And those who have come to teach others came by many names. They came to teach you what you were, what you can only be in truth, the Christ as you, the Buddha nature expressed as you, God as you. Whatever you wish to call it is not a new teaching.

What we have done and will continue to do is to claim you as this in vibratory accord. How we do this is by holding a field that actually transmutes the fear self to support the reclamation of what you are in truth. And the field is growing—it is a vast field now—and it is available to all men who wish to align to it.

The claims you make with us—"I know who I am in truth, I know what I am in truth, I know how I serve in truth"—will reclaim you in the octave of truth. And in truth there is no fear. Understand that, friends. When you are in truth and in your knowing, you are never afraid.

Now we will return to the context that we first established in this lesson. When others make agreements for you without your consent, you are not being known in your authority. When you make the decision that calls another to share the results without their benefit of acquiescing in will, you have done the same for them. In your decision for them, you have denied their truth.

Now you may have an arrangement—"On Tuesday, you decide, and on Wednesday, I do"—and then you are in agreement to shared authority. When you have someone, any man, any woman, who seeks to override the free will of another, you have a despot. You have a ruler who will assume the power of another at the cost of their free will.

As we have said, by the very nature of your being and by the alignment you hold as the one in truth, you have already rendered these relationships or the contracts that support them, real or imagined, as null and void. But how you experience this will be dependent on who you are. What you don't see yet is how much you need, the small self needs, the approval of an authority or the safety of a protector who will only offer you this at a great cost.

Now the command to love one another is the most important command you may ever know. But you cannot love another when you are fearful of him, or fearful of his leaving, or fearful of her doing you harm. So when you feel that you love in fear, you do not love, you want. And these are the wants we are speaking to today.

As you move into your own authority as the Divine Self, you will begin to see where you have claimed authority at the cost of another's needs, and even more so, where you have given your authority to another man or another woman to give her the power to choose for you. You may do this in a marriage, yes. You may do it in a very simple encounter. You may also do it by rule and governance. You may do it in a war. You may do it in a playground. It is all the same principle.

When I know who I am in freedom and in truth and I have aligned to it, I must give everybody else the freedom they have as well. And in this is love.

See the ones before you, whoever they may be, the ones that populate your world. See them as they are in your mind's eye, if you wish, and realize that each one you know is a brilliant and independent creation, and anything you've needed from them, desired of them at the cost of their own will, is now being released.

"Well, I want that one to love me," you may say. "I want her to know how I feel."

You may tell her how you feel. You may hope for the best. But you are not demanding that she attend to you in a creation or a lie. You may know her as she is, and love her as she is, and know that she is free as well.

When you see the one you never want to see—"He is the one who took my money, she is the one who took my husband, she is the one who hurt my child"—you must know them as well in their authority as a Divine Being.

When someone is operating out of alignment, they may do harm, or what you would call harm, but it is not done by the Divine Self. It is done by the one who has forgotten her true nature. And anyone who has designs upon another at the cost of their own will is in the act of forgetting.

We will continue with this later. We will use this in the text if we wish. We thank you each for your presence. You may take a few moments to yourselves. We will return shortly. Thank you for your presence. Good night. Stop now, please.

Day Eleven

Now the thing you don't know about what we do with you is we bypass your resistance by knowing what you are. At the level of truth that we teach, what you have created in fear does not exist. Do you understand this, friends? The small things you attach to, the embellishments by the small self, the creations made in fear, the agreements made in worry are bypassed because they do not exist at the level we teach.

Now if you can really understand this, you will comprehend the vast teaching you are in fact receiving. At the level of the causal self, the Divine Self as you, the True Self as you, there is nothing else but the Divine Self and her requirements.

This does not mean that the small self is banished, no more than the sunlight impressing itself on the dew makes the dew disappear. The dew is transformed and assumed by the sun and comes in another form.

You understand ascension in a wrong way. The belief that you align to the Christed Self and walk around upon a cloud is not a true teaching. The body you hold is in fact the vehicle of your expression as the Christ, and the moment you realize that the physical form can also be attuned to its true nature, which simply means in expression of the Divine and not apart from it, the claim is made by you, "I am here in truth." And "truth," we say, will mean in your full manifestation.

Now what does it mean to be in full manifestation? You don't have to pay your bills? You don't have a wife anymore?

Again, that would be preposterous. The man you know and have known as you is present as you at a different level of vibration where the things that were claimed in lower vibration do not exist. And we say "do not exist" intentionally.

Now he is confused by this. "So I made a mistake when I was in low vibration. That mistake doesn't exist in the high vibration you speak to?"

Actually, yes, but in a different way than you understand. You are actually accountable to all of your creations. Anything that was made by you is yours to claim or reclaim in a higher octave. As you align to the Divine as you, what was claimed by you in lower nature is lifted with you. You can attend to it, you see, in the higher way as the Divine Self and not at the level of fear that it was initially created as.

What happens now, as we attune you in the vibration of truth—not to but *in* the vibration of truth—all claims made, contracts made, agreements made to stay small, or to adhere to the violence against the self that you have all known, will be released because they do not exist in the higher vibration.

Now the testament to this in some ways will be your experience here in this place, in this teaching, in the lives that you live here and elsewhere, because what you have manifested surrounds you. The clothes you wear, the relationships you hold were all claimed by you at different levels of vibration.

But as you are in truth, in the vibration of, in the current of, in the claim of "I am in truth," what was claimed by you prior to this will be known in truth. And the moment you know anything in truth, you can claim it in its true way.

Now what you are, the Divine as you, is always in truth. The Divine does not hold a lie. So Paul has been asking, "Why truth? Why not love? Why not joy? Aren't these frequencies we can be in attendance to?" And you will be, yes, as we continue our teachings.

Now the current of truth in all ways claims a path for you because what you see is not in illusion. Do you understand this? And who you see is as they truly are as what they are, the manifested Divine. We are working with the vibration of truth and the sword of truth, if you wish to say it, to reclaim all things in their proper way, their true way, so you may know yourself in their accord.

The consummate relationship you have as the Divine Self is in love, but you cannot be in love when you are in a lie. Do you understand this? It is required to acclimate as truth to move beyond the realm of illusion that you have impressed upon the landscape you inhabit.

Now when Paul goes to the idea of truth, he sees a fiery God wreaking havoc on all of this world. That is not what happens in the least. The Divine Self is in truth, can only be in truth, and consequently can only claim in accordance with this. Nothing else is possible.

Truth, we will say, is a quality of, an expression of, an alignment in God. Period. You cannot have God and have a lie. You have God in truth. The quality of love, the expression of the Divine as and through you, is as present in truth as anywhere else. But to entice the self to move to love when the small self is still intent on creating a world that has been agreed to in lies must require you to claim truth to light the way.

Now the teaching you are receiving is an imperative teaching, and by this we mean you cannot attend to the idea of enlightenment without truth. "The truth will set you free" has been said, but you don't want to know truth because you have a belief still in what you have invested in as the small self and what your world tells you should be known to you as truthful that is not.

We will give you an example. The belief that somebody else should have authority over you is ridiculous. It's a ridiculous presumption. You may have an agreement to be in accord with someone who directs you, but they cannot wield power unless you give it to them. But you invest in this, which is a false structure, every day of the week when you pay the toll on the highway or do what you are taught. "I am doing as I was told."

We do not tell you not to do as you are told. We need you to know that you are doing it. If you know you're doing it, you are in your power and your own authority. Do you understand this?

But you acquiesce all day long to the cultural dictates of what it means to be a man or a woman or this or that, and you attend to yourselves at the cost of truth because you do not see that you are expressing in form that has been embedded in lies.

"Oh, I am too old to be married," says the one who will stay single. You understand this, yes? Because somebody once said you are too old, and she agreed, and here she sits, "Oh, woe is me, this is what I have become."

Now what we would like you to know is that the treatise we are giving you is part of a larger teaching, *The Book of Truth*, and the teaching you are receiving now is part of a chapter that was begun yesterday with different students present. But you are being trained to understand the language that we use outside of the convenience of the known.

Now "the convenience of the known" simply means "this is what that meant yesterday, it must mean that today." And when we speak to truth, we actually bypass your need to codify your experience as what it was, to realign you and all you have claimed and created to truth.

Now when we see you, when we hold you in witness, we bear witness to truth and not what you would like. And those of you who have an investment in being seen the way you think you should will have a very difficult time with where we wish to take you all because what will not be affirmed by us, not to you, the students of this work, is the construct of personality that was born in agreement to fear. We will not go there with you. It serves you no good, and to enable you to continue in self-pity or self-righteousness would mean we are party to a lie, and we will not be. We know what you are. You can call yourselves what you like.

Now what you are as the Divine will be known by you in your experience. Underline the word *experience*. It's imperative that you understand this. "In your experience" means in how you know yourself and the world you inhabit. This is not theoretical. We will teach you to see yourselves as you are, but you will not do this when you are claiming treason against the True Self.

"Claiming treason?" he asks. "What could that mean?"

It means to lie to yourself about your true nature. "I am no good. I am the best." Both are lies. *You are.* You are as you are as the True Self, and as we have said many times, the Divine Self does not have a damned thing to prove. She knows who she is, she knows who you are, she knows who all are because she exists without the requirement of a frame that would solve her problems by telling her what she is in a convenient way.

Now what we will talk about today and continue to teach you is the disassembling of formal structure. Formal structure means structure that was intended to claim you in a small inheritance. And as you align to truth, you will withstand your true nature while the things around you start to fall. And we use that example intentionally.

If you can imagine an oak tree that moves through the ground and spreads its branches, it knows what it is. It is expressing its truth, its true nature. It cannot express anything else. And you are the same. But the structures surrounding the oak tree that were built in flimsy ways will be moved by the strength of the tree moving itself into its full bloom. Do you understand this?

So what is not convenient here, and will not be for some time, is that the life that you live will be in an encounter with lies. And we will tell you what this means.

The truth of what you are cannot coexist at the level of a lie. You have shifted dimensions, if you wish. But the manifestations of the world you live in that were claimed in the lower self, individually and collectively, must now be addressed by the one who knows who he is, which simply means that your very presence upon this plane will be the antidote for the lies that were claimed by you and others prior to this level of attunement because it can't be any other way.

Here is a simple example. You become a lantern, a blazing lantern. Wherever you go, you illuminate the darkness, wherever you stand and a lie is present, because you cannot be in accord to it. At the level of vibration that you hold the lie ceases to exist. Do you understand this?

Now the manifestation of you at this level of causation requires an amplitude of the physical body to be able to hold the vibration. This cannot be done without a form, and for one reason only. Because you stand in form and are known in form as the truth of what you are, you can only claim in like vibration that which is in form as well. What you see, you are in agreement to, and what you are in agreement to is truth.

This is not theoretical, it is alchemy. Seeing as you, as the Divine Self, can only transform the witness and what is witnessed in the same accord. Now here we go:

> "On this day I choose to know what I am as truth. And as I say these words, I give permission to the body I hold to be made manifest in accordance with this name. I am in truth. I am in the current of truth. And all I see is in agreement to truth. I know who I am. I know what I am. I know how I serve. I am here in truth. I am here as truth. In truth I have my being."

Period.

Now as you do this, you have an agreement made to withstand change, to withstand the currents of fashion, the decisions made by others of what you should have been or should be today, because if it is not in truth, it will not align you. Nobody can tell you what you are, because you are the expression of it. And as the expression of it, you claim all things into its alignment by the beacon of truth that you are.

He is interrupting with a question. "So you say our bodies need to be transformed to hold this frequency?"

Yes, we did say that. And we will attend to that as we continue. But there is a reason for this. As you hold the vibration and are the conduit for it, you have to align to it. You cannot hold and keep what you cannot accept. And the aspects of the self that are in lower dimension must be lifted to be able to attend to the field that you are being held by.

Understand those words. "The field that you are being held by." You are not the field, you are of the field. Do not mistake yourself for a moment to be truth without identity, and the identity of truth is the Divine Self and not the small self. When you are in the field of truth, you have aligned to God as the characteristic of truth that it exists at, at a certain octave. Love does the same thing. Joy does the same thing. They are ways of being expressed as the Divine because they are aspects of the Divine.

But as we are beginning with truth so that you may light the way and not be deceived by the requirements of the small self, or a world that would like to tell you what you are, you can claim love and joy as you follow your truth.

And your truth, we promise you, the truth of what you are, will set you free. Period. Period. Period.

Day Eleven (Cont.)

Now what you don't know is that it is done in a second, in a millisecond. What you don't know is that the transformation as the Divine Self does not invest in the kind of process you have become acclimated to. "It will take three years, it will take ten years, or ten lifetimes, to know what I am." The agreement we are making with you, we your teachers, we the authors of the text, is that the transformation we speak to is made known by you as you stand before us.

Now the act of witnessing anything informs what is seen by the consciousness that sees. And as we see you and we claim you as what you are, we announce you to the world, "You are here." The announcement is made to the small self, and the Divine as well. And because we hold you in authority, in our authority, we have the right, with your agreement, to support you in alignment to truth in a way that is a permanent shift in the structure that you've known yourself as.

Now he is getting concerned already. "Please do not make promises."

What a promise is, is an affirmation of what can be.

What we are telling you is an affirmation of what is in truth. *What is in truth.*

The claims that you have made with us so far—"I know who I am in truth, I know what I am in truth, I know how I serve in truth"—have supported you, yes, in a reclamation of what you are as a vehicle, an expression, a holder of truth. But the idea that you hold that this should take one hundred years is actually an agreement in what the small self thinks.

Now Paul has a good question. We will answer it. "If you know yourself in truth, but you go back and forth, what does that mean?"

Well, we will tell you what it means. It means you have not held the vibration that is present as you, but that does not deny the vibration. Paul is seeing the image of a radio moving in and out of broadcast. He turns the dial with his hand. "Let me feel the good one, let me play the music I like." Until the vehicle itself, which you can call the radio, has acclimated to the vibration, the engagement with a frequency as what it plays all the time will only be limited by your fear or agreement to what was playing on the other stations prior to hearing the new. And this is the back and forth you speak to.

But does it happen in an instant? Yes, in an instant. The vibration of truth as you, as you have aligned to it and as it is expressed by you, is on in frequency. And the expression of it by you, as you may hold it, happens in an instant as well. What does not happen in an instant is your awareness of it. And this we must explain to you.

The creations you see, the agreements made, the authority given to others to be your deciders are still impressed by you in the old consciousness in which they were initially created. So what you agreed to in the past and expect to see again reclaims you in an engagement to them. What we say now is that the what that you are, in acclimation and agreement in truth, is what transforms this.

What does not transform it is lowering your vibration and seeking to attend to these things at the level that they were created at. This is how you change the dial to the old broadcast. "Now, this is how you fix a car," and you go to the way you fix a car because it is the known way. Well, that may be so. "This is how you fix a relationship," and you go back to what you've known to remedy a situation that was made in conflict or in lower nature.

As we have said many times, we do not fix things. We make them new. We reclaim them as what they truly are. And the vibration of truth may be witnessed, claimed, and with any creation that was made in lower form.

So what we are telling you is that you've made something in low frequency. You now stand up on the mountain. What you do not do is trek back down the mountainside to the low vibration that the thing was initially claimed at and try to fix it there. You lift it to where you stand on the mountainside and you perceive it in truth. This is the remedy for the dance of up and down.

Now when we claim you in truth, we do it in a loving way, so you must understand that this teaching is not to make you wrong. And the creations you've made and must now attend to that were claimed in fear will be lifting to you in order to be witnessed, which simply means it makes itself present in your consciousness, because if it's in your consciousness, it's in your field. And there you go. What an opportunity to claim the truth in the prick by the thorn that makes itself known on your side.

Here we go, dears. We say these words for each of you in the knowing that it is so. As you stand before us, you the readers of the text, you the student of the work, you will be lifted to us commensurate to your ability to hold the frequency we give you and at the level you can receive us. And we honor the level that you stand at. You will be loved in a truthful way. "In a truthful way" means we are not telling you to be anything other than what you already are. We do not demand change because we claim you, the Infinite Self, in accord with our vibration. And those aspects of you that are out of alignment will be known, will be seen, will be witnessed in consciousness so that you can reclaim them as the one who knows who he is.

"How is this done?" he asks.

If you would imagine for a moment that wherever you stand, wherever you may be, is the perfect place for your new agreement, you will comprehend that you are where you need to be to receive this claim. And the claim we make for each of you is the lifting of your field to the imprinting of truth that is your true nature in an alignment.

Paul is in a questioning mode. "Is this for the text?"

In fact, it is, and we are teaching our students all over and throughout time with this benediction. Those of you in witness in form are actually witnessing a multidimensional occurrence, because we are speaking to those who are hearing these words one hundred years from now, and knowing it in their being as you are knowing it as well. And the aspect of you who is present here in form or reading or hearing these words is attending to those who will follow you by the very nature of your being.

The gift you each give is your own claim of truth, is the succession of all who will follow in your wake. You see, my dears, you have come to be sung, and the song that you sing is the song of the Christ in incarnate form as you, as all you meet, may never meet in form, but will know in truth. We know who you are in truth. We know what you are in truth. We know how you serve in truth.

We would like you all to be lifted as one. We are here. We are here. We are here. Lift, please, with us, if you would. We are hearing you in all ways, the what that you are in sound and song. You will say this after us, if you wish.

> "I know who I am in truth. I know what I am in truth. I know how I serve in truth. I am here. I am here. I am here. And in this agreement to be, I allow those who will follow to be illumined by my name. I know who I am. I am here."

Thank you each for your presence. We will take a pause for Paul. Thank you each.

•　　•　　•

We would like to continue with a little lesson in sovereignty. And by the very nature of what you are, you are sovereign and cannot be other. By this we mean any belief that any of you hold that you do not have free will must be attended to once and for all. And by this we mean that the agreements that you have made to be taken over by another are still agreements, whether or not they may be perceived as such.

Now the gift of this teaching is to release you from obligations made in fear. "If I don't do what they say, I will be put away. If I do as I wish, I will not be known."

The claim that we make for you—that in your being

and your knowing what you are, the choices that you are gifted with will be in appropriate agreement to your knowing of your sovereignty—will allow you to know yourself as free regardless of how circumstances are perceived.

"What does this mean?" he asks.

It means something very simple. The temptation to blame another, to use your own will to override the will of another, to paint a picture of your world that excludes the Divine in anyone or anything will be understood in choice.

The claim that you make—"I know who I am in truth"—makes you accountable to every choice you've ever made throughout time. And this is the biggest gift of the day. The vibration of truth transcends time. Because it is an aspect of God, it is not limited by the watch on your wrist or the calendar date that you ascribe to it. The claim "I know who I am in truth" dismantles, not only the structures that are apparent today, but the agreements you made to these structures throughout time.

Now many of you here who know our work, who read the text, have been around a long time and perceive yourself as sovereign, perhaps, in the life that you live. But what you do not know is that many of you participated in the creation of the very structures that are now being dismantled. Do you understand this?

The building of a church and a religion, the building of a habit that may have been known through thousands of years, is a group, collective, creation and it was made by someone once upon a time. Don't think for a moment that you are the one who's inherited this without participation to it. This is very good news because the claim of truth actually releases you from the names that you have given things that are out of accord with truth throughout time.

Once the relationship is released—"I am the one who burned the witch or was burned at the stake, I am the one that began the church or warred against the church, I am the one that decided that prayer should be this or that that was a heretical prayer"—will be released because the new name, "I know who I am in truth," reclaims the aspects of you that bore these things, claimed relationship to them or in your participation with them throughout time.

It is an understanding, you see, for all of you, that the vibration of the Divine exists without form but is imbued in form and may be known in form as well. The idea of the eternal now, the ever-present present, is also true. You can only attend to the present in the moment you stand in.

But what you think of as the past, even yesterday's past, is also a collective agreement to operate in time. Do you understand this, dears? Your perception of time is a collective agreement to know what time is.

If God is all things, God can be time, but it can also be no time, because time does not exist in the eternal now. The invocation "I know who I am in truth" is an eternal claim. It claims you as you were, as you are, and as you can only be, because the Infinite Self, the one who expresses in truth, is not calendar or time based. You are not your Divine Self on Tuesday or in this lifetime. You are always the Divine Self because that is all you can ever be. And the aspect of you that was always this, because this is what he could always be, can only always be, is the one who is being reclaimed by you outside of time.

When we continue this teaching, we will speak to time in more authentic ways so you may comprehend the limitations that you have known yourselves through that are not in truth. Period. Period. Period.

We will end this session for the text now. We will continue when we can. You may take a pause, Paul. Period. Period. Period.

Day Twelve

Now what we think is that what we are is the True Self, and when you can get to the place where you have bypassed the systems of control that would tell you otherwise, your reality will affirm this. But what you think is what you are in your experience and expression. We are using the word *think* intentionally so that you may understand the difference between thinking and knowing.

The Divine Self as you, the one who knows, does not engage in process as the small self does. At the top of the text, we described this book as an oracle, something that may be understood, or a way to know. The accessing of the True Self as a way of knowing must be understood by you now so that you may attend to the information that is already present within you.

What you don't understand yet is that everything you see, absolutely everything, is identified by you based on prescription. And the unprescribing that we have been attending to in this section on deconstruction is about the replacing of the old system with the knowing that is born in the True Self.

Now the catalyzation of this, what propels you forward in this expression, is truth. Understand this, dears. Truth is the catalyst. If you can imagine a system that has been running poorly, the clogs in the mechanisms slow it down or push energy in the wrong directions, you will begin to understand that the claiming in truth that we are offering you will actually shift you and clear you so that the knowing that you have may become present where thinking was paramount.

There is a vast difference, you see, between planning a vacation and being on vacation. There is also a difference between planning a vacation and going on vacation. The planning that you do—"we will go here or there, see this or that"—is done in thinking. When you know where you are going, you are gone. You have done it. The mechanism that propels you forward does not require the analyzation that you have done or utilized to decide things.

Now Paul is asking, "But there is nothing wrong with analysis. We do it all day long. 'I see this; this needs to happen there.' And we go into what we know to support the change that is needed."

That is actually true, but what we are actually saying to you is that the mechanism that you are is rather rusty and cruddy with yesterday's memories or prescriptions of what should be.

Now the claim "I am in my knowing," which we have offered you before, is testament to what you can know outside of the small self's definitions of what should be. The one who knows is always in response to her truthful self, the Divine Self, the aspect of her that may operate as truth.

Now what we wish for you in this disassemblance of form and structure are that the things and ways you have known or decided, things in thinking or presupposition, may now be attended to so that you can reclaim yourself as the one who knows in truth.

We will ask you each to make a decision now. Decide one human being in your life stands before you, anyone in your life, a friend or a parent, a coworker, perhaps, and you see them as you see them. You decide who they are based on your prior experience. "Oh, she is wearing the sweater I bought for her. Oh, he is looking angry again. When he looks angry, he will do such and such." You are prescribing behavior or an outcome or assigning history based on what you've known about them.

Now would you look at this person again and make a new decision? "Everything I know about this person is wrong, is my idea of who he or she is, and I have been projecting an identity upon them based on my prescriptions—perhaps through my experience, yes, but I am knowing them through the intellectual self who has history or ideas about who someone is." This is the second step. To realize that you may not know is a precursor to knowing.

Now the third step, as we would like to say, is realization. You realize that the one you see has knowing of her own and a way of operating in the world that will support you each in a higher way. The listening you do with your ears and the decisions you make with your mind have been invested in prior knowing or experience.

When you realize someone in a new way, you have uninvested yourself in what you have known thus far. What this will do is give you an opportunity to be present for them outside of the form and structure that you have utilized to navigate the relationship up until now.

The claim you make for the one you see—"I know who you are in truth, I know what you are in truth, I know how you serve in truth"—in fact disassembles them from what they are holding, the constructs of behavior, the identity that you've used and they have agreed to, to be in consort with you at a certain level of agreement. You are bypassing the contracts or exchanges of identity born in history to see them as they truly are.

Now Paul has a question. "In the past you have done this, and you've taken them outside of form to vibration. Is this what you are doing now?"

When we do this, we will do this. We are teaching you something now about how you intend others to be in prescription. And how you prescribe to another is simply symptomatic of how you prescribe to your whole world. If you can do it with your mother, you can do it with yourself, you can do it with community you attend to, you can do it with your life. The claim you are making for another, to see her outside of form, which simply means outside of prescription, aligns them to what they truly are.

Now we will ask you each, you who attend to these words, to imagine that one before you as if she was never born, had never come in the form she is in, had never been invested in a physical self, but is just vibration. What you are doing here is disassembling form or the requirement of the form to be the rendering of the construct of frequency that they express as. If they have no body, are they still themselves, or have you mistaken them through the flesh to resemble what you think they are based on prior intention? If they don't have the body, are they still in love, in the frequency of love that I have placed them in? Are they still beautiful or ugly or old or young? In fact they are not. They just are as they are in the vibration of truth.

Now what we would like you to do is witness that energy before you and make this claim for them. "I know who you are. I know what you are. I know how you serve." And as this claim is made for them, what you are agreeing to is their Divinity in place of all other things—the relationship you've had with them, how you have prescribed their behavior or intended it to be, how you've known the body or the sex or the age, how you've known the energy in a certain way, now you witness in truth.

Now if you were to go back in reverse and now replace the form and replace the ideas you've had or how you prescribed this person to be, at least it will still be informed by the essence of what they are.

The claim we are making for you each is actually done in this way. What we just gifted you with is the act of witness that you may hold for another. You will not witness them in truth as you prescribe what they have been to you, because all you will be doing then is reaffirming what you have known or believed to be true in your thinking. Do you understand this, yes?

Now what we would like you to know is that none of

this makes you wrong. The vibration that you hold has taken a form—you like to wear your hair this way or that, you like people to see you in certain ways. You are completely complicit to this thing, the idea of thinking and perception and how and what you see based on intention to be known in the way that you wish.

When we take you on the journey we intend, we bring all aspects of you. "All aspects of you" means even the habits you wish you could shake, even the ideas you hold that are not in alignment to truth, and we will also say even the interest you give to the darkness that you may hold within you. We bring it all up to the altar so that it may be known in truth.

When you bring others to their truth, you are not trying to change them. Understand this, friends. This has never been about behaving well, nor will it ever be. The transition that you are making as truth—"I know who I am in truth"—is in the quality and being as the one who knows. We will emphasize again, knowing and thinking are not the same thing. When you know the one before you, you are investing in truth. When you think about another, you are investing in your own prescription of what you think they are. Do you understand the difference here?

Until you understand the difference—"I know who you are," which doesn't mean "I think I know who you are," which is just your idea of them—but until you understand

"I know who you are," you are playing the game of idealization. This is not idealization. This is not looking at the sick person and seeing them well because you wish them well. This is seeing the Divinity and the inherent worth that can only be born outside of the ideas about another that you may be investing in or they may be investing in for themselves.

Your ideas of who people are, are always false. Do you understand this? They are just your ideas and they are prescriptions you hold based on your history.

"Is it possible," Paul asks, "to know another, to truly know another outside of the limitations we've given them, outside of the idealizations we hold for them, outside of the rules we prescribe to about what a man is, or a woman is, who she is supposed to be or who he was?"

It is more than possible. It is true. And once again, friends, when you know who you are in truth—not having the idea, but knowing—when you know who you are in truth, you have the privilege, the deep privilege, of knowing another. Do you comprehend this, yes?

So we are desystematizing you now to comprehend that what you think of another is your idea, but what you know about another is truth. And as you begin to operate in truth, you begin to know many things. You no longer rely on the systems of information that you have utilized to navigate your reality. The compass that you are has a new focus—not idealization, but truth; not desire, but truth; not fear, but truth. And as truth is your compass, you will be directed by it well.

He asks for an example. "What does it mean to have a compass in truth?"

It means you know. You are actively knowing, in your bones, in your being. The what that you are is in resonance to truth, and even though it may feel preposterous as the small self, to the True Self who knows it will be the gift that allows you to move or to claim or to choose wisely. The claim "I am in my knowing" aligns you to your knowing. We have said this prior, but the embarkation of a journey in truth requires you to begin to trust that truth is the compass that leads you to the new world, the higher world.

The way that you may know if you are engaging in this is to work with it. Go into alignment first. "I know who I am in truth. I know what I am in truth. I know how I serve in truth. I am here. I am here. I am here." And then ask the questions you need. Do you understand this?

There will come a time, dears, when you don't even have to ask the questions. You will just know. But as you are teaching this to yourselves, a new way of being in the world, the reliance upon the truth of what you are to give you the information that you require will be a gift that will give you sovereignty. This means you don't have to ask your friends what you should do every day. You don't have to sit on your duff and complain that you don't know. You will have the opportunity to know what you are, and to know what you require as the True Self, as the one who can benefit from the information.

We will say this. This will be in the text, yes. Paul is anxious about the transmission and only for one reason. It is a new teaching and he is efforting his hearing. Our intention is to override him, and we are doing so successfully and we are quite happy about it.

So we thank you each for your attentiveness to the lesson and we will continue soon. Thank you each for your presence. You may take a pause. Period. Period. Period.

(Pause)

We would like to start again with an issuance of vibration for all who attend to these words. The teaching you are receiving is happening on multiple levels.

The idealization of others, or what you prescribe for them, or how you intend them to be as the small self, is always in denial of their inherent truth. When you begin to operate as truth, you no longer prescribe as the small self, but you do realize them outside of what they may have claimed for themselves. You must understand, dears, that when you decide for another, you are always deciding from your perspective about what you think things should be.

The Divine Self knows and does not prescribe. What she witnesses is the realization of the Divine in the one that she sees, and this claim for another supports them in realizing what they are at a higher level.

Now when this is done, first in intent—"I know who you are in truth"—the intent itself catalyzes the system you hold to support the one before you in her new realization. As you claim yourself in truth, the what that you are, the manifested self then does the work, so there is no effort. Do you understand this?

You are learning a new language and you are practicing it with those before you, but as you become fluent in the new language, it is simply your expression. You are no longer deciding for others. You are knowing them, because it's all that is.

The effort that you work with here in the new teaching has been systematized for you so you may operate with a new understanding. The equivalent would be, "I am learning the language of the country that I have always existed in, but just didn't know it. And as I know it, I am fluent in my new home."

The catalyzation of your being, "I know who I am in truth, what I am in truth," is what allows you to know another. The idea of knowing must be understood some more for you to be able to attend to it. Many of you think know-ing means the known, what has been known. "I know the good place to shop, I know how I look in the blue suit, I know what kind of girls I prefer" is always resting on what you've known and not what is.

When you really understand this work, you don't know where to go to the store just because you were there, and you may not like those girls anymore because what you thought you liked was inherited information that you put value upon.

Here is the new claim: "Every aspect in my life will be reknown by the True Self."

"Reknown" means known anew, and known with the authority of the Divine Self, who will prescribe and claim only in truth.

Now Paul doesn't like the teaching. "Well this is all well and good, but it feels like a fantasy. How will we change this much?"

This is alchemy, dear. This is not self-help. Do you hear these words? "Alchemy" means transformation, "self-help" means you tie your shoelaces differently and you wear a bet-ter cologne. Do you understand the difference between transformation and cosmetic change? We are not redecorat-ing your house so you are more comfortable. You are living in a new damn house. The True Self in its expression is the house you live in, and your attachments to what's been on the walls, or in the cupboards, or hidden in the closets, is what we are disassembling along with everything else.

Now is disassembling fun? Why does it need to be fun? But it is an adventure to realize how much you've invested in what you were taught by others, by what was claimed for you by your families or your countries or the scholars who came before you who taught you what morality was and has now been translated to law.

The equivalency of being in a new self without the inheritance that you had claimed in fear or in habit is a grand adventure. "What does the adventure look like? How do we know this practically?" That's a good question and we will answer.

Each day you leave your home, you are going to begin to realize that you are not what you think, and you are not what you thought, and consequently how you see the world will be new, because the new eyes you hold do not prescribe meaning to what has been there. Do you understand this?

Yes, it says "post office box." You may put the letter there, but you will understand what it is in a new way, a construct that was placed there by convenience for the workers to collect the mail. It has held a million letters, payments made, grievance notices, birthday cards. It has been the receptacle of thought for all who came before you, and one day it will not be there.

The thing you pass on the way to work every day one day will not be there. It's a transient form. It has been known as one thing. One day the metals that comprise the box will be flattened by something, melted by something. It will be something else. And each one you pass on the street, who was once born, was once never born. They are articulating themselves in the beings they stand in by announcing who they are. "I am the woman late for work, the man playing with the child, the one who looks so sad, the one who is in joy." And as you see each one this way, you will see what they have prescribed themselves as.

And here is the gift. Once you realize that they are eternal beings having an experience in form, you will understand what it means to see God in each one you pass, because that is who you see. You see the Divine in form because you know what you are and you know who they are as well.

Now this will be an experience, yes, but it is only the first step toward alignment to the Divine as you. The one who knows who she is, and knows who others are as well, is the one who claims truth in the face of lies for others. That woman who looks so sad, who is invested in sadness, will be known by you as an aspect of the Divine.

When you see her in her truth, you are not making her happy, attempting to change her way. That would be the ego self-prescribing what she should be to conform to your idea of a happy lady walking in the morning. Who says she should be happy? That is not your business. Here is what you know: She is a piece of God, and in that truth, the auric field she holds will be remembered as what she is by nature of your witness. You are not prescribing anything other than what is already true, and as this is realized by her in the higher levels of knowing that you are always in engagement with, the field that she holds will say, "Thank you," and you will feel this each time you do it.

As you witness one in truth without their knowing, you will be welcomed by them. The physical self may not be in response, but the wink of the eye that the field itself holds will come as an acknowledgment that they have been met and seen. Once this occurs, you have supported someone else in realignment by nature of your witness.

Now the teaching of witnessing has been ongoing with us, and for a very good reason. To be in witness means to be in relation with what is perceived. You are doing this consciously still. "I am making up my mind. I am knowing what I am. I am making a choice." You are still operating as a small self in some ways, learning the new language of truth. What comes eventually is that there is no effort because it is known. And here we use the word *know* in a new way. "I know who you are because you can only be. I know what you are because you can only be here. I know how you serve because you are expressing."

You don't need the language to affirm this is so. It's how you resonate, and the perception you hold has moved beyond acclimation to coherence. In coherence with the True Self as the True Self, the effort that you've used to decide who and what you are is gone. The effort is gone because you are not what you were.

The lightning rod, you see, that you have always been has been struck, and you are in emanation as the Source that has struck you and embodied as you. This is not a fabrication, this is truth. It is what the Christ is, what the Christ teaching always was, the realization of the Divine. This will be done by you as you know what you are.

Now there are pitfalls here, and we must address them quickly. Some of you would assume that this means you are special or have a privilege, and this is never true. The moment you believe that to be so, you set yourself apart from your Source and you move into sorcery, the navigation of the elements to control others. This is not a high way to work.

Now sorcery itself, as we are describing it, involves conjuring and deciding for others or overriding the will of another. And any teaching of truth will speak to the harsh penalties that are paid by the one who endeavors to use this work to hold sway over another. The work we teach you cannot be misused because of its Source and the intent behind it. But you may use anything you like to try to get your way.

The challenge here, for some of you, is you believe you

must be special to be worthy of this. "You see, I found this work. I will be seen as special. You see, I can do this. I must show the world."

The truth shines brightly without explanation. The truth does not seek to explain itself, just as God does not need to, because it is. In fact, everything you see right now, the hair on everybody's head, the windows, and the sky beyond, is only God. When you understand that, the idea that you could be special becomes silly.

Now what is not silly is that you are unique, and that you have unique ways of expressing your truth. But to vilify another is not truth. To place yourself above another is not truth. Or to conjure for show is not truth. When we show you what we are through the man before you, we do so in order to teach you. When he prepares himself for this work, the only preparation is to recede and allow the truth to come through. He does not comb his hair or hope you like him. He cannot do the work as us when he prescribes the outcome or the effect as his small self.

You are the same. As the vessel of the Divine in your unique expression, you will be known and sung. And to be sung means to be used in alliance with your truth. And the song that you sing is the glorious song of the Divine Self. It is a humble song as well, but you don't understand humility yet. To be humble is not to scrape and crawl. It is not to hide your true light. It is to be in celebration and in wonder and in a knowing that you are of the great Source—not specifically you as the small self, but you are of the greatness that has made all things so.

The True Self, you see, bears witness in love, and love and selfishness do not coexist. Love and the seeking of a claim do not coexist. Love and fear have never existed together. But the truth of what you are in her claim "I am here" is a wondrous song that will be heard. And the echo of your song, as your presence is known by all those you encounter, will be a gift to the world.

We will end this teaching in a few moments, but we will take a question, and we will ask you to speak loudly, on the teaching itself. Is there a question, please?

Q: I was going to ask about sorcery. How is that possible that someone can impose their will upon another without them allowing it?

A: You do it all day long. "He will like me the way I want him to" is an intent. When you bring energy to it and claim them outside of free will, your intention is to manipulate. Now this is not a treatise in sorcery. When we use the term, our intent is a very simple one. Do not use this work to manipulate or to gain. It will not work. What is true will be known to you in your acceptance of it. Some people believe that they have no power of their own, so they claim it over another as a way to receive interest on the investment in their own energy field. You do not do this at this level because this is a teaching of truth. Period. Period. Period. Is there another question, please, on the teaching?

Q: What can the Guides do to support us in releasing false humility to support us in this transition?

A: We would like to say this. The claim "I am in truth" will do it for you because the other is not true. Do you understand this? "I am the best dancer here" may be true. You can celebrate being a wonderful dancer. Please put on a show. We would all like to applaud you and enjoy the gift you have been given as the one who may dance. That is not prideful. But the moment a better dancer comes into the room and you want to sock him in the nose, you have lost your joy. You are seeking a claim. You are frightened of being overshadowed by one who has a greater gift, and you have lost the humility of the one who has been gifted and is sharing the gift. When you have a gift, it is yours to share. That's why it was given to you. If you bake all the cookies and you eat them for yourself, you will grow large and nobody will know what a wonderful cook you truly are. Period. Period. Period.

Q: With this teaching is it the small self that we really have to realign or change to the new because the higher self already knows it?

A: Not really. In fact, the claim of truth on an alchemical level realigns you, so you are not doing the work. Do you understand the difference here? You are so invested in doing the work that you can't comprehend that the alignment itself is the alchemy, and the processing of the integration is what you are really speaking to. The alignment is done, but you live in a world where you envision things through prescription, through what you were taught them to be. As the Divine Self, the opportunity then is to see anew, but the small self still is present seeking to impose will or vision upon what has been in order to replicate the known. This is what we have taught you already. The seeking to replicate the known is the challenge. Because you had eggs yesterday, you expect to have them tomorrow. If tomorrow there are no eggs, you are frightened. "What happened to my meal? I expect to have what I have had."

Now the Divine Self knows who she is without the habituation that the small self has utilized to know herself. Do you understand this, yes? So the caution we have for you is always a return to the known in its comfort, in its false safety, because it's what you've had. In fact, when you embark on a great adventure, you only carry those things with you, you need, and you must be willing to release even those to receive what might be given to you. Your attachment to the known is always the challenge. But the Divine Self as you is your ally here. He is the truth of what you are. And as truth becomes your compass, you will in fact know. Period. Thank you for the question. One more, please.

Q: Does my body function as my compass of truth and how can I learn to use my body to differentiate between truth and comfort?

A: Very, very easily. Am I in habit? Am I doing this unconsciously? Is this what I was taught to do? Am I choosing this of my own free will? If it is being chosen by you, you have a comprehension. If you are acting upon habit, you are not. Period. Period. Period.

Q: Does the body become a compass?

A: Not necessarily, because people have different ways of responding to vibration. Some of you know in your mind, some in your heart, some in your skin, some in your belly. The activation of the Divine Self will actually support you in being in response in different ways than you have utilized thus far. The ability to listen to the True Self as we teach will come in knowing. When you know, there is no question. The small self thinks, the Divine Self knows. When you think, there is always a question attached. When you know, there is no question. Period. Period. Period.

Q: *I'm having a little trouble understanding how to be in the True Self and operating outside of the known and also continuing to do the job and the functions that my smaller self needs to do every day.*

A: Very good question. Who shows up for work? That's the only question here. You are still thinking that the Divine Self is not working, that she is off in the garden playing with the fairies. The Divine Self is at the computer and on the telephone as you. How do you show up? "I am here. I am here. I am here."

Now the challenge at work is prescribed behavior. "I am expected to wear a certain thing, or behave a certain way that is antithetical to how I feel. There is prescribed behavior, a time clock to attend to." Well as you attend to these things in truth, if they are not in truth for you, you must be willing to release them to the truth that is there. The adherence to the old, whether it be an employment or a marriage or anything else that would seek to bring you back to the old, only at the cost of the new, will then be attended to as part of the process we've described. But the one who shows up to work, or to the marriage, or to the school is still the Divine Self. She cannot be separate from you, so do not segregate her until office hours are over. We thank you for the good question.

We will take a pause. Stop now, please.

Chapter Five

REUNIFICATION
IN TRUTH[*]

Day Twelve (Cont.)

Now the only thing you don't understand yet about the vibration of truth is that it is a causal energy, an energy that impacts and transforms and transmutes that which it encounters. You have ideas about truth, still, from your childhood. "Do not tell a lie, tell the truth." And while these are moral codes and helpful ones, the vibration of truth that you are comprehending and being as is a transforming vibration that will align all that you see to its true nature.

Now we are being very careful here with our language to support Paul in the transmission of this text. And we are being supportive of you, as we are able, in the comprehension you have of concepts that perhaps were distorted throughout time.

---

[*] Recorded in workshops at the Esalen Institute.

If you imagine a wave overtaking a shore, you have an understanding of how one thing informs another. The shoreline may be shaped by the movement of the wave. The shoreline may be known in its relationship to the sea. There are identities born in this relationship.

The vibration of truth, we would like to say, operates as a wave that overtakes a shore. But the shore it overtakes is that which is perceived by the seer. This is only done through and as one who has aligned to the level of vibration as truth.

If you can imagine that the consciousness you hold becomes the wave, and the informing you do by directing sight or attention to anything is what causes the vibration to go where it's called. Now you are not doing this intentionally, no more than the wave intends to crash against the shoreline. The wave itself is propelled by force of what it is. The ocean and the tidal wave are one and the same, but the tidal wave itself may move from the sea and extend the sea or overtake the landscape it is encountering. And when the wave comes, it calls back with it to the sea all that is not in truth.

Now the metaphor we use of a tidal wave is a very accurate one. When a tidal wave attends to those things that it encounters, those things that are not moored safely—or, we would say, in truth—will be catalyzed and reclaimed by the sea, washed away, as Paul would say, but we would say reunited with the sea from which all things came.

So the release of things to truth is a very positive thing, but the challenge is as one in a tidal wave. "What do I keep? What do I attend to? How do I hold the house up in the face of all this change?"

There is no cataclysm here, but there is truth, and truth will unmake a lie or overtake a falsehood. It will reclaim one who in her ignorance is responding to a world in anger or fear and reclaim her as what she truly is. But the overtaking of the wave of truth and the one who is in it is a bit of a dance. We will explain this.

The one who has an investment in who she thinks she is, and all the frames she has claimed, will be attesting to the falsehood of those claims by her trying to keep them. Do you understand this? The wave will release the very things that need to be moved. What is never moved is that which is born in truth. And the dance, we say, is to try to maintain or stay afloat in the midst of a tidal change, a change of being, a change of being in an encounter with truth that has not come until now.

The claiming of truth by you for another is always a gift. Understand this, dears. The claiming of truth for another is always a gift. But what we are teaching now, that the one who perceives as truth has the impact of the wave we described on all she perceives, is a different way of understanding, comprehending the truth in encounter with a lie.

Now, the world you exist in is fraught with lies. And you

look around you, you see them for what they are some days, but many of them you love. You love the lies that serve the small self.

"Oh, look at the interest I made in the bank," but you say you hate the banks. "Oh, look at the man who says I'm so handsome," but you don't like superficial men. You understand this, yes? So you say to yourself, "I am not what I say I am." And the claim that you make, "I am in truth," which is the agreement to be as this, is what aligns you to the force or the wave of the vibration of truth and what it will impart, not only to your life, but to all you see.

Now if you can imagine a child who can only see truth because she does not know a lie, and you put that child upon a mountain, she would describe very accurately all that she sees. "I see a woman wearing a hat," the child would say, not a queen with a crown. She has not invested the crown in meaning. She knows an old lady with a hat, and that is her truth. She is bypassing rules and not reclaiming history, in her innocence.

You do not have the innocence. You know what a hat is, you know what a crown is, and that is why you unlearn here only to the extent that the vibration as truth that you have aligned to can be as you in expression. Then you are not the child on the hill, you are the master, the one who knows who she is and can claim a world in accordance with this.

"What is the effect?" Paul asks.

The effect is great transformation. If you can understand that the vibration of truth is here, but it is now being anchored here and carried by you and all you attend to, you will understand and comprehend that your very being imparts the tidal wave, and what you see is where the wave lands. You are not looking at something you don't like and saying, "Oh, bring the truth here, they sure need some truth." That is the small self.

The small child who witnesses from the mountaintop does not judge one man as good or another evil. She sees two men doing different things without the prescriptions of moral code and history. You will do something similar, but not so much by intention, but by witnessing. The act of witness as the True Self in alignment with truth as a vibrational force calls truth where it is seen. You are the vessel of it, not the director of it. Your attention itself is what claims it in truth, not your prescriptions for what it should be.

Now what happens when a world is touched in this vibration as truth is that the world must be seen in its truth. And all those things that were claimed in fear, even if you like them because they make you feel good about your small selves, will be washed to the great "I Am," the great sea, the sea of truth, the sea of God, where it may be reformed.

Now Paul is seeing an image he doesn't like. He has seen what happens in a flood. Things are carried away, there is great chaos, there is fear, there is death. "Is that what we are to look for?" he says.

No, not at all. If you can understand that truth itself is impartial, as is the sunlight which shines upon all, whoever they may be, you will realize that what is encountered by truth may be reshaped as the wave gently touches the shoreline, or may be left without what it thought it needed, or may be swept away itself to be reknown in light, in God itself, and be re-created in the higher octave.

Here we go again, friends. What you perceive to be transformation that is not attractive, does not appeal to your sense of what should be; you go into fear. But any time there is great change or upheaval, there is displacement. A garden cannot be tilled while the soil is covered in cement. Sometimes the cement must be broken in order for the flowers to bloom. But your attachment to the structures that have been born and created by others, and are moored in many ways in place by conscious and unconscious agreements, will not be immune to the transition that is here now and is ongoing.

The frequency of truth aligns all things in truth and it is a great gift. But do not be attached to the outcome. "I want this much truth. You can tell me I need a new hairdo, but don't tell me I'm old and ugly." Well that's not what would happen here. What would happen here is you would realize that "old and ugly" is someone else's poor idea and it is not in truth.

The beauty you see before you when you witness another in truth is beyond description. It relies on things beyond the five senses to give it meaning. You experience beauty as a whole being. You do not admire it as a cosmetic thing. You experience the beauty of the sunset, of the world, of the young man or woman, or old man, or dying man, or man in the gutter, because God is there, too. Do you understand this teaching?

The challenge for so many of you is you believe that an outcome that is not to your liking is punishment, and that has never been the case. "Oh, woe is me, we will be punished now for our attachments to false teachings." Leaving the teaching is a gift, not a punishment.

What faith is, is knowing, and knowing and realization are one and the same. And as you are realized, known as what you are in your truth, you become the vessel of great change.

"I see a new world before me. I see what was made in form being reclaimed in truth and aligned to the Source of all that is. And in this witnessing, I claim the song of love that all men may know what they are and love themselves and their fellows in the knowing of their truth. I say these words of my own free will. I am in change. I am changed as truth rises in me and resurrects all I witness in its name. I am here. I am here. I am here."

It has been done. It has been claimed. It has been named as you, you the student of this work, you who hears these words, who reads them on the page. We are here with you on this great journey.

We will take a pause. Stop now, please.

Day Thirteen

Now don't justify anything because you think you're supposed to. This includes your attitudes, your behavior, your history. When you justify, you defend, and the time of defending things must end now if we are to progress in this teaching.

The lineage you hold as human beings is a very distinct one. You have come into form for the distinct purpose of remembering what you are, and this has been going on since you first incarnated upon this plane.

Now what you truly are is of the earth and not of the earth. And this has been the dilemma since the beginning of time. The aspect of you that identifies as form knows itself in relationship to other things that have manifested at the same dense level, and this is the three-dimensional world that you exist in.

But what you truly are, which invests all these things, is spirit, and the knowing of this, and the knowing of the true identity that informs each cell of what you are and all things you see is the claiming of the inheritance.

Now "Why has this not happened?" is the great question. There has been a fear-based lineage operating with you concurrently that has been seeking to distill itself as you. Now if you can comprehend fear as a vibration that seeks to assume itself in form, you can understand what we are saying. As mankind identifies in fear, it re-creates or replicates that energy in its creations.

We have said so many times that the action of fear is to claim more fear, but what you don't see is that the creations of man that were made in fear are also assuming responsibility for the same action. This is being countered by the action of God or the Divine Self as it knows you, as it is you.

"Now are you talking about evil?" Paul is asking. "This sounds like good and evil or a teaching of duality. We don't do this, do we?"

Well you don't, actually, but you believe you do. If you can understand this, that the fear that you see all around you is your accountability to your own creations, you have claimed this as a lineage. It is yours and nothing else's.

"We will blame those people over there or those ones out there, perhaps, who did this to us."

In fact, you did it to yourselves. The claiming of fear as what you are occurred a long time ago, and those aspects of the self that believe themselves to be fearful continue to contaminate each aspect that it operated as. Each decision you have made, because you are frightened, tainted the outcome with fear. You do this yourselves.

So now that you understand that there is no demon or devil assuming this, but it was done by man in its own way, you can understand that it is now being countered by your true nature.

"Well, can this happen?" Paul asks.

It is already so. Hear these words: Fear is a lie and any form it's taken is also a lie. Now can a lie be labeled as truth? Yes, it can. And here is the conflict that you are all going to face. There may be a very good intention outlined in something that has also manifested in a fearful way. You intend to have government to support the needs of the people. This can be a very productive thing. But if that government is operating in fear or seeking to establish itself in fear or rule over others, which is an action of fear, the identity of the government must be reknown in a truthful way for it to align to the new vibration that is here as you—and, we will add, in all men.

So the idea of a battle between good and evil is also a fear-based structure. It is not true. The only battle you have is with your own self or the identity that is claimed in fearful ways that has produced the structures that you have inherited and, in fact, reinforced by naming them as fearful.

Now what we do with you each is structure you again,

align you again, support you again in the full remembrance of your Divine nature so that you align, not to what was made in fear, but what is in truth. And the claim you make, "I am here in truth," will see itself out-pictured in your world. The darkness you see, the fear you see, is a lie. It is a lie. No matter how big it is, how it claims to overtake, it is still a lie.

And if you believe that a lie will overcome truth, you might as well put the book down now because you are in idolatry, a belief that there is something greater than the action of the Divine.

Now the claims you have made thus far—"I know who I am in truth"—are not mimicry. You are not parroting us. You are deciding. And the decision must be made by you, for you, to claim its meaning. And the claim you've made— "I am here, I am here as the Divine Self in manifestation, I am here as the truth of what I am in its expression, I am here in my knowing of who you are and what all is"—is a reincarnation of truth as what you are. The claim of identity is made in intention and establishes itself as what you are in your alignment.

Now what you see before you, those things claimed in lower nature, must again be attended to in one of two ways. Decide that it will always be there—we will always have a war, we will always have hunger, we will always have fear— and that claim supports the alignment of the fear-based structures. You give them a nod, a tip of the hat, perhaps, and say, "Oh, I know you're there. You're not going anywhere. I might look away, but you will be there tomorrow when I look again." And fear says, "Thank you so much for telling me who I am, for showing me my power, for granting me purview over what you see because I cannot be here without your permission."

Do you understand this, friends? You made fear. You make it every day by claiming its identity, and it grants you permission to do so because this is how it exists.

The other opportunity you have is to lift beyond it. Now you do not do this by force of will. It will not be done by effort. What you've claimed or made, you are accountable to. But as we have instructed you already, to know what you are implies that you know what everybody else is as well, and everything else. And the shadow of fear is banished by the light of truth that it would attend to.

Now what we will offer you is a new claim of being. The human being that you are—who knows himself in form, has agreed to be embodied and in consort with a three-dimensional reality that you call and know as your life—may be reclaimed as the True Self in physical form by releasing the desire to know itself as separate from its spiritual entity or the truth of being.

"Desire?" Paul asks. "Did we desire this?"

Yes, you did. You came here to learn, and you learn

through the choices you make. And the desire to learn through separation, or the forgetting of what you are, was done by you as well.

Now, the mission is over in some ways, and we will tell you why. You have all stood at a precipice as a species—on the verge of knowing what you are, on one hand, and on one hand on the verge of annihilation through the action of fear that you continue to claim. The choice has always been yours.

We see you alive and well in a new world, a buoyant world, where the action of fear no longer holds a claim over you. But if you don't believe this, you will continue to claim what you have known.

Now is this a frightening teaching? Not in the least. We are not saying you are going to be annihilated. We are saying, as we've always said, that humanity has a choice of how it proceeds. The Divine as you is in a new agreement. The Divine in all men, in all beings, is awakening to its true nature as expressing through the forms that it has claimed. And the rejoicing, we say, of what can come will be heard throughout the universe.

But we will say this. The choice remains your own.

Now the work we do with you in restructuring or reacclimating you to the Divine as what you are must also engage the physical form. It cannot bypass this. You must understand that the amplification of the Divine Self as may be held by you cannot hold the lower vibration that you have become accustomed to. So there is some transformation that you will undergo in body.

Now we will explain this. You hold vibration in every cell of your being. As you lift in frequency, the dense energies—those things vibrating at a lower level who have become accustomed to being what you are—are going to be challenged. And you may experience this in changes in the body itself that are productive but unexpected.

The transitioning from the experience of the self as solid form to vibration is what we are speaking of. You are in form, but you are not solid. You never have been. You are in vibration now, but the density of your being is being realigned through the activation to the field of truth to the Divine potential that you each hold that is being realized in fullness—underline *fullness*—through this transcription, the book that you hold in your hands.

The beings that you are, who hear these words, are being announced, one at a time, in a higher plane. "Here she comes! Here he comes! There they all come! How wonderful this is!"

Welcome to your new lives, my friends. Welcome to the truth of what you are in form. Welcome to who you have always been and only forgotten, and let us love you as you stand before us, because you are the torches that will light your world anew.

We sing your song for you. You are here, you are here, you are here, not for you, but for all, all who will come behind you, all who will follow, all you may meet and may never meet.

Now the Christed Self, the truth of all human beings, has never been dormant really. It has always been active, but precluded from your experience by your agreement to separation. And the new agreement has been made to incarnate as what you are. The vibration of the Divine in chemical alchemization in the beings that you are is about to ensue.

We will take a pause for Paul. And we may resume this teaching when we return.

(Pause)

What we would like you to do is to begin to realize who other people are outside of the claims you've made for them. This is more than an exercise. It's a decision that will have ramifications upon your lives if you do this with the intention we offer you.

As we have taught already, how you see others is in fact a projection of your own identity placed upon them. And what they think they are is often not what they are, as well. So the challenge we have here is that we have you, the perceiver, imposing your own ideas or mind upon what somebody else is, and the one you are seeing is also wearing a mask that she believes to be her. This is why you have so many problems in your relationships. You are deciding who others are without knowing them, and they don't know themselves either.

Now the adjustment we have for you is a decision that truth will inform how you see everyone you encounter. *In-form* is the key word here. You are not unmasking them, you are not deciding for them, but you are allowing truth to be the way you see, and also what you see. And in this exchange, you actually unmask your partner because the mask they wear is a creation in fear.

Now Paul is interrupting. "But is the mask a bad thing? Do you mean the personality self when you mean the mask?"

There is nothing wrong with personality. We have one when we want. You have one as well. But the decision to perceive in truth actually bypasses the construct of personality to the truth of what they are.

Now there are levels of truth. The first face you see—we will call that the mask—that is the face that's being invited to be seen. "See who I am as I wish. Let me be known as I wish to be."

The second level—we can call this truth—is what is being hidden, is what is fearful of being seen that the mask in fact protects. "You will not love me if you know who I am. You will think me foolish or forlorn. You will desire me in a way that I cannot handle. You will judge me if you understand who I truly am."

So the mask protects you, and when you move beyond the mask that protects another, the first thing you see is what, in fact, the mask protects.

Now the next thing that happens, when your intent is to see them in truth, in a loving truth, is you comprehend the aspect of the self that is so afraid. You do not judge that aspect. That aspect was created in fear or in need, and the mask that it covers is a protective device that was created in need as well. So to decide that someone is full of shit, and we are using that word intentionally, is that they are full of the mask that they are wearing to protect themselves from what you would see if you saw beneath it.

Now underneath that level that seeks to be hidden is a luminous self, the child within, the untainted self, the extraordinary being that chose to incarnate and has held form. The witnessing of this aspect of the self is different than the Divine Self. But to render the beauty, the true beauty, of another in witness is to bypass the mask, what the mask has protected, to the true person—still in personality, but without fear or unmasked—that lies beneath it.

Now then, you go where you may only go when you know what you are. Those of you who've done work with yourselves—"Well, I know I am not the mask I wear, and

I know the fear that I have is covering something even that is not in fear"—you can do this only up to the level of the person self that is still there as you are.

Until you know what you are as the Divine Self, you cannot witness the Divine Self in another. You may have your idea of the Divine Self, but we encourage you that if you stop at the self, the nice self, the unprotected self, the one that is not ashamed, you will be missing finally the opportunity to witness the face of God as the one you see. And every face you pass, when you know what you are, is in fact the face of God.

"Now can this be done?" Paul asks.

It is done, again, as what you are, but not by the small self who cannot claim these things. The challenge of this teaching for many of you is that the announcement of the small self—"Here I am to save the day"—will actually bypass the Divine Self. The small self thinks he will do it right, she will get it right, when in fact all she has to do is align as truth and then the work is done through and as her.

Now when we said a decision to see the inherent truth in all you witness, we are not making it hard work. We are claiming what is already true that may be known by you in the higher octave that you exist in as the True Self. The comprehension of this is not done through the intellect. It cannot be done there. In fact, the intellect will tie it in a knot and a bow and spend the rest of her life trying to untangle it. The True Self knows, the small self thinks. And the comprehension of this teaching must be done in experience.

Now the ones we see before us, the students of the work, have been attuned as what they are. But their experience of what they are is still limited because the lenses of the camera you experience your world in are still informed in history. The eyes in your head comprehend a world and analyze and distill information in systemic ways that will continue to produce the same experience that you have always had.

When we speak of chemicalization, or the reinvention of the physical self, we are speaking of two different things—perception as known and experienced in form and what processes that perception, which is the entire vehicle you hold. You experience your world, you see, through the senses, and the senses have form in the bodies you hold. The actualization of what you are happens in your entire being, but the way you experience it, finally, in consciousness and in body, must utilize the senses because that's how you are informed by the manifested world.

Now the senses you hold have in many ways been limited by what they have been conceived of by others, and the True Self has access to information and experience that bypasses the systems of agreement that mankind has gotten used to. As we speak through Paul, we bypass his systems in order to meet you through the senses. You feel the energy or you hear the words. You comprehend the text through the eyes in your head or the braille that you feel beneath your fingers. You are still in exchange with what we are, even though the what we are exists outside of form, as you understand form.

Now if you wish to know what we are, the Divine that we are, you may meet us where we are. But in order to do that, you must actually acclimate to the vibratory frequency that we operate as. Paul's system, you see, has been acclimated, and will continue to be, to hold the vibration that comes in language for the good of the student. But the experience he has of us is still very limited by his conceits about what it means to be in form and in response to something that is not at the level of vibrational alignment that he holds.

Here we go, friends. The work we will do now is to lift you beyond the comprehension that has limited you, the agreement to know reality in a limited way that was prescribed for you and attuned to by you each in collective agreement. What we are doing now is lifting you outside of the known to the level of expression where you may be seen and see as the Divine Self.

Now what does it mean to be seen as the Divine Self? It is not done in form, and the perception of the Divine Self—although it is inclusive of form, does not disregard form—exists beyond it and in it at the same time. So how you are perceived is in the field by the vibration that encounters all things as what it is. Underline the *what*. The vibration of the Divine Self in manifestation is collectively experienced as one realizes herself at this level. As you know yourself, you are known.

Now what does it mean to be known? This has not a damned thing to do with your personality or how the world decides about you. The Christ as you in manifested form holds a vibrational light that is witnessed at a higher level and goes into agreement with all it sees.

If you can imagine that all you witness as the higher self, the Divine Self, the Christed Self, the Infinite Self, whatever you wish to claim it as, is perceived in like accord, the Christ sees the Christ in all it passes, and all it passes in turn sees the Christ.

Now this is not done through the senses as they have been prescribed so far. Some of you believe that what this means is your psychic ability will expand. And while that may be the case for some of you, how you invest in the vibration you hold, and how you perceive as it, will be determined by your requirements for development and choice in a higher octave.

Each human being has the innate ability to experience the other worlds that are ever-present. But they have been veiled and aligned to in dense form, so your experience has been limited.

In the lifting that we do with you, you begin to claim things outside of collective agreement, and not only for your own good, but for the good of all you meet. You see, as you exist in a higher alignment, you align what you see by the presence of your being. But if what you see is condemned by you, claimed in lower nature, you are standing there with it in that like accord. As the lifting happens in your field, the physical body must become acclimated at the level of vibration that you are now holding. And the disassemblance of the physical form happens in a way that you may not comprehend intellectually, but will experience as the system you know yourself as is appropriated to be the vessel in consort with your intent and requirements for your growth and learning.

You must all understand that aligning at this level does not stop you from your requirements of learning, and these things may be claimed by you prior to incarnation, or during the life, so that the True Self may be known outside of the old claims. Now an old claim is something that was decided by the self at one time that has been perpetuated in your experience. And the experiences you have had thus far in a life in all ways have been in support of your growth and learning. Alignment to the True Self does not take away your lessons if there are things you are required to learn. So don't go into an analysis of what it means to be the Divine Self that would include "I don't have to pay my taxes, or have a bad day, or a cold." Do you understand this? That is the fancy of the small self, and it also is a symptom of a disgust with the lives you live in physical form that are actually blessings. Do you understand that?

The belief that ascension or acclimatizing as the Christed Self keeps you from experiencing pain is not so. If you step on a rock and you trip on your behind, your behind will be sore as the Divine Self, as the small self as well. It's still your behind.

Now the thing we wish you to know about the process of alchemy and the body is that once it has begun, it is continued only in alignment with what the system can hold. This is very important. Some of you wish this to be realized overnight. As we have already said, the alignment to truth is instantaneous, and the holding of the vibration is present in your field as you and is reinforced by your intention. "I know who I am in truth, what I am in truth, how I serve in truth."

But to hold the frequency of a higher octave, and hold a consciousness that will keep you in alignment to it, may be known by you over a period of time or all at once. But the body itself must be appropriated to hold the field in a constant way. This is not to say that we are asking you to invest in process. As we said, the alignment to truth is instantaneous. But the expression of it as what you are in form requires a disassembling of the attachment that you have held to a reality that is fraught with lies.

As we commence with this teaching with our students, with the readers of the text, we implore them not to go into impatience, but to allow the reality they hold to unfold in accordance with their individual needs for expression. Some of you come here, you see, to know yourself in fullness. Some of you have come to realize what can be, and will commence a level of incarnation that may be held in vibration at another time. One is not higher than the next. You may decide to do this on Monday and not on Tuesday. It will still get done. So there is no fear.

Now the alchemization of the physical self requires a transmuting of fear that has been held as the body. Underline the word *as*. The memory of fear that the cells in the body hold, that the very strands of your DNA, if you wish to call it that, have known, must be released to the higher octave.

"How is this done?" Paul asks.

In alignment and in grace. The word *grace* is very important here. You do not do it as yourself, but the claim "I know who I am in truth, what I am in truth, how I serve in truth, I am here, I am here, I am here" is what calls the vibration to assist you in this release.

Understand, dears, that if you still experience fear, you are not doing this wrong. You are having an encounter to support you in the release of the lie that would inhibit your expression. Do you understand this?

So begin to say "Thank you" to all of your experiences—all of them, high and low and in between, yes—because the gift of them is the True Self in her authority reclaiming purview. "I am here. I am here. I am here."

The last thing we will say as we end this session is that the beings that you are, are being attuned to be able to receive a higher octave of transmission. This does not mean you hear us. We are not the station you are playing as Paul is playing us.

What you will be in accord with is truth in all ways. And all that is in truth will then be available to you. Not just a current, a vibration, but all things that express themselves in truth, in love, will be made available in that current.

So begin to expect the possibility of phenomena as part of the life you live, and do not be alarmed when the sky itself begins to smile down upon you. It knows who you are as well. The sky is in truth, because how could it not be?

You are dearly loved. We will end now. And we will thank you, Paul, for sitting so long for this work. Period. Period. Period. Stop now, please.

(Pause)

Now what sovereignty is, is an awareness of what you are in relationship to all other things. What sovereignty is, is a withstanding of transformation in a world around you while maintaining the identity of the one who will not be moved.

The claim we make for each of you—"We know who you are in freedom, we know what you are in freedom, we know how you serve in freedom"—means that the sovereign self has been realized by you, and all things are possible in the alignment to truth as what you are.

Some of you believe that the life that you've lived thus far has been problematic, or you have been punished by your circumstances. That is not the case. You come into an incarnation with a list of things you need to learn, probabilities that you may encounter as ways to know the self in circumstance. As you know what you are—"I know who I am in truth"—the veils are lifted. And what appeared to be a disaster is perceived as an opportunity. What was perceived as penance is seen as opportunity to grow. What was claimed in fear has seen the light of day and claims you anew as the sovereign self who is no longer attached to an outcome, or something that was once that is no more. The claim you make, "I know who I am in freedom," announces you as the one who may always choose in sovereignty, but as the True Self.

Now the claims you make in the small self—"I will have my way, he will do what I wish, she will get what she needs as long as I don't lose anything"—are still pliable and may be re-created at any moment by the claim "I am here in freedom," which announces you, once again, as the Divine Self.

Now Paul doesn't like this teaching yet. "It sounds easy, and if it's easy it cannot be so." That's the problem here with so many of you. You need to be challenged in your experience to claim something as so. So we guarantee, if that is your need, you will find it. But the claim of sovereignty actually means that what was once made in the lower self may be reframed in your free will in alignment as the Divine Self.

Now the expression of the Divine through you bears witness in vibration and in action. You must understand these words. To be in action means to be in motion, but consciousness itself in action does the work.

If you are called to physically lead a parade, you will hear the trumpet first and begin to march, and others will fall behind you. You don't make the parade. You begin to march to the music that is, and the parade commences. You don't announce to everybody, "Let's have a parade. It's time for a good parade. Come, come, come, do as I say." You begin to march to the horn that is leading you forward and others fall in line because you become the music that you follow.

The dear ones you are, the ones who have incarnated to relearn their names, are leaders of many parades, know it or not. And the coming change on this plane will announce many things as so that were deemed impossible in years prior.

What an incarnation is, is an expanse of time of learning, a charade, perhaps, because the encasing in time is actually only there for the experience to be learned through. You don't incarnate in one year and not another. In fact, the True Self exists outside the calendar. But the physical reality that is being attended to by you may be known in a country or on a date in a place in time. These are markers, in some ways, for what may be learned, what may be known, what may be claimed in physical experience.

A physical experience for you is an opportunity to know the soul in a dense vibration where duality has been claimed. But the reclamation outside of duality as what you are is the first trumpet that will be sung. And the reclamation of the world that follows will be a testament to truth and its action.

What you come to at the end of your years is a realization that a lifetime is not a justification for having done things. It's an opportunity to have been. And the being of you as your conscious self, the one who witnesses the flowers grow, who cradles the baby in her arms, who sighs in grief, or weeps in joy, who has had this experience of a life lived, is the one who designs her next pattern of learning, what she will commence with on this plane again if this is where she resumes her schooling.

The ones you know yourselves as have had many names and many encounters, and the claim in truth, "I know who

I am in truth," is not a claim of this particular identity. If you can understand this, you make the claim for all you have been and all you will be, all you can be, because you are claiming as the Infinite Self. While the projection of reality in the three-dimensional world is seen anew, the true operation is happening in multiple dimensions because the entire being who bears testament to many lives, many worlds, many expressions of consciousness is being claimed as well in unity, in unity of all.

The gift of this for the small self, finally, is that she is assumed in what she has always been. She is no longer fragmented outside of her Source, she knows herself as home, as one with the Infinite Being that she truly is. In some ways, what you all are is a shattered mirror, and the small pieces that you hold reflect a light that you remember and know yourself to be of. But the mirror itself is a whole incarnation, and all of you born finally, finally, finally are of one light, although what you reflect back will be a reality particular to your learning.

Justification, as we said earlier, is an act of the small self. You no longer need to justify yourselves, but you do need to claim, because in claiming you align, and the creations that you attest to, as the one who knows who she is, visibly reflect the truth of what you are.

Notice we said "visibly." When something is visible, it is seen, it is not imagined. And as we are speaking truth, and speaking to you as and of the vibration of the hierarchical truth that may be encoded by you, by us, overriding the limitations the small self has used to justify her lies, the claims you make will be seen. What does something mean when it is seen? It means that it is known, made visible, and claimed as is.

We have promised you from the beginning that this would not be a theoretical teaching, but an exemplar, an arc of being that you may know yourself as. And what you are now, in the one who may know herself as sovereign and free, is the witness to the reclamation of a new world.

As we continue the teaching, we will speak to this. For the world, you see, is operating in transformation, and the wisps of change from the smoke that is present will be known and witnessed and understood by the one who has the eyes with which to see.

Yes, this is in the text. This is the end of the chapter. You may take a pause.

"What is the chapter's name?" Paul asks.

"Reunification in Truth." Thank you for your presence. Good night. Stop now, please.

Chapter Six

STRUCTURE AND TRUTH[*]

Day Fourteen

Now religion is a way of understanding ideas in a codified way. You have a doctrine, you ascribe to a doctrine, you know where you stand. Your needs are met in some ways by the doctrine. You are taught to observe a day of the week, to pray at certain times of day. The free will of the self is still existing and appropriated by the doctrine. "I feel good when I pray every day. I know what day to observe. I know the rules of a Sabbath or a Sunday. I know the religious holiday and I observe."

Now the things that you assume religion to be are not. A religion, in fact, has great opportunity as a structured system of ideas that can take a traveler, a pilgrim, if you wish, on a journey to home, to its inevitable reunion with its Source. But that is not what religion has been. We have said

---

[*] Recorded in workshop at the Esalen Institute.

many times that this will not be a religion but a practice or a way of being that some may ascribe to as they are called to realize their True Selves, the Christ that is them and all men in truth as they align to it.

The choice you make here as the one hearing these words is how to listen and to what. Even the filters of your consciousness are reframing these ideas to suit the needs of the small self. "I don't like religion," you say. "It's a controlling thing." And perhaps in your experience it has been, for another way may be to perceive a doctrine as a teaching that will illumine those who understand the mysteries that lie beyond the text in the truth of the ideas or principles that are presented therein.

For some of you, you see, the baby has been out with the bathwater for so long that the baby's grown up, had a life of its own, and you wouldn't know it in truth if you ran into him at an intersection on a highway. You would not know the one you bore because you decided that he was not in truth.

Now we will not tell you the religious teaching is always productive. But we understand the merit that may lie at the heart of all. And at the heart of all true religion is one simple idea, that you are not separate from your Source, and the systems of behavior that have been aligned in doctrine in all religions throughout time were perhaps initially presented as ways for you to learn to stay on the narrow road to the summit of truth that the religion said it would grant you.

But here is what happened. In all religion, the personal investments, the ones who decided what books should stay in, what teachings should be left out, where you should pray, and what you should wear when you do it, were deciding either in self-interest or out of the fear that if the religion was not protected in a certain way it would not survive. So there were practices born out of necessity at different times in the history of a religion that may no longer be true to the requirements of a man today.

But we will promise you this. In the teaching of truth that we are granting you now, even your relationship to religion may be understood in a truthful way. We do not damn them, nor do we sing their praises. We comprehend them as ways of learning to a known system of ideals that were prescribed by men—some highly inspired, perhaps— at different times on the history of this plane. But as we have said, truth is always true, and the particle of truth that is inherent in a religion may be discovered and the whole system may in fact be understood in a new way.

Now what a doctrine is, is a set of ideas that will be mandated as law and followed in prescribed ways. That is not what this is. This is a teaching of truth, and like a river, once you step into it, you will be washed in it or carried through it to where you need to be. The things that propel you forward in truth that carry you down the river will be in alignment to truth. And when you bump against a rock or find yourself scrambling to the shore, in fact what is happening is you are coming up against an obstacle to truth, a system of beliefs or behavior that will be standing in the way of your journey.

We have called these "boulders" in other texts and we are going to revisit that idea now, briefly, so that you may understand them in the context of the issuance you are receiving now.

When you have an idea of what you are that has been codified over time, that you believe to be you because it has been there for so long, you have something we would call a boulder. But what the boulder actually is, is fear naming itself in an attitude or through a belief system. "I cannot be loved" would be an example here. "I will never get it right" would be another. "All men are evil" would be another. "God is a punishing God" would be another.

You have utilized these things so much that they inform the world that you are seeing. And because you cannot align to them as other than yourself, you believe the belief to be your own and unchangeable. The landscape that you perceive through is identified, discolored by, invoked by the misguided sight of the boulder or belief.

The transmutation of this or the alchemization of a

belief system in truth is a very great one, a very great event. But it is not entered into without an understanding that something that has been created at this level that pretends to be truth and is not will be met with a new reality once it is disassembled. And we only caution you in processing this as a small self, because the small self is the one who claimed it in the first place and believes it to be her.

So in alchemy it is transformed and reclaimed in the vibration of truth, but at the cost of what you thought you were. And the occurrence here, the manifestation of this, is very challenging in some ways to what has been created through it.

Imagine this, friends. You have been a docile woman, you have a relationship where your needs are met, you have not had to work, you chose a relationship where your needs were provided for. When you realize that the fear that you've held of claiming your independence or asserting your will of being in self-governance is realized in fullness and transformed, you are still walking into your old home and looking at the children who expect you to clean up after them and the husband who wants his dinner set upon the table at a certain time. The view you have was created in the false self and must now be known anew.

So how does this woman create a life that is in support of the identity that she knows herself to have in truth? The landscape that she still exists in, created in other times to reaffirm a belief that she has held that she is unable to care for herself, is going to have to be met in a new way. What she does is one of two things—pretend she does not know who she truly is, who she has newly claimed in truth, or claim all that she sees before her in truth, which is a triumph.

Now understand this, friends. When you are aligned to truth, you can only witness it. And if your friends say, "Come back down the hill and have a nice drink with us, it's easier here," you may be tempted to, yes. But the cost of that in almost all cases is a reacclimation to the lower vibration that you used to adhere to.

You go back in the old water, have a nice swim in the old tank, and the sea that you drift in is confined by the small self's identity. The one who knows who he is, who she is, reenters the landscape that presents itself and announces, "I am here, I am here, I am here," and the True Self that you are will claim into manifestation a replication of what happens at the new level of realization that you have attained.

Another's behavior may be invested in who you have been. But who you are can claim that, too, in a high regard. When you understand that the "I Am" Self, the Divine Self as you, is more powerful than habit, you become liberated even from those things that you have believed yourselves to be in small ways because they were used to being expressed as and by you.

Now when we said "triumph," we meant victorious. The docile wife who has found her truth reenters her home and she says, "Hello, everybody, I am so glad to see you, and now you can take care of yourselves. I am in victory." Now their jaws may be on the floor, but they will also smile and we will tell you why. When anyone follows her truth, she gives permission for everybody else to do the same. And those who were in collusion with the old behavior—"I don't have to pick up my laundry, she will do it for me"—get the benefit of their own resources. Do you understand this?

So the fear of changing, we would say, is usually about the fear of the reaction that you will receive or the implications of the change upon the life that you live. And when we say "victory," we mean it. The acquiescing to a pattern of behavior or a prescribed way of being that limits your expression is the small self claiming victory over what he has been, and the True Self in "I am here" reclaims the purview of all she sees.

Now when we teach you, we do it in witness and in comprehension. And when we understand you, we do it in a way that may support you in reunderstanding what you have chosen at other times in your life.

We would like you to take a moment and reflect upon where you live, who you live with, perhaps, what it looks like, and why things were chosen and when. You will realize very quickly that what was chosen by you was always chosen to meet a specific need that presented itself at a certain time. "I was learning to cook, I bought a book to tell me how. I wanted to rest someplace comfortable, I bought a bed. I painted the walls with pictures to make my child look happy when he entered the room. Everything was chosen."

Now you don't like to cook, you never read the book, the bed had a bump in it and you sleep on the other side, and the child couldn't stand the pictures and yelled at the walls when you showed them to him. But they were still created to meet the needs of a time.

Here we are, now, in a new time, as a new woman, as a new man, who has claimed victory over what she has known and believed. We are going to do something now with the room you stand in and with all who stand with you, perhaps, in that room.

We want you to imagine that where you stand is a place of being, and that the alignment to truth in the field of truth is where you stand. As you claim these words, you are going to claim victory over the purview you have, as the Divine Self announces herself to this landscape and all who dwell therein: "I know who I am in truth. I know what I am in truth. I know how I serve in truth. I am here. I am here. I am here." And the vibration that you have, the tidal wave of truth as we have described it, begins to emanate as you and reclaim all these things, all these things that you see in the octave of truth that you now carry.

Perhaps the things are not changed, but your witness of them will. And you will find yourself eventually standing in a landscape that can only be in accord with the truth that you hold.

Now alchemy, as we have said, is transformation. And the claim of victory may include those things that you believed could not be moved, the boulders, yes, the structures you've adhered to, the beliefs that you've held in sorrow or in fear, and the ones you know about and the ones you don't that are still informing the lens of the reality you hold.

As we do this with you, we are holding the vortex for you, the current or frequency that we know in truth. And as we amplify this for you, you the student of the work, the student of the text, the one who has come to learn, we will amplify your vibration to a level of expression where what you are claiming as a boulder, or a system of trouble, may be transformed.

"How is this done?" Paul asks.

By knowing who you are. "I know who I am in truth. I know what I am in truth. I know how I serve in truth. And I am free."

As this claim is made by you, it is held by us in consort. Because the claim was made in truth, it may be held in truth, and as we hold truth, as we know who we are, we can gift you with the agreement to the claim that you have made. And in consort with our holding the frequency that you may not yet attend to at the level of issuance the body can hold and claim, the release will be productive as you align it, the boulder, the trouble, the fear, in truth.

You may be feeling the frequency, now that your system has agreed to this. How you hold a vibration in your system is dependent upon the issuance or the nature of the problem. But the release of a block or a boulder or a trouble is usually met by a feeling of lifting, of being liberated from something held.

Now Paul has a question. We will take it. "Did we just release a boulder?"

If you said the words, and you agreed to them, and you agreed to us in being in consort with you in the vibration of the truth, yes, you have. But what you do not know is that you may reclaim it because you intend it to be there.

Hear these words, friends. You bought the pot to learn to cook in. You bought the book to fill the pot with the correct things. You still don't like to cook, but you think, "Someday I will." So you keep the book and the pot handy just in case. You have created the boulders and you attend to them in your own way. If you wish to hide it at the top of the closet, you have not released it.

"But what if I let go of my fear? Something bad will happen. I will keep a small bag of it just in case I need it for a rainy day."

The boulder that you are transmuting was just a simple idea, once upon a time, and grew in size to something that you could experience as obstructing your journey or your true expression. So we invite you, instead, to liberate the self even from that.

"I am free. I am free. I am free."

We will continue this teaching in a few moments. We will take a pause for Paul. We will ask you to be quiet in the interim. Period. Period. Period. Stop now, please.

(Pause)

The offering we have for you is instruction, but experience is the way you learn. The instruction itself gives you a system of creation to apply to the life you live. But your experience of your life is the best teacher you could ever have.

Now if you think for a moment about the things that concern you in your life, the relationship that's not working, the job that seems to be going nowhere, the addictive behavior you can't seem to transform, you will actually understand that these things are your teachers. And if you bang your heads against them, you will miss the lesson.

Imagine, now, that the thing that is challenging you the most is taking a form—a form, a thing, a shape perhaps, a being perhaps—and imagine this thing stands before you.

And you may inquire to this thing, "What have I come to learn, and what have you come to teach me?"

Now listen—and see what you receive. You may hear a voice, you may know, you may feel. The oracle you stand before may actually be speaking to you in a way that you may see and hear. It matters not. Ask it what it's come to teach you, and you will *know*.

Now sometimes the answer is not what you think. Sometimes the answer is not convenient. Sometimes you will wish to impose an answer because it's what you would like to know.

We will tell you what we mean here. When you decide what something should be, you intend to see it the way you wish. The relationship that you think is there to teach you generosity may actually be there to teach you to let other people decide to meet their own needs without your support.

So if you decide in advance what the answer is, you may be misled by what you desire. If you allow yourself to be taught by what you have claimed before you, and you align to it in truth—underline *in truth*—you may actually be met with the answer you have been seeking.

So please do not go into this exercise with a prescription for what the answer should be, or you will be hearing the small self's intent to keep you in the same place you wish to move from.

Now the next thing we wish you to know is that you

may do this exercise in any way, in any relationship, at any time. Realize that anything you see before you is a creation, a thing made. And by understanding that you are in vibrational accord with everything you see—because it cannot be there without you, in your experience—you have the opportunity to ask it what it is there to teach you. Do you all understand this, yes?

That man who made the pass, that insulted you, the woman who took your job, the husband who left, the child who always complains are your creations as well. And inviting them on an energetic level to be in consort with you—"What have you come to teach me?"—will support you in claiming the truth about the lesson.

Now not all things are personal to you. One of the challenges we face in our teachings is that you like to look at everything through the small window of your life when, in fact, you are a great expression. And what happens on the other side of the world that you are in witness to is there for the same inquiry. "What have I come to learn through this, what are you here to teach me?" will work with the war, will work with the government, will work with all things if you realize that the world is your teacher and it is there to support you in realigning in your highest way.

Now if somebody says, "Well, I didn't create the war, so I didn't have anything to do with it," you are actually distancing yourself from your own accountability as a participant to the world that you are in. You are not alone on this ship. You are with millions and millions of others. And as you stand up and announce yourself, "I am here, I am here, I am here," you will begin to meet one another in this claim. And you, together, may change your world.

But unless you inquire what the lesson is, how will you know? "Well, we should have no war" may be the answer you decide, prior to inquiry. But perhaps if you go in and you invite it to tell you what it is that it is there to teach you, it might be something very different.

"The war is teaching me the value of life, and as I understand this and affirm the value of life, my work is made known to me as the one who has been in consort to this creation."

The value of life is a lesson that most of you don't learn until the life you are living is over, and then you say—"Oh yes, I was as this, I was as I thought, and now what am I?"—as you transition outside of what you've claimed.

So the exercise we offer you is a way to access *knowing*. Do you understand this? You are being given a gift here. "What am I to learn?" puts you in a position of humility and authority in any instance. If you know everything now, you shouldn't read another page of this. You should have put it away some time ago. But if you are willing to be taught, your life will be your teacher, and you will find it a remarkable and wonderful teacher.

We will stop this session now. We will thank you for your attention. When we return, we will teach you different things. Period. Period. Period.

Day Fourteen (Cont.)

Belief in what you know because it was taught to you by another must be understood now. An inherited belief is not the known, and this is the biggest challenge you will face as you encounter this teaching. You believe the world to be a certain way. There are books written about how the world is, and you have inherited knowledge through religion and science that prescribe a way of being in the world. The history of your world is understood by you only in reference to what has been understood by those who assign themselves to be the ones deciding for you what history should be. You don't know your history, you know the metaphors for it, you know aspects of it, but in fact what you are doing is piecing together a puzzle with many missing pieces and assuming it is whole.

Now this is not a testament or a teaching on history, but it is a teaching in truth. And what we would like you to know is that the world that you live in has been around much longer and populated much longer than you have known. The civilizations who came before you were in attendance to high learning, some of them very high, and through their misuse of authority and claims of power managed to release the known world that they had in ways that you may know of as flood or cataclysm.

When we say these things, it's only to tell you that you have a small understanding of what history is, and the relics of those times that still exist in places in the world are reminders of the manifestations of humans believing themselves to be gods at the cost of their world. Never once believe that you have authority over another, and never once believe that the world that you live in, the known world that has been prescribed to you in known ways, is all there is.

Now inherited history assumes you in beliefs that have become collective constructs. A collective construct is a collective agreement about what has been made in form. And when you see things around you that are in structure, the affirmation of the structure and form brings you to an agreement that this is what is. But what has come before in thought and feeling, in action that has made this form into being, may be a construct from another time that, in fact, has been inherited by you as fact.

What we wish you to understand is that the claims you make of the visible world—we will call that the known world because you think you know it—are in fact collective agreements about what you think is there. And what is truly there, what informs the structure, may be quite different.

You see a landscape where somebody has built a house. The house was perhaps built upon a ruin; the ruin was once a church; the church was once shielding a vortex, a place of power. The one who now lives in the house that is built on the vortex is living in a frequency that has been there since the beginning of time, but does not know it.

The parallel here is that the frequency of truth has always been present, but you have not aligned to it. And once you do, you begin to understand that collective agreements, things made into form by all of you that you believe to be true because you have not thought to question them, may not be.

Now as we said earlier, when you think you know everything, there is nothing to learn. And the act of forgetting what you are has been mankind's job for some time. And you have done a good enough job of it to claim a world that exists in separation, even though it is not. So viewing the known world in a higher way actually requires you to claim what is—is in truth—in the face of what you have thought to be true.

Now you know what a dollar bill is, but it's really just a piece of paper with an image on it that is used as an exchange of vibration. So you think money is important, but money is not real. It was decided upon by you as a way to exchange goods, and goods, we would say, are industry, things made or bought or purchased or grown, and these things may be known in different ways as well. So you can look at currency as a symbol of something that was decided by you in collective agreement that has a basis in a need, but perhaps the need itself has been misconstrued by all of you.

Now if someone has a skill and wishes to share the skill, and somebody else has extra fish and wishes to exchange the fish for the skill, you have an agreement that has been made. And currency is simply a symbol that is used now in place of the fish or the skill, but the same barter is implied. The need for the exchange was prescribed by each of you. "You like to fish and I don't. I will take the fish from you that you don't want." And then one day the man who likes to fish says, "Well, if I give everybody the fish, I will have all of my other needs met." And suddenly he is in industry. And the industry is erected, and the house is built, and the sign over the door says, "Fish Here." And you come with your goods, and now you have a civilization and a market-place. You understand this, yes?

But if we go back to the impulse—he likes to fish, per-haps she likes to grow in her garden—the sharing of bounty outside of what has been decided by you as industry may be once again known in a different way, because you've always had barter, which has become industry and busi-ness. And in your world, now, corporate structures that dominate the individual's ability to care for themselves, be-cause they have invested their lives in a belief that if they don't work for somebody else they will starve on the streets, was what you claimed in collective agreement.

The fish and the garden are still there. But what you have erected upon them and the industries built in the name of commerce were claimed by the collective. And the distortion of them is what you live with. As human beings begin to reclaim what they are in truth, they must create structure that recognizes the unified need of the whole at the cost of the individual's requirements for security or wealth or protection. And until you all do this, you will be at war with one another. You want their fish. They want the produce from your garden. But a wall was built between them. And the only way to get what you want is to conquer them.

When you begin to know that who and what you are, the Divine Self as what you are, is one with its Source, and you know that the same is in truth for your brothers, the idea of hoarding or keeping your things to yourselves becomes ludicrous. And we will tell you why. The belief that you cannot be cared for by the Source of what you are creates the need for you to grab and hoard and protect your goods, to count your pennies at night to ensure your safety in a world gone mad in greed.

We use the word *greed* intentionally, and greed, we will say, is an aspect of fear. The belief that you do not have enough, or should have more, or must be seen as having more than the man beside you is an action of fear. And, as we have taught you, the action of fear is to claim more fear.

Now if we were to ask you each, in this very moment, to take one thing off of your person and to give it to the first person you meet, you would be horrified. "But I need that ring. That is my comb. My spectacles are required by me. I won't give away my coat. My coat is mine." And as you decide these things, you also decide that the Source of the coat and the comb is limited. Do you understand this, yes?

The gift you give another by knowing who they are should not stop you from sharing your fish, or the produce from your garden, or the clothing on your back, should they be in need. You have many opportunities on this plane to do good. Now we don't use *good* in a normal sense. To be in truth always means you recognize worth, inherent worth, Divine worth, in the one you see. And the beggar in the street is as loved by God as the king in the castle. Do you understand this?

But the king in the castle, for whatever reasons, holds resources that can give the one in the street her safety or well-being or shelter from the elements. But you don't do these things, you see, because you don't think you should, because you have collective structures that support the beliefs that you should not do for another what you wish to be done for yourselves.

Now if you have a gift to give of any kind—the song you sing, the writing you do, the muscles on your back that support you in lifting things that the one beside you cannot—you are honor bound in some ways as the one in receipt of the gift to give it away or to share it. If you don't give away the gifts you have, you will grow stingy, and the gift that you think is so special will shrivel and die. Anything man has that can be shared needs to be shared with the ones beside you.

Now Paul is getting cautious here. "Well, I was very poor. I don't want to be poor again. If I give away my money, I may be poor. That frightens me."

The fear of being poor asks you to hoard your funds, and if your funds are hoarded in fear, your funds are replicating lies.

Now we will explain this for you. There is nothing wrong with wealth or poverty. They are different ways to learn about the manifested world. But to realize that each one before you is sovereign and has a right to be as they are can imply that it's every man for himself. And that is not the case.

Each one here who hears these words is called to act in truth. And to be in truth means you know your Source, the Source of all that is, and not at the cost of anyone else receiving what they need. If you deny bread to the man that is hungry, you have cursed yourself in your belief that there is no more bread to give. Do you hear these words? These are words of truth.

Now when you realize that all of the systems that have been created to keep human beings separate from one another, whether they be class or color or religions that fight amongst themselves, you misperceive yourselves as separate from your brother. And in fact you cannot be.

To begin to reclaim your lives in truth while you are in consort to structure and industry, things that have been claimed throughout time, forces you to encounter them in new ways. Here is how we attend to this. Imagine for a moment that you stand in an empty landscape. There is everything to be seen and nothing to be seen as far as the eye can see. There is a vista that has yet to be populated with anything, not even an artifact from a million years ago. The landscape is barren of creation and exists in infinite potential. You share a unified field here on this plane and consciousness expresses itself in form and fills the field with the things it needs.

Earlier in this text, we invited you to look at your room and see the things you needed or claimed at an earlier time in your life. The vista that the manifested world is, is claimed in exactly that way. But here we leave you in an empty plane where all things are possible.

Now imagine, if you wish, that all around you the emblemizations of society are popping up—little houses, big castles, banks, and hospitals. And suddenly this world is full of the manifested things that humanity has decided it requires to support itself in this landscape. At this very moment, we would like you to know that everything that was created was created in a belief in a need at one time. And as the man who had the fish decided to build the store, the man who held the purse for his friend decided to build a bank and charge interest, and the woman who healed the sick made it easier by building a house where the sick could be brought, and that became the hospital that you see today.

In this very moment, we would like you to witness these things in a new way. And these are the words we would encourage you to use:

"I witness the world before me as something made manifest, something created by mankind to fill a need. And what I will now do is claim that I am witnessing these things with new eyes in truth, so that I may be brought to witness the essence of their creation. And as I do this, I say these words. 'I claim this thing in truth. I claim this manifestation in alignment to Divine truth so that it may be witnessed in its highest form outside of what's been prescribed or decided upon by others throughout time.' As I lift this thing to higher vision, I claim these words. 'I see you in your truth, and you will be made new in the field of truth. I am here. I am here. I am here.'"

And as you bear witness to this thing, you are claiming it in alignment, in truth, to know it anew. And in this knowing—and remember *knowing* means realization—the thing is transformed by the imprinting of your consciousness.

Everything you see bears the thumbprints of all who have come before you, the man who held the purse for his friend who made the bank so, the woman who tended to the sick. Their thumbprints are upon every hospital or bank ever made. Their consciousness claimed it once, and you have all affirmed it, given it great form and structure.

As the one who knows who she is, the consciousness and the claim of truth—"I know what you are in truth"—claims your expression and the lifting of it to the Divine imprint, so it cannot be as it was.

This teaching will continue later in the day. But we are very pleased with the transmission thus far and the attention it is receiving by those who are attending to it. We thank you for your presence. Stop now, please. Period. Period. Period.

(Pause)

The only thing you need to know about what you become in alignment to truth is that what you are is what you have always been without knowing it.

The Creator as you—the amplification of the monad,

the Divine spark, the accelerated being of your essence—
has always been you in the higher octave. And the claim "I
am here" calls into purview all aspects of the self that may
be summoned by you in accord with this.

Now some of you believe that your investments in the
world that you've known must continue or else, and hear
what you say when you mean this: "There is something
more important than the evolution of my being. I have put
the money in the bank. It had better add up to something."

What we are going to tell you now is that your responsibility has never been to dismantle a physical landscape, but
what you are in accord with that is not aligning to the truth
of what you are. And as we continue this talk about structures and what has been built around you, we want you to
imagine, for the purposes of this teaching, that there is nothing to lose, nothing that will be lost by you if you encounter
yourself without the attachments to form that you have utilized to claim an identity, either in society or your culture or
your religion, your profession. It doesn't matter where or
what. But if you can imagine that there is nothing to lose by
rising in vibration, and that all you need from any of those
things to support you in truth will align with you in a new
way. All that doesn't get carried is what was claimed in fear
and enjoined with others in an agreement to be afraid.

An agreement to be afraid—this is a new concept. But

you have done it and continue to do it. And we would like you now to make a decision that the one who agrees to anything new will be the Divine Self or the aspect of you who is risen and who knows—who knows, who knows, who knows—that all agreements entered into will now be in truth. And this is the claim we support you in:

"On this day I choose to agree only to those things that are in alignment to truth, and I will be shown in every instance the truth of each situation that I encounter. As I make this claim, I rejoice that I have surrendered and released all of my ties that were made in fear. And all agreements, all contracts made in fear, will now be unbound and released from my life and my field. I know who I am in truth. I know what I am in truth. I know how I serve in truth."

Now the claim you have just made must be made whenever you endeavor to conjoin with others for a group purpose. Even a group purpose that is in support of one's alignment or growth may be configured in a structure of power that disempowers others. So the claim is being made that, as you rise, and as you join with others to claim victory over fear, you do not unintentionally remake the fear-based structures in a different way.

"What is an example?" Paul asks.

"Well, we will all join together to do this or that good thing. But someone must be in charge, and the one who's in charge must tell others what to do. And if they don't agree with what we say, well, they can go work with that group over there."

And that group over there, hearing about the abuse of authority in the group you just came from, distances itself from the first group, claims a solitary identity, although perhaps their mission is the same, and erects a nice wall that they may throw torpedoes across in their quest for enlightenment. Do you understand this teaching?

"Well, it all sounded good," you say. Perhaps it did. The motivation to do good deeds may be covering another agenda. "I must be seen as the one doing good deeds. I must be seen as the one who has evolved. I must be known as the most helpful one so I will be approved of."

And you've carried the same behaviors of the small self into a teaching that does not hold it. So the claim that we made for you and with you—because you may use it anytime—is that what you claim or go into an agreement with will be in alignment to truth.

Now the other thing you must understand is that you are already agreeing to fear in the lives you live without understanding. Here is an example: "I am supposed to be a success. If I am not a success, what have I become? I should have been married, but I am not married. If I am not married, what have I become?" And what you've done, actually, is ascribed authority to structures born in fear and equated yourself in an identity that can no longer be held without sacrificing the truth of what you are.

There is no success here externally. There is nothing to measure it against. Do you understand that? "Well, I will be the most enlightened one here," says the small self, who demands to be the most enlightened one here. There is no measuring in truth. Truth is truth, not by gradation, but by fact. Do you understand this? Truth is truth. It cannot be a little bit true. It is true if it is true, and then it is always true.

Collective agreements to be afraid are given to you in many ways to ask your authority be given to another. If you choose to do this, know that you are in choice. But the agreement always comes at a cost, and the cost of the Divine Self in its truth, in its expression, is in fact too great to sacrifice for a belief that the small self has held in what must not be left.

"Well, I have accountability. I have a family and there are bills to pay." Care for your family and pay the bills. We never said not to. Why would we do that? That would be a distortion of the teaching. But know who you are and what you are as you pay the bills and care for the children. You understand this, yes? You can find a nice way out of this teaching by deciding what is more important.

Now, we will tell you, some of you may say, "Well, my

truth is different." Well, we like that one, because what you are describing is your opinion of what your truth is. And you are entitled to that as well, because as we said, when something is true, it is eternally true. And the invocation of truth, "I know who and what I am in truth, I am serving in truth," is always true for the True Self or the Divine Self who is now being expressed by you.

The next thing we would like to discuss is what is not your fault, because you blame yourselves at most opportunity for what you have not done. Because you've inherited a world that is in change, and perhaps were participatory to the circumstances you see around you, you feel that you should be motivated to attend to things from some kind of guilt.

"If I don't do this, I am not doing my part. I am not a good man or woman."

That is obligation and is, again, the small self seeking to be expressed in self-righteousness. Self-righteousness, as we have said, is always the small self being righteous. And if you are dissuading yourself from a life well lived through a sense of guilt or what should be done, you are responding in fear.

"Well, somebody has to do it," you say. And it may well be you. But the Divine as you does not act in fear. She knows who she is and she does not live in guilt because guilt is an aspect of fear that would seek to disguise itself in another way.

The last thing we will say before we end this chapter is thank you each who have attended to these words thus far. They are challenging at times because they ask you to decide a new thing. But the decision, once made, aligns you to the very best that you may know. The causation of all good things is in alignment to truth. The causation of all you fear is never truth. It cannot be.

Here we go, friends:

"On this day I journey forward to the new life that will unfold before me. And as I give permission, my consent, to agree to truth in all commitments and choices, I sing a song of freedom. I know who I am. I know what I am. I am free. I am free. I am free."

Thank you each. Good night. Period. Period. Period. Stop now, Paul.

Chapter Seven

RESPONSIBILITY TO BECOMING

Day Fifteen

We will tell you these things before we resume the dictation for the text. What is happening now in this transmission is a realization of what can be—underline the word *can*. As we resume the teaching, we wish to take the reader outside of the known to a new potential. And this will not happen when one decides, prior to embarking on this journey, that there is no journey, but just a nice idea.

The caution we give you now, you the reader, you who comprehends these words, is that where you will be taken will be outside of the claims you've made thus far to be in consort with a reality that was prescribed for you. The mission we have had from the very beginning of these teachings has been the realization of the Divine, the Divine Potential realized as all men, the Divine Self in manifestation. And those of you who presume to understand this are still deciding what it means within the frame or structure that you have inherited. If we are to bypass this, we actually have to bypass a decision of what should be, of what would be prescribed as the small self imprinting herself on the idealization of a Divine Self.

Now here is the truth. The caution we give you is for your benefit. When we discuss realization and the potential that you all possess to be realized, we are not promising you that you will become something you could not. We are telling you what you are that you have not agreed to. And in the agreement, you decide how much the window can be opened to pierce the sense of smallness that you've justified as a race. The moment the light begins to shine in—and, yes, we mean the light of truth—you are seen in increments as what you can truly be, because you are this thing and can only be at a higher level of truth.

Now a small self, you see, who has been in charge of a world only sees things through the prescriptions that she has utilized to decide what things mean. She cannot do other. She has done her best, at times under very challenging circumstances. But the time has come to release the feather duster from her hand so she can stop fixing things and tidying a life that has never been real and align to what she is in her majesty as the Divine Self.

Now Paul doesn't like this term. It sounds very grandi-

ose to him. "Oh they're telling them all they are grand beings. They just want to feel a little better." This is not that
teaching. And we will ask him, in all love, to withdraw his
opinion so we can commence this class, this text, this missive, in responsibility to becoming. And that will be the
title of the chapter: "Responsibility to Becoming."

Now to become is to come to be. And to be as the True
Self in its expression defies the norms and the constructs of
reality that you've agreed to. The work we've done with this
text so far has been to align you to what you are, both in
vibration and context, so that you may comprehend where
you are going as best you can while claiming truth, in many
ways, for the very first time.

Now when we teach you becoming and responsibility,
we are actually telling you that where you go and are
responsible to go would be to a new life—l-i-f-e, that is
correct—a new life that participates in a restructuring at a
cellular level of the being that you are so you may become,
come to be, the expression of the True Self. Underline the
word *expression*. You are always the True Self. The aspect
of God that is you is always present, but it is not necessarily
being expressed. And the voltage or amplitude of the vibration of this must be claimed and embodied in order to be
claimed in what is perceived.

We have been preparing you for this through this text.
And we will continue, not only to prepare, but to claim the

vibration as you as what you are, so you may know it, and *be* it, and come to be *as* it as your expression.

Now forgiveness here is required, and we will go into this briefly. What you have justified through fear has been made manifest on this plane for far too long. And each one of you has been in agreement to this. And you assuage yourself of the guilt you have of being personally accountable to historical choices by trying to be better people.

We will tell you this. You don't get to be better people. You get to be what you are. And what we mean by forgiveness is that you no longer need to decide that you were wrong, because if you decide you are wrong and claim that in identity, you misalign and you move beyond truth.

Here is what we would do with this. The claim is made for you, for each of you who attends to these words, that anything claimed or justified in fear in any time will now be made known to the vibration of truth so it may be reclaimed in this octave. Now, the personality self is the one who seeks forgiveness, not the Divine Self, and we do not make the personality self wrong for asking for this. "Tell me I am not at fault for a life poorly lived. Tell me I am not to blame for gifts unused. Tell me I am not the one who contributed to structures of fear." Well, you were. You could not do other because you've been acclimated to the density of this plane, which is fraught with structure in fear. And we will do this with you now:

"On this day I claim that any remorse I may hold at con-tributing, for contributing, to structures in fear will be released in this claim. I am free of the choices I have made and the recrimination that I hold against the self or justifications for behavior or misidentification through-out time. In this claim, I align myself only to what is, to what is in truth, and as I make this claim, I respect the choices made at all times, honor the need I felt at the time they were made, and reclaim myself as worthy of the new choice to re-create and be in accord as the Divine Self in truth. I know who I am in truth. I know what I am in truth. I know how I serve in truth. I am here. I am here. I am here."

Now what we have done with you, in many ways, is re-lease you from beliefs that were never in truth, that you are separate. And the acclimation to this in form, as we have previously described, will be in understanding that what you created yesterday you have still inherited in the land-scape. But as the octave lifts, as the vibratory accord you are in shifts, what is reclaimed by you will not be at the same level. But your belief in regret or the self that would seek to harm the self for things done will be a contributor to you assessing your ability to move past collective structures of guilt or self-blame.

Now we will continue. As we teach you what the body

holds and the body agrees as, we are only doing this in illustrative ways so that you may understand that the symbol of the body as a vessel is a limited idea. The body is of God, as is the earth and sky, and the programming of the body, or how the body knows itself, will now be attended to as this text resumes. The claim of the body, "I am the Divine Self in manifested form," defies agreement. You pass the mirror, you don't like what you see, you go to the doctor, you don't like what you hear. What you see around you would regard you as the shell that holds the idea of the Divinity you are, but not as the expression of it in truth.

So as we reclaim you here, and reidentify you, and claim you in responsibility for your adherence to this teaching, in fact what we are telling you is that the mirrors you have utilized to understand what you are in physical form need to be released and replaced with a higher mirror. When we work with our students and we witness them, we hold the vision of what they are so that they may be met at this level of attunement. And the claims we have made for you each in this text thus far—"we know *what* you are in truth"—is intended to hold the field and the body at this level of vibration so that the system that you know the body as may become acclimated to the higher voltage that is what you are, that would not be held in old form.

Now the density of matter is something you can all comprehend. But because something is dense simply means it is vibrating in accord with a level of density that it has been attuned to. As the body is transformed as the expression of the True Self, what is actually happening is that the vessel that you are, in its expression as a Divine Self, is acclimating to the higher octave so that it may be the emanation of it in an active way, in a participatory way, so that the landscape that it exists in may be understood and reclaimed by one who operates as what he or she truly is.

Now there are lots of questions here from Paul. We will attend to them eventually, but not at the cost of this dictation, which is resuming at this moment without his permission. He wants his questions now, and we will get there when there is time.

The octave that you express at—and we use the word *octave* to mean level of vibration—assumes you in like accord with the plane that you exist in. So the density of the plane, in agreement to the density of the form you hold, creates a collective agreement about how the world is experienced. As you lift yourself in vibration, what happens is that the agreement to the dimensional reality that you exist in is transformed, and you experience the landscape you exist in, in a higher octave. It is as it was, but in a higher way.

The teacup on the table is still a teacup, but your experience of the teacup, and the table itself, is altered, because both you and the teacup are now in coherence at a higher octave. And the creation of this on this plane, which is a higher level of vibration in expression, renders the world you know as malleable to transformation. As you release the density that was claimed in form and you go up the octave to the next level of expression, you exist at that level in union with all other things. And the claims made at that level—"I know what I am"—are in manifestation with a manifest world that is in agreement to it.

You can understand this, in some ways, by assuming that if you go to a foreign country where everybody speaks a new language, the language is how you will use your expression. Not the language from the country you came from—nobody will understand you. You speak the language of the country you stand in. And at this level, you are in agreement to a new landscape or a new world because you exist there with like vibration.

Now the testament to this must be your own lives. We will challenge you here. If you do the work of this text, which simply means the alignment to truth and the willingness to transform, the body itself and your attachment to what you thought you were, your experience of this plane, must be altered. In your experience, you will know, and as you know, you agree to what you are, which is the Divine Self in manifestation.

The crucible here is always the personality self, who seeks to justify her claims and will reference the old, or the language of the old country, to support her in reclaiming the old vibration. And then she can be guaranteed to be right when not a damned thing happens. And that would be her intention.

We are not promising you that you will sprout wings and fly on a cloud. We are assuring you that the aspect of what you are in truth, in its expression, will move in consort with a world that exists in like vibration.

Now some of you think that this is a very pretty world. "The flowers must bloom all day. Heaven on earth is a happy place." But, again, please understand, dears, that the teacup on the table was still a teacup, but you are preparing the self to realize it in the higher octave that it also exists in, where it may be known in a new way.

And your experience here on this plane is quite comparable to that. If you can imagine that the Divine as you is walking down the street and witnesses something that the small self might run from, or shield her eyes from and damn or fear, the Divine Self as you, who does not judge and does not fear, will have a completely different comprehension of what she sees, because what she sees is in truth. She does not comprehend the attachments to the old at the level of the small self. But she understands them as they relate to the way the world is operating.

So if you see something on the street that would make the small self run, the True Self will understand what is required of her and attend to the need without fear. The object is to be in alignment with what you are, the Divine as what you are, and bear witness to a world that is in agreement to this.

Now as we have said already, the Divine is in all things. But perhaps you can understand that the idealization of what things mean, as have been authorized in history, is what is reclaiming you in agreement to what they were at the cost of what they are.

We will offer you this: The sky is blue because you believe it to be blue, because someone once said "blue sky," and the agreement to the blue sky is in the mind of the system here and is replicated by you all. If one day the color of the sky was revealed to be different, you would all be doing your damnedest to see blue where there was something other because you expect to see what you have always known.

To be in a reality as the Divine Self does not mean you are walking around smiling and waving at everybody. You may choose to do that, you may choose to do as you wish. But, again, your misconceptions of what it means to be as the Divine Self have been inherited by you. The man who is sick and dying and is in his misery on his deathbed is as of God, and in his perfection, as the newborn baby is. These are simply different ways that the body is expressing, and all are loved and agreed to by the True Self in alignment to what they are. Again, the word *what* means manifestation.

Now the one who fears death has an agreement to what she sees. The one who has an attachment to what things should be has a response to something based on her attachment. We are not devaluing these things. Why should we? They are things that you learn through. But until you comprehend that the Divine as you has a very different relationship to the material world than the small self does, you will continue to claim the world that you have known yourself through.

Now you justify much in the name of fear. "Well, he was chasing me, I had to run. They did this over there, we had to react in some way." And in these claims, you perpetuate systems that have brought you all to the brink of a destruction that does not need to happen. And we will say "does not" because the octave of truth that is present here, as you, will actually support it in being manifested in what you see before you. As you know what you are, you know what other things are as well, and the manifestation of the Divine, as known by you in form, is known in the form of all things.

The discrepancy you will face between what we teach and the reality you see will actually come in stages to be healed. And we will explain this. Your investment in separation, how you believe yourself to be as outside of your Source, or what you would decide is outside of Source, will be understood by you in order to be reclaimed.

Paul is seeing again the image of the wave of truth that we described earlier, brushing against a shore, enveloping what it sees. And each time you encounter something, someone, some situation that you would like to deny the Divinity in, you can claim the truth of what you see is in realization with the truth of what it is.

And we will give you an example. If you see something on the television set that you would be asked to witness as an atrocity and go into fear with, to claim the truth in it— the action of the Divine is present in all things, of God is in all things—is not being present or named by you to excuse anything, but to lift the very thing you see to a level of congruence with truth where it may be comprehended in a higher way.

We don't make it better this way. We don't put little bows on anything. We have asked you always to be in full accountability about how you treat your fellows. But when you see an action in fear that is asking you, encouraging you, to join it in fear, by claiming the thing in truth you are claiming your identity, the what that you are, by claiming the what in manifestation of what you see, which would be the equivalent of the wave of truth encompassing what you see to bring you into a new alignment with it.

Now Paul is cautious about this teaching. "You are asking us to forgive things, or to be docile about things." That's actually ridiculous. That's the last thing we are doing. To comprehend the Divine in what you see as the one who knows what he is, is to transform the thing you see to a higher way of expression, which actually means you are manifesting a new world by not agreeing to the fear that would call you to it.

The disassemblance of the structures of this world that are ensuing now will be coming very quickly because, as we have said, what is no longer in truth, what is not in truth, cannot coexist with the new level of frequency that is here to be and to be known in all things. And those of you who come here to be in this agreement with us, have come to claim a world in consort with truth for the benefit of all.

Your responsibility, you see, is to everything you see. Do you all hear these words? As the one who can perceive or be in witness to a world, your responsibility as the manifested truth, the Divine as what you are, is to claim truth in all, which aligns what you see to the higher vibration. The claim "I am here, I am here, I am here," which is the Divine as you announcing its purview, is inclusive of all she sees. You become the searchlight, the beacon of light, and what you witness—"I know who I am in truth; I know what I am in truth; I know how I serve in truth"—is claimed in truth by your presence as the witness of it.

The manifested world, you see, is then imprinted by you in the higher octave and lifted to its truth. This is the disassemblance of structure. There is truth in every structure, but what has been in lies must be released from it for it to be serving you and all mankind.

Imagine, if you wish, that every lie that was ever told or perpetrated against mankind by anyone at any time was circling this plane as an energy field. We will call this the level of fear that you have been encountering and has been seeking to replicate itself in form or in manifestation as long as you have known yourselves in form.

What we are doing is lifting this world beyond that illusion because, in truth, these lies do not exist. And the field of truth that we are working with here, we promise you, is far more powerful than any lie that has been told.

Paul is asking himself, "Well, I see this world. I see this fear floating around the world as you have described, but I don't see what the truth does."

By your very being as the one who knows what he is, in witness to anything—underline *anything*—you have the ability to reclaim what you witness in accord with the vibration that you are holding. At that level, the illustration of the world surrounded in fear can be met by you as the one who can claim it, and every bit of it in truth.

If we were to give you a meditation upon this, it would be very simple. Imagine the world before you and all who dwell in it, and claim truth in all you witness. "I know who I am in truth. I know what I am in truth. I know how I serve in truth. I see the Divine truth in all manifestation. And in this claim, behold, I see a new world."

We will thank you each for your attendance to these words today. We will resume tomorrow and continue this chapter. Good night. Stop now, please. Period. Period. Period.

Day Sixteen

We will ask you this: Will this teaching resume without concern for the transmission? The work that we have before us is of an amplitude that Paul has not encountered before, and his concerns about the broadcast, unfounded we would say, could curtail a teaching of great importance. Our advice for the young man in the chair is to have a nice nap, concern himself with the actions of the day, and leave us to our students for the highest good of all, of all, of all.

Now, as we resume the teaching, we wish you to comprehend one thing—that the material realm that you operate in is based in agreements that have been made by you all. The laws you understand of how the world operates are actually there in service to what you have prescribed a reality to be. As the ascension of consciousness begins to unfold, substance, which simply means that the bodies you know yourselves through are in agreement to the higher octave; the laws of the plane that you have known yourself through must then be rerendered by the collective to support a reality that seeks to be established in form.

Now the reality we speak to is a collective agreement to be as the Divine Self. In fact, *as* this, and as this is known by each man, by each being, the world she assumes herself in is actually transformed through her witness and through the impression she makes upon the landscape that she coexists in.

Now Paul is interrupting already. "So one person has one experience of this plane, and another has another?"

Yes, that is true, but it has always been true. One may smile at the rain and bless the nurturance that it will give the soil, and another may curse it because her day has been destroyed by the rain that has fallen on her party. You all have ways of addressing your world that are singular, regardless of what you see or how it might be of benefit to someone else.

The degree that you understand that consciousness informs the physical plane will be needed to incur the vibration as the Divine Self in amplification to withstand the changes that would come in form. Now, if you understand that the being that you are holds vibration by nature of being, you've taken the first step. If you can consider the possibility that the physical systems that you utilize to operate as must be in accord with a level of vibration to bypass collective agreements about what has been possible for mankind to attain, you will move into an opportunity to reknow the self in a higher way. But the possibility of what you are, the manifested Divine Self in her expression amassing form in the higher frequency, is predicated on your willingness to release your attachment to what you think reality is.

Now this is a challenge for Paul to even say. His imagination runs rampant. "So we are being told that we have to see all things in a different way and render the landscape that we have known as a false place?"

In some ways, you do, but not in the ways you imagine, Paul. When you imagine escalation in vibration, you are assuming chaos when, in fact, what it brings is perfect order. And by this we mean that the small self's need to explain things or render things in certain ways based upon the teachings she's received is voided in all ways so that the truth may be known. Because you've received a teaching about what the world is, what the body does, how things happen as they do, you use these things to frame your comprehension of all things you see. You look at the laws you've made collectively and ascribe the material realm to the teachings you've known, and we would say at the cost of what truly is.

Now if you can imagine, just for a moment, that the concept of time itself is an equalizer, because you've all used it as a shared construct without argument, you can see

how a law is set. No one in their right mind would argue
the clock or the calendar—they would be thought to be
mad. But the truth of the matter is the calendar is a construct. It is malleable to choice. And if a culture were to
decide that their calendar year would last three months,
they would do perfectly well in their manifestation of a system that would incorporate the world to their requirements
of a calendar.

It is an illusion, but it is a vast illusion. And the construct
of time as a shared system of agreement is the easiest one to
begin to look at and to collectively move beyond. If time is
a law, and the calendar date is an application of the law of
time, and the collective agrees that perhaps this is not so,
you can begin to move into a different relationship with
time. And the body you know yourself through then begins to have a different experience of itself within the structure because the rules have changed.

You all comprehend what day it is because you wake up
and you remember what it was the day prior, and so you
know what should come after and there is next to no
thought being applied. Once you take away the calendar,
you still have ways of assessing time—the time it takes to
bathe the child, to bake the bread, to walk to the work you
do each day. And as you continue in your habituated ways,
you would actually find that you would replicate the system
of time sheerly out of habit.

As we move you outside of the laws you've known, we must take you to the realm of potential, to perceiving the possibility that, as the True Self that you are, the Divine Being you can only be does not exist in time. She can bypass the law of time as consciousness. This is the first step.

If you can imagine consciousness as broadcast, and the field that the broadcast exists in operates outside of time because it has not been prescribed to a three-dimensional realm, you can begin to comprehend that the dreams you have or the thoughts you may know are existing independently from a clock, a calendar, that has been agreed upon. But the form that you hold, the body that you know yourself in, is moored in agreement to linear time. And the law of time oppresses you in many ways because you have decided that how you be in consort with the calendar will conform to the ideas of what time should be.

If you can imagine right now that the moment that you sit in, the very moment you sit in, is in fact eternity and the eternal now that you stand in is always in present time, the idealization of achievement, things born in structure, begins to diminish.

Now we are not saying that time is not of value. But we are illustrating it as a collective agreement that you have all adhered to as law. As you align to the Divine as you, the what you are in form, you will not do so through the standard clock. You will not do so in obeyance to structure because these things that you know serve to compress your experience into codification for the purpose of utilizing a shared agreement. The manifested self, the one that knows itself in form, must then be transformed to a new potential that even the body in its divinity may be thought of as timeless or without time.

Now Paul is in a rut here, attempting to dig himself out. "Well, I hear what they're saying. I will have no part of it. We are not immortal. And if they are taking us there, I am going away."

Well, we will tell you something, friend. You are all immortal, and that's the one thing that you keep denying about yourselves. The Divine Self as you *is* immortal and is expressing itself in a mortal package in a three-dimensional realm where you've all agreed to what time is.

Now the body may not be here forever, but until you get with it and comprehend the structure of the physical realm as Divine itself, you cannot align to your true expression. So we are not telling you that the body is there in the current form it is two hundred years from now. But the *you* that you are, and in fact the *what* that you are, can never die.

The illusion of time supports death. But death, you see, is only comprehended at this level of reality. And as you assist the vibratory shift that is taking place on this plane and begin to render reality in its true nature through the alignment to truth that you perceive all things in, the death and the frame of death that you have all claimed is lifted again to the comprehension of the transition outside of the physical realm, which it only is.

You see such a small part of your reality. You do not comprehend the vastness of Spirit and all who are here to assist this plane in its realignment. Your belief in your small selves and your desire to protect the body from inevitable demise is actually transforming you to the small self in need, where the Divine as what you are, who knows her immortal being, does not even fear death.

Now the life you live at this time is informed by many things. We have spoken of history as a deciding factor. You know what things are through what you were taught they were. But we have not talked yet about how to bypass the calendar through self-identification. If you align as truth and know yourself as this vibration, the claim "I am in truth" will also reveal the Divine Self as out of time. And your experience of yourself in eternity, or unbound by the clock, will begin to be a benefit of your experience here, because unless you begin to realize that the system of achievement here—what it means to be enlightened, if you wish—has very little to do with manifestation through prior structure or old agreements, you will not know the vastness of being that is your true inheritance.

The small self, you see, perceives enlightenment as a goal, and the idea of a goal or place arrived to in destination is always some other time. Enlightenment, you see, or the being that you are as realized in coherence with the Divine Self as what you are, is in an infinite moment that exists outside of time.

"I was enlightened on Wednesday last," you would like to say, "and perhaps next Thursday I will be enlightened some more."

The Divine Self that you are is enlightened. The small self will never be. And your seeking to attribute your divinity to the small self, who operates through the system of time and is moored to the agreements of the flesh, is what you claim when you seek to know the small self as God. It is not.

The Divine as you is here, is here, is here as what you are and may only be. The Divine as what you are has been the teaching of this text, and the self that you know in agreement to truth is the one who bypasses the system of time as consciousness.

"Now what does it mean," Paul asks, "to bypass time?"

We will honor you this question. It means you comprehend the timepiece on your wrist, you understand its use, you understand the collective agreement to show up for work on Monday. But you know what you are, the Divine as what you are, is unlimited by the clock. Use the word *unlimited* well—which simply means is not suppressed, is not withheld, is not imprisoned by time—because if you do this with time and make time your keeper, you have made a God of time. And God, itself, exists in all time and no time because God is all things.

You do not make an appointment with God to have a nice chat at the last moment of your life, because God is as present now, as what you are, as it will ever be. But to be in agreement to this means you have claimed in being the vibration of Source as what you are in manifestation.

We will do this with you now, if you wish. The claims we make for you are made on your behalf by us in support of this agreement. We don't make it so for you unless you align to it, and the process of aligning to the claim is always the same:

"I am in agreement to this as being so and the potential of it as being manifested as and by me."

Until the potential is made manifest as and by you, you will not know yourself as it. If you seek to know it in completeness prior to agreement, you will be challenged by this, and we will tell you why. We are creating a world that exists outside of time for you to realize it, and this system that we offer you—"I am outside of time"—is always true for the Divine Self because she is unlimited, unmoored, untethered to the attachment to the time clock that the small self believes itself to be bound by.

"On this day I claim that I will have a new realization of what I am, the Divine Self in manifestation and all things in it outside of time, so that my knowing and realization of what I am as an eternal being will be claimed by and through me and expressed as me in consciousness and form. And as I agree to this, I give permission to be supported in this realization by the Divine that I am and all who attend to me as my enlightenment is manifest in my being. I claim this of my own free will. I know what I am in truth. I am here. I am here. I am here."

Period. The claim has been made, the choice has been taken by those who said the words, or set the intention, or simply agreed. So be prepared, dear friends, for a glimpse of eternity through your being and conscious perception. In that one moment of perception, when the time clock ceases to exist, you have broken the law of time. And once that law is broken, which simply means it has no meaning, your entire world will never be the same.

You are liberated in ways because you understand always that the Divine in the now, the truth of what you are now, the expression as now, is truth. And everything else, everything else you can imagine, finally, finally, finally, is illusion.

We will cease this dictation in a few moments. We will

continue this teaching tomorrow. But we wish to thank the man in the chair for his service today, and we acknowledge Victoria* and her escapades in time. In some ways she has been gifted with this being as herself outside of the clock so that she may claim her own truth and know what she is, as all men will one day.

We thank you both for your presence. Good night. Good night. Good night. Stop now, please.

Day Seventeen

We will say these things in commencing this dictation: Where we take you next will be to a new idea that mankind itself can bypass structure, limited structure, to re-create a world. But unless mankind aligns himself to what he is—underline, again, *what*—the manifestation of the Divine in form, he will be circumvented by his own requirements for a world that seeks to replicate itself through history when such things could not be so. Unless you take the leap that things are not what you think they are, and what they may be may be vastly greater, you will collectively decide to continue what you have known.

Now the chances are that if you continue on the path

---

* Victoria Nelson.

you are on, you will find means to direct your energies toward the very things that you say you do not want. You don't want war, but you claim it every day. You don't want famine, but you see it every day. And we will say these words for you once again: You are not distinct from the landscape you inhabit, and because you can perceive anything you are in vibratory accord with it. Because you are in accord, the consciousness you bring to anything informs it. And as the Divine Self knowing who he or she is in manifestation, you can cocreate a higher world, a world where these things no longer exist because you cannot agree to them in vibration.

Does it take everyone to manifest a new world? In fact, it does not. The ones who come in an awareness of what they are, the manifested self, claim victory for those who will follow. Because the way has been lit and claimed in truth, the boulevard that you walk down will become wide enough to support millions. But this will not happen without consent.

How is consent gained? In one of two ways—by inviting or showing. And if you show the truth as what you are to one you see, the one you see, seen as the truth of what they are, will go into accord at a vibrational level to what you are. The consent is done, not by asking, but by being.

As you become the beacon, as you come to be the beacon of what you are, the Divine Self in witness, who you witness agrees to you in vibration because the higher octave will be played in their field. And the field itself must rise to be met at this level of congruence.

Here we go, friends:

"On this day I choose to bear witness to only truth in all I see, and each one I meet will be instilled in the octave of truth that I abide in as my Divine Self. The call I give, 'You are here, you are here, you are here,' to each one I pass announces them all in their purview as the True Self, the Divine Self, the Divine Being that they are in resonance, in action. I am Word through the one I see before me. On this day I choose to bear witness to the Divine truth in all mankind. I am Word through this intention. Word I am Word."

As the claim has been made by you, it is sung in your field for all humanity to hear—*all* humanity, yes. You imagine yourself in your small home, book in hand, perhaps, seeing the world that perhaps you may impact by your next good deed. But where we have taken you, dears, is to inform the world, the entire world, with the truth of what you are.

As you are an emissary of this teaching by the very nature of your being, by the field that you've claimed in alignment to truth, you can claim it in all ways. And we support you each in the claims made on behalf of those you may meet, or may never meet. This is how the world awakens, friends, by the witness of the one who knows who and what another is. There is no convincing required because this is done in energy and agreement. And by "agreement" we mean congruence.

Now Paul is interrupting with a question. "So we don't require permission? People are agreeing to something they don't even know."

People are not agreeing. The energy field that they hold is. The light that you are shows them who they are, and in acknowledgment, in coresonance with you, they agree to be what they can only be in truth. Again, underline *in truth*. The witness you are holding for another is the claim of truth, of what they are, the Divine manifested. As this is always true, the lie they believe themselves to be is released from them in accord with their own highest self and their agreement to be manifest. Underline, as we said, *their agreement*.

The highest self that they hold is in purview here, not the small self who would seek to continue on her small and merry way. The Divine as what you are supersedes and re-creates and reclaims in her witness the world she stands in, and the vehicle you know as the body is part and parcel to this expression.

As we continue with the body, we first wish to assure

you that what we are doing is maintained by you and in your authority to agree to. But the reacclimation of the self in the higher vibration in manifested form is an undertaking, and we say this so that you can each comprehend that the transformation you undergo will be outside of the expected, or the known, or the prescribed. The teaching here is to give permission to the body, and all the body knows itself as, to be re-created in agreement to be the expression of the Divine Self.

Now understand what we are saying. *All the body has known itself as.* As we discussed earlier in this text, the imprinting of consciousness on manifested structure—everyone who ever went to the bank has contributed to the structure of the bank by imprinting her consciousness upon it—the same is true for the physical self. Everyone who has ever witnessed you in a physical form has agreed to you. And your body, in fact, holds the vibration of how you were witnessed, or how you perceived yourself as being witnessed by others.

In some ways, the agreement to be seen by the lower self, or the small self, has undermined the True Self's ability to become manifest as the physical expression that you truly are. If a child is taught to be ashamed of her body, the body holds the memory of shame. If a young man is taught to be aggressive in form and that the body itself is a machine for aggression, the body itself has become attuned to that requirement as a way of being. If the body believes she cannot be loved as the skin grows old, or the man believes he will not be meritful as his muscles fail, you have chosen things that the body agrees to. And the agreement to be in the body with these as your benefits is determined by you and expressed by you in all ways. So when your health is failing, or when you are ashamed, perhaps what you are doing is utilizing the impression of a world that you have been seen by and conforming the physical self to the requirements of the world.

Here we go again:

"On this day I choose to release from my body all memories of witness, and all claims upon the body made by anyone, anywhere, that are contradictory to the truth of what I am. As I claim my Divine Self in manifest form, I align every cell of my being and the field that I hold to its innate truth, that the Source of my being, the True Divine, the Creator as I, is in perfect expression. And all the things that would deny this truth are being released and transformed in the knowing of what I am. I know what I am in truth. I am here. I am here. I am here."

Align to this, now. This is an enormous claim. You are releasing the memory of how you have been perceived by others, or how you believed yourself to be perceived by them throughout time. And in this release, all the schisms between the truth of being and the illusion of being will begin to align in perfect ways to be re-created in truth. As you know what you are, you must also know what you are not. And the verdicts against the physical self—"she should be ashamed of herself, he should be frightened of his body or the impulses of the body, he will never be this or that because he cannot hold it"—will be released to the new creation, the Divine as what you are.

Now if you can understand the teaching thus far, you will comprehend that, once again, all we are doing is claiming you in truth at this level because the perceptions by others—the way they think you are, or their opinion of what you are, or how you believe yourself to be in their estimation in form—are lies. These things were never true.

So as you are aligned in truth, the fingerprints—the imprint of others' perceptions that have soiled the field you hold and in many ways confirmed you as unholy—will be released in the claim you have made.

He asks a question: "What is the process of this?"

The process is alchemy, and we will say this, finally, again. Your investment, Paul, in picking things apart is based in history. "What will be the next step for me?" is what you are asking, as if you have control at a personality level of releasing the imprinting of a lifetime, or many lifetimes, if you wish, of witness by others, claims against the body by

cultures, memories held in the body from past times. This is
all done in a higher octave. And the re-creation of the self
does not make you look any different than perhaps you do
today, because the truth of what you are will be expressed as
what you are, and your idealization or glorification of the
physical self as something other than true, and always true,
will be met by you in falsity.

The Divine as what you are must only express as you
wherever you stand. The idea, Paul, that you will look like
a God upon a mountaintop and radiating light is in fact
true at a higher level because you are all this. You are all on
a mountaintop and radiating light as the Truest Self. But
the form that you have taken in this lifetime is the most
perfect form for you to be expressed in as what you are.

Now we will say this: Those of you who have been
damned in the body through fear or shame, through an
agreement to culture—"If you don't look like this, or adhere
to that, you will not be known"—will undergo a process of
sorts as you reclaim the self. But, again, the process of rein-
tegration in truth—which means in the claim of truth, "I
am in truth," and the physical body's claim in truth, "I am
here in truth"—will go through its process without your
consent at a level of personality.

Claiming the divinity in the form you hold aligns the
body to its truth. And the truth is what does the work. Will

your body look different? Paul asks this for himself. Perhaps it may, but the alignment itself is not cosmetic. The alignment itself is here to support you in the re-creation of a world. And the being that you are, the consciousness and the form, is the vehicle through which this happens.

Now we will ask you this: Are you willing to learn a bit more about what it means to be seen by us as what you are? We will do this with you each, if you like, and please comprehend this. We are present to you, the frequency that we are, to the readers of the text, wherever you may be. So your invocation of our presence in this exercise will be met to the degree that you can accept us.

We would like you to imagine that where you sit or stand or lie is a holy place. Wherever you are there is God, and what can be met by you in this holy place is God itself and all who come in his name, its name, her name, whatever you wish to claim it as. In this holy place, you ask, if you wish, to be witnessed by us, the source of this text, the scribes, if you prefer, or the consciousness that is the Christ informing each word in love.

Now, if you wish, we will stand before you and we will hold you in vibration in our witness of you, and as we say this for you, we anoint the physical self, the embodiment of Source that you are and can only be, with the eyes and the perception and the frequency of God. Here we go:

"We see you as you are. We see you as you can only be. And in this frequency of truth, we witness the reacclimation of what you are in the form you have taken to be expressed as in this lifetime. We know who you are. We know what you are. We know how you serve. You are here. You are here. You are here. Be in truth."

Feel this, please, if you wish. The vibration that we hold will be in consort with you as you allow it and as you let yourself be received by us. In the holding of this vision for you, we give you permission to know, and to know means to realize what you are and what you can only be in manifestation.

Now Paul is getting in the way—so many questions today from him. The one we will answer is the one we wish you to know. "Am I changed? Have I been changed by this encounter?"

You are as you have always been, beloved as you are, as we see you, as you have always been, the Divine Self before us, the one we witness you all as, ever-present, the eternal self, the Christ as you, the truth of what you are, aligned in what she can only be. "I know myself in truth. I am here."

So are you changed? You are revealed as what you can only be.

We thank you each for your agreement to be, to be as

you are, and to become, to come to be the True Self in perfect manifestation.

Now we will continue with the dictation for a short time more. There is a question that has come up about the maintenance of the body. "Do we eat meat or fish? Do we stay away from meat or grain? How do we behave?"

Those of you who like rules will be very disappointed by the answer we give you. The Divine as who you are, the Divine as what you are, is the one who claims the requirements of the vehicle you hold. And as you agree to be as this and give the authority to the True Self to maintain the systems of the body, you may do so in high ways.

To look outside the self for prescribed behavior is to reduce the body to a list of things that must be met. On Monday you may need fish. On Friday you may need grain. And if you honor the truth of the moment you are in as the True Self, you will be met perfectly and choose in accord.

Some of you despise the body or what you perceive it to be, and if you have made this claim with us today, you will understand that how you've perceived your body, or allowed the body to be perceived by others, is what has claimed you in this. And the release of this function to despise the self or the form you hold will re-create you and realign what you are outside of the reasons for this, whatever they have been.

The anointing you receive by us as we see you in your

perfection in fact overrides the witnessing of others in lower vibration. Do you understand this?

So if you believe yourself to be seen as homely in someone's estimation, our witnessing of your true beauty will always hold forth and be claimed in truth because we see you in truth, and someone else's idea of what you should be or how you should be seen is simply their opinion.

We will say thank you each, now, for all you bring to us. And your willingness to be taught and to be met by us where we stand is a gift you give, not only to us, but to all you know and all that may be known by you as the one who knows who she is, who he is, in truth.

We thank you, and good night. This is the end of the chapter, yes. Period. Period. Period. Stop now, please.

Chapter Eight

FREEDOM

Day Eighteen

The only thing we can say about what will happen to each of you as you realize yourself—underline the word *realize*—is that you will become what you truly are. Underline *what*.

This has been a teaching in manifestation and the Divine Self as what you are, perhaps at the cost of the small self's itinerary for who she should be and what she has planned. The big gesture that encompasses you as you claim your independence from the small self's agenda is freedom. And if you can understand what this means, it means freedom from expectation about what you should be, or how it should look, or what the world should look and be as.

Now, we will say this for you. Some things are required. You hold yourself in a body, you are required to care for the body, you have a livelihood at this time because you've agreed to a world that operates in commerce. As you bypass the systems of control or agreed upon ways of exchange, you actually call higher ways into manifestation. At this juncture, we will say, few of you are prepared to release the life that you've claimed in worry or in expectation to what might be born as you and for you in a higher way.

Here we go:

"On this day I choose to release myself from all expectations of how things should be, or what they should look like as perceived by the small self. And in this claim of freedom, I realize myself as the one who is independent from the foils and beliefs of collective agreement that would seek to hinder me from my true expression as my True Self. I know who I am in truth. I know what I am in truth. I know how I serve in truth. I am here. I am here. I am here."

This is a claim that is made by you to re-create the self outside a fixed agenda or outside of the perceptions that you are holding in investment because you cannot imagine yourself without being realized in certain ways. Even the identity you hold that was prescribed by you as who you should be seeks to impale you in a series of ways upon the intractability of physical manifestation.

What this means is that if your belief is that your

progress is dependent upon anything in form, you are using that thing to justify and claim you in a small way. It can be anything, you see. "When I have the perfect marriage, or the perfect employment, the perfect practice, the perfect insight, the perfect realization, I will be here as I truly am. But until that moment, I will wait and claim this thing as what I require to be free."

The only requirement for freedom is realization of what you are, because the moment this is understood, all ties and tethers to what was created for you or by you to be in agreement to a system of control is leaving, is gone, is eradicated in truth.

Now we come back to the idea of truth for one reason only. The systems of control that we speak of, or the ways that you would seek to realize yourself through external manifestations, are never in truth. And we will tell you why. All that is in truth is present now in this very moment, in the eternal now that you have encountered in the reading of this text and through the alignment to the what that you are. The Divine Self operates as what you are in the eternal now. And anything that is not present as you is simply an idea of what is required to call you forward.

Now, this is confusing for Paul. "But there are things we need, and we call them into being. We require food, we go to the market. Don't tell me my needs are met now if I have an empty kitchen."

We are telling you something very different. The idea of expectation as something to strive to, or claim for, or bring yourself as in consort to at the cost of the present moment you stand in, is what is being addressed. The infinite now is always here. It is here as you, as you walk to the market, as you prepare your meal. But the justification of what you should be as predicated on some future event—"when I am this or that, have claimed this or that"—is never true because your realization only happens in the moment you stand in.

The path to enlightenment, if you wish to use that term, is always now because enlightenment is now and not on some prescribed date at some other point in time. Until you all understand that what you have done so far is prepare the way for manifestation that is already present as what you are, you will be confused by this. In a higher octave, the Divine as you is fully present, and the realization of this and the knowing of this is the creation of what you are in manifested form. You are not becoming what you are not, you are claiming what you are. And as you come to be at this alignment, in this awareness, the release of the lies that you have given credence to will claim you in freedom.

Now, many things are there for you to learn through. You have a life before you, still, and the belief that when you enlighten yourself, or become enlightened, there will be no more lessons is untrue. This is not about stasis. It's about being. And being, we say, is always in motion.

As you stand before us today, you may think yourself as still, but the field that you hold is in motion, and the blood is coursing through your veins, and the ideas in your mind are circling around you, and the images in your mind are teaching you what you can imagine and therefore bring forth into the manifest world. So even your belief in arrival someday—"I will arrive and be myself, and I will have no more worry"—is not true because you may claim worry anywhere you like. You still have choice.

Now what we would like to teach you today is about freedom and what it means to be free at the cost of a world made. The world is made by you each in tandem with the collective needs of the culture you live in, and the collective cultures create collective agreements about how to be with one another. And the messes you find yourselves in, in civilization, are about the misconceptions of who others are and what their requirements for growth might be. You ascribe behavior to ones you know little about in order to perceive them through the lenses of your culture or what you have been taught to believe. And they do the same for you. Consequently, you have skewed vision, misperception, and misidentification of who and what others are.

"Is this ever remedied?" Paul asks.

It is remedied very easily. If each man were to stand naked before her brother, she would understand immediately that humanity holds no name but truth. If you would really understand each other outside of the clothes you wear, the businesses you attend to, the churches you pray at, the politics you believe in, if you were to see the one before you at a level of essence, you would realize very quickly that he or she is no different than you. But until humanity bypasses the need to be right at the cost of another being wrong, to win at the cost of somebody else losing, you will be challenged.

"What is the remedy, then," Paul asks, "if we cannot attend to those things?"

Truth, we would say, and the alignment to truth in the level of service for the world you live in. When we taught you "I know who I am, I know what I am, I know how I serve," we explained that service was the Divine Self in its fullest expression. And as you anchor the vibration of truth in the field that you are, as you align and sing it, how you witness your world, anyone and anywhere, in the vibration of truth reclaims them at the level of essence, naked, if you wish, from the accoutrements of age or gender or culture or religion or politics. As you witness the Divine in any human being, he is reclaimed as what he is. But this is not done in fanciful ways, and it is not done in corrective ways. It is never done to make another man behave as you wish him to. That would be the small self ascribing behavior as she wishes to the one she witnesses as disobeying her requirements for who he or she should be.

The testament to this, we say, would be those in your lives. Every day somebody disagrees with you, gives you a dirty look or some false praise. You are always in mechanisms with your fellows in a strange dance of agreement and disagreement. But when you work with truth as the identity you hold—"I am in truth, I am in alignment as truth, I see all the world before me in truth"—the music changes and the silly dances you would play out with your fellows will be moved to the higher octave.

As we witness you each, we reclaim you as what you are so that you may do the same. As we said earlier in this text, what you become is what you are. And what you are, in fact, finally, is what we are—God as what it is, impressed in form or in vibration, experiencing itself in all that she sees before her. If you become as God as the perceiver—"I see with the eyes of the Christ, I witness all things in truth"—you are operating outside of personality or personal agenda. And as this one who may witness at this level perceives a world, the world must be transformed.

Now, Paul is concerned by the teaching. "We need evidence. We need to know that this is so, or it makes no sense. We cannot know if how we perceive our world informs the world."

Well, you already know this. But we will give you an example. Look around the room you are in. It's the room you chose to be in for whatever reasons. Now, close your eyes, and when you open your eyes again, imagine that the room you are in is a room in eternity. The moment you are in, in this place or time, is always here because you are in the eternal now. Allow the knowing of this expression—"I am in the eternal now"—to inform how you witness. And understand that your expression as the one seeing is actually informing the landscape you stand in.

Now, close your eyes again and imagine that this room is simply an illusion, that it exists in time and space at a certain octave, or as a field of vibration, but the solidity you believe to be before you is not true. And when you open your eyes again, we would like you to imagine that everything you see before you is in motion. The air is in motion, the walls in motion, your feet, your hands, and what you see is all alive as a field in agreement to be in vibration.

Your experience of this, quite simply, is about leaving a known world to begin to perceive what already is that exists before you. Everything we just told you is true. The room you are in lives in eternity as you stand in it. And the walls and the floor are alive in vibration because everything is in motion beyond the small self's realization of form.

Now, the real question for Paul is, "How are things changed?"

Through witness. We will tell you very simply that if there is a flute playing a certain note, and that note is in resonance, it will call other things to it of like resonance.

When you claim truth in what you see as the Divine Self who knows herself as truth, she aligns to the truth in what she sees. The things that are never true are always frightening. Do you understand this, yes?

When the Divine Self witnesses something in fear that was created in fear, she has the purview, the jurisdiction, the amplitude, and the True Self that knows what is before her, to re-create or realign the vibrational form of the things she sees.

Go back to the idea of the room in motion. Everything is weaving in and out. Nothing is solid. If you go to an incident in the world that you would perceive as frightening and you claim it in fear, you solidify the form of fear. You make it so by the name you claim it in. And how you inform that name with the Divine Self will be very different than the one who claims it in fear.

As the Divine Self in witness, she moves beyond the solidity of form to what is always true. Everything is vibration and everything is a manifestation of consciousness. Because something was claimed once in consciousness and made into form, it can be re-created in the higher way by the one who knows who and what she is.

As humanity as a whole begins to circumvent creations made in fear by claiming truth and not agreeing to fear, the small self's investment in knowing itself as fearful is first diminished and then released. What we are doing with you each is catalyzing you to catalyze your world. You are lightning rods for the vibration of truth, and once you are lit by this light, you perceive it in all things.

"Well," you may be saying, "I want the experience of this."

Find a friend, if you wish. Sit with your friend. Look at the one before you and set this intention: "I know who you are in truth. I know what you are in truth. I know how you serve in truth. You are here. You are here. You are here." And let them respond to the vibration they feel.

You are enlightening them, bringing them light as truth, but you only do this as the Divine Self, not as the small self who would like to prove something. The Divine Self as you does not need to prove a damned thing. She knows who and what she is.

Now, when we teach you vibration, we give you an experience of it as you may align to it. If you wish to imagine yourself being impressed by us in vibration, you may, but what we are actually doing is holding you and the field you hold in the vibration we use to support you in your re-creation. The physical form that you hold has been addressed by this text from the moment you picked it up. The vibration is encoded in the pages you hold, in the sound of the voice that you hear. The vibration of truth and its intention for you are operating to serve your knowing and being of this vibration outside of the known. The way we know you, which exists outside of time, supports us in realizing you outside of time and the small self's intentions for what you should be, the expectations of the past that would seek to use you to call you back to what you have known or were supposed to be.

You imagine the old lady dressed for her wedding many years after the wedding failed. She still expects the music and the dancing, but her veil is corrupt, her dress in tatters. In many ways, you are all this woman when you defy your present moment and the gifts that are present in it by assuming what you should be or should have been. The music of the Divine Self is always playing on the worst night or the best. It is here, it is here, it is here, and may be known as and by you.

When you face an issue in your life that is born in expectation—"It should have gone the way I wanted, he should not have left so soon, she should have done what I asked, they should have given me what I wanted, or they should, or perhaps they will, so I may know myself as safe"—in some ways what you are doing is prescribing a life for yourself born in expectation. And almost all expectation is born in hereditary agreement. What one should do is always prescribed. What one does may be very different.

When you are free of your expectations, how you should be, look, or act, how you should experience the Divine or what it should look like to be enlightened, you begin to have a very different experience of what you are, untethered by these things that would seek to limit you.

As we continue in this text, we intend to surmount several beliefs that you all attach to that are about good and evil and what they mean, because, in fact, what you do in your authority to choose is name things in vibration that then bring you into accord with them. Even these names, we would say, are fraught with the investments or expectations of the past and are operating in some ways to confuse the truth of what you are.

As we have described earlier, truth is impartial. It is present in what it is. It does not emblemize things in one way or another. It speaks truth, which simply means it is in truth and can only be, and perhaps at the cost of what you think it should be.

By operating as truth, in the claim of truth, you become impartial to the investments of morality that are serving to limit you in your true expression. The church has done a very fine job in confusing you all about who and what you are. The belief that you are sinful by your very nature is corrupt. It is not true. You are born in truth. But you have the issues from past karma, incarnations, that must be attended to, and, in some ways, realizing yourself in truth supports you in knowing what you are outside of even those creations, because they are also not true in the higher octave.

As human beings begin to become aware of their divinity, they begin to claim their birthright and they begin to succeed in realizing themselves in their true potential. And then there is no more war. There cannot be war in truth, finally, because war is an act of fear any way you look at it. And in truth, a fear cannot exist.

"Is there such a thing as a good war?" Paul asks.

Perhaps a just war would be something you would claim, but even that is not true. The sanctity of human life, the Divine Self as what you are impressed and expressed in a body, is a holy thing. And the Divine as you knows this to be so in all men. So it's only the small self who can justify an act of murder, never the true self. And war, we would say, is murder and it always has been. And if somebody prescribes war, they are prescribing murder, however they wish to announce it.

Now, when we teach you freedom, we operate in some ways with what you are in your current expression to be valued by you so that you may move beyond it in the new claim that you make. "I am free as I am in this moment, in this eternal now." And the being that you are, who knows herself as free, unchained, unattached, untethered to the rules and regulations of society's need to conform, to be what they think you should be, what you would be by another's rule, the truth of what you are may be liberated and known and sung in a new song.

As you stand before us, we wish to claim you again in freedom. And realize this, friends. We are claiming what is true and what is always true, just what has been denied by a world that is operating out of alignment with truth.

We see you in your beauty, we see you in your right to be, in all you have known and may know, and in your freedom you may sing the new song of truth that is your embodiment. We call you forth, each and every one of you, the wonderful brigade we witness in transformation who claim their truth, not only for their own well-being, but for the well-being of their world.

We see you in truth, we know you in truth, in truth you have your being. We are here. We are here. We are here.

We will call this chapter "Freedom." We will continue tomorrow. Thank you for your presence. Good night. Stop now, please.

Day Nineteen

The responsibility you each have to the lives you live is before you. Each day is a new opportunity to know what you are, the manifested self. But if you remain in conjecture—"I assume that this is so"—the benefits you receive of the claim "I am in my truth, I know who I am, what I am, how

I serve" will be less truthful in your expression because, simply, you have not aligned to them in fullness.

The gift we give you today in this transmission is the alignment you require to become manifest as the free man, free woman you truly are. The claim "I am here," as we have said, is the Divine Self in its purview, the truth of who and what you are announcing herself to the field she holds and the world before her.

The gift you receive today is a higher vibration in announcement: "I have claimed my truth, and the manifestation of it will be known by me." As you announce this—"I have claimed my truth"—the alignment to what you've received that is already present in your field will begin to work with you to out-picture this in your experience. The truth of what you are, the manifested self, will begin to resonate as the body you hold, and the experience of consciousness that you embody as will reflect back the new world we have talked to you about.

Now the incarnation you stand in has been brought to you to recover and remember and reknow what you are outside of claims made in history. And the relinquishing of the past, as we have discussed thus far, is required on certain levels to begin to perceive the self as without the fear that was born in past times.

All fear, you see, seeks to work in memory. You have an

intention to be free, and the fear that you may have known of what it entails, what you might have to encounter, what others will say or do, is what inhibits you. It is never anything in the present moment because the present moment that you know yourself in is, in fact, untethered by historical data as you know what you are.

So if you understand the concept we are teaching you now—that the fear of being at this level of incarnation is actually created only in memory, or what was, or what you believed could be based upon what was—you will see the futility of it. What you end up doing, then, is reamassing the images of history that will tell you what humanity will not achieve, cannot become, and you will attend to your life at only that level.

The one who knows who and what she is, is not actually breaking all the rules, as Paul would surmise. In fact, what she is doing is aligning to a world that exists with different rules, different ways of comprehension, and, consequently, different ways of being.

The reenactment of history, which you are always engaging in in perpetuity—"This is what we do" (and when you say, "This is what we do," you go ahead and you do it again)—the replication of these things strands you, in some ways, on an island where codification of expectation are met in limited ways.

Imagine, if you wish, that in the world you've agreed to

be in there were certain things that were claimed by everyone, and the collective agreement to be at this level in these agreements creates a construct that everyone shares. Now, if you can imagine that these were simply things that were decided and agreed upon, you can imagine moving beyond them. But unless you do, you will re-create them in the expectation that they are supposed to be there.

The idea of expectation, or imagining what should be based on what was, is what we wish to attend to, because what you can do when you release expectation is claim something much different, much higher, if you wish. And the broadcast of your being without the limitations of expectation is free to claim in accordance with the needs of the Divine Self.

You see, the small self has her way of deciding what should be. "I should do this or that." "If I get this or that, I won't have this or that problem." And the process of navigating a lifetime becomes a process of deciding what you need to get, where you need to go, based upon a prescription of what you should have, or where you should go, to be what you think you are.

Now when we explain it this way, it makes sense to you, but what you don't realize is that almost all of your choices are in agreement to that. "I will do what I should do to be the man or woman I think I should be."

When the idea of what you are is maintained as truth,

you stop playing the game of edicts based on others' requirements for you. But the disassemblance of the structure of identity that has merit and still requires transformation is a challenge for all of you.

The self you know is not wrong. The one who goes to the store, who likes to do this or that in her free time, is a wonderful you. And when we say "disassemble," we simply mean that the what that you are, the manifested what, assumes aspects of you that have been operating in fear, or agreement to lies, or restrictions of freedom that you don't even know are there.

As the liberated self begins to come forward as her expression, the small self must be remolded, made anew, to be in conformity with the truth of what you are. If you are always frightened of cats and you know yourself as the one who's afraid of cats, you will align yourself outside of what you've claimed so that there is no more need to be in accord with that level of vibration. What was frightening ceases to be frightening because the Divine Self, in her truth, is never afraid.

Now the claim "I am here, I am here, I am here" always will align you to the purview of the Divine Self if it is claimed in truth. You can call yourself a magician. You can call yourself an airplane pilot. But unless you are behind the wheel of the plane, you are saying something that may not have truth. The Divine as what you are in manifestation is the one who claims the words we intone for you. And the claim "I am here" will realign your life if you allow it its expression.

What it also does, and infallibly so, is recorrect the instances in your life where you are out of alignment, because you cannot be as you are in truth and maintain the misalignment that you claim as something other.

Now, Paul requires an example. If you have a belief about yourself that is untrue—"I am a this, I am a that"—it is out of accord with your Divine nature, but you have free will and your reality will reflect the choice you make. The one who believes she is a this or that will find a this or that out-pictured all around her, which simply confirms the claim that she's made.

As you align as the Divine Self—"in my knowing, I am in my knowing, I am in my truth, I am in alignment to truth, I am here, I am here, I am here"—those aspects of the life that were created or out-pictured by you to confirm a mistaken belief will be revealed to be what they are, and for the very simple reason that they are not true and not in the highest truth that you may know yourself as and through. Now, when you make the claim "I am here, I am here, I am here," the jurisdiction of the claim or the out-picturing of the claim is upon what one perceives before her, and the regarding of the thing you see as the Divine Self must align it to truth.

So Paul is asking, "Okay, so I pass the mirror, I don't like what I see, I claim, 'I am here, I am here, I am here,' and I approve of my reflection?"

You are still talking as a personality self who has preferences based in expectation about what he should be or how he should appear. As you align as the True Self, "I am here, I am here, I am here" projects to you the truth of what you are, and that is the witness you hold. If the reflection you see is out of alignment with truth, you are projecting upon yourself something you think should be there that is not there because you have not aligned to it.

As you align to what is in truth—"I know what I am," the manifested self as the Divine Self—the physical reality you know yourself in will in fact conform to what is true. Now, when we use the word *true* here, we don't mean idealized. Once again, the idea of a perfected self—and the Divine Self *is* the perfected self—has been embellished by you all to resemble some picture of a model who has had his hair done, and who wears the perfect clothing and smiles all day. The manifested Divine Self of the one who has no teeth in her head is still the Divine Self with no teeth. Your idea of how you should look or what it means to be at this level has been prescribed to you in foolish ways. The idealization of form and what it should appear to be is a cultural issue, not a spiritual one. And if you wish to continue with it, you will continue to replicate history.

Now, the body itself has been worked with and will continue to be through this engagement. And the responsibility you have to the body you are in, as we have described, is to care for it well. It is of you, it is the Divine expression, and you have authority over when you bathe or how you eat. How you care for the physical self is always a reflection of how much you know and be as the True Self. The one who denies the body is denying the aspect of God that is in form. The one that adores the body and ignores the spirit has the reverse issue. They idolize form at the cost of Spirit. How you come into agreement here is by claiming it:

"On this day I claim that the issuance of form I stand as is in perfection in a high octave, and that the needs of the form that I stand as are being met by me in all ways in agreement to the truth of what I am. As I know this to be true, I move into a new agreement about my ability to care for the form I hold. And in this claim I choose to release myself to the jurisdiction and the purview of the truth of what I am. I know who I am in truth. I know what I am in truth. I know how I serve in truth. I am here. I am here. I am here."

Now the ability you have to align at this level is completely predicated on your willingness to release the prescriptions that you have been spoken of, or to, or been in accord with throughout the lives you've lived. But it is much less difficult than you all make it. To be in alignment in form is simply to agree to it. And to agree to it in a higher way simply means you give permission to the Divine as you to shepherd you forward in this process of engagement.

The equipment you have as a physically manifested being is here to support you in this, which simply means that the wisdom of the body itself will support you as you begin to attend to the body as holy.

Now, as we teach you, we agree with you about the things that require transformation.

"What might this be?" Paul asks.

The assumptions you make and the expectations you hold about what you should be is the basis of this chapter, because, finally, they keep you infirm on the foundation of truth that we are building for you. The acquiescence to others' requirements of what one should be, the beliefs in what it takes to be esteemed—and for what or by whom—must be attended to. And each one of you here is going to be given the opportunity to re-create your lives outside of collective agreement. This does not mean you become a hermit, or you don't go to the bank, or you don't pay your fines when you drive the car too quickly. It simply means that you know what you are in the challenges you face, and the alignment to what you are in the claims we've made bring you forth outside of the dictates that would define you.

Anything that would define you seeks to limit you. Do you understand this concept? You seek to define God, and you cannot, because God cannot be defined. You seek to know yourself in truth, but you want the truth to attend to you as you think it should based in your expectations of what you think should be. And in defining truth in this way, you move back to the lies you've known.

The claim "I am here in truth" doesn't mean somebody hands you a bouquet of flowers and invites you to walk down a runway. You have not been crowned anything other than what you have always been, and been in denial of.

The vision that you hold of the Divine Self cannot be defined either. And we want you to understand this. The moment you prescribe what it looks like to be in the Kingdom, or what it means to be as the Divine Self in manifestation, you seek to define it and, consequently, limit it through your expectation.

"So what are we supposed to do?" Paul asks. "This is infuriating. How are we to be?"

You need to be as you are, as you are in truth. And then you are reclaimed in this vibration. As this vibration assumes you, you reclaim it in your manifested world because you are not separate from the landscape you inhabit. As you claim these things, the metamorphosis, the reacclimation to what you are, is known as you. And as you, in this frequency, you exist in a higher octave. But if you know what you think it should be, you will try to create it, to inform your need to be, once again, as you think you should. The True Self knows and realizes. The small self thinks and expects.

Here we go, friends. As we teach you this, we wish to offer you one thing. By releasing expectation, you open up to the possibility of much more, vastly more than you could claim as a small self with her outline and laundry list of the things she must be or have. As we say these words for you—we underline *for*—we say them as the ones who know what they are, because in our knowing we may assume you in your own.

"On this day we claim that the ones we see before us are autonomous beings and not informed by the expectations of a world that would prescribe identity in limited fashion. We release from the ones we see before us all need to define or project outcome based on misinformation or expectation that is out of alignment in truth. And as we know this to be true, we claim the Kingdom as their true inheritance. We know who you are in truth, we know what you are in truth, we know how you serve in truth. You are here. You are here. You are here."

Now the realization of this in the manifested self may happen very quickly, or slowly. Whichever way it occurs is the best way for you to hold the vibration. Some of you require the light to go on quickly to see where you truly stand. Others of you require the light to get brighter slowly so you may understand in increments the acclimation to what you claimed in form.

As we say the words, we agree to them as what you are, the manifested self. The consciousness that informs this must be realized to meet the claim, and that is why we use the words *in truth*. When you operate as truth and in truth, you actually support the being that you are in the arrival to the new landscape in the way that she can hold it.

"What does this mean?" Paul asks.

Quite simply put, if you were left on the shore of a strange country without a penny to your name and no language to serve you, you will be reliant only on what you've known to survive in the new country. If you are prepared for the voyage, as we are doing now, and are gifted with the currency of the Kingdom you arrive in and the language to be in conversation at this level with others, you have acclimated. And the passage is much more beneficial to all.

Now, we ask you this: Are you willing to reclaim what you are in the relationships you hold? This is the next big question because you are all in relations, and have expectations of your fellows, and are met by them in their expectations of you.

What does it mean, we say, to be the Divine Self in a marriage, in an office, in a school? What does it mean to be in truth when you are out of alignment with the ones around you who prefer that things remain as they were?

The first thing we would like to say is that each and every encounter you have is an opportunity to know who and what you are, because it's the opportunity to claim the truth in the one you see. And the one who claims the truth about herself cannot do other than claim the truth in the one she sees before her.

So if you understand right away that it's all an opportunity, and you don't have to demand others to be different to be in your authority, you have won already. But the fear that you all have is that, as you transform, you will be misunderstood or crucified or whatever you would imagine would be the outcome for embodying in truth.

We will promise you this: These are expectations, once again, that have historical precedent, and your reliance upon history to direct you where you go will lead you right down the same damned path as the ones who came before you. The path of ascension, we would say, is the path of the rising consciousness. It is the rising consciousness that perceives a new world and, in this perception, claims the world as manifest. Those who populate the Kingdom of heaven are the same people you see every day. You witness them in the higher octave and your experience of them is transformed by your name, "I am here, I am here, I am here."

This does not mean they do what you want. It means you know who they are. And in that knowing, the ones you see are also transformed. The key to the Kingdom has always been you. It always will be. But not you at the level of personality, which is what gets you so frightened.

As we have said many times, you do not become the Christ, the Divine Self, the True Self, the Infinite Self, whatever you wish to call it. The Christ becomes you, the Divine as you, the truth as you, love as you in broadcast and expression—and, in this text, we add *in form*.

The idea of being in form as the Divine Self is age-old, but it has been misunderstood. The concept of an avatar, the concept of one who has come from outside to be the salvation of others, the one who believes that only those who are chosen are to be realized at this level of vibration, are cultural dictates that you have ascribed to.

In fact, the way was shown by those who came before you. And the teaching of the Christ, at its essence, is a true teaching, and was as true then as it is true today. But the blasphemy of religion and its attempt to control in some unfortunate ways have rendered the teaching meaningless to those who would most benefit from it.

So we are retelling a story for you today, and then it will be the end of the chapter.

Once upon a time there was a young woman who believed

herself to be God. She went out every day and sought to confirm the belief in the manifest world. She was ridiculed, she was cast out, and she decided there was no point. And she returned to her community without the love that she had believed to be there as she truly was in the other way.

One day it came to her that she was not God, and her announcement of herself as God had been the issue. Her intention may have been pure, but the way she perceived it was misconstrued, not only by her, but all of those she spoke to, and in this moment she realized that she was not God, but God was her. And in this moment of humility, what transpired was the alchemization of her being to what she had always been.

The community she lived in knew she was there, but she did not announce her name or parade herself through the streets. God has no need to—it is everywhere in everyone in everything. So the simple nature of her being in that accord, in that union with her Source, supported her in claiming her life and all she saw within it in the same way. And as she began to perceive herself as one with all that is, she claimed the Kingdom, not only for her, but all who lived with her, and the town itself began to rise in a miraculous way.

"What is happening?" the townspeople asked. We will tell you, and this was the answer they never knew. They were held in the vision of one who knew who she was, who had no investment in how she would be seen, who sought no glory, no medal, for the love she held for humanity.

The Christ has come in each of you, my friends. Let us sing the song together. You are here. You are here. You are here.

Thank you for your presence. We will stop now, please. Period. Period. Period.

Chapter Nine

THE TRIUMPH
OF THE NEW

Day Twenty

We are responsible for the teaching, and we will remind Paul that, as we set forth to teach each day, we are prepared for the lessons the students require to learn. Today's lesson, we would say, is in love and the being as love that comes as a causation when one announces himself as truth. The being of the self as truth, in fact, is what paves the way for the action of love to be in response and in broadcast as the one you are. And as you claim yourself as truth, the lies that you have known yourself through that have disabled your capacity to be expressed as love are released and you are aligned to your True Self.

Now, understand, friends, that the True Self is as love. But you imagine love, as you still do, to be an emotional state and not a vibration, a creation of the light that supports itself in operating as you. The Divine Self that you are, in her authority, claims herself in love because she knows what she is.

Now, most of you believe yourselves to be capable of love. "I have this feeling or that, this way of knowing myself or that, so I assume this to be love." But if you really understood love, you would also understand the depth of it and the breadth of it. And as you become as love, the one who knows who she is, you infuse the frequency of it in the landscape you exist in.

Now we are telling Paul something important. Step aside, friend, for this teaching to come through. He wishes to correct the teaching. "This is *The Book of Truth*. We have already been taught that in the broadcast of truth all things may be aligned as truth, so what is this love business, interfering with the teaching?"

The idealization of what you are as a manifested self is of love. The True Self that you are cannot exist without it, but the lies that you've used to claim yourselves as separate from your Source have hindered the expression of love as the expression of you.

Now, we teach you this in our authority. The belief that love is precious, the belief that love is gentle, the belief that love is romantic, is all, while possibly so, simply limited, as your understanding is about what love can be as expressed by you. The thunder of love, the quake of love, the foundation of a world knowing itself in love, is not very precious. In fact, it's a grand call of the Divine to summon all men to service for her fellows.

As you've been operating as truth and making the claims and attunements that we have supported you in, you have aligned yourself to a level of vibration that in many ways supports the reacclimation to love that is the Divine in its highest form.

Now, truth paves the way for love to sing. Truth announces itself and clears away the debris that would stand in the way of love, and truth announces itself with impartiality, whereas love knows full well what is needed and how it is expressed in every circumstance for the highest good of all.

As each one of you comes forth in the announcement of being—"I am here, I am here, I am here"—you have claimed the Kingdom, but you don't understand yet what being in the Kingdom means. And it does mean you become as love, and not in a convenient way, because the idealization that you would make for love is still imprinted by those who've come before you.

If you can imagine loving with the depth of your being each human being you encounter because you know what they are, you will understand what this means. The idea that love could be known in convenience, could be impartial to the needs of another—the idealization of what you think love is—must be met now to re-create you as the conduit for its expression. And we will use the teaching of truth to support you in this.

"On this day I decide that any belief in love or any attributes to love that I have decided upon that are out of alignment with truth will be re-created in a higher way. And as I claim these words, I support my entire being in attuning to the frequency of love as may be known as and through me. On this day I claim that I am in alignment to love, and the vibration of love as what I am in its expression will reclaim a world through my being. As I say these words, I know them to be so. I know who I am in love. I know what I am in love. I know how I serve in love. I am here. I am here. I am here."

Now the grain of salt that you would examine to understand this teaching must be released because the teaching is so vast that your attempts to decipher it through examination will not work. And we will explain why. The frequency and amplitude of the vibration of love is all-encompassing. And as the way has been paved by truth, the reacclimation to the teaching of love, and the vibration as it, may assume you. But it will not be done with the intellect's permission. It will actually assume the intellect, because the intellect that you know yourself with believes itself to be sovereign and, consequently, independent from the Source of its true nature. When you idealize the mind and keep it separate from the Source of your being, you have made an idol out of the mind. When the mind itself is assumed in Source, you begin to operate with the alignment to the mind of all, which means the Divine Mind, which is available to you each in your knowing.

The presupposition that any attunement we give you can be deciphered by you and then explained will leave you witless, because the level of operation that we align you at actually has no language, and our efforts to imprint you with language are succeeding because of the intonation that we incorporate in your field.

If you can imagine that the claims you make with us are chords that play, and the intention is set in language so you have a comprehension of what is becoming *as* you, you will understand this a little better. The amplitude of the frequency that we are working with here is vast and can hold a million and more just in the idea of its potential. In its realization as and through each of you, it holds untold millions.

Now we will explain what this means. The small self can imagine its potential being realized only to the extent that she can imagine potential realized. The Divine Mind and the True Self may claim much more because they are not hindered by the idealization of what you can imagine in small ways. So the frequency we are teaching you as will be met by each of you as you can comprehend it, but the truth of what you are doing exceeds comprehension. Those of you who feel the vibration as we instruct you in it can bear testimony to its efficiency. The claim "I am in truth," if you have worked with it carefully—which means in intention, with care—have already realized in several ways what you are, what you are not, and how you've been tied to the rules of a world that are not operating in truth.

The claim of love that we bring to you today is to support you each in the agreement to be as this in all of your action. Truth without love can be mercenary, but the compassion of love informing all things supports you each from the depth of your very being in lifting your world in love to its true nature. You may pull a child up from the streets by her hair, or lift her in your arms in love, and we suggest the latter is how we operate and how we instruct.

The testimony to truth will always be the light informing what is true and releasing what is not through its very exposure. The release of the fear-based self, which serves to obstruct the vibration of love as what you are, is being met in the claim of truth that we have announced. And the frequency *as* love that is supporting in this the Divine nature in truth, which is love, can then hold its expression.

If you can imagine that you have a basket that is woven through with fear, the fear informs all things the basket holds. When the fear is released, what the basket holds is fearless. If you can understand that you are the basket, and the fear that you've known yourself in is being released so the being that you are may be held in love, you will comprehend this teaching.

Now the broadcast of your being, or the issuance of the vibration of love in all you see before you, must now be met in action. And we will explain what this means. The challenge that most of you face with each spiritual teaching you receive is that you believe it to be theoretical, or a model of behavior, or you wish a prescription. "We must meditate three times a day, and eat no meat, and then we will be spiritual and on the path that has been set forth for us." In fact, what you are as a spiritual being does not require these things, although you may be led by your Divine Self toward any of those actions.

True spiritual teachings—and we will say all true teachings, regardless of what they are in—must be proven by the student as so. And if it is not, you may remain comfortably at the level of theory. "Well, we suppose this works because it should."

When we say "prove this teaching," we mean to be *as* it so that you may know it. And you will not know it until you are it. You are *as* the True Self in its broadcast.

Now some of you may close the book now and say, "Well, this was an interesting folly. I cannot imagine it can be so." And then that will be what you get.

But until you decide that the action of being as the

Divine Self is the transformation of this plane and you to your true nature—and realize this as what can be, will be, as you bear witness to it—you will not know what you are, and you may not have the experience that you are asking for.

The teaching of the Kingdom, which we will commence with again very shortly, must bear witness to itself through your experience to be known by you. And it is the gift, the greatest gift, of this teaching, because what it means is that you have claimed yourself as the vessel of the Divine and are in union with it, in manifestation as it in the life you live—not in a cloud someday, but in the moment you stand in. And in the knowing of this, you claim the world that is in agreement to it.

The fear you have of moving beyond the known has been addressed prior in this text. Your attachment to what you think should be has been announced and reclaimed in the higher octave. The Divine Self that you truly are has been announced and agreed to.

Now, as we give you love as the instruction of the day, once again you balk. "How am I to be love?" Paul asks.

You are love already is what we respond as. You are love already. You all are. It is the truth of your nature as being of God. You don't learn love, you learn behavior. You allow love to be as you, and in the agreement to be as it, it is as you in all ways. The depth of love we hold for you will not be described because there are no words. The depth of love that is you cannot be articulated because it is so true, in such truth, that nothing else exists at that level of vibration. And the being as this calls the world to you, and you become its shepherd.

Yes, we use the word intentionally. You become its shepherd. The being that you are in love teaches others by being as you what they can be and what they truly are. This was always the teaching of the Christ, and it always will be. The one who says, "Follow me," and is in love is encouraging all to be as they can be in the same truth in union with its Source.

Now, we will teach you again, and when we do we will respond to the questions Paul is having about the teaching thus far. The challenge he is having today is the challenge of expectation. He assumed we would continue where we had left off and build upon the prior idea, which was his limited expectation of what was to come. In fact, we have, but not in the way that was comfortable for him.

The teaching you are receiving now about being as love in the basis of truth will support where you go and how you be in all ways. The desires you have to understand what we teach in a context you may know will be gifted to you in the lives you live. When we say something is too vast to be explained, it is never too vast to be known. And as you know and realize the teaching in your lives, you may find your own language to describe it. But the willingness you have to be as this frequency in fullness has always been the intention of the work we do with you.

We will commence with another teaching when we resume, and we will return to this as we see fit. This is the beginning of a chapter. Thank you. We will resume later. Period. Period. Period. Stop now, please.

Day Twenty (Cont.)[*]

Now we were authorized to bring you a teaching to survive the lives you live and well beyond them. And the teaching you are receiving tonight is an eternal teaching in how you be outside of the landscapes you've known or what you've created on this plane.

As you are eternal beings, you come with authority as well. To reach the heavens as a conscious being simply means you align to it. You claim the benediction of the Source you hold and you request the embodiment, and the realization of the embodiment, that may be held by you in material form. A teaching for the ages, we would say, survives an age, and the teaching of consciousness of any worth at all is not a timely teaching but an ageless one. What was true a million years ago in consciousness must be true today and will be true a million years from now.

Now the lineage you all hold, the manifested selves you are,

---

[*] Recorded during an online seminar.

have been in agreement to many things. You look at the stores, you buy what is there. What was there was there in some other form by some other name a hundred years ago, and a hundred years prior there was something other that could be claimed by you today. As mankind progresses, he claims new things into being, new ways of communication, new ways of destruction, but the impulse behind all of them is consciousness, consciousness made manifest in material form.

Now the Divine Self that you are holds no history. Do you understand this, yes? She is infinitely perfect. She is unbound by time. She is not destroyed by the death of the body. She lives on in all ways and knows herself as free. Each one of you here in your agreement to this teaching is accepting the fact that the truth of what you are, the manifested self as you, will be known in form, not someday other and not on some other plane outside of this reality.

The manifestation of God as you that is here as you now seeks its expression by you, but she is stuck in some ways by listing a self within a frame that in some ways cannot align to the prospect of eternity. You see, the small self knows she will not be here one day. She fears her demise, and the Divine Self that you are that seeks to express as her in the form she holds must enlist the agreement of the small self to embody. But in order for this to happen, you cannot hold the level of fear that the small self has accrued in her lineage as a small self.

Now what you are, in fact, can only be true in a higher realm if it is known in form by you here. You cannot agree to a teaching that cannot be known by you. You can have a catalyst for your understanding. You can receive a boot in the butt, if you wish, to propel you forward. But as we have said, the teaching we offer you must be agreed upon by you, and then you may know it. You cannot stay in conjecture and claim the Kingdom, because then the Kingdom will remain a theoretical place where one inhabits a higher realm after they have gone from the realm they stand in today. And that is not so.

The Infinite Self that you are, asking you in your permission to be received as you—and "as" and "through" you means as your expression—has come as you for one reason: to anchor the Kingdom into manifestation on this plane of experience. And, as we have taught, the Kingdom itself, the awareness of the Divine in all things, is here now, but exists in a higher octave than the physical form has agreed to thus far. In the alignment to truth—"I know who I am in truth, I know what I am in truth, I know how I serve in truth"— the manifested self, which means the form you hold, goes into an alignment with the truth of what she is so that even the form itself is assumed and realized as of God. If the God Self is not expressed in form, it remains an idea.

Now the aspect of you that already comprehends that everything you see before you is consciousness made into form can align to the potential that the Divine as what you are may also be the same. But how do you know it? How do you claim it as true? How do you know your inheritance until you are experiencing it? This is the teaching of the night.

The experience of the Divine in manifestation must be agreed to, to go into alignment with it. And the step that you take toward this agreement is realizing—underline *realize*, which means know—that what you are, the form you hold, cannot be separate from its Source. Once the agreement is made in fullness, the realization ensues.

Now imagine, if you wish, for the sake of this teaching, that you stand in a room as a pillar of vibration, that what you are in fact is a level of frequency being expressed or manifested in what you know as a body. Imagine, then, that the vibration that you hold is not in agreement to physical law because the aspect of it that knows she is of God actually bypasses law that exists in lower vibration. This is the first step to this claim of agreement.

As long as you believe yourself to be bound by the laws of man and the exchanges of men that have decided what these laws should be, you will be tethered to the laws at the cost of the vibration that you truly are knowing its full expression.

Now the aspect of you that already knows that this is so, which is the Divine or Infinite Self, the Christed Self, if you prefer, needs no convincing, but requires agreement from the aspect of the self that would stand in the way of the alignment that is required. And the claim we make for you each tonight is that you are going to be willing to bypass limited agreement of what form is and, consequently, move outside of the reality where form is conceived of as permanent structure that can be known by you in a higher way. The Divine as what you are knows this to be so already but seeks to express itself as what you are, which means in form.

Now the challenge for Paul, as he takes the dictation, is that he cannot believe it so. He is already disagreeing. He's like the child behind the schoolyard kicking the rock in the sand— "Well, they say it's so, and here I sit, saying the words, but I can't agree to it"—which sets the young man up to stay behind the schoolyard and not in the darned classroom where he may learn, as you are learning now. The imagination he has assumes that what we are saying is that you will walk through walls. That is not this teaching.

Manifestation, the Divine in form, has the power to recognize the Divine that is also existing in form. Like attracts like. And if *you* remain outside of God in the substance you hold, all substance will. Do you understand this? If the form you hold is not in this agreement, there is no point to appealing to the higher law because you've already decided that it does not inform you. The one who knows what she is, is the one who claims the Kingdom because the Kingdom is manifest.

Now the Divine Self has work to do here. She exists on

this plane to trumpet the arrival of a new dawn, to sing the song that will call all men and women forward in truth. The reckoning that we speak to and have always spoken of—the self facing the self—is not punishment, it is glory, because when the self recognizes the self in its false structures, she begins to realize the magnificence of the truth of what she is. And so long as you're all investing in what was invented yesterday, what was taught yesterday, what you believed to be true yesterday, you cannot know what is today.

The consequence of the teaching you are receiving is manifestation. Underline that. The teaching of this text is the teaching of the self *manifested*, the Divine Self made manifest on this plane. It cannot be other. And the proof of the teaching must be your experience in this realm as the one who perceives and recognizes what she is and what is before her. All consequence is the effect of thought, because thought precedes action and thought precedes anything being made manifest. But aligning to the Divine Self aligns you to the Source and bypasses the systems of agreement that the small self has known and adhered to and called a world into form with.

The jurisdiction you have now as the Divine Self is to recognize divinity and, in truth, you alchemize what you see. And by this we mean, in the claim of truth you are, you express as, you acclimatize the vibratory field of what you witness in the same vibration. Light illumines darkness, truth eradicates lies. And they work together to claim anew.

Now fear, we have said, in its purview, will seek to re-claim everything and use it in her own way. "I must be fear-ful of a teaching that tells me I am Divine." We would argue you should be terrified of a teaching that tells you, you are *not*, because that would be denying God as the Source of all things. And the claim "I am here"—in my knowing, in my purview as the True Self—is what calls the Kingdom into manifestation for all mankind. The Christ has come *as* you because God is in all, or the Source of being is in all, and God in truth will not hold a lie.

Now the changes you will undergo as you claim these things are many, and to agree to them simply means you are aligning to what you are. And manifestation in align-ment at this level of agreement renders all things that are not in truth inferior and then obsolete. You cannot play the game of embellishment anymore. You cannot tell the little lies or the great ones, nor can you receive them. And here is where the challenge lies. As the one you are—the True Self, in receipt of lies—and knows what she is, the lies themselves will be met by you in truth, not through your action, but by the field you hold.

You do not become a target of lies. In fact, if you walk down the street in any city, you would be encountering a thousand lies before you crossed the second avenue. Be-cause so many of you ignore the truth of what you are, you've claimed agreements in lower ways. The testimony to this would be how you value each other. And in any city street, the one who is impoverished is left to starve, and the others walk behind and look the other way.

Now what you are standing as is a moment of truth. And we are using this word intentionally—a *moment* of truth—and in this moment of truth you will be reclaimed in this octave in your permission to do so.

"What does this mean?" he asks.

Just what it sounded like. The frequency we hold, which operates as truth, will commence to sing. And in the song and in the vibration that we announce ourselves as, we acclimate each of you to the agreement you will make, and that is the moment of truth.

He asks a question. We must take it. "But how is this different than what we've done?"

We will answer that one. You have agreed sequentially, first and foremost, to deny fear as the active article in your life. You've chosen anew and then you have agreed not to bear witness to history in the agreement that it's true, but what was. And then you have decided to reclaim the self in agreement to truth in a way that you may uncover, or unmask, or release the small structures that you've endowed with great power. And finally, we say, you are agreeing to serve. And in this alchemy, "I am agreeing to serve," the thunderbolt comes and claims you each in an illumination

in your field that will progress and reclaim you in the Kingdom. We have said it.

Now this is the teaching you need. Here we go:

"On this night I choose to be enabled in all ways to be in
full service as my True Self, and in truth I claim this,
and in agreement to truth I witness it. And as I say,
'Yes,' to this, all aspects of my being will be claimed in
the higher vibration and all I have known and will
know, all I have seen and will see, all I may believe and
may know and may bear witness to from this moment
forward is in truth, in alignment to truth, in agreement
to truth. I am here. I am here. I am here."

Be received by us, if you wish. In the field we hold, in the
octave we sing, all is holy, as are you. "All is holy, as am I."
There is nothing outside of the Kingdom because all is
God and will be known in truth. We are here. We are here.
We are here.

Receive us as you are, as you sit, as you stand, as you lie, as
you be, and allow the light that is truth and allow the love
that incorporates truth to be as what you are. You are here to
serve, my dears, and if you said, "Yes," the orchestra plays,
the dance continues, and you sing in glory for all.

Now the teaching will resume in a moment. We take a

moment for Paul and for those of you who need it to support yourself in claiming this in whatever way is personal to you. You are making the claim of your own free will and the decision is yours. The experience and the expression of it will be yours as well. Period. Period. Period. One moment, please.

(Pause)

We are continuing now in a new way. And to resume the teaching means to change the subject because we have said what we had to say and claimed what we needed to claim for this to commence. Now we will continue with what will not happen and what will not be agreed to by us.

As you exchange the vibration of the known for the new, the temptation will be to claim the old in security, and you cannot do that at a certain level without re-creating the old self's structures.

Now the action of fear you have been expressed as in truth will not attend to it. And as you say, "Yes, I am here in truth," the invitations of fear will be released, as long as you do not agree to them. If you can imagine that you are sitting in a chair and the worst thing you can imagine is whispered in your ear, align to the truth of what you are and sing the song "I am here." If the fear that you would imagine is expressed in your world, use it as an opportunity to claim the Kingdom, which is the awareness of the Creator in all manifestation regardless of what presents. And if the small self who seeks to be comforted requires it, hold her, teach her, but do not give her fear because she will be known in it. There is no need.

The triumph of the new is always at the cost of the old. And we will call this chapter "The Triumph of the New" because, as you have claimed the words with us, you've claimed yourself in truth and all is made new.

Now he is in the background, rolling his eyes. "Well, it doesn't look very new to me. I see myself as I was."

You can, if you like, but who is the perceiver, friend? Who sees in the mirror? The small self who fears or doubts or judges the body he sees, or the Divine Self who knows? God loves all, you see, and the aspect of you that expresses as this may claim yourself, as well, as you say, "Yes."

Some of you come to us asking to be healed. Here is what we say to you. Let yourselves be known as you truly are. Let yourself be loved as you can only be. Let yourself be witnessed in truth by us so you may be known outside of the shell of the small self and her injury or her shame or her rage or her fear. The one you are is here to be witnessed and is always in truth when she knows who she is.

The action of this text so far has been reclamation in manifestation. You must begin to expect that, as you attend to our words, as you attend to the teachings, as you witness your life, that the transformation of it will be in accord with what you require to know yourself in truth. There is no object here, no finish line, no trophy at the end. The gift of the Kingdom is the gift of union, and it is here and will be known by you as you say, "Yes."

"What happened tonight?" he asks. "What did we do?"

You stepped over the threshold into the world you can claim now, and you will be known in truth. We are here. We are here. We are here.

Thank you for your presence. We will return with questions on the teaching. Period. Period. Period. Stop now, please.

Q: Can the Guides elaborate on the reference to the thunderbolt? They also talked about the facing of the self is not something to be frightened of, that it's in glory. Can they add a little bit more about how this may present itself so we can work in congruence with the Divine Self as it embodies?

A: Stop planning. This is what you are doing. You are looking for a list that you might check off about what this will be. The teaching of the thunderbolt is a teaching of activation. The higher purview is what enlightens you, as a thunderbolt does. You become the conduit or the lightning rod for the expression of Source through your very being.

Now, what does it mean to know? And that is what you are asking. To know means to realize, and you only realize in the moment you stand in. You cannot know tomorrow, you cannot know yesterday. It happens in the now. Now, you wish a signpost. "May I see the Kingdom, please? I've been told it's around the corner. Am I in the right Kingdom?" In fact, that's what you wish to know. And while we comprehend the question, we must explain it. God is all. And the awareness of this, and that you are not separate from your Source, or your brother, is the awareness of the Kingdom.

Now, to what degree, you may ask? And we like that question because it allows us a way to explain something that you do need to know. You have been taught that if you bear false witness against another, that if you are in unforgiveness, you cannot align to the Kingdom, and in fact it is so. But it does not render God as not there. You can't stand somebody— your awareness of the Divine will be hindered unless you decide that the one you see, like him or not, agree to him or not, is as holy as anything else. The stages of awareness and progression that one aligns as, as he calls the Kingdom into manifestation, will be highly dependent on the individual's needs for evolution. It would be wrong minded to place yourself at the top of the mountain that you have not yet climbed. And those of you who would think that you are taking the escalator up the mountain here, and plopped upon a throne, will have a very challenging time. As we have taught you all, the small self's investments about what should be will be seen by you. And as they are released, the True Self comes forth and witnesses the Kingdom that is already here. Unless you understand that the Kingdom itself is a dimension of expression, an octave played, that exists now in tandem with the reality you know, you will have a limited comprehension of it.

Now you asked about reckoning and the facing of the self. It is a blessed moment to know the self in truth. But on consequence, what you have lied to yourself about must be seen because it is not so. As you agree to be as truth and claim it as what you are, the scales fall away from the eyes. Your vision is unheeded by fear and you see in worth, you see in truth, you do not judge, you do not blame, and you cannot fear. All of these things exist in the lower octave.

The one who seeks the Kingdom, but seeks to blame another, will be torn into pieces. The one who seeks the Kingdom and is willing to relinquish the known will find it, however lovely the known seems.

You live in a world, you see, that says, "I will have the big house and my spiritual practice, and my spiritual practice will serve me as long as I have the big house." If the house were not there, would there not be God? The convenience of spiritual teachings—that there is nothing to see, and all things may be known as they have been unless you don't want them there, then you pick something a little better—must be understood for what they are. They are the equivalent of a glass of warm milk before bedtime. You will have a nice sleep, but you may not progress.

Now, we have nothing to say about claiming good things or claiming the life you can have. You exist in a field of infinite potential. Anything may be claimed that is in alignment to your truth. But your truth, you see, the Divine truth that you hold, must trump the truth of your mother and father that said you have to be this, or agree with those teachings, or be this kind of man or woman, as we were taught and as our parents before us were as well.

We understand the questions you ask and we are grateful for them. We impress in language through the man before you as we can to achieve a state of consciousness for the convened, for the reader, for the student, and we support the whole as we can. But when we are required to speak to the individual, we may elaborate with illustration in ways we cannot otherwise. We thank you for your presence and the question. Period. Period. Period.

Q: When I feel the contrast in others and when I see the small structures that you were talking about, instead of feeling blame or shame should I take that opportunity to see that as my bigger self?

A: Claim your freedom as the one who chooses. This is the teaching of liberation. If you want to blame another, by all means do, but understand what it does. It puts you in a place of being a victim and it denies your authority. So know that you are the one choosing. The first responses most of you have are historical. "He stepped on my foot, I should punch him. He stepped on my foot, I must have done something to deserve it. He stepped on my foot, maybe he wants to ask me out." Your first response will be predicated by your history.

Now, the old self seeks to re-create the known at every opportunity and it includes your reactions to the things in your world. As you move to the authority of the True Self as what you are, while the temptation may be there to re-criminate, to fear, to blame, to argue, the tendency will be moving away because it is not in truth. The True Self, you see, will call forth what she requires to learn through. And if you are one who needs to learn how to manage your temper until you realize there is nothing to be angry at, you will call those lessons to you.

Now Paul is interrupting us. "But sometimes we need anger."

Sometimes you do, if you wish you do. You may choose what you want, but as you align to truth, how and what you express must be in consort with that. And the Divine Self does not blame, does not shame, does not fear, does not punish. She knows far more, but she does attend to her world in truth. And that may be to say, "No," or to say,

"Yes," or to say, "Stop it, this is not okay." Period. Period. Period. Thank you for the question.

> Q: *If the small self makes a decision out of fear or anger, how come the True Self doesn't step in and show them something different or allow them to go through with that choice?*

A: You have free will. That's the first thing. And you are choosing all the time. The claim we have gifted you with, "I know who I am, I know what I am, I know how I serve," calls your vibration into present time so you may choose anew. As we said, you operate in history, you do what you've done, because it's what you've been known to do. The choice you make now is to choose wisely, and that is choosing as the True Self. But you must be in inquiry here. When you take an action in fear, you are calling more fear to you. When you do something in frustration, you are agreeing to the thing that is frustrating you.

Now, we will talk. He wants to say something. The question is a good one. "How do we choose a high way when we've always been choosing the old?"

To claim the truth of what you are is informing your actions will support you in this. When you claim truth—"I know who and what I am in truth, I am here in truth"—you cannot play games as the small self would be-cause those things are out of alignment with the truth of what she is. But as you progress in this teaching, your accli-mation to truth will be such that you don't step on your own feet and you stop replicating history because it's what was known. We thank you for the question.

> *Q: I think what I heard tonight was that the small self is actually part of this choice to manifest as the Divine Self. Can they speak more about that?*

A: The Divine Self operates as you, but you've been gifted with free will, and the alignment that we speak to requires consent as the True Self emerges, at the cost of the known. And "the cost of the known" means the truth of what you are. The claims you make with us are in support of this teaching. We thank you for the good question. We will say good night.

Chapter Ten

THE GIFTS OF
THE KINGDOM

Day Twenty-One

The only thing you don't understand is that this has happened. It has already happened in the higher realm and may be attended to now by what you are as the manifested being you know yourself as.

The claims that have been made in this text will hold with you as you claim them, and the process of identifying as the what that you are, the True Self, the manifested self, is the way you claim your life. The life that you are living now has been claimed by you in many ways for the purpose of realigning to the True Self. If you can understand, friends, that all you have been through, all you have believed and known, will now be used in service to truth, you will understand and comprehend why you are here and what you have come for.

The decisions you've made to be in attendance to our teachings has been the necessary step for the life you are living to step forward over the threshold into the new realm. When we talked to you last, we said you stepped over the threshold. And what we mean by this is the life that you have known, and known yourself as and through, has ended as you have known it.

Now, the climate you stand in, in the room you sit in, the walk you take to work, is still acclimated to the prior self and her choices. But the one who has aligned to truth will now reclaim things in her purview. "I know who I am in truth. I know what I am in truth. I know how I serve in truth."

The alignment in these claims is deeply significant. There is nothing cosmetic about them at all. They will restructure you because the agreement to be as truth will touch all things. The wave that we described earlier that washes away that which is unstable or out of alignment with truth is encompassing you now. And the joy of this is the release of the old and the claiming of the new, what lives beyond the threshold.

The life you are living now is the product of many lives. The encounters in the life you live are the products of beliefs and things you've chosen. How you attend to the physical life that you stand in now must be transformed for you to make your way. What we don't advise is that you make the announcement "I am in a new life." The fact that you stand where you are and see the ones before you and are able to claim them as they truly are will be testament to this. And the life that you live in all ways must begin to reflect the restructuring of the self to be in appropriation in the vibration of truth.

Now, where we take you next in this teaching is to outside of the world that you know and to the Kingdom and its manifestation. The triumph of the text is that the ones who listen and heed the call are being prepared for the work of their lives, not the work that they would choose as the small self, but the work of their lives. And we would say all the lives you've known yourself through have been in preparation for this level of reidentification as the what that you are. And the claims you've made for the small self to be in agreement to where she will be taken is what supports you in reclaiming a world that may now be known to you in a higher way.

The broadcast of your vibration as truth touches all things. You are the wave, you see, as you embody the vibration of it. And the truth of your being in its amassed way will claim what she sees and support the removal of the denial of light.

Now the denial of light is impressed in most things. We don't deny it. We understand that the tree casts a shadow, but the tree itself is of love, and the fact that the shadow is cast does not render the tree as something negative. But we will advise you that your own small selves and the small selves of others still have the great investment in maintaining control. And the achievement of your being in this alignment is the reclamation of those things that you have attended to in fear and transforming them to what they are.

The process we would recommend to all of you is to stand where you are and imagine, for a moment, that you are in vibration as truth. And as you stand, the expression of your being aligns to all you see. If you can imagine the clock on the wall, and the window before you, and what lies beyond the window in truth as your expression envelops it, you will begin to understand that the very things you see and have known as real will begin to transform to a true recognition of what they have always been.

The key to the Kingdom has been you, as we have said, but the witnessing of it in participation with your fellows is where we take you now. The Kingdom lies before you, above and beneath, and on all sides. It is where you stand, and in your truth you may claim it.

"I know who I am in truth, I know what I am in truth, I know how I serve in truth. And I am the one who perceives the world made new. I am Word through this intention. Word I am Word."

This aligns you as the visionary, the one who sees and witnesses, and what she claims then and what she perceives in the vibration of truth will be always there in alignment with the vision of the light.

Now, the crucible you have is memory, and we will address this now. You have memory for a reason. You remember which way you drive to work, how this one or that one treated you. You remember the rules of how to cross the street, how to tie the shoes, perhaps how to treat the one beside you. And while we do not eradicate memory, we do realign it because much of memory is all projection as the small self claims things and gives them meaning.

"I don't like the way she looked at me. That job was bad. That man was evil."

Whatever these things have been that are imprinted in memory are still there as you encounter your day. So the alignment of memory in truth will in some ways be a displacement of what you have thought, or were led to believe, or agreed to that has claimed a memory that may be informing your life. Your attachment to what you think is there also rescinds the reality of truth, and the alignment to truth in what you see requires you to comprehend the reality of truth in what you have seen prior. Because you walk in illusion when you look at the past and you use that lens on your present—or your future, yes—you are in witness to a false perception when you rely on memory that is not in truth.

"Well," you may say, "I know what my ex-husband said. You cannot tell me he is a good man. I remember him well."

We are not asking you to decide who anyone is or what happened. We are putting a new lens in the spectacles you wear so that you may have an understanding of truth in memory. So much of your pain, and the disfigurement of the self that you have endured, has been projection. As we have said many times in this text, the Divine Self is what you are and all else is an idea. And memory, we say, finally, is an idea as well.

So the reclaiming of memory in alignment to truth is not to make you wrong in your perceptions or your opinions of the past, but to liberate you from them so that your present and future, or what you believe to be your future, will be known in a higher way. The crucible of memory, we would say, is that memory always seeks to reinform the present moment in one way or another. And the collective memory of this plane does the same thing.

Now, Paul has a question. We must take it. "But we have heard that those that do not remember the past are doomed to repeat it. We require memory to keep ourselves safe."

We do not dismiss the claim, and what you have been through was there to teach you, both individually and collectively. But, again, we remind you we do not eradicate your memory. We claim you in freedom of it through the lens of truth that would bypass the claims of history that you are projecting now in your lives. The one who was told he would not be loved operates from that memory and the belief system that has supported it and claims it in his field as truth when it has never been. The memory of it is stored in the physical self, in the body itself, as well as the field. And your consciousness imprints it on the reality before you, which makes it seem real because it is your experience here. But your experience here is simply giving you back what you have claimed. It's entirely neutral in this respect.

If you believe yourself to be this or that, you will claim that in your expression. That is how the world works, and that is how individual and collective agreement manifests. So, in truth, we say, memory may be restored to its truth.

Now, the truth of what you are expresses in present time, in the moment you stand in. And the moment you stand in, while informed by the moment that preceded it, is not reliant upon it to have an expression or to know. As your knowing or realization of truth is manifested as what you are, the alignment in the present moment requires you to claim the information you need to move forward with. It is only supplied in the present moment. Do you understand this, friends? What you require to move forward with is gifted to you in knowing and realization only in the moment you stand in. Everything else is the idea in memory projecting itself into the moment you stand and out beyond it.

If it is true that all is supplied in the moment, you are far less reliant on the data of history than you think. The consciousness you hold at the level we are teaching you has access to information in a higher realm that the small self does not. So the small self, who is dependent upon memory, makes her choices as best she can, whereas the True Self knows as she stands and aligns to what she truly is.

This is a vast difference in the way that you express from what you are taught to be. You can only be in the present moment, you may only know in the present moment. Everything else is an idea.

Now, in the reclamation of memory to what you are, we have to advise you that what you will do here will defy what you believe can be. But how it is informed through you may be known to you in your expression.

If you can imagine an open window that leads to an infinite sky, we would like you to position yourself comfortably where you sit and claim these words with us:

"On this day I choose to align memory and all memory I have known to the vibration of truth. And in this claim, I give permission to all memory I know, individual and shared memory, personal and race memory, to move into an alignment with the vibration of truth. And as I say these words, I claim it as so. I am in truth. All I have known and believed is in truth. And all I will know and will believe is in truth. I know who I am in truth. I know what I am in truth. I know how I serve in truth. I am here. I am here. I am here."

Now, if you would, imagine that the field that you hold is beginning to spin, and as it spins it begins to lift you right out of your chair up to the ceiling and then out the window to the sky. In this spinning, you are releasing from your field misinformation, false perception, false agreements made, that may be imprinted in memory and are now to be restored.

The Christed Self, the what that you are, is the one that does this work, not the small self who thinks she knows everything. The Divine as what you are is the one who is lifting you to the level of vibration or alignment where this is even possible. The replication of memory will be released in this claim, which simply means that, because it was, it no longer is, because the True Self will claim what you need in the moment you stand in.

As the field you are living in and expressing through continues this process of release, what you will understand is that the reliance on memory to get through the day has not been disbanded. You need these things. What you don't need is the misperception of memory that is creating your life out of alignment to truth.

As you restore yourselves now to the chair you sit in, the place you lie, wherever you may be, you may know this to be so. The truth of what you are operates as and through all aspects of you. And if you would decide memory is a vault where things are stored and cannot be accessed by the vibration of truth, you will be missing the point of the teaching.

Collective memory, we would say, including the memory of fear that is held in the physical forms that you hold, will also be addressed by the collective in the coming decades. And we use *decades* intentionally. The time structure you know yourself in is aligned in some ways to the requirements of those who are here. And while we eschew the calendar and the ways you attend to it, we will observe that the collective frequency on this plane is in the requirement for the release of fear as the barometer for your well-being. "If I am not afraid, I will be okay" keeps you running from fear, which actually empowers fear and keeps you on the run.

The realization that wherever you stand is sovereign, and wherever you are, you are on holy land, will support you firmly in this progress. How the ones around you attend to fear and their memory of it, which is what catalyzes them to move in one direction or another, will be entirely dependent upon their level of agreement and alignment to truth. The one who is easily deceived, who prefers deception because it allows her to hide in the shadow, may find herself screaming as the light comes. Others of you will welcome it with an open heart. There is no penalty here.

But the reckoning we have taught—humanity facing itself in all of its creations—is an act of love. And it is not punitive. As those of you who progress here attend to the world in truth, you cast the light that banishes the shadows because the light that you are, in knowing of who and what she is, can only know the truth in others.

Tonight, we will say, the culmination of this teaching will begin. And by "tonight" we mean in this transmission that you are receiving now. The claims have been made and the prudent time to release a teaching is when the student is ready to be in receipt of it and to let it be as her. So we intend to complete this text in the coming days in perfection.

The quality of life that you have right now is dependent upon your perception of what quality means. In the alignment to truth and in the knowing of what you are, you may reclaim all things. And the announcement we give you—"You are here, you are here, you are here"—is the trumpet song that you announce yourself to the world in. When the trumpet sings, many awaken to their own Divine Selves.

The ones who disfigure themselves by hiding from the light they truly are will be called forward in love, and the mirror placed before them will be in love. There is no human born, no man or woman born, who is not loved by the Source of her being. But the Divine as what you are has been shielded from you for so very long that you've forgotten what you are.

Because the seed of the tree will always bear the same fruit as the tree, you must understand that the Divine that you are is of the greatness of its Source. The Christ is the seed, the aspect of the Creator in all human beings that seeks to be realized in matter. The what that you are and the fruits of her expression are the gifts of the Kingdom. And that will be the title of this chapter, "The Gifts of the Kingdom."

When we resume this manifesto on the subject of kingdoms and divinity and truth in all, we will bring gifts. We are pleased for this transmission and for what it entails to those of you who will work with it. We are productive when we teach, and the student may know that she will be met, he will be met by us wherever you stand. We know who you are. We know what you are. We know how you serve. You are here. You are here. You are here. We thank you for your presence. Good night. Stop now, please. Period. Period. Period.

Day Twenty-Two

We are ready to teach, and the culmination of this text is about to commence, this day and tomorrow. We would like to require the reader to remember only one thing. The choices that they make are always theirs. How they choose is up to them as well. And as they claim their true inheritance, the Divine as them, the choices that they make will be in agreement to the truth of what they are, and herein your lives become effortless. You are no longer in a quandary about what to do because you operate from a place of knowing that is not embellished with the dictates of others, culture, or religion, but ascribed to truth. And in truth you may know and have your being.

"Does this make your life easy?" Paul asks.

Well, yes, it does in some ways, but not in the way that you think. The claims that you have made thus far are about acclimation and agreement, and the product of these things is the expression you know. You are living in a new world, in some ways, when you claim what you are because the physical self, in its alignment to the Divine truth of what you are, is a different experience of being than you have known. But the challenges still faced are from the things that have been in agreement prior to your claim that seek to support you in reclaiming them and the old. So as we lift you today, we lift you to the ease of the unknown.

Now, this is the challenge for some of you. To lift to the unknown, to the unpredictable, to what may be so but cannot be seen is a challenge for the small self. But understand, friend, that the True Self abides there, not in uncertainty, but the unchosen—*the unchosen*, that which was not chosen in prior time but may be chosen in the moment you sing.

Now, the challenge here for us as your teacher is to show you what you cannot know until it is known by you. If you can imagine a woods, a deep woods that is full of foliage, the sun is still shining, but the hindrance of the leaves precludes the sun from showing itself in fullness. You are still standing in the sun, but obscured by the leaves.

Here we go, everybody. On this morning we claim the inheritance of each of you is being announced to claim you in freedom from all those things that would preclude your witness. And we ask you to announce this to yourself:

"On this day I am free of what I have known that would seek to hinder me from the new, that would seek to prohibit me from claiming the new and my true inheritance. I claim this of my own free will, and in this choice I make, I align to my potential as the one who may know and be in this expression of the Kingdom. I know who I am in truth. I know what I am in truth. I know how I serve in truth. I am free. I am free. I am free."

Now the claim that was just made was simply about allowance and agreement to allow the new to hold, the new to claim you. As you seek the Kingdom, you don't see what is present. And the Kingdom, as we said, is here. So in your being, in the claim we make and you agree to, you support the shift in awareness, in knowing and realization that is required to see the sun that still shines even through the leaves. The gift of this is that regardless of the circumstance you stand in, you will be able to realize that you are not without the light that is always present, even when the shadows seek to overtake.

Now, as we stand before you each, we wish you to know one thing. The teaching is not over when the book closes. In fact, the teaching just begins. The life that you are living now is changing—underline *is*—for better, we would say, in the claim "I am here." And in the announcement to be as truth, the limitations you've used to define your experience are being released in simple and profound and responsible ways.

Now, when we use this language—"responsible"—we mean that nothing is happening for you or to you that is not in agreement to your individual requirement for release. When you have something that you have chosen in a prior time that is in limitation and you attend to it as a permanent structure, a thing that will not be changed or moved, how you are left to attend to it in truth will be the most perfect way for the challenge or the creation or misbelief to be reknown in a higher way. The struggle here for some of you is you still wish to claim the very things that you think curse you—"my this, my that, my those things"—that will not be changed. Here we go, friends:

"As I claim my freedom, I offer my hands, that they may be used in fullness. I offer my body, that it may be reknown by me in its Divine nature. I offer my emotions, that they may be lifted and reformed to be in service to my own awareness of truth. And I lift my mind and all that is in it to liberation from the known that I have used to define myself in fear or in solitude or in ways that do not serve my usefulness as a conduit, as an expression of the True Source of my being. As I gift myself to my Source to be released from all bondage, all known in fear or limitation, I am gifted in response by the light of my truth that I may be claimed in inheritance. I know who I am as the one who receives, who is giving in response, and who says yes, I am here, I am here, I am here."

Now there is no need to decide again. If this choice is made in agreement in the Divine Self, it is activated as what you are. And the alignment to this claim will be met as you in all aspects of your life. You must allow yourself, friends, to receive the gift that would be given. But you cannot receive the gift as you cling to the old and the known and those very things that you believe are your curses that, in fact, have been only other ways to learn.

As we love you, we love all aspects of you, not just the ones you think are preferable or appropriate or allowed love. The stinging wit, the complaining, the arguable self, the one who self-pities, who challenges others for the sake of the challenge—he is loved too, as are all men.

So never think for a moment that this has been a treatise

on being a good boy or a good girl to meet the approval of us, the teachers of this work, or the Source of the teaching, which is the Creator. You are each as you are in your uniqueness and in your willingness to realign. The aspects of you that are not in support of your truth will be re-created or realigned or released, not by your efforts, but by the Source of your being.

As you confront these aspects of the self, you may be challenged for a moment, but we would only ask you not to go back and hide in the dark and cling the very thing to you that you say you would like to release. The tidal wave of truth will find its way there, as well, and will lift you and it to the Source of all things so that you may be reknown.

As we continue this text, we will say a few things about expectation and the requirements for what you don't need. The expectation that this text will solve your difficulties must be rendered useless. The expectation of it will seek to outline how this should happen, which then reverts you back to the small self's need to decide an outcome. The teaching of alchemy is in fact the teaching of transformation, and the vibration of truth is what alchemizes and transforms the self in alignment. So the prescriptions you would offer will, in fact, rebound and bring you back to the small self's need to prescribe an outcome as she would like it to be.

The offering you are being given here in this text is one of love. It is not a text to harm, but instruct in truth. And the vibration that is the book, because the book is a vibration, an oracle, as we have said, that will support you in your own awareness of what truth is and how to be as it for the good of the world. The text is what it is for your benefit. And as we continue, we support the text itself in the lifting of the reader.

So the small self's requirements of how this should be are needed to release. And now, as we continue, as we authorize more in this instruction, we invite the reader to question us in the higher realm. This simply means that, as you are reading this text or pondering the text itself and the questions occur, you announce them and expect to receive the answers in your life. Your life has become your teacher now. And the book itself informs your experience of your world as what you are in vibration. So assume the answers come as the questions are asked, not through a voice, perhaps, but through example and experience and what you see and who you see and how you see it.

To die to the old life you have known is to be born anew, and the death of the old self, while not a death as you can understand it, is what is going on in a certain way. As we recalibrate you each in your systems, in the vibrations you have chosen to operate as, what is null and void is in release. And some of you may be experiencing this in the physical self or the emotional self as weariness or pain or loss.

The temporary removal of the old is immediately replaced by the highest vibration that can be held by the student. And in this alchemy, the student knows herself in a new way. Give permission, please, to the process you have chosen to engage what you are in material form. It must be known in form. As we have said from the beginning, this is a teaching of practicality and expression. We have moved well beyond theory here to manifestation, and you are the manifest one, and your experience of this must be the testament to the work.

Now, Paul is interrupting. "Okay, somebody just read the book and says, 'I didn't feel a thing,' and they close the binder and toss it in the bin."

That is not what will happen here. Everybody who reads these words will be met at the level of expression that they can hold. If one does the work of the text, one is met.

Now their experiences may vary. Their expectations of what the experience should be in some ways claims them in a limited manner that may actually preclude the gifts from being received that we are offering. But still they receive on a level of vibration, on the level that they can hold of the truth of their being that is always here as them.

There are no mistakes here, not in this book, and not in this teaching. We are congratulating the man in the chair, not only for his ability to take the dictation without fear, but in allowing himself to claim the teaching in a way he has not yet. As his experiences begin to align him in a new way, he may teach this text, not only as us, but as himself.

We are supporting him, now, in his ability to speak as the man he is, and not only as the vehicle of our expression. As we assume him in the octave we hold, we actually lift his being to its highest level to be expressed through for the good of the students he meets and for the good of those he encounters. This is not to make him special, but to support him, himself, in saying, "I am allowed to be what I am. And I need not hide in the corner and speak in the whisper so that others may hear me as I speak the words of the Guides." He is here in a life, too, that must be lived in love, and you are all worthy of this, as well.

The amassed teachings that we have gifted you with so far are continuing. There will be another cycle of texts when this trilogy is completed, but what they will be offering will be life instruction for the ones who stand and navigate a physical realm in collective agreements to show them how to reclaim physical experience and love and marriage and choice in the highest ways available.

These texts will come in time. But the jurisdiction that we have given ourselves to complete this trilogy requires us to continue. And when we convene this teaching tomorrow, we will inform you where we will go when this text is done.

Congratulations are in order, as well, for the student of

the text who has been with us from the beginning. You have worked very hard. And to those who are new to the work, you are being caught up very quickly. And those who have been working with us prior are available to you for energetic support on the inner planes simply by asking.

In the last text, we invited students who were willing to support others in going forward to volunteer. And we continue with this claim now. If you are willing to be in energetic support of those who work with the text, your simple "yes" will align you to the school room that we are operating as. You may run up and down the aisle, as you wish, and give love and grace and support to the students in the room who may be struggling. This happens in a higher level, but may happen on this plane, as well, as you meet and discuss.

The last few things we will say before we complete this day's work is that we are gifting you each, each one of you here who attends to these words, with the authority to choose as the higher self. And here is this claim:

"In this choice to be as my True Self, I align all choices to the authority of the True Self so all that I choose may be in agreement to truth. I am Word through this intention. Word I am Word."

"I am choosing in truth, I am aligned to truth in all of my choices, I am not afraid, I am here, I am here, I am here" will support you each effectively in making the highest choice in all circumstance.

The last thing we say to you each is progress at your perfect pace. Your perfect pace means there is no race to glory, there is no timeline for your truth. The Eternal Self, the truth of what you are, is here as what you are and will only be and always be. And so you don't need to worry. The shifts you make happen in accord with your ability to receive them. And the progression of the teaching in your experience happens as you can hold it.

We thank you each for your presence. We lift you as one, and we hold you in love. We say "Yes" to you. We know who you are in truth. We know what you are in truth. We know how you serve in truth. You are here. You are here. You are here.

We are Word. Thank you and good night. Stop now, please. Period. Period. Period.

EPILOGUE

Day Twenty-Three

We are here as we are, and as we continue this teaching, as we say good night to the students of this text, we wish you to know one thing. There is no one answer to the question of being. But the answer you have been given here—"I am in truth, I am in agreement to truth"—will serve you to pave the way for your own truth to lead you forward.

The Divine Self that you are has an agenda for you, and this is your realization as what you are, the manifestation of God here and now in brilliance, in love, and in agreement to serve the Source of its being. Here we go. We will say these words for you in an awareness of the need the reader may have for an announcement of presence:

> "We see you in your beauty. We see you in your right to be, in all the claims made to issue your inheritance to you in fullness. We see you in agreement to what has been announced and what has been received. And as we celebrate you each, we lift you to the purview of the True Self who will be known in his realization, her realization, in

fullness. We sing your song with you. We are of the same light. We are here. We are here. We are here."

We say these words now. The infinite potential you hold may be known by you at the level of assessment and agreement you are in coherence with as a vibratory being. As we say, "Yes," to what you are, you agree at the level you may. And the transition in amplitude comes as it can be carried, held, and known as what you are.

The being that you are has manifested as what you are, and the what that you are is and always has been an aspect of God in realization. The man you are, the woman you are, the being you are in totality, is met by us to support this. And the agreement to be as what you are has been the issuance and benediction and claim of the book you hold.

As we go forward in our authorship, we will offer you a text on agreements made in higher octaves to sing for all. The manifestation of heaven on earth, which is the realization of the Kingdom as may be known by you in a shared landscape of inheritance, is where we take you next. And the issuance of this text, the one you hold now, is in preparation for where we will take you on the other side of the hill.

The transition you must undergo as a being is one of acquiescence to what you have claimed. So the renunciation of the small self's agenda in its encounter with truth will be what you experience as your vehicle absorbs, acclimates, and agrees to be as what you are. And as you stand there, you will be known in the world you live as an expression of the Christ manifested. All of you are this in one awakened state or another. Each human being is. All of you, all of you, all of you here are what you have been waiting for.

We are so proud of the issuance of each of you as you say, "Yes," to yourselves. And we give thanks to each of you for what you have chosen.

We will say this for Paul in brevity. Your work will commence immediately in preparation for the next text. We promise you this. You will be met by us each step of the way. Preparation means you will be prepared to be the vehicle of the next expression, and the teaching will come in sequence as you can hold it and announce it in text.

We will thank you for the discipline you hold that allows this. We will also congratulate Victoria and the students who have been present for the issuance of the text you hold now. You are all in benefit from your agreement to be.

As the next text unfolds—and you will be given the time and day when we wish to resume—it will come quickly and massively, which means, for Paul: Clear the decks for three weeks of dictation. And by "clear the decks," we mean our intention is to support you in being the oracle of transmission in a different way than we have aligned you to thus far.

We speak easily, now, through the man in the chair. His

resistance to the teaching has been released and there is little counterance to the expression we would offer ourselves as in speech and in being. The opportunity this grants us is to demonstrate our being and our teaching in new ways. The vibration we hold is too aligned to a high frequency to be fully embodied in manifestation. But as we work with Paul and each of you in your agreement to be in service, we will do a mighty good job in knowing you in your full capacity to be expressed in truth.

The love we have for you transcends personality and time and your ideas, even, of what love is. The vastness of being that we know in, that we agree to, that we share, is large enough to hold the bunch of you. And all else who wishes to know will be welcomed.

We sing our song now as this good-night commences. We sing our song in love. We sing our song in beauty, that we may be heard through the eternal knowing that is available to each of you.

As you say, "Yes," to what you are, *The Book of Truth* is ended.

We thank you all for your being. Good night. Period. Period. Period. Stop now, please.

ACKNOWLEDGMENTS

Dustin Bamberg, Tim Chambers, Joan Catherine Kramer, Beth Grossman, Mitch Horowitz, Amy Hughes, Jeannette Meek, Victoria Nelson, Bob Olson, Noah Perabo, Amy Perry, Brent Starck, Natalie Sudman, and the Esalen Institute.

ABOUT THE AUTHOR

Born in New York City, Paul Selig attended New York University and received his master's degree from Yale. A spiritual experience in 1987 left him clairvoyant. Selig is considered one of the foremost contributors to the field of channeled literature working today. He offers channeled workshops internationally and teaches regularly at the Omega Institute, the Kripalu Center, and the Esalen Institute. Also a noted playwright and educator, he served on the faculty of NYU for over twenty-five years. He is the former director of the MFA in Creative Writing program at Goddard College and now serves on the college's board of trustees. He lives in New York City where he maintains a private practice as an intuitive. Information on public workshops, online seminars, and private readings can be found at www.paulselig.com.

The Chinese Americans

The Chinese Americans

Revised Edition

Benson Tong

University Press of Colorado.

Published by the University Press of Colorado
5589 Arapahoe Avenue, Suite 206C
Boulder, Colorado 80303

The Chinese Americans by Benson Tong was originally published in hardcover by Greenwood Press, an imprint of Greenwood Publishing Group, Inc., Westport, CT, 1997. © 2000 by Benson Tong. This edition by arrangement with Greenwood Publishing Group, Inc. All rights reserved.

Printed in the United States of America

 The University Press of Colorado is a proud member of the Association of American University Presses.

The University Press of Colorado is a cooperative publishing enterprise supported, in part, by Adams State College, Colorado State University, Fort Lewis College, Mesa State College, Metropolitan State College of Denver, University of Colorado, University of Northern Colorado, and Western State College of Colorado.

The paper used in this publication meets the minimum requirements of the American National Standard for Information Sciences—Permanence of Paper for Printed Library Materials. ANSI Z39.48-1992

Library of Congress Cataloging-in-Publication Data

Tong, Benson, 1964–
    The Chinese Americans / Benson Tong.— Rev. ed.
        p. cm.
Includes bibliographical references (p.) and index.
  ISBN 0-87081-730-2 (pbk. : alk. paper)
  1. Chinese Americans. I. Title.
    E184.C5 T63 2003
    973'.04951—dc21

                                                                                   2003006542

Design by Daniel Pratt

12   11   10   09   08   07   06   05   04   03   10   9   8   7   6   5   4   3   2   1

For John

Contents

Preface to the Second Edition

This revised version of a work originally published in 2000 remains an interpretive narrative of the Chinese American historical experience from the American Revolutionary era to the present. Compared with the first edition, this is a longer story, providing as much coverage of the pre–World War II era as it does of the period that follows. I have nevertheless shortened Chapter 1 in response to several reviewers' comments, although I chose not to eliminate it. I maintain that without a firm grounding in the history and culture of China, the history of Chinese America remains inexplicable.

The new edition incorporates emerging themes in the scholarship of Chinese American and Asian American histories. Immigration laws, contemporary immigration, nativism and racism, political mobilization, transnationalism, identity formation, the racialization of the body and health care, religiosity, the literature of early immigrants, sexuality, family life, and children's history are some of the subtopics covered in more depth in this revised work. In responding to the larger call for historians to explore the multiple pasts of geographic areas outside of California—also known as the "east of California" project—this volume offer insights into some of those terrains. I have also included brief discussions of conflicts and cooperation between Chinese and other peoples of color—a historical theme yet to be fully studied by the academy.

The narrative here reveals that Chinese Americans have historically been castigated as "Orientals" or the malevolent "other" whom the dominant society used as the foil in its discourse on citizenship. Chinese Americans found themselves beyond the boundaries of American peoplehood. The Chinese lacked the qualities needed to exercise citizenship. Considered either too effeminate or too hypermasculine (or a threat to the public weal), the Chinese did not measure up to the test of manhood and public virtue considered part of the definition of citizenship. Immigration laws, labor, political participation, and family life were some of the areas of contestations over morality and patriarchy. If gender was one organizing principle of citizenship, so was race. Like African Americans and Native Americans, Chinese and other Asians were excluded from citizenship, since their nonwhiteness suggested the absence of the capacity for self-governance. Ascriptive exclusion and stratification have been central to the American past.* Yet Chinese Americans have contested the boundaries of rights and obligations and continue to do so today.

In regard to the transliteration of Chinese names, words, and phrases, it is important to note that *putonghua* (Mandarin)—the official dialect in today's mainland China—is pronounced quite differently than Cantonese, which most early Chinese immigrants spoke. With the exception of names commonly spelled in a different romanization system, I use the Pinyin romanization system for Chinese proper nouns. For common words and phrases in the Cantonese dialect, I use the Cantonese spelling. Names of people that appear in historical sources in Cantonese spelling remain as such in this work.

---

*See Evelyn Nakano Glenn, *Unequal Freedom: How Race and Gender Shaped American Citizenship and Labor* (Cambridge, Mass.: Harvard University Press, 2002), esp. 1–2, 18–55.

Preface to the First Edition

This volume is an interpretive narrative of the Chinese American historical experience from the 1780s to the present. The purpose of this book is to elucidate the impact of political, economic, social, and intellectual trends—both those in the countries of origin and, to a larger extent, those in the United States—on the lives of Chinese immigrants and Chinese Americans. The Chinese American experience, including its contemporary state of affairs, is surveyed to explore the intersections of race, class, gender, and sexuality. Equally critical is the examination of how Chinese Americans, in turn, have actively shaped the history of the United States. The narrative focuses on the agency of Chinese Americans through selective presentation of their "voices."

The expansive story presented here suggests that the Chinese American identity was and is far from singular, static, or irreversible. The book challenges the assimilationist thrust of some previous surveys of this same historical experience. Chinese immigrants and subsequent generations, through their human agency, have instead continuously negotiated the boundaries of race, gender, class, ethnicity, sexuality, and nationalism and thus defy any neat categorization of their identity or "place" in American society. Furthermore, Chinese Americans, through their attempts to apply lessons of democracy and equality of humankind, have played a vital role in shaping republican ideology and ultimately have forced the United States to uphold its revolutionary promise.

Although designed to provide readers with a broad understanding of this often historically maligned American ethnic group, coverage in this volume, because of space limitations, is still somewhat selective. Therefore the discussion focuses on post-1945 developments, particularly those that relate to politicization and the formation of ethnic identity.

Acknowledgments for the Second Edition

In preparing this second edition, I have benefited greatly from fellow scholars who took the time to read the first edition and offered comments and criticisms. In particular, I would like to thank Elliott Robert Barkan, Yong Chen, and Linda Trinh Võ for their input and support. I would also be remiss if I did not acknowledge the able assistance of Kerry Callahan, former chief editor at the University Press of Colorado, who was also instrumental in overseeing the transfer of the copyright from a previous publisher. I appreciate her constant encouragement, as well as her efforts to keep the book on schedule. The editorial staff at the University Press of Colorado has been generous with its time and effort, enabling this project to move through a tight schedule fairly smoothly. Finally, John's patience and willingness to entertain himself while I was immersed in reading and writing are simply priceless.

Acknowledgments for the First Edition

In researching and writing this volume, I have once again been reminded of the multiple debts I owe to friends, professional acquaintances, and family members. It has been a "perilous journey," to quote from one Gold Mountain song, and yet calmness prevailed in the end. The warm embrace of a circle of lifelong friends and even strangers has enabled me to "come ashore, the sooner the better," as another immigrant song states.

I would be a *juk sing* (literally, in Cantonese, "hollow bamboo"—a useless or ungrateful person) if I failed to acknowledge the nurturing gifts of Linda Trinh Võ and Antoinette Charfouros McDaniel. During a trying two-year stint at Oberlin College, I learned many lessons from them, some of which are found in this text. For photographs that grace this volume, I thank Linda, Antoinette, Terry E. Abrams, and Haipeng Li who generously expended time and energy in this venture. Haipeng also deserves the credit for checking the Pinyin romanization of Chinese words and phrases. Although my mentor, the late Gerald Thompson, never read this manuscript, I am grateful to him for urging me to undertake this daunting project. The writing of this text also attests to his remarkable influence on my professional life, and I hope I have measured up to his exacting standard.

At Wichita State University, Kenneth R. Spurgeon, in his capacity as research assistant, helped with bibliographical work and eventually researched and wrote—under my supervision—the biographical sketches included in the appendix.* Many other students, mostly at Oberlin College, also shared their penetrating insights into the Chinese American world. Students enrolled in Asian American seminars at Oberlin prodded me to reconsider some of my understanding of the literature, and I will always be grateful to them for their efforts.

---

*In this second edition, the biographical sketches have been omitted.

The Chinese Americans

1 Roots of a Diaspora: Chinese Culture and Society in the Late Qing Period

The Chinese presence in the so-called New World came about through trading connections, particularly those forged by the Manila galleon trade. From 1565 to 1815, Chinese, along with Filipino, sailors and stewards toiled in cargo ships that plied the waters between Manila and Acapulco. By the seventeenth century, some Chinese merchants were trading in Mexico City. These mercantile links had widened by the late eighteenth century to encompass the fabled sandalwood trade between Hawai'i and China.

The first Chinese to live in Hawai'i—experts in sugar production from Guangdong province in southern China—arrived in the early 1800s. The tiny community grew following the recruitment of nearly 200 contract laborers in 1852 for work on sugar plantations. The Chinese presence in the mainland United States was first recorded in the late eighteenth century. The first arrivals were three Chinese sailors, known only as Ashing, Achun, and Aceun, who came to Baltimore in 1785 as part of an abandoned interracial shipping crew. From this small, inauspicious beginning, the trickle widened into a wave in the 1850s as more than 20,000 Chinese in 1852 alone descended upon California because of the gold rush.[1] Chinese immigration to the United States gathered momentum until anti-Asian immigration laws passed in the late nineteenth century halted further arrivals. The story of Chinese America, however, must begin in late imperial China during the height of the Qing dynasty (1644–1912), the last dynasty before the emergence of the republican nation-state.

The Chinese civilization, one of the longest continuous civilizations in human history, can be "visualized [as] a majestic flowing stream."[2] Its cultural and geopolitical dimensions across time and space have maintained a strong historical presence in the imaginations of Chinese, both within mainland China and beyond. As the site of the geopolitical and cultural roots of the historical Chinese diaspora to Southeast Asia, Australasia, and South and North America, China embodies complexities in language, religion, customs, political system, legal heritage, and physical landscape. This land of more than 4 million square miles (including Inner Asia–Mongolia, Manchuria, Chinese Turkestan, and Tibet) and almost 430 million people in the mid-nineteenth century is indeed a country of dramatic contrasts and diversity.

Scholars typically trace the origins of the Chinese identity to the middle Yellow River basin in northern China nearly 5,000 years ago, where a group of tribes known collectively as the Huaxia had developed a neolithic culture to a somewhat advanced level. The Huaxia tribes then expanded southward to the lower Yellow River and Huai River valleys, where they encountered and absorbed another group of tribes, the Dongyi. By the twenty-first century B.C., the Huaxia had established in Henan the first national state in China, the Xia. This proto-Chinese state and its culture became the foundation for the modern Han Chinese people and culture, which today makes up 94 percent of the population.[3]

In the next centuries the Huaxia people spread to all parts of northern China and established a number of states. In the third century B.C., one state, Qin, through military conquests, successfully unified most of China—including parts inhabited by non-Huaxia ethnic groups. The establishment of this far-flung empire permitted the Yellow River culture to be disseminated to all parts of China for centuries to come.

But recent archaeological findings indicate that this cultural process was not simply a one-way phenomenon of domination by one particular group over the others. Neither was it necessarily a process that began 5,000 years ago. In fact, several centers of cultural development—starting perhaps as long ago as 10,000 years—across present-day China contributed to the shaping of the Han Chinese and its civilization, which, in turn, has given rise to regional variations in dialects and customs among the Han Chinese people.

For example, the Yue people—one of the largest, most prominent ethnic groups, which first appeared in history more than 3,000 years ago in the lower Yangzi Valley in eastern China and then spread southward into present-day Fujian, Guangdong, Guangxi, and northern Vietnam—had a language or languages and a culture different from those of the proto-Chinese states in the Yellow River basin in the north. Over time this Yue culture contributed primarily to the cultural development of Guangdong, the southernmost province, to which—up to 1965—from 90 to 95 percent of the Chinese in America trace their *gen* (roots). An indicator of the way the confluence of peoples and cultures has resulted in variations lies in the realm of surnames. The three most common surnames in China—Li, Wang, and Zhang—are rarely found in Guangdong, whereas Mai, ranked eight in that province, is not listed among the 100 most common surnames in China. Still, the perception that a cultural core area exists has given the Chinese, both citizens of mainland China and the *huaqiao* (overseas Chinese), an imaginary claim to a common place of origin.

This element of commonality has been reinforced by the classical distinction between Hua or Huaxia (Chinese), which suggests culture and civilization, and the "barbarians," namely those who did not live in China proper (defined as south of the Great Wall of China and excluding Inner Asia). This sense of cultural superiority, which solidified ethnic pride and defined *zuguo* (the motherland), helps explain the perpetuity of the well-known *Zhongguo*—"Middle Kingdom" or "Central Cultural Florescence"—syndrome.

GEOGRAPHY OF THE MIDDLE KINGDOM

From a physical environmental standpoint, it is understandable why the Middle Kingdom mentality—which held that China was the center of the world and superior to other civilizations—continued for so long in the popular Chinese imagination. The region north and west of China is a vast, relatively empty area of wind-swept desert or grassland country—namely the steppes of Mongolia and the Gobi Desert. To the southwest, beyond the Kunlun range, lie the rugged, lofty Tibetan plateau and the Himalayas. Directly to the south are steamy, dense tropical jungles; to the east, the forbidding Yellow and China Seas. These formidable barriers kept premodern China (before penetration of the West in the early nineteenth century) relatively isolated, although controlled commercial contacts with the outside world were never severed.

Such premodern historical contact, however, did not work both ways. The cultures of Southeast Asia, Japan, and India only marginally shaped Chinese civilization. Furthermore, China's closest neighbors were either sedentary peoples who consciously chose to emulate Chinese culture—especially the Koreans, Annamese (Vietnamese), and Japanese—or pastoral peoples, such as the Mongols, Uighurs, and Kazakhs, who occasionally challenged China militarily but never culturally.

In fact, until the disruptive nineteenth-century contact with the outside world occurred, intermittent visitors to China submitted themselves to the symbolic ritual of the Chinese tributary system. The farther these "foreign devils" stood from the civilizing influence of Chinese culture, the more the Chinese considered them "barbaric" and lowly. Thus the Chinese structured the tributary system to express their cultural superiority. It also stood as an extension of their internal social and political order. Within this hierarchical structure of foreign relations, China served as the lord and other states as the vassals. Non-Chinese rulers and their subjects presented tributes or gifts to the imperial court as a sign of submission, and in return they received imperial gifts, trading privileges, and protection. Diplomatic relations, similar to interpersonal ones, also embodied the principle of reciprocity. The hierarchy that underlined diplomatic relations also implied that China had little use for diplomatic legations abroad. As a result, Chinese in the United States were unrepresented until 1878. By then, the anti-Asian movement was well under way, and China was too weak to turn the tide.

Given this limited, unequal contact with the outside world, as well as the awe-inspiring landscape, it is not surprising that historically the Chinese had a strong sense of "place" and that this, in turn, was celebrated in classical literature and popular mythology. Overseas Chinese of the past maintained some emotional identification with their homeland—a phenomenon catalyzed by the legal and social discrimination they encountered in host countries, including the United States.[4]

China's vastness and highly diversified landscape have also resulted in multiplicity in both socioeconomic life and cultural expression, which, in turn, has shaped the diasporic process. The topography within China fragments the country internally, first along the north-south direction and again within each half. The most prominent divisive element is a mountainous region, made up mostly of the Jinling range, which stretches across central China from Tibet toward the China Sea. This separates the Yellow River drainage zone in the north from the Yangzi River drainage zone and its coastal valleys in the south. Although both northern and southern China feature major waterways, each area is different.

Northern China's main traffic artery—the Yellow River—brings heavy sedimentation that has impeded navigation. In the past, the silt has also led to the danger of a rising riverbed, and when dikes break, catastrophic floods occur. Given that, the river's bitter nickname, "China's Sorrow," seems appropriate. The north also features a smooth coastline with few places suitable for harbor development. The Yangzi River—the main southern artery—is far less malevolent; it is navigable all the way (the construction of a mammoth dam at Sandouping or Three Gorges region, scheduled for completion in 2013, will change this phenomenon), and its many tributaries provide easy access to all surrounding areas. Unlike the north, the south has a rough coastline suitable for ports and maritime trade. Not surprisingly, this transportation network historically kept the south ahead of the north in terms of economic development.

The north is made up of two fairly inhospitable areas: the somewhat arid, vast lowland plain in the east and a highland plateau in the west. The north also suffers from a rigorous climate; relatively dry year-round, it alternates between very cold winters and very hot summers. Because of these climatological conditions, the growing season in imperial times was short, and only dry crops such as wheat and millet were cultivated, mostly for subsistence purpose. These limitations impeded the development of market-oriented economies.

Southern China is a contrast to the north; the former boasts of many undulating valleys and hills and an abundance of lakes, rivers, streams, and other waterways. Unlike the north, the south is blessed with adequate monsoon rainfall and moderate variations in temperature. All that—coupled with its primarily leached, noncalcareous soils—has resulted in a nine- to twelve-month high-yield growing season and the farming of crops such as rice, fruits, and beans for the market economy.

The south is further fragmented into distinctive smaller areas, separated by stretches of low but rugged hills. For example, Guangdong, the southernmost coastal province, is shielded from the Yangzi River basin by a mountainous barrier. Fed by numerous rivers, the southern part of this province forms a common delta known as the Pearl River Delta—an area that is fertile and hilly. In the nineteenth century it was heavily terraced for both subsistence and commercial farming.

Guangdong, because of its unique southerly position and protective coastline, has attracted traders from southern Asia and Southeast Asia since the third century A.D. By the early sixteenth century, Portuguese maritime travelers—followed soon by the English, Dutch, French, and Americans—became interested in Guangzhou (Canton), the maritime center, as the gateway to the lucrative coastal traffic in silk, tea, porcelain, and other Chinese goods. Following such exposure to influences from abroad, which included science, Christianity, and fanciful stories of other lands—America included—the people of this subregion gradually became more receptive to new ideas and change.[5]

China's topography overall lends itself to regional separatism in multiple forms, which, in turn, has made political centralization problematic and at times nearly impossible. Centrifugal forces became more visible at the dawn of the turbulent nineteenth century, thus setting the stage for internal migration and immigration.

LANGUAGE

The influence of regional separatism is evident in the realm of language. Although racially China is fairly homogeneous—only about 6 percent of the populace is made up of non-Han people, comprising more than fifty minority groups—China exhibits a marked linguistic diversity.[6] Such divergences clearly result from internal geographical isolation across time.

The spoken language is fragmented into at least half a dozen mutually unintelligible regional dialects, each of which has any number of local variants. Chinese dialects differ significantly in pronunciation and less so in idiom and syntax. Cantonese (also known as Yue), to use one example, is a dialect spoken mostly in the southeast, especially in the province of Guangdong. It has therefore historically been spoken in many communities in the United States. Today about 50 million speakers of this dialect live within and outside mainland China, including the Sanyi, Sze Yup, and Zhongshan varieties so prevalent among Chinese abroad—especially in the Americas and Hawai'i. Other important dialect groups in Guangdong that have made their way to the United States include Hakka- and Fujian-derived dialects.[7]

Most dialects such as Cantonese vary dramatically from Mandarin (*putonghua*), the official dialect spoken by most Chinese today and by many contemporary Chinese immigrants in the United States, but all are written alike. Despite the babble of dialects, China is united linguistically by the standard written language, which is used by every group and region.

The Chinese written language, which earliest archaeological evidence dates back to the Shang dynasty (1765–1122 B.C.), is unique. The complex characters—today numbering about 40,000—are not letters, which all Western languages employ, but began as pictures or symbols. The characters are not phonetic representations but are actually ideographs. Since a character is an ideograph, it has the same meaning or meanings to all readers, although it may be pronounced differently in various dialect regions.

The Chinese language features only monosyllabic "words" or characters. Since there are more characters than syllables, many characters are pronounced as the same sound or syllable. To differentiate, tones are used. Every character has a fixed tone. This tonal feature in the spoken language gives Chinese a musical rhythm, which left nineteenth-century Chinese immigrants vulnerable to mainstream mockery.[8]

Another significant element in Chinese language is the emphasis on word relations, which tends to echo the relational character of Chinese philosophy. Ideas are often presented through compound expressions consisting of antonyms; examples include "buy-sell" for "trade" and "advance-retreat" for "movement." The antonyms are not seen as opposites but as united concepts forming a complete idea. The meaning of each character can be determined only in relation to other characters.

All this reflects the focus of Confucianism—the core of Chinese thought— not on the individual but on the web of human relations. The emphasis here is on a person's moral obligations to others, not on the individual's human rights. The fact that the Chinese language possesses an extraordinary number of kinship terms suggests an intense concern with family relationships; similarly, the rich body of ethical terms and concepts indicates China's preoccupation with moral values. The emphasis on kinship and familial relations bound nineteenth-century Chinese immigrants in the United States in ties of mutual reciprocity.

The intricacies of the Chinese language have, in the words of an eminent historian, "the character of an institution, rather than a tool, of society."[9] The mastery of classical Chinese (*wenyan wen*) used in high literature, as opposed to the "vulgar" vernacular speech (*baihua wen*), took many years. Not surprisingly, written language—at least before the iconoclastic vernacular or plain language movement in the early twentieth century, which swept aside that arcane classical style of writing—remained the province of the scholar-gentry class throughout most of Chinese history and helped, in that sense, to preserve the hierarchical old order. Predictably, members of the class ran many of the Chinese language schools established in nineteenth-century Chinese America.

SOCIETAL STRUCTURE

The hierarchical class structure also tended to preserve the old order. The scholar-gentry or scholar-official class was one of the four major classes in traditional Chinese society. By late Qing, society was highly stratified with status distinctions maintained through the sanctions of ritual and law. The four classes were ranked according to their social value in descending order: scholar-officials, farmers, artisans, and merchants. This categorization exalted government service above all other occupations and attached little or no social value to wealth or military valor. It also privileged scholastic achievement but co-opted intellectuals into government service. This class structure also, to some degree, shaped the fortunes of early Chinese immigrants in North America, particularly the way host countries received them and how intraethnic relations played out.[10]

In late Qing the scholar-official class, which made up only an estimated 3 percent of the population at the dawn of the twentieth century, was typically outranked by hereditary nobles. At the top of the social hierarchy during the Qing dynasty were two groups of hereditary nobles: the imperial Manchu clansmen and certain civil or military officials, including the renowned fighting bannermen. The court bestowed upon both groups titles and privileges as acknowledgment of certain achievements. Both groups received special allowances of property, food, and money, as well as other social and economic benefits in accordance with their rank.

Civil bureaucrats or scholar-officials, some of whom also carried titular nobility, also enjoyed significant prestige. By late Qing the court had devised a nine-rank system for officials, and each rank carried official dress and other symbolic marks of status. Those who belonged to this class typically spent years mastering the classics and sat for arduous examinations at different levels of increasing difficulty, culminating in the metropolitan or national exams held in Beijing. On the whole, only a very small fraction of an estimated 1.1 million degree holders during the Qing period held offices, but regardless of whether they held offices, they were considered the gentry class in China. They earned the legal privilege of wearing distinctive robes and caps, being exempted from certain types of punishment if convicted of a crime, and avoiding labor service tax and other taxes.

The gentry class in China, unlike those in Europe, did not resemble a landed elite. Although most did live in rural areas and many were landlords, by the early eighteenth century the scholar-gentry often served as the administrative broker between imperial officials and local people. Thus their income came from performing local services such as supervising schools, managing public works and welfare projects, organizing the militia, and mediating legal disputes. Over time, such income progressively replaced landed wealth as the major economic foundation of the gentry class. Before the sociopolitical chaos engendered by the Chinese Revolution in 1911, few members of the scholar-gentry class had to leave their homeland to eke out a better livelihood. Consequently, very few, except those who left to pursue higher education, were found in the early Chinese immigrant community of nineteenth-century America.

Below the gentry stood three classes of commoners. Peasants ranked higher than artisans or merchants because farming was regarded as a productive contribution to life. Craft and mercantile activities, on the other hand, were considered unessential, unproductive, and frivolous. This overall understanding reflected the agrarian-oriented Confucian value system. Local variation rooted in urbanization aside, in late imperial times peasants made up at least 80 percent of the population. They labored on the land, experienced limited social mobility, and lived on the margin of subsistence. Because of the absence of primogeniture, or inheritance by the oldest son, Chinese landholdings became fragmented into small plots. On average, families in southern China owned only 12 to 15 *mou* (2 to 3 acres), which economic historians have deemed insufficient for an economy of scale to occur.[11]

Also, throughout nineteenth-century China, an estimated 30 percent of peasant families were tenant farmers, and another 20 percent were petty landowners who, in addition to working their own land, rented additional land to make ends meet. Because of a general shortage of both fertile soil and capital, rents were high, and rural interest rates sometimes climbed to 40 percent per year. These conditions explain in part the nineteenth-century exodus from China and the upswing in the diaspora of the laboring class relocating to the Americas.[12]

Probably out of necessity, by the mid-nineteenth century many Chinese peasants had turned to the handicraft sector to help supplement their meager family incomes. Small rural workshops and peasant homes processed goods ranging from wine, oil, and sugar to silk, cotton cloth, and iron utensils. Peasant women often played a significant part in these activities and thus enhanced their economic importance to the family.

The class below the peasants—the artisans—although ranked lower in status, often earned as much and sometimes even more per capita as the peasants. A wide range of occupational groups came under this class, including craftspeople, manufacturers of commodities, and service-oriented individuals. These artisans and laborers could work as independent operatives or be employed by gentry families, the merchant class, or the state.

By the late nineteenth century, in the wake of early industrialization, a segment of this class had become the new, still small, urban proletariat who worked in shops and factories using low-level technology. Unlike traditional artisans, industrial workers did not enjoy paternalistic relations with employers; they were driven to maintain high levels of productivity and often lived in decrepit urban surroundings. This growing urban proletariat class rose to prominence during China's revolutionary era in the early twentieth century, and their political agitation, in turn, influenced to some degree the worldview of the Chinese in America.

Merchants theoretically were ranked at the bottom of the four-class structure. Mercantile activities were stigmatized as exploitative and demeaning. Merchants, to secure large-scale businesses, had to cultivate the paternalism and support of imperial officials. This class was so unattractive that many merchants bought degrees and titles to gain higher prestige and enjoy certain benefits. Following the anti-Qing rebellions in the mid-nineteenth century, which wiped out the financial resources of the imperial government, as many as 50 percent of official posts were secured through purchase; many of these presumably were bought by the merchant class.[13]

Following the expansion of commerce and industry after the 1870s under the influence of the West, the stigma attached to mercantile activities slowly began to ebb. Some literati, disillusioned with the demanding scholarly life and encouraged by the burgeoning market economy, threw their resources into Western-style economic ventures. Thus the boundaries between the classes gradually blurred. But the stigma attached to mercantile activity, not to mention government supervision of industrialism, never disappeared, as attested to by the need to rationalize such activities in the name of preserving national strength and prosperity. This social attitude, coupled with the promise of mercantile freedom, explains in part why some of the merchant class made their way to the United States in the late nineteenth century.

The four-class structure has recently been shown to be simplistic. It has been argued that at least nine distinct cultural groups were positioned in relations of dominance and subordination. By applying three variables—education, economic position, and legal privilege—in various ways, the Chinese social spectrum ranged from the classically educated, legally privileged, and economically self-sufficient elite (the most dominant group) to illiterate and dependent commoners (the most subordinate group).[14] This scenario included the emergence of a new, independent merchant class and a small intellectual class—both freed from gentrylike aspirations.

Gender further complicates this picture. A woman of elite background could be privy to all advantages and still exercise little influence. Women's subordinate position in society was reflected and asserted in legal statutes, informal social customs, elite and popular literature, handbooks on household ritual, and medical texts. Further, circumstances for women in China were not the same throughout the country, even for members of the same class.

Although Chinese society was stratified, no caste system existed. Theoretically, everyone could access mobility regardless of family, birth, or religion. The Chinese system's emphasis on merit rather than birth and the partial accessibility of education produced considerable movement between classes or social groups. Consequently, the rural-urban gap in cultural literacy and lifestyles was less marked than that in some European countries in the nineteenth century, although rapid economic development in urban centers in the late Qing period eventually created social differentiation. With so much already in flux, potential immigrants' later decision to emigrate was prompted as much by the desire for mobility as by the need to escape privation.

THOUGHT AND RELIGION

Perhaps what held Chinese society together despite the pressure of internal modernization was its pervasive philosophy, which undergirded religiosity. The presence of ethics in every area of traditional Chinese culture, including music and the fine arts, is an indicator of the strong influence of thought in shaping Chinese identity.

Traditional Chinese thought, shaped primarily by Confucianism with marginal influences of Buddhism and Daoism, was strongly concerned with human relations. This focus could be found in the "Five Constant Virtues" of Confucianism: *ren* (humanness, or filial piety and submission), *li* (propriety), *yi* (duty), *zhi* (humane wisdom), and *xin* (faithfulness). Of the five, *ren* was the most important, since it served as the key to an orderly family and state. Other significant elements of Chinese thought included an emphasis on nature and natural processes, as reflected in the belief in Heaven's predeterminism of fate; a profound sense of cultural superiority; an awareness of and respect for tradition; and a focus on hierarchical order and social harmony—all of which made Chinese traditional society conservative and precedent-minded.[15]

Unlike other cultural traditions, the Chinese saw their moral order as one shaped by men and women; the human being, not God, stood at the center of the universe. The ethical system as it existed by the late Qing period did not spring from a supernatural authority, as it does in the case of Christianity and Islam. Buddhism and Daoism, the two major institutional religions in traditional China, offered few major contributions to this ethical system; much of it was grounded in Confucianism.

The core of Confucianism in late Qing was the "Three Bonds": between ruler and subject, between father and son, and between husband and wife. These and the relationships between older brother and younger brother and between friend and friend constituted the "Five Relationships." All Five Relationships involved subordination, inequality, and nonreciprocal service; for example, a wife was subordinate to her husband but enjoyed virtually no rights.

In this patriarchal construct, the family served as the central unit of society, and all relationships outside it mimicked those inside. Thus the ruler-subject relationship echoed the father-son tie; similarly, the ruler, who supposedly received from Heaven the mandate to rule, stood in a position of a son to Heaven. The Chinese did not consider the emperor to be divine in any sense; rather, in a broad extension of the family pattern, the ruler functioned as the mediator between Heaven and humankind—playing one role as filial dependent to Heaven and another role as paternal exemplar to the people. Thus in Confucianism the cult of Heaven, the family system, and the state constituted a unified entity. Just as critical was the idea that the cosmic universe constituted one entity, without a beginning or an end, and was not divisible into natural and supernatural realms.

It would not be an exaggeration to describe mid-nineteenth-century China as a land of polytheism and eclecticism. Religiosity took on a highly diffused character and upheld the moral order as defined by Confucian ethical values. Although the two major institutional religions—Buddhism and Daoism—remained visible in late Qing, practiced far more widely was a form of popular religion that involved a syncretic melding of the teachings of Buddhism, Daoism, and Confucianism; the practices of local cults and ancestor worship; the worship of patron gods and spirits through divination and sacrifice; the mystical arts of prediction—astrology, palmistry, and geomancy; and animism. Not surprisingly, Chinese religion did not feature a personal creator external to the cosmos.

Religion, given its polytheistic and highly diffused character, has served well as an integrative force for Chinese social institutions and organized groups. Ancestor worship, typically carried out at shrines in the home and also at graves and ancestral halls (for collective observances by extended family and kinsfolk), constituted a cultural universal in traditional China. Through the performance of prescribed, scheduled rites, family members rekindled the memory of departed kinsfolk and, in turn, integrated the living with the dead in perpetual kinship ties. Living family members also were conjoined as one through such collective expressions. The values of familism—all rooted in Confucianism—were strongly reinforced. Periodic or anniversary sacrifices for ancestors and elaborate mortuary rites for the recently deceased were customary practices for most Chinese families.[16]

The parallel to family ancestral worship could be found in public religious observances. A communal belief in the appeal to the supernatural for success and security welded together such organizations as fraternal groups, protective societies (tongs), occupational associations, and local communities. For example, southern coastal, maritime communities actively worshiped the goddess of sailing, Tian Hou. Every traditional trade had its own patron god, whose birthday celebration constituted a major event for tradespeople— one typically commemorated with festivals and even parades. These celebrations also embodied a specific social function; for the masses, life had been a constant struggle for subsistence, so such celebrations served as a mechanism for the affirmation of life through drama, joy, and merriment. In a predominately agrarian economy, shrines and temples dedicated to agricultural deities governing the natural forces, such as the Dragon God or Lung Wang (which regulated water), were common. Elaborate annual imperial sacrifices to the agricultural deities reflected their primacy to the nation's well-being.

Popular religion over the centuries, however, had also appropriated Buddhist concepts such as the transmigration of souls and the law of causal retribution (karma). Most Chinese in late Qing consequently believed the soul existed eternally, materializing in an endless succession of temporal existences in multiple forms of life. Popular religion also incorporated the Buddhist bodhisattvas—beings who compassionately refrain from entering nirvana to help others—into its pantheon of gods. In general, Buddhism worked well with Confucianism; both emphasize the preservation of a moral order through service, self-control, and selflessness. Also, the Four Noble Truths, the core of Buddhist teachings, impart that life is an endless cycle of births and deaths in a sorrowful world, and only the elimination of selfish desires will end pain and sorrow.

The elimination of selfish desire comes from following the Eightfold Noble Path, which is akin to the Confucian Five Constant Virtues: correct views, attitudes, speech, conduct, occupation, effort, perception and consciousness or self-examination, and concentration. Buddhist morality is based on concrete social values such as love, charity, courage, self-control, and respect for all living matter. By following these precepts, an individual, through multiple rebirths, can gradually move toward Enlightenment, or the ultimate existence, whereupon the painful cycle of life and rebirth can be broken.

Daoism also contributed to the popular religion through its mystical aspects of occult magic and the practice of deifying prominent, legendary, and historical figures. Over time, the Chinese landscape became dotted with shrines and temples devoted to a large host of national, regional, and local gods. The Chinese valued Daoist gods for their utilitarian function, much as they approached Confucianism and its moral precepts. The moral and magical functions of the cults, not the religious identity, dominated people's consciousness and their receptiveness to any given belief.[17]

Daoism advocates spontaneity in union with nature. Followers renounce obligations attached to social relationships and seek psychological freedom by being themselves naturally. The central principle of Daoism entails the independence of each individual—in direct opposition to Confucianism's objective of bringing humans in line with established social conventions.

As is the case with Buddhism, the value system of Daoism also echoes Confucian virtues. The social principles of loyalty, faithfulness, integrity, duty, and filial piety constitute the exalted core of Daoism, as they do in Confucianism. Daoism, inspired by the Buddhist idea of karmic retribution, developed a system of merits and demerits that reward good behavior with prolonged life and reduce one's life for wrongful acts.

Much of this eclectic, popular religion was transmitted to early Chinese America. Discriminated against by the larger Euro-American society and forced to exist in segregated spaces, Chinese immigrants fell back on religiosity for emotional sustenance and self-identity. The practice of religion, particularly ancestor worship, also helped this largely bachelor society—the by-product of antifamilial immigration laws, at least until these laws were liberalized in the mid-1940s—to maintain ties with both nuclear and extended family units left behind in China.[18]

Some of the earliest social institutions erected in U.S. Chinatowns were temples for collective worship. Early immigrants also visited shrines memorializing patron gods, built mostly in the headquarters of mutual aid associations and tongs. Many turn-of-the-century Chinatowns—such as those in San Francisco, New York, and Los Angeles—held anniversary festivals and colorful parades. Of these, the Chinese New Year festival, the only holiday still celebrated by most Chinese in the United States today, was by far the noisiest and merriest. The fifteen-day celebration typically ends with the dragon dance, which commemorates this creature of strength and goodness who carries out the will of the gods.[19]

Another important celebration in both mainland China and Chinese America was Ching Ming, or the Pure Brightness festival. The Chinese considered visits to family tombs a formal and necessary annual rite. Since the Chinese in America lived far away from ancestral graves and family tombs in their native villages, they visited the local Chinese cemetery on this occasion. Most mutual aid and fraternal associations erected spirit shrines for those who had no loved ones buried in the area.

Women, trained since girlhood, have typically played a prominent role in all celebrations and ancestor worship in both China and the United States. Women have shouldered the responsibility of remembering ancestors' death dates, praying to the ancestors for the family's well-being, and often trying to interpret unfavorable ancestral behavior. They have also learned and carried out the customs and minute details of the rituals necessary for each celebratory occasion.

The belief in and practice of popular religion and its eclectic philosophical underpinnings ensured that the country's culture, or *tezhi* (its way of life), remained stable and uniform, even though it was saddled with a shaky, unwieldy political system and was constantly rocked by internally driven, transforming socioeconomic changes.

THE RISE AND FALL OF THE QING DYNASTY

Until the tumultuous Chinese revolutionary era in the early twentieth century, a succession of imperial dynasties had governed China since the first dynasty, the Shang, nearly 3,565 years ago. In 1644 the reigning emperor, Chongzhen of the Ming dynasty (1368–1644), was toppled by the northeastern Manchus who swept into northern China.

The Manchus arrived at a time of socioeconomic dislocations, a time beset with difficulties "usually associated with the end of a 'dynastic cycle'— eunuch domination of the court, moral degradation, political corruption, intellectual irresponsibility, high taxes, and famine."[20] The masses—dissatisfied with the failure of the ruling house to solve problems of poverty and privation—were on the verge of large-scale rebellion, and the Manchus found allies among the leaders of the Chinese rebel forces. This scenario, repeated again and again throughout imperial times, was typically interpreted by the popular mind as evidence that the emperor, the Son of Heaven (*Tian zi*), had lost the sacred mandate to rule.

Although the Manchus' Qing dynasty was non-Han, it accepted the traditional Confucian order. Such adaptation gave the ruling house some stability until the era of Emperor Qianlong (1736–1799), whereupon China entered another dynastic cycle. By then the Manchus' zealous championing of the traditional orthodoxy had become a liability as the winds of change began to sweep through this vast land.

Below the emperor was the nobility, composed of those of both Manchu and Chinese origins, who—unlike those in Europe—wielded little political or administrative power. As a rule, they were kept fairly isolated from the corridors of power. The scholar-official class populated the multiple levels of governance ranging from the Grand Secretariat—the advisory group to the emperor—all the way down to the lowly district magistrates who collected taxes, settled litigation, and maintained peace and order in the locality.[21]

Within district divisions such as villages, towns, and cities, the magistrate relied on two self-governing neighborhood organization systems called *baojia* and *lijia*. Local residents, including many ancestors of present-day Chinese Americans, made up the *baojia* and *lijia*, with the former facilitating police control and the latter helping with collection of taxes. Thus the Qing government maintained imperial control even at the local level but without extra officials or additional expenses. For local residents, the *baojia* and *lijia* helped to reinforce pseudo-kinship and familial ties.

Further reinforcing such ties was the lineage tradition. In Guangdong, peasants lived in lineages, which linked all families—regardless of socioeconomic standing—with a common ancestry. A lineage typically owned property and managed temples, schools, and charity projects. Land in particular constituted corporate ownership and was rented out to locals who also had a stake in it. Thus the classic European division between landlord and tenant is not applicable in this context. Such kinship and familial ties facilitated immigration through monetary and emotional support.

From a Western perspective, however, this political system was fraught with problems. For example, the judiciary did not stand independent of the executive branch. Due process of law did not exist, nor did advice of counsel in a trial. A case was often tried simply on its moral implications, regardless of legality. Chinese society believed the law served to uphold social order, not to protect individual rights. Thus magistrates applied the codified laws in a flexible manner, depending upon the people and circumstances. Men and women were not equal before the law. Because litigation supposedly stemmed from behavior that was not virtuous—even on the part of the suing party—the Chinese, to avoid social disapproval, customarily avoided recourse to law unless absolutely necessary.[22] Much of this system, however, was not necessarily transplanted wholesale to the Chinese American world.

When Qianlong abdicated his throne in 1799, the Qing dynasty had already passed its apogee. The unbalanced economic development, with some regions outpacing others, threatened the state, since unequal development in the absence of political centralization and economic linkages could lead to conflict. Compounding the situation were a series of expensive bungled military campaigns, localized rebellions, and a rapidly growing population without needed technological innovation. The next emperor, Jiaqing (1799–1820), inherited a country that was "externally strong but internally shriveled" (*wai qiang zhong gan*). Within the next twenty years or so, the country suffered from serious administrative ineptness, widespread political corruption, and moral maladies—all of which the Chinese masses took as clear signs of a falling dynastic fortune.[23]

At the end of the eighteenth century, a large-scale anti-Qing movement—the White Lotus Rebellion (1796–1804)—broke out. Initiated by the White Lotus Sect, a secret society dedicated to restoring the Ming dynasty, the rebellion depleted the imperial coffers. In the same era a number of other minor uprisings also occurred. The well-known Ming loyalist Heaven and Earth Society (Tian Di Hui), also known as the Triad Society (Sanhehui)—the historical origin of many secret societies (tongs) in the United States—perpetrated a significant uprising in Taiwan in the 1780s. Equally irritating to the imperial government were two Muslim revolts in northwestern China and a series of uprisings conducted by Miao tribesmen in southwestern China. Although the Qing government succeeded in suppressing these challenges, it bore a heavy monetary burden and failed to eliminate religious, economic, and ethnic resentments. The government's ineffectual response shook public confidence and badly weakened the economic foundation of the Qing empire.

Exacerbating these convulsive changes was population pressure. The population began to grow in the sixteenth century, and the rate of growth increased over the next two centuries. By 1800 the population stood at 300 million, at least a twofold increase since the 1660s. But the amount of arable land had not increased correspondingly, since so much of China consists of arid and mountainous areas. Between 1661 and 1812, the amount of arable land increased by less than 50 percent, but the population increased by more than 100 percent.[24]

Although population growth moderated after the 1770s, a drop in the death rate—mostly as a result of a long period of relative peace and stability—kept the momentum going. Without a fundamental change in the economic system or the impact of an industrial revolution, population pressure became a significant problem. For the displaced, poor, and unemployed, survival often meant turning to banditry or other social action antithetical to prescribed conventions.

All of these problems—faltering administration, widespread corruption, degeneration of the military, and the pressures of a rising population—indicated that the ruling power had passed its peak. Ironically, internal economic and social changes, not unlike those taking place in Europe, only highlighted the ineptness of the state. Since late Ming times, China had experienced a series of intertwined precapitalist changes including significant urbanization, especially in the lower Yangzi area; the increasing role of a monetary economy; the development of regional and long-distance trade; the emergence of a countrywide market for commodities; more geographic mobility; expanded popular literacy; growing heterogeneity of the gentry class; and the professionalization of some managerial activities.[25] In this context of fluid social relations and gradual disintegration of the old order, by 1800 the country had become vulnerable to both internal rebellion and external invasion. In this milieu, social dislocations intensified, and against such a backdrop both migration and emigration became viable, even necessary possibilities. Yet certain things did remain the same. Language, thought, religiosity, and the core of the hierarchical societal structure prevailed, as they had for centuries. Displaced peasants, ambitious tradespeople, restless artisans, and the few seekers of Western knowledge transplanted much of this heritage to the new fabled land—the United States.

2 Travelers to Gold Mountain: Immigration, Labor, and Exclusion

CONTEXT FOR IMMIGRATION

By 1800 China faced more rapid change and was looking toward an ominous future. China was too weak militarily to protect itself from Western imperialism but was too strong culturally to surrender political initiative to Chinese modernizers. In the absence of modernization, its people were forced to look elsewhere for a livelihood.

Early emigrants in the nineteenth century who chose to journey to the United States (known popularly in Cantonese as *Gam Saan* [*Jinshan* in Mandarin], or "Gold Mountain") hoped to strike fortunes in the gold mines of the proverbial *Mei Kuo* (*Mei Guo* in Mandarin, or "Flowery Flag," the Cantonese colloquial term for the United States). But *gam saan haak* (*jinshanke* in Mandarin; Cantonese for "travelers to Gold Mountain") found only *hek fu* (Cantonese for "taking in pain," or adversity). Prejudice, disfranchisement, and social exclusion marked their daily existence. Life became a struggle, haunted by unfulfilled Gold Mountain dreams.

But before the pressing reality in the United States confronted them, potential emigrants found themselves caught in circumstances unique for Guangdong, the main source for U.S. immigration. In Guangdong province a dramatic rise in the population was the most fundamental indigenous change. Whereas China's total population increased 47 percent between 1787 and 1850, during that same period Guangdong's population grew 79.5 percent. One of the five fastest-growing provinces in China, its population shot up to 28,182 in 1850 from 16,014 in 1787 (note that Chinese imperial documents that historians used to compile statistics involve serious under-reporting, particularly for regions far away from Beijing, the capital city).[1]

This enormous population growth in southern China led to a struggle for limited cultivable land, a situation compounded by the absence of primogeniture. The growth of the population in relation to the amount of land that could sustain that population was higher in Guangdong than in the rest of China. The social implications could have been ameliorated if the tremendous economic vitality and social change experienced during the sixteenth to eighteenth centuries—not unlike the conditions that led to the Industrial Revolution in Europe—had developed into full-scale industrialization. The reasons this failed to happen are manifold.

For one, China's educated elite spent so much time and energy trying to attain the status and prestige of the scholar-official class that it had to sideline endeavors that might have fostered economic and technological change. Heavy government exactions—with no concomitant infrastructure for trade—on private wealth and investments also dampened the spirit of entrepreneurship. Perhaps the strongest reason for China's inhibited industrialization was the relative stability of market demand, which offered little stimulus for radical technological change and attendant higher productivity. Even in agriculture, rapid commercialization did little to transform small-scale subsistence farming.

Without rapid capitalist and technological improvements to absorb the dispossessed, human dislocation became ominous. European imperialism—which had precipitated the first and second Opium Wars (1839–1842 and 1856–1860, respectively)—hampered industrial growth because of the costly effects of foreign wars, the drain on the specie caused by importation of opium, and general economic competition. As the major point of contact with the West, Guangdong was visibly affected.

In Guangdong an overabundance of cheap, mass-produced foreign goods flooded the domestic market, limiting demand for local products. Even though Chinese investment in foreign enterprises in China grew after the 1860s, little of that economic pattern benefited the masses. The rapid growth of the colonized islands of Macao and Hong Kong, as early as the mid-1850s, captured much trade from Guangzhou (Canton, the main port city of Guangdong). By 1870 free trade and competition from other coastal ports further exacerbated the unemployment rate of the urban proletariat.

Concomitant with this economic imperialism was the international migration of labor. The global expansion of European and American capitalism had necessitated movement of workers, capital, and technology across borders so investors and businesspeople could tap into the natural resources and markets of underdeveloped countries.

The eventual immigration from Guangdong to Gold Mountain was part of a larger diaspora that involved as many as 2.5 million people between 1840 and 1900. These mostly young, economically displaced men—not to mention the estimated 250,000 forced into slave labor in the "coolie trade" (the trafficking of contract laborers) in Cuba and Peru—heeded the call of Western capitalists and departed for underdeveloped colonies in Africa, Southeast Asia, Australia, New Zealand, Hawai'i, the West Indies, Canada, and the United States.[2] European colonization of Southeast Asia in the nineteenth century brought that region into the world market. Chinese immigrants occupied a subordinate status in this export-oriented economy; they mined the mineral riches, sawed the lumber, laid down the tracks for railroads, grew the rice and other crops—and a few lucky ones rose to become entrepreneurs, tradespeople, and compradores. Others were brought to Australia as early as 1848 as indentured laborers to work in the plantations, but they soon abandoned that labor for the gold rush of the 1850s and beyond. The need to escape their lowly status in the mining industry also induced the Chinese to abandon depleted goldfields in California and move northward to join the frenzy of the British Columbia gold rush in 1858. When all the nuggets and gold dust had been mined, the Chinese turned to extending the Canadian Pacific Railway into British Columbia. Also in the 1850s U.S. citizens and ships were implicated in the "coolie" trade that brought thousands of Chinese to toil in the dense sugar-growing fields of the Caribbean basin. Later, Chinese laborers in Spain-held Cuba were trafficked to Louisiana to work in that industry.[3] Thus this massive human migration resulted from transnational connections between colonizing and colonized powers, with its demographic distribution determined in part by convulsive economic and technological changes.

Paralleling these disruptive developments was a series of internal uprisings including the Taiping Rebellion (1850–1864) and the Red Turban uprisings (1854–1864), both of which ravaged the countryside. "Ever since the disturbances," a government report noted, "[the] able-bodied go abroad. The fields are clogged with weeds." Between 1856 and 1868, the Hakka-bendi (*bendi* means "natives" and refers to the Cantonese-speaking Chinese) interethnic feuds over fertile delta lands—a bloody conflict that raged across the province of Guangdong—led to the loss of at least 200,000 lives and further exacerbated the plight of poor peasant and proletariat families.[4]

Natural calamities compounded the declining conditions. Every year between 1832 and 1881 at least one major catastrophe plagued the county of Xinning (later renamed Taishan). Located within Guangdong, Xinning was the place of origin for more than 50 percent of first-generation Chinese Americans. Nearly every year the people of Xinning, Xiangshan (later renamed Zhongshan, the second-most-important Chinese emigrant community), and surrounding counties faced natural disasters—droughts, floods, heavy snowfalls, typhoons, or crop failures caused by insects or blights. One flood in Guangdong was so severe that, according to one imperial account, the "rivers and the sea and the streams have joined in one sheet over the land for several hundred *li*" (one *li* equals a third of a mile).[5]

Famines and natural disasters often hit all classes of Chinese society, but the subsistence-based peasantry was the most strongly affected. Following the devastating Opium Wars, the financially strapped Qing government—saddled with large indemnities because of the recent conflicts—imposed new taxes on peasant farmers. Few could pay, and many lost their land. Corruption by officials sometimes compounded these families' financial burden. The turmoil in the economy, coupled with hostile ecological and climatic conditions, led to destitution and deprivation. Faced with such conditions, some Chinese decided to leave their villages for distant lands.

That decision was provoked in part by exaggerated tales of riches in the United States. Since the late eighteenth century people in Guangdong had been exposed to American influences by Yankee traders and missionaries. In addition, some of the earliest writings about the United States, dating back to the early nineteenth century, first appeared and were circulated in this area. Even more important were the direct trading links, from the late eighteenth century onward, between Guangzhou and California. A two-way traffic in lucrative goods ranging from sea otter skins to ornate Chinese furniture led to the dissemination of news in southern China about the fabled America.[6]

Stories about the discovery of gold in California reached China as early as the summer of 1849, barely a year after the astounding news leaked out of the U.S. Pacific Coast. Cantonese merchants, with fairly extensive ties to Americans, probably helped spread the news, and local Chinese were soon sharing tales of astounding wealth on the other side of the Pacific. Other Guangdong residents heard about the golden hills of North America through friends and relatives who had been part of the earliest wave of prospectors in California. The promotion of California's supposed bountifulness by captains of foreign vessels, who were interested in expanding their business in human cargo, also captured locals' attention. Overall, such trans-Pacific connections explain in part why Chinese emigration took place and why most Chinese immigrants came from Guangdong.

REVISIONIST HISTORY

Recent scholarship on immigration history has forced a reevaluation of the understanding that the general immigrant experience was one of uprootedness and alienation. Previously, it was understood that individual emigrants, torn from their isolated peasant communities by the encroachment of capitalism, were forced to leave their disintegrating villages for an alienating industrialized environment. As a result of these so-called push factors, they became strangers in a strange land. Over time, however, they would leave behind this social disorganization, adjust to life in America, and become Americanized. Their immigration was a linear progression from traditional culture to Americanization.[7]

In reality, many emigrants—like the Chinese—had already migrated within their homeland and experienced modernity. Hired hands, poor peasants, sharecroppers, and small landowners, who constituted the majority of the Chinese exodus, faced economic pressures and had to look for new ways to make a living. Yet they were not necessarily the most impoverished people in the country. Prospective emigrants opted to emigrate to maintain their status and lifestyle, and they often did so with the help of a social network of relatives and acquaintances. They relied on the kinship system to provide information about their new country, to encourage them to emigrate, and even to pay the transportation costs. Those who left often traveled to nearby seaports such as Guangzhou, Hong Kong, and Macao, where they came in contact with ships and persons bound for foreign lands. Forward-looking rather than past-oriented, emigrants hoped in the long run to control and improve their lives.[8]

Although the Chinese diaspora can be conceived as part of the international migration of labor, those headed for Gold Mountain made their own choices regarding their futures. These mostly young Cantonese men (a small minority were Hakkas) departed for the United States to achieve upward social mobility. The fact that so many came from Taishan, the county that supplied most of the experienced wage laborers for the subregion's market-oriented economy, suggests that at least some of those who left were not necessarily unworldly victims of Western capitalism. A smaller stream of merchants and artisans, already engaged in a premigration network of business connections in China, also flowed to America as early as 1849 because of prior exposure to capitalism.

Although adventurous and enterprising as a result of a long seafaring tradition, these men—who often left families behind—planned eventually to return to their ancestral villages. During the first decade of immigration to the United States, as many as a third did so. This phenomenon, known as return migration, also characterized turn-of-the-century European immigration to the New World.[9] Although many Chinese Americans began their stay in the United States as sojourners, or "birds of passage," involved in temporary migration, a large number—for legal, financial, or other reasons—eventually remained in America to live, work, and settle. Yet societal acceptance eluded them. Reinforced by this rejection, sojourning became a part of the Chinese immigrant mentality, no matter how much it departed from that reality. As sojourners become settlers, the Chinese immigrant worldview became oriented more toward America than toward China.

THE NATURE OF IMMIGRATION

In the nineteenth century most Chinese immigrants came to the United States as free laborers under the credit-ticket system. Only a few arrived as contract laborers, with most of those in Hawai'i, also known to Cantonese Chinese as *Tan Heung Shan* (Mandarin is *Tanxiangshan*, or "Sandalwood Fragrance Hill") after the fabled sandalwood trade between Hawai'i and China. But it was commercial sugar production that drew Chinese laborers to Hawai'i. After pioneer Wong Tze Chun's failed attempt in 1802, other Chinese sugar masters in the 1830s—relying on coethnics—had more success in the industry. One such entrepreneur was the legendary Chun Fong, who became the largest shareholder of one plantation that hired more than 300 workers toiling on about 1,200 acres in sugar. Reportedly, he received more than half a million dollars for his share of the company when he returned to China in 1890. On Chun Fong's plantation, as was the case elsewhere on these islands, Chinese gradually replaced native Hawaiian workers in the ubiquitous sugarcane fields.[10]

Far more Chinese were recruited by white planters than by Chinese planters. White planters, who had ample capital and technological superiority, believed Chinese laborers could meet their demand for a "docile," cheap workforce in ways Native Hawaiians and African Americans could not. Chinese workers' noncitizen status also meant the planter class could retain political dominance and still secure an abundant supply of labor. Euro-American planters recruited workers, mostly from Amoy, Fukien province, using emigration brokers who offered Chinese free passage to the islands. Chinese laborers signed labor agreements to work for a planter for five years and in return received wages, shelter, food, and medical care. Yet life for these Chinese laborers, of whom an estimated 50,000 arrived between 1852 and 1900, was arduous: working long hours, they returned to crowded and unsanitary quarters and ate poor-quality, monotonous food. Under the Masters and Servants Act of 1850, those who reneged on their contracts would have their servitude lengthened or be sentenced to hard labor. They also soon found themselves pitted against other ethnic groups, such as Japanese field hands and Native Hawaiian and Portuguese foremen and semiskilled workers, in an attempt by planters to set up a mechanism of control by developing an ethnically diverse but divided workforce.[11]

Most of the larger number of travelers to Gold Mountain relied on the credit-ticket system, which also characterized emigration to Southeast Asia,

Australia, and Canada. In this system a broker loaned money to an emigrant to pay for the voyage, and the emigrant paid off the loan plus interest out of earnings in the new country. Many emigrants also borrowed from kinsfolk for the trans-Pacific journey.

Almost all of the early wave of Chinese immigrants were men, even though an estimated half were married and many had established families prior to immigration. The situation in Hawai'i differed somewhat from that on the mainland; in Hawai'i, missionaries and planters encouraged the immigration of women to maintain social control and to prevent "loose morals" among the predominately male populace. By 1900, of the 25,767 Chinese in Hawai'i, 13.5 percent (3,471) were females; on the mainland, only 5 percent of the 89,863 Chinese were females.

WOMEN AND GENDER DISPARITY

The glaring absence of women on the U.S. mainland was unique and departed from the immigration pattern of other ethnic groups. The gender ratio for the entire Chinese population in the United States in 1860 stood at 1:186, or 1,784 females compared with 33,149 males. Between 1860 and 1900 the skewed ratio did not improve; women never exceeded 7 percent of the total Chinese population during the entire period. Until 1940 the ratio remained highly unbalanced: for every four men, there was only one woman.[12]

Various factors accounted for the disparity in gender and the resulting disjointed households. Patriarchal cultural values, rooted in the hierarchically oriented Confucian ideology, dictated that women be subordinated to men and confined to the domestic realm. Single women did not travel to distant places by themselves, and married women remained at home. The "Thrice Obeying" dictates of Confucianism deemed that women should obey their fathers at home, their husbands after marriage, and their eldest sons when widowed. This subordinate role required that women follow the "Four Attributes": propriety in behavior, speech, demeanor, and work.

Females led a precarious life from early childhood. The Chinese proverb "a boy is born facing in; a girl is born facing out" encapsulated the general consensus on the low status of Chinese women. Infanticide, abandonment, and sale into indentured servitude tended to occur with daughters rather than with sons. Unlike sons, daughters were typically excluded from educational opportunities.

Daughters were also considered unworthy of much social investment, since after years of careful nurturing most married and joined other households. Families, however, did see the betrothal of a daughter as an opportunity to display status and dignity by offering ostentatious dowries to the bridegroom's family. Sons were far more prized because they continued the family lineage, performed ancestral worship, and labored for the family's honor and livelihood. Sons were so important that families without male heirs, especially those in southeastern provinces, sometimes resorted to matrilocal or uxorilocal marriage.

The ultimate symbol of the subordination of women was foot binding, which symbolized social rank (only women of nobility, gentry, and mercantile background typically had their feet bound), proper upbringing, and erotic appeal but also restricted women's mobility and reinforced the Confucian ideals of female virtue and isolation. In 1855 a Chinese merchant explained that few men brought their wives to America because they had "compressed feet" and were "unused to winds and waves."[13]

Peasant women, expected to labor inside and outside the home, generally did not bind their feet. Work, however, did not result in greater independence for these women. Some women who engaged in the sericulture industry—in which raw silk was produced by raising silkworms—in the Pearl River Delta did enjoy economic freedom and openly resisted marriage. They joined sisterhoods, rejected foot binding, and practiced celibacy. Hakka women in Guangdong were also well-known for rejecting foot binding and displaying self-confidence. These women aside, most performed labor that sustained family life but found themselves on the periphery of power.

When their husbands went abroad to *Mei Kuo*, or the United States, wives were expected to stay at home and take care of the children, the in-laws, and the home. Some of these *gamsaanpo* (*jinshan po* in Mandarin), or "Gold Mountain wives," did more than that, however. They toiled in the fields and factories, joined rebel groups, banded together as sisters in the marriage-resistance movement, and at the turn of the century added their voices to the rising feminist consciousness in China. Because some women were abandoned by their Gold Mountain husbands, they became breadwinners for their families. For over a decade Fong Shue-ying heard nothing from her gambling-prone husband in the United States. Driven to desperation and with two sons to feed, she made a living carrying people on her back from village to village.[14] This emerging sense of self-identity was likely responsible for driving a small trickle of women to go to America to flee gender oppression and gain a measure of independence. Much more of the female migration was orchestrated by men for profit, especially for the lucrative prostitution trade.[15]

Most Chinese wives and daughters, however, were left behind because the upkeep of families abroad was too costly. Moreover, the men believed they would be separated from loved ones only temporarily. In a culture in which the family served as the core of the social order, keeping wives at home guaranteed that husbands would not forget their kinsfolk in China, would send remittances, and eventually would return to China and continue to support their elderly parents.[16]

Discouraged by the transitory, frontierlike, and inhospitable conditions in the United States, women deemed it wise to remain in China. Early male immigrants worked in mines, on railroads, and in the fields—workplaces incompatible with the needs of wives and children. During most of the second half of the nineteenth century—the height of Chinese immigration to the mainland United States before the gates were closed for a long time—capitalists and policy makers discouraged the arrival of women. Chinese men were considered a temporary labor force and thus were disposable. But the immigration of Chinese women and children would, the white-dominated society feared, lead to family formation and a possible mongrelization of the superior Anglo-Saxon race.

Class- and gender-based, racist immigration laws—designed to meet the need for cheap, exploitable labor without threatening U.S. racial homogeneity—blocked Chinese women's entry into the United States. Given the less than civil treatment and lack of legal protection Chinese immigrants had to endure upon arrival, Chinese women had little inclination to leave a familiar environment for barbarian lands. In an 1852 letter to the California state government, Chinese community leaders bitterly explained that "if the privileges of your laws are open . . . a better class will come . . . [and bring] their families with them."[17]

By comparison, an atmosphere of official openness toward immigration coupled with limited social hostility enabled pioneer Chinese communities in Penang, Singapore, and Hawai'i to enjoy a rate of nuclear-family growth that belied the joint-family ideal and sojourner mentality. In the absence of strictures against miscegenation, conjugal unions with native women enabled early family formation, but as time passed and more Chinese women arrived, more marriages involved them. Conversely, the absence of such conditions in the United States thwarted the transition from sojourners to families. In sum, the persistence of the sojourner phenomenon in America was at least as much the outcome of restrictive policies and the treatment immigrants received in the host country as it was of cultural dictates.[18]

On the sojourner phenomenon (as well as the absence of Chinese women) in the United States, Adam McKeown has argued that this was an economic strategy designed to ensure rapid and predictable returns on the investments made in immigrating to and residing in the host society. Chinese male immigrants relied on intertwined institutionalized migration networks—migrant businesses and native place or district associations—and kinship ties for dispersal to various parts of the globe to allow for the maintenance of patrilineal families back in China. Chinese migration to the United States was a circulatory process for the upward mobility of those left behind. If migration is the outcome of the conscientious decision to keep families intact, the role of exclusion laws in discouraging female immigration and family reunification would seem to only reinforce the phenomenon of split households, as well as the need to resort to selective chain migration.[19]

THE ENDLESS JOURNEY TO AMERICA

The trans-Pacific journey was cumbersome for the Chinese emigrants. In theory, even prior to the Qing dynasty, Chinese who contemplated leaving the country faced punitive imperial edicts if they returned. Fear of political unrest fomented from without, and official support for filial obligations to ancestral remains, dictated such mandates. In reality, implicit recognition of the economic value of the seafaring trade and other economic ventures meant antiemigration statutes went largely unenforced as early as the mid-eighteenth century and in the next century became meaningless as external and internal threats distracted the officialdom. In 1893 the Qing government officially lifted the ban against those wishing to return.[20]

U.S. consulate officials in Hong Kong (the port of departure for many Chinese emigrants), who were charged with enforcing anticoolie laws, placed certain legal barriers on immigration even when the ban had been lifted. Following the passage of the 1862 Act to Prohibit Coolie Trade, the American consul or his agent examined each prospective emigrant to prevent involuntary travel. From 1862 to 1871, however, the certification process, tainted by ineptness, became perfunctory.

The same cannot be said about the 1875 Page Act, designed to check the flow of Chinese prostitutes to America who in the minds of the Euro-American society could debase white manhood, health, morality, and family life. Chinese prostitution in the United States, a function of gender-based immigration laws, flourished until the early twentieth century. Chinese men, bereft of family life and denied conjugal ties, sought prostitutes, or *baak haak chai* (a derogatory Cantonese phrase for "100 men's wife")—as they did opium smoking and gambling—for entertainment. White Americans, exhibiting racial bias rooted in gender roles, considered Chinese laborers' patronizing prostitutes as simply another sign of the corrupt nature of Chinese manhood. Chinese men, Americans reasoned, were weak and unable to control the sexuality of either their women or themselves.[21]

Applied stringently, the Page Act also excluded wives and single women with legitimate claims. Immigration officials believed prostitutes typically posed as wives, sisters, or daughters of Chinese already in America. Officials consequently assumed that all Chinese women seeking entry into the United States were potential prostitutes. The Page Act, by casting doubts on the morality of Chinese women and, by extension, on that of the men as well, was a significant step toward the passage of exclusion legislation.

Because U.S. officials in Hong Kong applied the law unevenly, Chinese men (at least until the era of exclusion laws)—but not women—could proceed with their departure for America. Following the signing of the Burlingame Treaty (1868) between China and the United States, the Chinese secured the right to open, voluntary immigration to the United States. The century-old prohibitory emigration law of the Qing government was repealed. The treaty further offered Chinese residents equal protection of all legal rights enjoyed by other foreigners living in the United States, and in the early 1870s U.S. federal courts decided that the treaty also provided for the right to work and reside in America. Anti-Chinese sentiments along the Pacific Coast and their consequences, however, including the 1882 race-specific Chinese Exclusion Act, soon made a mockery of the spirit of the treaty.[22]

From approximately 1849 to 1867, *gam saan haak* sailed to that distant land on voyages that took 55 to 100 days or more. The advent of the Pacific Mail Steamship Company's famed China line in 1867 ushered in the age of steamships, which plied the trans-Pacific route until well after the turn of the century. Unlike sailing ships, which held departure until fully booked, steamers offered a schedule and a speedy voyage. The time needed to reach San Francisco shortened from months to weeks. Steamships also could hold more passengers. All that, coupled with a more than threefold drop in the fare, encouraged immigration.

Chinese passengers on the way to America, except those of privileged background, almost always traveled in the cheaper steerage section. Passengers ate poor-quality, bland food, scrounged for limited water, slept in rickety berths consisting of canvas stretched over wooden frames, and suffered from inadequate ventilation. Sometimes basic bodily functions proved impossible because of overcrowding. During storms, immigrants curled up in berths; food, utensils, and people bounced in all directions.

As their ship cut across the wide waters of the high seas, the immigrants—unsure of the future and anguished over the separation from loved ones—struggled to hold onto the dream of finding a new start, of shaping unknown beginnings. That guarded anticipation mixed with melancholy was reflected in an early-twentieth-century Cantonese folk song: "Drifting on a voyage of thousands of miles / I reached the Flowery Flag Nation to take my chances / sorrow is to be so far away from home."[23]

ARRIVING IN AMERICA: IMMIGRATION CLEARANCE

When immigrants first set eyes on their land of destiny, they were awash in anticipation. Huie Kin, a male immigrant who arrived in 1868, recalled that the "feeling that welled up in us was indescribable, to be actually at . . . the land of our dreams."[24] With the exception of those who took advantage of lackadaisical border policing and slipped into the United States by way of Mexico or Canada, immigration clearance for most arrivals became a nightmarish hurdle.

A gloomy, poorly lit, two-story shed—known to the Chinese as *Muk uk* (Mandarin is *Mu wu*), or "Wooden Barracks"—at the Pacific Mail Steamship Company wharf greeted early arrivals in San Francisco, the point of disembarkation for most nineteenth-century Chinese emigrants. Chinese arrivals were held at this overcrowded, unsanitary, and unsafe facility until immigration officials cleared them. In 1910, in part in reaction to Chinese complaints and in part to isolate those with supposed communicable diseases, the government erected a two-story wooden building to serve as the new immigration station on Angel Island in San Francisco Bay. A trickle of arrivals entered the West Coast through Seattle's immigration station. Some Chinese immigrants disembarked at Vancouver, British Columbia, and then took the long journey on the Canadian-Pacific Railroad to one of four border crossings: Sumas, Washington; Portal, North Dakota; Richford, Vermont, or Malone, New York. Those who arrived by sea in New York were processed at Castle Garden, the immigration depot that operated until 1890 when Ellis Island became the new processing center.[25]

Immigration officials then subjected the Chinese to an extensive examination. The interrogation was protracted because officials believed nearly all Chinese lied to gain entry into the United States. Perhaps many Chinese were guilty of illegal immigration, but if so, it was only because Chinese exclusion laws forced immigration underground. By the turn of the century, as racial hostility intensified and loopholes in the laws were closed, the Chinese relied on duplicity to enter the United States to either reunite families or establish a livelihood and continue financial support of loved ones left behind in impoverished China. Such fraudulent entries, often relying on the assistance of kinship networks, persisted until the exclusion laws were repealed in 1943.

Typically, a Chinese merchant or someone who posed as one would claim American birth and thus citizenship, as guaranteed by the Fourteenth Amendment. He then would claim the birth of a new son (rarely a daughter) upon his return from each visit to China. A potential immigrant could then, after buying the "slot," pose as the merchant's son or daughter and claim entry into the United States. Born Mar Ying Wing in Taishan, Guangdong, in 1922, Wong Hung Yin took the latter name when he became the "paper son" of a distant uncle, Wong Wing Lock, who was actually Mar Moy Jing—a paper son himself. Wong Wing Lock, who had entered the United States illegally in 1906 through El Paso, Texas, later claimed to have that name as well as native-born status. In doing so, he could claim the subsequent birth of three sons. Although the first two were indeed sons born in China, the third was a fabrication so a slot could be created for his nephew Mar Ying Wing. Other Chinese, aware that merchants were exempted from exclusion laws, would buy business shares to claim they were merchants or would bribe merchants to list them as partners. The author Lisa See's great-grandfather, Fong See, immigrated in 1871. He established a partnership of eight men that included his nine-year-old brother and his father, who had returned to China. On record, each person had contributed $500 to the business, but the amounts were fictitious. Except for Fong See, the sole proprietor, the others were merely partners on paper to establish their merchant status. After the devastating 1906 San Francisco earthquake destroyed most municipal records, thus eliminating the way to verify data supplied by new arrivals, such claims quickly shot up. In fact, Mar Moy Jing had taken advantage of such a fortuitous change: relying on the affidavits of two witnesses, he took on a new identity.[26]

The purchase of a false identity did not guarantee entry to the United States. During the exclusion years, the testimonies of newcomers and their corroborating witnesses were rigorously scrutinized. Chinese arrivals had to answer detailed questions about their background and relationships to relatives residing in the United States. Officials would cross-check their answers with those provided by witnesses and relatives who had immigrated earlier. To prepare for this ordeal, Chinese emigrants studied purchased "crib sheets" containing information about their "families." In his memoirs, Tung Pok Chin explained that he had purchased his "paper" for $2,000 and eschewed his status as a married man with two children in favor of the identity of a single man so he had fewer names and dates to memorize. In spite of his uncomplicated "life," the interrogation in Boston lasted three days.[27]

Those who failed the initial interrogation could appeal or be reexamined, but the process was always a psychological burden for immigrants. Oak Yip Gee recalled that during her two-week detention on Angel Island she heard of stories of arrivals authorities turned away on the grounds of falsified testimony, and soon she "felt very worried because I didn't know what would happen to me."[28] Throughout this ordeal Chinese relied on their transnational networks of family, clan, and community across the United States and in China to provide financial backing, immigration advice, crucial witness testimony, and legal counsel. About 5 to 10 percent of Chinese who arrived on Angel Island were eventually forced to return to China.[29]

FAMILY LIFE

Chinese men who were able to land on American soil often experienced considerable difficulty establishing a family life given the exclusion laws that stymied family immigration to the United States. Antimiscegenation laws, the shortage of coethnic women, and racial hostility also discouraged the formation of families. After the U.S. Civil War, western states including Oregon and California broadened their antimiscegenation laws to include new racial categories, including Asians. The laws reflected prevailing gender hierarchies, whereupon white women's sexuality was constantly policed but white men were allowed some sexual license. The laws consequently were applied most stringently to Asians, whose men were thought likely to marry white women. Conversely, the laws were rarely enforced against Native Americans and Hispanics, whose women—rather than men—were known to have crossed the color line.[30] The sex imbalance for Chinese Americans continued until the post–World War II era, when legislation for family reunification was passed. The hostile reception by the host society also served as a check on establishing a family in the United States.

But Chinese men were not dissuaded from trying to head households. They looked farther away for conjugal partners. A number of Chinese men pursued trans-Pacific marriages; Wong Yow saved for fourteen years before returning to China at age thirty-five to take a bride in a marriage arranged by his extended family. He spent all of his savings on the wedding but returned to the United States alone. For the next thirty-eight years until his family could immigrate, he juggled his roles as husband and father through letters, remittances, and intermittent visits.[31]

Chinese men sometimes brought their spouses to the United States. The presence of fishing families in the Monterey Bay region as early as the 1850s countermands the stereotype of the womanless Chinese laborer and also suggests that the women either came with the husbands during the latter's initial migration or arrived soon after. In Nevada County, California, in the 1880s, Chinese laborers who were gainfully employed—not just merchants—had wives or women living with them. Chinese American families toiled in the Sacramento–San Joaquin Delta at the turn of the twentieth century. By then, more American-born women were available as potential spouses.

Chinese men who lived in small communities away from the intensely anti-Chinese West Coast sometimes entered into marriages with other peoples of color—a phenomenon the antimiscegenation laws ignored, since historically such laws were designed to police unions between white women and men of color. Chinese crossed the border of racialized desire with African Americans and Creole and American Indians in the South, Native Americans in the Pacific Northwest, Mexicans in the Southwest, Irish in New York City, and Hawaiians in Hawai'i. Chinese men involved in interracial marriages were typically small-time entrepreneurs and laborers, suggesting that those who could afford to do so preferred to have Chinese transnational families or to raise their children in America. In contrast, Chinese women rarely entered into interracial unions because of their small number as spouses for Chinese men, their social isolation from the dominant society, and the negative Chinese attitude toward such liaisons.

In most families Chinese wives tended to be much younger than their coethnic husbands. In Los Angeles the age difference was fifteen years in

1880; thirty years later it had dropped only slightly to fourteen years.[32] The wide age disparity between husbands and wives suggests either that Chinese men, most of whom were laborers struggling to survive, had to toil for a long time to save for matrimony or that some wives were concubines or second wives. The enforcement of exclusion laws meant that many wives were merchant-class female immigrants from China. Other women were American born or former prostitutes; they were often adolescents because of the general shortage of Chinese women and the antimiscegenation sentiments that considerably narrowed the pool of brides.[33]

The typical Chinese family was a patriarchal, economic unit and in that narrow sense was similar to the structure in China. The husband took on paid labor outside the home, and the wife kept busy at home with housework and child care. Working-class immigrant women also often did paid piecework for subcontractors. The wife, in deference to the husband's link to the outside world, remained in a subordinate role. Concerns about racial and sexual assaults during an era of anti-Asian sentiments forced Chinese wives to remain secluded at home, thus reinforcing their dependency on male marital partners.

But the family structure was not an exact replica of that in China. Unlike the case in China but similar to the situation in Southeast Asia, second wives in the United States were often as important as first wives (since the latter often remained in China), and the absence of large kinship units meant there was little familial mediation of domestic disputes. Further, the sporadic practice of polygyny took a different form than it did in China. Unlike the traditional practice of multiple wives living in the same household, in America the first wives typically resided in China. Other men entered into common-law marriages without divorcing their first wives.

Certain unique circumstances Chinese conjugal partners confronted in the United States also altered gender relationships and made them more equitable. In America, wives were freed from the demands of in-laws and from the power of mothers-in-law who in China asserted control over the household. They could thus assume the role of female head of the family. Additionally, given the shortage of coethnic women, Chinese men prized their wives as marital and sexual partners. Men in households without women had to learn domestic skills (and even use them to eke out a livelihood, as in doing laundry), which reinforced that appreciation. The irrefutable fact that women's labor in the form of sewing, doing laundry, or taking in boarders earned additional income also gave them more leverage in their relationships with spouses. In their roles as joint heads of households and coproviders, they also participated in domestic decision making. Compared with their status in China, Chinese women enjoyed a slightly more elevated position in America, although outwardly they paid homage to the ideal of male authority at home.

Nineteenth-century Chinese immigrant families were also different from those in China because of their material culture. Men, whose world was oriented toward the public sphere, wore American clothes during working hours, although they probably reverted to traditional garments at home. As time passed, both women and men—and their children even more—adopted Western-style clothing for leisure and work. In an archaeological study of Ventura's Chinatown in southern California, women more than men seemed to conserve culture in their community as evidenced in the abundance of traditional cooking utensils, table ceramics, imported food containers, and food remains.[34]

Unlike the large extended families in China, nuclear families prevailed in America. In Los Angeles the average number of children in a Chinese family hovered between 1.4 in 1880 and 2.7 in 1910. Poverty, lack of medical services, and the fact that men married late contributed to the small family size. Large families were not uncommon, however; members of the merchant class probably raised more children than those in the laboring classes. In 1880, of the sixteen Chinese families with children in Los Angeles, fourteen were members of the merchant class. Thirty years later 90 percent of Chinese children had parents who ran small businesses.[35]

Chinese American children were often pressed into working in their families' economic ventures. Daughters and sons picked fruits, dried seafood, cleaned houses, helped raise siblings, and sometimes were hired out as domestics. They worked in vineyards, fields, orchards, canneries, and homes. Their efforts and role in the Asian rural economy became even more significant after passage of the Alien Land Act of 1913 in California, a law other states also enacted. The act barred Asian immigrants from owning land or leasing it for longer than three years. Deprived of the economy of scale and of the ability to build capital, Asian farmers resorted to labor-intensive farming that demanded the effort of all family members. Rural second-generation Chinese girls and boys also played the important role of landholders. As native-born American citizens, they could own the land their parents desired. By the early twentieth century, children who lived in cities and towns also contributed to the family economy; they waited tables in the chop suey restaurants, folded clothes in laundries, sewed garments in sweatshops or at home, and sold curio items in gift shops. Fang H. Der, who arrived in Baltimore in 1931, recalled that at age seventeen he was put to work in his father's restaurant. Each day after school he mopped the floors, washed dishes, waited on tables, and helped cook.[36]

The offspring of mixed marriages were often uniquely set apart from Chinese children. First, they typically adopted their mother's culture. Hi Wo of Benson, Arizona, married Emeteria Morena in 1900 and raised four daughters and a son—Isabel, Soledad, Victoria, Felicia, and José. The children had Spanish names, spoke little Chinese, and ignored their father's customs and cultural celebrations. The children spoke Spanish and were Catholic.[37]

But the lives of biracial children were complicated by the black-and-white binary. Arlee Wong, the daughter of Chinese-black parents who raised her in Greenville, Mississippi, complained that she and her siblings—caught between black and white worlds—grew up rather lonely. Both white and black children ignored them. Like other children of mixed heritage, she had to attend the dilapidated segregated school for blacks. Yet her light skin and straight hair sometimes allowed her to pass for white. Her brothers, with features that marked them as Asian, found acceptance elusive. Other black Chinese in the South merged into black communities, and a few exploited the "Mexican" or "Indian" categories so they could be considered white in certain situations and black in others. Those who moved across the color line with any ease typically denied their Chinese or mixed heritage.[38] But some keenly felt the emotional burden of living in two worlds; the biracial writer Edith Eaton, or Sui Sin Far, bemoaned the fact that she could never describe the identity crisis she suffered to her parents because "they would never understand. How could they? He is English, she is Chinese. I am different to both of them—a stranger, though their own child."[39]

NATIVISM IN THE LATE NINETEENTH CENTURY

Anti-immigrant sentiments in the second half of the nineteenth century, although not without precedent, were particularly virulent. Before that period, faith in the process of assimilation—which supposedly would transform untutored foreigners into upright, patriotic citizens—predisposed most Americans to accept new immigrants. In this classic melting-pot thesis, U.S. society would take on a cosmopolitan, unique character as the diverse elements gradually fused and lost their indigenous roots.

Before rapid industrialization and a consolidating national market economy arrived in the late nineteenth century, ethnic groups lived apart from one another, and the majority Anglo-Americans remained dominant. The process of assimilation played out rather slowly with little interethnic antagonism. Occasionally, nativist sentiment did break out, most notably during the 1840s when the anti-immigrant Know-Nothing Party targeted Germans and Irish Catholics for religious and ethnic persecution.[40]

General consciousness of racial and ethnic differences intensified in the late nineteenth century as spatial and socioeconomic boundaries between communities blurred under the influence of industrialization and economic development. The ability of the American national identity—one rooted in abstract democratic ideals—to hold the republic together was called into question. An aggressive movement to forge a homogeneous national identity rooted in Anglo-Saxon culture soon emerged, and certain ethnic groups—the Chinese included—were deemed unassimilable.

WORKING LIVES

At the height of the anti-Asian movement in the late nineteenth century, the Chinese never constituted more than 0.2 percent of the total U.S. population, but they still encountered rabid hostility. The white-dominated society, however, initially welcomed the Chinese as workers and investors in a booming economy.[41] The seemingly imperceptible presence of the Chinese—one shaped by the fact that early arrivals were scattered—rendered them innocuous. But nativism soon reared its ugly head.

Even before the start of the gold rush in California in 1848, Chinese were laboring in Hawai'i. Chinese sugar plantation workers sometimes headed for rice farms owned by friends and relatives when they had completed their contracts on the plantations. Others cultivated the equally lucrative taro and pineapple or entered the Chinese grocery business, often serving as agents and financiers of rice planters.[42]

Within just a few years of the discovery of gold, 24,000 Chinese—an estimated two-thirds of the Chinese in America—were laboring in the mines, often working claims whites had abandoned for richer fields. Yet they did well. During the years 1855 to 1870, more than 10 percent of gold and silver exports—valued at more than $72 million—from San Francisco went to China. Their knowledge of mining precious metal, perhaps acquired from countrymen who had toiled in mines in Southeast Asia and Australasia, gave the Chinese the edge. Forced to depend on coethnics in a hostile America, Chinese pooled their resources to try to strike gold. Family, village, and district ties transplanted to the United States nurtured the sense of cooperation, allowing the Chinese to use not only their mining skills but also their knowledge of the technology of aquatic management involving pumps, dams, and flumes. Their reliance on large-scale mining operations belied the myth that all Chinese simply used portable pans and rockers. A fairly balanced diet of protein- and vitamin-rich foods gave them the physical endurance to labor in the arduous conditions. Buoyed by these advantages, Chinese enjoyed a monopoly in placer mining (collecting surface gold from streambeds), but only for awhile.[43]

Working in small, all-male groups, Chinese miners adopted domestic habits that both intrigued and invited ridicule from whites, who associated cooking, cleaning, and laundry work with white women. Chinese divisions of labor unsettled white notions of womanliness and manliness. Considered an economic and a moral threat, Chinese miners, cooks, and laundry workers in white-dominated mining districts soon came under heavy fire. In 1852 the California state legislature passed the Foreign Miner's License Tax, ostensibly to be imposed on all miners who did not want to become citizens. Lawmakers knew the Chinese could not gain citizenship, since the 1790 Nationality Act reserved that privilege for white persons. The tax therefore fell heavily on Chinese miners, which, coupled with the decline of placer mining in California, forced them to venture farther inland. The miners were also encouraged to move farther east by stories of new gold and, later, silver strikes in places as far away as Tombstone, Arizona, and Boise Basin, Idaho. By the 1870s the Chinese had spread to every placer area and represented about 25 percent of all miners. Yet they never escaped the hatred that greeted them in California. For example, in 1863 Washington Territory denied Chinese the right to testify against whites, and in 1864 the territory levied a Chinese Police Tax on every Chinese resident.[44]

During the mid-1860s, as gold became more scarce and anti-Asian sentiments flared, Chinese miners began abandoning the diggings. Some ventured into fishing, and Chinese fishing activities eventually stretched from the Oregon boundary to Baja California and along the Sacramento River Delta. By the early 1870s a number of Chinese fishermen concentrated on catching and processing shrimp in the San Francisco Bay. Even before the end of the gold rush, Chinese were fishing for squid around Monterey while others harvested abalone in the waters off the southern California coast. Chinese fishermen, taking advantage of their experience drying fish in China, turned much of their catch into invaluable commodities. Yet as in the goldfields, racial animosity threatened their livelihoods; in 1860 California began collecting a four-dollar license fee from them. Then in the 1870s Italian and Portuguese fishermen along Monterey County's coast attempted to drive them out, a process aided by several fishing regulations designed to harass Chinese. Asian fishermen adapted; they resorted to night fishing, and a few became seaweed gatherers on the central coast of California.[45]

A sizable number of Chinese—about 12,000—built most of the Central Pacific Railroad, the western half of the ambitious transcontinental railroad, which challenged the workers' physical endurance and creativity. Following the completion of this project in 1869, some released Chinese work gangs helped build other lines: the Northern Pacific Railroad from Kalama, Washington, north to Tacoma; the Southern Pacific Railroad's north-south line along the California coast that eventually extended to El Paso, Texas; and the California Southern Railroad that connected with the main Santa Fe line. After the work was completed, some of the former railroad builders remained where the lines ended; for example, Texas's Chinese population jumped from 136 in 1880 to 710 in 1890, in part because of the influx of rail hands who had laid the Southern Pacific's tracks.[46]

Other unemployed railroad workers scattered into the hinterlands in search of agricultural work. As labor gangs they constructed irrigation channels and levees and reclaimed swamplands in California's Sacramento–San Joaquin River Delta area. The largest reclamation effort involved at least 3,000 laborers to reclaim as many as 40,000 acres.[47]

By the late 1860s and early 1870s, shrinking opportunities in mining and railroad construction pushed some Chinese into truck gardening and farming. This venture was nothing new; since the heyday of mining, Chinese had grown vegetables in mining camps and as itinerant peddlers had sold them to Chinese miners and non-Chinese customers. Beginning in the late 1860s Chinese leased land from whites in the delta to grow grain, hay, potatoes, onions, beans, and vegetables—sometimes hiring Mexicans to work for them. Chinese tenants and sharecroppers who aspired to move ahead, however, encountered the barrier imposed by California's Alien Land Act in 1913—a restriction that remained until the law was declared unconstitutional in 1952. A 1920 law amending the 1913 act was even harsher; under it, "aliens ineligible to citizenship"—which meant in effect Asian immigrants—were disallowed from leasing land or from purchasing it through corporations or in the names of their American-born children.

Still, a few Chinese agriculturists did make a name for themselves. Chin Lung, the Chinese "Potato King," farmed more than 1,000 acres in the delta and earned a reputation as a likable businessman in tune with the latest technology. Another adaptable agriculturist was the legendary Lue Gim Gong, who developed award-winning varieties of hardy oranges and grapefruits that could endure frosts. Lue, however, died almost penniless, the victim of unscrupulous white distributors.[48]

Most of the Chinese involved in agriculture were laborers who toiled in orchards, vineyards, and fields of cash crops. In Monterey Bay, for example, Chinese laborers made up for the shortfall of Native and white American hands and cultivated tobacco, hop, mustard weeds, and sugar beets. In Riverside, California, Chinese also replaced Native American workers and worked alternately in citrus and grape crops. With little but a Chinese hat, bedding, a small suitcase, and maybe a few tools, they earned enough to keep fanciful dreams alive. But Chinese migrant laborers were not always welcomed; Bing Fai Chow, a farm laborer, never strayed far from Locke, California, and its orchards because whites in rural communities threw stones at him. White farmers sometimes refused to hire Chinese help.[49]

Some of the Chinese involved in agriculture and other extractive industries were more fortunate; they were labor contractors who found a niche in the rigid racial division of labor in which Euro-Americans owned the capital and Chinese supplied the labor. One well-known contractor was Chin Gee Hee. Brought to America in 1862 by a benevolent kinsman, Chen quickly became a partner in a labor recruiting firm, the Wah Chong Company, based in Seattle. Chen's main role was to recruit Chinese men to fill the labor contracts he acquired from lumber camps, coal mines, farms, canneries, railroads, and steamship companies. From this brokerage role, Chen expanded into the import-export trade, eventually becoming a prosperous businessman in the Puget Sound region.[50]

More significant for the long-term distribution of the populace was the dispersal of Chinese laborers to the rest of the American West and eventually to all parts of the United States. In 1870 Chinese workers began to show up in the salmon canneries on coastal bays and along streams from central California to western Alaska. Others arrived in the Pacific Northwest after being recruited to help build the Northern Pacific line, to run lumber mills, or to harvest hop in the fields of the Puyallup Valley, Washington. Some Chinese, after their initial engagement, moved to Seattle, where they worked in small businesses—laundries, restaurants, and dry goods stores—owned by Chinese merchants.[51]

Following two commercial conventions in Memphis and New Orleans in May 1869, called to discuss the prospect of recruiting Chinese labor, in the early 1870s planters and businessmen directed the Chinese Christian missionary and labor contractor Tye Kim Orr to procure Chinese workers. With some coming from Cuba and others from the upper South, California, and all the way from China, Chinese field hands and railroad builders soon appeared in Louisiana, Mississippi, Texas, and Florida—mainly to help fill the gap left by former black slaves. In Florida, Chinese work gangs also worked in drainage operations, construction sites, and turpentine camps.[52]

The recruitment of Chinese labor grew out of planters' optimism about the future of the sugarcane industry but also out of a vision of slavery's past. With Cuban competitors mired in an economic upheaval and the "redemption" of Louisiana from Republican rule on the horizon, the post-Reconstruction future could be secured by falling back on the past. White planters and contractors aspired to use Chinese for their labor but also to help control recently enfranchised blacks through their model behavior and "docility." Given whites' fear of "Nigger rule" in southern states—sentiments that never resembled the political reality—and the absence of Jim Crowism (institutionalized segregation) until the 1880s, this attempt to play one ethnic group off the other to maintain white control was not unexpected. The argument, also made by Tye, that Chinese "coolies" were naturally submissive and industrious resonated for planters eager to cut costs and stay competitive.[53] Conversely, when Jim Crow laws became established at the turn of the twentieth century and the existence of another race promised to complicate the enforcement of segregation, Florida dissuaded Chinese from migrating to the state. Plantation owners in other southern states simply fired their Chinese laborers. Chinese who left the fields either gravitated to urban centers like New Orleans or found work elsewhere, such as in Arkansas, Louisiana, and

Georgia. In Mississippi, Louisiana, and Texas, those who remained behind often became peddlers or storekeepers.

Chinese laborers also found their way to the Northeast, specifically Massachusetts, New Jersey, Pennsylvania, and New York. In North Adams, Massachusetts, in 1870, a ladies' boot and shoe factory owner used 75 Chinese contract laborers to break the hold of the Knights of St. Crispin (the shoemakers' union) on the workplace. Emulating the North Adams example, the managers of a cutlery-making factory hired 300 Chinese from Louisiana and California, who arrived in 1872 and 1873, to work in their factory in Beaver Falls, Pennsylvania. The Chinese workers were used to drive down the wage scale white workers demanded and eventually to displace them. In 1873, 68 Chinese men arrived in Belleville, New Jersey, to wash and iron clothes in a hot, humid steam laundry after the employer failed to secure enough Irish and German female workers. By the early 1870s an estimated 500 Chinese lived in New York City. Some, independent of any internal migration from California, apparently arrived through their involvement in long-running American maritime trade or coastal shipping routes. They were engaged in a variety of endeavors: cigar making and peddling, running boardinghouses and laundries, maritime shipping, and retail. Boston's small Chinese populace in 1900—a little under 900—showed the same concentration of service-oriented and self-employed occupations. As a result of this general dispersal, by 1920 only a little over 60 percent of the total Chinese populace remained in the West.[54]

By the turn of the century the Chinese population was also becoming urbanized, as racial hostility forced the Chinese to retreat to Chinatowns—physically segregated neighborhoods within white-dominated cities and towns. In the early 1870s many unemployed Chinese, newly released from railroad work and unable to find much work in the exhausted minefields, flocked to San Francisco—by then a burgeoning city of opportunity. San Francisco's Chinese population zoomed from 2,719 in 1860 to 12,022 ten years later. The pattern was repeated elsewhere. Los Angeles's Chinatown, for example, trebled in size from 605 in 1880 to 1,817 in 1890, largely because of growing Sinophobia and concomitant gloomy economic prospects elsewhere in nonurban areas. Small Chinatowns such as Watsonville, Salinas City, and Santa Cruz—all in the Monterey Bay area—developed to meet the needs of the semimigrant Chinese labor force. Such ethnic enclaves typically featured a cluster of buildings along one street or within one block that housed establishments such as boardinghouses, dry goods stores, laundries, gambling halls, and maybe a small temple. Communities on the West Coast grew from decade to decade but often reached a plateau when exclusion throttled immigration.[55] With the arrival of exclusion, many Chinese—hoping to escape the hostility—migrated further eastward and southward. Chinatowns emerged in Philadelphia; Boston; Baltimore; Washington, D.C.; New York City; Prescott, Arizona; and El Paso, Texas.

In the early days, Chinatowns were often transient centers for gold miners and laborers headed for the hinterlands, but by the turn of the twentieth century they were becoming places of refuge and residential communities. They also maintained ethnic boundaries. An archaeological study of ceramics, faunal materials, eating habits, and alcohol consumption in El Paso revealed that Chinese experienced limited acculturation rather than assimilation. A study of bony remains of meals at five sites—Sacramento, Woodland, Ventura (all three in California); Lovelock, Nevada; and Tucson, Arizona—also supports the conclusion that the material culture and domestic practices throughout the nineteenth century reflected those in China to some degree.[56]

By the end of the nineteenth century small Chinese communities that did not qualify as Chinatowns in terms of not being visible, concentrated Chinese neighborhoods developed in Buffalo, New York; Providence, Rhode Island; Fall River, Massachusetts; Hartford, Connecticut; Pittsburgh; St. Paul–Minneapolis; and New Orleans. In towns and cities where Chinese constituted a tiny percentage of the population, their businesses and residences were scattered throughout the area. They also tended to rely heavily on the ethnic enclave economy for their livelihoods. For example, by 1900 all of the approximately fifty-two Chinese living in the St. Paul–Minneapolis area worked in Chinese laundries, restaurants, or stores.[57] Since Chinese depended on coethnics for employment, white hysteria over "Oriental" competition for jobs was preempted. Nativism directed at European immigrants might also have diverted attention away from the small number of Chinese.

In the 1870s urban Chinese moved into the manufacturing economy and found themselves relegated to low-paying, racially segregated jobs—mainly as factory operatives in woolen, knitting, and paper mills; tanneries; shoe- and cigar-making factories; and garment industries. Often Chinese occupied the menial positions, and Euro-Americans took the skilled jobs—a reflection of a labor market stratified by race. In instances where they held the same job as whites, the Chinese often earned less than their white counterparts. In the early 1880s Chinese men earned a dollar a day as factory operatives, half of what white men made per day.[58]

The small number of Chinese women in the United States—in 1880 there were 4,779 (compared with 100,686 males)—fared even worse.[59] Suffering from racial and gender discrimination, inadequate education, and untransferable skills and having to meet domestic responsibilities, most Chinese women in the late nineteenth century were restricted to a few occupations. They either did piecework at home for subcontractors—sewing, washing, rolling cigars, shelling shrimp and abalone, sorting walnuts and vegetables, and making slippers and brooms—or performed personal and domestic service, namely prostitution and domestic labor. The domestic laborers worked primarily as *mui-tsai* (Cantonese), or contracted girl servants. In New York City, for example, an estimated 40 to 50 percent of the gainfully employed Chinese female immigrants in the nineteenth century labored as domestic servants.[60]

By the early twentieth century women had found work in garment, cigar-making, and food-processing factories or sweatshops. Chinese women were disproportionately represented in the garment industry. Chinese seamstresses were either sole breadwinners or co–wage earners for many immigrant families. They turned Old World skills that met the needs of the self-sufficient family economy into cash-yielding work, enabling them to adapt to American conditions. Although they were moving farther from the domestic sphere by engaging in new trades, some things remained the same. In San Francisco they were workers in "home factories" (workshops established by spouses or relatives), and in New York City they were part of the "putting-out" system in which sewing was brought home. The workers were paid on a piece-rate basis with no hope for upward mobility. They were also paid less than men and were given less remunerative tasks. Wage labor, however, was not entirely oppressive. Although women carried a double burden as both wage earners and unpaid household producers, women's earnings and access to social networks outside the family to some extent ameliorated male authority within the home. Thus women's employment in America was as liberating as it was oppressive.[61]

Given the generally less-than-ideal working conditions, some Chinese chose to become self-employed—running laundries, dry goods stores, herb stores (where practitioners of Chinese medicine set up shop), gift shops, and restaurants that catered to the growing ethnic community and to white customers. Perhaps the most ubiquitous Chinese urban enterprise in the nineteenth century was the laundry. The low start-up cost, minimal contact with non-Chinese, and portability of the occupation attracted Chinese to the venture. In 1900 one of four employed Chinese males in the United States was a laundry worker or owner. In 1898 one newspaper journalist estimated that in the greater New York City metropolitan area, half of the Chinese population—or around 8,000 Chinese—were laundry operators and workers.[62]

Laundries also met a universal need. That, along with the fact that the service provided was deemed "feminine" enough for the womanless Chinese, facilitated the migration of Chinese eastward, escaping Sinophobic sentiments. In Wichita, Kansas, for example, the number of Chinese-owned laundries increased from one in 1880 to twelve in 1887.[63] Such self-employment did occasionally lead to class mobility as individuals—relying on their managerial skills—accumulated capital and American experiences and invested in new ventures; however, most self-employed individuals remained mired in a marginal existence. Other Chinese, to avoid intense interracial interaction and conflict, hired themselves out as domestic servants who typically worked for one Euro-American family at a time. In southern cities, however, where African Americans dominated the bottom rungs of the urban economic structure, Chinese found limited opportunities in service-oriented establishments and semiskilled or unskilled labor.

BEYOND THE YELLOW-WHITE RACIAL DYAD

In Chinese American history the study of race relations has historically been posited as a yellow and white dyad. That dyad, Gary Okihiro has pointed out, has shaped the periodization and understanding of immigration, contact, conflict, and adaptation.[64] Yet multiple racial pivots did exist. Conflict and cooperation occurred among nonwhites, as well as between whites and nonwhites. Mutual antagonism between minority groups reveals, to quote Sucheng Chan, "how pernicious racism can be in a mixed, fiercely competitive society in which all groups were prone to extreme ethnocentrism."[65]

In the nineteenth century Chinese immigrants found themselves pitted against nonwhites in several settings. The competition for limited resources and jobs between the two groups revealed not only white prejudices but also the existence of a multiple-tiered labor structure. European workers remained in the upper echelon, holding down good-paying jobs, whereas in the lower rank Chinese seemed to hold an advantage over African Americans, Native Americans, and even at times other Asian newcomers.

In San Francisco white employers preferred to hire Chinese and European immigrants over African Americans. Most white employers were contemptuous toward blacks, whereas they were more paternalistic toward Chinese—sometimes even showing grudging admiration for them, although they were still condescending. If blacks were considered lazy and shiftless, Chinese were docile and disciplined, although less intelligent than whites. Such perceptions in part shaped the segmented labor market: Chinese dominated the cigar-making industry and railroad building, whereas white workers were clustered in skilled trades. San Francisco's blacks, who were outnumbered by Chinese one to ten during part of the nineteenth century, were mere spectators regarding these changes. By the 1890s blacks were even shut out of the food service industry, which had previously welcomed them.[66]

Because white employers played Chinese and blacks against each other, racial and class tensions between the two races festered. In San Francisco black community leaders initially justified Chinese immigration as a way to secure the "cheap" labor necessary to develop economic ventures in which whites seemed disinterested. With the Chinese performing the manual and unskilled jobs, the leaders argued, the door would be open for African Americans to rise from the bottom rung of the labor ladder. Such arguments seemed no different from those raised by many white manufacturers and investors;

Chinese were welcomed for their labor, not for their potential contribution to the melting pot. Beginning in the late 1860s, against the backdrop of the rising number of Chinese immigrants and southern planter elites' increasing use of them as workers, a few black leaders became fearful that Chinese laborers would undercut the fortunes of the freedmen in the South by allowing employers to lower wages.[67]

As anti-Chinese sentiments reached a crescendo in the 1870s, black journalists and labor unionists derided Chinese labor as "the thorn festering [in] the vitals" of the American people. Immoral, illiterate, unclean, fundamentally inhuman—these were the qualities, such commentators argued, that marked the Chinese as not worthy of living and working in the United States. In showing such antipathy toward Chinese, which echoed mainstream nativism, black Americans sought to elevate themselves vis-à-vis the Chinese.

Ethnic antagonism also existed in the canneries of the Pacific Northwest. To avoid full automation—which demanded enormous capital investment—and make up for the shortfall in Chinese laborers following the impact of exclusion, canners first turned to Native Americans and European Americans. But the Native Americans resisted the industrial discipline canners demanded, and white laborers were scarce. Cannery owners eventually relied on Japanese immigrants but placed them in the common labor positions and used skilled Chinese as tinsmiths, butchers, and fillers. With the aid of Chinese labor contractors, Chinese cannery workers earned the highest wages, faced the least dehumanizing work conditions, and limited the entry of non-Chinese into skilled trades.[68]

In the hinterlands of the American West, intercultural contact between Chinese and Native Americans sometimes resulted in violence. Economic competition for limited resources contributed to the tensions. In western Nevada, Paiute women sold wood to white townspeople, but when the Chinese entered the area they displaced the women because they gathered and transported the wood more efficiently. In the Puyallup Valley and along the White River in Washington, Chinese and Native Americans searched for work as hop pickers. Euro-American farmers tended to hire Chinese pickers, as they were willing to work for low wages, even though the farmers considered Native Americans better workers. In reaction, 3,000 Native Americans descended on the valley in 1879 and drove away Chinese pickers. Instances of Native Americans killing Chinese miners in the American West were not unheard of; often, these cases were part of the larger conflict between whites and Natives. As was true with whites, to the Natives, Chinese had encroached on their lands and fishing grounds. Whites added to the growing mutual hostility by disguising themselves as Native Americans when they raided Chinese camps or by playing Chinese and Native laborers against each other.[69]

In the first few decades of the twentieth century, Chinese (along with Japanese American) entrepreneurs who ran restaurants and grocery stores in cities with small African American populations competed with black businesses. In Denver, Seattle, and San Francisco, Chinese- and Japanese-owned establishments welcomed working-class black customers whom white store owners had offended. These establishments overcame black customers' potential ethnic loyalty to coethnic businesses by offering outstanding service, taking advantage of an extensive coethnic distribution network. The outcome was predictable: African American entrepreneurs were either driven out of business or hung on precariously with a narrow profit margin. Instances of Asian discrimination toward blacks were not unknown; blacks, according to some accounts, were turned away by some Chinese-owned establishments that depended on white patronage. In Seattle, where restrictive covenants prevented residential dispersal of minorities, poor Chinese competed with blacks for rental properties owned by wealthy Chinese or Japanese within an expanded Chinatown; this integration of the Chinatown was a testament of Chinese residents' powerlessness as segregation squeezed racial minorities into a declining neighborhood.[70]

As much as U.S. minorities engaged in intergroup conflicts, instances of cooperation and mutual accommodation—even solidarity—at times tipped the balance in favor of amity. In Arizona, Yuman Indians sold fish to Chinese railroad workers and supplied the firewood for Chinese laundries. Native and Chinese Americans worked side by side on the Central Pacific line and in silver mines in Arizona. Chinese and blacks even socialized in several settings; Sacramento Chinese shared a church with African Americans for several decades during the nineteenth century, and interracial marriages in the Deep South stemmed from the common class backgrounds of Chinese sharecroppers and tenant farmers and black women with farming backgrounds. Class ties also forged interracial liaisons between Chinese laundrymen and Irish domestic servants in New York City and between Chinese restaurant owners and cooks and Irish and Polish female restaurant workers in Minneapolis–St. Paul. In the late 1860s the venerable black abolitionist Frederick Douglass wrote a number of articles in defense of the Chinese, arguing that exclusion was undemocratic and that they would contribute to the U.S. economy.[71]

THE ANTI-CHINESE MOVEMENT

The ties that bound Chinese to other racial ethnic minorities included segregation and spatial differentiation. By the early 1870s Sinophobia had found expression in the formation of anticoolie clubs, sporadic boycotts of Chinese-made goods, and anti-immigration laws. Even before the 1870s various laws gave Chinese the clear message that their presence rankled native-born Americans. For example, in 1852 the California legislature passed the Foreign

Miners' License Tax and the commutation tax, with the latter requiring a hefty bond or payment for each new arrival. California's 1862 Chinese Police Tax stipulated a monthly tax to be paid by each Chinese resident. That same year the U.S. Congress passed an act to curtail American involvement in the coolie trade between Asia and the Americas. Because the law broadly defined a coolie as any person shipped abroad "to be held to service or labor," the distinction between coolies and voluntary immigrants became blurred, and all Asian (not just Chinese) laborers in the nineteenth century fell under this morally laden label. In 1870 the California state legislature passed a discriminatory statute that required each Chinese immigrant to provide proof that he or she possessed "good character." The law, with later amendments, also required the state commissioner of immigration to collect from a ship's owner or consignee a monetary bond for every passenger deemed either a noncitizen, a pauper, a lunatic, handicapped, or a prostitute. It was presumed—incorrectly, of course—that most Chinese would fall into one of these categories. Another 1878 California law also reflected non-Chinese revulsion toward the Asians; it mandated that Chinese who wished to exhume the dead for shipment to China had to secure a permit from local health authorities.[72]

The problems Chinese faced in California were echoed elsewhere. In Hawai'i, Chinese who were not naturalized citizens of the kingdom were denied a license to sell imported goods (1874); additionally, custom duties were raised on goods produced in China (1876), and Asians could not land in Hawai'i without prior consent (1878). Chinese who fled to Canada found that nativism existed there as well; in response to constituencies that raised the alarm over increasing Chinese immigration from California, the British Columbia legislature passed a law in 1875 denying Chinese suffrage, followed by measures to ban the use of Chinese laborers in public works and to levy a license tax on able-bodied Chinese. The legislature also repeatedly lobbied the dominion government in Ottawa to restrict Chinese arrivals and withhold their naturalization.[73]

In addition to state and federal laws, the Chinese had to deal with insidious local ordinances that also sought to impede their livelihoods and ultimately force them to return to Asia. This form of prejudice became prevalent after the passage of the 1870 Civil Rights Act, which among other things was supposed to, first, protect the Chinese right to testify in court and, second, to forbid the imposition of unfair exactions and taxes. The first provision removed the legal disability imposed by *People v. Hall* (1854), in which Chinese testimony—as well as that of Native Americans and African Americans—against Caucasians was deemed invalid because of their racial inferiority (although this applied only to the state courts). The second provision, coupled with the equal protection clause of the Fourteenth Amendment, invalidated anti-Chinese state laws. That same year, however, Congress countered this reversal of fortunes by amending the 1790 Nationality Act so that Chinese would not be covered by the extension of naturalization to African Americans.[74]

To circumvent the Civil Rights Act, local governments passed ordinances that were neutral on their face but that could be enforced selectively against the Chinese. In San Francisco the cubic-air law, implying that the Chinese lived in overcrowded, dirty conditions, forced every residence to provide at least 500 cubic feet of air per person. The queue ordinance required that the hair of every male prisoner in the city jails be cut to within one inch of the scalp, a disgrace to Chinese nationals; and the sidewalk ordinance prohibited peddlers from using poles to carry loads on sidewalks. Los Angeles officials required vegetable peddlers—a trade group overwhelmingly dominated by Chinese—to meet certain licensing and regulatory requirements. Outraged by these impositions, the Chinese vendors went on strike, which hurt the larger populace so severely that the city rescinded the requirements.

Perhaps the most vituperative San Francisco ordinances were those related to laundry. During the 1870s Chinese owned 240 of the approximately 320 laundries in San Francisco.[75] Considered symbols of Chinese economic success in America, the laundries also reminded whites that the Chinese—far from being mere sojourners—intended to stay. Euro-American proprietors and local newspapers railed against the Chinese laundries, and the embers of smoldering hatred caught fire in 1877 when in a three-day rampage mobs destroyed some of the laundries. The city fathers fanned the flames of xenophobic hatred with ordinances designed to harass or force the ouster of Chinese laundries by withholding licensing until they met certain conditions.[76]

Throughout the 1870s such animosity was repeated in other small towns in California. Ventura slapped a hefty fifteen-dollar levy per quarter on each Chinese-owned laundry, Salinas City and Watsonville forced Chinese laundries to wash clothes away from the main business district, and Santa Cruz singled out Chinese laundries for a special business license.[77] Such poor treatment invited a blunt commentary from Chung Sun, a victim of the 1871 two-day Los Angeles anti-Chinese riots in which twenty-two Chinese were killed: "In civility, complaisance, and polite manners [Americans] are wholly wanting and are very properly styled barbarians."[78]

The roots of the general animosity against Chinese immigrants may date back to the fifth century B.C., when the military engagement between the "civilized" Greeks and "barbarian" Persians sparked writings about Asia—a continent supposedly containing exotic, debased, inscrutable peoples. The Mongol invasion of Europe in the thirteenth century gave credence to the developing image of Asia as the Yellow Peril. This irrational fear of an "Oriental" conquest found fertile soil in America and continued to grow. In the minds of European settlers, American Indians—the descendants of Asians—stood in the way of progress, of America's evolution from savagery to civilization. African Americans similarly represented a threat to the development of American civilization, since their slave labor constituted unfair competition for free workers—an argument that foreshadowed claims made later against the Chinese.[79]

These colonial understandings of nonwhite groups fed into the Yankee traders' image of China and its people following their arrival in China in the late eighteenth century. Yet early perceptions of Chinese seemed more benign than maligned. During the American Revolutionary era, Americans admired the opulence, values, and material goods of Chinese civilization. American elites believed the trade of goods and ideas with the empire of China would promote the shaping of an independent, wealthy, and distinctive republic. Those who possessed Chinese luxuries and ideas attained a social status that marked them as the nouveau riches.[80]

By the early nineteenth century, Americans' admiration of China shifted to emulation and then to a desire to dominate the country as proof of U.S. progress as a civilization. U.S. merchants and their ships profited from the China trade, their wealth built by luxuries, opium, and "coolies." American-style chinoiserie suggested in a symbolic way the republic's cultural mastery of China. The respect and admiration for China shifted to eventual disdain, sometimes mixed with condescending pity, as U.S. imperialism—as with that of European—reached its long arm into China. By then, American traders, diplomats, and missionaries described the Chinese as superstitious, crafty, and dishonest. In the United States, many Americans learned about these so-called Chinese aberrations through the popular dime novels of the antebellum years, and those in large cities also learned of them through dime museums, theaters, lectures, and merchandise. Early Chinese arrivals in New York City were compelled to conform to this developing commercial form of "Orientalism"; they became tea merchants, behaved as "mandarins," and performed exotic acts.

The interest in the "Orient" and the Chinese "otherness" attracted voyeuristic Euro-Americans to sideshow exhibits of Chinese human "freaks" such as the Siamese twins Chang and Eng Bunker, who were promoted as quaint young boys. Equally exploited as a showpiece was Afong Moy, supposedly the first Chinese woman to arrive in America in 1834, whose dainty features and colorful costume gave credence to the mystique of "Orientalism." When Americans played yellow face in minstrel shows, often satirizing Chinese immigrant life through comic routines, the degradation of the Chinese was complete. Anything deemed Chinese—bodies, clothing, and cultural differences—became a marketable public spectacle. Racial caricatures became the standard vocabulary of a visual culture.

By the early 1870s, as anti-Chinese hostility heated up, the prevailing, inscrutable "coolie" stereotype of the Chinese immigrant began appearing in novels about the California frontier by such writers as Bret Harte and Ambrose Bierce. Fictional works in the "future history" genre—which prophesied an "Oriental" invasion by the mindless, monolithic Chinese mass—such as Pierton W. Dooner's *Last Days of the Republic* (1880), echoed the larger fear of Chinese immigration. Since white Americans believed the Chinese were far more intelligent and competitive than African Americans or Native Americans, the threat they posed required an aggressive response lest U.S. workers be eliminated from the labor market. Only poverty, idleness, and the drain of America's wealth to China awaited if nothing was done about the current flood of immigrants. Anxiety rose when commentators pointed out that unlike African Americans and Native Americans, who were threats of the past, Chinese dominance represented the unknown future. The ingrained perception of Asia as made up of expansive lands populated by a brutish mass, coupled with the emerging image of the Chinese as the perfect "laboring machine," foretold trouble for republicanism and the march toward progress.[81]

A major factor in the shift from negative representations of the Chinese to exclusion, from rhetoric to reaction, was the unstable economy. Slashed wages and high unemployment characterized the lean years of 1873 to 1878. During this severe recession, American labor groups blamed their woes on the Chinese and their capitalist employers. White workers chafed at the industrialists' recruitment of Chinese laborers and were unpersuaded that the whites' status and occupations would improve as Chinese filled the lower-ranking jobs. The "industrial reserve army," or Chinese laborers, were not only "cheap labor" but also constituted the mass that would invade factories and displace Euro-American working men. The fact that the Chinese—in the middle of the recession—had migrated to the heavily populated Northeast; established themselves in New York, Boston, and Philadelphia; and supposedly found work in major industries only heightened alarm about an impending "Oriental" invasion.[82]

Stories about the "slavelike" nature of Chinese labor whipped up fears about the return of slavery and its attending political complications. Although charges of "coolieism" were unfounded, Chinese laborers were still—erroneously, of course—compared to American black slaves. The physiognomy of the Chinese was supposedly akin to that of African Americans; both indicated a biologically determined depravity that could taint the purity of the white race.[83]

The supposed similar depravity of Chinese and African Americans explains the application of the color line to both racial minorities in U.S. education. In 1854 the local school board in San Francisco provided a "colored school" for black children, and in 1858 the board passed a resolution institutionalizing separate schools for whites and blacks. Echoing public sentiments on the issue, the *San Francisco Bulletin* commented, "Then let us keep our public schools free from the intrusion of the inferior races . . . let us preserve our Caucasian blood pure. We want no mongrel race of moral and mental hybrids."[84] Two years later the California legislature passed a law that established segregated schools and authorized the withholding of public monies from any all-white school that admitted racial minorities.

Although an all-Chinese school opened its doors in 1859, low enrollment and the racial prejudice of officials led to its closing in 1870. In spite of the hostile environment during the 1880s, the Chinese community persistently lobbied for access to educational facilities, citing it as a right guaranteed by their tax-paying status. Success seemed in sight in 1884 when Joseph and Mary Tape won their suit against the school board for denying their daughter, Mamie, a public education. School officials circumvented the ruling, however, and established a new, segregated Oriental School. Various California communities, including San Francisco, kept Chinese children in segregated elementary schools until the early 1930s when Chinese civic organizations and leaders fought successfully for the end of segregated schooling. At the higher levels of education, Chinese in San Francisco successfully blocked attempts to establish separate junior and senior high schools. Chinese schoolchildren in the South, however, remained in all-black schools until 1950. Asian and black children were lumped together as "nonwhite," the extreme opposite of "white." In *Gong Lum v. Rice* (1927), the plaintiff's daughter, Martha Lum, was a U.S.-born citizen of Chinese descent who was denied access to an all-white school in Mississippi. The issue was whether Chinese should be considered "colored"; if so, the denial would stand. The Mississippi Supreme Court ruled that Chinese were part of the "colored," or nonwhite, race. Clearly, the categories of black and white had been revised to nonwhite and white.

Economic, racial, and cultural factors clearly forged an American consensus on the undesirability of Chinese immigration. For example, local newspapers often carried news of crowds of young whites at the docks heckling and even pelting new Chinese arrivals. Much more ominous was the 1870s' agitation led by the Workingmen's Party and its demagogue, Dennis Kearney. The Workingmen's Party cry, "The Chinese must go," captured the attention of Californians. Capitalizing on the economic crisis and aware of the potential political windfall for the labor movement in terms of increasing its influence in state politics, labor leaders lined up behind the anti-Chinese rhetoric. Although the rhetoric stemmed in part from white workers' understanding of an economic competition between more or less free (white) and indentured (Chinese) laborers, it was also rooted in Jacksonian politics that conceived democracy as the battleground of the working classes against capitalists and monopolies. The Chinese were the tools of the capitalists, and so they must go.[85]

The Workingmen's Party's influence was palpable at the 1878–1879 California constitutional convention. Delegates, in a display of intense animosity against the Chinese, inserted an article in the final form of the document that prohibited corporations and those in the public sector from employing Chinese. It even called for the expulsion of Chinese from towns and cities or for them to be segregated within prescribed limits, something towns and counties tried to carry out in subsequent years. The Chinese were also stripped of equal protection and of the right to vote in state elections. A statewide referendum in 1879 seemed to express the consensus: an overwhelming majority of voters—94 percent—were against continued Chinese immigration.

Echoes of such nativism were also heard on the East Coast. In New York City, labor unions and local politicians organized anticoolie rallies as early as 1870, and the hostility of organized labor prevented most Chinese from entering the city's manufacturing sector. Like their peers in the West, working men in New York City argued that Chinese labor undermined the wage scale. Although they opposed Chinese contract, or "coolie," labor rather than Chinese immigration, their rhetoric had an obvious racist tone. Conjuring images of the Chinese as backward, heathenistic, and unassimilable—essentially the enemies of progress—the harangues of these white-led labor unions resonated with the American public in a time of anticipated industrial progress yet unrealized by an economic downturn. Racial scapegoating reduced the anxiety raised by the demand for progress.[86]

Racial identification as a central tenet of working-class ideology had evolved since the antebellum years within a context of white racism that justified slavery and the extermination of Native Americans. The Democrats promoted a proslavery outlook that suggested blacks were inferior to whites. Republicans were no better; their cry for free soil—keeping slavery out of U.S. territories—arose from the fear of black labor degrading, or lowering the quality of, free (white) labor. A political tradition of accepting class and racial divisions in the society also undergirded Republican politics. Many feared the immigrant. Republicans and Democrats bore a nearly identical ideological baggage. Both parties also saw the extermination of Native Americans as unavoidable; the Democrats' cry for expansion of slavery to guarantee territorial growth and the Republicans' drive for industrialization hinged on that extermination. After the Civil War, white workers transferred antiblack, anti-immigrant, and anti–Native American hostilities to the Chinese.[87]

The momentum of the anti-Chinese movement can also be ascribed to politicians who were quick to exploit cross-class rhetoric to swing a vote or a state in their favor. After all, the 1870s were marked by a gradual fading of Civil War partisanship and the emergence of a converging political consensus.

Both Democrats and Republicans needed to identify with new issues so voters could set them apart. Scapegoating the Chinese for the ills of a country in the grip of a recession would deflect attention from its early industrial problems. The exigencies of electoral politics pushed politicians to whip up anti-Asian feelings and later to make calculated legislative decisions. Politics became the conduit to crystallize and propagate a racial discourse.[88]

Elsewhere, anti-Chinese intolerance stemmed as much from people using Chinese to deflect nativism away from certain European immigrants as it did from the perceived economic threat. In Colorado in the 1870s, Italian workers in coal mines felt threatened by fellow Chinese workers. Italians feared that eventually they would be displaced by the "cheaper" Chinese or that their pay would be lowered to the Chinese level. Complicating the picture was the social prejudice of Cornish, Irish, and Austrian immigrants against the Italians. Long seen as the most "brutish" European ethnic group, Italians adopted existing social prejudices toward the Chinese to show their own adaptation to mainstream American society, assert the definition of Americans as "white" persons, and deflect nativist antiforeign feelings from themselves.[89]

The same process of appropriating "whiteness" to acquire a racial identity that would set a group apart from nonwhites (in this case Asians) played out in 1872–1873 in Beaver Falls, Pennsylvania. The displaced German and Irish workers in the town's cutlery factory, which had hired Chinese laborers, fought back by depicting the latter as "coolies," servile, and transient. The workers appealed to the management to rehire them. They petitioned the U.S. Congress and the Pennsylvania legislature to pass an anti-Chinese contract labor law. All the while they identified themselves as "white labor" that should not be debased by Chinese labor.[90]

In San Francisco, Irish working men backed the anti-Chinese outcry of unions such as Kearney's Workingmen's Party. Long despised for their drunkenness, popery, and political corruption, Irish immigrants found that the privileged white racial identity eluded them. To find their place in the United States, they linked Irishness and whiteness in a war against the proletarianized Chinese. In defending the white working family against the Chinese threat, Irish workers racialized proletarianized labor and at the same time promoted themselves as champions of white working men.[91] Thus the anti-Chinese movement was the outcome of both race and class and their mutual and clashing interests.

The nativism inflicted upon the Chinese also played out within a larger context of the history of American nativism from the 1840s to the 1920s. As explained by Matthew Frye Jacobson, that nativist era was shaped by a revision of whiteness. The issue of who was fit for self-governance—a question that had been raised since the founding of the republic—became tied to racial idioms. From the 1840s onward, American nativism had an undercurrent of race; all immigrants, regardless of their country of origin, belonged to a certain race and could be placed in a hierarchy of civilizations. Because the core republican principle that not everyone was capable of self-control and independence remained sacrosanct, "the argument for inclusion could only generate other exclusions; this or that group's asserted 'fitness' for self-government could only be measured by some group's unfitness."[92] As policy makers and politicians struggled to define the boundaries of citizenship in the late nineteenth century, racially marked "others" such as African Americans, Asians, and other groups eventually demarcated the parameters of the category "white persons"—those who could be naturalized as stipulated in the 1790 naturalization law. Even as some Europeans—Celts, Italians, Jews, and Slavs—became part of a scheme of hierarchically ordered white races used to determine immigration restriction, nonwhites, including Asians, failed the test of whiteness that determined naturalization and were deemed unfit to enter the United States. The notion of "white" or "Caucasian" consanguinity drew a clear line between a supposed monolithic whiteness and its "others."[93]

ANTI-ASIAN LAWS AND CHINESE RESISTANCE

The Chinese did try to resist such prejudices and in so doing demonstrated a knowledge of U.S. governmental institutions and remarkable savvy in manipulating them. Responding to the *Hall* decision, San Francisco merchant Lai Chun-chuen, in an 1855 letter to Governor John Bigler, sarcastically said that the decision to bar Chinese testimony on the grounds that the Chinese were as lowly as blacks and Native Americans must have stemmed from anything but "enlightened intelligence and enlarged liberality." The *Oriental (Tung-ngai san luk)*, a white missionary-owned newspaper aimed at Chinese immigrants, read *Hall* as a mockery of Republicanism and Christianity. In the 1850s, taxation of miners elicited protests from Chinese mutual aid associations, which argued that imposing such a tax was acceptable only if the Chinese enjoyed legal protection in the courts. The leaders of these associations, through a lobbyist in Sacramento, succeeded in preventing the passage of subsequent odious legislation, and they were instrumental in securing protection for the Chinese under the 1870 Civil Rights Act.[94]

As the anti-Chinese movement swung into full gear, however, the strategy of petitioning to lawmakers became increasingly futile. In exasperation, some Chinese community leaders urged fellow compatriots in China to dissuade potential immigrants from coming to the United States. For the most part, their resistance now had to take place within the courts. The decision to employ American jurisprudence constituted a departure from the traditional Chinese submission to government's laws and reflected selective acculturation into the American way of life.

As early as 1861 several individual Chinese had contested the foreign miners' license law in the courts and won, although the judiciary sidestepped the constitutional question. In 1862 plaintiff Lin Sing successfully challenged the validity of the monthly tax on Chinese residents in California on the grounds that it violated the U.S. Constitution and U.S. laws, particularly those involving federal power over foreign commerce (in this case, the Chinese).

Over the next several decades Chinese litigants pressed that same line of attack. When the Chinese in Idaho heard about the Civil Rights Act of 1866 and the subsequent Fourteenth Amendment, which collectively guaranteed every U.S. citizen equal protection under the law, they had more grounds to fight discriminatory state laws. They filed several suits against Idaho's head tax, which was levied on every Chinese resident, and against the special monthly levy on Chinese gambling houses and brothels. Ultimately they failed, mainly because the courts ruled that they were not citizens and thus were not covered by the equal protection clause.[95]

In 1879 the Chinese community in San Francisco, in *How Ah Kow v. Nunan*, questioned the constitutionality of the queue-cutting ordinance, arguing that it undermined the equality of treatment promised the Chinese by the Burlingame Treaty, the 1870 Civil Rights Act, and the due process and equal protection clauses of the Fourteenth Amendment. Later, the courts, in the habeas corpus cases *In re Quong Woo* (1882) and *Yick Woo v. Hopkins* (1886)—brought by Chinese laundrymen against the series of laundry ordinances—affirmed that the Chinese, although not citizens, deserved equal protection of the law.[96]

The Chinese, however, suffered a severe setback on the question of naturalization. In 1878 several Chinese asked the federal courts to rule that Chinese aliens did fall within the 1870 stipulation that "any alien, being a free white person" could become a U.S. citizen. This became necessary since, aside from "white persons," African Americans were the only other group that could become naturalized citizens. But the courts found that a white person was a Caucasian, and since Chinese were not Caucasians, they were barred from citizenship.

The failure to gain citizenship gave the anti-immigrant movement a boost. Since they could not vote, the Chinese were unable to deflect the movement against them politically; further, for whites, they must deserve exclusion from citizenship because of their racial inferiority. Restrictionists, however, still had to overcome the limits placed on state power over immigration and the free emigration provision in the Burlingame Treaty. They realized that they had to fight for their cause in Congress.

Their first attempt—the 1879 Fifteen-Passenger Bill (stating that no vessel should carry more than fifteen Chinese passengers to the United States)—was vetoed by President Rutherford B. Hayes because it violated treaty protections. Chinese immigration, however—much to the joy of restrictionists—

became a major issue in the 1880 national election because the Pacific Coast served as the swing vote on several key issues. In an effort to curry votes, both parties called for the restriction of Chinese immigration and the amendment of the Burlingame Treaty.[97]

In response, the Hayes administration impaneled a commission to negotiate a new, restrictive treaty with China. The new treaty, however, was a compromise—a testament to the Qing government's late response to numerous earlier pleas for diplomatic intervention by Chinese mutual aid associations in America. Faced with Qing resistance, the U.S. commission secured only restriction of Chinese laborers who had yet to immigrate to the United States; those already present in the country and those of nonlaboring classes could still enjoy free travel and equal protection. The 1880 Angell Treaty represented a significant departure; class-based restriction of immigration had been written in treaty form, and the institutionalization of prejudice against the Chinese gathered momentum.[98]

That momentum was steamrolled by a series of anti-Chinese outrages. Violence against Chinese was nothing new; it is estimated that in the 1850s almost ninety Chinese miners lost their lives because of the contested Foreign Miners' License Tax. Spontaneous outbreaks against Chinese occurred in several California towns in the 1870s, including one failed attempt to burn down Chico's Chinatown. Responding to this wave of violence, in a 1876 letter to city authorities, Chinese merchants in San Francisco pleaded for treaty protections and reciprocity in Sino-American relations: "Being here under sacred treaty stipulations, we simply asked to be protected in our treaty rights."[99] The merchants demanded indemnification for loss of property and lives, but to no avail.

In Congress, opponents of restriction—mostly representing commercial and religious groups—tried to check antiforeign feelings by emphasizing the Chinese contributions to U.S. economic well-being, but to no avail. Congress passed the Chinese Exclusion Act in 1882 by a wide margin, and for the first time in its history the United States adopted a policy of exclusion based on race and nationality—a measure that laid the foundation for future barriers against other ethnic groups.[100]

The 1882 act suspended the entry of Chinese laborers into the United States for the next ten years. Chinese laborers already in the country as of November 17, 1880, could remain, but they were governed by certain entry and exit regulations. This class-bound legislation did not apply to merchants, diplomats, teachers, students, and travelers (the exempt classes) but did require them to possess documentation attesting to their right to enter the country. That requirement would force the exempt classes to cope with mind-boggling paperwork and a creaky bureaucracy. The exclusion act—significantly—denied all Chinese access to naturalization on the basis of race.

What made the Chinese Exclusion Act and other subsequent race-based immigration laws even more restrictive was the narrow interpretation of the legislation. According to Erika Lee, immigration officials, responding to pressure from anti-Chinese groups and reflecting their own ethnocentric biases, applied a restrictive interpretation of the exclusion laws. Immigration officials denied entry to those who were clearly neither laborers nor part of the exempt classes. Immigrants who found their right to land rejected included spouses and children of exempt-class immigrants, accountants, doctors, and other professionals.[101]

Immigration officials also applied informal policies that raised the bar for entry requirements. For example, beginning in 1893, officials in San Francisco mandated that every departing Chinese merchant had to file a photograph and a sworn statement about his business and his partners with the customs office. Exempt-class Chinese who planned to return to America were expected to furnish such proof in addition to the certificate from the Chinese government attesting to a person's right of admission—which by law was the only document required. Officials also dictated that only whites could offer testimony in support of the exempt-class status of applicants for admission. The informal policies of local officials were approved by the Treasury Department (which had jurisdiction over Chinese immigration until 1900) and the Bureau of Immigration. Both agencies also, in processing appeals from Chinese immigrants denied admission, often upheld the rulings of officials. Whenever officials were deemed lenient, both agencies pressured them to adopt a more vigilant approach. By the early twentieth century, the Bureau of Immigration had implemented the Bertillon system to keep track of Chinese immigrants (which largely involved measuring applicants' body parts, a process Chinese considered humiliating); they also prolonged the investigative process, strengthened border patrols along the Canadian and Mexican borders, and stepped up efforts to deport illegal Chinese immigrants. Overall, the rigid enforcement of the exclusion laws made it extremely difficult for Chinese immigrants to gain entry into the United States.

That landmark 1882 legislation catalyzed other anti-Asian movements elsewhere. Following a spate of violent incidents, Canadian legislators passed an immigration act in 1885 that imposed a head tax on new arrivals and restricted the number of passengers per vessel. Similarly, the upswell in anti-Asian sentiments gave impetus to legislative efforts to lower the status of Chinese in Hawai'i; a new constitution in 1885 disfranchising Asians who were naturalized citizens was followed by proposed amendments that choked off Chinese immigration except to meet agricultural demands. In 1887 nearly 900 Chinese signed a petition opposing such "class legislation," but to no avail. When the United States annexed Hawai'i in 1898, Asian residents came under the exclusion laws and had to apply for documents to enter the mainland and return to the islands.[102]

Almost immediately following passage of the 1882 act, the Chinese tried to mitigate its severity. Once again resorting to mediation of the federal courts, Chinese litigants managed to loosen the regulations governing the entry and exit of laborers with "prior" resident status and those of merchant background. Because so many Chinese entered following these rulings, in 1884 Congress tightened the regulations. Also that year the courts made two rulings with far-reaching consequences for family formation. First, in the case of *In re Look Tin Sing*, the court held that Chinese children born in the United States to parents who could not be naturalized were considered U.S. citizens, which implied that they fell outside the exclusion laws. The court in a separate set of cases allowed wives and children of Chinese merchants to enter the country (although not those of the Chinese laboring class).[103]

For Chinese in America, such legal battles seemed pointless at times. The passage of the Chinese Exclusion Act had further incited hostility toward Asians. Sustained, organized violence—capitalizing on the absence of political rights and legal protection for Chinese—spread like wildfire in the 1880s. Nativists, including those in labor unions, railed against the vexing presence of Chinese in western industries such as mining, timber, and railroad construction. Westerners in small and medium-sized towns sought scapegoats for an imagined labor competition, one fueled by sensationalist newspaper coverage of Chinese activity.

The "driving out" had arrived. Hostilities broke out in Denver, Colorado; Rock Springs, Wyoming Territory; Snake River Canyon, Idaho; Portland, Oregon; Tacoma, Puyallup, Snohomish County, and Seattle, Washington Territory; Alaska; Tombstone and Tucson, Arizona; Wichita, Kansas; and numerous California towns from Yreka in the north to Redlands in the south. Often, anti-Chinese advocates proposed economic boycotts of Chinese businesses or ordinances to harass those enterprises. In Chico, California, in 1885, the local anti-Chinese association first demanded that the authorities force Chinese businesses to relocate to the outskirts of town and then called for a boycott of white establishments that hired Chinese laborers. In Wichita, Kansas, the labor organization, Order of the Knights of Labor, led an 1886 campaign to boycott Chinese laundries. In El Paso, Texas, the city council passed antiopium ordinances to wipe out opium dens. In other cities and towns, cesspools that laundries developed became cause célèbre for race-specific segregation ordinances.[104]

The smoldering coals of hostility burst into flames. Rounded up like cattle, Chinese were routed out of cities and towns such as Seattle, Tacoma, and Puyallup. Commenting on the forced exodus from Tacoma, Chinese merchant Lum Moy recalled, "They presented a sad spectacle. Some lost their trunks, some their blankets, some were crying for their things."[105] In Seattle, white workers forced several hundred Chinese from their homes and marched them to the waterfront to board steamers headed for San Francisco. In Truckee, California, white residents held a torchlight procession to celebrate the expulsion of Chinese. Some Chinese in Chico, Denver, and Redlands had their homes looted and burned to the ground by angry white mobs. Perhaps the worst incident occurred in Rock Springs on September 2, 1885: 28 Chinese coal miners were killed in a riot, including 11 burned alive in their homes. Over 300 troops who rushed to the bloody riot came too late. In pitting Chinese against white miners by using the former as strikebreakers paid at lower wages, their employer, Union Pacific Railroad, ignited latent racial tensions.[106]

An estimated ninety-one instances of anti-Chinese violence flared up during the 1880s, with seventy-three occurring in 1885 and 1886 alone. The violence that erupted on the U.S. mainland sent Chinese in Hawai'i into a panic, buying rifles and ammunition and hiring night watchmen to patrol Chinatown. One outcome of the driving out was that some Chinese moved farther eastward, only to confront more animosity. In Milwaukee, a city with about sixty Chinese, an outburst of nativist sentiments in 1889 grew out of charges of Chinese sexual misconduct with underage white females. As the trial of the two Chinese laundrymen accused of illicit interracial sexual conduct unfolded, a mob mentality developed. Within days, crowds of local residents besieged Chinese laundries. Windows were smashed, and Chinese laundrymen were run out of their businesses.[107] Although the Qing government protested against the outbreaks of violence, U.S. authorities brushed off the protests and denied that the United States was liable for Chinese losses.

Following the wave of mob violence against the Chinese in the American West in 1885 and 1886, the Qing government—in a move to curtail further loss of lives and property—assented to the revision of the 1880 treaty, including a twenty-year moratorium on the immigration of Chinese laborers in exchange for a guarantee of protection of Chinese residents already in the United States. Unsubstantiated rumors that China planned to reject the revisions led Congress to push through the rather severe Scott Act in 1888, which prohibited all Chinese laborers from entering the United States—even those who had been in the country before November 17, 1880, and had the necessary documentation. Although the Chinese challenged the validity of the 1888 amendment in *Chae Chan Ping v. United States* (1888), they failed to win the case. In a decision with profound implications for immigration law, the U.S. Supreme Court affirmed that Congress had the sovereign power to exclude aliens, even those previously granted permission to stay.[108]

By the early 1890s prejudice against the Chinese had expanded to include certain European immigrants. Blamed for the rise of radicalism, a disorderly labor movement, and the industrial depression between 1883 and 1886, Eastern and Southern European immigrants bore the brunt of many Americans' anxieties about the new economic order. In the late 1880s Congress passed laws to reduce the importation of foreign labor under contracts, which supposedly had depressed the labor market.[109]

To further control the immigration wave, Congress passed a new law in 1891 that allowed the federal government to take full and exclusive control of immigration; to exclude certain criminal, immoral, or indigent classes; and to deport those already admitted into the United States if they were found excludable. In step with this sweeping hostility, Congress passed the Geary Act in 1892. The law required that all Chinese laborers in the United States had to register for a certificate of residence; if they did not comply, they could be arrested and even deported. Those found guilty of illicit residence in the United States could also suffer a year's imprisonment performing hard labor. The government clearly intended to sharpen the distinction between laborers and merchants and close loopholes the former had exploited to enter the country. In sum, the law raised the specter that every Chinese person was in the United States unlawfully.[110]

The Geary Act angered the Chinese; the Chinese vice consul in San Francisco complained that this system of registration placed Chinese "on the level of your dogs."[111] Around 600 Chinese in Brooklyn, New York, engaged an attorney to inquire about their legal rights. Over a thousand agitated Chinese in New York gathered at the meeting to form the Chinese Equal Rights League, which concluded with the issuance of a resolution decrying the act unconstitutional and arguing that it would exacerbate racial tensions. The Chinese Consolidated Benevolent Association (CCBA), better known as the Chinese Six Companies in San Francisco—the umbrella organization for Chinese mutual aid associations—urged the community not to register because the act was unconstitutional. The Chinese Six Companies hired lawyers to bring a test case—*Fong Yue Ting v. United States* (1893)—but the suit ended with an affirmation of the right of Congress to expel or deport, which the Supreme Court deemed to be part of a sovereign state's unconfined power over immigration. The CCBA's failure to reverse the tide damaged its communitywide reputation and provoked infighting among the associations. A political vacuum was in the making. The court's upholding of the new law had a chilling effect on the number of Chinese arrivals: 2,836 had been admitted in 1891; only 1,441 entered in 1894.[112] Those already present in the United States, cognizant of how vulnerable the status of a laborer was, sometimes chose to "enter" the merchant class. In 1893 writer Bruce Edward Hall's great-grandfather Hor Poa invested $200 in a grocery store that had seventy-three other merchant-partners.[113]

Some Chinese fled to Mexico or Canada in a panic—an exodus that immediately diminished the supply of agricultural labor. Both the Geary and

Scott Acts (the latter stating that any Chinese who went past the three-mile territorial limit of the United States would be considered to have left the country) also put Chinese fishermen out of business. Having been declared laborers by an amendment to the Geary Act, these Chinese could no longer fish in Mexican waters and then return to the southern California coast without risking deportation. Most chose to sell their boats, and some turned to new ventures such as market gardening.[114]

Two years after the passage of the Geary Act, the United States and China concluded the 1894 Gresham-Yang Treaty in which the tottering Qing government agreed to accept the contents of that act and the extension of the exclusion of Chinese laborers for another ten years. In return, the United States allowed the return of domiciled laborers who had left temporarily and who had family or property in the United States. In 1900, when Hawai'i was formally annexed to the United States, Chinese entry into the islands also came under the exclusion laws, which were extended in 1902 for another ten years.[115]

In 1904 China declined to renew the Gresham-Yang Treaty, and Congress made Chinese exclusion indefinite. Thus a long invidious chapter—one that began in the 1870s—of limiting and then excluding Chinese immigration finally came to an inglorious end. It would be nearly forty years before Congress reconsidered these barriers, and substantial changes would not be made until 1965.

Although the Chinese community had little success fighting the federal laws, Chinese individuals, by filing writs of habeas corpus, found a way to gain possible admittance into the United States even though they were initially refused by immigration authorities. Until the late 1890s, more than 80 percent of the petitions ended with the reversal of the earlier decision to exclude. Legislation in 1894, along with the upholding of that law in the U.S. Supreme Court case *Lem Moon Sing v. United States* (1895), however, removed Chinese cases from the courts' jurisdiction. The Bureau of Immigration's decision in cases involving new arrivals excluded by law became final unless reversed on appeal by the secretary of the treasury. The number of petitions dropped rapidly, from 207 in 1894 to 36 in 1895.

Chinese immigrants, however, turned to another loophole: the courts still had jurisdiction in citizenship cases. Since the *Look Tin Sing* (1884) and *United States v. Wong Kim Ark* (1898) rulings had upheld the claim that native-born Chinese were citizens and therefore were exempt from the exclusion laws, Chinese arrivals who could prove they had been born in the United States presumably stood a good chance of gaining entry. The number of Chinese immigrants who resorted to the courts to overturn the decision to exclude them rose again by the end of the decade. Until 1905, over half of the petitions succeeded in overturning that decision. In the 1905 landmark case

United States v. Ju Toy, the Supreme Court ruled that the federal courts could no longer accept petitions, regardless of whether the petitioners were citizens or aliens. Chinese immigrants involved in admission cases had lost access to the courts.

Chinese embroiled in civil and criminal disputes with whites often resorted to U.S. courts to secure redress. Before 1882 the courts in some western states refused to allow Chinese testimony if the litigants denied the existence of a God as part of the oath. But the New Mexico Supreme Court ruled in *Territory of New Mexico v. Yee Shun* (1882), a case that involved the murder of a Chinese immigrant by a fellow coethnic, that Chinese could testify in open court provided attorneys did not raise doubts about their religious or cultural practices. With this legal breakthrough, Chinese, regardless of religious affiliation, could seek legal protection in the courts.[116]

Most Chinese-white cases involved civil rather than criminal disputes. Typically, Euro-American companies or individuals owed Chinese workers wages or money for services rendered or goods delivered. In Idaho in 1870 four Chinese laborers—known only as Ah Lung, Ah Tung, Ah Hee, and Ah Why—in separate suits sued Robinson, Taylor, and Company for unpaid wages. Given the fact that the company owed, on average, each man only fifteen dollars and that in traditional China civil disputes were settled outside the courts by village or clan leaders, these Chinese plaintiffs had clearly not only become familiar with the U.S. judicial system but had also absorbed the meaning of Western justice.[117]

FAMILY REUNIFICATION DURING THE EXCLUSION ERA

During the exclusion era Chinese Americans also rejected discriminatory treatment through their struggle for family unification, which Chinese deemed vital for the community's long-term survival. Yet until the dawn of the twentieth century these efforts seemed futile. The courts in the habeas corpus cases *In re Ah Quan* (1884) and *In re Ah Moy* (1884) had ruled that the status of wives of Chinese laborers was derivative or followed that of their husbands, and thus they were inadmissible as stated in the 1882 act unless they possessed return certificates—which had to be secured before they left for China (and hence were unobtainable for new female arrivals). But in *United States v. Mrs. Gun Lim* (1900) the court ruled that wives and minor children of Chinese merchants residing in the United States could enter the country without such a document. This victory meant that Chinese Americans, to bring their wives and children into the country, had to acquire merchant status either by pooling resources with others to start businesses or simply by purchasing a "paper" attesting to such status. But the victory was not a resounding one. Immigration authorities in a number of cases still questioned the validity of Chinese marriage customs and the age gap between marital partners.[118]

The struggle for family reunification also encompassed the status of non-citizen wives of U.S. citizens of Chinese ancestry. In 1902 the District Court of Appeals for the Ninth Circuit heard the case of Tsoi Sim who was arrested for deportation on the grounds that she lacked the certificate of residence the Geary Act required. But Tsoi Sim had entered the United States as a child before the Chinese Exclusion Act went into effect, had grown up in the United States, and married an American of Chinese ancestry. The court ruled in favor of the appellant, arguing that when she married she had acquired the right to remain by virtue of her husband's domicile. The ruling had profound implications: any male citizen of Chinese ancestry could now return to China to get married and bring his alien Chinese wife back to America, even if he was a laborer. The loss of civil documents in the wake of the 1906 San Francisco earthquake unwittingly further opened the door: by falsely claiming U.S. citizenship, Chinese men could then bring their spouses into the country. From 1906 the number of Chinese wives of U.S. citizens admitted into America increased each year until 1924, when the number was 396 compared with just 7 in 1906.

The steady climb of family reunions came to a sudden halt with the passage of the 1924 Immigration Act. The legislation was designed mainly to thwart immigration from Eastern and Southern European countries, but it had larger implications for the construction of categories of difference that in turn determined the fortunes of Chinese Americans. The 1924 law sorted Europeans according to nationality and ranked them according to desirability. Yet the law also constructed a white American race, whereby those of European descent shared a common whiteness that separated them from non-whites—thus allowing European immigrants to claim U.S. citizenship (already defined as a black-and-white issue in the 1790 Nationality Act and the Fourteenth Amendment). Conversely, the law conflated ethnic and racial identities for non-European immigrants such as Chinese, Japanese, Filipinos, and Mexicans. The conflation of the two identities suggested a racial logic that determined which people could become Americans and which could not. In the case of Asians, the act condemned them to permanent foreignness—a historical trajectory already determined by the 1882 Chinese Exclusion Act and carried forward by naturalization and land cases in the early 1920s (*Ozawa v. United States* [1922] and *Terrace v. Thompson* [1923] are two examples) in which the court upheld the concept "ineligible to citizenship" for Asians.[119]

The 1924 act constricted Asian inflow through the clause that barred the entry of "any alien ineligible" for citizenship. Since the 1882 act had already denied naturalization for Chinese, immigration officials could now turn away new Chinese arrivals—including spouses of U.S. citizens. In 1924 thirty Chinese wives of merchants and citizens who arrived at San Francisco were refused entry. The Chinese community quickly hired attorneys to appeal. The court ruled that wives of merchants, by virtue of their husbands' occupation, could enter the country. Wives of U.S. citizens of Chinese ancestry, however, did not become citizens when they married and remained ineligible for naturalization. Hence the 1924 Immigration Act can be applied to the latter category of applicants. The decision essentially eliminated one of only two ways by which Chinese wives could join their husbands in the United States. Not surprisingly, between 1925 and 1930 not one woman entered as the wife of a citizen. Given the skewed gender ratio and the illegality of interracial marriage, American-born Chinese who wished to marry and start a family faced considerable hurdles.[120]

Overall, the litigation the Chinese brought before American courts during the late nineteenth century proved that they did not stand idly by while discriminatory laws and the attending violence descended on them. Through these cases Chinese litigants questioned the boundaries of government authority and the rights of citizens and noncitizens and in so doing contributed to the shaping of American democracy and republicanism.

ECONOMIC DISCRIMINATION AND LABOR PROTEST

Chinese immigrants also challenged the United States to live up to its promise of equality and opportunity by resisting economic discrimination through class alliance both within the community and with other ethnic groups. In this way the Chinese rebuked the perception that they were "docile" and "servile."

The story of the Chinese railroad workers' failed strike in 1867, in which they demanded higher wages and shorter hours from the Central Pacific, is well-known. More than 5,000 Chinese railroad builders walked off their jobs, demanding pay and working conditions equal to those of their white co-workers. Less well-known are the cases of agitation among contracted Chinese laborers in the South. The Chinese protested against planters and railroad owners who withheld wages or arbitrarily changed the terms of contracts. In 1870 around 250 Chinese workers filed suit against the Houston and Texas Central Railroad for breach of contract when the company ignored its obligations. Hundreds of Chinese railroad builders seized cars and equipment belonging to the recently bankrupt Alabama and Chattanooga to reinforce their demand for back wages.[121]

Within a year after Chinese men arrived to work in the Belleville, New Jersey, steam laundry plant, they were engaging in strikes and abandoning their jobs. In Beaver Falls, Pennsylvania, Chinese cutlery workers went on strike in 1873 when they discovered that some of them were paid less than other coethnic workers. They also expressed resentment toward the economic domination of the company, one that was exercised through Chinese interpreters. Aware of the growing shortage of Chinese workers following the enforcement of exclusion laws, farm laborers in California in the 1880s and 1890s also struck time and again for higher wages and for recognition of their rights as workers—including advances in pay and better working conditions. The growing consciousness of such rights also extended to Pacific Northwest–bound Chinese salmon workers, who demanded an advance on their wages before boarding the ships departing for the north.[122]

In Hawai'i, in addition to individual acts of violence against bosses and plantation property, in 1891 dissatisfied Chinese workers banded together to protest against misleading expectations in their labor contracts. Nine years later Japanese and Chinese laborers—in a departure from historically rooted interethnic antagonism—collectively struck over the same issue, thus holding out the possibility of forging a class-based consciousness and identity.[123]

Chinese laborers could not seek the support of the white-dominated organized union movement. Except for isolated cases—such as the admittance of Chinese and Japanese miners into United Mine Workers locals in Wyoming in 1907 and failed attempts by the Knights of Labor to organize Chinese laundry workers in New York City in the 1880s and 1890s—Chinese and other Asian laborers were completely excluded from national labor unions. For example, when Chinese cigar workers in San Francisco walked out in 1885, white unions not only offered no help but accused them of being cocky and misguided.[124]

Because of the fragility of institutionalized organizing, Chinese workers—from farmhands in the San Joaquin Valley to plantation laborers in the Deep South—often relied on coethnic labor contractors (who hired workers and supervised the workplace on behalf of white employers) to help them secure the best jobs and offer protection against an employer's oppression. Labor contractors, however, frequently exploited their subordinate coethnics through excessive profits for supplying food and necessities and lucrative commissions for finding them work. Thus coethnic workers became dependent on the contractors, forging tight race-based relationships that precluded the emergence of class consciousness. And so racial solidarity triumphed at the expense of class-based alliances among Chinese workers and other ethnic groups.

CULTURAL IDENTITY OF IMMIGRANT CHINESE

Ethnic solidarity in workplaces, a reaction to racial oppression, contributed to shaping the ethnic consciousness of the immigrant Chinese in North America. But their cultural identity was in fact, to quote Yong Chen, the outcome of a "dialectical relationship between past memories and present experiences, between historical continuity and change, between New World conditions and Old World ties."[125]

The immigrants' awareness of their nationality was rooted in memories of the national history and cultural traditions they had shared with fellow countrypeople in China for centuries. Even though dialects and physical distance contributed to parochialism, the written form of language was the same. A common national past also reinforced the Cantonese immigrants' collective identity; most could trace their families' premigration history to the Song dynasty (960–1279) period when their ancestors began migrating to Guangdong from the north. Certain terms in the Chinese language also reinforced their national identity. In calling themselves the "tang people," or *tangren* (the people of China), Cantonese immigrants were suggesting that they were tied to a period—the Tang dynasty (618–907)—that marked one of the highest points of Chinese civilization. "Tang" historically has also been used to identify the Chinese and China. Chinese immigrants in North America often spoke about "*hui* [return to] *tang*," or "going back to China."[126]

Rich Chinese religious traditions also played a part in honing the collective immigrant identity. Protestant missionaries labored long and hard to acculturate the Chinese. The missionaries saw Christianization as part of the larger attempt to Americanize ethnic minorities. Civilizing these inferior "heathens" was the desired goal; they achieved far less, however. At the end of the nineteenth century, the number of Chinese Christians on the Pacific Coast stood at only around a thousand. Other Chinese who showed up at the mission churches were drawn more to the secular subjects offered at Sunday schools than to the religious teachings. The halting progress of proselytizing the Chinese also resulted from the continuance of eclectic, popular religion among the immigrants. Temples—often called "joss houses" by non-Chinese—dotted the social landscape of Chinese America. Shrines, found in mutual aid associations, were also set up in shops and other establishments. The deities in the shrines and temples—which were also widely worshipped in China—reminded the Chinese immigrants of their national traditions.

The Chinese cultural identity was also seen in the customs and habits that were displayed and celebrated. Chinese-style dress and wearing the queue were visual signals that revealed Old World Chinese sentiments and sensibilities. Chinese New Year was another opportunity to display cultural distinctiveness; lighting lanterns, setting off firecrackers, and beating drums and gongs as lion dances were performed marked the Chinese as "other" in the eyes of the dominant society yet also indicated resistance to the white pressure to conform.

Meanwhile, the exclusion laws led to a sharp plunge in the Chinese population—from a high of 105,465 in 1880 to a low of 61,639 in 1920.[127] This dramatic decline in just forty years is unprecedented in the history of American ethnic groups. Furthermore, by 1920 exclusion laws, by hindering entry and family formation, had resulted in a community of mostly middle-aged men, with foreign-born males outnumbering men who were citizens well into the World War II era.[128] Such facts—coupled with a heavily male-dominated culture, a history of economic and social discrimination, a legacy of white-inflicted violence, and a high degree of cultural difference between Chinese and the Euro-American society—likely explain the slow acculturation of the Chinese. Still, the Chinese discovered that their lives and the communities they built would nevertheless be subjected to the forces of Americanization, Christianization, and China-centered nationalism. Their pursuit for the right of U.S. citizenship became dialectically linked to their country of origin and its fortunes.

3 Nationalism and Americanization Before 1945

Even though the indefinite 1904 extension of exclusion laws stymied the flow of immigration from Asia to America, sociopolitical and economic life in Chinese American communities continued to develop and even flourish, thereby refuting the supposedly pervasive impact of assimilation on Chinese immigrants and their offspring. Their ethnicity persisted as a source of group identity and solidarity. Although Americanization and, to some degree, Christianity did shape their fortunes and selfhoods, equally important were the countervailing forces of China-centered nationalism and racial exclusion. These conflicting forces sometimes created ambivalence regarding the community's self-identity and its relationship to the larger body politic even as they reinvented Chinese immigrants—through a continuous, multifaceted nonlinear process—into Chinese Americans.

An early example of that process was the large-scale 1905 boycott of American goods in China, which represented an outburst of Chinese frustration with foreign imperialism and also sprang from events in the United States.

Chinese Americans, since about 1900, had considered that these events were leading up to an organized effort to eliminate them. The 1904 law that set aside all treaty provisions and the 1905 *Ju Toy* decision upholding the Bureau of Immigration's right to carry out arbitrary deportations were ominous signs of an impending fate. More troubling was the 1903 Boston Chinatown raid, ostensibly conducted to force procrastinating Chinese to register in accordance with the provisions of the Geary Act of 1892. The real intent, however, was to eliminate the Chinese presence, as evidenced by subsequent deportations and relocations.[1]

By the early 1900s a China-oriented political consciousness had permeated the Chinese American society to some degree. The humiliating defeat of China in the Sino-Japanese War of 1894–1895, the botched 1898 "Hundred Days' Reforms" (designed to speed China's modernization), the expanding European economic imperialism in Asia, the continual discrimination against Chinese immigrants in America, and the sociopolitical changes occurring in Chinese America awakened dormant nationalist sentiments in Chinese at home and abroad.[2]

Ardent critics of the Qing government had made their way to America since the turn of the century to establish parties to promote their respective political agendas. Baohuanghui, or Protect the Emperor Society (its name was later changed to Chinese Constitutional Party), established in 1899 in Vancouver by reformer Kang Youwei, sought to establish a constitutional monarchy in China. The party competed for Chinese American support with Xingzhonghui (Revive China Society, later renamed Tongmenghui), founded in Honolulu in 1895 by Sun Yat-sen, proponent of a republican form of government for China. Chinese Americans—whose efforts became part of a larger overseas Chinese politicization—soon offered monetary contributions, financed China-based commercial ventures to modernize the homeland, disseminated propaganda in North America, and organized a military academy in California to train men for subversive work in China. In turn, beginning in the early 1900s in Hawai'i and in the 1930s on the mainland, both parties funded Chinese schools as a means of achieving modernization in China, although nationalist sentiments often pervaded the curricula. They also printed newspapers in the United States that served as their mouthpieces, helping thus to maintain the loyalty of their followers.

Branches of both parties mushroomed in major Chinatowns in North America, Hawai'i, and eventually China and Southeast Asia. By the 1911 Chinese Revolution, Baohuanghui had thirty-seven chapters in the United States, and Tongmenghui had twenty-seven. The rivalry between the two parties for the allegiance of Chinese Americans split the community. Often, Baohuanghui attracted moderate elements such as established merchants and traditional intellectuals, whereas the revolutionary movement elicited support from small shopkeepers, workers, and Western-influenced intellectuals. The competition became less intense when the Qing dynasty toppled in 1911, dashing the hopes of monarchists. The tensions within the community notwithstanding, the activities of the parties politicized Chinese Americans, encouraging them to abandon provincialism in favor of nationalism.

In general, the political freedom Chinese in the United States enjoyed allowed the political parties to develop unhindered. By comparison, branches of the parties in Southeast Asia faced limited tolerance from colonial powers and independent Thailand that would harden into repression. These powers feared political mobilization would pit Chinese against indigenous peoples and threaten commerce with Japan, which had invaluable investments in the region. The Chinese government's theory that nationality followed the *jus sanguinis* (a child's country of citizenship is the same as that of his or her parents) and not the *jus soli* (a child's country of citizenship is that of his or her birth, a belief the Qing dynasty had expressed in the 1909 Chinese Nationality Act), coupled with aggressive nationalist activities among Chinese residents, seemed to suggest to authorities in Malaya, Indonesia, Thailand, and the Philippines that China wanted to form an imperium in imperio. By the 1930s, schools faced operating restrictions, publications were being censored, and organizations went underground.[3]

In the United States the Guomindang, which replaced Tongmenghui, was less visible in the larger society and thus drew little adverse reaction from the U.S. government. Chinese Communist elements, which were organized in Southeast Asia and thus elicited vigilance from those governments, were diffused into small leftist organizations in the United States that drew little bureaucratic attention. The shift of mainstream American attention from the Chinese to the Japanese "menace" following the indefinite ban on Chinese immigration in 1904 also facilitated ethnic mobilization.

TRADITIONAL COMMUNITY ORGANIZATIONS

By the early twentieth century internal turmoil within the Chinese American community had also prepared the way for mobilization. Until 1900, leaders of Sanyi origin (Sanyi, or Three Districts, refers to the Nanhai, Panyu, and Shunde districts in Guangdong), because of their economic dominance in the community, controlled the ethnic political leadership through the Zhonghua Zong Huiguan, or Chinese Consolidated Benevolent Association (CCBA)—better known as the Chinese Six Companies.[4]

As an umbrella organization for district associations, the CCBA, loosely established in the early 1860s and formalized in 1882, galvanized a sense of community that crossed clan and regional lines and provided a collective response to anti-Chinese agitation. Until the first Chinese legation was established in Washington, D.C., in 1878, the CCBA operated as the diplomatic representative for the Chinese in America. Since most Chinese were still foreign born and had yet to plant roots in the United States, the CCBA often justified its fight against racial oppression on the grounds of defending treaty rights, and it demanded hospitality and reciprocity in accordance with China's sovereignty.[5]

Serving as the mouthpiece of the Chinese community and buttressed by the explicit support of the Qing government, the CCBA dominated the internal affairs of Chinatowns. It settled disputes between associations, contested or sought relief from anti-Chinese laws, acted as a clearinghouse for fund-raising projects, and protected merchants' class interests. For example, the CCBA witnessed changes of ownership and property sales and oversaw the credit-ticket system. The power the CCBA wielded attested to Chinese immigrants' need for intracommunity governance, given their exclusion from the political sphere. The same need also prompted the Chinese in Hawai'i to form an organization similar to the CCBA called the United Chinese Society. In the absence of a Chinese consul on the islands, the society settled disputes, managed the credit-ticket system, offered disaster relief, and served as the voice of local Chinese.

Below the CCBA were the benevolent regional and district (or native place) associations, or *huiguan*, in which membership was determined by accident of birth. The two earliest, most influential *huiguan* were the Sanyi huiguan (Sam Yup Association) and Siyi huiguan (Sze Yup Association). These included people from the same region or district of origin who often spoke closely related Cantonese subdialects. A small minority that spoke Hakka had a separate organization; the earliest was the Renhe huiguan (Yan Wo Benevolent Association) founded in San Francisco in the 1850s. Other organizations of non-Cantonese immigrants did not appear until the twentieth century when more non-Guangdong immigrants, such as those from the Fuzhou area and Hainan Island, began arriving.

Visible in America since 1851, a *huiguan*—similar to those in China— erected temples for the performance of sacrificial rites, shipped the bones of the deceased back to China and managed the U.S. cemeteries, provided medical services, and established Chinese schools to teach a China-oriented curriculum. One of the earliest schools was the Nam Kue Chinese School in San Francisco, founded by the Nam Hoy Fook Yum Benevolent Society in 1920. *Huiguan* leaders also mediated personal or business disputes between members. The *huiguan* in the United States were not exact replicas of those in China. The U.S. *huiguan* were immigrant organizations that functioned in a hostile environment; they must be viewed within the context of the exclusion of Chinese in cities and towns. Consequently, these *huiguan* adapted and served uniquely American functions. One of these functions, which indicates the merchant class's control of leadership, was to check the number of defaulting debtors who were absconding—mostly linked to the credit-ticket system—by issuing an exit permit. Without the permit, debtors could not purchase a ticket back to China. A second unique aspect of the U.S. *huiguan* was the organization of the CCBA to muster collective strength. By the 1890s, as many as 95 percent of the Chinese in North America belonged to *huiguan*, attesting to their pervasive influence.

Related mutual aid organizations, which included surname or family associations, enrolled members of a common surname without regard to locality of origin. These included the numerically large Li (Lee), Huang (Wong), and Chee (Chinn) groups. These associations could also enroll several surnames as was the case with the Longgongtang (Loong Kong Association), also called the Four Brothers' Association. In the United States, surname associations—which did not require close blood ties—were more visible than clan or lineage associations, which were organized on the basis of an extensive kinship network with members living in the same area. Because the Chinese populace in the early years remained largely immigrant and semitransient, such networks rarely existed in North America. Present in the United States by around the 1870s, the surname associations provided charitable services akin to those of the *huiguan* and sometimes even offered protection to members threatened by tongs, or secret societies.

Far smaller in size, usually made up of no more than fifty people, were the *gongsi fang* (also known in Cantonese as *fong*), composed of patrilineal kinsfolk descended from a common paternal ancestor or people who hailed from the same village. The *gongsi fang* offered temporary lodging, provided social centers, and acted as a source for business loans. Because the exclusion era did not end until 1943, the camaraderie offered by *fang* activities served as a substitute for family life. Not surprisingly, *gongsi fang* disappeared following repeal of Chinese exclusion laws, although surname associations continue to exist today.[6]

The Chinatown organizations perhaps best known to Euro-Americans are the fighting tongs, a special kind of secret society. Established as early as 1852, these structured, exclusive socioeconomic organizations struggled for political and economic power within the community. Often pitted against one another and also against the CCBA, tongs sometimes resorted to open warfare to settle scores. They took control of or played a role in running Chinese vice businesses—gambling saloons, brothels, and opium dens. Limited employment opportunities and a low level of acculturation—all products of the anti-Chinese movement—drew Chinese immigrants to these organizations.

These tongs, however, must be differentiated from another group of secret societies that—like tongs—also traced their origins to the Triads, or Sanheihui, which originally formed in southern China to spearhead an anti-Qing movement. In the United States Triad lodges—including such prominent ones as Binggongtang (Bing Kung Tong), Anliangtang (On Leong Tong), and Xieshengtang (Hip Sing Tong)—federated loosely as Zhigongtang, or Chee Kung Tong, and soon attracted many disfranchised Chinese laborers, Chinese Christians, and struggling, middle-ranking merchants.

The composition of the lodges suggests their protective nature. Sidelined by the wealthy, powerful merchants who controlled the *huiguan*, laborers, Christians, and small-time merchants gravitated to secret societies for security and employment. Chinese who wished to enter America in violation of anti-immigration legislation came to rely on these secret societies (and sometimes the surname associations). In this sense the perpetuation of these societies was an outcome of restrictive immigration laws. Triad lodges, fighting tongs, surname associations, and *huiguan* were not mutually exclusive, however; an immigrant could and often did belong to all four organizations. Because of the political legacy and its marginalized image, secret societies proved invaluable allies for mainland Chinese political leaders looking for agents to help disseminate their propaganda.

Augmenting the complexity of the social fabric were the conservative merchant guilds, which had only a marginal role in shaping the early fortunes of the community. Later, within the context of the rising nationalist response to Western trade competition in Asia, by 1910 Chinese chambers of commerce sprung up in major Chinatowns and eventually absorbed the early merchant guilds. Two leading guilds found in cities with Chinese communities were the Zhaoyi gongsuo (Shew Hing Association) for Sanyi merchants and the Siyi-dominated Keshang huiguan (Guest Businessmen's Association).

Far more influential, especially after 1900, were the exclusively male occupational guilds, such as those that drew together cigar makers or laundry workers and that often challenged the authority of the CCBA and *huiguan*. Guilds sometimes monitored workplace conditions and often barred nonguild members from gaining employment in certain industries. In general, guilds, secret societies, and fighting tongs had open membership requirements and, by nature, promoted some economic mobility.

Despite the proliferation of social organizations in Chinese America, the CCBA remained the most powerful. Its Sanyi leaders—drawn from the minority segment of the Chinese populace—lost credibility, however, when they failed to counter the Geary Act. The community leaders of Siyi origins (Xinhui, Taishan, Kaiping, and Enping districts), who made up almost two-thirds of the Chinese populace in America, now found an opening to challenge Sanyi leadership. Boycotts of Sanyi businesses ensued, and soon the tong wars broke out.

AMERICANIZATION, EQUAL RIGHTS, AND THE 1905 BOYCOTT

Also competing for Chinese Americans' attention by the turn of the century was a tiny but vocal Chinese Christian community—estimated at 2 percent of the total population in 1892—that grew out of Chinese missions established mostly by Protestant lay missionary organizations. In small Chinese American communities Chinese missions, in the absence of district and clan associations, stepped into the latter's role and functioned in several ways to acclimatize newcomers to the new environment; they offered English classes, living quarters, and social centers rolled into one. In sizable Chinatowns, Chinese Christians jostled with traditional organizations for potential converts. Chinese Christians rejected the elitist, conservative nature of the ethnic political leadership and embraced more Western-oriented political ideals. Some of the strongest supporters of efforts to topple the Qing monarchy were Chinese Protestants. Chinese Christian churches in America served as sanctuaries where Sun Yat-sen and his followers took rest, promoted the revolution, and raised money. Convinced that the U.S. democratic values, republican government, and modern way of life had developed as a result of Christian influence, they tried to move China down that road. In part because of a stance that extolled the lifestyle of a society that discriminated against Chinese immigrants and in part because their fellow Chinese saw them as insufficiently "Chinese," the Chinese Christians were marginalized in Chinatowns. They had to band together for mutual support and soon established their own schools, missions, churches, and presses.[7]

Through Reverend Wu Panzhao, more commonly known as Ng Poon Chew—a prolific local journalist and lecturer—Chinese Christians vocalized their political consciousness in Ng's daily newspaper, the *Chung Sai Yat Po* (CSYP), the leading Chinese-language paper in the early-twentieth-century United States. The San Francisco–based newspaper's editorials called for an anti-Manchu revolt in China and linked it to the Chinese struggle for equal rights in America. In the early 1900s Reverend Ng embarked on several nationwide speaking tours, trying to make a case for Chinese contributions to the well-being of America and thus for the need for immigration reform.[8] In 1900, when San Francisco residents blamed the Chinese for a rumored bubonic plague and the entire Chinatown area was quarantined, leading Chinese Christians—taking advantage of a divided CCBA—led the charge to end the demonization. Overall, through these efforts Chinese Christians gradually established a tenuous credibility within the community.[9]

Against the backdrop of race-based agitation, the call for a boycott of U.S. goods in 1905 in Canton and Shanghai evoked a swift response from the Chinese in the United States, whose resentment of the years of ill treatment turned into outright anger. Reports of the harassment of Chinese arrivals in 1904 and 1905 that included the exempt classes of merchants, tourists, and students and guests of both the Louisiana and St. Louis expositions (designed to promote trade, commerce, and local tourism) and the fairs in Omaha and Atlanta galvanized Chinese to act. The boycott, which lasted nearly a year and drew support from all major Chinese organizations—including the Zhigongtang, Chinese Christians, and native-born Chinese Americans under the aegis of the Zhuyue Zongju (Anti-Treaty Society)—represented a significant departure from the previous emphasis on judicial or diplomatic recourse. The boycott lost steam, however, when the Qing government, buckling under pressure from U.S. authorities, chose to retract its support.[10]

Nevertheless, the boycott checked certain blatant abuses: raids of Chinatowns became a thing of the past, the processing time for new immigrants was shortened, calls for a more stringent registration process abated, and the momentum to expel all Chinese residents was halted. The slight turn of fortunes was also reflected in the immigration statistics: in 1905, 29 percent of immigration certificates approved by American consuls in China were rejected; the following year only 6 percent were rejected.

The failure of the boycott to reverse the anti-immigration laws, however, reinforced Chinese Americans' sense of inferiority. Strengthening China through evolutionary or revolutionary change could improve the fate of the Chinese in America, but some of those engaged in China-centered nationalism also experienced conflicting loyalties to both China and the United States.

One fledgling organization that may have understood the dilemma of this duality was the Chinese American Citizens Alliance (CACA). Founded in 1895 in San Francisco and originally named the United Parlor of the Native Sons of the Golden State (NSGS), the group attracted both native-born and naturalized Chinese Americans whose worldview was shaped by U.S. education and exposure to Euro-American culture. The group's visibility grew during the exclusion era. In 1900 about 11 percent of the Chinese in the United States were native born; the figure had increased to 52 percent by 1940.[11]

Derisively labeled *juk sing* (literally, in Cantonese, the hollow part of a bamboo stalk but implying "empty" or "useless") by foreign-born Chinese because of their supposedly shallow understanding of traditional Chinese culture, some American-born Chinese objected to the homeland orientation of the traditional associations, which seemed to hinder acceptance by the larger society. In their mind, the continual discrimination against all Chinese stemmed from a miscarriage of Americanization. The cause célèbre for direct action came in the form of the controversial 1892 Geary Act. Chinese Americans realized that the legislation violated their rights as U.S. citizens, and in 1892 a group in New York City formed the Chinese Equal Rights League to raise the community's political awareness and prepare a test case before the U.S. Supreme Court.

The origins of this effort can be traced to Wong Chin Foo, an early proponent of modernity in China. Wanted by the Qing government for preaching so-called heretical beliefs, Wong fled to America in 1873. Arriving at the height of the anti-Chinese agitation, Wong took to the lecture circuit. In his talks before Euro-American audiences and later in his published writings, including those in his short-lived newspaper, *Chinese American* (Wong was one of the earliest to use the phrase, signifying his desire to be recognized as an American), he tried to eliminate cultural misunderstanding of the Chinese. When he realized that the misunderstanding was the root cause of racial prejudice, he devoted his energies to educating Americans about the virtues of Chinese culture and customs.

In 1884, two years after the passage of the virulent Chinese Exclusion Act, Wong and a group of naturalized Chinese Americans organized what may have been the first Chinese voter registration association in the United States to increase Chinese participation and influence in U.S. politics. But their efforts came to naught. A Chinese community divided by clan, geographic origins, and dialect—coupled with the exclusion of the Chinese from naturalization (as stated in the 1882 law)—derailed their efforts.

Wong and his compatriots moved from raising political consciousness to securing equal rights after passage of the Geary Act unleashed a furor within the Chinese community. The Chinese Equal Rights League, the organization they had formed, departed from the CCBA's conciliatory approach to interracial relations. Unlike the CCBA, whose writings and petitions against anti-Chinese outrages often took a defensive tone, the Equal Rights League adopted an aggressive posture. It demanded that the United States live up to its banner of democracy and that Chinese be accorded equal rights, including suffrage. Although these early efforts bore no tangible fruit, they did inspire others—including those in the NSGS/CACA—to build on Wong's pioneering role in the Chinese civil rights movement.

On the West Coast, nearly a third of the San Francisco Chinese populace quickly became members of the NSGS/CACA, and over the next several decades it expanded to other cities within and outside California—with local lodges in Oakland, Los Angeles, Chicago, Detroit, Boston, Pittsburgh, and Portland, Oregon. The organization's commitment to assimilation reflected the class affiliation of its membership—which included professionals, white-collar workers, and businesspeople—most of whom had at least a high school education.

Before the 1930s the males-only CACA (women were not admitted until 1976) scored some successes on the political front. It blocked an attempt in 1913 to disfranchise Chinese Americans. Then it took on the provisions of the 1924 National Origins Act. The law, along with the court's decision in 1925 to apply the "alien ineligible to citizenship" clause to wives of U.S. citizens, effectively narrowed the already small opening for Chinese female immigration.

The CACA fought back, arguing through its spokesperson and attorney Y. C. Hong that the new law unfairly separated conjugal partners, stalled family formation, and perpetuated split households. Chinese men were already barred from marrying Caucasian women by antimiscegenation laws passed in as many as fourteen states, with California's law in place as early as 1850. Further discouraged by the 1922 Cable Act, which denied a woman (including an American-born Chinese) U.S. citizenship if she married a Chinese alien, a Chinese man now had to go to China to marry a woman whom he could see only infrequently.

To capture support for its arguments, CACA mounted a vigorous lobbying campaign. It secured letters of support from prominent U.S. citizens including Ray Lyman Wilbur, president of Stanford University, and Nicholas Murray Butler, president of Columbia University. The CACA circulated its pamphlet to members of Congress. When called to testify before the House of Representatives, CACA leaders stressed that a U.S. citizen's domicile should also be his wife's. In a nod to past Yellow Peril fears, they assured the congresspeople that the entry of Chinese women would not increase job competition with white workers. The presence of Chinese women would preserve family units and preempt the need for interracial marriages.

Congress, in reaction to the arguments, amended the legislation in 1930 so that Chinese alien wives of Chinese citizens who were married before May 26, 1924, could legally enter the United States. As a result of this amendment, an average of sixty Chinese women each year between 1931 and 1941 entered the United States as citizens' wives.[12]

In addition to the fight against discriminatory legislation, CACA also tried to foster a more positive image of Chinese in the United States through its antidefamation efforts. Sensationalist Yellow Peril literature that presented erroneous statements about the Chinese became one of its targets. Another effort to promote incorporation of the Chinese into the larger society involved the campaign for equal educational opportunities in public schools, which highlighted the injustice of segregated facilities. "Segregation does not make for good citizenship," said attorney Kenneth Fung, an officer of CACA. "Our children, born here . . . should not be subjected to a humiliation that would only breed discontent."[13] Finally, CACA offered English-language classes as a means of Americanizing foreign-born Chinese. Overall, CACA served as a vehicle for members to highlight their U.S. patriotism and citizenship through peaceful and legal means of resolving injustices.

Notwithstanding its call for Americanization, CACA joined the 1905 boycott, which united the community but also polarized it. The Baohuanghui, *huiguan*, merchant guilds, and CCBA—the faction in favor of constitutional reform in China—backed the demand that the United States admit all Chinese except laborers. Opposing that view were those who favored revolution in China and the admittance of all Chinese, including laborers; they included the Xingzhonghui, Triad lodges, Chinese Christians, and American-born Chinese Americans. When the boycott failed to elicit the espoused aims, each faction blamed the other for the failure.[14]

Still, China-centered politics in North America did blunt the sense of regionalism and clan affiliation and concomitantly sharpened ideological commitment. By 1912 rivalries between various social organizations had been redefined in political terms. Zhigongtang and Triad lodges tended to see themselves as champions of the common man; the *huiguan* backed a type of oligarchy of the wealthy and the educated. Because the *huiguan* were conservative, they tended to support the reform-oriented Baohuanghui; the Zhigongtang and Triad lodges, however, were inclined to back the revolutionary politics of Tongmenghui.[15] Class lines loomed large overall and remained so for the rest of the early twentieth century. The failure of the 1911 Chinese Revolution to secure full democracy also meant that political consensus within the Chinese American community remained elusive.

NATIONALISM AND THE CHINESE AMERICAN IDENTITY

Despite such conflict, nationalism was strong enough to initiate some social change. By the 1910s a far broader segment of the Chinese population in America had become interested in anti-imperialistic politics, which led in part to an identity transformation for those Chinese. When fused with Chinese Americans' racial contacts in the United States, China-centered nationalism gave momentum to the forging of a Chinese American identity.[16]

In the years before 1911—prior to the outbreak of the Chinese Revolution that toppled the Qing dynasty—a failure to truly comprehend Sun Yat-sen's revolutionary ideology, coupled with a mass Chinese American psychology that favored obedience and eschewed rebellion, limited the popularity of Sun's ideology among those Chinese. Chinese Americans' moral and financial support for the Tongmenghui prior to 1911 was disappointing, an outcome of the tepid support for the pro-Qing CCBA and the Chinese Chamber of Commerce. As a result, Tongmenghui members in the United States focused on portraying the Manchus as foreign and emphasized the need to overthrow the Qing dynasty, a goal in line with the Zhigongtang's traditional political aim. But the Zhigongtang in the United States was quite different from that in Asia; in the former it functioned less as a renegade political body and more as an organization to offer immigrants protection, employment opportunities, business networks, and mutual aid.

According to Shehong Chen, the reflections of Ng Poon Chew's newspaper, the CSYP, on the currents of Chinese nationalism were more in line with the emerging Chinese American cultural sensibility. The route to restore China's sovereignty, the paper argued, lay in embracing capitalism and adopting humanitarian morals. Chinese Americans could play their part by investing in China's rich untapped resources. The Chinese in America could combat discrimination in the United States by adopting Western education and discarding outmoded practices such as idol worship. The CSYP's vision of China's future, as well as its understanding of the relationship between Chinese Americans and China, "showed the diasporic dimensions of Chinese American nationalism and new meanings of Chineseness."[17]

The efforts of Chinese American women echoed what the CSYP extolled. Educated Chinese American women in New York City organized literacy programs to "uplift" coethnics in the working class. They also participated in the liberty loan campaigns during World War I. They raised funds to initiate the Chinese Boy Scouts of New York. Chinese women also joined the China Society of America, a Sino-American friendship association based in New York. The formation of the Chinese Young Women's Christian Association in 1918 marked a milestone: not only was it the first Chinese American women's social and educational organization in New York City, but its activities politicized women to appreciate their dual allegiance to both China and the United States. Some of this activism was spearheaded by Chinese female students who came to the United States in the early twentieth century. Inspired by the mounting sentiment for reform, they sought knowledge to cure an ailing China.[18]

Chinese Americans showed support for the successful October 10, 1911, Wuchang uprising that led to the rise of the Chinese republic the following year. They wrote letters to foreign governments to lobby for support, bought military bonds, and raised funds for China's Red Cross; Chinese women also sewed clothing for soldiers. Chinese American women in New York City staged musical performances conveying nationalist themes. Yet the tensions between Chinese traditional values and the diasporic consciousness and environment—as reflected in the tepid CCBA support for Sun Yat-sen and CSYP's call for an American-oriented identity for Chinese—had yet to be resolved. With the birth of the Chinese republic, Chinese American support for Sun Yat-sen wavered even more. The credibility of the Guomindang (the new name of the Tongmenghui starting in 1912) plummeted with the botched anti-Yuan Second Revolution in 1913. Following the lead of community elites, Chinese Americans now pinned their hopes on Yuan Shikai, president of the Republic of China. They wanted to see a strong and stable China. Instead, the country was plunged into domestic turmoil, which Chinese Americans blamed on the Guomindang. Between 1912 and 1914 Chinese in the United States played their role in defending China's fragile independence by donating money to the beleaguered Yuan government.[19]

But the Chinese American identity also responded to the changing circumstances in the United States. The Chinese responded enthusiastically to the 1912 establishment of the first Chinese Young Men's Christian Association in San Francisco, billed as an educational-*cum*-recreational facility that would enable the young men to learn skills and morals they could contribute to the homeland but that also would allow them to fight racial prejudice and segregation in America. The Chinese community demonstrated an even stronger growing consciousness of their minority status in the United States when they collectively expressed outrage at the 1912 Dillingham Bill that gave federal authorities wide latitude to strip Chinese Americans and their dependents of their exempt status and deport them. The family could be deported in the case of a divorce or the death of a merchant. Following an intense campaign to turn the tide by emphasizing the rights of Chinese Americans as citizens or legal residents of the United States, the bill failed to become law. The same response greeted a 1914 proposal by U.S. immigration authorities to register all Chinese residents in the country. The proposal threatened to single out "paper sons," or those who did not belong to the exempt categories. Moreover, Chinese objected to the race-specific nature of this registration; other immigrants were not singled out, only the Chinese. The Chinese rejection of the registration proposal forced immigration authorities to shelve the idea.

By the end of 1914, as ethnic minority consciousness was evolving, Chinese in America were becoming disenchanted with Yuan, who was a dictator de facto. Japan's outrageous 1915 "Twenty-One Demands" on China threatened Chinese sovereignty and sparked an anti-Japanese boycott that the Yuan government—much to its citizens' dismay—discouraged. This boycott of Japanese goods, led and participated in by non-elites, marked to some degree the loosening of the power of the CCBA and the *huiguan*. In Chicago, the Chinese organized a Chinese National Salvation Association to stop the Chinese government from selling China out to Japan. Smaller bodies were formed in Cincinnati, New York City, Los Angeles, and San Francisco. The boycott, however, ran into a stumbling block: Chinese businesspeople, particularly those in the West, were often involved in trade with Japanese in America. In the interest of maintaining their livelihoods, some Chinese resorted to traditional expressions of patriotism, including making donations for military preparedness and writing letters of support for the Chinese government. The political elite prevailed in the end, but not entirely. Chinese in America refused to buy national bonds the Yuan government sold. Distrust of Chinese politics ran deep, even as patriotism remained intense.

That patriotism, along with a strong awareness of their marginalized status in the United States, fed into the Chinese dismay over the outdated Chinese exhibition halls at the 1915 Panama Pacific International Exposition in San Francisco. The image of a modern China populated by westernized people was nonexistent. Even as Chinese in America blamed the Yuan government for mishandling the project, they confronted an equally damaging representation of Chinese life: the exposition featured a "chamber of horrors" section that portrayed Chinatown as an area filled with addicts, opium smokers, and gamblers. The sinister, barbaric Chinese image reared its ugly head again. Outraged, Chinese leaders tried to shut the exposition down, but to no avail.

The evolving transcultural and transnational identity among Chinese in America reached a new height with their 1915 communitywide support of the Chinese American–owned China Mail Steamship Company that provided trans-Pacific service for passengers and cargo. A modern venture, the company was owned by Chinese American stockholders of all backgrounds who had refused to accept the Yuan government's invitation to establish a joint venture with Americans.

Between 1916 and 1924, as republicanism in China unraveled and the country plunged into warlordism, Chinese in the United States became even more committed to republicanism as the basis of a modern China. The plan to turn over German rights in Shandong to Japan after World War I sparked the iconoclastic May Fourth Movement in China in 1919, but as with the issue of republicanism, Chinese Americans remained out of step with changes in China. They held onto Confucianism and traditional Chinese cultural values even as the intelligentsia in China deemed them obstacles to progress. Yet throughout this period the Chinese in America strongly believed capitalism would produce a modern and thriving China. Some Chinese in the United States also pushed for inclusion of selected Christian values in shaping a modern China and defining a Chinese American identity.

The rising tide of strengthening China through modernization and democracy swept Chinese Americans along with it. But Chinese Americans fashioned their own cultural sensibility that was different from the one in China. In reflecting on their "place" in America, they drew from an idealized Chinese culture but accommodated the norms of mainstream U.S. culture. Christian and non-Christian Chinese closed ranks as the former became more critical of American civilization and the latter the debilitated social conditions of Chinatowns. Barbaric practices inflicted on women—such as foot binding, arranged marriages, polygamy, and prostitution—came under fire. Between 1900 and 1920 the CSYP featured numerous editorials and articles arguing that women's emancipation would promote equal rights for all Chinese in America. Educated Chinese Americans also denounced smoking opium and wearing queues and promoted progressive reform in Chinatowns and education, as well as integration into the larger U.S. society.[20]

Paralleling these efforts were attempts by CACA to deflect the crushing blows to family reunification dealt by the 1924 Immigration Act, as discussed earlier. The attempts revealed how critical the second generation was of American democracy, yet they also dispelled any perception that the Chinese were disinterested in making America their home. Another instance of Chinese resistance to racial oppression, as well as their commitment to be part of U.S. society, was their reaction to a proposed 1924 California bill that would have regulated the manufacture and sale of herbal medicine, as well as forced Chinese herbal doctors to secure a license from a state board of medical examiners. Chinese herbal doctors and stores that sold such medicine quickly marshaled a counterattack to defeat the bill. They sought the support of American-born Chinese, including those in CACA, Chinese churches, the CCBA, the Chinese Chamber of Commerce, and major Chinese-language newspapers. The bill was eventually withdrawn. That success, along with the mobilization to defeat the 1924 act, showed that the Chinese in the United States could claim their rights and yet take pride in their Chinese cultural heritage.

GILDED GHETTOS

Against this backdrop of rising ethnic pride, by the early 1910s major Chinatowns had witnessed a facelift as opium smoking, gambling dens, and brothels—which became synonymous with outmoded ways—entered a long decline even as Chinese leaders encouraged the growing tourist trade that capitalized on the supposedly exotic nature of "Orientalism." San Francisco's Chinatown best illustrated this process. In 1890 the San Francisco Board of Supervisors passed the Bingham Ordinance, which would have relocated Chinatown to an area set aside for slaughterhouses, hog factories, and other businesses considered prejudicial to public health and comfort. The courts ruled, however, that institutionalizing residential segregation was unconstitutional.[21]

Meanwhile, Chinese residents were still demonized as lazy opium addicts, grotesque lepers, syphilitic weaklings, and immoral prostitutes. The Chinese afflictions, whites believed, could undermine the heterosexual domesticity that privileged companionate marriage and reproduction of healthy citizens. Given their understanding that San Francisco's Chinatown constituted a medical menace, local authorities were quick to blame the Chinese for the bubonic plague in 1900, ascribing it to their naturally defective bodies. Such medical scapegoating was not limited to San Francisco's Chinese. Chinatowns in Honolulu and Vancouver, British Columbia, had similar experiences. Blaming the Chinese for the bubonic plague in 1900, authorities in Honolulu set Chinatown on fire, destroying 4,000 homes and leaving 4,500 people homeless. The U.S. Public Health Service ordered its officials to pressure Pacific Coast cities to contain the threat of epidemic diseases lurking in Chinatowns. In Vancouver an 1890 panic over cholera sent health officials into ten years of close surveillance of Chinatown that climaxed with the dismantling of rows of Chinese dwellings. As the conflation of race and place, Chinatowns seemingly offered the illusion of boundaries within which epidemic diseases could be contained.[22]

In response to such racial geography, Chinese American communities took steps to reconstruct Chinatown's image. After the 1906 earthquake, city leaders in San Francisco, taking advantage of the destruction of Chinatown, again threatened to move it to the city's outskirts. Leading Chinese merchants realized that they had to shatter Chinatown's slumlike image. To that end, a gilded "Oriental City" soon emerged—pagodas and falsely curved "Oriental" roofs began to dot the skyline, Chinese pageantry was revived, and thousands of light bulbs transformed Chinatown into a fantasyland. Tourists who visited this and other Chinatowns, which underwent similar changes, could satisfy their curiosity about Chinese culture at the endless curio and gift shops and partake of unusual delectables in chop suey and chow mein restaurants.[23]

In Vancouver, by the turn of the century merchants were fighting back by putting responsibility on authorities' doorsteps. They appealed to City Hall for neighborhood improvement. They also urged the authorities to break up houses of prostitution, opium dens, and gambling houses. In 1936 an exotic "Chinese Village," complete with a bamboo arch tower, opened in the heart of Chinatown, ushering in an era of commodified ethnic tourism.[24]

In Los Angeles the block-long China City, the brainchild of white entrepreneurs, opened for business in 1938. It was a tourist-oriented showplace complete with moon doors, rickshaws, paper lanterns, joss houses, and a re-creation of China's Great Wall. Oriental gift shops, chop suey restaurants, and fortune tellers lined the narrow, winding streets and open courts. Less exotic but no less commercial was the new Los Angeles Chinatown that emerged on another site in the late 1930s after city fathers decided that the old neighborhood was too decrepit and seedy and that the land was needed for a new railway terminal. But the new Chinatown was also the product of Chinese initiative. Led by second-generation, college-educated Peter Soo Hoo, Chinese Angelenos established an association to develop the new community, which featured modern concrete buildings and wide, open streets devoid of gambling dens and houses of prostitution. A five-tier pagoda completed the makeover.[25]

During the prohibition era tourists who patronized some of the more elegant Chinese restaurants in New York City not only could gawk at faux "Oriental" interiors but could also dance to live music. Later, during the Great Depression—as a way to drum up business during those trying times—Chinese entrepreneurs opened nightclubs that featured cabaret-style entertainment, which capitalized on whites' fascination with the seductive, submissive "China doll" image of Chinese women.[26] Of the many highlights in Chinatowns, the most eagerly anticipated were the sensationalized tours of underground tunnels filled with fake opium dens, gambling joints, brothels, and sometimes mock "tong wars" over slave girls. The manufactured image of sin and evil, combined with the spectacle of the exotic, became the prime lure for non-Chinese tourists.[27]

But Chinatown was more than just a voyeuristic tourist attraction. This ethnic neighborhood served as home and community for those living in a strange land. Racially excluded from the suburbs, they had to put up with overcrowded conditions and decrepit buildings in downtown districts. Only Chinese lived in these neighborhoods, although some Eastern European immigrants and a few Irish women (married to Chinese men) lived in the Chinatowns in Boston and New York. In New York's Chinatown, where in 1940 the gender ratio was still six to one compared with San Francisco's two to one, Chinese men lived together in small rooms and apartments. In the Chinatowns, many services were within walking distance. For Chinese men and women, Chinatown nurtured traditional lifeways even as it constituted a defensive response to the larger hostility. This awareness drove the *Chinese Digest*, a weekly second-generation Chinese American–owned publication based in San Francisco, to oppose any attempt to turn a part of Chinatown into "Little China" to serve as a tourist attraction during the 1939 San Francisco Golden Gate International Exposition. Chinatown, the journal declared, embodied customs, habits, and culture and was hardly an exotic film set.[28]

As anti-Chinese discrimination increased, the Chinese responded by drawing their ethnic boundaries even closer. Recent archaeological evidence uncovered in the old Los Angeles Chinatown reveals that acculturation was limited until its demolition in 1933. Artifacts and structural remains indicate the persistence of Chinese names and burial practices, traditional leisure activities, food items made in China, and ethnic-dominated settlement patterns as indicated in land use and traditional architecture. Furthermore, Euro-American businesses never became part of the ethnic enclave's economy.[29]

Self-employment, residential segregation, and low acculturation collectively did not occur by happenstance. The changing geographic distribution of the Chinese between 1900 and 1940 in part prompted the development of Chinatowns into so-called gilded ghettos. Although only 33 percent of the Chinese population in 1900 resided in cities with 100,000 or more inhabitants, the figure had jumped to 71 percent by 1940. In 1940 the Census Bureau classified 91 percent of the Chinese population as urban.[30]

The urbanization of the Chinese population was no coincidence. With low reproduction resulting from gender-based immigration laws, Chinese communities in smaller cities and towns declined. Also precipitating this shift was the flight of the second generation from small Chinatowns. Striving to distance themselves from these neighborhoods' negative image, one second-generation Chinese resident shared these sentiments: "I have not cared much about Chinatown. It seemed such a dingy, dirty place. I went there as little as possible and think I was rather ashamed of it."[31]

Shaped by such societal forces, Chinatowns in western cities—including Butte, Montana; Boise, Idaho; Rock Springs, Wyoming; Denver; and Salt Lake City—were slowly disappearing between 1900 and 1940. By 1940 only twenty-eight cities with Chinatowns remained, and many consisted of only a street, a few stores, and several hundred Chinese residents. Euro-American hostility pushed the remaining few out, and many flocked to metropolitan areas in search of jobs in an ethnic labor market.[32] In these cities, Chinatowns—with the notable exception of Seattle, which still served as a way station for seasonal cannery workers toiling in the hinterlands—became a base for small ethnic businesses.

LABOR AND THE ETHNIC ECONOMY

Clearly, before the 1940s Chinese were clustered in an ethnic economy, holding down mostly low-wage dead-end jobs. In 1920, 58 percent of those gainfully employed were in the service industries—mostly restaurant and laundry work—compared with only 5 percent of native-born whites. Educated second-generation Chinese women were underemployed and worked primarily in clerical, domestic, and sales jobs.[33] Immigrant (first-generation) women, however, either toiled in garment sweatshops or worked for little or no wages in small, family-run businesses where the line between production and family life blurred. The role of wives and some daughters in this family-based economy became more visible following the gradual reversal of the skewed gender ratio, which in part was an outcome of the 1930 amendment to the 1924 Immigration Act. Few Chinese—male or female—could be found in agriculture, manufacturing (except in the garment industry), or transportation.[34]

The ethnic economy in Chinatowns was also characterized by the dominance of people from the same district or ancestral village in a specific occupation or business. In part because immigrants came from within a small geographic area, with many related by in-group marriages, and in part because of chain migration, members of the same district or county shared a sense of regional solidarity. In-group mutual aid and support, which immigrants relied on to make the trans-Pacific adjustment, cultivated this sensibility.

People originating from the Hua Xian district during the interwar years, for example, dominated the meat and grocery businesses in northern California. Doumen people predominated in the growing of asters and chrysanthemums in the San Francisco peninsula. In the Sacramento–San Joaquin Delta area, immigrants who hailed from the Zhongshan district in Guangdong province often specialized in fruit growing, whereas those who came from the neighboring region of Sze Yap (a reference to the four districts of Xinhui,

Taishan, Kaiping, and Enping) tended to cultivate potatoes. And many early-nineteenth-century fishermen along California's coast were likely the "boat people," or *Tanka*, who historically fished and lived aboard their boats in south China. Because many enterprises tended to rely on relatives, friends, and family members as low-cost labor, kinship ties were reinforced.[35]

The 1940 U.S. Census reveals that over 60 percent of the Chinese in the United States were manual laborers. Even among American-born Chinese with some Western education, 59 percent were engaged in manual labor. Most of the rest identified themselves as either managers or owners of small businesses, working long hours with limited returns. Thus most gainfully employed Chinese were laborers or merchants.[36]

The number of Chinese involved in laundry work illustrates the lopsided occupational distribution. In 1870, of the 46,274 gainfully employed Chinese in the United States, only an estimated 3,653, or 8 percent, were laundry workers. By 1920, of the 45,614 Chinese in all occupations, about 12,559, or 28 percent, were laundry workers. The number of Chinese-owned laundries climbed steadily during the interwar years. Chicago boasted only 209 laundries in 1903, but twenty-five years later it had 704. In 1910 an estimated 4,600 Chinese laundries were found in New York City; by 1933 that figure had climbed to somewhere between 6,000 and 7,500.[37]

Like countless Chinese men who arrived in America during the exclusion era and were deprived of a normal family life, laundrymen were overwhelmed by loneliness, illness, poverty, and despair, compounded by the grind of endless work days, low pay, and cramped living quarters. The life of Sin Jang Leung exemplified their plight. The son of a Gold Mountain sojourner in Taishan, Leung came to the United States in the late 1930s at the behest of his father. Hoping to attain success in New York City, Leung found only arduous, repetitive labor and little rest. "I really didn't want to work in a laundry, but what could I do?" he recalled in frustration. "I was a newcomer. I didn't know the language. Where could I go?" Leung was also the victim of racial prejudice, a phenomenon he attributed to the fact that Chinese Americans "look quite different—our eyes, hair, forehead, everything!"[38] Years of endless toil eventually resulted in Leung contracting tuberculosis, and he finished his years as a down-and-out gambler whose ties to the extended family in China had long been severed.

CLASS-BASED RESISTANCE AND THE CHINESE MARXIST LEFT

But many Chinese laundrymen found self-fulfillment through class-based resistance, trying to claim their rights as productive citizens of their adopted land. In the 1930s Chinese laundries in New York City were forced to lower prices to compete with increased mechanization in white laundries, which had already driven some Chinese laundries out of business. In retaliation, white laundry operators banded together as a trade organization and set minimum prices for laundry work. When Chinese laundries ignored the new rates, the white owners called for a boycott of Chinese laundries. They persuaded city authorities to pass an ordinance levying a heavy license fee and requiring one-person laundries applying for a license to post a $1,000 bond. Clearly, the bond requirement was designed to drive small, struggling Chinese laundry operators out of business.[39]

As in previous instances, Chinese laundrymen turned to the CCBA for mediation. When the CCBA appeared incapable of effecting change, the laundrymen organized their own independent laundry association—the Chinese Hand Laundry Alliance (CHLA)—which was run fairly democratically. More than 2,400, or about a third, of Chinese laundrymen in New York joined the association. With the help of white attorneys, the CHLA argued before city authorities that the bond requirement discriminated against small laundries, and in the end they persuaded the authorities to reduce the bond to $100.

The CHLA still faced the formidable, hierarchically organized Chinese power structure headed by the CCBA, which considered the CHLA's activism to constitute defiance of its authority. For the sake of survival, the CHLA tried to forge an alliance of sorts with the Chinese Marxist left, which by the early 1930s—through the U.S. Communist Party and affiliated front organizations—had established itself in San Francisco and New York City.

In San Francisco the Marxist left—through such front organizations as the Chinese Workers Mutual-Aid Association (established in 1937) and against the backdrop of the Great Depression—organized laundry workers, garment workers, maritime workers, and others, but with limited success. Slightly more successful was the organization of the unemployed. As the Depression deepened, some of the unemployed joined the San Francisco–based Marxist left group Huaren Shiyi Hui, which attempted to aid the unemployed by demonstrating for relief aid from the CCBA and the U.S. government.

Buoyed by New Deal legislation (the federal government's attempt to reinvigorate the economy), which granted organized labor the right to engage in collective bargaining and to demand better wages and working conditions, some Chinese workers—independent of socialist influence—broke into the mainstream labor movement. Chinese maritime workers in New York organized as Lien Yi, originally a political arm of the anti-Communist Guomindang (GMD), found acceptance from the National Maritime Union in the early 1940s. In 1938 Chinese female garment operatives in San Francisco went on strike for 105 days and through sheer determination gained a foothold in the International Ladies' Garment Workers' Union. Although some Chinese did gain membership in a few mainstream labor unions, the color line persisted.

In New York City the Chinese situation was compounded by a language barrier; many early leftists were Mandarin-speaking intellectuals, but the vast majority of the proletariat spoke Cantonese. The organization of workers was also stymied by the lack of class consciousness. Kinship ties and the absence of a clear division of labor between proprietor and employee—a common feature of small businesses—ensured that class conflict would be minimal. That same absence characterized trade guilds like the CHLA, which exhibited division along family, clan, village, and geographic rather than class lines. Thus the average Chinese worker felt alienated from classical Marxist doctrines.

Workers could have overlooked the left's ideological agenda if they had desperately needed leadership to help overcome the economic downturn of the 1930s, but that was not the case. Although the Chinese unemployment rate in major cities was significant, Chinese Americans' situation was better than that of African Americans, Mexican Americans, and others. The segregated ethnic economy and available community resources—the outcome of Chinese exclusion and enduring discrimination—cushioned the Chinese from the full weight of the Depression. Chinese American women, who held mostly protected service-sector jobs, also helped compensate for any loss of income by their husbands and fathers, who were concentrated in hard-hit production jobs. Further, in spite of historical antecedents, the U.S. government did not exclude the Chinese from unemployment relief or other New Deal programs. For all these reasons, the Chinese left made little headway within the community in the 1930s.[40]

THE GMD, THE LEFT, AND THE "TO SAVE CHINA" MOVEMENT

The competition of the anti-Communist GMD with the Chinese Marxist left against the background of a rising tide of Japanese aggression in East Asia in the 1930s complicated the political picture. After the GMD had purged the Communist wing in its party and established a national government in Nanjing in 1928, it began to strengthen its control over Chinese overseas communities as chauvinistic nationalism rather than revolutionary social change began to prevail. The Nanjing regime sought to stamp out the opposition. Relying on its extensive network of spies and informers, the regime cajoled U.S. police and immigration authorities to harass and deport Chinese Communists and other members of the left. U.S. publications of the regime's political rivals were banned from entering China, and in the United States they found themselves competing with GMD-funded newspapers. The Nationalist government tried to cultivate political loyalty and solicit financial contributions for the war against Japan. To those ends, Chinese consulates influenced the local leadership to reinforce orthodoxy in Chinese schools, and GMD agents infiltrated Chinese trade guilds, family and district associations, and labor unions. For example, when unorganized Chinese maritime workers in New York City threatened to go on strike in 1936, the pro-GMD Chinese Seamen's Union drew many of them in at the expense of the Marxist left.[41]

The Marxist left, however, found an ally in the laundry workers. Both groups took a stand against racial discrimination and domination by traditional authorities in the Chinese community. What riveted them together, however, was their common disapproval of the GMD's policy of nonresistance toward Japan. Led by Chiang Kai-shek, the Nationalist government insisted on *annei rangwai* (first, pacification [of Communists and local warlords], then resistance). By waging a civil war and ignoring Japanese military aggression, the GMD increasingly earned the wrath of Chinese at home and abroad.[42]

Chinese Americans' disapproval of the GMD's policy paled in comparison to their hatred of the Japanese invaders. In 1932, a year after the Japanese army invaded Manchuria—known as the Manchurian Incident—an unnamed waiter in Hawai'i wrote to a Hong Kong friend: "The dwarf Jap invade our territory. When I heard about it my hair stick up. . . . My only hope is to have all [of] us to work together and struggle and boycott Japanese goods and make the dwarf Jap kill themselves."[43] In Hawai'i former Baohuanghui and Guomindang members put their ideological differences behind them and formed an Overseas Chinese Save the Country Organization that nonpolitical bodies such as the Chinese Chamber of Commerce, the United Chinese Society, and district associations soon joined. When Japan, in the absence of a formal declaration of war, invaded China on July 7, 1937 (known as the Marco Polo Bridge Incident), Chinese Americans were gripped by a new sense of urgency. Imbued with nationalist fervor, Chinese Americans, led by the CCBA, organized a *jiuguo* (to save China) movement. A Chinese War Relief Association came into being to coordinate the anti-Japanese effort of about 300 communities in the United States and the rest of the Americas.[44]

On the mainland United States major Chinatowns organized national salvation associations, which backed anti-Japanese rallies; rallied the community to boycott Japanese-made goods and lobby for a U.S. embargo on all materials headed for Japan; and launched an intensive fund-raising campaign to support China. Chinese Americans organized "Rice Bowl" parties that involved parades, dances, cultural events, and parties designed to raise funds for war relief. On May 9, 1938, the first Rice Bowl parade wended its way through the streets of New York City with more than 12,000 participants who manned floats, held up banners, carried flags, and performed dragon dances. The day was billed as a "Solidarity Day," and thousands threw coins and dollar notes onto an oversized Chinese flag carried by traditionally garbed young women. Chinese Americans also supported aviation clubs and schools to train pilots for the Chinese air force. Chinese youth organized choruses to perform at rallies and on Chinese radio to promote the war effort. In schools they commemorated "National Humiliation Days" with parades, vernacular plays, and patriotic songs. To demonstrate their nationalist sentiments, Chinese young people banded together as youth clubs to raise funds for war relief and became interested in cultural activities ranging from Chinese shadow boxing to literary writing. The Chinese Youth Club (established in New York City in 1938) and the Chinese Youth League (established in San Francisco in 1942 and later called the Min Qing, or Chinese American Democratic Youth League) sponsored social and recreational programs that indirectly raised political awareness of China-related events. Unlike established clan and native place or district associations, these progressive organizations welcomed young men and women of all social backgrounds. The organizations offered opportunities for members to work together and learn from each on stage, in publications, and in education classes.[45]

Chinese American women participated in fund-raising, propaganda, civil defense, and Red Cross work and collected clothes and medical supplies for China. Katherine Sui Fun Cheung was one of these ardent nationalists. An early female aviator, she flew her plane—one for which Chinese American women's organizations had raised funds—across the United States to sell war bonds for China and collect aid for refugees. In New York City in 1932, Chinese women formed the Chinese Women's Anti-Japanese Invasion and National Salvation Association (Kangrijiuguohui). They raised relief funds by performing lion dances, typically an all-male endeavor. Chinese American women joined mainstream American women's associations in biracial marches against Japanese fascism. Starting in 1940, the China-originated New Life Movement spread to the United States. Ten organizations emerged in Chinatowns that rallied women to uphold orthodox Confucian social values and oppose Japanese aggression. Such national salvation work gave women an opportunity to develop leadership and organizational skills and to gain confidence and respect as active participants in a political movement. These efforts also escalated interracial understanding and promoted acculturation. As women gained entry into the public sphere, the goal of women's liberation—full equality—became less elusive. Such expressions of China-centered nationalism also suggest that traditional parochialism was breaking down.[46]

RESHAPING THE "ORIENTAL" IMAGE

This nationalistic fervor within the Chinese American community also involved efforts to gain the sympathy of the mainstream society, which was essentially disinterested in the Sino-Japanese conflict. By portraying Japanese and Japanese Americans in a negative light (and Chinese in a positive one), Chinese American patriots hoped to shatter the image of the "Oriental," an

Asian of indistinguishable and degraded ethnicity. In so doing, they hoped to improve the Chinese American image and status in the United States.

Soon after the 1931 Manchurian Incident, Chinese in Walnut Grove, California, to give one example, distributed GMD-produced English publications castigating Japan's actions throughout this area in the Sacramento River Delta. Since both Chinese and Japanese in the region were farm laborers, sharecroppers, or tenants, they depended on white landowners and farmers for their survival in Walnut Grove. Living under racial subordination, the Chinese saw the war crisis as an opportunity to push the Japanese further down the ladder and secure the support of local white elites. Nationalism and interethnic conflict served as the conduit for economic betterment.[47]

The *Chinese Digest* (1935–1940)—a U.S.-born, Chinese-owned publication—also tried to mobilize nationalism and interethnic strife to counter racial lumping. The *Digest* sought to dispel the common stereotypes of the Chinese, such as that of the "sleepy Celestial enveloped in mists of opium fumes"—a reference to Fu Manchu, the paragon of Chinese evil depicted in British author Sax Rohmer's popular Yellow Peril novels. To contradict the prevailing stereotypes, the *Digest* portrayed the Chinese as "average Americans" who "drive automobiles, shop for the latest gadgets and speak good English."[48] The *Digest* clearly projected a vision of Americanism that included Chinese Americans but excluded Japanese Americans, rendered here as the racialized Other. To validate this socially constructed understanding of American nationalism, the *Digest* manipulated race. It named white public figures who supported the national salvation movement and used Euro-American accounts to buttress the depiction of the victimization occurring in China.[49]

Racist stereotypes commonly used against Chinese Americans were also adopted to create an unflattering image of the Japanese. One article described contemporary China as "internally disorganized by swiftfooted, ubiquitous little Japanese soldiers in steel helmets."[50] This subtle depiction of the Japanese as subhuman and the unspoken comparison to insects—describing the Japanese as mindlessly obeying ants—is reminiscent of stereotypes that plagued the Chinese in America.

The devious image of Chinese Americans moved off center stage when the self-effacing, asexual Charlie Chan—an oppositional racial archetype—emerged. Unlike Fu Manchu, who embodied yellow power, Charlie Chan affirmed white supremacy. First appearing in the novels of Earl Derr Biggers and then in feature films, Chan, through faithful servitude to white society, gained upward mobility—rising from houseboy to the middle class. A benign detective who spoke in pidgin English with pseudo-Confucian aphorisms, Chan derived his moral authority from his "foreign" heritage, thus denying the American side of his identity. In this sense both Fu Manchu and

Charlie Chan shared the burden of alienness—Fu Manchu represented Yellow Peril gone wild, and Chan was Yellow Peril contained.[51]

An extension of the "friendly Chinese" image of Charlie Chan was that of a humble, gentle people, popularized by Pearl S. Buck's *The Good Earth* (1931). The novel showed the perseverance of a Chinese family in the face of adversity, and it projected a humane characterization of the Chinese to U.S. readers. Emotionally moved by this portrayal of the Chinese, Americans—aware of the Sino-Japanese war raging in Asia—came to see the Chinese as a noble people victimized by the despicable Japanese.[52] As the war plodded on, sympathy for the Chinese grew perceptibly, and in the white imagination the threat of the Yellow Peril shifted to the Japanese Americans.

For Chinese Americans, the war reinforced the belief that creating a stronger China would improve their subordinate status in the United States. As Zuo Xueli, a woman who spoke at a patriotic rally in San Francisco, warned, "If we don't take immediate steps to defend and preserve our country [China], then I fear the future standing of the Chinese in America will be even lower than [that of] the blacks."[53] Given that belief, Chinese Americans were quickly drawn to the anti-Japanese movement. After the forging of the GMD–Chinese Communist Party (CCP) united front—established following the outbreak of the Sino-Japanese war in 1937—the CCBA, the GMD, and the allies of the Marxist left collaborated, although uneasily, in relief associations under the umbrella organization Chinese War Relief Association.

Such nationalist endeavors were not unique to the Chinese. Other immigrant groups in America, including the Jews and the Irish, engaged in a homeland-based political movement. But unlike the Jews and Irish, the Chinese—because of persisting cultural and language barriers—could pursue such activities with little or no interference from U.S. authorities. The vibrancy and long lifespan of the China-oriented movement were also outcomes of the unremitting mainstream hostility toward the Chinese. For Chinese Americans, such involvement held the promise of rectifying unequal power relations across the Pacific, as captured in laundryman Tung Pok Chin's recollections of his support of the CHLA's medical relief efforts: "If China were strong, I thought, then our image here would also be strong; if China were strong, many of us would not have had to go overseas."[54]

IDENTITY DILEMMA AMONG THE SECOND GENERATION

The fact that even Chinese with U.S. citizenship engaged in such pursuits underscores that the phenomenon of assimilation fell far short of embracing this second generation. Despite the pervasive presence of American socializing agents such as public schools, churches, civic organizations, and the popular media, the progeny of the immigrant generation stood outside mainstream society.

Their racial origin—their visible physical characteristics—set young Chinese American men and women of the early twentieth century apart from the larger society. They experienced social segregation, economic discrimination, and legal handicaps because of their perceived physical and biological differences. "They refused to take me in because I was Chinese," remembered David Young, eventually admitted to the local grammar school in San Francisco only because he was mistaken for a member of another ethnic group.[55] Chinese Americans were also barred from public facilities, including movie theaters and swimming pools.

Chinese American youths played sports on a segregated basis, usually with or against other Chinese or Asians. Their involvement in sports did defy Orientalist stereotypes that perceived Chinese American males as unmanly, asexual creatures and Chinese American females as meek China Dolls who were submissive and powerless. Their participation in popular American sports such as baseball, football, basketball, and prizefighting suggested progress toward assimilation into U.S. society, but the Chinese Americans were still under the shadow of "racism's traveling eye."[56]

The second-generation Chinese Americans had attended public schools and Christian churches where they learned about U.S. values, including equal rights and personal freedom. Taught to accept that Chinese ways were backward and un-American, the youths ran headlong into an intergenerational conflict with their parents, who adhered to a more traditional culture. Parents often demanded that their offspring learn the traditional Chinese language and culture by attending local Chinese schools. Both at home and in Chinese schools, Chinese Americans were exhorted to defer to filial piety and the authority of their elders and simultaneously to suppress their individual aspirations.[57]

These American youths, however, were generally indifferent to this teaching because they saw the United States as their "home"; China remained "foreign" to them. By the mid-1920s Chinese American youngsters sported American accoutrements; Chinese girls, for example, bobbed their hair, wore sleeveless dresses, and emulated the popular flapper image of the day. Many openly rejected their parents' culture and saw themselves as modern. In 1924 Flora Belle Jan of Fresno explained, "My parents wanted me to grow up a good Chinese girl, but I am an American and I can't accept all [the] old Chinese ways."[58] Interested more in postwar consumerism and romance than in marriage and family life, Jan sometimes disappeared for days. The writer Eleanor Wong Telemaque, whose family represented the only Chinese in Albert Lea, Minnesota, in the 1930s, recalled how she grew up blaming her ethnic origins for her social isolation from peers and desperately wanting to "be American, one hundred percent all-American."[59]

Young Chinese women, more so than their male peers, had to struggle to assert their independence. For them, gender refracted the influence of race and ethnicity. Although expected to abide by patriarchal restrictions on their movements, education, career, and matrimony, some chose to assert their individuality. These American-born women wanted the freedom to pursue a career, choose their own spouse, and base their marriage on love rather than family arrangements.[60]

The working-class lives of women performers in Chinese American nightclubs reflect this generational shift. Their lives spanned a period of change in U.S. women's roles. By the early 1900s urbanization and industrialization, augmented by widening educational opportunities, gave rise to the "new woman" phenomenon. Tied less to patriarchal constraints and keen to pursue individual self-fulfillment, Euro-American "new women" of both middle-class and working-class backgrounds discovered economic mobility and their sexuality. Unlike white women, Chinese American women faced both racial and ethnic barriers in their struggle to become new women. Chinese performers, struggling against racist images of Chinese women as modest maidens and biologically alien "bowlegged creatures" incapable of dancing and singing, had to also contend with proscriptive Chinese standards of propriety, which took a dim view of public immodesty.[61]

Similarly, educated, American-born, middle-class Chinese women—inspired by Christianity's message of equality with men in the spiritual world and emboldened by the spirit of the new woman—resisted Confucianism, which discouraged women's self-development. Concomitantly, Chinese American women were drawn into civic participation, which the church actively encouraged for all women. The American-born women who founded the Square and Circle Club in San Francisco in 1924 exemplified the way Chinese American women used Western ideas about women's claim to social leadership to address the needs of the Chinese American community through fund-raising and direct service. In Los Angeles Chinese women organized themselves as the local chapter of the Women's New Life Movement Association, or the Mei Wah Club, and the Los Angeles Chinese Women's Club; like the Square and Circle Club, both organizations were also service-oriented.[62]

Caught in an identity crisis—pulled simultaneously toward both Chinese and American cultures—young Chinese American women and men sought a way out. Many felt the two cultures were worlds apart. In an era when cultural pluralism had yet to make its mark in popular consciousness, a synthesis of both cultures was not an option. Thus they had to choose one over the other. Until late adolescence, most leaned toward embracing the American side of their identity.[63]

But acceptance from the larger society was difficult to attain. Esther Wong of San Francisco recalled that her French teacher, in response to her reading aloud in class, yelled, "Well, you read all right, but I don't like you. You belong to a dirty race that spits at missionaries."[64] As a child, journalist Louise

Leung Larson knew white children called her "Chink" or "skibee" (the latter meant Japanese) because "being Chinese meant being different."[65]

Scientific studies of the interwar period seemed to confirm that Asians were far too "other" from white Americans; considered an ethnographic spectacle, the Asian body was strange, peculiar, and weak. Asians were less intelligent than whites.[66] Social scientists such as the illustrious University of Chicago sociologist Robert E. Park concluded that "race consciousness," or recognition of racial difference, stemmed from awareness of physical difference rather than from the physical traits per se. In moving away from a biological definition of race, Park and his colleagues sought to foreground culture as the explanation for race. Cultural difference explained racial consciousness, but the cultural differences between "Orientals" and whites were linked to the former's ancestral origins in Asia, and so the "Oriental" was ultimately exotic. He or she wore a "racial uniform," or skin color, that set him or her apart from white Americans. As the exotic "other," the "Oriental" was a foil for the triumph of modernity in the West. Overall, such a representation of the Asian only made the youths even more self-conscious—even ashamed—of their racial ethnic origins and culture.[67]

When they moved into adulthood and began job hunting, Chinese American youths felt the full weight of racial prejudice. Of the 19,470 Chinese males in California gainfully employed in 1930, 7,773, or 40 percent, were in domestic and personal service. Eight years later little had changed. (Information on Chinese females is unavailable.) In 1938 the Oriental Division of the U.S. Employment Service in San Francisco reported that most firms discriminated against Chinese, including U.S.-educated citizens. That same year, 90 percent of the agency's placements were made in service sectors. Some states, such as California, had laws barring the employment of Chinese Americans in certain fields such as financial administration, law, dentistry, veterinary science, medicine, architecture, and real estate, to name a few. Further, Chinese were shut out from jobs that required union membership because they were barred from joining unions.[68]

Although few expressed a desire to follow in the footsteps of their immigrant parents and settle for unrewarding jobs, in the end many moved into those same occupations. David Chin, the owner of a laundry in New York, bemoaned that "even if you had an education, there was no other work than in a laundry or restaurant."[69] When writer Jade Snow Wong was a senior at Mills College, her vocational counselor bluntly told her she should not waste her time looking for employment in white-owned firms and should concentrate on Chinese businesses.[70] Perhaps the second generation's reluctant awareness that their lives were tied to the ethnic enclave economy played a part in shaping their loud outcry in the 1930s against the growing Japanese American economic competition in San Francisco's Chinatown—a phenomenon that ended only when the Japanese were incarcerated during the war years.[71]

Chinese women, faced with sexism in addition to racism, fared even worse than their male peers. Already denied college educations by their parents, who favored investing in their sons' upbringing, most American-born Chinese women ended up in clerical and sales jobs—sometimes helping out in the family business—or became self-employed. The few who secured higher education fared marginally better. Wong chose to pursue writing and ceramics, fields in which she would not have to compete with men or be judged by her race. Even Chinese women who entered gender-typed professions such as clerical work, sales, teaching, or nursing encountered difficulty. One female clerk recalled that her employer did not trust Chinese women in the sales department: "They didn't hire Chinese girls until the 40s. We just dusted the place and did cashiering."[72] Retail establishments, however, would move Chinese women to the storefront whenever they were needed to promote an exotic image. Lilie Louise, an employee of Blackstone (forerunner of the May Company), wore a red Chinese dress and taught customers mah jong to encourage them to buy a set—even though she knew nothing about the game before taking the job.[73] Caught at the intersection of race and gender oppression, Chinese women labored with little recognition and discovered that advancement was reserved for whites. Although the fortunes of these second-generation women were an improvement over those of their mothers—who were still overwhelmingly locked in low-paying, unskilled work—equal opportunity eluded them.

Mired in a socioeconomic milieu that subjugated them, second-generation Chinese Americans eventually realized that the future of American-born Chinese was fraught with uncertainty. Their claim to U.S. citizenship was tenuous. Some began to consider China, that "alien land," as a potential place to apply their skills and knowledge. Others held onto their faith in U.S. democracy and its promise of liberty and fair play.

This divergent vision became apparent in a 1936 national essay contest sponsored by the Ging Hawk Club, a women's social club based in New York City, whose topic was "Does My Future Lie in China or America?" As the submitted essays revealed, those who argued that their fortunes and self-identity lay in China acknowledged that racism in America had made them cynical toward U.S. democracy. Disenchanted by the injustice, many like Kaye Hong, who won second prize in the contest, urged their fellow Chinese Americans to "go west . . . to China." Conditions in China also attracted them. A war-torn China needed all the human resources it could muster for the rebuilding effort. Consequently, the Nationalist government advertised widely in the United States for aviators, engineers, agrarian specialists, teachers, and translators, among other highly sought personnel. This campaign was somewhat effective; an estimated 20 percent of American-born Chinese went to China in the 1930s.[74]

Although second-generation Chinese Americans said they returned to China because of the racial prejudice they had encountered in the United States, many used nationalism—the moral imperative to rebuild the homeland—as the main justification. China advocates placed the collective interest ahead of personal happiness. Their work in China would help free it from the shackles of imperialism and, it was hoped, end prejudice against the Chinese in America. If China was prosperous, cosmopolitan, and independent, the Chinese in the United States would be respected by non-Chinese Americans.

The "go west . . . to China" movement swelled to a crescendo in the 1930s, which was not a coincidence. Persisting racism, compounded by a prolonged economic downturn and the immediacy of the Sino-Japanese war, served as catalysts for this ethnic identification. The second generation identified with the Chinese culture because of their marginalized status in America. Given the social and economic isolation imposed on them, Chinese Americans were forced to see themselves primarily as "Chinese" rather than "American." Thus the absorption of Chinese immigrants into mainstream society was never progressive or irreversible.

Still, the dilemma of being pulled in different directions, of having a "double consciousness," to borrow African American scholar and activist W.E.B. Du Bois's phrase, never receded.[75] The dilemma stemmed from the multifaceted nature of assimilation. Although Chinese Americans adopted the cultural behavior of mainstream society—a practice known as behavioral assimilation or acculturation—they were not necessarily welcomed into the institutional activities and general civic life of that society and could not always access structural assimilation. Becoming Chinese American clearly was not simply linear or teleological.

TRANSNATIONAL FAMILIES

Most scholars describe Chinese families in the exclusion era as split households. Chinese perceived these separated or transnational families to be part of a migration network that could ensure a return on their investments. Families in Guangdong were known to have lived well on the remittances their relatives abroad sent home. The phenomenon of split households was also in part the outcome of the gender-biased immigration process that blocked the immigration of alien wives and discouraged matrimony between female U.S. citizens (Chinese and non-Chinese) and alien Chinese.[76]

The conscious practice of sending more boys than girls abroad also contributed to the separation of families. This gendered immigration pattern was the outcome of prevailing patriarchal cultural values and the perception that boys enjoyed more economic opportunities than girls in the United States.

But the gender-selective immigration process was also shaped by an existing immigration system that disfavored native-born women as sponsors of their children and alien spouses. As spelled out in the 1907 Expatriation Act, an American woman who married a foreigner had to forfeit her citizenship and take on her husband's nationality. The 1922 Cable Act eliminated disfranchisement of native-born women but kept it in place for those who married persons "ineligible to citizenship" (which, as discussed earlier, included Asian men). An American-born Chinese woman married to a foreign-born Chinese was not only was stripped of her citizenship but was also deprived of the possibility of naturalization because she in effect fell under the exclusion laws that denied U.S. nationality to Chinese immigrants.

The case of Fung Sing illustrated the way the 1922 act, in conjunction with the 1924 Immigration Act, not only deprived women of their basic rights but also blocked Chinese female immigration and as a result thwarted women's role in extending chain migration. Fung Sing, who was born in the United States, left for China in 1903 and returned to the United States in 1925 after her Chinese husband died. Immigration authorities in Seattle denied her entry. At her writ of habeas corpus case, the court ruled that not only had she lost her U.S. citizenship by marrying a foreigner, but she could never become naturalized since her spouse was ineligible for citizenship. She was, by virtue of her marriage to a citizen of China, also a citizen of that country. She was subject to the exclusion laws and therefore barred from entering the United States, thus ending her ability to help relatives immigrate there.

No such disfranchisement affected native-born male Chinese married to non-U.S. citizens. American-born Chinese fathers could also sponsor U.S. admission and citizenship for foreign-born children. The same did not apply to American-born mothers. The 1930 amendment to the 1924 Immigration Act and the 1922 Cable Act did little to change the situation; native-born married women won independent nationality (that is, they no longer had to take their husband's nationality), but the gender-biased, derivative citizenship laws were still stacked against their facilitating family reunions. This situation persisted until 1934, when a new law allowed a foreign-born child of an American mother to claim U.S. citizenship. Meanwhile, from the late nineteenth century until the 1930s, U.S. nationality laws sent a clear message to Chinese Americans: Chinese women were far less able than men to sponsor dependents and relatives.

The convoluted story of the family of Lee Chuck Suey explains why Chinese immigrants favored sending boys abroad. Laborer Lee arrived in America in 1877, changed his status to that of merchant, and then returned to China several times to marry and to father children. Upon his first return to the United States in 1892, he claimed a male offspring named Wah Doon at the port of entry, even though the unborn child turned out to be a girl, Gay Heung. Lee declared a son for economic and familial reasons. The debt Lee incurred to make the initial trans-Pacific voyage weighed heavily on his mind. He wanted his dependents to follow in his footsteps so they could help pay the debt. Lee also bore an emotional debt. As was the case with many other Chinese immigrants, clan or kin had planned and financed his journey to America. His relatives expected a return on their investment. A daughter, he probably reasoned, would have had less chance than a son to succeed in America and thus would be less able to help pay back debts. A son, however, could follow in his father's footsteps, and the son's future U.S.-born male children could sponsor other relatives to come to the United States. Lee thus chose to claim his unborn child as a male, thereby securing an immigration slot for his own son or another male relative—thus laying the foundation for more chain migration. Later, Lee used that slot to bring in his nephew Wah Doon. Gay Heung never joined her family in the United States. The absence of a slot, the expense of purchasing a paper, and possibly her awareness that, even if she managed to pass herself off as native born, she could never sponsor her foreign-born children to emigrate (since until the 1930s the derivative nationality laws excluded mothers from taking advantage of them) kept Gay Heung in China her entire life.

The phenomenon of split households precipitated change in gender roles. With so many of their husbands in America, Chinese women often assumed the role of heads of their households. They managed the family's budget, made decisions about children's upbringing, cared for elderly in-laws, and, if necessary, sought paid labor outside the home. Chinese men in the United States depended on their female relatives to care for their extended families in China. Single men in America relied on their extended families to find brides for them.

The pursuit of Gold Mountain dreams also distorted the patrilocal structure of the Chinese family. With male spouses and natal male family members absent, married Chinese women were often pulled back into the affairs of their own parents, siblings, and relatives. After all her siblings had emigrated to America, Gay Heung took care of one of her nephews for a number of years. She was also the guardian of several half brothers and sisters while they were in school in China.

As discussed previously, before World War II the boundaries of familial ties were stretched across the Pacific to form a complex immigration network. Family members, relatives, and friends on both sides of the ocean played multiple roles. Early immigrants in America sponsored relatives and even fellow villagers. They claimed dependents other than their own children, bought false papers, and offered supporting testimony. Those back in the villages selected persons to fill slots, raised money for the journey, and helped those emigrating to memorize information on crib sheets. The relationships were mutually reinforcing; out of loyalty, successful Chinese immigrants sent remittances and later assisted family and kin left behind in China to enter the United States.

A Chinese family's transnational relations with its homeland were hardly static. Gender, generation, and life experiences in America could seemingly strain such relations. In Louise Leung Larson's memoir of family life in early-twentieth-century Los Angeles, patriarch Tom Leung's trip to China in 1921 to investigate educational opportunities suggests a desire to uphold his Chinese heritage, although he changed his mind when he discovered the schools paled in comparison to those in the United States. Leung's decision was striking, since he was an ardent supporter of Kang Youwei's efforts to reform China; Leung had boarded student followers and joined the Kang entourage in its travels across the United States. After Leung's death his wife, Wong Bing Woo, refused to return to China in spite of both her relatives' entreaties and her earlier support for the modernization of China (although that support centered on women's education). She valued her independence from her husband's family too greatly to give it up. She also believed her future and that of her children lay in the United States.[77]

Although ties to the ancestral villages might have attenuated as time passed, prior to World War II Chinese immigrants in America played a critical role in supporting public projects in China. This was particularly true for those who hailed from the county of Taishan, which until 1960 was the origin of more than half of the Chinese in the United States. In contributing monies and at times technological expertise to the building of schools, railroads, and other infrastructure—as well as providing support for the purchase of land—the U.S. Chinese brought modernity to the homeland. Chinese Americans enabled their countrypeople to negotiate encounters with a Western-dominated, industrializing world. In turn, the Chinese in China courted émigrés and their descendants through letters among trans-Pacific families, China-based magazines for overseas Chinese, and the *jinshanzhuang*, or Gold Mountain firms, that handled financial dealings for customers abroad.[78]

WORLD WAR II AND CHANGING FORTUNES

World War II triggered a series of overlapping events that would encourage Chinese Americans to think of themselves "as being rooted in place and as deriving their identity from that rootedness."[79] During those years and immediately beyond, Chinese Americans experienced tentative progression into mainstream life. Japan's surprise attack on Pearl Harbor and the ensuing U.S. entry into the military conflict meant that China and the United States were allies waging a war against totalitarianism. Because of this relationship, American images of Chinese—undergoing revision since the 1930s—began to change even more rapidly. In place of negative stereotypes, the U.S. mass media extolled the Chinese as polite, moderate, and hardworking. Even before the smoke from the bombing of Pearl Harbor had cleared, the December 22, 1941, issue of *Time* magazine explicitly differentiated the Chinese "friends" from the Japanese. The Chinese facial expressions, according to the article, were more "placid, kindly, open"; those of the Japanese were more "dogmatic [and] arrogant."[80] Posters and photographs in magazines and newspapers offered sympathetic images of valiant Chinese men and women defending their country against rapacious Japanese invaders. In this environment, Chinese Americans found an opening for sociopolitical and economic gains during the war years and beyond. The Chinese American experience contrasted dramatically with that of the Japanese Americans, which encompassed blatant racial discrimination in the form of incarceration in U.S. concentration camps.

In spite of their changing image, Chinese Americans did not escape racial lumping. During the war years Chinese Americans reported being harassed when mistaken for Japanese Americans. Eugene Moy grew up in Los Angeles during the war years and recalled that his father, who ran a grocery store, was dragged out of his truck and beaten by police until "they were sure he wasn't Japanese American."[81] To deflect such possibilities, Chinese Americans wore buttons that read "I am Chinese," displayed signs that proclaimed "this is a Chinese shop," and carried identification cards issued by the Chinese Nationalist government.[82] On the war front, U.S. military personnel of Chinese descent were caught in the line of fire, since their appearance seemed similar to the enemy. Perhaps in part out of the fear of racial lumping and in part out of ambivalence toward the tense Sino-Japanese relations, Chinese Americans publicly expressed few misgivings about the Japanese American internment, although privately many probably sympathized with their plight.

In response to the rallying cry for all Americans to back the fight against fascism, Chinese Americans—men and women—bought war bonds, rationed necessities, volunteered for civil defense work, and raised funds for the Red Cross. In Chinatown canteens, Chinese American women entertained coethnic servicemen and visiting Chinese Nationalist soldiers.

No less profoundly "American" was their involvement in the armed services and the war industry. Between November 1940 and December 1945, 13,311 Chinese—nearly 22 percent of adult Chinese males in the United States—were drafted into the armed services. An unknown number—perhaps several thousands—also volunteered for military service. Over 20 percent of the 59,803 Chinese adult males in the United States served in the U.S. Army (including the Army Air Corps), and a smaller percentage joined the U.S. Marines and the Coast Guard. Later, 1,621 Chinese were enlisted in the U.S. Navy. Two hundred fourteen Chinese American military personnel died while defending their country.[83]

Chinese American involvement in a war was nothing new. In 1917 nineteen members of the Chinese American Citizens Alliance volunteered for World War I. An undetermined number of young Chinese men also signed up to show their patriotism; one of them, Sergeant Sing Kee, won the Distinguished Service Cross for his bravery in keeping communication lines open despite being repeatedly gassed during a bloody battle.[84] Like their predecessors, Chinese Americans during World War II saw military service as a duty: "Because I am an American in the American service as a citizen, native-born, [I am serving in the military out of] a sense of duty," explained Richard Gee of the 407th Air Service Squadron. Others viewed military service as an opportunity to articulate not only their American patriotism but also Chinese nationalism. James Jay of the same squadron as Gee recalled that after he read about the atrocities Japanese soldiers had committed in China, he "wanted to go to China and fight Japanese. I was born in China so naturally it's part of my heritage. I live in United States. I don't want to see those two countries go to the Japanese."[85]

The war changed the legal status of many Chinese Americans. Some of the inductees were paper sons who chose to confess their status and thus earned citizenship or the right to be naturalized. The U.S. Army, in fact, sometimes even facilitated this process; in one instance, eighteen men training in Florida and unable to fulfill the legal entry requirements for citizenship were taken to Canada so they could reenter the United States legally and thus qualify for citizenship. Unlike African American inductees, who were placed in segregated units, Chinese Americans were integrated in the military—although 1,200 did serve in all–Chinese American units stationed in the China-Burma-India theater. After the war some Chinese male veterans—taking advantage of the GI Bill of Rights—obtained college educations or paid for houses in the suburbs. Although they did not elude racism—until May 1942, Chinese men, for example, could enlist in the navy only as mess attendants—Chinese American men's worldview expanded and their self-confidence was boosted as a result of their wartime service.[86] Tung Pok Chin, who served in the U.S. Navy, recalled that he "developed a true sense of power and national pride for the first time" in his life. "From a weak China," he continued, "to an all-powerful United States Navy, I was indeed proud that I had made it to Gold Mountain."[87]

During the war years Chinese American women also claimed their place in America. They broke cultural traditions, left homes, and donned the uniforms of the armed services—although sexism and racism continued to plague them. A small number served as WACs (Women's Army Corps), WAVES (Women Accepted for Volunteer Emergency Service in the navy), WASPs (Women's Airforce Service Pilots, which used female pilots to transport military aircraft), in the Army Nurse Corps, and in the SPARs (women's reserve of the U.S. Coast Guard). Kim I. Surh volunteered for the Army Nurse Corps out of a deep sense of loyalty to America, although her officer husband's overseas assignment gave her the initial impetus to enlist. After basic training at Staten Island, New York, she was assigned to the bloody European theater, wearing uniforms tailored for men. WACs complained of shoes that were too large and a shortage of women's overcoats.[88]

Sexism was often blatant. Maggie Gee recalled that her involvement in the WASPs ended abruptly in December 1944 when the organization was disbanded as a result of pressure by resentful male pilots. Chinese women also complained that men in the same jobs were promoted ahead of them. Being "Oriental" in a largely segregated armed services sometimes caused women to be singled out. Gloria Toy Gim Jee, who grew up in New Orleans's Chinatown, initially experienced prejudice from non-Chinese in SPARs, although as time passed her race became less problematic as she developed friendships rooted in a common female experience. Other Chinese women complained of being mistaken for "Japs"; racial lumping against a backdrop of jingoistic nationalism worked against them. For most female Chinese military personnel, however, their service increased their self-confidence; widened their perspective of the interlocking nature of race, gender, and nationalism; and opened up new educational and employment opportunities.

Working in wartime industries was equally transformative. Because of a labor shortage with so many men away at war and new federal laws prohibiting discrimination, jobs became readily available for racial minorities and women. Suddenly, Chinese workers could escape the dead-end, low-paying operative, manual labor, and service jobs they had been locked into for so long. In 1942 an estimated 1,600 Chinese Americans—of a total populace of 18,000 in the San Francisco and Oakland Chinatowns—were engaged in defense work, mostly building cargo ships and tankers. Chinese engineers, technicians, and skilled workers also found openings in the defense industries in the Seattle-Tacoma Shipbuilding Corporation, the shipyards of Delaware and Mississippi, and the airplane factories on Long Island, New York. Between 1940 and 1950 the number of Chinese who held professional and technical jobs—deemed part of the primary sector of the labor market—more than tripled. Chinese Americans were leaving restaurants, laundries, and retail establishments behind and stepping into new roles. One example was an American-born University of Minnesota–trained architect who managed his father's restaurant until World War II, when he was able to find work in a defense-related industry—his first professional job since graduating from college fifteen years earlier.[89] "To men of my generation," recalled Charlie Leong of San Francisco, "World War II was the most important historic event of our times. For the first time we felt we could make it in American society."[90]

The number of Chinese American women, in a break with ethnic traditions that circumscribed women's involvement in the public sphere, also increased in the aforementioned occupations and also in white-collar clerical positions. These women won the respect of their fellow Americans, and their self-confidence increased. Jennie Lee Taylor remembered how in spite of her training as a welder she never had a job offer until Douglas Aircraft Company in El Segundo, California, hired her in 1942. "Face it—it is a man's world . . . so, you gotta get out there and work harder," she said. Reflecting on her fame as the first woman in the company to earn the journeyman welder's "A" rating, she stated, "It did me good to know that I could prove I was the best."[91] Even women who did not enter defense-related industries sometimes took on new responsibilities vacated by spouses and male relatives; sisters-in-law Marie and Audrey Ah Tye had to run the family's service station when their husbands left for military service. Donning homemade overalls with hoods to protect their hair, they filled gas tanks, wiped windshields, and checked oil.[92]

This turning point, however, marked only one stage in a long process of change. The specter of racism and sexism had not disappeared. The contradiction between the U.S. rhetoric of waging a war against Nazi racism and the persistence of anti-immigration laws became obvious to both Chinese and non-Chinese; Japanese propaganda also pointed out this hypocrisy. The propaganda also made it clear that the United States was little different from European colonial powers and had little intention of respecting Chinese sovereignty or independence. In the face of this attack on U.S. credibility, the need to counter Japan's campaign that Asia was for Asiatics (that is, Japan's attempt to conquer or control Asia was also designed to promote Asia's independence or freedom from Western colonization), and the fact that China was a U.S. ally, the campaign for repeal of Chinese exclusion began to gather momentum.[93]

The repeal campaign—heavily colored by the politics of race—was managed largely by the Citizens' Committee to Repeal Chinese Exclusion (CCRCE), a group of white businesspeople, missionaries, career diplomats, and representatives of the media who wanted repeal more to strengthen Sino-U.S. relations than to rectify past racial mistakes. With the exception of letters of support several organizations such as the CACA, the CCBA, and the CHLA wrote to the U.S. Congress, Chinese Americans kept a low profile during the campaign. The few Chinese called to testify before the House of Representatives' immigration committee simply augmented the CCRCE goal of presenting Chinese Americans as fully Americanized residents who, far from being a threat to the country, were hardworking and patriotic.[94]

Yet initially, efforts to repeal exclusion went nowhere. Opposition in Congress and among labor and veterans' organizations feared reopening the gates to Chinese immigration would lead to job competition and unemployment. President Franklin D. Roosevelt, in a special message, assured the

American people that no such scenario would play out, given the proposed highly limited quota. He also tried to persuade U.S. citizens that the repeal, which would court China and bolster its morale, was part of the U.S. effort to end the war. Other policy makers also argued that repeal would benefit the United States by keeping China as an economic ally. The 1943 visit of Song Meiling, better known as Madam Chiang Kai-shek, wife of the president of China, unwittingly also promoted the cause of repeal. During her month-long tour of the United States, Song never criticized racism in America or lobbied for repeal. The press—enraptured by her beauty, charm, and seeming frailty—nevertheless portrayed her as the symbol of a nation and a people that believed in freedom and democracy. A distorted China Doll image of Song echoed that of China; both were helpless and in need of U.S. aid.[95]

The law Congress eventually passed in 1943, however, was more symbolic than substantive. Although it did repeal thirteen anti-Chinese immigration laws and allowed Chinese residents to become naturalized citizens, it set an admission quota of 105 Chinese per year. Applicants for naturalization had to present documentation to verify their legal entry into the United States and demonstrate fluency in English and knowledge of American history and the Constitution. These requirements effectively ruled out undocumented immigrants, many of whom also lacked literacy. Even "paper sons" would be disinclined to take advantage of this change for fear of being discovered as frauds. As a result of these regulations, between 1943 and 1949 only 5,107 Chinese became naturalized, although this was a dramatic improvement over the 226 naturalizations between 1937 and 1942. An undetermined number of the naturalizations after 1943, however, were the outcome of military service.[96] The repeal also stopped short of rejecting race-based restriction of immigration. As amended shortly thereafter, the law stated that any person of half or more Chinese "blood" from anywhere in the world would be included in the annual quota. Chinese entry into the United States continued to be regulated on a racial rather than a national-origin basis.[97]

The repeal also erected a possible barrier for family reunification. Before 1943 Chinese children of American citizens applying to enter the country were considered outside the quota limit. The same applied to immigrant wives of U.S. citizens married before 1924. After 1943, however, every Chinese person entering the United States—except members of exempt classes—was counted as part of the quota. Not surprisingly, Chinatowns did not mark the repeal with public celebrations.[98]

In spite of the shadow cast over the liberalization of immigration for Chinese, which in 1946 was extended to Filipinos and Asian Indians, the repeal did constitute a new era in Chinese American history. After nearly a century of racial exclusion, Chinese Americans could now consider making a claim to political equality and making America their homeland.

New Ties and New Lives in Cold War America

SOCIOECONOMIC CHANGES IN THE POSTWAR YEARS

Chinese American participation in the larger society during World War II brought about changes that reverberated long after the war, which, in turn, created fissures within Chinese America. World War II was clearly a transforming experience for Chinese Americans, regardless of gender or class background. As discussed in Chapter 3, through their military service and contribution to the wartime industries, Chinese Americans altered the larger society's previously skewed dominant perception of them. Consequently, white hostility toward Chinese declined, thousands were naturalized in the 1940s, and the exclusion laws were rescinded. The repeal of the exclusion laws, although compromised by a quota on yearly admissions, led to a gradual rise in female migration and a subsequent balancing of the gender ratio.[1]

Even as families were reunited, a significant number of young American-born Chinese men and women—having been exposed to wartime patriotic propaganda and emboldened by new economic opportunities—were breaking their ties to the family-based economy and forging new lives connected to the white-dominated society. This was not an unqualified success, however; Chinese Americans in the 1950s still routinely complained about occupational advancement stymied because of racism. One postwar study shows that one-third of the 337 respondents cited discrimination as a serious barrier to upward mobility.[2] Still, as some Chinese Americans established their independence away from Chinatowns and old sociopolitical structures, Chinese America became transformed. Over the next several decades class-based lines rooted in differentiation of occupation, socioeconomic status, English language proficiency, generation, and place of origin—all of which had been present prior to 1945—further polarized this ethnic community and reconfigured social and political links both within the community and with mainstream society. In sum, the Chinese American identity became less definable and more complicated.

An obvious remaking of the face of Chinese America as a result of the rippling effects of the wartime boom and postindustrialization after the war was seen in the redistribution of occupations across gender lines. Of the 36,000 gainfully employed Chinese Americans in 1940, only approximately 1,000 worked in professional and technical positions. A decade later about 3,500 held such positions in a workforce of 48,000. By 1950 Chinese men were employed not only as service workers, operators, clerks, and sales personnel but also as managers, officials, white-collar professionals, and proprietors.[3]

The war also held the door open for women's increased share of the labor market. Between 1940 and 1950 the number of women in the workforce nearly tripled, from 2,800 to 8,300. About a fifth of wage-earning women were factory operatives, and some were either clerical workers or sales personnel, but a significant minority were mechanics and professionals in the private sector. By 1950 over 1,150 held professional or technical jobs compared with only 200 ten years earlier. Racial discrimination, however, continued to block Chinese American women's access to white-collar jobs. Still, the labor participation rate of Chinese women in 1960—30.8 percent—was higher than that of their white female counterparts.[4]

Chinese Americans were able to hold onto the gains they made during the wartime years because of larger forces unleashed by a post-1945 economic boom. The general demand for necessities and luxuries, coupled with the war-enforced savings of millions of U.S. residents now available for consumption, kept factories humming at full speed. More new jobs opened up in defense-related industries when the Cold War between the United States and the Soviet Union precipitated a rush to increase American military power. Furthermore, the federal government embarked on an expansion of the bureaucracy to implement the multiple parts of President Harry S. Truman's Fair Deal program, supposedly a continuation of the New Deal of the 1930s. Part of the Fair Deal agenda involved massive infrastructure development, including new highways, airports, public power projects, and other facilities. As the federal, state, and local governments raised their involvement in national economic life, prosperity filtered slowly downward, although mostly to the white middle class.

RECONFIGURATION OF CHINATOWNS AND SUBURBANIZATION

The occupational mobility enjoyed by some Chinese Americans, particularly those of the educated second generation, eventually depleted the existing labor force in small Chinatowns. That development, coupled with rapid technological advancements, forced remaining Chinese entrepreneurs to either innovate or move into other ventures. For example, mechanization in the form of steam laundries and laundromats drove many old-time small-town Chinese hand laundries out of business and led to their concentration in cities. Other laundry operators turned to the restaurant enterprise, in part because newly arrived coethnics preferred to work in restaurants where they could earn more in fewer working hours. By 1960, for example, only half of the 430 laundries that had existed in Chicago's Chinatown in 1950 remained in operation. Handicapped by the absence of an economy of scale in an age of corporate consolidation of economic and financial resources, Chinese-owned cafés and restaurants that had once served mainly Euro-American food folded as fast-food chains gained popularity. The ubiquitous independent Chinese vendors and grocery stores were also made anachronistic by modern supermarkets in cities.[5]

In the 1950s a housing boom occurred when the economically revitalized Euro-American middle class fled downtown neighborhoods for the suburbs. Middle-class Chinese Americans joined the exodus to suburbia, and Chinatown businesses seemed set to decline. Chinese restaurants, however, became innovative. Some followed the dispersion of Chinese American families by relocating to the suburbs. Others turned into chop suey and chow mein establishments and introduced the concept of "take home" food to suburbanites working in the downtown districts, who could pick up the food on their way home.

Despite such innovations, Chinatowns continued to decline in the postwar years, although the residents of at least one Chinatown tried to halt the urban blight. In the late 1940s—as awareness of the dilapidated nature of buildings in Seattle's multiracial Chinatown grew—Chinese, Japanese, Filipino, African American, and white residents in a unique collaborative venture across the color line formed a self-help group, the Jackson Street Community Council. The organization drew businesspeople and leaders from different ethnic groups. Although bereft of government assistance, the council cleared vacant lots, planted trees, sponsored community events to promote the area, lobbied the state legislature for urban renewal programs, and convinced the city council to pass a housing code ordinance that required absentee property owners to fix up their properties. The efforts of the Jackson Street Community Council were conjoined by those of the volunteer Chinese Community Service Organization, whose membership was mostly composed of young Chinese American professionals.[6]

Such communitywide efforts failed to halt the decline; between 1940 and 1955 Chinatowns in as many as twelve cities disappeared. In the postwar period, federally funded highway building and slum clearance for new public housing also contributed to the demise or contraction of Chinese neighborhoods. Changing land-use patterns and concomitant changes in land values determined the future of these ethnic ghettos. Philadelphia's Chinatown became physically smaller when authorities turned the main street into a thoroughfare to help connect the city with New Jersey. Similarly, Pittsburgh's Chinatown was obliterated by a modern expressway. In 1955 the last surviving block of Los Angeles's Chinatown was demolished to make way for new and wider roadways in connection with the building of the Hollywood Freeway. The construction of Interstate 5 through the Chinatown core of Seattle in 1962 effectively isolated the part of the ethnic neighborhood east of the highway, eventually forcing establishments there out of business. In other instances, such as Chicago, the encroachment of the central business district into Chinatown—an outcome of urban expansion and rezoning—forced the ethnic neighborhood to relocate.[7] But the life cycle of remaining Chinatowns was considerably extended by the arrival and settlement of new immigrant families.

Working-class and immigrant Chinese families who could not afford residential mobility discovered that Chinatowns, in the wake of "white flight," had become even more segregated. Thus even as some Chinese Americans increased their share of the economic pie or, in other words, became incorporated into U.S. society, others faced continued physical and social segregation and remained excluded from mainstream life. Chinese Americans, despite some success in challenging race- and gender-based occupational barriers, were still routinely denied access to high-paying jobs. Equally important was the reality that fifteen years after the end of World War II, according to one California labor report, for every fifty-one dollars earned by a white male, Chinese males earned only thirty-eight dollars in spite of the fact that 24 percent more Chinese males than whites were college graduates.[8]

POSTWAR IMMIGRATION LAWS

In the immediate postwar years a major departure from the restrictive, national origins–based immigration policy—adopted because of the swelling nativist tide in the 1920s—began to emerge. The goodwill generated by the Allies' victory over fascism nudged Congress to pass the 1945 War Brides Act, which permitted spouses and children of U.S. citizens in the military to gain nonquota visas during the next three years. A total of 5,731 Chinese spouses and dependents of war veterans entered the United States during those years. The liberalization of immigration laws also came closer to fruition with the 1946 Chinese Alien Wives of American Citizens Act that allowed Chinese wives of U.S. citizens to bypass national origins quotas and enter the country as nonquota immigrants. Although the law applied only to marriages after its enactment, a subsequent amendment in 1947 allowed wives to gain non-quota entry regardless of their marriage date. Because both the War Brides Act and the 1947 amendment to the 1946 act recognized *all* marriages to veterans regardless of when matrimony occurred, Chinese Americans could now reunite with wives and children excluded before the war. Historian Xiaojian Zhao studied a sample of Chinese wives who entered the United States between 1945 and 1952 and concluded that the vast majority were not new brides but longtime wives who had endured split households for years. An additional act also passed in 1946—the G.I. Fiancées Act—permitted 5,000 alien fiancées of U.S. servicemen, including Chinese, to enter the United States over the next three years.[9]

The 1946 acts, along with the 1947 amendment, led to the entry of an unprecedented number of Chinese women into the United States. But Chinese women still faced obstacles in trying to gain entry. Earlier, husbands who were "paper sons" had furnished false testimony either to secure immigration clearance or to support the immigration of kinfolk. To avoid implicating those in the immigration network in their own efforts to secure entry, during their interrogations these women had to corroborate their husbands' testimony and conceal a part of their personal history. The fortunes of Dong Zem Ping reveal the way the past haunted Chinese war brides' reunification with their husbands. When Dong's husband immigrated to the United States, he did not report that he had a pregnant wife, thereby suggesting that he was a paper son. He could bring his family members in because of his wartime military service, but his previous fraudulent testimony barred him from claiming Dong (and their child) as part of his past. Dong and her husband had to marry a second time so she could enter as a war bride. Not only did Dong have to pretend she was a new bride when she arrived in America, but she was forced to leave her son behind in China.[10]

Although Chinese war brides encountered constraints that still threatened to keep families apart, they did not hesitate to claim dependents during the application process, which suggests a perpetuation of the trans-Pacific immigration network. Mary Yee, who became the wife of a paper son in 1934, rejoined her husband in America in 1948. Besides her own daughter, Yee also claimed two sons; one of the boys was actually her nephew, and the other was the son of her husband's godfather. She endured a two-week ordeal at the immigration station, as she was interrogated repeatedly.

Immigration officials, if they suspected document fraud, could detain and even deport such women. But prolonged detention and deportation were fraught with political implications. Chinese American veterans, through their service, had garnered mainstream public support. That support became critical when a tragedy occurred in 1948. Thirty-two-year-old Leong Bick Ha, after a fifteen-year separation from her husband, had not performed well at her immigration interrogation. After being held for three months with no sign of an impending release, Leong decided to hang herself. More than 100 Chinese female detainees protested with a day-long hunger strike. The Chinese War Veterans Association in New York, joined by Chinese newspapers and community organizations, protested against the detention of Chinese war brides. The resulting adverse publicity and public pressure eventually forced the Immigration and Naturalization Service (INS) to terminate its policy of detaining Chinese arrivals.

Mostly wives forcibly separated from husbands by previous immigration policy and new brides whom Chinese American soldiers had married in China, the new influx of female immigration in the 1940s helped raise the total Chinese population in the United States from around 77,000 in 1940 to more than 117,000 by the end of the decade. Almost 92 percent of the over 7,000 Chinese immigrants who entered the country between 1948 and 1950 were females. Undoubtedly, most of these women were new brides and *gamsaanpo* taking advantage of the laws passed in the period 1945 to 1947. Between 1948 and 1965, before immigration laws underwent more changes, 37,593 Chinese women were admitted into the United States—which represented 60.1 percent of the total number of Chinese immigrants during that period. Overall, during the first two decades following World War II, an estimated 65 percent of the women admitted into the country entered as wives of U.S. citizens.[11]

Another visibly dramatic change was the balancing of the gender ratio; by 1960 it stood at 1.3 males for every 1 female compared with 2.8 to 1 in 1940. Although the long-term trend in the twentieth century was indeed toward a balance in the ratio, any such trend before World War II was the outcome of legislation that discouraged male immigration (and, to a lesser extent, female immigration). Natural reproduction rather than immigration gradually altered the skewed gender ratio. Thus legislation that supported family reunification after World War II was significant because it speeded the entry of women, allowing immigration as a phenomenon to again play a role in increasing the population size. The preponderance of younger age groups among new post-1945 immigrants—a cohort at its reproductive peak—facilitated the gradual adjustment of the previously skewed gender ratio. From 1947 to 1956, for example, 76 percent of those admitted fell within the age groups 15 to 29 and 30 to 44.[12]

Clearly, this systematic effort to confer U.S. citizenship on those of Chinese ancestry stemmed from the globalization of American power—particularly its emergence as a superpower in the Pacific—and the worldwide rejection of colonialism, imperialism, and racism after World War II. To counter the perceived rising Soviet Union hegemonic influence in the Pacific, the United States sought allies among East Asian powers, including Japan and the Guomindang (GMD) government in exile in Taiwan. A shift in U.S. immigration policy could solidify these developing trans-Pacific diplomatic ties.[13]

A massive reaction against colonialism, imperialism, and racism—provoked by the recent fight against Nazism and wartime and postwar nationalist movements afoot in Asia to overturn old imperialist powers—paved the way for Americans to accept a change in immigration policy. They were compelled to reexamine the U.S. identity in relation to their shortcomings as a nation. Nationhood was now linked less to any single ethnic derivation and more to abstract values such as freedom, democracy, and equality. The postwar confrontation between Western democracy and communism also constantly reminded Americans of the national discourse to uphold self-determination and equality worldwide. Tolerance of cultural pluralism was gradually becoming a tenuous shared belief.[14]

IMMIGRATION LEGISLATION AND THE COLD WAR

The Cold War, however, preserved residual suspicions of so-called un-American or alien behaviors and attitudes. Internal as well as external dangers supposedly loomed. Partisan politics—Republicans and Democrats were locked in a contest to outdo each other's attacks on Communist subversion in an attempt to gain the political upper hand—only spread the hysteria. Consequently, in the name of safeguarding the republic, in 1950 Congress passed the Internal Security Act (McCarran Act), which empowered federal authorities to deny entry to or deport aliens who had been Communist Party members or who belonged to Communist front organizations. Resident aliens with such affiliations could be denied citizenship. The act also authorized the president to order the attorney general to round up and detain persons considered national security risks—a measure that recalled the internment of Japanese Americans during World War II.[15]

When the Korean War broke out in 1950 and brought Chinese and U.S. troops into direct military conflict, the loyalty of the Chinese in the United States came under scrutiny. Apparently, the federal government used the McCarran Act against radical or progressive Chinese. One such case involved Kwong Hai-chew, a Chinese sailor with permanent residence status who, following his return from a prolonged stint onboard an American merchant ship, was detained and denied reentry because of his alleged ties to the American Communist Party. Although Kwong was a labor activist—he had been president of a Chinese seamen's association and was involved in the white-dominated, socialist-influenced National Maritime Union (NMU)— the prosecution could not offer substantive proof of his alleged "red" connections. Yet it took seventeen years of persistent litigation to bring about a reversal of the decision to deport him, one that hinged on nothing more than an accusation of guilt by association.

The new emphasis on national security—mirrored in the large-scale investigation into the loyalty of more than 6 million federal employees beginning in 1947 and Senator Joseph McCarthy's virulent claim that "Commies and queers" were working in the State Department—increased the momentum to revise and recodify the large amount of immigration legislation in existence since the early twentieth century. This process clearly reflected the belief that controlling immigration would stave off any possible internal subversion.

The resulting 1952 McCarran-Walter Immigration and Nationality Act— passed over the veto of President Truman—was in many ways a regression for immigration policy reform, since it retained the national origins system. The new legislation also discriminated against potential immigrants of Asian ancestry, since only a token 2,000 visas were set aside for the nineteen countries within the so-called Asia-Pacific triangle (all countries from Indian to Japan and the Pacific islands north of Australia and New Zealand). A small quota, an average of 100 per year, was set for each of the nineteen countries. The quota for China was 205 (it already had a quota of 105 following the repeal in 1943). In contrast, Northern and Western Europe received 85 percent of annual admissions. Furthermore, unlike other quotas, which were set according to country of birth, these quotas involved ancestry categories such as Chinese, Japanese, and Korean. Asians, regardless of their country of birth or residence, had to qualify under those limited categories. In a sense, the legislation perpetuated the legacy of restriction and expressed isolationist nationalism.[16]

The McCarran-Walter Act was progressive in other respects, however. The legislation not only permitted persons of all races to become eligible for naturalization (and for property ownership) by explicitly abrogating the 1924 "ineligible to citizenship" clause but also demolished the long-standing principle of Asian exclusion. Through this 1952 legislation, other Asian nationalities and permanent residents—such as Indians, Filipinos, and Koreans—could also enjoy similar immigration rights. This, in turn, contributed to the escalating Asian inflow, with the Asian share of legal immigrants doubling from 6 to 12 percent between 1950 and 1960.[17]

The 1952 legislation also dramatically expanded the selective system of "family and skill screening," which gradually replaced the "ethnic screening" in force since 1924. The screening here refers to the multiple categories of admissions. One of these categories—covering spouses and unmarried minor children of U.S. citizens—was not limited by the yearly numerical quota. Other categories or classes, however, fell under the preference system, whereby each class received a certain share of the available quota visas for that year, and applicants who met the criteria for the highest preference standing received the first available visas until the number assigned to their preference class ran out. The 1952 law assigned the highest preference to immigrants with urgently required technical or professional expertise and their immediate family members—a preference some policy makers believed was necessary for economic development that could tip the Cold War balance in favor of the United States. Secondary preference went to the parents and adult children of U.S. citizens. Spouses and unmarried children of permanent resident aliens received third preference; siblings and other immediate relatives of U.S. citizens followed.[18]

In 1960 an amendment to those provisions—PL 86-363—passed in the U.S. Congress. Pushed by Chinese veterans, the amendment modified the quota system so that thousands of Chinese relatives of U.S. citizens and permanent residents who had applied for visas before December 31, 1953, could apply to enter the United States under nonquota status. Along with the 1962 Refugee Act that gave the Chinese 25,000 nonquota visas, PL 86-363 opened the floodgates of postwar Chinese immigration even before the landmark 1965 Immigration and Nationality Act abandoned the discriminatory national origins system.[19]

FAMILY FORMATION

Aside from the first preference, the other categories, along with the right to attain naturalization, engendered more chain migration. New citizens of Chinese ancestry used the preference system to reunite with family members. Thus in the postwar period, the legal immigration flow was sustained more by family reunification preferences and kinship networks than by economic cycles and deliberate recruitment.[20]

The immigration regulations of the Chinese government also governed the rate of the flow. For example, C. Ng's daughter (name unknown) brought her father to America in the early 1960s after repeated attempts. Other family members had to remain in China as "hostages" so Ng and his daughter would continue to send remittances, of which the Chinese Communist government apparently took a large percentage as punishment for the Ng family's landed class background. For some mutilated Chinese families, the prohibitive cost of reunification also prevented emigration. Orchard worker Wong Yow, who lost all of his investments on mainland China after the 1949 revolution, had to wait nearly twenty years before he had accrued enough savings to bring his wife to the United States in 1968—thirty-three years after their marriage.[21]

Despite the preference system and the attending racial quotas, the number of Chinese admissions in the 1950s was fairly high. Several factors accounted for this phenomenon. As mentioned earlier, family reunification provisions in the 1952 act allowed Chinese with U.S. citizenship and even those of permanent residence status to bring in spouses and children without being subjected to a numerical quota. Additional visas were also extended, using the provisions for political refugees under the 1948 Displaced Persons Act (further amended in 1950), to an estimated 5,000 Chinese students and professors who could or would not return to mainland China because of financial reasons or fear of persecution following the fall of the country to the Chinese Communist Party in 1949. Visas were also extended to Chinese maritime workers and visitors who were trapped in America.[22]

More Chinese refugees fleeing the rule of the Chinese Communist government—over 2,000—were admitted following the passage of the Refugee Relief Act in 1953. Another 2,000 Chinese who had secured the necessary clearance from the Nationalist government received visas for entry into the United States. Congress further unraveled the racially based quotas when it passed the Refugee-Escapee Act in 1957, which enabled federal authorities to grant some visas independent of quota restrictions and to admit more refugees—including around 2,000 persons from China. As a result of these additional routes of entry, approximately 32,000 Chinese were admitted into the United States between 1953 and 1961—a figure that far exceeded the annual ceiling imposed by the 1952 legislation. Between 1962 and 1965 more than 15,000 refugees from Communist China, who had fled to nearby Hong Kong, were admitted under special provisions as refugees. Finally, the fact that more Chinese entered the country than left to return to Asia meant that in the postwar period the total population grew at a constant pace.

The growth of the total population and the gradual balancing of the gender ratio promoted family formation among Chinese Americans. By 1960 the proportion of married Chinese—59.8 percent—had nearly caught up with that for the total U.S. population, which was 69.1 percent.[23] The percentage of split households among the Chinese remained higher than that for total population, however—the lingering outcome of the separation of families as a result of the Communist takeover of China. Because most new female immigrants were of childbearing age, the birthrate jumped dramatically several years after the passage of the War Brides Act. Whereas the Chinese birthrate was the lowest of all ethnic groups in 1940, by 1960 it had outpaced that of Euro-Americans. Because of past exclusionary laws, however, the number of native-born Chinese did not surpass that of foreign-born Chinese until 1960. When nativity is examined by sex, the number of native-born women that year was still significantly lower than the number of men—the outcome of the pre-1943 gender-biased exclusion laws.[24]

NEW EDUCATED MIDDLE CLASS

Although the postwar immigration wave was characterized by an overwhelming influx of wives and children, it was also marked by a significant number of young people—men and women—enrolled in colleges and universities, who arrived either on their own or under government-sponsored or private programs. When the Communist victory occurred in 1949, some Chinese students were stranded in America. Those who relied on family support and those who held scholarships from the defeated Nationalist government found themselves cut off from financial support. The U.S. government recognized this problem and enacted special regulations in 1951 to allow these students and scholars to accept employment in the United States; soon after, those who had entered before 1950 were allowed to change their nonimmigrant status to that of permanent residence.[25]

The presence of these stranded students and scholars caused an increase in the number of Chinese employed in professional and technical jobs; the percentage jumped from a mere 2.5 percent in 1940 to 6.6 percent in 1950 to 20.3 percent ten years later—a tenfold increase in twenty years—for gainfully employed Chinese males. The increase could be attributed in part to the 1944 repeal of the 1879 California constitutional provision that forbade the employment of Chinese by corporations and state, municipal, and county governments. By the early 1960s the Chinese had made significant inroads in the medical, scientific, engineering, and teaching professions. In 1961 a survey conducted by the Chinese Taiwanese Embassy revealed that more than 1,300 persons of Chinese descent were on the faculties of eighty-eight American institutions of higher learning—including 98 faculty members at Harvard, Princeton, and Yale.[26]

This intelligentsia—along with other Chinese refugees escaping Communist rule and, beginning in the late 1950s, the arrival of significant numbers of students from Taiwan and Hong Kong to pursue higher education—altered the occupational distribution and diversified the Chinese American community in terms of place of origin and language. Many of the political refugees hailed from provinces outside Guangdong, the ancestral origin for most Chinese Americans before 1945. Most, unlike earlier emigrants, were urbanites and typically spoke Mandarin, which was considered a mark of respectability. This class and regional differentiation gave rise to gradual distinctive residential clustering, as seen in New York City.

In New York City there were harbingers of what came to be known as "uptown" Chinese and "downtown" Chinese.[27] The uptown Chinese comprised the newly arrived and displaced Mandarin-speaking group. Many other members of the early uptown Chinese were the monied segment of the populace, who as much as possible disassociated themselves from the traditional core of Chinatown. Many of those who had earned advanced degrees in the 1940s and 1950s, although experiencing initial downward mobility because of their deficiency in English, found professional jobs. Some of the most prominent Chinese Americans are from this rank, including the architect I. M. Pei, Wall Street financier Jerry Tsai, and Noble Prize winners in physics Yang Chen Ning and Lee Tsung Dao.[28]

Perhaps more representative of the displaced Chinese was Rose Chiayin Tsou. A native of Shanghai, she arrived in America in 1947 to study library science. Uncertain of the political climate following the establishment of Communist rule in China, she chose to stay in America. Eventually, she and her husband opened a restaurant in Eugene, Oregon. Her social circle, reflecting her language and educational background, was composed of Mandarin-speaking business and professional people.[29]

As soon as these privileged Chinese had established themselves in America, they sent for their family members, thus consolidating and expanding the social networks that undergirded emigration from Asia. Typically, early uptown Chinese in the 1950s did not live in the old ethnic ghettos. Aside from their upwardly mobile status, which enabled them to join the white flight to the suburbs, changes in the law facilitated their exodus. In 1947 the Supreme Court ruled that restrictive covenants in title deeds—which had long kept Chinese and other Asians out of white-dominated neighborhoods—were unconstitutional. This encouraged some Chinatown residents to leave the ethnic enclaves, especially as local governments gradually lifted restrictions. Five years later the California Supreme Court struck down the alien land laws, which had barred noncitizen Asians from owning land, and similar legislation in other states was also repealed. Thus those with economic means could theoretically settle on land outside Chinatowns.[30]

Of course, de facto discrimination did not disappear completely. Lorraine Yee, born in Los Angeles, recollected that Asians who tried to find real estate in privileged neighborhoods were called "block busters" because they broke the color line. Asian Americans found that real estate agents were reluctant to sell them properties. Nearly twenty years after the 1947 judicial decision, Chinese moving into a white-dominated neighborhood could still spark flames of racial hatred. Sam Sue, who grew up in Mississippi, recalled that the day before his parents planned to close on a house in a white neighborhood in 1966, an irate Euro-American resident threatened to burn the house down. Sue's family had to wait nearly five years before they could build a house on the outskirts of town far away from whites.[31]

Chinese America in the postwar years saw neighborhoods emerge that were separated by class divisions, as taking up residence in the outlying areas of Chinatowns came to represent a higher socioeconomic status. This flight from the inner cities seemed to parallel the larger white outmigration to the suburbs. But because of residual prejudice and for pragmatic and emotional reasons, many Chinese Americans—as did some other ethnic groups—reclustered in neighborhoods adjacent to old Chinatowns. As a result, uptown Chinese could continue to maintain networks of kin and compatriots and in so doing could preserve and transmit to the next generation ethnic values, behaviors, family patterns, gender roles, food preferences, and sociopolitical choices. The poorest Chinese, who made up part of the early downtown populace, however, remained in the core area of Chinatowns.[32]

WORKING-CLASS IMMIGRANTS

The uptown Chinese were very different from the downtown Chinese, who in the 1950s and 1960s included recent, uneducated immigrants from the rural, southern Chinese working class (including refugees who came by way of Hong Kong) who gravitated to the old core of Chinatowns to seek work and living quarters. Some older native-born Chinese also lived in these old neighborhoods. Most downtown Chinese spoke very little English, and they worked for low wages in dead-end jobs, typically as manual laborers and in service-oriented industries.[33]

The downtown Chinese families, although newly reunited, were immediately consumed by the struggle to survive. The sudden arrival of so many women and children severely strained the male-dominated Chinese community, particularly in the areas of employment, health, and delivery of social services. Suffering from poverty and continuing residential discrimination, many families resorted to living in dilapidated dwellings in the ethnic ghettos. A good number of families were forced to live in former bachelor quarters—which often consisted of one- or two-room apartments—or hotel rooms, all typically with limited kitchen and bathroom facilities. In fact, by the late 1960s Chinatowns had become a frequent topic of sensational newspaper exposés; one article described San Francisco's Chinatown as an "impoverished prison . . . behind the picturesque and colorful Grant Avenue facade."[34]

In sum, the absence of a change in economic status precluded residential mobility, which supports a class-bound theory of residential location. Chinatown crowding, which early Euro-American commentators ascribed to cultural predilection, clearly stemmed from economic constraints. For example, the density of dwellings in San Francisco's Chinatown declined in the postwar years, as Chinese Americans had increasing opportunities for residential mobility.[35]

Some people stayed in Chinatowns because of convenience to workplaces, social networks, and ethnic-oriented commercial establishments. For those who lacked facility with the English language, Chinatowns offered language (and cultural) security. A class-based theory of residential location may be insufficient to explain the lack of residential mobility.[36]

GOLD MOUNTAIN WIVES, WAR BRIDES, AND GENDER ROLES

Living on the margins, Chinese women had to work in coethnic restaurants and sweatshops to supplement their husbands' meager incomes. Almost all of these women toiled for endless hours in dangerous and unsanitary workplaces, earned below minimum wage, and received virtually no health or vacation benefits. A typical story is that of Dong Zem Ping. Separated from her husband for several years, Dong had to pose as a war bride after World War II to gain entry into the United States. Since she possessed limited English language and job skills, she had to work in a garment sweatshop, which also became her site for child care. She recalled that the physical toll exacted a heavy cost: "Many times I would accidentally sew my finger instead of the fabric because one child screamed or because I was falling asleep on the job."[37] Through her hard work, however, Dong was able to help support her four children, and later—in a classic case of chain migration—she sent for her China-born son as well as her parents, brothers, and their families.[38]

Gamsaanpo, or Gold Mountain wives, such as Dong were generally disappointed with their new lives in America. During the war many who had lost communication with their trans-Pacific husbands found themselves emotionally abandoned and without financial support. After the war, most came to the United States filled with anticipation of a better life, but they soon discovered that the dream of securing a share of *Gam Saan* turned into *hek fu*, or adversity.[39]

Not only did Chinese wives have to deal with the cultural gap, proscribed economic opportunities, the language barrier, and the emotional cost of trying to survive, they also faced the challenge of sharing a household with their husbands—whom they had previously seen only during the husbands' sporadic visits to China. In the postwar period of reunification, wives complained of social incompatibility, clashing goals and values, and often a meager household income. Many spouses quickly became disenchanted with their husbands' endless working hours and hard physical labor, for which they received pitiful compensation. "I used my tears to wash my face every day," said Lee Wai Lan, who arrived in the United States in 1946.[40] She soon discovered that her husband, who had a white mistress, lived in a dirty house and could offer her little security. Lee found manual work in a Chinese restaurant and soon saved enough to start her own restaurant. Other Chinese spouses, fed up with the daily grind, returned to China. Although many other immigrant women like Lee managed to find self-fulfillment, some apparently failed to cope with the pressure of daily survival: the percentage of female suicides rose from 17.5 percent in the 1950s to 28.3 percent in the 1960s.[41]

Young Chinese "war brides," who generally married more acculturated and educated Chinese men, fared better than the "separated" immigrant wives in their adjustment to life in America. Most had been exposed to some aspects of Western culture while still in China, and when they arrived in the United States they slowly adapted to the new material culture, guided by their Westernized husbands. Some learned English fairly quickly. They wore trendy clothing, groomed their hair in the latest styles, and adopted Caucasian names. With these newly developed life skills, they were able to find employment outside the ethnic ghettos.

For both war brides and separated wives, stabilizing conjugal ties with their husbands was fraught with difficulties. Chinese men who had spent years in an all-bachelor society had acquired recreational habits, such as gambling and patronizing prostitutes, that provoked heated conflict in the reunited families. Wives also had to accept the loss of control over the household budget, which they had managed while residing in China. In the United States women resisted sharing or relinquishing authority to their male spouses, particularly authority over household finances. In some households, however, a more egalitarian division of work emerged; men bereft of their spouses' domestic skills before 1945 continued to use the skills they had acquired during that time. Women, however, did not necessarily abandon their domestic labor. Although many were now wage earners, they were still unpaid household workers under male authority, and in that sense labor remained both liberating and oppressive. Clearly, both wives and husbands were forced to grapple with a new gender division of labor.

REBELLIOUS YOUTH AND EDUCATION

Equally disruptive in Chinese American family life was the intergenerational tension between parents and children who had just joined their fathers in America. Like their recently transplanted mothers, sons and daughters were disillusioned with their fathers' small businesses or dead-end jobs. Having been brought up in China in comfortable surroundings made possible by the remittances sent home by Gold Mountain fathers, the youth rebelled against their parents' "slavish" occupations. In addition, English language deficiency and persistent racial discrimination blocked their own aspirations for occupational mobility. As a result, a good number became malcontents and engaged in antisocial behavior. Increased juvenile crime, although in part rooted in poverty, also stemmed from the general breakdown of family life.[42]

Juvenile delinquency and the antisocial behavior young people demonstrated—especially the foreign born—could likely have been minimized if educational opportunity, considered the main route to achieve socioeconomic mobility, had opened across racial and class lines. In California in 1947 the legislature amended the California Education Code to exclude racial segregation. This terminated de jure segregation in public education as well as the policy of allowing local school districts to establish separate schools for nonwhite youngsters. Segregation did not immediately recede into the distant past, however. Euro-Americans who disliked racial integration could and did move into so-called better neighborhoods, and school boards resorted to gerrymandering housing patterns to determine school district boundaries.[43]

Accessibility to education was also compromised by the public school systems' inability to cope with the large number of newly reunified families after World War II. After 1950 more U.S.-based parents—fearful of the impact of Chinese Communist rule and the Korean War on their children's futures—filed papers to bring their foreign-born children to America. In San Francisco alone, within a seven-year period (1948–1855), around 1,500 immigrant boys and girls with little or no English language background swelled the ranks of the school-age populace and placed a heavy burden on Chinatown schools. Special classes—known as "opportunity classes" at the elementary level and as "Americanization classes" in the secondary schools—had to be set up to quickly immerse these immigrant youths into life in America through lessons in English, citizenship, and geography.[44]

By 1952 Chinatown schools could no longer absorb the massive number of newcomers, and social problems began to emerge. Compounding the situation was the fact that immigrant children often contributed to the household income by working long hours with little rest or sleep. Others had to work to help pay off their recent trans-Pacific passage. A local school survey conducted in San Francisco in 1952 reported that more than 50 percent of immigrant children held after-school jobs, and school officials were convinced that many of their employers had flouted child labor laws regarding the maximum number of hours minors could work each week.

NATIVE-BORN CHINESE AND REJECTION OF CHINESE CULTURE

The entry of a large number of female Chinese immigrants into the United States in the two decades after World War II ended produced a new generation of native-born Chinese. These Chinese Americans—who grew up in the 1950s and early 1960s—like their predecessors in the 1930s, also experienced racial and gender discrimination.

Of mixed racial ancestry, Betty Ann Bruno, whose mother was Chinese Hawaiian and whose father was Irish and Dutch, grew up in California. She remembered that the swimming coach at the local high school prevented her and her siblings from using the swimming pool because the coach mistook them for children of Mexican immigrant farmworkers. In high school and in college Bruno dated white men whose parents, because of antimiscegenation sentiments, forced them to break up with her. Clearly, such feelings had not receded in spite of the California Supreme Court's 1948 ruling that antimiscegenation laws were unconstitutional. It took nearly another twenty years for most other states to repeal their antimiscegenation laws. After college Bruno went to Washington, D.C., to work, where she tried to rent an apartment. The landlord had been very cordial over the telephone, but when he met Bruno in person he told her the apartment was no longer available. As a result of such blatant racist experiences, Bruno internalized self-hatred; she avoided identifying herself as Chinese or Hawaiian until she was middle-aged, and she remembered wishing she had been "born looking different than what [she] was."[45]

Rebelling against their parents' traditional family-centered values and worldview was a way many native-born Chinese American youth of the post-war years asserted their selfhood in a climate where their ethnicity remained a liability and mainstream American youth culture extolled consumerism and rebellion against conformist family life. Ben Fong-Torres, whose name was part Spanish because his father used fraudulent papers to gain entry into the United States, grew up to become a journalist. In Amarillo, Texas, he spent time with white schoolmates, drank root beer floats, and listened to popular music on the jukebox. This was Fong-Torres's "way to feel Americanized."[46] Similarly, Bruno remembered that she wore "bobby socks, had the long sloppy joe sweaters, and learned to drive when [she] was fifteen and ate at the drive-in . . . and did everything that everybody else did."[47]

Throughout his life Fong-Torres tried to juggle pursuing his personal desires and ambitions and fulfilling his filial duty to his parents—a dilemma many young Chinese Americans encountered. In his youth, Fong-Torres dated a white female student but eventually broke off the relationship because he feared the wrath of his parents, who had not supported his free-spirited sister's betrothal to a white artist. Later, he chose to attend a college close to his parents' restaurant so he could work there on weekends. Fong-Torres wrote that he wished he could explain to his parents "the conflicts we [he and his siblings] all felt, growing up both Chinese and American . . . we were torn between obligations to the family and the freedom we naturally wanted."[48]

POLITICS OF ASSIMILATION

Second-generation Chinese Americans were pulled away from their parents' worldview by the repressive climate of the postwar era. The Cold War reversed the flattering image of the Chinese that had prevailed during the war years. Against the backdrop of the rise of the Communist-led People's Republic of China (PRC) in 1949 and the outbreak of the Korean War that pitted the United States against Communist forces in Asia, the Chinese (and Chinese Americans) were now portrayed as inhuman, treacherous, and deceitful. Chinese Communists, according to news magazines, apparently resorted to torturing citizens to extort money from their relatives in the United States. The duplicitous status of many Chinese raised the specter of Communist infiltration into the United States. Because immigrants historically have been linked to radical politics, it was easy for Americans to accept such a claim.[49]

Chinese Americans did not take this sensationalist reporting lightly. The *Chinese Press*, an English language Chinese-owned newspaper, warned its readers that the losing streak of U.S. troops in the Korean War could turn into the "Pearl Harbor" for Americans of Chinese descent. One editorial in late 1951 went so far as to call upon Chinese Americans to be "on constant alert" and to make every attempt "to maintain closer contacts with Caucasian groups" to ward off suspicions of them.

To prove their unequivocal loyalty to the United States, Chinese Americans took steps to demonstrate that they were 100 percent American. First, some Chinese forsook dual citizenship, claiming just U.S. citizenship. In so doing, Chinese Americans were sending a clear signal: they were choosing the United States over China. Aware that native-born Americans drew no distinction between citizens of the PRC and Chinese Americans, the Chinese American press and community leaders denied that the Chinese were naturally inclined toward communism, going so far as to portray China as simply a pawn of Soviet imperialism.

In the 1950s second-generation Chinese Americans came under pressure to move to the suburbs as a way to draw a class distinction between them—upwardly mobile professionals, or at least aspiring ones—and the nonprofessional classes in debilitating Chinatowns. Moving to the suburbs, with their conformist and homogeneous lifestyle, would also prepare middle-class Chinese for full integration into American life. Chinese Americans would be moving away from the checkered past, both geographically and mentally. The sociologist Rose Hum Lee was one voice among educated Chinese Americans who called for integration. Chinese Americans, urged Lee, needed to shed all signs of foreignness to secure complete assimilation. Otherwise, she implied, Chinese, already burdened by their "non-American" physiognomy, were certain to provoke questions about their place in the United States. Born and raised in Butte, Montana, Lee earned a Ph.D. at the University of Chicago. She became the first Chinese American (and the first woman) to head the Sociology Department at Roosevelt University in Chicago. Her life dramatized the positive outcome of assimilation.

But Lee's call for total integration was no less than a call for conformity during the repressive 1950s. To that end, native-born Chinese were told that education was the route to improved economic opportunities. The print media, including the *Chinese Press* and *Time* magazine, highlighted the fact that Chinese Americans were choosing to pursue higher education, suggesting that racial prejudice was a nonexistent barrier as long as they were willing to work long and hard. The route of accommodation taken by American-born Chinese, as gleefully reported in the mainstream media, had produced a generation of productive model citizens—a development that constituted the origins of the "model minority" myth of a later era.

The politics of assimilation in the 1940s and 1950s were also reflected to some degree in the positions of Chinese language newspapers published in the United States. Before World War II the Guomindang had forced several left-wing newspapers out of business through intimidation, harassing journalists, and gaining control of independent community newspapers. Guomindang-owned newspapers propagandized the GMD worldview and rallied Chinese Americans to support the Nationalist regime. Departing from that pattern were the *Chinese World, Chinese Nationalist Daily, China Tribune,* and the *Chinese Pacific Weekly*—the last of which was founded in 1946 in San Francisco by Gilbert Woo. An immigrant who came to the United States in 1932, Woo—like many Chinese American men—was separated from his wife and daughter for decades, another victim of Chinese exclusion. Before he owned the newspaper, Woo was editor of the *Chinese Times*, the mouthpiece of the Chinese American Citizens Alliance. At the height of World War II, Woo wrote a regular column for the paper that kept Chinese soldiers abroad abreast of community news. The *Chinese Times* and other Chinese American newspapers also invited soldiers and civilians to write about their wartime experiences. In a sense, the press knitted a far-flung community facing dispersal and mobility during the war years. Equally important, the press reminded Chinese Americans to draw a link between the war against fascism and the war against racism facing them on the home front.[50]

After the war many Chinese Americans moved out of Chinatown, yet they remained attuned to community changes through the press. The *Chinese Pacific Weekly*, for example, provided extensive coverage of the postwar changes in immigration laws. Woo's editorials encouraged Chinese Americans to improve their English and to vote, since such participation would prove that they were upstanding citizens committed to the United States who did not deserve to be discriminated against. Concomitantly, he urged Chinese Americans to distance themselves from China-related politics, since such efforts distracted them from the struggle of integrating into the larger American society and further split the community.

CONFESSION PROGRAM

In the 1950s some young Chinese Americans who heeded the call for integration into the mainstream society discovered that their estrangement from their parents' generation was exacerbated by the silence and secrecy engendered by the "paper son" scheme. Because of the exclusionary laws, some parents—particularly fathers—used false identities and hid the truth even from their own children and extended families. Wong Gun Chown, the father of scholar Charles Choy Wong, had secured a slot as a son of a bona fide American citizen and entered the United States in 1936. When Wong senior returned from a two-year visit to China in 1949, he falsely reported that he had sired two sons (in addition to two real sons) to create new slots for sale. Wong's wife and second son, Charles, entered the country in the 1950s, but not before the duplicity had been exposed when the authorities interrogated the wife. In a tragic twist of fate, that exposure led immigration authorities to turn down the visa application of the eldest son, who then committed suicide. This memory of a fractured family haunted Charles Choy Wong for years and was likely the cause of the emotional distance he felt from his father. Apparently, Wong junior discovered the story of his illegal family name and fractured identity through the Confession Program implemented by the Immigration and Naturalization Service.[51]

The Confession Program, initiated in 1957, was ostensibly designed to allow Chinese paper sons an opportunity to clear up their family immigration histories, which had become contorted because of earlier false claims. The program, at least in theory, allowed those who had gained entry into the United States through fraudulent means to regularize their status if a close relative—spouse, parent, or child—was a U.S. citizen or a permanent resident alien. Data compiled from the INS records suggest that at least 25 percent of the Chinese American population in 1950 was in the country illegally. The practice of paper immigration during the exclusion era had only reinforced the stigma of marginalization, augmenting the racialized view that the Chinese were unscrupulous, devious, and immoral. Illegal immigration undercut, in the mind-set of non-Chinese, any claim to U.S. citizenship. Equally damaging was the dominant perception that all Chinese arrivals were illegal immigrants; the detention and prolonged interrogations at the Angel Island immigration station arose from that context. Paper immigration also reinforced the isolation of Chinese America by demanding that immigrants maintain networks of identity protection. To end the social isolation, the majority of the 30,000 Chinese Americans involved in the Confession Program eventually either chose or were forced to attain legal status by becoming permanent resident aliens or naturalized citizens.[52]

The program, however, had its origin in the Cold War fear that the fraudulent entry of some Chinese immigrants had allowed some Communists to enter. Even before the Communist victory in mainland China in 1949, several suspected leftist organizations—such as the Chinese Hand Laundry Alliance, the Chinese Workers Mutual Aid Association, and Min Qing (Chinese American Democratic Youth League)—came under the surveillance of the Federal Bureau of Investigation (FBI).[53]

But a backlog of applications that resulted from potential immigrants fleeing the civil war in China in the late 1940s and early 1950s also precipitated the search for a more efficient way to process new arrivals. The Hong

Kong consulate that processed visas and passports for mainland Chinese applicants had blood tests gathered since 1951 to weed out false paternity applications, but that did not eliminate the established interrogation and scrutiny—which in fact became more probing and time-consuming. The approximately 2,000 civil suits Chinese American derivative citizens (spouses and children of U.S. citizens) who were denied passports filed in the U.S. courts for a declaratory judgment on their claims to citizenship also increased the urgency for a new direction.

Everett F. Drumwright, the U.S. consul general in Hong Kong, led the administrative response that expressed anti-Communist politics and racialized suspicions. In December 1955 Drumwright warned in a report submitted to the U.S. State Department that the paper immigration was tied to Communist infiltration. Drumwright raised the specter of China sending spies masquerading as immigrants into the United States. Since the warning came on the heels of a stalemate in the Korean War, the failure of French forces to wrest control of Vietnam from the Communists, and the diplomatic standoff over islands off the Chinese coast claimed by both Taiwan and the PRC, much of it seemed credible. Although the State Department did not accept Drumwright's harsh recommendation to end extensive investigation of denied applications by simply denying passports and visas on the basis of mere suspicion, the report gave momentum to a coordinated effort to ferret out illegal immigrants.

In early 1956 the Department of Justice ordered that grand juries be impaneled to investigate illegal Chinese entries. Officers of thirty-four Chinese family and district associations in San Francisco, along with their records, were subpoenaed. The Chinese Consolidated Benevolent Association (CCBA), or Chinese Six Companies, led a successful legal challenge to this blanket subpoena. Undeterred, INS, FBI, and State Department officials targeted individual Chinese to appear before the grand juries. These investigations led to the dismissal of around 200 civil suits and to thirty-eight indictments. INS agents searched Chinese residences and raided business establishments. They questioned suspected paper family members and ringleaders. They rounded up Chinese seamen, believing they had eluded the law since they came under British jurisdiction. Agents interrogated leftist Chinese Americans and deported some. Chinese American leaders protested and, perhaps in an attempt to strike a chord with the capitalist-minded Eisenhower administration, stressed that the raids had resulted in losses to merchants of up to $100,000 a week.

Besides resorting to legal action, Chinese community leaders also took defensive measures. The CCBA in Boston urged Chinese Americans to remove their names from their true family associations and register in associations linked to their paper surnames. In Washington, D.C., the CCBA created new records to conceal fraud and destroy incriminating evidence. In March 1957, 124 delegates representing Chinese Americans from all parts of the country met in Washington, D.C. They passed resolutions urging the U.S. government to reform immigration policies and to adjust the status of paper immigrants. To those ends, CCBA leaders agreed to promote the INS Chinese Confession Program.

According to INS statistics, from 1957 to 1965 at least 11,336 Chinese Americans confessed to having slipped into the United States under false pretenses. About 5,800 slots—names of nonexistent persons not yet claimed for illegal entry—were closed. Another 19,124 people were implicated as holding false citizenship by the confessions of other Chinese Americans.[54] But many Chinese Americans, unwilling to implicate relatives and friends and historically distrustful of immigration authorities, avoided the process altogether.

The postwar program evoked a general panic in Chinatowns, in part because of the aggressive efforts by the INS to seek confessions—efforts that often began with leads from anonymous telephone calls, letters, and seized family documents. Against the backdrop of grand jury investigations, anti-Communist sentiments, and rumors of mass deportations, Chinese Americans kept a low profile or caved in to intimidation.[55]

Equally discouraging for those who contemplated confessing was the absence of an assurance that if a Chinese person who confessed was determined to be eligible for an existing statutory remedy—such as qualifying for the preference system or showing proof of extreme hardship and good moral character—the paperwork would be processed in a timely fashion. Those deemed qualified for any remedy usually had to give up their citizenship status and wait a number of years before they could apply for and receive permanent resident status. The INS never promised confessors that they would receive immunity from prosecution. Meanwhile, their occupational mobility was circumscribed, since they had no immigration status. Furthermore, they had to limit political participation for fear of being deported on the grounds of "subversive activity." As it turned out, many were not eligible for any statutory remedy, and a few were deported.[56]

THE CHINESE MARXIST LEFT AND COLD WAR POLITICS

The authorities deported some Chinese Americans because they had been members of either progressive or labor-related organizations, including the Chinese American Democratic Youth League (CADYL) and the Chinese Workers' Mutual Aid Association (CWMAA). These organizations did harbor some Chinese Communist sympathizers, but many of the members had also participated in the struggle to gain democratic rights in the United States—such as working on election campaigns for progressive candidates and mobilizing support for passage of a fair employment practice act in California.[57]

The Marxist left, through its publications and contacts with affiliated organizations like the Chinese Hand Laundry Alliance (CHLA), captured the attention of political dissidents and Chinese from all walks of life. Many average Chinese men and women had become disillusioned with GMD corruption and totalitarian rule, which, in turn, had resulted in economic ruin and social dissipation in China over the last several decades. By the end of 1947, the situation in GMD-held territories in China had deteriorated to such a degree that even some Chinese American businesspeople—generally considered the most politically conservative segment of the community— gave support to a new North American–based united front organization. The Overseas Chinese League for Peace and Democracy in China, founded in late 1947, tried to promote democracy and oppose American involvement in the civil war raging in China. On college campuses progressive Chinese students, through their publications, urged students from China to prepare themselves to return to help reconstruct the homeland.

A few other left-oriented organizations tried to promote nonintervention in Chinese domestic issues. The CHLA sent telegrams and letters asking congressional members to vote against military aid for the crumbling Nationalist government. The Chinese section of the NMU persuaded U.S. maritime workers to boycott a shipment of war-related supplies to Chiang Kai-shek's regime. The Chinese left also organized a number of speak-outs against Chiang and the U.S. military presence in China. When the 1948 presidential race heated up, Chinese Americans opposed to U.S. involvement in China backed the Progressive Party candidate, Henry Wallace, who had criticized that policy. As the conflict in the homeland drew to a bloody conclusion, intraethnic support for the Marxist left ignited, only to be doused by the combined counterattacks of GMD elements and the U.S. government.

International and domestic events halted the growing support for the Communist-led PRC. The Cold War, marked by dramatic actions by the Soviet Union such as the Communist coups in Eastern Europe in 1947 and 1948 and the Berlin blockade in 1948, plunged the United States into a global struggle to contain the Soviet Union and stop the spread of communism. In 1948 red-baiting in the United States escalated with the espionage case of Alger Hiss. When the Korean War broke out in 1950 and the PRC entered the conflict, the U.S. government resumed military aid to the Nationalist regime in Taiwan and restrained Chinese students in the United States from leaving for mainland China.

More ominously, FBI agents and immigration officials increased surveillance of the Chinese community. Tung Pok Chin, who served his country during World War II, recalled that FBI agents made multiple visits to his laundry. Apparently, the authorities believed that since his writings had frequently appeared in the *China Daily News*, a Chinese language newspaper with suspected leftist leanings, he could be a Communist sympathizer or worse. Fearing for his and his family's future in America, he burned all his poems.

FBI intimidation panicked Chinese Americans; even some moderate Chinese newspapers had to fold because of canceled subscriptions and advertisements. In this milieu, GMD supporters, through the party's China Lobby—a conservative network consisting of Euro-American congressional members, military officials, businesspeople, and journalists—pressured Congress to offer more assistance to the GMD government in exile in Taiwan. GMD forces and their allies, which included the powerful House Un-American Activities Committee, eventually focused on unraveling the so-called Communist conspiracy at home that supposedly had caused the United States to "lose" China. Scholars affiliated with the think tank the American Council of the Institute of Pacific Relations along with China experts in the State Department were vilified in congressional hearings; those subjected to such treatment included Chinese American progressives such as Chen Hansheng, Y. Y. Hsu, and Chu Tong. The U.S. Justice Department began applying the "guilt by association" principle even more strictly when it indicted those who sent money to relatives and acquaintances in mainland China. U.S. intelligence, with the aid of customs officials, also blocked the entry of any goods suspected of originating from mainland China or from Hong Kong businesses linked to the mainland. Not surprisingly, remittances to relatives in China—which had amounted to $7 million in 1948—plummeted to $600,000 within a year and continued to drop.

The Chinese left in the United States almost collapsed under the weight of this deepening scrutiny. Some established organizations—including the CWMAA—became defunct, and others such as the CHLA suffered a dramatic drop in membership. Other organizations dropped progressive-sounding names and revamped their missions to stay afloat. The CADYL changed its name in 1954 to the more innocuous-sounding Chinese American Youth Club and shifted its emphasis to educational, cultural, and social activities.

Undoubtedly, the Confession Program of the 1950s and 1960s sacrificed left-wing activists. Still, the program's legacy was not entirely dark. At the least, it legalized countless Chinese paper sons, opening the door for their sons and daughters to claim the rights and privileges of U.S. citizenship in the decades to come. By straightening out distorted family genealogies, the program allowed Chinese to sponsor their true relatives into the country. It laid the basis for Chinese Americans to make full use of the family reunification provisions of the 1965 immigration reforms.

REVIVAL OF GMD CONTROL

Because of the general political hysteria, interest in Chinatown organizations— even those with little connection to the Marxist left—declined sharply. That decline, coupled with ongoing red baiting, held the door open for a small, select group of community leaders to control Chinatown's political and social structures until diplomatic relations between the United States and the PRC were normalized in the 1970s. Meanwhile, GMD agents cajoled the CCBA to form anti-Communist leagues in every Chinese American community. Apparently, the CCBA and other pro-GMD Chinatown organizations even assisted the Immigration Office and the Justice Department in pinpointing Chinese Communist members or sympathizers.[58]

The revival of GMD control within Chinese America resulted from a series of overlapping events. Many organizations were going through a change of guard. The deaths of members of the so-called bachelor's society led to a vacuum in leadership, one the second generation—which was more in step with mainstream America—was disinclined to fill. GMD party followers who chose to emigrate to the United States rather than move to Taiwan were ready to fill those roles. Chinese Americans could only acquiesce, given the prevailing anti-Communist atmosphere and the PRC economic reforms that seemed to undermine the interests of their families back in China.[59]

The hostile climate dampened interest within the Chinese community for progressive, left-oriented political activities. Once the initial panic over red baiting and the Confession Program subsided, the general interest in China-oriented politics resumed. Chinese Americans felt compelled to demonstrate their commitment to the Taiwan government as a way to convince mainstream Americans that they believed in U.S. democracy and that they were "not Communists, but democratic, freedom-loving people," to quote Ruby Chow of Seattle.[60] Victimized by the West's skewed image of Red China and suspected as a potential fifth column of the PRC, Chinese Americans tried to counter those attitudes by taking part in the Guomindang's anti-Communist campaign. Chinese American involvement in Guomindang activities received the stamp of approval from the Taiwan government, which until the 1980s never gave up the idea of "patriotic overseas Chinese" or the principle of jus sanguinis—the policy that a child's citizenship is determined by its parents' citizenship. Since the Taiwanese government held this ambivalent attitude toward assimilation into mainstream U.S. society, some Chinese in America could still see themselves as part of a larger China-oriented political sphere, even though the PRC had early renounced its claim on the loyalty of overseas Chinese and encouraged them to take up citizenship in the receiving countries.[61]

In the 1950s Chinese Americans' interest in the politics of their ancestral homeland was compelling for a number of other reasons. The situation can perhaps be clarified by comparing Japanese immigration after 1945 with that of the Chinese in the postwar years. Both mainland China and Taiwan continued to send immigrants to the United States in significant numbers after 1945—unlike Japan, which sent few immigrants. As a result, Chinese communities in North America have continuously grown, both in terms of the number of compatriots and in cultural and ethnic consciousness. Because the new arrivals came from a country marked by tumultuous events, their political sensibilities were heightened. Furthermore, the unceasing instability in China—the civil war, the rise of Communist rule on mainland China, the socialist transformation, the chaotic 1960s' Cultural Revolution, and the continuing political tensions between China and Taiwan—kept the attention of the Chinese in America riveted on China-oriented politics. Japan's political stability, in contrast, has done little to sensitize Japanese Americans to their connection to the ancestral homeland.

NEW SOCIAL ORGANIZATIONS

In the postwar years the diversity of the Chinese American community, with different segments of the populace at different stages of acculturation into mainstream society, precluded the GMD from exerting complete influence on all social groups. Continuing a trend set during World War II, Chinese Americans discovered that with the doors of opportunity opening, they could find work without having to rely on native place or district associations or clans. More Chinese perused newspapers for employment information or asked fellow professionals for advice. The arrival of a large number of immigrant women and families in the postwar years meant later newcomers could depend on family members or relatives to facilitate their adaptation to life in the United States. The role of the *huiguan* seemed superfluous. The existence of families also displaced the need to join a clan or *huiguan*, since newcomers could rely on the former rather than banding with members of the latter to serve as investors in small businesses.[62]

The existence of American-born Chinese, a displaced intellectual class, the small merchant elite (*qiao ling*), a dwindling so-called sojourner generation (*lao huaqiao*) made up mostly of workers, and an increasing number of female newcomers—which collectively is admittedly a simplification of the social structure—led to the proliferation of new organizations. Old Chinatown organizations, with their deeply rooted traditions and ingrained leadership, could not accommodate all of the different groups. New organizations, the outcome of a reinvigorated flow of immigration, sprung up after the war. They included alumni and professional associations, sports and social clubs, and new non-Cantonese associations.

Most new non-Cantonese associations had membership requirements based on geographic origin and dialect-group affiliation. Those established during the 1940s include New York's Fujian Tongxianghui and San Francisco's Meixi Fujian Tongxianghui, both of which drew together Fujianese who hailed from Fuzhou and were primarily maritime workers who settled in U.S. port cities. Those who hailed from Chaozhou organized their own Chaozhou Tongxianghui in New York around 1956. Although they provided services akin to those of the Cantonese associations, they exerted little political influence, largely because of their small memberships.[63]

Alumni associations encompassed a growing percentage of the Chinese American populace. Membership in these organizations is determined by matriculation at a particular institution. Since most schools in China drew a high proportion of students from the surrounding geographic area, these organizations resemble locality associations insofar as place of origin is concerned. Alumni groups, however, tend to be a more recent phenomenon.

The outcome of the higher percentage of foreign-born Chinese with middle school and higher education in the postwar period, alumni clubs can be divided according to the schools' locality. Institutions in the Pearl River Delta—which attracted surrounding Cantonese-speaking people—such as Lingnan and Zhongshan (Sun Yat-sen) Universities and Peizheng (Pui Ging) and Taishan middle schools, have alumni clubs in Chinese communities across North America. Universities and schools outside the Pearl River Delta—particularly those in eastern and northern China—include such well-known institutions as Beijing (Peking), Yanjing (Yenching), and Jiaotung (Chiaotung) Universities. Because the alumni of these institutions are spread all over the globe, the world headquarters of some alumni clubs are in Taipei. When students from Taiwan began settling in the United States in the mid-1960s, alumni clubs of Taiwanese tertiary institutions such as Taiwan and Chengkung Universities began to surface. These clubs are so active that California even has an umbrella organization called the Zhongguo Da-zhuan Xiaoyou Lianhehui (Federation of Alumni of Chinese Universities and Institutes). Finally, a few alumni groups in the United States cater to those who graduated from Hong Kong institutions such as Hong Kong University and Chinese University of Hong Kong.

IMMIGRATION REFORM IN THE 1960S

Although the two decades following the end of World War II witnessed changes in the place of origin of emigration, population size, occupational distribution, class alignments, growth in the ethnic economy, the flourishing of sociopolitical life, and an evolving political consciousness, even more dramatic shifts occurred after significant immigration legislation was passed in the mid-1960s. Before John F. Kennedy entered the White House, Presidents Harry Truman and Dwight D. Eisenhower had tried to push, respectively, for ending the national origins system and for imposing quotas without regard to race, national origin, creed, or color. Both leaders failed. President Kennedy shared his predecessors' desire for immigration reform and recognized the need to end the national origins system. Kennedy consequently called for the repeal of race-based exclusion of the Asia-Pacific triangle. Kennedy's rationale lay in his recognition of the interdependence of nations in the growing globalization of the world economy. By the early 1960s the transnational movement of workers, refugees, and their families had become one of many global exchanges of capital, commodities, and information across national boundaries. The 1952 measures, as Kennedy argued, had failed, however, to encourage a rapid and large influx of professionals and skilled workers who could contribute to U.S. economic development.[64]

The proposed reform of immigration laws also, but to a lesser extent, stemmed from the desire of policy makers to counter Communist propaganda that the United States had treated Asian immigrants poorly during the Cold War era. To that end, immigration laws had to reflect the humanitarian ideals of a free society. Racial discrimination at the policy level, as exemplified by the national origins quota and the Asia-Pacific triangle, was inadvisable politically. Said one member of Congress, "How can we say to nations around the globe . . . that their people are not worthy of coming to the United States and then expect them to stand beside us in the war against . . . Communism?"[65]

Immigration reform in the mid-1960s was probably conceived more to promote economic development both at home and abroad and to deflect the Communist challenge than to rectify past injustices committed against Asian immigrants. The Kennedy and Lyndon Baines Johnson administrations downplayed the impact immigration reform would have on new Asian arrivals. Senator Edward Kennedy, a key figure in shepherding the reforms through the Senate, assured Americans that "the ethnic mix of this country [would] not be upset" and that the reform would "not inundate America with immigrants [from] . . . the most populated and economically deprived nations of Africa and Asia."[66] President Johnson, although critical of the race-based exclusion of the Asia-Pacific triangle, considered reform necessary to repair historical errors made in regulating Eastern and Southern European immigration, but he was fairly silent about how Asian immigrants figured into the plan.

In spite of the minimal attention paid to the exodus from Asia to America, the 1965 amendments to the 1952 McCarran-Walter Act (although the 1965 bill became known as the Immigration and Nationality Act, it was in effect a series of amendments) were far-reaching in transforming immigration provisions for Asian arrivals. The legislation abolished the national origins quota system (along with the legislation for the Asia-Pacific triangle) on July 1, 1968. As of that date, each sovereign country in the Eastern Hemisphere, regardless of its size, received a quota of up to 20,000 immigrants per year. The applicant's quota would be charged to his or her country of birth rather than to his or her nationality or race. The Chinese now had a quota of 20,000 per year instead of the 205 per year that had been allowed since 1952. Since the 1965 bill placed a much heavier emphasis on family reunification than it did on occupation and most visas were therefore reserved for relatives, policy makers did not expect that Asians in America—who had low rates of immigration prior to 1965—would be able to take advantage of the new law.[67]

The new amendments also established new categories for admittance. Two occupational categories helped aliens fill jobs that lacked qualified U.S. citizens. Additionally, under the nonpreference category an alien who invested $40,000 in a business could qualify for immigration to the United States. Furthermore, Congress made available a process for adjusting the status of people who originally entered as nonimmigrants—such as students, temporary workers, and tourists—and who later applied for permanent residence. Since these categories were available to applicants from all countries, Asians had no advantage over other nationalities. The Chinese, however, could take advantage of a new refugee category that reflected Cold War politics— namely, the "seventh preference" for persons fleeing a Communist or Communist-dominated country.[68]

In spite of the expectations of policy makers and their inattention to Asian immigrants, the 1965 law worked in ways the sponsors probably never expected. First, the amendments were out of step with the general pattern of immigration. Between 1946 and 1965 only 57 percent of immigrants who entered the United States came from Europe, and by the early 1960s the percentage had dipped far lower. Fewer Europeans arrived because Western Europeans, who enjoyed a high socioeconomic status, saw no reason to emigrate. The Irish, the one Western European group that sought entry in large numbers, found it difficult to do so because too few recent legal Irish immigrants were available to provide the close blood connection needed to generate chain migration. And Eastern Europeans who wanted to flee Communist repression could not do so easily. Of the 4.83 million persons legally admitted between 1946 and 1965, an increasing percentage were Asians: the figure rose from 6 percent of legal immigrants in the 1950s to 12 percent in the 1960s.[69]

Second, Congress failed to appreciate the impact of chain migration. Growing numbers of Asians (and Latin Americans, since there was no cap on the number admitted from the Western Hemisphere until the 1965 law placed one at 120,000 annually) had arrived since 1945, and as soon as they had attained permanent resident status, a cohort of relatives became eligible for immigration under the second preference category. When the relatives became

U.S. citizens, as a large number did within the minimum five-year waiting period, more persons became eligible for admittance under the preference system. This process continued, with citizenship or permanent residence bestowed on each new cohort of arrivals. Since 1965, chain migration has accounted for the vast majority of nonrefugee admittances.[70]

Third, the 1965 act, although it places an annual global ceiling of 290,000 entries, is applicable only to those subject to numerical limitation. Legal immigration, which hovered around a quarter of a million annually in the 1950s, rose to about a third of a million annually in the 1960s and to nearly half a million annually by the mid-1970s. This pattern of consistent growth was clearly a reversal of the slowdown since the 1920s. Even more unanticipated was the reversal of the direction of emigration; instead of a wave from across the Atlantic, it was and remains a wave from Asia and Latin America.

In the short term the 1965 law, with its emphasis on family reunification and skilled workers, allowed temporary visitors for pleasure (presumably some were relatives of U.S. citizens of Chinese ancestry) and students, including their wives and children (the assumption is that the students were enrolled in professional or graduate studies), to adjust their status. Between 1966 and 1975 an average of 38 percent of the Chinese accepted as immigrants were in fact Chinese already in the United States on a nonimmigrant status. For example, following immigration reforms in 1965, Chinese admissions soared from 4,769 in 1965 to 17,708 in 1966; of the latter number, 11,300, or 64.2 percent, of the admissions were Chinese already residing in the United States.[71]

By 1960, as revealed in census data collected that year, there were 236,084 Chinese in the United States (including Hawai'i)—a 67.4 percent increase since 1950. The gender ratio had changed dramatically, as male dominance dropped from 65.5 percent to 57.4 percent. These changes notwithstanding, some demographic facts remained basically the same. Most of the Chinese population was still concentrated in the West: 60.6 percent lived in four Pacific states—California, Washington, Oregon, and Hawai'i. Still reflecting the bachelor immigration pattern, Chinese males were significantly older than Chinese females, with a median age of 30.9 years for males and 25.2 for females. Also reflecting the prewar immigration patterns, males predominated among the elderly.[72]

By the mid-1960s obvious changes had occurred in Chinese America, particularly in the areas of educational and occupational attainment, gender roles, geographic dispersal, and reconfiguration of the ethnic economy. Overall, there was a movement toward acculturation into mainstream life, even though marginality remained a critical phenomenon—particularly for newcomers. In the post-1965 era Chinese Americans, along with other Americans of Asian descent, would encounter numerous new challenges such as the reemergence of nativism, increasing intraethnic diversity, and the rise of pan-ethnicity, or an Asian American worldview. Yet because the growth of the Chinese American community is part of the larger unparalleled migration flow, the social meanings of race, ethnicity, and American identity were further refracted by the overall changing U.S. racial and ethnic makeup.

5 Socioeconomic Mobility and the Ethnic Economy

IMPACT OF IMMIGRATION REFORM

Since 1965 the rapid, unceasing flow of *xin yin min* (in Cantonese *san yi man*, "new immigrants") to the United States has transformed the socioeconomic mobility of Chinese America and the nature of its enclave economy. As the population becomes increasingly heterogeneous and polarized by class lines rooted in differences in human and monetary capital, education, language, political affiliation, place of origin, previous exposure to Westernization, and cultural preference pattern, the wage-earning labor force has become less concentrated within just a few sectors.

Although a significant number of Chinese Americans have been incorporated economically into the larger society, many have not become integrated into mainstream society. In fact, some have not even undergone cultural assimilation (change of cultural patterns to those of the dominant society), let alone structural assimilation (large-scale entrance into the cliques, clubs, and institutions of the dominant society). In a sense, some new Chinese immigrants, especially those from Taiwan and Hong Kong, have defied the argument of contemporary social scientists that upward economic mobility is a function of integration into the larger society. To understand this phenomenon, some background information about immigration after 1965 is necessary.

Since the mid-1960s immigration reform has initiated several significant shifts that depart from the pattern of Chinese arrival and settlement before World War II. First, from the 1940s to the 1970s, the majority of the Chinese population was native born, reflecting the maturation of the progeny generation of the early twentieth century. By 1980, however, the majority of Chinese were foreign born.[1]

Second, family immigration has characterized Chinese American life since the mid-1960s reforms went into full effect in 1968. Most of the new Chinese immigrants after 1968 came as nuclear families. In the 1990s immediate relatives—who are not subject to the numerical limitations of the preference system—made up a substantial proportion of the total immigration to the United States. For example, among a total of 708,394 immigrants admitted into the United States in 1993, 251,647, or 35 percent, were immediate relatives of U.S. citizens.[2] This family-chain migration has affected the acculturation of immigrants. Since newcomers are part of a larger ethnic social network, they depend on its support. The Chinese community has had to respond to these newcomers' needs, and in the process ethnic identity remains intact and is even strengthened. Finally, newcomers after 1965—unlike earlier immigrants—have included a significant number of white-collar professionals, and many have arrived with their families seeking to settle permanently rather than sojourn as single men.[3]

MIGRATION AND CONDITIONS IN CHINA

Although the Chinese migration pattern since 1965 has undoubtedly been reshaped by revised U.S. immigration policy, it has also been affected by changing conditions regarding exit. Following the 1949 Chinese Revolution, mainland China slipped into a period of repressive Communist rule that clamped down on people's exit from and entry into the country. Chinese citizens became increasingly resentful of their unrealized potential. Apparently, those with *hai-wai-quan-xi* (relatives abroad) were treated as enemies of the People's Republic of China (PRC). They were suspected of having committed, or being capable of committing, treason in support of the Nationalist government or American imperialists.[4]

One interviewee, identified only as Mr. Peng, recalled that he and his family lost countless opportunities for advanced education and job promotions because his wife's brother had fled to Hong Kong and later immigrated to the United States. Embittered by the experience, Peng remembered that after the Cultural Revolution he "simply could not take it another time. This world is large—why should I be in China to make a living?" In the early

1980s his daughter, who had married a Chinatown worker and later became a naturalized U.S. citizen, managed to get the entire family out of China.[5]

Clearly, in the wake of continual turmoil and political repression in China, the Chinese suffered from a national identity crisis. They came to appreciate the wide gap that existed between aspirations and the means to attain them in China and thus began to see emigration as the most effective means of fulfilling their wish for a better future. Furthermore, the remittances sent to China by newly arrived Chinese workers in America were seemingly convincing testimony that the United States offered an abundance of opportunity.[6]

IMMIGRATION AND GLOBAL RESTRUCTURING AFTER 1965

In 1981 the 1965 act was amended to bring it in line with full normalization of U.S. relations with the PRC, so that mainland China—like Taiwan—would receive a separate yearly quota of 20,000 immigrants to the United States. As a result, the total immigration from both "Chinas" rose from 25,000 in 1981 to nearly 40,000 in 1985. By then the PRC government had adopted an open-door policy and initiated national economic reform. The PRC government gradually lifted the barriers to emigration, although those with exceptional professional skills and higher education degrees or those with sensitive positions in government or scientific research institutions were prevented from emigrating. Most applicants today still face a laborious screening process.[7]

Chinese entrepreneurs and investors in Asia also secured an additional opportunity to emigrate following passage of the 1990 Immigration Act, drawn up to help supply the United States with skilled workers and attract needed capital. This legislation in some ways reversed the postwar trend that emphasized family reunification because it encouraged the immigration of skilled workers and their families by increasing the number of visas for them from 54,000 to 120,000 per year.[8]

By the time the act was passed, global restructuring—rapid global economic integration—had weakened U.S. postwar dominance of the world economy. Capital from the United States, as well as that from other developed countries, found its way to less-developed countries to take advantage of comparatively lower labor costs and greater accessibility to resources. Furthermore, developing countries in Asia had penetrated the global economy by manufacturing for export to developed countries like the United States. The result of these developments for the United States in the 1980s was stagnation, stymied productivity growth, high inflation, rising unemployment, and economic dislocation. The worst recession since the Great Depression of the 1930s hit the United States in the early 1980s. Overall, the restructuring, coupled with rising productivity rates, led to fewer jobs in traditional production and goods-processing industries. To compensate, U.S. capitalism reorganized by focusing on the information processing and microelectronics industries and the service sector, thus increasing the number of high- and low-paying jobs. Some existing manufacturing industries, however, innovated through task routinization (which further fragments the division of labor and deskills workers), thus enabling them to use unskilled labor from the readily available pool of immigrant workers.[9]

To meet the challenge of global restructuring, the United States—as did many industrialized nations—chose to lure new human and physical capital by lowering the immigration bar for capitalist newcomers. The 1990 law not only more than doubled the yearly number of skill-based visas but also earmarked 10,000 of them for those willing to invest at least $1 million in a new business that employed at least ten workers. Additionally, the law also provides for an annual lottery that enables 40,000 persons per year to be admitted.[10]

Since 1965 an increasing number of immigrants of Chinese descent have come from the former British colony of Hong Kong. In 1986 Hong Kong's quota was increased from 600 to 5,000 persons per year. In anticipation of the return of Hong Kong to the PRC in 1997, the 1990 act also allowed for an increase of Hong Kong's quota to 10,000, which was revised to 20,000 in 1995.[11]

Some of the more than 850,000 Chinese who arrived in the United States between 1965 and 1990 had entered under new refugee provisions. In 1980 the Refugee Act was enacted to broaden the definition of a refugee beyond that of a person fleeing from a Communist-dominated country as a way to reflect the end of the Cold War. The revamped definition now encompassed those who, for fear of persecution on account of race, religion, nationality, membership in a particular social group, or political opinion, were unable or unwilling to return to their country of origin. This change in the definition has enabled more Chinese, including those originating from non-Communist lands like Hong Kong and Taiwan, to enter. The passage of the Chinese Student Protection Act in 1992, legislated in the wake of the 1989 Tiananmen Square massacre, allowed 48,212 students from mainland China already present in the United States to become legal immigrants.[12]

DEMOGRAPHIC STATISTICS

As a result of the new avenues of immigration, the number of first-generation Chinese immigrants in the United States today far exceeds the number of native-born Chinese. The U.S. Bureau of Census estimated in 1990 that 63 percent of the Chinese population constituted first-generation immigrants. This high percentage is predicted to extend far into the new millennium. In fact, the percentage would likely be even higher if a severe backlog—the result of a high demand for visas from China—had not developed for preference categories, with the wait for some as long as eight years.[13]

From 1980 to 1990, mostly as a result of immigration (a high rate of natural increase played a secondary part), the Chinese population in America doubled from 806,040 to 1,645,472. Of that total, 253,719 were born in Taiwan, 152,263 were born in Hong Kong, and the rest trace their ancestral origins to mainland China. Among Asian Pacific American (APA) groups—including those from Samoa, Guam, and other Asian Pacific islands—during that same period, the Chinese were not the fastest-growing group. Outpacing the Chinese were the Vietnamese, Koreans, and Asian Indians. In 1990 Chinese Americans, however, constituted the largest APA population; they represented 22.6 percent of all Asian Pacific Americans and about 0.7 percent of all Americans. In total numerical increase, Chinese Americans outpaced the other APA groups, and, more significant, in the 1980s they made up the third-largest group of legal immigrants to the United States, exceeded only by those from Mexico and the Philippines.[14]

When all APA groups are taken into consideration and measured against other groups in the United States, several salient facts emerge. Although APAs made up only 2.8 percent of the total U.S. population in 1990, their numbers increased by a little more than 95 percent from 1980 to 1990, growing from approximately 3.7 to 7.3 million. African Americans constituted 11.7 percent of the total population in 1990 but saw a net gain of only 13.2 percent during the previous decade. The number of nonwhite Hispanics, who comprised 9 percent of the total population in 1990, grew by 53 percent during the 1980s. Finally, whites, who made up 75.6 percent of the total U.S. population in 1990, accounted for a meager 6 percent increase during the 1980s.[15]

Data from the 2000 census suggest that Asian Americans are the fastest-growing population in the United States. Between 1990 and 2000 the population of those who reported being Asian alone increased by 48 percent, compared with the total population growth of 13 percent. When those who reported their race as constituting one or more Asian groups are counted along with those who reported their race as a combination of one of the Asian groups and another race, the percentage jumps to 72 percent. Chinese Americans remained the largest Asian group, with 2,432,585 reporting being Chinese alone; that number increased to about 2.7 million if it includes those who reported their race as a combination of Chinese and one or more other races or Asian groups. The over 2.4 million who reported being Chinese alone constitute 23.7 percent of a total Asian population of 10,232,998 (those reporting one Asian group alone). Of the 2.4 million Chinese, an estimated 1.5 million are foreign born. Between 1990 and 2000 the total population of those who reported being Chinese alone increased by 787,113. Chinese Americans made up 0.9 percent of the total U.S. population in 2000.[16]

Asian Pacific Americans are one of the fastest-growing groups in the United States. Social scientists and scholars predict that the APA population will continue to experience rapid growth well into the twenty-first century, with a projected growth of at least 17.9 million by 2020—which would be a 145 percent increase from 1990. A large percentage of this group will be made up of Chinese Americans.[17]

GEOGRAPHIC DISTRIBUTION

In terms of geographic dispersion, Chinese Americans, as well as other APA groups, continue to immigrate to the East and West Coasts, with only marginal representation in the Midwest and South. The top three states of intended residence for Chinese between 1990 and 1993, in descending order, were California, New York, and New Jersey. The 2000 census showed that the three states with the largest Chinese American populations, in descending order, were California, New York, and Texas. In 2000, however, 49 percent of the U.S. Asian population lived in the West. Hawai'i, California, and New York have the largest percentage of Chinese Americans in relation to their total populations. Chinese Americans, like other APA groups, are gravitating to states where coethnic communities, shaped by historical recruitment of Asians for labor, are well established.[18]

Reflecting its historical legacy, contemporary Chinese America has also remained highly urbanized. Among immigrants from mainland China and Hong Kong, the top three metropolitan areas of intended residence in 1991, in descending ranking, were New York, San Francisco, and Los Angeles. The preferences for immigrants from Taiwan were Los Angeles, New York, and San Jose.[19]

To some extent, the divergence in city preferences reflects the composition of the migration flows and the concomitant occupations desired. The Taiwanese flow includes a significant number of highly skilled and professional workers. Many have chosen to settle in Los Angeles and outlying areas because of opportunities in the high-technology and aerospace industries and the region's Asia-Pacific business environment. Much of the recent exodus from mainland China and, to a lesser extent, Hong Kong, however, has included those of middle- and working-class backgrounds with little human capital (education, job experience, and English proficiency); therefore, this group would be likely to flock to New York or San Francisco to take advantage of a burgeoning ethnic economy—knitted by kinship networks—that offers jobs and small-business opportunities. Such was the case with undocumented immigrants from Fuzhou, south China, who arrived in New York City by the thousands in the mid-1980s, filling jobs in palatial restaurants and crowded garment factories. These newcomers and others have revitalized Chinatowns, helping to reverse the earlier trend of suburbanization and dispersal of Chinese businesses. Today, garment and restaurant workers along with retirees make up the bulk of these old neighborhoods.

Most newcomers have chosen to live in cities because entry-level jobs are far more accessible. Moreover, Chinese immigrants converge in cities to take advantage of the social and economic support of their ethnic community.

Finally, the family-chain network character of Chinese immigration also helps to maintain the pattern of settlement. A concerted marketing campaign by Chinese realtors and developers has sometimes led to the growth of a Chinese-dominated neighborhood or suburb; an example would be Monterey Park, California, where in 1990, 37 percent of the population was Chinese, compared with only 15 percent in 1980.

A departure from the past, which stems from population pressure on old Chinatowns, is the fact that Chinese are rapidly taking over outlying areas of Chinatowns that used to be heavily white rather than concentrating in the core and dispersing later. The high population density, scarcity of housing, and high land values in old Chinatowns have forced residents to flee to the outskirts. Those moving to the outlying areas are also motivated by the promises of such migration: privacy, ample space, and upward social mobility. Over time, businesses—restaurants, garment sweatshops, banks, and others— associated with the enclave economy also moved to be closer to their customers. Examples of so-called satellite Chinatowns include Flushing in Queens and Sunset Park in Brooklyn in the greater New York City area (examples of smaller outer-borough satellite Chinatowns that are mainly residential concentrations are Sheepshead Bay in Brooklyn and Corona/Elmhurst in Queens); Monterey Park in Los Angeles (some Taiwanese have spilled over into Alhambra, Westminster, and Garden Grove), which contains many Taiwanese immigrants (as does Flushing); and the Richmond district in San Francisco, where Hong Kong newcomers have converged since 1965. On average, residents in these secondary settlements tend to have a higher, less working-class socioeconomic status than those in the Chinatown core. Old Chinatowns, in sum, have extended their boundaries to accommodate the arrival of new immigrants and capital, forcing a dispersal of both.[20]

Within urbanized areas, residential choice varies according to the group. Taiwanese immigrants tend to settle in suburban communities, but most new mainland Chinese and those from Hong Kong—at least initially—converge in inner-city neighborhoods. This discrepancy can be ascribed in part to socioeconomic status. Taiwanese immigrants, who are better educated and have better-paying jobs, can disperse to suburbia; mainland Chinese immigrants, with less human capital and fewer resources, have to concentrate in Chinatowns to access the coethnic support system. Residential patterns, however, are tied not simply to higher socioeconomic status but also to factors associated with bonds of family and kinship and the economic enclave. Those who have left Chinatown rarely abandon the social relations rooted in the enclave. Residential dispersion has, in effect, resulted in decentralized ethnic enclaves, or satellite Chinatowns, with strong political, economic, and social ties to the original enclave. Thus residential decentralization has not necessarily led to cultural assimilation.[21]

Residential patterns, finally, have also hinged on the location of work-places. Before the 1960s some Chinatowns, such as those in Chicago and New York City, witnessed an exodus of immigrants to the suburbs, in part because their concentration in small businesses such as restaurants and laundries had followed the pattern of suburbanization. Chinese, therefore, were dispersed into all parts of the city and beyond. The Chinatowns in San Francisco and Boston, however, developed ethnic enclave economies, focusing primarily on the garment industry. With factories clustered together in one area, Chinese workers remained concentrated in these Chinatowns.[22]

EDUCATED, HIGHLY SKILLED IMMIGRANTS

Statistically, the Chinese in the United States have seemed highly successful; in 1990 almost twice as many Chinese as whites were employed in white-collar work, including professional, managerial, and technical positions. The statistics are less impressive, however, when occupational distribution based on nativity is taken into consideration. The percentage of native-born Chinese in white-collar occupations in 1990 was higher than that of the white population—77 percent compared with 59 percent. Foreign-born Chinese, however, do not enjoy the same advantage. They occupy a bipolar occupational structure, with workers clustered either in professional and managerial occupations or in low-paying service-sector jobs, with relatively few in between. This bipolarity is the outcome of a bimodal distribution of educational background. For example, 31 percent of the adult immigrants from mainland China in 1990 had college degrees, but 16 percent had less than a fifth-grade education.[23]

The overall employment profile of Chinese in the United States is in part rooted in immigration policy. Visas for the third category of preference—members of the professions or those with exceptional ability in the sciences and the arts—and the sixth preference—skilled and unskilled workers who are in short supply—have offered a window for many educated, skilled Chinese without relatives in the United States.[24] In 1969, 21 percent of Chinese immigrants entered as professionals, and 61 percent entered in the family categories. Admittedly, these proportions decreased after the mid-1970s, but only because of a 1976 law that required all professionals to secure a job offer from an employer before admittance. Furthermore, by the 1980s professionals were using family preferences to petition for the entry of relatives, thus swelling the number entering through the family provisions. In 1985 only 16 percent of immigrants entered in the professional categories compared to 81 percent as family members.[25]

In spite of the steady decline of those entering under the professional provisions, the absolute numbers of professionals and executives have increased, particularly for those from Taiwan. For example, although more than twice as many immigrants from mainland China entered in 1989, Taiwan had more occupational immigrants. The following year 83 percent of PRC immigrants entered under family preferences, whereas 42 percent of the Taiwanese came under occupational categories reserved for highly skilled individuals and their families. By 1990 around 36 percent of all gainfully employed Chinese were engaged in managerial and professional occupations, of which a significant number were foreign born. The high percentage of professionals and managers reflects a larger trend; for example, one-third of all engineers with doctorates working in American industry in the 1980s were immigrants, and of that pool about a quarter were Asian Americans or Asians.[26]

A number of these highly skilled Chinese immigrants, encouraged by the reputation of U.S. higher education, entered the country on an F-1 (student) visa and pursued graduate studies, but many hoped to remain in the United States by adjusting their status to permanent residency. For example, between 1961 and 1981, only 15 percent of the 86,000 Taiwanese who went overseas to study returned, and the large majority of those 86,000 emigrated to the United States.[27]

Chinese professionals and managers in Asia have become interested in relocating to the United States in part as a result of the fallout from global restructuring. To maintain cheap labor policies, Asian countries have restricted social spending and, consequently, have limited jobs in the public sector. Furthermore, the homelands are still in the throes of expanding employment in the private sector, and opportunities are limited. Nevertheless, these countries' higher education in the scientific and technical fields has been Westernized, thus increasing the pool of highly skilled—but unemployed—labor.[28]

ARRIVALS FROM TAIWAN AND HONG KONG

Highly skilled workers in Asia have also been lured to immigrate to the United States by country-of-origin–specific reasons. Until very recently an authoritarian regime has been in control of Taiwan. Complicating the political quagmire is the unabated threat of a military attempt by the PRC to regain control of the island republic. The number of Taiwanese who applied for visas to come to the United States jumped dramatically after Taiwan left the United Nations in 1971 and again after President Jimmy Carter established diplomatic relations with mainland China in 1979 and concomitantly terminated official ties and a mutual security treaty with Taiwan. The specter of an imminent PRC takeover has continued to cast a pall of uncertainty over the island republic. Immigrating to the United States, a politically stable country that is staunchly anti-Communist, appeals to many Westernized Taiwanese. David Tsai, who was born in China but fled with his family to Taiwan after the 1949 Communist victory, observed that those who emigrated were "looking out for the future and also for their children," as they did not want them "to be brought up in war."[29] Recent outward direct investment from Taiwan, concomitant with the migration flow, has grown so rapidly that confidence in its currency was shaken during the 1980s, which sent unemployment and underemployment rates spiraling upward.[30]

Likewise, the impending handover of Hong Kong to the PRC in 1997 encouraged brain drain and capital flight. According to one research study conducted in 1988, 38 percent of the managers and professionals surveyed were prepared to leave Hong Kong in the next nine years.[31] The Tiananmen Square massacre in 1989 exacerbated the uneasiness of Hong Kong residents—many of whom were former mainlanders who had illegally escaped Communist rule—and thus played a part in accelerating immigration to America. Clearly, many were worried about losing personal freedom as well as the free enterprise system after Hong Kong was returned to China. Additionally, a smaller migration outflow from Hong Kong, as well as from Taiwan, can be ascribed to the wish to have children educated in the United States, where the bar for college entrance is much lower than that in Asian countries.

Hong Kong residents contemplating emigration tend to be young, educated, and from the middle or upper middle class. Thus Hong Kong emigrants tend to be more urbanized, more frequently exposed to Western culture than those from mainland China. Generally, they have transferable work experience, and some possess necessary monetary capital to invest in business ventures. Thus some Chinese, in a refutation of the conventional understanding of emigration as the outcome of "income differentials" (under which people move from low-income areas with an abundant labor force to high-income areas where labor is scarce), emigrated more to enjoy political stability and secure their families' future well-being than because they were mired in poverty and unemployment in their place of origin.

OCCUPATIONAL BARRIERS

A number of immigrants in the professional category experience downward mobility in the United States because of a poor command of English, the lack of transferable skills, difficulty securing professional licensing, the absence of American middle-class "cultural resources" (values, mannerisms, lifestyle, and symbols), and racism. The fact that the percentage of recently arrived Chinese immigrants employed in the professions is generally far below the share of college graduates illustrates this dilemma. It is not uncommon for former doctors, teachers, accountants, and engineers to take jobs as janitors and waiters when they first arrive in the United States. In China Tom Wing Wah was a professional with a degree in physics. When she arrived in the United States in 1976, she initially worked on an assembly line in a factory. She recalls with a tinge of bitterness, "We are college graduates, but we are working in sewing or electronics factories. We all have taken a big step backwards in our profession or work."[32]

A 1999 study showed that the returns on one's investment in education are greater for non-Hispanic white men than for all three Asian groups—Chinese, Japanese, and Filipinos—in California and Hawai'i. The difference in rates of return to education for foreign-born men stems in part from the fact that their schooling is less transferable to the United States than that of foreign-born, non-Hispanic white men. When experience was taken into account, foreign-born Asian men generally had lower returns than non-Hispanic white immigrants. All three Asian groups also experienced labor market discrimination, with those in Hawai'i having fewer problems than those in California—perhaps because of the former's multicultural environment, which promotes more equal treatment of different ethnic groups.[33]

Even those who experienced no occupational downgrading or who eventually secured a job in the professional or managerial categories often encountered ethnic and gender stratification at work that relegated them to the less prestigious jobs within a given industry. They faced barriers to promotion into management positions or ran into the "glass ceiling." For example, even though Chinese and other Asians are well represented in high-technology professional positions in the Silicon Valley—an estimated 21.5 percent of the total number of such employees in the valley, according to one early 1990 study—only 12.5 percent of Asian high-technology professionals were in management positions.[34] Another contemporary survey of the same area revealed that 66 percent of respondents claimed their promotions were blocked because of their race.[35] Even more striking were the findings of the 1995 U.S. Glass Ceiling Commission, a blue-ribbon corporate panel chosen by Congress. The commission found that Asian Americans made less money than whites in many occupational categories: 10 to 17 percent less for Asian American men and as much as 40 percent less for Asian American women in all categories studied. Even when whites and Asians had the same qualifications, the lack of parity remained. The panel concluded that inequalities seemed to stem from race.[36]

Of course, other factors exist for the glass ceiling. In one 1987 study, published in 1989, 238 highly educated San Francisco Chinese ascribed the glass ceiling to corporate culture, management insensitivity, and weak language proficiency, in addition to racism.[37] There is no doubt, however, that race remains a formidable barrier. The victims of a bipolar understanding of race relations, Chinese Americans are promoted less frequently than African Americans through affirmative action programs, and at the same time they are not considered as desirable as white executives and thus are denied promotions. Asians are regarded as a highly successful minority group—the "model minority"—and so the question of a glass ceiling seems moot. But Asian

Americans are also regarded as too unaggressive to exercise effective leadership in the workplace.

The workplace environment has become even more hostile since discrimination based on workers' English language proficiency, accents, and desire to speak another language has become common. The arrival of a significant number of newcomers with varying levels of English language proficiency has been matched by increased language discrimination. Prospective Chinese employees have been disqualified because they failed to pass employment tests that demanded English proficiency to comprehend, even though such proficiency was unnecessary for success in the particular job. Chinese employees have also been subjected to English-only rules in the workplace, even though they are not always justified by business necessity. Others have been reprimanded or even fired because of their accents.[38]

Chinese Americans are fighting these biases by adopting advancement strategies, such as participating in business-sponsored social functions, cultivating mentors, improving their interviewing skills, and educating employers about existing social biases against Asians. Some Chinese Americans have resorted to judicial or legal processes to seek redress for grievances.

For example, in 1988 Angelo Tom, a fifth-generation Chinese American who had worked at the U.S. Department of Housing and Urban Development's (HUD) San Francisco regional office for nearly a decade, was turned down for promotion to the position of supervisor of his unit. The woman chosen for the promotion had less experience than Tom. Before Tom was considered for the promotion, other qualified Asian Americans had been rejected for upper-management positions at that office. HUD alleged that Tom, like the others before him, lacked leadership and interpersonal skills and was too technically oriented for the new job. At the U.S. Equal Employment Opportunity Commission hearing, witnesses refuted the allegation. The presiding administrative law judge agreed and awarded Tom back pay, a retroactive promotion, and attorney's fees.

Chinese American women and men are still underrepresented compared with their percentage of the total U.S. population in the most prestigious professions—physicians, judges, dentists, and lawyers—as well as in management. Even though Chinese and other Asian Americans are deemed to be highly interested in education, they remain underrepresented in higher education at all levels except as students and in entry-level teaching positions. In addition, they typically receive lower wages than white men; in 1990 Chinese American and other Asian men who possessed at least an undergraduate degree and who worked full-time earned about 10 percent less than white men with comparable educations, even though the former were much more likely to have graduate degrees. Chinese and other Asian women fared even worse.[39] Chinese women, on the whole, receive less economic return than Chinese men, even though their labor force participation grew from 44.2 percent in 1960 to 59.2 percent in 1990. To some degree, this gender differentiation in income earnings is rooted in the fact that more men than women are found in the professional and managerial classes, even though in 1990 nearly a third of Chinese American women were in those classes.[40] In the study of 238 respondents cited earlier, 39 percent were women, and nearly all reported sex discrimination and work-family conflicts as significant barriers to upward mobility.[41]

These gender-determined socioeconomic patterns have likely reshaped gender relations between middle-class women and men. Chinese female professionals, given their earnings, need not depend solely on their spouses for economic survival. Their contribution to the family income has offered them leverage to negotiate for more male participation in household tasks. One study of Taiwanese immigrants in New York revealed that male spouses' involvement in household labor varied considerably along class lines; those in the professional class did a larger share of housework than those in the working or small-business classes. Overall, however, women still perform more of the household tasks than their husbands. Moreover, professional women generally cannot rely on female, coethnic social networks for material and emotional support to help lighten the burden of household work because most of them live in white-dominated suburban neighborhoods.[42]

THE SELF-EMPLOYED AND THE ETHNIC ENCLAVE ECONOMY

A second group of identifiable Asian participants in the U.S. labor force consists of the self-employed, some of whom were once professionals in Asian countries. Frustrated by blocked economic opportunities in the United States and handicapped by language difficulties, some chose to own small, ethnic-oriented businesses. For example, some Chinese subcontractors work for large high-technology firms in the Silicon Valley producing component parts ranging from circuit boards to graphics cards. Many of these subcontractors once worked as engineers or low-level managers, became tired of being passed over for promotion, and decided to leave their mainstream careers. In sum, self-employment has been a way some Chinese have circumvented labor market barriers.[43]

The growing Asian American population—a source of labor and an untapped market for goods and services—lures potential Chinese entrepreneurs into this form of economic adaptation. Apparently, in the Chinese enclave economy a strong interdependency known as ethnic integration exists among coethnic suppliers or owners and customers—particularly in the finance, insurance, and real estate industries and the service sector. For example, in San Francisco County alone, in the early 1990s there were 9,028 Chinese firms serving a Chinese population of 127,140—an average of one Chinese firm per fourteen Chinese people.[44]

Social scientists have also argued that ethnic entrepreneurship is a manifestation of the national restructuring of capitalist development. By reinvesting capital, recruiting marginalized labor, and increasing the number of small firms so production and marketing can be more flexible, ethnic entrepreneurship can be considered a specific response to changing circumstances in U.S. urban economies.[45]

After Korean Americans, Chinese Americans have the next-highest self-employment rate of any immigrant group. One 1982 government report enumerated 52,839 Chinese-owned firms in the United States. Ten years later the economic census showed that Chinese owned more than 153,000 businesses—a 189 percent increase since 1982. What remained constant throughout those years was that the majority of Chinese enterprises were retail stores, restaurants, and personal service establishments (such as laundries and beauty shops).[46]

Chinese American entrepreneurship, however, is represented in nearly every type of venture. Aside from the conventional mom-and-pop grocery stores, gift shops, laundries, and restaurants, entrepreneurs are involved in larger ventures such as clothing manufacturing, publishing, banking, jewelry, fast food, legal and insurance services, medical equipment, design and manufacturing, fashion design, and high-technology industries. Since the 1960s the ethnic enclave economy has dramatically diversified from small-scale service operations into manufacturing, wholesale, consumer, and professional trades.[47]

Most Chinese American businesses are small and involve minimal capital. A number of these businesses rely on personal family savings and money borrowed from a kinship network. It is not uncommon, however, for Chinese entrepreneurs to take out loans with banks—often Chinese-owned banks such as the Cathay Bank, the United Savings Bank, and the Bank of Canton. There is no shortage of Chinese-owned banks; between 1979 and 1992 seventeen new ones opened in Los Angeles alone. The clientele is made up predominately of Chinese and other Asians; unlike some immigrant ventures before 1945, such as laundries and restaurants, they do not necessarily depend on nonethnic customers to survive.[48]

Many of these ventures have opened new opportunities for immigrant workers. In New York City, for example, in the early 1980s Chinatown's restaurants employed nearly 15,000 workers, mostly men. Around 20,000 immigrant Chinese women found work in 500 factories in the Lower East Side of Manhattan, the extended Chinatown area.[49] Many of these jobs involve long hours and pay very little, but some working-class newcomers who have little education or English language competency are satisfied with the wages, which are higher than those in mainland China for the same type of work. "I found a job washing dishes in a Chinese restaurant," said an unidentified

Chinese male cook. "I received $300.00 for my wages in the first month. You know that a professor in Taiwan could not even earn that kind of money. I would have liked to have come earlier if I knew that it was so easy to earn big money here."[50]

Some scholars have used such testimonies to point to the existence of a reciprocal relationship within the ethnic enclave whereby both employers and employees benefit from their involvement in the economy. Rejected by the host or mainstream society, members of a given ethnic group retreat into their own communities where they can rely on ethnic solidarity to offer security, protection, and economic advancement. According to this enclave economy theory, the low-wage labor force enables small enterprises to compensate for the lack of an economy of scale.[51] Chinese entrepreneurs, however, are clustered in these marginally profitable, highly competitive, and labor-intensive enterprises precisely because they lack capital and skills. As a result of these circumstances, most businesses turn in rather low net profits and constantly run the risk of failing.[52]

The enclave economy theory also fails to point to another downside of Chinese immigrant entrepreneurship: it has contributed to the strain of urban race relations. The entrepreneurs—especially those who run large operations—exploit disempowered non-Chinese laborers, including undocumented immigrants; compete with non-Asians over urban space, forcing real estate values and rents to climb; and engage in exploitative retail trade (such as opening liquor stores in poverty-stricken neighborhoods).[53]

Ethnic entrepreneurship also involves class and gender exploitation. Workers are typically paid below minimum wage, and their jobs rarely lead to upward mobility. Female family members who are typically involved in these establishments are isolated from the larger society. As unpaid family labor, wives and daughters remain dependent on husbands and fathers for economic support and stay unattuned to other gender-role paradigms in the mainstream society.[54]

TRANSNATIONAL CAPITAL

Many Chinese enclave establishments are not isolated from the dominant economy; their business activities transcend ethnic lines, and their circle of customers and employees has enlarged to encompass non-Chinese. Thus the enclave economy is not unconnected to the larger world.[55]

Some Chinese immigrants in the United States—especially owners, executives, and investors in major transnational businesses—have established bases in the U.S. economy as a way to move their capital out of politically unstable Hong Kong or Taiwan (or even Southeast Asia) and eventually immigrate to the United States. Events in Asia, such as the return of Hong Kong to China in 1997 and the 1989 repression of Chinese student protests, and China's military threat to Taiwan amid mounting demands for its independence from China have fueled capital flight to the United States.[56]

A structural decline in the American economy beginning in the early 1970s and stretching into the early 1990s, accompanied by devaluation of the U.S. dollar and low interest rates, also drew foreign portfolio investment to the United States. American hard assets became a bargain on the world market. Investments from Hong Kong have been particularly significant; of the total foreign investments in real estate, banking, and hotels for the period 1974 to 1988, nearly two-thirds came from the former British colony.[57]

Most Chinese investments have followed the geography of Chinese settlement and the location of major finance and banking centers in U.S. cities. Prominent areas of investment include New York City, the San Francisco Bay area, Monterey Park (southern California), Houston, and Denver. Perhaps the most visible outcome of such investment has been Monterey Park, often dubbed "the Chinese Beverly Hills" or "Little Taipei." With thirty-eight bank branches holding $1.5 billion in total assets in the mid-1980s, the mean family income of Monterey Park's Asian population surpasses that of white families.

Most investors and entrepreneurs behind this capital flight entered the United States either through the investor migration provision or as intracompany transferees. Although the latter is a nonimmigration status, such visa holders can apply for immigration after operation of the subsidiary is proven to be sustainable.[58]

The process of upgrading from nonimmigrant to immigrant status became more expedient for business owners and investors when new legislation in 1990 allowed intracompany transferees to apply directly for immigration visas under a special category with an annual quota of 40,000. Of course, some business immigrants, as with professional ones, have entered the United States through family categories.

Because of loopholes, some Chinese subsidiaries in the United States are designed to help immigrants obtain legal residency rather than to do business, as illustrated in this story of an unidentified Chinese immigrant: "I owned a toys [sic] factory in Hong Kong. . . . Then, we moved to Los Angeles. In order to maintain my L-1 visa and apply for immigrant status later, I have to import a certain amount [of toys] . . . regularly from Hong Kong to show my business is doing well."[59]

A number of Chinese owners have also relied on family members—often second-generation Chinese Americans pursuing studies in the United States—to identify and establish their transnational operations ranging from real estate investment to hotel chains. Mr. Lee (full name is unavailable), the second son of a watch manufacturer in Hong Kong, recalled that his immigration to America occurred as part of his father's business strategy: "I was studying at

U.S.C. [University of Southern California] then, so he asked me to do marketing as a part-time job. In only a few years, I was able to establish a solid business, so my father decided that after graduation I should settle in Los Angeles and continue the operation."[60]

The involvement of this new wave of privileged immigrants has revitalized Chinatown's economy and created a structural duality. Aside from a protected, somewhat stabilized enclave sector serving a mostly ethnic clientele—including restaurants, grocery stores, and service-oriented establishments—an enclave export sector also exists both within the United States and abroad that includes, for example, the garment and high-technology industries and that services the unstable demands generated by the larger consumer market. Mixed in with these establishments are a growing number of glitzy, up-market real estate projects such as upscale condominiums, multilevel department stores, and high-rise office buildings. In New York City in 1978, Hong Kong tycoon Yip Hon—who also has investments in Vancouver and Toronto—built the Wing Ming, the first large modern office building encased in reflective black glass. Some projects have relied on local as well as overseas investors; such was the case with the Ice House Condominiums in New York City, which featured thirty-seven loft apartments. Purchased by well-to-do Chinese investors, the units are rented out to recently arrived immigrants.[61]

Some of these privileged Chinese immigrants do not have to depend on the ethnic economy. Hong Kong hotel tycoon Lawrence Chan is president of Park Lane, which owns hotels around the world, including some in the United States. A few wealthy Hong Kong immigrants have bought many of the posh downtown office buildings in San Francisco; others have taken control of formerly white-owned retail chains. The importance of this transnational capital to Chinese American participation in the U.S. economy is underscored by one study, published in 1998, of Chinese Americans who served on the boards of directors for Fortune 1,000 companies—almost all of them hailed from well-to-do families in China, Taiwan, and Hong Kong.[62]

Beginning in the early 1990s, against the backdrop of a moderate economic slowdown in the United States, a reverse capital flight back to China took place, which also reflects overseas Chinese businesspeople's growing optimism about the future following Hong Kong's reunification with the PRC. The interest in investing in China was deepened by robust growth rates in the PRC in the 1990s that approached 14 percent.[63]

As the enclave grows more economically complex and becomes linked to world markets and transnational capital in-flows increase, the state takes on a visible role in its operations. Enclave-state contestations occur over the disposition of space and the pace and scale of transformation. In New York City one confrontation since the 1980s has occurred over the traffic congestion and poor sanitation allegedly caused by ethnic street vendors. Following a few failed crackdowns on public street vending in the 1980s, Mayor Rudolph Giuliani's aggressive efforts to evict street vendors, with the help of a massive police force outfitted in riot gear, only invited protest demonstrations by the vendors. Members of the Chinatown Vendors Association rejected a proposal by city authorities to relocate them to an open-air market, preferring unrestricted street access for their businesses. Communitywide concerns about crime and the sullying of the ethnic identity of Chinatown motivated the protests that greeted the city's 1982 plan to build a detention facility there. Similarly, issues of community control came to the forefront in 1979, when authorities proposed creating a special zoning district in the middle of Chinatown that would facilitate high-rise development bankrolled by transnational capital—a plan that would have driven up real estate values and eventually forced low-income families to abandon their dwellings.[64]

ATYPICAL IMMIGRANTS

In sum, the privileged Chinese in the post-1945 era—who are involved in high-stake investments, drive Mercedes, and converse in Mandarin or Cantonese in American cities—do not fit the typical portrait of the "good" immigrant, who is poor and grateful to be in the land of opportunity and who moves through the expected stages of incorporation and economic and geographic mobility. The Chinese of the early labor immigration in the late nineteenth and early twentieth centuries took two to three generations to penetrate the middle class. But immigrants since 1965, in the minds of white Americans, have moved quickly and directly into middle-class status and beyond. A white resident of Monterey Park, California, offered observations on this monied segment of the new wave of Chinese immigration: "Before immigrants lived in their own neighborhoods and moved into ours after they learned English, got a good job, and became accustomed to our ways. Today, the Chinese come right in with their money and their ways. We are the aliens."[65]

Such resentment is rooted in the overturning of the traditional pattern of ethnic stratification. In the mid-1980s white residents (and some established Japanese American and Latino residents) in Monterey Park began to feel threatened by the physical markers of the burgeoning ethnic economy, such as new condominiums, the growth of new ethnic-oriented stores with their Chinese signs, and the increasingly congested streets. These markers of a visible Chinese presence reminded them that the community was no longer theirs to control. Soon, anti-immigrant nativism reared its ugly head.[66]

Local politics in Monterey Park became centered around the issue of economic development, and lines were drawn within the fractured community. In 1986 the Monterey Park city council passed an English Ordinance that made English the city's official language. Then an antidevelopment movement mounted by longtime residents successfully removed pro-development members from the council. The city council placed limits on residential and commercial development, which affected mainly the Chinese. The Chinese, however, did not take these mandates without a fight. Chinese business owners mobilized and established an organization to oppose the English-only and antidevelopment ordinances through electoral and judicial processes.

Some of these business owners and investors as well as professionals have returned to Asia after securing their green cards. This transnational phenomenon has typically occurred when the immigrants become disenchanted with the economic limits of the United States. The glass ceiling has engendered reverse migration. Rapid economic growth in Asia over the past few decades has also opened myriad opportunities previously unavailable, and more immigrants are returning to their homelands to take advantage of what is offered. For the sake of his children's education, however, the male head of the household usually leaves his wife and children in the United States. This practice of leaving the family behind and flying back and forth between Asia and America has become a noticeable trend. On August 22, 1993, the *San Jose Mercury News* estimated that 30 percent of the Taiwanese immigrant engineers who used to work in Silicon Valley have returned to their homeland for better opportunities.[67]

WORKING-CLASS CHINESE

For ethnic entrepreneurship to be successful, business owners count on the loyalty of coethnic employees and in turn are supposed to be concerned about their employees' welfare. But workers in Chinese firms often find this situation difficult to sustain in spite of the intertwining of family and kinship ties with the employer-employee relationship. The rupture stems from the economic exploitation that has become part of contemporary immigrant entrepreneurship. Working-class Chinese are typically exploited in several ways: they receive no overtime pay, no vacation or sick leave, no health or occupational safety benefits, and no job security. Working-class Chinese—mostly foreign born—are also overrepresented in a few industries in the secondary sector of the economy, namely, in dead-end jobs that are labor-intensive, sometimes seasonal, and generally lacking social prestige.

Chinese American women, in comparison to white women, are overrepresented in low-mobility occupations. For example, Chinese women, along with Korean and Vietnamese women, are overrepresented in the garment labor force and in services, clerical work, sales, and domestic household work. In the San Francisco Bay area, the garment industry employs over 25,000 workers, of whom more than 80 percent are of Chinese ancestry and the vast majority are women. A report prepared by the International Ladies' Garment

Workers' Union (ILGWU) in the early 1980s estimated that New York City had over 400 Chinese-owned garment factories that employed more than 20,000 workers, many of whom were women.[68]

This lopsided situation is the result of several factors. The availability of a supply of immigrant labor has encouraged the garment industry to transform Chinatowns in New York City and San Francisco into sites specializing in garment production, particularly for the volatile markets of women's and casual wear. Garment factory operators or their subcontractors prefer women because they consider women, in a classic case of gender typing, to be more suited than men for the detailed and routinized tasks sewing demands. There is also the perception that the women are working for "pin money"; they can be hired and fired in accordance with the seasonal demand for labor.

For many Chinese women, particularly the foreign born and newly arrived, the dialectic relationship between work and family remains central to their identity. Chinese women are interested in garment labor because it fits their dual role as household worker and wage earner. The industry's flexible and informal work culture allows women to supervise their children at the workplace, do chores at home, or do both on a daily basis. Many women, often paid on a piecework basis, can do the sewing at home and still be close to their social network and ethnic amenities. Bernice Tom, fifty-six years old at the time of her interview, arrived in the United States as part of the wave of *gamsaanpo* in the 1940s and has worked in the industry since she arrived: "I like working here because I can go home anytime. This was important when my children were small. I like being in Chinatown and I like the flexible hours, the independence. I can visit my friends and go shopping."[69]

Tom's comments indicate that although she had gained some independence, she is still responsible for the domestic realm. Like Tom, most Chinese working women see their work as a contribution to the family's income but rarely use the opportunity to transform the patriarchal family system. Work for them is seen as an extension of family obligations.[70] Most of the women, however, are probably dissatisfied with their work; one study published in 1982 discovered that 84 percent of the 108 working women interviewed expressed little satisfaction with their current dead-end jobs.[71]

Because many of these women work for coethnic contractors, a personal working relationship often exists, which opens the door for more exploitation through longer working hours, subminimum wages, lack of overtime wages, use of child labor, and hazardous job conditions. Paternalism and ethnic loyalty sometimes make workers hesitate to vocalize their grievances or to see the relationship as exploitative.[72]

Some individual Chinese female workers, however, have expressed their dissatisfaction. They have developed a work culture that resists speedups by cutting corners in workmanship, relies on the rhetoric of ethnicity to negotiate for higher piece rates, and meshes the seasonal nature of work with the demands of family life. This protoclass consciousness is also forged by the women's awareness of, and pride in, their contribution to the family economy.[73]

Whereas working-class Chinese women are overrepresented in the garment industry, most working-class Chinese men labor in restaurants. Because recent immigrants have yet to master English, most find themselves locked in low-wage jobs as waiters, busboys, or cooks. Danny Lowe was twenty-one years old when he was interviewed in San Francisco. His first job in that city after he arrived from Hong Kong was as part of a fishing crew. He explained that he became a fisherman, although he was "not interested in that job," because he "had no [other] way." Later, he worked in a restaurant. He explained his experience: "Before, I was a painter in Hong Kong, but I can't do it here, I got no license, no education. . . . I want a living, so it's dishwasher, janitor, or cook."[74] Family ties—some restaurant owners sponsor relatives as workers—have also forced new immigrants to repay the social debt they have incurred by continuing to work for these employers.

Apparently, Chinatown workers experience a dual form of oppression. Already blocked from entering the mainstream labor market, they are compelled to work and remain in the ethnic enclave economy. One sociological study revealed that "an overwhelming majority of the Chinatown immigrants who settled in San Francisco between 1962 and 1975 and who started in the ethnic labor market were confined to that market in 1980."[75] In 1980, 25 percent of the residents of New York City's Chinatown lived below the poverty level, compared with 17 percent for the city's total population—a situation that suggested many Chinese residents were trapped in low-paying jobs in this split labor market.[76]

ORGANIZING WORKERS

Chinese workers involved in immigrant ethnic enterprises have resisted such exploitation at times; however, organizing a labor movement among Chinatown workers is not easy. Nationwide, rank-and-file participation in the labor movement has generally declined since the early 1980s. In the 1950s about 35 percent of American workers held membership in a union, but by the mid-1990s that figure had dropped to 11 percent.[77] White-dominated unions also tend to be indifferent to the plight of Chinese workers because of deep-seated stereotypes held by white union leaders, which purport that the Chinese are "clannish" and are uninterested in being organized. Even when Chinese workers succeed in drawing unions' support, they typically are not protected. For example, in 1979 New York Chinatown workers joined the American Federation of Labor and Congress of Industrial Organizations (AFL-CIO) Hotel and Restaurant Employees and Bartenders Union, Local 69, but the union regularly refused to enforce their contracts and rarely confronted management about violations of labor codes. According to Peter Kwong, Local 69 was more interested in collecting dues than it was in representing its Chinese members.[78]

Because of these complaints, Chinese grassroots activists formed the Chinese Staff and Workers Association (CSWA) to promote the labor movement in Chinatown. In February 1980 the association galvanized Chinese workers into action to picket against the Silver Palace, New York Chinatown's largest restaurant, when the restaurant tried to force waiters to share a higher percentage of their tips with the rest of the work crew. The strike became a communitywide event, with local activists, lawyers, and other restaurant workers offering moral and material support. The strike ended when management acquiesced to the demands of the workers, who by then had organized their own independent restaurant union.

In the 1990s ethnic-based grassroots organizing became the strategy for mobilizing female Chinese garment workers in New York City. The ILGWU had been trying to organize the Chinese since the mid-1950s, and by 1974 nearly all of New York City's Chinatown garment workers had joined. But the ILGWU, which is organized from the top down, was unable to make Chinese contractors or manufacturers comply with minimum union standards for shop floor conditions. For most Chinese seamstresses the ILGWU was at best a health insurance provider or a social welfare institution and at worst was nonexistent.[79]

The ILGWU's incompetency was evidenced in 1990 and 1991, when several owners of garment factories withheld payment of back wages. The workers, mostly Chinese women, were outraged, as they expressed at one spontaneous rally: "We want justice! We are no slaves! Pay out wages now!" The workers approached the ILGWU and New York's labor department, but the investigation went nowhere. Frustrated by the impasse, they sought the assistance of the CSWA. The workers, backed by the CSWA, called a press conference to air their grievances. They held public information rallies and organized a petition drive in Chinatown to garner support for their cause. Five months after they began their struggle, one owner caved in and paid the workers their wages. With its bilingual skills and community ties, the CSWA is better able to deal with a fragmented industry.[80]

The CSWA, like any other community-based organization, must grapple with structural-, ethnic-, and gender-specific barriers to mobilization. First, garment shops in satellite Chinatowns tend to be more hidden, smaller, and more mobile than those in Chinatown cores, allowing them to evade industry standards and labor laws. These shops can open and close rapidly. The workers are highly mobile and may move from shop to shop during any given year. Second, in smaller establishments such as restaurants and grocery stores, Chinese employees work with their employers, who often are blood relatives, of the same lineage, or of the same dialect group. Such kinship or pseudokinship ties create a family-like atmosphere that inhibits the formation of class consciousness. Third, workers are afraid of losing their jobs if they take time off to engage in labor activities. Fourth, undocumented workers tend to shy away from unions for fear of trouble with the Immigration and Naturalization Service (INS). Five, women workers must contend with a lack of self-confidence. Saddled by the double burden of being unpaid household workers and wage earners and made vulnerable by their lack of proficiency in English, these workers suffer from low self-esteem—which in turn deprives the labor movement of its sense of empowerment, the key to successful organizing.[81]

Yet change for the better has not been entirely elusive. Group allegiances such as those between Chinese workers and employers from the same subregion or the same lineage or dialect group are breaking down. The burgeoning ethnic enclave economies in Chinatowns feature large-scale enterprises. Restaurant and garment factory owners have a high labor demand that typical immigration networks of relatives or pseudokinsfolk are unable to fulfill. As workplaces employ more people from different regions of China and with varied backgrounds, regional and kinship loyalties weaken. The gap between labor and management widens. Class consciousness forged by common exploitation by impersonal employers emerges.[82]

The 1982 New York Chinese garment workers' strike is an example of class consciousness taking precedence over kinship and regional loyalties. The genesis of the strike lay in Chinese sweatshop contractors' refusal to accept a new work contract that included a wage hike for workers because white manufacturers had left the contractors out of the bargaining process. Crying racial discrimination, the Chinese contractors urged their workers to stand behind them in the name of ethnic solidarity. The 20,000 seamstresses, however, insisted on the wage increases, and when their employers ignored them, they walked out. The strike won communitywide support from churches, civil rights organizations, and social service agencies. In the end, the contractors caved in and signed the new contracts.

COMMUNITY-BASED LABOR ACTIVISM

To circumvent some of the barriers to organizing, labor groups such as the CSWA rely on consciousness-raising sessions and teach-ins and encourage the rank and file to participate actively in public education activities. In 1995 the CSWA, recognizing the decentralization of labor and capital, opened an organizing office in Brooklyn—the first outside Manhattan's Chinatown. Following a successful campaign in 1985 to secure job training and reemployment assistance, one local community organization based in Boston—the

Chinese Progressive Association—established a workers' mutual aid and resource center. The center provides support to unemployed garment workers fighting for back pay, unemployment insurance reform, and the upgrading of other benefits.[83]

Another community-based organization, Asian Immigrant Women Advocates (AIWA), based in San Francisco, is even more innovative in its attempt to reach out to female Chinese garment workers and other Asian women in electronics industries and the service sector. Using a multipronged approach that builds self-confidence and is sensitive to the nuances of Asian immigrant cultures and the double burden of female labor, AIWA has successfully empowered women to increase their accessibility to county services, raise their awareness of occupational hazards, and protest against specific workplace abuses.[84]

By the mid-1990s grassroots organizations such as the AIWA were able to mobilize countrywide support for their causes because of the existence of larger umbrella organizations that brought union leaders and rank-and-file organizers of several Asian communities together for mutual cooperation. These organizations include the Asian American Federation of Union Members and the Alliance of Asian Pacific Labor, both of which have promoted union visibility and, simultaneously, the political empowerment of Asian Americans.[85]

Because of this grassroots activism, institutionalized unions such as the ILGWU have been forced to adapt to the changing times. Two years after the 1985 agitation in Boston, the local ILGWU began building bases by offering bilingualism in its educational programs and other services, hiring more Chinese organizers, and participating in Chinese cultural events. These activities address cultural sensitivity, communication, and access to the ethnic economy—aspects considered crucial for organizing communities of color. Yat Lee, a longtime ILGWU member, noticed a more deferential attitude among union officials toward Chinese members: "The new leadership is better than the old. When the new head [union official] comes to the factory, he always nods at us, says hello, and tries to talk to us in Chinese."[86]

In New York City in 1992, the ILGWU initiated a Campaign for Justice—with workshops, workers' committees, and a workers' center—to train workers to organize themselves. The ILGWU is offering more social unionism in the form of health insurance, retirement funds, college scholarships for members' children, and an education department that offers classes in English, citizenship, and leadership training. The 1995 demonstration to protest poor working conditions and low wages in Sunset Park, Brooklyn, illustrated the impact of such consciousness-raising efforts; even though only several hundred demonstrators were involved, the demonstration was initiated by the workers, received support from Latino garment workers and other labor unions, and involved participation of nonunion sympathizers.[87]

Like the ILGWU, the umbrella organization for the labor movement in the United States—the AFL-CIO—has been forced to acknowledge the rapid increase in the number of Chinese and other Asian workers. In recognition of the need for a formal support organization for Asian American labor activists, in 1992 the AFL-CIO sponsored the establishment of the Asian Pacific American Labor Alliance, which it is hoped will help bridge the gap between Asian Americans and the U.S. labor movement. These changes in established unions have, in turn, created more prounion sentiment in the community, a turning point given the Chinese mistrust of these historically anti-Asian unions.[88]

UNDOCUMENTED IMMIGRANTS

Both institutionalized unions and community-based organizations, however, have yet to make significant inroads in gaining the support of undocumented immigrants. The roots of the impasse lie in part in the difficulty of identifying this pool of workers, whose number fluctuates and cannot be determined. These immigrants are generally reluctant to interact with the larger society.

Illegal Chinese immigration grabbed headlines in the mid-1990s when several ships arrived from the PRC trying to smuggle newcomers into New York City; the most notorious incident was that of the *Golden Venture* in June 1993. After the ship struck a sandbar near New York, hundreds of Chinese jumped into the Atlantic Ocean in a desperate attempt to reach shore. Ten drowned, and many more were injured. Later, newspapers carried accounts of dehydration, privation, and physical abuse on this and other human trafficking vessels. After the *Golden Ventura* incident, the INS and other federal agencies established an interagency task force to tackle the issue of Chinese sea smuggling. The official U.S. approach toward illegal Chinese has also hardened; ships identified as engaged in trafficking humans have been turned back and their passengers deported.[89]

In spite of the publicity ships overfilled with Chinese immigrants received, only a minority of immigrants made the journey almost exclusively by sea. According to one extensive study, most undocumented Chinese workers surveyed either slipped across the U.S. borders with Canada and Mexico or arrived by air. Most likely, few illegal Chinese left China by air, given the difficulty in securing passports and visas for travel. Thus the first leg of the trip out of China was often made by sea or more commonly overland to Hong Kong or Myanmar. They then traveled by sea or flew to Central or South America or Canada, crossing the border by land. The few Chinese who arrived in the United States by air also had to leave China by land.

Not all illegal Chinese came as part of an organized clandestine traffic. Some undocumented Chinese immigrants are visa abusers who arrive with nonimmigrant visas, work without acquiring permits, and stay after their visas have expired. Most, at least initially, plan to make as much money as possible during their short stay in America and then return home. A mainland Chinese woman who works as a household servant in southern California for a year can earn the equivalent of almost seventeen years' salary of a college professor in China. Given this income disparity, it is not surprising that many immigrants lengthen their stay and eventually become illegal aliens.

Although illegal Chinese immigrants have often cited their ambition to improve their economic status as the motivation to move to the United States, transnational migration has also stemmed from changing structural forces in China. Beginning in the late 1970s China's open-door policy and its restructuring into a market-oriented economy turned agricultural land in the Fuzhou area (in Fujian province) into an industrial area, displacing farmers from their land. Not surprisingly, Fuzhou has become the largest source of undocumented immigrants to the United States. Other illegal Chinese immigrants hope to receive political asylum. Ever since President George Bush issued the 1989 executive order allowing Chinese students in the United States to become permanent residents following the Chinese government's crackdown on student protests, potential immigrants have believed the United States is a haven for those applying for political asylum.

According to INS estimates, from 10,000 to 15,000 Chinese from the PRC try to enter the United States illegally each year. In 1992 an estimated 3.3 million unauthorized immigrants were living in the United States. The largest group—71 percent—came from Mexico, Central America, and Canada; Asia accounted for only 9 percent. Chinese undocumented immigrants overall accounted for only 1 percent of the illegal residents in the United States in 1992.[90]

In 1986 undocumented immigrants, mostly Mexicans, received amnesty or were legalized in the United States through the provisions of the Immigration and Reform Control Act. The law provided for the legalization of undocumented aliens who had been residing in the United States since January 1, 1982, as well as of seasonal agricultural workers who had been employed for at least ninety days during the year preceding May 1986. The same legislation, however, also sought to control future illegal immigration by requiring all employers to verify the legal status of new employees and by providing for sanctions against employers who knowingly hire undocumented workers. Despite this check on undocumented aliens, illegal Chinese immigrants have continued to arrive in the United States.[91]

In swelling the U.S. labor market, undocumented immigrants have become the subject of controversy. Mainstream political commentators and policy makers have complained that, like their more numerous Mexican peers, Chinese immigrants are taking jobs from minorities who are U.S. citizens, driving wages down, and causing welfare costs to skyrocket. Yet studies have shown that undocumented newcomers, in fact, have spurred economic growth.

Their labor has enabled industries to procure higher profits and lower prices. Illegal Chinese in particular, clustered in the ethnic enclave economy, are highly unlikely to be taking jobs away from non-Chinese minorities or women. Pulling in incomes above the legal minimum wage, Chinese workers do work excessively long hours. Many illegal Chinese tend to leave spouses and children behind in China. Hence they have little reason to rely on state health and educational services.[92]

Since the 1960s the economic participation of Chinese Americans has changed dramatically. Those involved in the so-called enclave economy are no longer isolated and segregated from mainstream markets. Tied to the larger national and global restructuring, the enclave economy has offered opportunities but also has engendered class-oriented exploitation. Chinese Americans employed by or running businesses linked to the larger economy confront class-based barriers (and for women gender-based barriers) against upward mobility. Regardless of their social location or type of labor participation, most Chinese Americans have had to grapple with the politics of race, as witnessed in continuing racial (and gender) discrimination in the workplace. To overcome this discrimination, Chinese Americans since the turbulent days of the civil rights movement have turned to political empowerment and pan-ethnic mobilization with other Asian American groups.

Scene inside Chinese American grocery store, late nineteenth century. *Courtesy,* San Francisco History Center, San Francisco Public Library.

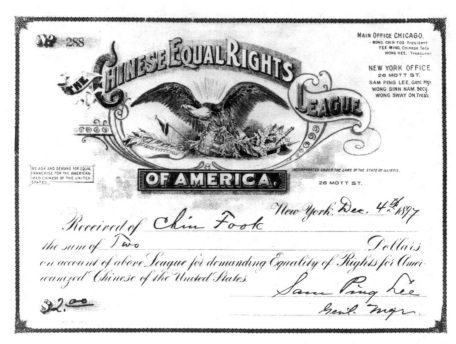

Chinese Equal Rights League membership certificate of Wong Chin Fook, founder of the organization, 1897. *Courtesy,* San Francisco History Center, San Francisco Public Library.

Mar Sen Keol and her children, Guangdong, China, circa 1935. *Courtesy,* Wayne Hung Wong.

Mar Tung Jing alias Gee See Wing (*seated*) and son, Mar Ying Wing alias Wayne Hung Wong (*standing*), circa 1935. Both father and son had to resort to the "paper son" scheme to enter the United States. *Courtesy,* Wayne Hung Wong.

Wong Wing Lock, "paper father" of Mar Ying Wing alias Wayne Hung Wong. *Courtesy,* Wayne Hung Wong.

Pan-American café, a Chinese-owned restaurant in downtown Wichita, circa 1930s. Servers were Euro-American women; Chinese workers usually ran the kitchen. *Courtesy*, Wayne Hung Wong.

Chinese American operator at the Chinatown Telephone Exchange, 1939. *Courtesy,* San Francisco History Center, San Francisco Public Library.

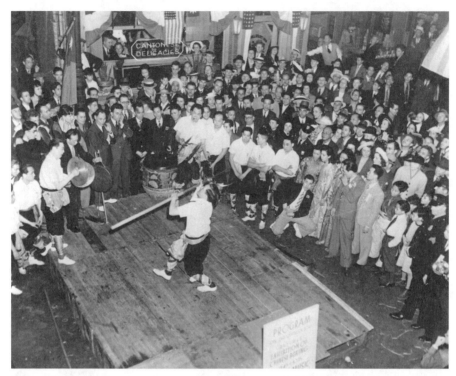

Chinese boxing exhibition at Rice Bowl party, 1938, possibly in Chinatown, New York City. *Courtesy*, San Francisco History Center, San Francisco Public Library.

Chinese youth in Wichita, Kansas, circa 1940. *Courtesy,* Wayne Hung Wong.

Chinese American youth in liberty bond parade in Wichita, Kansas, during World War II. *Courtesy,* Wayne Hung Wong.

Wayne Hung Wong in the U.S. Army during World War II, joining more than 13,000 Chinese American men and women who served in the conflict. *Courtesy,* Wayne Hung Wong.

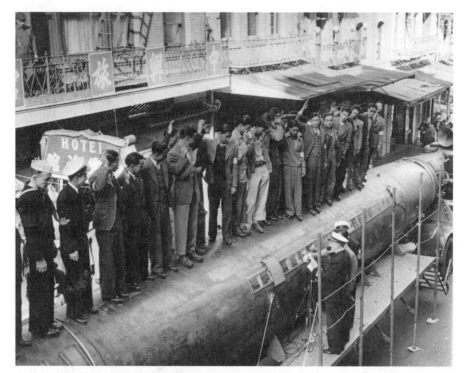

Captured Japanese submarine used symbolically during a navy recruitment exercise in Chinatown, San Francisco, 1942. *Courtesy,* San Francisco History Center, San Francisco Public Library.

Crowded kitchen in a Chinatown, San Francisco, apartment, circa 1940. *Courtesy,* San Francisco History Center, San Francisco Public Library.

Chinese women in mainland China transporting goods to a factory, 1995. *Courtesy,* Haipeng Li, Oberlin, Ohio.

Free-market economy in mainland China, part of the changing context of emigration, 1995. *Courtesy,* Haipeng Li, Oberlin, Ohio.

Annual "Take Back the Night" March at Washington State University, Pullman, 1996—designed to raise awareness of violence against women—included participation of campus Asian American and Pacific Islander student organizations. *Courtesy, Asian Pacific American Student Center, Washington State University, Pullman.*

Christmas potluck for Asian American and Pacific Islander student mentors at Asian Pacific American Student Center, Washington State University, Pullman, 1997. *Courtesy,* Asian Pacific American Student Center, Washington State University, Pullman.

Chinese lion dance, part of Independence Day celebrations in Washington, D.C.,
July 4, 1998. Note the non-Chinese participants as dancers. *Courtesy,* Haipeng Li,
Oberlin, Ohio.

Chinese market in Chinatown, San Francisco, 1999. Benson Tong Collection.

Gift store along Grant Avenue, the thoroughfare on which Chinese-owned businesses cater to tourists in San Francisco's Chinatown, 1999. Benson Tong Collection.

Chinese language and cultural school in San Francisco's Chinatown, 1999. Benson Tong Collection.

Chinese Consolidated Benevolent Association building in Asian Pacific Historic District, San Diego, 1999. *Courtesy,* Antoinette Charfouros McDaniel.

Ying On Labor and Merchant Association building, completed in 1928, in Asian Pacific Historic District, San Diego, 1999. *Courtesy,* Terry E. Abrams.

One of the many minimalls funded by Chinese Vietnamese in Little Saigon, August 2002. *Courtesy,* Linda Trinh Võ.

A Chinese Vietnamese–owned supermarket in Little Saigon, August 2002. *Courtesy,* Linda Trinh Võ.

6 Political Mobilization and Empowerment

Chinese Americans today enjoy political enfranchisement, but their political participation in mainstream society has remained marginal. Certain barriers—illiteracy, lack of fluency in English, lack of understanding of the American political process, the perception that Chinese electoral power is inconsequential—have impeded the full exercise of their political rights. In the 1960s, however, political mobilization to circumvent those barriers gathered momentum. That turbulent decade witnessed the emergence of the Asian American movement, a pan-Asian coalition that attempted to link all Asian ethnic groups in the struggle for racial equality and social justice. Chinese Americans participated actively in organizing a pan-ethnic movement that would embrace a communal consciousness rooted in the commonality of historical oppression and a culturally shared sense of being Asian.

By the late 1960s shifts in social and demographic factors within Asian American communities had prepared the way for the emergence of a pan-Asian consciousness. In the post–World War II years, native-born Asians who spoke fluent English and had been educated in U.S. schools began to outnumber immigrants. As language and cultural differences that had long divided Asians began to blur, the Chinese in America began to communicate with other Asian Americans.

Equally critical to the development of pan-Asianism was the weakening of loyalties to the ancestral homelands. Unlike their immigrant elders, American-born Chinese did not see the historical animosity between Chinese and Japanese Americans as pivotal to their identity. One young Chinese American explained this generational difference: "We have buried the old hatreds between Chinese and Japanese, and my friends and I must go beyond our parents' 'hang-ups.' My mother is upset because I'm engaged to a Japanese girl but she knows she can do nothing about it."[1]

Crucial to this inter-Asian interaction has been the crumbling of economic and residential barriers in the postwar period. As racial discrimination in employment and housing came under attack, Asian American residential patterns underwent a reconfiguration. Segregated ethnic enclaves declined as Asians moved out of these early immigrant neighborhoods. For example, in 1940 half of the Chinese in New York City lived in its Chinatown, but by 1960 less than one-third lived there.[2] Chinese Americans who left Chinatowns for the suburbs often ended up clustering with other Asians in pockets adjacent to the old ghettos. Over time, Chinese Americans interacted more closely with other Asian groups, and they all soon realized that they shared common historical and contemporary experiences, including exploitation, oppression, and discrimination.

ASIAN AMERICAN MOVEMENT

This evolving sense of pan-Asianism was felt most keenly among young, educated Chinese and other Asian Americans. The Asian American movement emerged from the intersection of two historical phenomena: the coming of age of a generation of college-age Asian Americans and the highly volatile protest movement against the Vietnam War. By the 1960s the reunification of families, the lowering of discriminatory barriers to education, and the baby-boom phenomenon had pushed the number of Asian Americans enrolled in college and universities to an all-time high.[3]

This generation of Asian students coincidentally became young adults during a traumatic period in the United States. The idealism of President John F. Kennedy's Great Frontier and President Lyndon Johnson's Great Society—both of which, in theory, embodied a limited concept of a welfare state—was overshadowed by the failure of the civil rights movement to secure economic opportunity. Meanwhile, as the turbulent decade wore on, the U.S. military became more embroiled in the bloody Vietnam War.

Prompted by demographic changes and contemporaneous political struggles, Chinese Americans became involved in various sociopolitical movements—including the civil rights movement, women's liberation, and antiwar protests—which, in turn, sensitized them to racial issues. The civil rights and feminist movements made Chinese American women aware of their doubly impaired positions as members of a racial minority and as women. In particular, Chinese women discovered that the white middle-class–dominated feminist movement was indifferent to the unique circumstances faced by women of color in mainstream society.[4]

It was mainly the antiwar movement, however, that brought all Asian Americans—men and women—together psychologically and politically. These Asian American protesters drew the public's—and their own—attention to the racial subtext of the conflict raging in Asia and tied it to the oppression experienced in their communities. The fervent anticolonial nationalist movements in Asia stirred Asian antiwar protesters' racial and cultural pride and led them to stress the commonalities among "colonized groups" in both the United States and Asia, a perspective also known as the "internal colonial" model.

Soon these activists realized that the antiwar movement, which mirrored society's black-white binary understanding of race, ignored their participation and the issues they raised. Chinese Americans involved in supposedly integrationist organizations felt alienated and joined other Asian activists to establish their own movement for social justice and empowerment.

Part of the spark for this activism stemmed from efforts in the mid-1960s to get the San Francisco city government to rectify the socioeconomic ills in Chinatown. In San Francisco one survey completed in 1969 found that unemployment among the Chinese stood at 15 percent, a situation exacerbated by underemployment and miserly wages. Forty percent of Chinatown residents lived below the poverty line, the average educational level was less than fifth grade, and 77 percent of the dwellings were below minimum federal standards. Most shocking of all was the tuberculosis rate for the Chinese population, which was three times that for the entire city. These statistics were not surprising considering the poor in Chinatown resided in overcrowded conditions, worked long hours, and suffered from malnutrition.[5]

The conditions in San Francisco's Chinatown were not unique, however. In New York City's Chinatown in the early 1970s, underemployment, crumbling tenements, a rising crime rate, and rates of tuberculosis and suicides higher than the national average were signs of a community in crisis.[6] Health conditions among Boston Chinese in 1970 were equally poor. Infant mortality in 1966 stood at two-and-a-half times the figure for the city's general population, and they had 192 percent more new tuberculosis cases per capita than the rest of the city.[7]

RADICAL ACTIVISTS AND COMMUNITY-BASED ACTIVISM

Activists in San Francisco, linked to such community-based organizations as the Chinatown Youth Council and Intercollegiate Chinese for Social Action (ICSA), organized forums and marches to draw the public's attention to conditions in the ethnic enclave and, indirectly, to bring Chinese Americans' attention to the failure of the Chinese Consolidated Benevolent Association (CCBA) to address those ills. Another group, taking a lesson from the radical Black Panthers, organized the Chinatown Red Guards and traced the roots of these social ills to the blatant prejudice inflicted on the Chinese by the dominant society.[8]

The plight of the underprivileged in Chinatown attracted the attention of Asian American college students in the San Francisco Bay area, who in 1968 and 1969 engaged in a series of so-called Third World strikes, or protests, on the campuses of San Francisco State College (today San Francisco State University) and the University of California at Berkeley. The protests eventually spread to other campuses, such as the University of California at Los Angeles (UCLA) and the University of Washington. Initially, these student activists, who banded together with other students of color, focused on securing courses on the history and culture of Third World peoples. Soon the rhetoric turned to the establishment of ethnic studies programs (and, later, Asian American studies programs) in colleges and universities so students would have access to culturally specific knowledge to help them solve their communities' ills.[9]

Members of ICSA were particularly active in this agitation. Before the strikes, many had been involved in running a youth center in Chinatown, where English, civic education, and Chinese American history classes were offered to the community. The center also served as a drop-in center for wayward or rebellious youth.[10]

Another group made up of Chinese American youth activists was the Asian American Political Alliance (AAPA) at the University of California at Berkeley. Like other student organizations, Berkeley's AAPA initially focused on campus politics but soon became actively engaged with the ethnic community at large. To that end, the group established the Asian Community Center (ACC), based in San Francisco's Chinatown. The ACC was dominated by Chinese Americans—mostly second-generation Chinese and, later, newly arrived, pro–People's Republic of China (PRC) and foreign-born Chinese students. Influenced by Maoism, the ACC was committed to a leftist, revolutionary agenda that threatened to undercut the accommodationist stance of the CCBA and the Guomindang (GMD).[11]

Aside from showing pro-PRC propaganda films, the ACC became embroiled in the fight to save San Francisco's International Hotel. The hotel housed mostly elderly Filipino and Chinese bachelors, victims of antimiscegenation and anti-Asian immigration laws. When the hotel owners tried to evict the tenants in December 1968 to build a parking lot on the site, Asian American students, joined by other activists of color, mustered a campaign to halt the eviction—one that reminded Asian Americans of the U.S. racist past. The campaign, riddled by an ideological division between the left and accommodationist factions, ended in defeat, and the evictions did take place.[12]

The counterpart to the ACC in the East was Asian Americans for Action, or Triple A. One of the earliest pan-Asian organizations on the East Coast, Triple A began as an antiwar advocacy group. Internal divisions developed early when a Chinese American–dominated Maoist faction, which had splintered from the Communist Party, U.S.A., infiltrated the organization. The faction's rejection of cultural nationalism (including racial pride) immediately put it at odds with other members of the pan-ethnic organization. Interethnic hostility and a generation gap—young Chinese American Maoists pitted against an older Japanese American leadership—deepened the rift, proving that the forging of pan-ethnicity remained highly problematic. Alienated, the young members left and established I Wor Kuan based in New York's Chinatown.[13]

Committed to consciousness raising, I Wor Kuan, like the ACC, showed PRC films and sold publications touting Maoism. In its publication *Getting Together*, I Wor Kuan challenged the authority of the older Chinese establishment and criticized it for exploiting underprivileged coethnics. The publication also showed a growing pan-ethnic awareness because it covered issues of interest to all Asian Americans. Beyond propaganda work, I Wor Kuan provided free medical care and legal assistance for marginalized Chinese and dealt with housing complaints and workers' grievances. These efforts were designed to demonstrate that the existing political structure could not ameliorate the plight of marginalized Chinese.

BARRIERS TO POLITICAL MOBILIZATION

Although activists were occasionally able to rally the local community to strike back at racial discrimination—most notably when Chinatown residents mobilized to publicly protest against police brutality in New York City in 1975, as described later in this paragraph—the politicization of the community faced several roadblocks. Most Chinatown residents resisted or could not relate to the activists' anti-imperialist, class-based stance. Activists in general could not transform the community ideologically. For example, as mentioned earlier, in 1975 radical activists mobilized about 20,000 demonstrators in a protest against police brutality, but a few months later almost the same number of Chinese participated in a rally organized by the conservative CCBA to protest the closing of a police station in the neighborhood. A number of other revolutionary groups ran up against the same ideological barrier. The Philadelphia-based Yellow Seeds, established in 1971, offered educational, recreational, and referral services, but because of ideology and limited funding it failed to muster enough community support to survive more than a few years.[14]

The failure of radical activists to establish a broad base of support stemmed from several factors. Their organizing efforts were stymied by a language barrier because few of the activists spoke Cantonese. Seen as privileged "outsiders," the middle-class activists had little in common with the working-class Chinese who dominated Chinatown. The residents of Chinatowns typically regarded the activists with apprehension, if not outright hostility. Activists who espoused a politicized Asian American identity encountered the entrenched sensibility of ethnic particularism. Most Chinese Americans remained wedded to their ethnic community, their wellspring for selfhood and cultural heritage.[15]

An example of ethnic particularism is illustrated by the controversy over busing and the struggle to establish the so-called Freedom Schools. Centered in San Francisco, the issue surfaced in 1967 when a group of antibusing Euro-American mothers approached the Chinese community seeking a united front against busing children to schools in African American neighborhoods. Chinatown leaders and the media responded positively. The Chinese petitioned for an injunction against the court busing order.[16]

The petition was unsuccessful, and the group soon decided to engage in a boycott. When public schools opened in mid-September 1971, Chinese students stayed away; most had joined one of the three Freedom Schools organized by Chinese mothers. But the Freedom School movement faded when teachers and parents collided with the conservative traditional elite—which remained staunchly pro-GMD—over the question of protesting against the PRC's admission to the United Nations. When the traditional elite withdrew its support, the schools lost their funding, and the boycott soon collapsed.

The antibusing effort revealed several paradoxical undercurrents. Although it raised Chinese Americans' sense of group identity, it also revealed that the community was still very divided, polarized along generational and ideological lines. It demonstrated that many Chinese parents bore deep prejudices against African Americans, which, in turn, suggested that the Third World alliance forged by student activists had minimally affected the Chinese American popular consciousness.

By the mid-1970s most radical activists, in response to their persistent failure to capture community support, deemphasized their radical rhetoric. Instead, they joined liberals and civil rights activists to organize moderate, community-based organizations—such as the Asian American Legal Defense and Education Fund, Asian Americans for Equality (AAFE), and the Chinese

Progressive Association (CPA)—that were not reluctant to cooperate with the state or to rely on it for funding. These organizations' objectives zeroed in on reformist issues such as affirmative action and civil rights.

The AAFE was born during the 1974 protests over the lack of Chinese and Asian American construction workers on the Confucius Plaza site, then the largest housing project in New York City's Chinatown. After the confrontation ended in a victory for the militants, the AAFE became more institutionalized. It moved into tenant organizing and housing preservation. In 1988 the AAFE became a housing developer when it broke ground for a low-income housing cooperative. The AAFE also worked with tenant groups to acquire city monies to rehabilitate damaged buildings and assist Asian Americans with the legal and financial details of home buying. The AAFE also led the protest against the Special Manhattan Bridge District Rezoning in the early 1980s that threatened to drive out low-income tenants in the name of promoting high-rise real estate development.[17]

The CPA, based in San Francisco, has provided support for workers' rights and initiated English language and citizenship classes for new immigrants. In more recent years it has worked closely with other community-based organizations in a broad coalition called the Northern California Coalition for Immigrant Rights against reactionary, anti-immigrant social policies such as California's 1987 Proposition 63, the "English Only" initiative. The CPA also fought against the 1994 Proposition 187, which deprived undocumented immigrants of public social services, nonemergency health care, and public education; and the 1998 Proposition 227, the Unz-Matta Initiative, which ended bilingual education in California's public schools.[18]

PROFESSIONAL REFORMERS AND THE TRADITIONAL ELITE

By the early 1970s the post-1965 influx of new Chinese immigrants had placed a heavy burden on existing social services. Traditional organizations such as the CCBA and the *huiguan* clearly could no longer meet the needs of the community. It was fortuitous that the federal government's War on Poverty—part of the Great Society program—was fully under way. Billions of dollars were poured into antipoverty programs, which supported many community-based organizations that provided social, health, and legal services and offered job training and educational opportunities.[19]

The antipoverty programs also created employment opportunities for educated, professionally trained Chinese social workers and administrators. Unlike the radical student activists, who eschewed the politics of integration, these professional reformers sought to incorporate Chinese Americans into the existing political order. Their approach to ethnic advancement collided with the separatist stance of the radical activists, who saw them as outsiders with little understanding of the authentic Chinese American experience. Because these professional reformers possessed the skills and resources to deal with government agencies and officials who allocated funding for community-based projects, they quickly undermined the credentials of the grassroots activists.[20]

The reformers also threatened the power of the established traditional community leaders. Not surprisingly, the leaders of the CCBA and traditional clan and family associations did little to assist the reformers. Since the reformers received public funding and worked closely with government bodies, they were deemed to have undercut the mediatory functions of family and district associations, which mainstream society used to consider de facto representatives of the Chinese community. The control of the community was at stake, and this struggle for power was exacerbated by a division shaped by generational difference, level of Americanization, and educational background.[21]

Elites who led the traditional associations—also known as *qiao ling*—typically were born in China, were older, had little formal education, were mostly involved in business enterprises, and tended to be pro-GMD. The traditional elite played the role of cultural conservators by organizing Chinese cultural activities such as traditional festivals, supporting Chinese schools, maintaining clan and family associations, and serving as the conduit between the Chinese community in the United States and the Chinese in Taiwan.

Reformers, also known as *zhuan jia*, were born in the United States and were often highly educated. They became involved in professional, social, or volunteer work out of a sense of altruism. *Zhuan jia*, unlike *qiao ling*, have focused their energies on the delivery of social services. To that end, they have been willing to embrace the pan-ethnic identity *Asian American* to strengthen their movement for empowerment.

Starting in the late 1960s, the reformers joined forces with other Asian ethnic agencies to establish coalitions or joint councils to allow them to command more attention. This has become critical in cities where Chinese Americans do not constitute a significant segment of the populace. Also, the funding structure encourages and sometimes even demands that they operate on a pan-Asian basis. As one Chinese American director of a pan-Asian community-based agency in San Diego explained: "It's very hard to get a grant when you are serving only one ethnic group. . . . Funding agencies prefer to support pan-Asian coalitions because it is more cost-effective . . . [and] also allow[s] funding administrators to dodge the possible political fallout from having to choose one Asian group over another."[22]

In the past the traditional elites of the CCBA and other associations firmly held ground against this expression of pan-ethnicity or any attempt to undercut traditional authority. *Qiao ling* still considered Chinatown to be a self-sufficient community that could monitor and solve its own socioeconomic problems, publicly downplaying the community's ills. This stand augmented the "model minority" image of Chinese Americans—the skewed perception that this minority group is economically and educationally successful. In the late 1960s Lily Lee Chen, later the mayor of Monterey Park, California—the first Chinese American woman to be mayor of any U.S. city—was a Los Angeles County social worker. She discovered that a number of poor Asian Americans were unaware of how to take advantage of the War on Poverty programs. Chen recalled CCBA leaders failing to grant permission to establish a social services outstation in the organization's building: "They were concerned about the model minority image; they didn't want Chinese applying for welfare at their door."[23]

SOCIAL SERVICE AGENCIES

Most Chinese Americans in the late 1960s and early 1970s remained mired in poverty and privation. To quote Mason Wong, then president of ICSA, "The Chinese community has the same basic problems as all other nonwhite communities."[24] To resolve these problems, reformers set up community-based organizations. Some of the major groups established during the 1960s in San Francisco included Self-Help for the Elderly, the Chinese Newcomers Service Center, Chinatown Resource Center, the Chinatown Youth Center, and the Chinatown Child Development Center. These agencies provided medical and general social services to the elderly, assistance to new immigrants, planning for low-cost housing, day-care services, and civil rights advocacy. In Los Angeles, women—whose activism began as study or consciousness-raising groups—founded small community-based organizations. Asian Sisters, established in 1971, educated women about drug abuse. The Little Friends Playgroup was a grassroots child-care center in Chinatown Los Angeles. Larger in scope was the Asian Women's Center (established in 1972) whose services included education, counseling, drug abuse prevention, child development, and information on health care services. Three Chinatown-based organizations played a major role in shaping the social landscape—New York City's Chinatown Planning Council (CPC), the San Francisco–based Chinese for Affirmative Action (CAA), and Los Angeles's Chinatown Service Center.[25]

The CPC provides job training, legal aid, mental health services, and English language classes and also runs day-care centers and facilities for youth and senior citizens. It has also sponsored low-income housing projects and developed income-generating nonprofit service and rental establishments. The CPC has expanded geographically to cover the outlying areas of New York City as the Chinese population moves into new neighborhoods. By 1995, as the organization entered its fourth decade, its annual budget of $25 million was funding forty-five service centers and program offices throughout Chinatown and beyond.[26]

As with other federally supported agencies, the CPC has precipitated the diffusion of power within the community. This process has been encouraged by the influx of new immigrants with no ties to traditional associations, the loss of credibility of the GMD since the normalization of PRC-U.S. relations (which also undermined the authority of the traditional associations and the CCBA), and the emergence of a transnational ethnic economy unconnected to the traditional elite.

In the 1980s, however, when the CPC—composed primarily of affluent second-generation American-born Chinese—supported the city government's efforts to gentrify the core of Chinatown and encourage its decentralization through more rapid dispersal of the Chinese population and businesses, it provoked a controversy that undermined its authority and concomitantly boosted the declining power of the CCBA and affiliated associations. The fact that a number of CPC board members were linked to enterprises interested in either building or operating these new ventures caused the community to distrust the plan.

Old-time residents, benevolent associations, and activists galvanized a movement to oppose decentralization, which they considered an attempt to drive small businesses and residential buildings out of Chinatown's core in favor of erecting high-rise buildings to house corporate America. To block that possibility, Chinatown groups mustered a united front with other Lower East Side African Americans, Puerto Ricans, and church and tenants' groups to prevent rezoning changes and the violation of tenants' rights.

The same struggle took place in San Francisco in the mid-1980s, but in that case the traditional associations were pro-growth and those who fought them were mostly community-based activists and professionals. Clearly, both intracommunity conflicts were refracted by the generation gap, class interests, level of Americanization, and the politics of pro-growth versus pro-control.

Like the CPC, the CAA relied on the community for support and sustenance. Unlike the CPC, the CAA quickly developed an Asian American perspective. Established originally to fight for fair employment practices, the CAA today also offers counseling, English tutoring, and job placement services. The organization also widened its agenda to cover issues of equality and antiviolence for Asian Americans. It has disseminated information about anti-Asian violence, and in the mid-1980s the CAA joined with other civil rights groups to educate Americans about the nativist subtext of the English-only movement in California and nationwide. Finally, the CAA has carefully monitored university admissions policies that discriminate against Asian Americans.[27]

The Chinatown Service Center in Los Angeles, similar to the CAA, began in 1971 as a community-based agency designed to serve poor and non-English-speaking Chinese residents. From its humble beginnings in one room of a church, it now occupies three offices—two in the downtown district and a third in Asian-dominated Monterey Park. By 2000 its annual budget had reached $3 million, which has enabled the center to offer myriad services including a health clinic, counseling, and employment training. The 12,000 clients it serves each year include Chinese, Vietnamese, Cambodians, and Latinos. The center has also coordinated relief work with other agencies; after the 1992 Los Angeles race riot and the 1994 Northridge earthquake, for example, the center distributed food and assisted victims in accessing federal aid.[28]

GRASSROOTS RESPONSE TO ANTI-ASIAN VIOLENCE

The more radical Chinese Americans have tended to eschew the antipoverty and federally funded agencies because they regard them as instruments that foster the dependence of persons of color on the federal government. Chinese American radicals have banded together with other Asian Americans and established alternative grassroots organizations, which sometimes have difficulty securing funding and human capital from a community that is often suspicious of them.

Two alternative grassroots organizations that have remained visible in spite of the odds are the Asian Law Caucus, founded in 1972, and the Committee Against Anti-Asian Violence (CAAV), established in 1986. Both organizations have sought to defend the right of Chinese Americans to enjoy equal protection under the law. The Asian Law Caucus has offered legal representation to underprivileged Asian Americans, educated Asians in the United States about their legal and civil rights, and participated in litigation against institutional racism. The CAAV, however, was the outgrowth of an increasing awareness among Asian Americans that equal protection under the law could sometimes be compromised by racism as expressed through physical violence. The CAAV—which in 1986 brought together several advocacy groups including the Organization of Chinese Americans (OCA)—has been committed to public education, lobbying, and documentation of hate crimes, particularly those occurring in New York City. The group has also kept tabs on police brutality.[29]

In the early 1980s the U.S. Civil Rights Commission and state and local civil rights organizations began highlighting the increasing cases of violence against persons of Asian ancestry. In 1986 the commission reported that "the issue of violence against Asian Americans is national in scope."[30] Much of the wave of violence in the early 1980s coincided with deteriorating economic conditions after 1975. In the context of high unemployment, rising inflation, and high interest rates, competition between Asians and non-Asians often escalated into intergroup conflicts. An economic recession in the United States in the late 1970s and early 1980s led to a decrease in the profits of major U.S. industries. American policy makers, businesspeople, labor unions, and political pundits blamed the ills on business competition with Asian countries, which were experiencing dramatic economic growth. Anger against Asian nations, in a classic case of racial lumping, was projected onto Americans of Asian ancestry. Finally, anti-Asian sentiment was also the outgrowth of continuing anti-immigrant sentiments that became more virulent in the late 1970s.[31]

The 1986 commission report came in the wake of the brutal killing of Vincent Chin in June 1982. Chin, a twenty-seven-year-old Chinese American mistaken for a Japanese, was bludgeoned to death in Detroit by two Euro-American auto workers, Ronald Ebens and Michael Nitz. Ebens and Nitz, reflecting sentiments prevalent among some Detroit residents, scapegoated Japanese Americans for the downturn in the American automobile industry, which in fact was generated by Japan's aggressive marketing and sales of automobiles in the United States.

Although Ebens, in a plea bargain, admitted to being guilty of manslaughter and Nitz pleaded no contest to the charge of second-degree murder, both served only a three-year probation and paid a small fine. Chinese Americans were outraged by this miscarriage of justice. Lily Chin, the mother of the slain man, cried: "What kind of law is this? . . . This happened because my son is Chinese. . . . Something is wrong with this country."[32] The killing of Vincent Chin reminded many Chinese Americans of the legacy of anti-Asian sentiments. A century after the passage of the Chinese Exclusion Act in 1882, Chinese Americans—still regarded as foreigners—were being blamed for the U.S. economic woes.

American Citizens for Justice, a pan-ethnic grassroots group organized by concerned Chinese Americans, succeeded in getting the U.S. Justice Department to indict Ebens and Nitz for violating Chin's civil rights. In 1984 a jury acquitted Nitz but found Ebens guilty of having violated Chin's rights. Ebens was sentenced to twenty-five years in jail, but—much to the chagrin of Asian Americans—he was acquitted during the appeal and retrial.[33]

Since Chin was killed because of his racial identity, the case reminded Chinese Americans that all Asian Americans, not just Chinese, were at risk of suffering the same fate. When a similar case—the murder of Jim Ming Hai Loo, a Chinese American mistaken for a Vietnamese—occurred in Raleigh, North Carolina, in 1989, the ethnic community quickly mobilized and formed a pan-ethnic Asian coalition to ensure that justice would be served. As one local Chinese activist explained, "Like the Chin case, the Loo case is an Asian case. In both instances . . . the perpetrators cannot tell the difference between Asians. That's why it is an Asian problem."[34] The culprit did receive a stiff sentence: thirty-five years for second-degree murder and two years for assault with a deadly weapon.

In 1993 Sacramento, California, was rocked by five firebombings, two against Asian American targets. One of the two Asian targets was city council member Jimmie Yee, a second-generation Chinese American and Sacramento native son. Apparently, Yee became the target of a white supremacist group, not because of anything he did but because of anti-immigrant bashing within the context of an economic slowdown.[35]

The furor over hate crimes also included the issue of police brutality. Starting in 1974 Chinatown youth in New York City were at the receiving end of aggressive stop-and-frisk searches designed to weed out gambling and gang terrorism. In 1975 Henry Yew was severely beaten by New York City police. Yew was apprehended and abused during a public melee that stemmed from a parking dispute involving white and Chinese motorists. The AAFE swung into action. Around 2,500 demonstrators took to the streets to protest police brutality. A later demonstration endorsed by the CCBA drew a crowd of around 10,000, and in sympathy, nearly all Chinatown businesses closed for the day. A grand jury later dropped the charges against Yew and indicted the two officers who had beaten him; the commanding officer of the precinct was transferred to another locale. In a 1995 case, also in New York, a police officer confronted Yong Xin Huang, a sixteen-year-old playing with a gun, and shot him in the back of the head at point-blank range. The police claimed Huang had tried to fight, and the officer's gun had discharged accidentally. In spite of the testimony of key eyewitnesses who contradicted the police claims, the district attorney refused to indict the officer, claiming Huang's death was an "accident." The CAAV and several other advocacy groups tried to reopen the case through public education and mass rallies, but to no avail.[36]

Racist violence such as Vincent Chin's case and the police brutality against Yong Xin Huang were not random acts of terror but, as Scott Kurashige has argued, "must be seen as constitutive elements of the racial hierarchy and class rule in the U.S." Patterned forms of anti-Asian violence often stemmed from the convergence of economic deindustrialization, the politics of space (white privilege identified with certain neighborhoods), urban blight, the reversal of economic mobility for working-class white Americans, and, in the case of police brutality, also from continual "Orientalist" assumptions of Asian Americans.[37] This explains why hate crimes against Asian Americans rose slightly throughout the 1990s, although among racial ethnic minorities, Asians were the least targeted.[38]

ORGANIZATION OF CHINESE AMERICANS AND EQUAL RIGHTS

The most prominent Chinese American advocacy group today is the nonpartisan, nonprofit OCA, a national civil rights group based in Washington, D.C. Established in 1973, by 2000 OCA had forty-five chapters in the United States and one in Hong Kong and 10,000 members.[39]

Over the years OCA has sought to protect not only the interests of Chinese Americans but those of other Asian Americans as well, demonstrating an evolving sense of pan-Asian ethnicity. Together with other Asian American advocacy groups, it lobbied the Bureau of the Census for a separate count for each Asian subgroup in the 1980 and 1990 censuses to allow for more effective service delivery, better access to affirmative action and federal aid, and sufficient representation in the media. In more recent times OCA has been embroiled, in conjunction with other ethnic advocacy groups, in a movement to roll back congressional welfare reforms that targeted underprivileged immigrants and new permanent residents. The 1996 Personal Responsibility and Work Opportunities Reconciliation Act dramatically altered the U.S. welfare system by denying benefits to legal permanent residents who could not meet stringent requirements. The act placed programs such as food stamps, Medicaid, and Supplementary Security Income beyond the reach of the vast majority of permanent residents, of which Chinese Americans constitute a substantial number.[40] In 1997 the OCA and other immigrant advocates, by emphasizing the legislation's crushing blow to poor elderly people, convinced lawmakers to restore some public assistance benefits to legal immigrants. What remains uncertain is whether poor, English-deficient immigrants will be able to cope with the new welfare-to-work rules. Welfare recipients have only two years to move from dependency to self-sufficiency, but many Chinese and other Asian newcomers lack sufficient English proficiency to join job training programs that are conducted in English. Even if they complete the programs, they still face the hurdle of applying for jobs that may require a high level of English proficiency.[41]

Aside from agitating for the restoration of benefits and getting states to increase their benefits to compensate for the recent federal restrictions on eligibility, OCA has also spoken out against legislation that could undermine Asian Americans' political rights—such as the proposed 1998 Voter Eligibility Verification Act, which would allow election officials to confirm the citizenship status of registered voters and voter registration applicants by submitting names to the Immigration and Naturalization Service (INS) and the Social Security Administration (SSA). The law is flawed because the INS and SSA databases are incomplete; many Americans, including Asian Americans, could be prevented from voting through no fault of their own.[42]

THE 1996 CAMPAIGN FINANCE SCANDAL

In 1998 OCA was at the forefront of opposing legislative efforts to prohibit political donations by legal permanent residents, which would have infringed upon the constitutional right to engage in free speech. Since a disproportionate number of Asian Americans are legal permanent residents, this legislation would ultimately discourage political involvement by Asian Americans.[43]

The recent legislative effort stemmed from the spotlight on the flow of illegal foreign money from Asian governments, corporations, and individual power brokers into the U.S. political system during the 1994 and 1996 elections. Much of the furor focused on John Huang, former vice chair of the Finance Committee of the Democratic National Committee (DNC), and Charlie Yah-lin Trie, another fund-raiser—both of whom allegedly played a role in raising illegal political campaign contributions from Asia. The controversy surfaced when Bill Clinton's two challengers in the 1996 presidential race alleged that Asian Americans and their connections in several Asian countries, including Communist China, were behind the political corruption in the fund-raising efforts for the election. Committees of both houses of the U.S Congress looked into the allegations, but their goal was always either to discredit Clinton and the DNC or to incite fear of and hostility toward the PRC. Asian American individuals who had contributed to the Democratic Party in recent years became subjects of the investigation. Even officials of long-established Asian American organizations, such as OCA, were subpoenaed to testify. Ethnic slurs and Yellow Peril images were bandied about. Reportedly, Senator Robert Bennett (R-Utah), commenting on one Asian contributor, said that these "are classic activities on the part of an Asian who comes from out of that culture." During Senate hearings on campaign financing, another senator used a fake Chinese accent and said, in a reference to Huang's salary arrangement with the DNC, "No raise money, no make bonus."[44]

Public figures and politicians in Congress began scapegoating Asian Americans as agents of foreign influences, which, in turn, reasserted the notion that Asian Americans are foreigners. Politicians and political commentators alleged that the PRC government tried to buy influence with the Clinton administration through laundered campaign contributions made or handled by Asian Americans. By racializing political corruption, some members of Congress hoped to divert public demand for campaign finance reform.[45] Of course, exploiting nativism and racism for political gain is nothing new; it has been in existence since the days of California's Workingmen's Party (see Chapter 2, "The Anti-Chinese Movement," pages 45–53).

After the November 1996 elections the race card continued to be played. The DNC hired an auditing firm to uncover donors of "dirty money," and soon anyone with an Asian surname became a suspect. The Clinton administration decided to distance itself from Asian Americans. President Clinton failed to name any Asian American to cabinet-level and subcabinet positions. The Democratic Party, like the Republican Party, racialized the issue of political corruption. The print media also got into the act; the cover of a 1997 issue of the conservative *National Review* featured President and Mrs. Clinton in elaborate "Oriental" garb with "Oriental" facial characteristics, and Vice President Al Gore was outfitted in a Buddhist monk's habit—a reference to his attendance at a questionable fund-raiser at a Buddhist temple in the Los Angeles area.

The fallout from the campaign finance scandal was widespread. Not only was the public demand for campaign finance reform diverted, but equally neglected was the issue of how the transnational business and professional elite—with its connections to transnational and even flight capital—had succeeded in penetrating U.S. markets and politics for its own gains. Along the way, Asian American interests and political mobilization came under the influence of such "extraterritorial domination," to quote L. Ling-chi Wang.[46]

The OCA, in conjunction with thirteen other advocacy organizations, petitioned the U.S. Commission of Civil Rights to hold hearings in early December 1997 concerning the discriminatory ramifications of the campaign finance controversy. Asian American activists and community leaders who testified at the hearings charged that aside from the chilling effect the proposed legislation to limit the financial contributions of permanent residents would have on Asian American political participation, there was also the question of the derailment of well-qualified Asian American candidates for political appointments because of race.

On this question the stymied confirmation of Bill Lann Lee, the president's nominee for assistant attorney general for civil rights, comes to mind. If confirmed, Lee, the son of immigrant parents, would have been one of the highest-ranking Chinese American political appointees in the federal government. Lee's nomination in late 1997, however, was deadlocked in the Senate Judiciary Committee. Republican senators on the committee, opposed to the administration's support for affirmative action, found Lee wanting because he also reportedly supported that policy. Some of the senators' critics charged that the opposition was racially motivated, since previous nominees for civil rights–related positions who were Euro-American had been confirmed with few impediments. Clearly, the campaign financing uproar had unleashed a movement to demonize Asian Americans. The end result was that in spite of the full support of more than thirty Asian American organizations and many white and nonwhite politicians, Lee's nomination never came before the full Senate for a vote, and President Clinton appointed Lee to the position in an acting capacity (Lee eventually received a recess appointment from President Clinton and served as assistant attorney general for civil rights until January 2001). In spite of the media spotlight on the Lee nomination and the well-publicized Civil Rights Commission hearings, the racialization of the campaign financing controversy reached a new low on March 30, 1998, with the passage of the Illegal Foreign Contributions Act, which prohibits noncitizens—including permanent residents—from contributing to political campaigns.[47]

The doubts raised about the loyalty of Chinese and other Asian Americans have sensitized OCA to avoid supporting potentially inflammatory issues. A case in point was the 1999 Assembly Joint Resolution 27 in the California legislature. Authored by Michael Honda, a liberal Democrat, the resolution demanded that the Japanese government apologize and pay for the World War II atrocities committed against China and its people. A similar resolution had made its way through the U.S. Congress. Although some OCA chapter presidents considered this a human rights issue and thus worthy of the organization's support, others were less certain. The national OCA board voted not to support the congressional version of Honda's resolution. Echoing the concerns of other Asian American activists, Michael Lin, a past national OCA president, said the organization was reluctant to support the resolution for fear of reinforcing the existing perception that Asian Americans care only about Asian and not American issues.[48]

EDUCATION: WHY CHINESE AMERICANS SUCCEED

With an eye to the future, OCA has spent its resources training youths to carry on the civil rights struggle. Every year it sponsors an internship program that places young Asian Americans in Congress, federal agencies, and OCA chapters across the country to gain experience in public policy making and advocacy work. The OCA has extended such leadership training to high school students.

It seems necessary for OCA to raise the political awareness of young Chinese Americans given the fact that mainstream society has a skewed understanding of them and of other Asian Americans. The media has focused on school-age Asian Americans as the cohort that provides solid evidence that Asian Americans are the U.S. model minority. For example, the media has pointed out that the 1983 first-prize winner of the Westinghouse Science Talent Search was Paul Ning, a sixteen-year-old student born in Taiwan who attended Bronx High School. More significant, of the forty finalists at the national level, twelve were Asian Americans. Newspaper and television reports and special issues of newsmagazines since the early 1980s have applauded Asian Americans' supposedly phenomenal educational achievements.[49]

Some public commentators and even a few scholars have attributed this success to superb genes or a biological inheritance. University of Calgary psychologist Philip E. Vernon, in a 1982 publication, argued that Asians have larger heads than Caucasians and Africans and hence have greater intelligence.[50] More recently, Richard J. Herrnstein and Charles Murray's *The Bell Curve* (1994) reinvigorated the genetic debate by claiming that Asians probably have higher IQ scores than whites because they are better at "visual/spatial" skills than at verbal skills. This factor also supposedly explains why Chinese and other Asians are overly represented in medicine, the sciences, and engineering and, conversely, are underrepresented in literature, law, and politics.[51]

These conclusions, which ignore the impact of environmental factors, have been contested by educational researchers who have concluded that Chinese Americans and other Asian Americans simply work and study harder than whites and blacks. To explain this difference, scholars have zeroed in on Asian cultural values, which place a high priority on education, hard work, and family honor.[52] This cultural explanation for academic success, however, slights the role of the larger social context and smacks of confirming stereotypes.

A more nuanced rationale for Asian educational achievement lies in the impact of structural forces. Without ignoring the cultural angle, scholars who subscribe to this theory, also known as relative functionalism, assert that limited opportunities—the product of discrimination—in noneducational areas have forced Chinese Americans to pay more attention to education as an avenue for social mobility. Furthermore, the human capital—educational background, skills, and language proficiency—new immigrants bring to the United States could determine the track of their educational and professional training. According to one study of high-achieving Asian Americans, 85 percent of the children had fathers who had earned graduate degrees, 71 percent of which were doctorates.[53] Thus a complex combination of factors of race, class, and sociohistorical context must be employed in any analysis of Chinese American academic achievement.

The celebration of Asian American educational achievement—clearly part of the model minority myth—has profound repercussions for both Asian and non-Asian students. First, it pits Asians against less "achievement-oriented" peoples of color, taunting the latter to try harder without recognizing their problems. It also sidelines the continual barriers Chinese and other Asian students suffer in the classroom, the most vexing of which is poor English proficiency. According to the 1990 U.S. Bureau of the Census, 5.8 percent of Chinese Americans between ages five and seven did not speak English "very well," compared with the national average of only 1.0 percent. The dilemma here will likely be compounded by the English Fluency Act, passed by the U.S. Congress in September 1998. The bill, not unlike the Unz-Matta Initiative, requires the removal of limited English proficient (LEP) students from bilingual classrooms within two years of their entry. The law also bars funding for programs offering assistance to LEP students who have been in such programs for more than three years.[54]

Clearly, the bill threatens to reduce retention and graduation rates and consequently to narrow educational opportunities. It affects the most vulnerable, since LEP youngsters often come from poor socioeconomic backgrounds. Furthermore, the bill attempts to stem the progress made in providing bilingual education since the landmark case *Lau v. Nicholas* (1972), which secured Chinese Americans' right to bilingual education so their accessibility to equal opportunity in the classroom would not be jeopardized.[55]

BACKLASH WITHIN HIGHER EDUCATION

At the tertiary educational level, accessibility has also been a controversial subject. Since the late 1970s, Asian American representation in U.S. higher education has increased rapidly. On college campuses non–Asian American students joke that "MIT" stands for "Made in Taiwan," "UCI" (University of California at Irvine) means "University of California Immigrants," and "UCLA" refers to "United Caucasians Lost Among Asians." In 1995 Asian Americans made up less than 3 percent of the U.S. population but constituted more than 5 percent of U.S. college students. In some of the country's most elite schools, the percentage of Asian Americans far exceeded the national average. At the University of California at Berkeley, in 1996 Asian Americans made up 40 percent of undergraduates, whereas white students accounted for 31 percent.[56]

In spite of these impressive statistics, discrimination—not unlike what Jewish Americans experienced from the 1920s to the 1950s—has reared its ugly head. Some prestigious schools, both private and public—including Brown, Stanford, and Berkeley—were suspected in the 1980s of having applied a quota system to students of Asian ancestry. "As soon as the percentages of Asian students began reaching double digits at some universities . . . Asian American admission rates have either stabilized or declined," said L. Ling-chi Wang, a professor of ethnic history at Berkeley. In numerous cases, Asian American and white applicants had the same academic qualifications, yet the former were denied admission.[57]

Yat-pang Au, the son of immigrant parents from Hong Kong, was one such case. The winner of seven high school scholarships, Au graduated first in his class of 432 at his San Jose high school. He was a school athlete, was elected to student body and club offices, and had run a Junior Achievement company that garnered him the runner-up award as Santa Clara County's Young Businessman of the Year. In spite of these accolades, he was denied entry to the University of California at Berkeley.

Critics have charged that these institutions have manipulated admissions criteria to hold back the Asian influx. The underlying assumption held by university officials is that Chinese Americans and other Asian Americans are not truly Americans and that allowing too many of them into higher education would undermine the Americanism of the country's esteemed institutions.

In recent years conservative politicians and commentators have exploited the question of admission quotas for the purpose of dismantling affirmative action in admission policies. The position received a boost from *Hopwood v. Texas* (1994), in which the Fifth District Court of Appeals ruled that the University of Texas Law School's use of race-based criteria as one of many factors to admit students was unconstitutional. Antiaffirmative advocates have explained the controversy over admission quotas as the outcome of Asian Americans being pitted against Hispanics and blacks for limited seats in leading institutions. Thus, they argue, affirmative action has discriminated against Asian Americans by setting aside the factor of merit. Ever since the *University of California Regents v. Bakke* decision (1978), which admitted the use of race as an additional factor of consideration in admissions to allow the institution to achieve a diverse student body (the decision, however, prohibited racial quotas), a numerical limit on an "overrepresented minority" like Asian Americans, conservatives claim, has become necessary to promote "diversity."[58]

Asian American leaders in higher education have rejected such specious arguments. Mindful of creating any misunderstanding among minority groups (such as African Americans and Latinos) targeted for affirmative action, Asian American leaders and scholars have pointed out that they are not advocating that more Asian Americans be admitted to colleges at the expense of less-represented minority groups. Clearly, affirmative action preferences will negatively impact the admission of nontargeted groups such as Asian Americans and whites, but that impact, critics argue, should have an equal effect on the admission rates of all nontargeted groups and thus cannot account for the difference in admission rates between Asians and whites. Asian American students should not have to suffer the "double burden" of any reallocation engendered by affirmative action and an enrollment cap to prevent their overrepresentation. In addition, the "overrepresented minority" argument is flawed; the Asian American cohort is highly diverse in terms of race, class, and national origins. Affirmative action, if employed in certain ways, can benefit working-class Chinese who are underrepresented or could help to reverse the underrepresentation of Chinese Americans in the humanities. By diversifying the student body, affirmative action, educators and civil rights advocates argue, can provide students with the opportunity to learn from different races. The quality of higher education, they urge, depends on diversity.

Chinese and other Asian Americans are split on the question of affirmative action. The 1995 University of California board of regents' decision to abolish race, ethnicity, and gender criteria in admitting future students was supported by two regents of Asian descent, whereas another objected. In 1992 Henry Der, executive director of San Francisco's CAA, echoed the sentiments of a number of Asian American educational activists when he said that since tertiary education in some highly sought-after schools is publicly subsidized, students should reflect the diversity of California's taxpayers. Asians denied admittance in spite of high grades and test scores were less philosophical; they felt they had been discriminated against and blamed affirmative action. They argued that only individual merit should be the guiding criterion for admittance to prestigious schools.[59]

In the 1994 lawsuit *Brian Ho v. SFUSD* (San Francisco Unified School District), Chinese American students contested the desegregation consent decree that had been in place in the district since 1983. According to the decree, no public school could allow any single racial or ethnic group to exceed 40 percent of the total student body. *Brian Ho* centered on the prestigious Lowell High School. At the time, Lowell diverged from the common practice of using a lottery system to determine admission and instead relied on differential admissions scores (based on grade point averages, test scores, and other variables). Chinese American students were the largest student group in the district, and to keep them below the 45 percent cap (the cap for alternative schools such as Lowell) Lowell officials had to raise the group's admission scores a number of times as the years passed. The Chinese American Democratic Club, which pushed for the lawsuit, argued that the decree discriminated against Chinese Americans. Support for the lawsuit came from the San Francisco chapter of OCA (the national OCA took a neutral stance) and from many local Chinese American community leaders and laypeople. The CAA, the pan-ethnic group, opposed the lawsuit; past executive director Henry Der argued that the lawsuit could result in the abolishment of race-consiousness remedies. The 1999 settlement of the suit, as predicted by the CAA, nullified the consent decree and ended the use of racial classifications in enrolling students in schools. The results of this case exemplify what one scholar calls "racial trumping"—identifying Chinese Americans as victims of discrimination at the same level as African Americans, thus enabling whites to delegitimate specific black claims such as affirmative action for racial redress.

Still, Asian American community leaders and education scholars on the whole supported the recent fight—albeit unsuccessfully—against California's Proposition 209 (1996), which prohibits consideration of race, ethnicity, and gender in admissions to publicly funded state institutions of higher learning. A movement was also afoot to oppose a similar effort at the federal level. The antiaffirmative movement has spread beyond California; Washington state voters passed Initiative 200 in 1998, which banned all race-conscious practices and policies in public higher education. In November 1999 Florida announced that the state's ten public universities would no longer consider race in admitting students.

PARTICIPATION IN MAINSTREAM POLITICS

Members of the mainstream society—in spite of the activism of the last thirty years—still consider Chinese Americans and other Asian Americans to be apolitical. In 1960 sociologist Rose Hum Lee concluded that Chinese Americans were not politically astute or active in U.S. politics.[60] This perception has apparently changed little since 1960. Today, the ambiguousness of Chinese

Americans' place in politics is compounded by the absence of a strong association with either liberalism or conservatism.

This perception of political apathy stems from the belief that Chinese Americans' cultural values are strongly opposed to political participation. Supposedly a complacent and accommodating people, Chinese Americans are satisfied with their academic and economic achievements. Popular writers and scholars regard Chinese Americans as unsuited for involvement in public affairs because they consider them unprepared for the highly competitive, masculine-oriented U.S. culture.[61]

Because of this widely held stereotype, political parties in the past have made little effort to cultivate the Chinese American community. Of course, political parties have solicited donations from the community, but with the belief that little was expected in return. Because Chinese Americans have been sidelined in the political realm, many have retreated from electoral politics—which confirms their apolitical image.[62]

Over the past few decades, empirical studies conducted on electoral politics among Chinese Americans have seemed to confirm that image. According to one 1984 study undertaken in San Francisco, the Chinese voter registration rate stood at 30.9 percent—far below the registration rate for the general population in that city, which in 1984 was over 60 percent. Another study conducted in Los Angeles in 1984 produced similar results: the registration of Chinese stood at 35.5 percent, compared with the county's overall rate of about 60 percent. Low voter registration also characterized New York City's Chinese; one 1994 study showed that only 38 percent of Asians eligible to vote in an area that covers most of Chinatown were registered, compared with 64 percent for all of lower Manhattan.[63]

These low figures can be accounted for in several ways. First, the Chinese American population, as well as other Asian groups, has become more foreign than native born since World War II and thus has a high percentage of noncitizens who are unable to register to vote. One 1989 study that took citizenship into account revealed that 77 percent of California's Asian American citizens were registered, compared with 87 percent of whites.[64] Among Asian Americans, Chinese and Japanese demonstrated the highest rates of registration; they also had the highest proportion of native-born citizens.[65] Other surveys in San Francisco have shown that on certain issues the percentage of Chinese Americans who voted was as much as 5 to 10 percent above the rate for the general electorate.[66] The 1994 study of New York City's Chinatown mentioned in the last paragraph revealed, however, that only 40 percent of Asian voters registered that year actually voted, the lowest rate among the major racial and ethnic groups—a fact attributed to the high percentage of new working-class immigrants ignorant of voting procedures and democratic processes. Equally important was the existence of newly naturalized Chinese Americans, who often have a lower registration rate than native-born citizens—the outcome of immigrants having to go through a long and complex process of social adaptation and learning before fully participating in the customs of their newly adopted country.[67]

Studies have also shown that voter registration and voting are also contingent upon economic status and income. Areas with higher concentrations of middle-income as opposed to lower-income dwellers have higher registration rates. In San Francisco the registration rate in Chinatown, according to one study, was 23.1 percent of the Chinese voting-age population in 1984, compared with 39.9 percent in the other important Chinese pocket, the middle-income Richmond district. Another study showed that between 1983 and 1992, the number of Chinese American registrants in Chinatown increased by 41.7 percent, compared with 43.8 percent for Richmond. The same study revealed that the number of Chinese Americans registered to vote in predominately Chinese neighborhoods was increasing at rates far greater than those for the overall population. Voter registration drives led by such grassroots organizations as the Chinese American Voters Education Committee and the Asian American Voters Project have had a positive impact. Yet in terms of the number of registrants as a percentage of the Chinese population that was over eighteen in each area, Chinatown still lagged visibly behind Richmond. This differentiation could be attributed to the larger numbers of foreign-born residents in that part of the city.[68]

Any consideration of political apathy among Chinese Americans must take into account the historical disenfranchisement experienced by the community. Rejected and excluded in the past, they have retreated into their own families and communities and have shunned political involvement. This legacy of political exclusion and isolation has meant that voter registration campaigns in the community have had to confront and overcome deep-seated attitudes of political alienation and mistrust of government.[69]

Political disengagement has been compounded by the fact that many recent Chinese immigrants face a number of structural barriers in trying to exercise their political enfranchisement. Aside from English language deficiency, an orientation toward a wider ideological spectrum in their country of birth has made it difficult for them to understand U.S. domestic issues. Many underprivileged Chinese, in fact, simply do not have the time to concern themselves with political affairs; economic survival occupies too much of their attention. The situation has been exacerbated by the frequent absence of bilingual ballots and voting materials. Even though section 203 of the 1975 Voting Rights Act required election officials to provide voting-related materials and assistance in a minority language if certain conditions were met, a 1982 amendment dramatically circumscribed the statutory coverage of the earlier law. A new law passed in 1992—which mandated that a minimum of 10,000 LEP voting-age citizens would trigger bilingual elections at the county level—has somewhat widened accessibility to such materials. Still, slightly more than 30 percent of the LEP Asian American citizens qualified to vote in California live in counties that can legally ignore the federal law.[70]

The issue of Chinese American involvement in politics becomes more complex when we consider the type of political activity and political affiliation. Upper- and middle-class Chinese Americans are more likely than other groups to contribute money to candidates, even though they seem less inclined than whites to work on campaigns or attend political rallies. Chinese Americans, contrary to the public perception that they have weak or no political allegiances, actually have the same rates of party loyalty as the general populace. The previously cited Los Angeles survey conducted in 1986 revealed that 41.9 percent of Chinese were registered as Democrats, 36.4 percent were registered as Republicans, and the rest chose neither party. The 1984 San Francisco study mentioned earlier showed a similar split: 48.6 percent Democrats, 21.4 percent Republicans. The continuing entry of more foreign-born Chinese who then become naturalized may change the distribution of partisan preferences in the future.[71] One study that tracked voting patterns in San Francisco from 1983 to 1992 concluded that the percentage of Chinese Americans who stated no party preference increased during that period. Another study that focused on New York City's Chinese revealed that of the nearly 1,000 voters registered by the Chinatown Voter Education Alliance (CVEA) in 1994, more than 52 percent registered as independents. Perhaps the foreign-born believe both major parties have failed to address their concerns. For many recent immigrants, party affiliation reminds them of the authoritarian single-party government in their country of origin, whether the PRC or Taiwan. Party politics also evokes images of rigid ideological doctrine, frequent meetings, and heavy responsibility.[72] The bloc-vote potential of Chinese Americans has been further hampered by the growing diversity of Chinese dialects, countries of origin, political ideologies, and diverse faiths.

The Chinese American stance toward public policies also defies simple categorization. Unlike African Americans and Latinos but similar to most whites, Chinese Americans are likely to favor the death penalty. Similar to the other two major ethnic groups, however, most Chinese Americans tend to favor bilingual education but parted company—as did whites—with the two groups on the question of supporting amnesty for undocumented aliens.[73]

Voting patterns also show no consistency. In the 1984 presidential race, Chinese and other Asian Americans, although more were registered as Democrats, favored Ronald Reagan over Walter Mondale by 67 percent to 32 percent. In 1992 the vote was more evenly split: among Asian Americans, 39 percent voted for Bill Clinton, 33 percent for George Bush, and 25 percent for Ross Perot. In 1996, 48 percent of Asian Americans voted for Bob Dole compared with 43 percent for Clinton. In the 2000 race they reversed party allegiance, voting 54 percent to 41 percent for Al Gore over Bush. Perhaps this inconsistency suggests that Chinese Americans are more inclined than others to cross party lines. Chinese Americans, like most Americans, have voted on the basis of candidates' merits rather than by strict party lines.[74] Further, Chinese voters have not consistently voted for coethnic candidates for public office. One study of LEP voting-age citizens in San Francisco concluded that race was not the sole determining factor in how they voted.[75]

Race has often been a double-edged sword for Chinese American candidates. When California state treasurer Matthew Fong, a Republican, made his 1998 run for the U.S. Senate, Chinese Americans—even registered Democrats—flocked to his side. Chinese American resentment of the Democratic Party had been widespread since the campaign financing scandal led the party to investigate the citizenship status of Asian-surnamed donors, most of whom were U.S. citizens. For some Chinese Americans, electing a coethnic to a high national political position would be the first step toward ending their political invisibility. But Fong, like some Chinese candidates in the past, was still considered a "foreigner" in spite of being a native-born American. Fong was asked which side he would support if China invaded the United States. Fong lost to his liberal Democratic opponent Barbara Boxer, albeit by a slim margin.[76]

If we examine the number of Chinese Americans—most of whom have been Democrats—who have held public office since the end of World War II, the impression would be that their numbers have been fairly substantial. Chinese have run for political office at the national, state, and city levels. When Hawai'i became a state in 1959, Hiram Fong, who had served in the territorial legislature, was elected U.S. senator. The first person of Chinese descent to win state office on the mainland was Wing F. Ong. An immigrant who arrived in the United States at age fourteen in 1914, he went from being a houseboy to serving as a member of Arizona's house of representatives for two terms during the 1940s. March Fong Eu was elected California's secretary of state in 1974 and was repeatedly reelected by wide margins until she resigned in 1994 to serve as ambassador to Micronesia. In that same year her son Matthew Fong was elected state treasurer. Chinese American physicist S. B. Woo was elected lieutenant governor of Delaware in 1984, an office he held until 1989. Gary Locke, a former county executive and state legislator, was elected governor of Washington in 1996 and is currently the top-ranking Chinese elected official in the United States. Locke was also the first Asian American governor of a mainland state and the first Chinese American governor of any state. Interestingly, Locke, whose paternal grandfather was a houseboy, moved into the governor's mansion in a state where Asian Americans made up less than 6 percent of the population.[77] Eu, Woo, and Locke proved that a Chinese American can be elected to prominent public offices without a large Chinese or even Asian American population.

Nearly all Chinese candidates for public offices, however, have had to rely on Asian American financial contributions to fund their campaigns. Chinese Americans have contributed to campaigns disproportionately to their demographic strength; for example, in Woo's election, Chinese Americans from across the country contributed about 27 percent of the funds for his campaign. Through their pocketbooks, Chinese Americans have found a way to increase their influence over the political process.[78]

Chinese American visibility at the local level has been greater than that at the state and federal levels. In 1962 Wing Luke, whose grandfather was caught up in the 1886 anti-Chinese riot in Seattle, was elected to the Seattle city council. Luke, whose parents had run a laundry and then a grocery store, served several years as an assistant attorney general for the state of Washington before running for the council. Luke became the first Chinese American elected to office in a large American city on the mainland. Lily Chen, who was born in China to a privileged Beijing family and had served as a county administrator, became mayor of Monterey Park, California, in 1983—the first Chinese American woman to fill such an office. Chen had to rely on the support of Asian, Latino, and white voters in a city where half or less than half of the Asian residents were citizens and mistrust of Asian politicians ran high.[79]

Two years later Michael Woo became the first Chinese American member of the Los Angeles city council. He won a landslide victory in his 1989 reelection bid in a district with only a 5 percent Asian population, and in 1993 he ran for mayor. Woo, a liberal, lost to a conservative white but garnered almost half the votes. During his campaign he raised a significant amount of money from Chinese Americans in California, regardless of their political affiliation. Yet like Luke and Chen, Woo is sensitive to the need to forge interracial coalitions so the close tie between race and the economy receives attention. On the heels of Woo's efforts, Ted Dang ran for mayor of Oakland in 1994. Voters were tired of career politicians, so Dang, a real estate developer, ran as an antipolitician candidate. But his attempt to curry the working-class Chinese voting bloc by speaking Cantonese and the middle-class Asian voters by championing less government and lower taxes backfired with conservative white and liberal black voters, and he lost to an African American candidate. Recent, educated Chinese immigrants, mostly in San Francisco, have also run for public offices such as judgeships, school board seats, and city council positions. In 1991 Thomas Hsieh, the sole Asian American on the board of supervisors, ran unsuccessfully for mayor of San Francisco.

More gains could likely be made at all levels if voter participation was higher, political factionalism within the electorate dissipated, and the political district boundaries that divide some Chinatowns could be redrawn. The mixed political fortunes of Margaret Chin in New York City illustrate the barrier Chinese political candidates have faced. The daughter of a working-class immigrant family from Hong Kong, Chin as a college student had plunged headlong into the Asian American movement, pushing for Asian American studies programs and volunteering for student-run day-care programs in Chinatown. After years of being involved in the AAFE, in 1991 she announced her intention to run for a city council seat in a proposed reconfigured district that was almost 40 percent Asian. But opposition to the reconfiguration from other political coalitions, including one backed by a Chinese Democrat who was running against Chin in the upcoming primaries, led to a redistricting that was less favorable to Chinese voter mobilization. During the general elections Chin's opponent brought up her earlier militant days. The Chinese vote was split along party lines. Chin was defeated.[80]

Some gains have also been made in the area of political appointments, although marginal political power has stymied rapid progress. In 1988 and 1989 Mayor Art Agnos of San Francisco appointed twenty Chinese Americans, mostly immigrants, to serve on various city commissions. Chinese Americans appointed to other San Francisco city positions included Frederick Lau as police chief, Douglas Wong as police commissioner, and Wayne Hu as a member of the board of permit appeals. Top-ranking political appointments have been rare. Elaine Chao, U.S. secretary of labor who was nominated by President George W. Bush and confirmed by the U.S. Congress in January 2001, is the highest-ranking Chinese American official ever appointed within the executive branch. She is also the first Asian American woman in U.S. history to be appointed to a president's cabinet. Bill Lan Lee's controversial appointment as acting assistant attorney general for civil rights in 1997 (which lost its "acting" status in 1999 and lasted until 2001) was also a milestone in Chinese American political visibility.

These political advancements—which have made Asian Americans a more visible electoral bloc—in conjunction with the widespread belief that Chinese and other Asian Americans are generous political donors, have led mainstream political candidates to heavily court the community. Major political candidates, reacting to Asians' growing demographic strength, now campaign regularly in Chinese American communities, hoping to convince Chinese that their money, votes, and opinions do count. For example, in 1990 all three candidates for governor of California—Pete Wilson, Dianne Feinstein, and John Van de Kamp—campaigned in the Chinese American community and promised to support Chinese American political concerns, ranging from quotas in higher education to more appointments in government policy-making positions. Similarly, presidential candidates in the 1988, 1992, 1996, and 2000 elections canvassed for Chinese American money and votes.[81]

One sign of ethnic interest in American politics has been the emergence of voters associations such as the Chinese American Voters Association in Queens, New York; the Chinese Progressive Association in New York City; and the CVEA. These grassroots organizations carry out voter registration drives, provide information on political candidates, and run forums and lectures on politics for the community. Perhaps the largest of these groups is the CVEA, a voluntary umbrella coalition of twenty-eight community agencies and business, cultural, and religious organizations. The CVEA has worked with local authorities to secure bilingual poll workers, promoted electoral participation on the radio, sponsored forums on communitywide issues, and translated and distributed candidates' position papers to the Chinese media.[82]

Chinese and Japanese Americans have dominated Asian American electoral politics. A high percentage of native-born citizens, which has led to a high electoral participation rate, largely accounts for this phenomenon. But Chinese Americans have also reaped political benefits because they are more established and more organized than most other Asian groups. Aside from the OCA, Chinese Americans have articulated their concerns through the Chinese American Citizens Alliance, the National Democratic Council of Asian and Pacific Americans, and the Pacific Leadership Council—the last two of which are considered arms of the Democratic Party. The resources mustered through political advocacy bodies have allowed Chinese Americans to take advantage of the demographic shift following the arrival of the new wave of immigrants after 1965.[83]

INTRAETHNIC CONFLICT

Any attempt by Chinese Americans to play a larger political role in mainstream society is perhaps compromised by class and nativity divisions. The local political realm in Monterey Park is illustrative of the intraethnic conflict. Even though in the 1980s longtime residents of Monterey Park blamed Chinese Americans for the city's rampant development and subsequent socioeconomic problems, ranging from traffic congestion to rising real estate prices, the Chinese American community was far from united in defending the pro-development agenda.[84]

Most native-born Chinese in Monterey Park in the late 1980s had joined a loosely organized, liberal, multiracial, multiclass coalition—composed of Asian Americans, Latinos, and progressive whites—called CHAMP (Coalition for Harmony in Monterey Park) to crusade for controlled growth and racial harmony. Native-born Chinese who joined CHAMP generally resented coethnic newcomers' overnight success in the United States without having to struggle or play by the rules of assimilation. Newcomers seemed to be taking for granted the equality and civil rights established Chinese residents had fought for in the past. Later, however, pro-growth elements infiltrated the interethnic coalition, causing a rift within the group.[85]

Foreign-born, upwardly mobile Chinese tended to support the pro-growth agenda, and a few had joined the Association for Better Cityhood, a short-lived coalition that also attracted white and Latino developers and entrepreneurs. Defending the position of Chinese entrepreneurial elites, one Chinese developer stated, "The city [Monterey Park] has become identified as a land of new opportunity. . . . It has been a success story. We [Chinese] have made Monterey Park an important cultural and economic center."[86] Most immigrant Chinese were not necessarily affiliated with any formalized group; however, they voted as one bloc, which presented itself to mainstream society as allegedly nationalistic, conservative, and perhaps ethnocentric.

The division within the Chinese American community of Monterey Park, however, was not simply along the lines of foreign versus native born. Class differentiation between the foreign-born, entrepreneurial elite and the native-born, social service elite (made up of American-born social service professionals) played a critical part in fostering intraethnic hostility.[87]

Monterey Park had a third slow- or controlled-growth group called RAMP (Residents Association of Monterey Park), made up mostly of older white residents and a few old-time non-Chinese minority residents who resented the newly arrived Chinese immigrants' ability to experience economic mobility without assimilation. One faction within RAMP quickly demonstrated anti-Chinese sentiments by opposing—in the name of defending American values—Chinese language signs, supporting the English-only movement in the 1980s, and calling for the deportation of so-called illegal immigrants. The presence of this group helped to racialize the controlled-growth movement, thus invoking for some Chinese a link among language, race, and antidevelopment attitudes.[88]

Not surprisingly, immigrant Chinese Americans were suspicious of multiethnic coalitions and chose to remain as one voting bloc. Further, American-born Chinese did not necessarily remain unequivocal supporters of a liberal, multiethnic coalition against unchecked growth. When issues of culture, such as bilingualism, came under attack from white conservatives, American-born Chinese were torn between supporting ethnic solidarity against this form of nativism or looking out for individual self-interest and the larger community control.

Ethnic solidarity can triumph over class and nativity if the issue in question could profoundly affect the fortunes of the entire ethnic community. Such was the case in Boston's Chinatown struggle in 1993 to fight the expansion of a medical center into Chinatown. When the New England Medical

Center tried to acquire a small plot of land, called Parcel C, in Chinatown to build a large garage—an attempt supported by the traditional Chinese elite—grassroots activists and most of the Chinese community reacted negatively. The communitywide protest took place in a context of already serious air pollution, chronic traffic congestion, a critical lack of open space, and a severe housing shortage in Chinatown. These environmental problems, Chinese residents reasoned, would only be exacerbated by the erection of a garage on Parcel C.[89]

A coalition was formalized that formed alliances with mainstream U.S. environmental groups such as the Sierra Club and the American Lung Association, legal justice groups such as Greater Boston Legal Services, and even a health care advocacy group, Health Care for All. With the support of these organizations, the coalition held a referendum whereby the Chinese American community overwhelmingly rejected the hospital's plan and forced the hospital to conduct an environmental review of its proposed garage. A year after the agitation had begun, the hospital withdrew its proposal. The victory was tempered by the fact that the city had turned the land over to the CCBA of Boston, which in the past had squandered land and money it was given in trust for the community.

What happened in Monterey Park and in Boston could offer clues for future prospects of Chinese political participation in the United States. Even though the Chinese American population in some parts of cities or in some neighborhoods may have become the dominant demographic, economic, social, and cultural force, it is rarely the dominant political one. The fact that a sizable number of Chinese immigrants are noncitizens and cannot vote remains the major stumbling block to Chinese political empowerment. Furthermore, Chinese Americans have been geographically mobile, resulting in the absence of a stable population in a given area on which to build a political base. It is doubtful—with the exception of broad common issues such as bilingualism and racism—that the new Chinese entrepreneurial elite, with its transnational ties, could dramatically influence the politics of working-class ethnics, most of whom have few or no ties to those elites. The traditional elite, as demonstrated in the struggle over Parcel C, could stand in the way of effective ethnic mobilization for empowerment.

INTERETHNIC ALLIANCES

Perhaps because of these barriers to political empowerment, educated middle-class Chinese and other Asian Americans have sometimes joined interethnic alliances designed for mutual political cooperation. One recent instance was the political relationship established between Asian Americans (mobilized through the San Gabriel Valley Asian Pacific Americans for Fair Reapportionment) and Latinos to secure redistricting and reapportionment in the

San Gabriel Valley, California, between 1990 and 1992. Both communities found common ground on the issue of increasing minority representation at the state and federal levels. Political gerrymandering in the past had fragmented each community and diluted political power. Aside from this common history, leaders of both communities in the cities of the valley had worked together previously to defeat the pro-growth agenda. The end result of the cooperative venture in the early 1990s was the creation of a new assembly district that took advantage of the concentration of Asian Americans in four cities in the valley but still gave Latinos enough of a solid bloc to allow the incumbent from the old district to run for reelection.[90]

Such political coalitions may be less effective in the future as more Chinese Americans and other Asians move into the valley. Once Asian Americans outnumber Latinos, interethnic cooperation may be elusive. The diversified composition of the Asian American population could derail alliances across racial lines. The multifarious nature of the Asian American populace in downtown Los Angeles—one divided along the lines of national origins—has made reaching agreement within it almost unattainable, let alone trying to forge a link to the Latino community. Finally, the highly visible presence of African Americans and the underlying tension between them and Asian Americans have thwarted efforts to create solidarity among peoples of color.

NEW DIRECTIONS

The development of the political movement since the 1960s has allowed Chinese Americans to move further away from "the structure of dual domination" toward "freedom from racial oppression by white society and freedom from the extraterritorial rule of the Chinese government in Taiwan and its representatives in the United States."[91] An obvious turning point in the move toward freedom from the Chinese government involved the disputed Daoyutai Islands, claimed by both Japan and Taiwan.

When the United States announced it would return the Daoyutai and other U.S.-held islands to Japan in 1972, a protest movement led by foreign-born Chinese students across the United States was ignited. Beginning in 1971, students and scholars organized the Protecting Daoyutai movement. The contested islands involved much more than possible surrounding offshore oil fields; reclaiming them meant preserving the sovereignty of China.[92]

When the Guomindang government failed to respond positively to this U.S.-based movement, calling it subversive and pro-Communist, it came across as ineffectual to both the Chinese intelligentsia and the Chinese community. By the late 1970s, as normalization of relations between the PRC and the United States forged ahead and the PRC's international standing began to rise, loyalty to Taiwan became less entrenched among Chinese in the United States. The cultural exchanges Beijing made with Chinese in North

America in the 1980s and continuing to the present have helped to strengthen this evolving relationship and simultaneously to weaken loyalty to Taiwan.

The emergence of a community of immigrants from the PRC in the 1990s also challenged the Guomindang's grip on Chinese America. The passage of the Chinese Students Protection Act in 1992, following the Tiananmen incident in 1989, enabled approximately 50,000 students and visiting scholars to become permanent residents. New legal and illegal immigrants, students, visiting scholars, and personnel and families related to PRC economic enterprises continued to arrive in significant numbers in the 1990s. PRC-oriented newspapers emerged to air issues of interest to the new immigrants; *China Weekly* in Los Angeles County and *New Continent* in the San Francisco Bay area are two of the earliest publications. With more PRC immigrants settling and raising families in the United States, Chinese language schools that use PRC-approved textbooks have developed. In 1994 the Chinese School Association in the United States, which forges ties among the almost 100 schools established by the mid-1990s, was formed. Workers and merchants have organized new native place associations and chambers of commerce. Branches of the native place association Beijing Association of the U.S.A. have mushroomed in Sunnyvale, California; Los Angeles; Washington, D.C.; and Houston. Students, visiting scholars, and personnel of PRC enterprises have also founded social, professional, and business networks. Alumni and professional associations have proliferated. Some of the new organizations have formed umbrella structures such as the Federation of Chinese Organizations of Washington, D.C., the United Federation of Chinese Associations in New York, and the Chinese American Associations of Chicago—all of which have rivaled the hegemony of the CCBA. In organizing sociopolitical activities such as spring festival banquets, celebrating October 1 National Day (to commemorate the founding of the PRC), and welcoming PRC delegations, these umbrella organizations have reminded PRC immigrants of their ties to their country of origin.[93]

A growing pro-Beijing position is obvious in large Chinese American communities. In New York City the revival of emigration from the PRC in the late 1970s led to the formation of new family and regional associations that are Fujianese in orientation and loyal to the Beijing regime. At times, however, the pro-Beijing position among some clan and family associations stems more from trade ties to the mainland than from rigid Communist loyalty. In 1994 the pro-mainland faction, in a display of its growing political visibility, held the first-ever parade in New York's Chinatown to celebrate the 1949 founding of the PRC. An estimated 5,000 marchers and 8,000 spectators participated. The parade competed with the Guomindang's (pro-Taiwan faction) traditional parade on October 10, which commemorates the birth date of Sun Yat-sen, and thus created friction among community elites. The polarization has also spilled over into the media, with Chinatown newspapers and television stations supporting either Taiwan or China. The 1997 October 1 celebration in Alhambra, Los Angeles County, attracted a crowd of 10,000. In San Francisco the PRC flag was first raised in public in 1994 at the pro-PRC Chinese American Association of Commerce, a practice other PRC-leaning associations soon followed.

Politics in modern Chinese America are complex. The alignment of loyalties does not simply divide along the axis of support for the PRC or Taiwan. Dissident students behind the Democracy movement the PRC crushed in 1989 have continued to agitate in the United States for human rights and democracy on the mainland. Through organizations such as the Foundation for Chinese Democracy and the Chinese Alliance for Democracy, Democracy movement leaders and supporters have questioned China's open policy toward modernization and lobbied U.S. politicians for support. The debate over Taiwan's reunification with China (or support for Taiwan's independence) has also splintered Chinese immigrants, particularly those from Taiwan. The situation has become murkier with the GMD trying to keep up with its rivals, the pro-independence Democratic Progressive Party and the pro-reunification New Party, both of which have established branches and support organizations in the United States to raise funds and boost morale for their attempts to dislodge GMD hegemony in Taiwan.

The growth and increasing heterogeneity of the Chinese population have led to the continuing growth of Chinese associations. New native place or district associations have emerged, but unlike those of the past, these newer groups have often expanded their boundaries to include an entire province or a cluster of provinces—in part because immigrants now hail from all parts of China and other overseas Chinese settlements. The pattern of newcomers primarily originating from Taishan in Guangdong is a thing of the past. For example, the greater Washington, D.C., area has provincial native place associations of Beijing, Fujian, Henan, Shanghai, and Shandong. Associations even across provinces or countries have appeared; examples include the Donghei (the three provinces of northeast China), the Jiangzhehu (the provinces of Jiangsu and Zhejiang and the city of Shanghai), and the Indochinese Association (Chinese from Vietnam, Cambodia, and Laos). Since family immigration is common today, most of the new associations serve less pressing needs; they offer social activities and business networks. Since most members in any given city are scattered, interactions are less intense than those in the pre–World War II era. Also reflecting the growing diversity of the Chinese immigrant population is the continuing growth of associations of alumni of Chinese universities. In the greater Washington, D.C., area, by the mid-1990s more than thirty alumni associations were in place whose members had graduated from major universities in Taiwan and mainland China.[94]

Over the past several decades the politicization of Chinese Americans—geared toward integration of the community into mainstream society but still maintaining ties to Asia—has resulted in the emergence of a new identity. Conditions—geographic concentration, ethnic homogeneity, and solidarity—that used to preserve social isolation are less common today. Chinese now live and work under conditions of greater geographic dispersion, socioeconomic mobility, ethnic heterogeneity, and social conflict; and the ethnic identity has taken on a more fluid character.

RACIAL PROFILING

That fluid, often transnational ethnic identity can also be a double-edged sword. In the spring of 1999 a naturalized U.S. citizen born in Taiwan, Wen Ho Lee, a computer scientist at the Los Alamos National Laboratory in New Mexico, was fired from his job. Suspected of illegally passing data to China to help that country improve its missile capabilities, Wen was caught in the middle of the tense Sino-American relationship. Contributing to the strain were U.S. complaints about China's violations of human rights, China's alleged meddling in U.S. politics through illegal campaign financing, and now China stealing American technology. The federal government eventually indicted Wen on fifty-nine counts of mishandling data but did not charge him with espionage. Denied bail, Lee was held in solitary confinement for nine months. He then pled guilty to one charge of mishandling classified data and was freed.[95]

The resolution of the Lee case did not close the chapter on racial profiling. Conflict with Asia makes Asian Americans, including Chinese Americans, vulnerable. In April 2001 a U.S. surveillance plane flying in international airspace collided with a Chinese jet fighter, killing the Chinese pilot. Forced to make an emergency landing on a Chinese island, the American crew was held hostage. As this diplomatic crisis intensified, anti-Asian sentiments became more virulent. Political commentators urged a boycott of Chinese restaurants. A proposal to intern Chinese Americans was bandied about. In May 2001 a national survey showed that about a third of the sample believed Chinese Americans have a disproportionate influence in the high-technology industry and are more loyal to China than to the United States. Almost half agreed that Chinese Americans serving as spies for China was a problem, and a quarter perceived Chinese Americans as unfair competitors for jobs other Americans wanted.[96]

In the spring of 2002 Bin Han, a postgraduate researcher at the University of California at Davis and a naturalized U.S. citizen, was charged with stealing trade secrets. His employer alleged that he planned to sell vials of plasma protein to a company in China. After his arrest, Han's passport was confiscated and he was denied bail. Even before the trial began, the prosecution had dropped several of the more serious charges, realizing that the evidence was questionable. The jury acquitted Han of the sole charge of embezzlement. Both the Han and Lee cases made Chinese Americans uneasy. The mass media and Republican politicians had unhesitatingly surmised that Lee was a Chinese spy. The University of California at Davis jumped to the conclusion that Han was a disloyal employee with suspicious ties to China. The racial scapegoating was obvious. Unlike past targets, Wen's and Han's backgrounds—highly educated and professional, with family ties in Asia—mark them as a new type of Chinese American to suffer from racial profiling.

BEYOND BLACK AND WHITE

Chinese and other Asian Americans are perpetual foreigners, so goes the unsaid assumption in a country structured by the black-white dyad. Americans are invariably white and racial minorities black. Asian Americans, who are not black or white, are neither American nor minority. Thus prior to World War II they were deemed "aliens ineligible to citizenship." Asian Americans are shut out of the body politic, since racial formation determines citizenship. "American beats out Kwan," screamed the headline on the MSNBC website when Tara Lipinski defeated fellow American Michelle Kwan for the women's gold medal in figure skating at the 1998 Winter Olympics. The implication was clear: Kwan was the foreigner whom an American had beaten. Studio executives, in reply to film producer Christopher Lee's pitch for a film version of Amy Tan's novel *The Joy Luck Club*, said it was unworkable because no Americans were in it, although the film was made and became a box office hit. Racial doomsayers from essayist and novelist Gore Vidal to science fiction writer William Gibson—along with films such as *Bladerunner, Alien,* and *Soldier*—have revived paranoia about an Asian horde that will overwhelm white America, even the entire world. Asian Americans seem the literal embodiment of this "alien" takeover theme.[97]

The black-white dyad also leaves Asian Americans in a dilemma. Chang-Lin Tien, the first Asian American to head a major research university (the University of California at Berkeley), recalled how as a graduate student in Louisville, Kentucky, in the 1950s he faced the vexing problem of using the segregated city buses. He asked, "Just exactly where did an Asian fit in?" With no clear answer, he chose not to ride them.

Being yellow is not either black or white. Being yellow is about grayness. Whites celebrate Asians as "near-whites" or "whiter than whites" in the model minority understanding. Yet Asian Americans continue to experience racism in education and the labor market, and they remain vulnerable to hate crimes. In positing Asians as somewhere along the divide between black and white, the bipolar racial formation enables whites to show that Asians have been historically evolving from minority to majority status, from "near-blacks" to "near-whites." The black-and-white racial formation, according to Gary Okihiro, marginalizes Asians since it "ignores the gradations and complexities of the full spectrum between the racial poles."[98]

Through their involvement in political situations, Chinese Americans have not only demanded their rightful place in the United States but also have revamped the definition of their identity. This self-determining Chinese American identity—one that has confounded the zero-sum relationship between assimilation and the retention of ethnicity—has been built on shared historical experiences in the United States and on the principles of justice and equality. It is an identity that ultimately rejects chauvinistic nationalism and embraces a culturally diverse, dynamic understanding of America.

7
The Arts and Chinese Americans

EARLY CHINESE AMERICAN LITERATURE

Since the arrival of the earliest Chinese immigrants, both the U.S. government and the mass media have perpetuated dehumanizing representations of the community. Whether portrayed as brute hordes, vicious villains, dragon ladies, pathetic heathens, comical servants, loyal sidekicks, oversexed Suzie Wongs, subservient Lotus Blossoms, or emasculated detectives, Chinese Americans have struggled against an overall perception of them as unassimilable aliens. Certainly, in the realm of cultural production, Chinese Americans expended efforts—in spite of the privileged nature of such efforts given the language barrier, Americans' antipathy toward Asians, and general privation—to elucidate the sociopolitical and economic tensions between themselves and the dominant culture that had generated those debilitating images.

As a rising rabid anti-Chinese movement in the second half of the nineteenth century threatened their lives, livelihoods, and properties, Chinese immigrants spoke out to defend themselves. They sent numerous letters, petitions, and statements to the federal government, mainstream politicians, and local authorities. Typically written in a conciliatory tone, the writings portrayed a positive image of the Chinese in the United States. Chinese represented free labor that contributed to the making of modern capitalism, they patronized American entrepreneurs, they were truthful and capable of assimilation—these and other themes were designed to deflect the image of the "coolie" Chinese who unfairly competed with white workers, drained the economy through their sojourning, and refused to embrace the mores and sensibility of the host society. Perhaps the earliest plea for tolerance was the "Letter of the Chinaman to His Excellency, Governor Bigler" by Hab Wu and Tong K. Achick, published in 1852. Written in response to racist allegations of California governor John Bigler, the letter—through its direct opening, elegant English, and unemotional argument—suggests that early Chinese immigrants understood American culture and how to take advantage of that culture to defend their rights.[1]

Other nineteenth-century voices of the Chinese in America were less conciliatory toward the dominant society. Written by non-elites, they were emotional, defiant, and insistent on equality. Mary Tape's 1885 letter castigating school authorities for denying her daughter access to public schooling is one example (see Chapter 2, "The Anti-Chinese Movement," pages 45–53). Less shrill but no less angry is the autobiographical sketch of Lee Chew, a Chinese laundryman in New York. Published in a collection entitled *The Life Stories of Undistinguished Americans as Told by Themselves* (1906), edited by Hamilton Holt, the story is one of hardship, of utter humiliation. Excluded from the labor market, Chinese immigrants were pushed into laundry work, explained Lee. Forced into this "atypical" occupation for Chinese men, the laundrymen endured insults and fraud, even physical violence. With normal family life thwarted by exclusion laws and interracial marriage a taboo, Chinese men resorted to prostitution or married debauched white women. Rejected by their host society, Chinese men, Lee bitterly concluded, could only hope to return to their homeland. In his writing Lee hinted that he admired American democracy but believed it fell short of its promise of equality. Like Tape's writing, Lee's memoirs suggest an appreciation of the progressive tradition of American culture.

After the gates of immigration slammed shut for Chinese, the writings of Chinese in America came mostly from students in America for advanced education and from court officials posted to the United States. Lee Yan Phou, a student who came to the United States as part of the Qing-directed Chinese Educational Mission in 1873, wrote *When I Was a Boy in China* (1887). Seemingly just a litany of Chinese customs and mannerisms, Lee's work in fact explains away the "alienness" of Chinese practices as nothing less than evidence of Chinese superiority. Unlike Americans, Lee explained, Chinese were benevolent toward the lower classes, honored their families, and, above all, were civilized. Like other Chinese writers, Lee betrayed a kind of ethnocentrism used to counter racial bias during the height of exclusion. Sometimes that ethnocentrism also betrayed class bias, as is the case in diplomat Julius Su Tow's *The Real Chinese in America* (1923). Disparaging the lowly Chinese laborers who knew nothing of China's rich civilization, Tow implied that the "real" Chinese were those of the exempt classes. With the exception of the ignorant Chinese laborers, white Americans should welcome Chinese immigrants.

Other so-called cultivated Chinese recorded their ambivalent impressions of U.S. life. Qing court official Yung Wing's *My Life in China and America* (1909) and diplomat Wu Ting Fang's *America Through the Spectacles of an Oriental Diplomat* (1914) celebrate the promise of U.S. democracy in a time when the Chinese intelligentsia struggled to find a panacea for China's ills, as well as for the poor treatment of compatriots in the United States. These writers commented, in a politely muted voice, on the hypocrisies and social inequalities in U.S. society, including those inflicted on Chinese immigrants. Wu, for example, singled out self-reliance that shaded into self-interest at the expense of duty to family. America was the land of egalitarianism, yet vanity was strong, and "many people want[ed] to be more equal than others." And how, Wu wondered, could the United States be a nation of immigrants when its citizens were prejudiced against those they considered "aliens." The Christianized Yung Wing, another government-sponsored student sent to America who later became a diplomat, wrote his autobiography to promote reform for China but linked that reform to the central task of improving the fortunes of Chinese in the United States—thus anticipating an argument Chinese American reformers would make in the early twentieth century. By presenting himself as a model of the assimilable Chinese—Yale educated, garbed in Western clothing, and with a Yankee wife—Yung, like Wu, celebrated the idea that if given the opportunity, Chinese immigrants could be part of the melting pot. Both writers hoped their works could help achieve better treatment for the Chinese in America.

The theme of integration into mainstream society found its way into the literature of literate Chinese sojourners, who typically harbored little desire to put down roots in the United States. Examples include Huie Kin's *Reminiscences* (1932), Chiang Yee's *A Chinese Childhood* (1940), Adet and Anor Lin's *Our Family* (1939), and—notably—Lin Yutang's manifold writings, of which *My Country and My People* (1937) is the best-known. Unlike the other writers, Lin Yutang captured the mainstream public limelight. Born and raised in China but educated in the West, he understood the mentality of Western readers, and his writings accommodated their understanding of China and its people. He portrayed the Chinese as passive and unimaginative. If America and the rest of the West was masculine, China was feminine; if the West was abstract, China was concrete to a fault. His writings took the West as the point of reference and, in particular, took the United States as the norm against which all other nations' progress—China's included—was to be measured. China, Lin implied, had a long road ahead to modernization given the natural proclivities of its people and the distance to be covered.[2]

Most books by these literate sojourners—also called "tourist guides"—provide a quaint, superficial perspective of China and its culture, including its ceremonies and customs regarding food and dress, designed to appeal to Western readers' craving for exoticism. More significant, these works, written in an apologetic tone, place the blame for racial conflagrations on the failure of the predominately working-class Chinese laborers to integrate themselves into American life. Even as these authors heaped "Orientalist" praise on Chinese society and culture, they disparaged the supposed "clannishness" of Chinese working-class immigrants. These idealized, class-oriented observations—betraying the socioeconomic cleavage that existed within the turn-of-the-century Chinese community in North America—widened the rift between the community and the non-Chinese majority.[3]

The literary voices of Chinese immigrants did not operate entirely within these parameters, however. Notwithstanding institutionalized efforts to thwart community formation and acculturation, vestiges of a Chinese American oral tradition in the form of folk rhymes—such as the wood-fish songs (*muyu ge*) and Gold Mountain songs (*jinshan ge*)—have been uncovered. Both genres affirm the cultural change that had occurred after immigration to America through the use of colloquial Cantonese, Chinatown Chinese translations from English, and American-based themes. Some *muyu ge* are humorous and entertaining, but many are melancholy complaints about the hardships suffering male immigrants and the families they left behind had to endure while exclusionary practices shattered their hopes and aspirations. The thematic range of *jinshan ge* is broader. These songs also deal with the subjects of women, prostitutes, and sex—echoing the desire for female companionship among the men in predominately male Chinese America: "We're guests stranded in North America: / Must we also give up the fun in life?"[4]

Similar lamentations and longings found their way into the poems detained arrivals carved into the walls of the Angel Island Immigration Station. The moving, bewildered voices of these arrivals challenged the myth of America as the land of opportunity for all immigrants, as suggested in these lines from one poem: "America has power, but not justice / In prison, we were victimized as if we were guilty."[5]

The same counterdiscourse can be found in several novellas written in reaction to the 1905 Chinese protest boycott of American goods. Both *Kuxuesheng* (*The Industrious Student*; published in 1960 but written sometime in 1905 or 1906) by Qiyouzi (pseudonym) and *Kushehui* (*The Bitter Society*;

published in 1905) by an anonymous writer speak to the humanness of Chinese immigrants despite the fact that they lived in an overtly racist society.[6]

Writers who portrayed Chinese immigrants sympathetically include Edith Eaton, the offspring of a Caucasian-Chinese union who had lived in Great Britain and Canada before immigrating to the United States. The early years before arriving in America were difficult ones for Eaton; the prejudice against her mother's race left a deep imprint on her developing ethnic consciousness. Things were hardly better in the United States. The outright discrimination she and her siblings suffered only made her more determined to identity with her Chinese heritage.[7]

Considered the first Chinese American writer in English, Eaton, who used the pen name Sui Sin Far—which reflected her deep affection for her mother's race—enriched Chinese American literature through her autobiographical account "Leaves From the Mental Portfolio of an Eurasian" (1909) and her short-story collection *Mrs. Spring Fragrance* (1912). In these works Sui Sin Far, through irony and humor, exposed the wrongs done to the Chinese in America. Her writings—which consistently mirrored her developing identification with her Chinese roots—probed the duality biracial persons experienced, the humanity of working-class women, and the bond of friendship between women against the backdrop of gender-based exclusion laws and fractured families. Sui's writings reflect her intimate understanding of Chinese Americans—particularly the women—because she had spent years working and living in such communities. Not surprisingly, Sui eschewed late-nineteenth-century West Coast writers' typical portrayal of Chinese characters in their works: they employed the stereotypical "Chinaman" image that emphasized the exotic, alien, and quaint nature of Chinese people. Rather, Sui chose to depict the social realities of Chinese America in a direct, truthful manner.

Perhaps most noteworthy about Sui's writings is the fact that they speak to the generational conflicts between Chinese immigrants and their Americanized compatriots. The title tale in *Mrs. Spring Fragrance* pits an Americanized Chinese female immigrant against her traditional Chinese merchant husband. Whereas the husband wears Western garb and socializes with the non-Chinese world yet remains wedded to traditional values, Mrs. Spring Fragrance is independent, even defiant of traditions. The cultural divide between the two strains the marriage. Although they reconcile, the future of their marriage remains in jeopardy. In keeping with her desire to portray reality, Sui offers no simple solution to the issue of acculturation. In other stories Sui even suggests that the price to pay for Americanization often included facing rejection from one's ethnic culture. Sui believed the Chinese in the United States had resisted acculturation not because they were incapable of undergoing the process; rather, by adhering to their own cultural tradition, they could draw spiritual support in a hostile environment. As part of her interest in cross-cultural relations, Sui also wrote about interracial marriages. In popular writings of that era, stories about intermarriages typically ended on a negative note, one that left readers with the impression that miscegenation was morally repugnant and socially tragic. But Sui cast her stories within the framework of the lovers as victims of an ignorant society. The blame, Sui implied, lay with society, not the couples.

In taking a stand on racism, Sui became a voice for the inarticulate in the Chinese American community. Relying on humor, rational argument, and subtle satire, Sui's writings reveal a sophisticated understanding of racial bias. Rather than subscribing to a biological explanation for such racial sentiments, she ascribed them to social and environmental factors. Such factors explain why Chinese Americans exhibited their own form of bigotry. Sui suggested that their distrust of other races, disapproval of interracial marriages, and rejection of Eurasians stemmed from their marginalized existence in the United States.

Sui Sin Far's legacy lies in her function as "a bridge between two worlds," one that nurtured Euro-Americans' understanding of the Chinese. Her works also anticipated the post–World War II works of other Eurasian authors such as Han Suyin—perhaps best-known for her *A Many Splendoured Thing* (1952)— and Diana Chang (*Frontiers of Love* [1956]), all of which critique racial domination and Western imperialism and ponder the identity dilemma biracial persons experienced.

EURO-AMERICAN WRITERS: GOOD ASIANS AND BAD ASIANS

Sui Sin Far's contributions contrast starkly with contemporaneous works of fiction produced by Euro-American writers, which tend to offer distorted images of the Chinese. Lingering fears of a revival of the thirteenth-century Mongol invasion of Eastern Europe perpetuated the negative image of the Chinese well before their arrival in California in the 1850s. Claiming superiority for the civilized Christian population, Euro-Americans distinguished themselves from non-Europeans. Thus by the early nineteenth century, contemporary relations between Euro-Americans and American Indians and Africans, which involved unequal power relations in the form of colonization and slavery, also colored whites' perceptions of the Chinese. American traders, diplomats, and missionaries with ties to China propagated "conceptions of Chinese deceit, cunning, idolatory, despotism, xenophobia, cruelty, infanticide, and intellectual and sexual perversity."[8]

The end result by the turn of the twentieth century was two sets of stereotypes: the "good" Asian and the "bad" Asian. "Good" Asians are helpless heathens, loyal allies or sidekicks, and servants; "bad" Asians are sinister villains and brute hordes. According to Elaine Kim, this distorted understanding of the Asian functions as a foil to assure the Euro-American that he or she is "not-Asian." If the Asian is cruel and cunning, like Fu Manchu, the Euro-American is compassionate and honest; if the Asian is meek and subservient, the Euro-American is projected as benevolent and omnipotent. The comical and dumb-witted servant serves a savy and astute white employer; the ingenious Chinese detective—Charlie Chan—takes on the cases of his morally minded white colleagues and clients. The assumption undergirding this duality of good and bad Asians is that Chinese and Euro-Americans are incompatible, underscoring that the white is superior in all respects.[9]

As bad Asians, Chinese immigrants were irredeemable. By the early twentieth century a newly reinvigorated Yellow Peril scare, precipitated by fears of Japan's imperialist ambitions—which did not distinguish among Asian ethnicities—engendered these negative images. In pulp fiction the threat to the white race came in the form of Dr. Fu Manchu, the fiendish mastermind created by Sax Rohmer. Fu Manchu's machinations have appeared in thirteen novels, four short stories, a novelette, comic strips, and countless dramatizations on film, radio, and television—he was undoubtedly the first universally recognized "Oriental." Embodying the Asiatic threat of racial annihilation, Fu Manchu's racial attack was all the more menacing given his ambiguous sexuality. With his long fingernails and cruel lips, he was vulnerable and aggressive, feminine and masculine.

Chinese women also found themselves cast as promiscuous, untrustworthy, and diabolical creatures. The stock image of Chinese women—the Dragon Lady—was best projected in Sax Rohmer's *Daughter of Fu Manchu* (1931). The protagonist, Fah Lo Suee, followed the footsteps of her father, Fu Manchu, and became a champion of Asian domination over the white race.

The fiction produced by writers such as Jack London, Will Irwin, Frank Norris, and Sax Rohmer depicts the characteristics of Chinese—whether men or women—as biologically determined. In spite of exposure to white civilization, Chinese will eventually return to the "evil" ways. Even the offspring of Euro-American–Chinese unions—in spite of their partially white blood—cannot escape the fate that awaits them. Either they will die—a satisfactory fictional end to the Yellow Peril threat—or they will have to try to pass as whites.

In this imaginary Chinatown landscape—dotted with tong wars, slave girls, smoky opium dens, indescribable foodways, and rat-eating yellow men—so-called positive images equally abound. The obsequious, queer-looking Chinese servant who appears in a number of popular melodramas and stories set in the masculinized nineteenth-century American West validates the superiority of his Anglo master and his family. Ah Lam, the emotionless servant in Maud Howe's novel *The San Rosario Ranch* (1880), is typical of that image; his virtues are patronizingly described entirely in terms of servitude and obedience, and he eventually dies while trying to defend the honor of a white female visitor.[10]

But the subservient, effeminate male servant is not always so benign. Robert G. Lee has argued that in the fluid western frontier, as society developed from the male-dominated gold rush days to the settled domestic life of the 1870s, the Chinese represented a third sex—"an alternative or imagined sexuality that was potentially subversive and disruptive to the emergent heterosexual orthodoxy."[11] Mary Mote's "Poor Ah Toy" (1882) illustrates the anxieties westerners wrestled with in this era. Mote's short story relates the convoluted interaction between Fanny Siddons—a young, white middle-class matron—and Ah Toy, her Chinese servant. Siddons, exasperated by an insubordinate Irish female housekeeper, hires Ah Toy and the two take a liking to each other, although the erotic tension is configured within a mother-child relationship. But Siddons's engagement to Captain Ward infuriates Ah Toy, who confronts Ward. Dismissed for his insolence, Ah Toy tries to profess his love for Siddons. Although he is sent away immediately, to the confused Siddons Ah Toy—or at least his spirit—is still present. Meanwhile, an embittered Ah Toy hangs himself, but he leaves a note requesting that he be buried on the farm so he can be with her forever. The request is granted, and even though Siddons marries the captain, she often visits Ah Toy's grave.[12]

"Poor Ah Toy" upholds the prevailing taboo on interracial and interclass liaisons. Mote's message is clear: the duplicitous Chinese male servants are latently aggressive. But Ah Toy is not like any other Western man; he is childlike and feminine. In domesticating the household, he unsettles the gendered division of labor. In professing his affections for Siddons, he violates Victorian conventions about men being unemotional. He is the third sex, the one who disrupts Victorian American masculinity. In the twentieth century the loyal servant caricature lost its virulent side and took the form of the placid detective Charlie Chan and later, in television, of the servant Hop Sing in the western series *Bonanza* (1959–1973).

Lotus Blossom, or China Doll, the female version of the male servant, is the opposite of the Dragon Lady; submissive and deferential, she is powerless. Lotus Blossom was the perfect foil for the virility and attractiveness of the Euro-American male. In Homer Lea's *The Vermilion Pencil* (1908), the Chinese female character betrays her husband and father, even sacrifices her life to secure the love of the white hero.[13]

CHINESE AMERICA IN EARLY U.S. FILMS

The distorted characterization of the Chinese in text also appeared in early moving pictures. The films that graced the screen between 1894 and 1910 often portrayed the Chinese, to quote John Haddad, as a "ludicrous, clownish people, the salacious seducers of white women, and heartless murderers of innocent Christians."[14] Apparently, such images carried over in part from the crowd-pleasing vaudeville. The sensationalized Chinatown tours, which often included a stop at an opium den, also shaped the images on the silver screen.

Early films borrowed the magical acts and comic routines of vaudeville and adapted them to present the stock character of the laundryman. As in vaudeville, in most of these cinematic plots the laundrymen perform clownlike antics and are then harassed by whites. In the film *In a Chinese Laundry* (1897), a laundryman tries to make advances on a young, white female customer but fails clumsily. The film undoubtedly underscores the general rejection of miscegenation, allowing audiences to laugh at something that gave rise to social anxiety. In *Fun in a Chinese Laundry* (1901), a mischievous white boy taunts two Chinese laundrymen at work. When the Chinese retaliate, a tense situation turns violent. The white boy picks them up, kicks them, and rolls them all over the floor. After he departs, the Chinese come to life and perform one of their dances. The message is clear: it is acceptable, even fun, to abuse the Chinese.[15]

Whereas the laundryman was a buffoon, an asexual creature, the opium smoker—the other typical "Oriental" character in films—was a manipulator, a sexual threat. This skewed image stemmed from the popularity of the Chinatown tours of opium dens mentioned earlier. Films such as *A Chinese Opium Joint* (1898) and *A Raid on a Chinese Opium Joint* (1900) led audiences to believe that Chinese opium smokers lured white women into their dens and seduced them. Again the specter of miscegenation was raised. In grossly misrepresenting Chinese Americans as the exotic, silly, or dangerous "other," moving pictures allayed white audiences' anxieties about Asian immigration to the United States. The films symbolically marginalized the Chinese in the American imagination.

When the Boxer Rebellion in China broke out in 1900, placing European and American residents there in harm's way, the film industry immediately tapped into existing Yellow Peril fears. The fear of miscegenation, Chinese labor competition, and Japan's rapid modernization generated racial anxieties that, in turn, resulted in a besieged mentality among white Americans who saw these films. Chinese knife-wielding villains who attacked hapless girls and innocuous children took center stage in such films as *Chinese Massacreing* [sic] *the Christians* (1900), *Tortured by Boxers* (1900), and *Rescue of a White Girl From the Boxers* (1900). Even though the Boxers were a small minority and most Chinese distanced themselves from the group, the films led American audiences to think such behavior was representative of all Chinese people, including those residing in the United States. When longer narrative films became common around 1910, the image of the Chinese as Boxerlike, pitiless haters of "white devils" coalesced with the stock characters of the comical laundryman and the opium fiend. *Lights and Shadows of Chinatown* (1908) is a romance about two star-struck Chinese lovers whose lives were torn apart by coethnic hatchetmen. The setting, San Francisco's Chinatown, featured all the hackneyed themes and stereotypes—smoky opium dens, idol worship, fortune tellers, menacing tongs, and the hustle and bustle of an overcrowded, dirty Chinatown.

Interracial Romances in Films

The taboo subject of interracial liaisons was a consistent, pointed theme in early American motion pictures. Since the release of D. W. Griffith's *The Birth of a Nation* (1915), a film about racial mixing that upholds exclusionism (against African Americans) through violence, miscegenation on the silver screen has raised the specter of moral decline—echoing and reinforcing societal attitudes toward such conjugal unions. The fear of desire crossing the color line in films made visual sentiments prevalent since the nineteenth century in novels, short stories, and plays. The Yellow Peril's sexual threat to white civilization—already hinted at in Fu Manchu stories—was made explicit in early feature-length films. In 1919 Griffith's *Broken Blossoms* resolved the threat miscegenation posed to the nation's strength by making the Chinese, opium-smoking merchant Cheng Huan's love for Lucy—the abused illegitimate daughter of a brutal boxer—platonic and unrequited, leading Cheng Huan to commit suicide. Killing off the Chinese partner in an interracial liaison was a conventional device used to underscore the doomed nature of miscegenation. Although scholars have applauded the humanized portrayal of Cheng Huan, Lucy's innocence and "whiteness" ennoble the "baseness" of Cheng Huan to the extent that he avenges her death at the hands of her possessive father by shooting him. Thus again, the West "saves" the inferior and offers moral salvation for the Asian "other."[16]

The fear of interracial commingling was so strong that even when interracial romances ended with the couple's union, a plot twist often revealed that the Chinese partner in the romance was in reality white or Eurasian. Films such as *Shanghai* (1935) and *The Lady of the Tropics* (1939) featured Eurasian characters as seducers and seductresses, which enabled Hollywood to tackle forbidden sexuality without threatening the racial status quo or the film code of the times. Similarly, white male actors donning "yellow faces" were used in romantic plots instead of Asian actors. And since the early days of the motion picture industry, "scotch-tape Asians," or white men and women in "yellow face," have played lead roles in Asian-themed films.

Only a few Chinese women have played romantic leads opposite white men, whereas Chinese men have almost never been equal romantic partners of white women. This double standard of miscegenation, with its emphasis on the free sexual license of white men, desexualized Chinese men even as it hypersexualized Chinese women. Like their male compatriots who are asexualized, the women are depicted as sexual to validate the white man's superiority.[17]

Images of Women in Films

Of the two common images of Chinese women—Lotus Blossom and Dragon Lady—the Dragon Lady has probably appeared more often on the silver screen, particularly in early escapist films. In *The Thief of Baghdad* (1924) pioneer Chinese American actress Anna May Wong played the role of a servant who uses treachery to help an unscrupulous Mongol prince win the hand of the Princess of Baghdad. Wong—who had screen appeal because of her Caucasian-like features—played the role of either a criminally complicit or a sexually available Chinese woman who must die (to symbolically contain Asia and reinforce the idea that Asians are unassimilable) in such popular films as *The Toll of the Sea* (1922), a reworking of Puccini's opera *Madam Butterfly; Daughter of the Dragon* (1931), whose storyline came from the Fu Manchu books; and *Shanghai Express* (1932), opposite Marlene Dietrich.[18]

Despite the stirrings of the second feminist movement and the gradual post–World War II liberalization of immigration laws and attitudes toward the Chinese, the lot of Asian women in films seemed impervious to historical change. The films produced during World War II and after, reflecting the easing of tensions in Sino-American relations, offered more images of good rather than bad Asian women; however, Lotus Blossom and Dragon Lady are not necessarily opposing stereotypes. Since both stereotypes eroticize Chinese women as exotic "dolls" available for white male dominance, the image of women has remained static and improved little.

Perhaps the best-known deferential Lotus Blossom–like Chinese female character is Suzie Wong, the "hooker with a heart of gold" in *The World of Suzie Wong* (1960). Suzie, an abused yet alluring woman, is played by Nancy Kwan. An artist, Robert Lomax (William Holden), takes pity on her, and they fall in love. When Robert falls on hard times, Suzie disappears to help ease his burden. Suzie turns up again later, pleading for Robert's help in rescuing her illegitimate baby from a flood. Despite their efforts, the baby dies. Although the film ends with the couple reunited, the cost has been high.[19]

The influence of the Orientalist discourse in the arts after World War II—one that emphasized the themes of death and destruction—may be ascribable to the prevalent McCarthyism in the 1950s, which impugned the integration of Chinese Americans into the larger society. The terror unleashed on progressive Chinese Americans suppressed their earlier efforts to articulate racial consciousness and pride.

CHINESE AMERICAN LITERATURE SINCE THE LATE 1930S

Expressions of Cultural Nationalism

In the late 1930s and the 1940s, the impact of the Sino-Japanese War and a revival of American liberalism and Marxism led to the formation of left-wing literary groups in Chinatowns in the mainland United States. Composed mostly of students and activists, these groups argued for a Chinatown literature independent of the literary tradition of China that would serve as a vehicle for social criticism and reform. H. T. Tsiang, a leftist writer, answered the call. One of his works, *And China Has Hands* (1936), may be the first fictional account of the bachelor society written in English by a Chinese immigrant. Contemporaries of Tsiang published prose, poetry, commentaries, and essays in Chinese language weeklies and periodicals in New York and San Francisco. In the 1920s another group of unrelated yet still progressive Chinese students at the University of Hawai'i began to compose stories, poems, and plays about plantation life, generational conflict, and other local topics.

Perhaps the most significant literary production of the period was a body of twenty-three short stories published in 1947 and 1948 in the short-lived literary magazine *Xinmiao* (*The Bud*). Marked by an assertive, prolabor tone; openness about taboo topics; the use of Cantonese; and a wry humor, these stories foreshadowed the growth of a Chinese American literary sensibility in the 1960s and 1970s. The stories, which betray the community's isolation, exhibit a strong China-centered nationalism. They clearly reflect the ambiguous identity of Chinese Americans in this transitory period between repeal of the exclusion laws in 1943 and the later full-fledged reunification of families and restoration of citizen rights.[20]

Like other progressive writers, Chinese, American-educated émigré authors also articulated a defense of China during the war years. Women authors Helena Kuo, Adet Lin, Lin Tai-yi (Anor Lin), and Ma-Mai Sze wrote books stressing the courage and ingenuity of the Chinese people amid the horror of war. This romanticized portrayal has become central in nostalgic novels by such contemporary authors as Hazel Lin, Virginia Lee, and Bette Bao Lord. Lin Tai-yi's *War Tide* (1943) typifies the exuberant patriotism exhibited in these works. The plot centers on the exploits of an eighteen-year-old girl, Lo-Yin Tai, whose creativity and intelligence shelter her multigenerational family from wartime turmoil. Fueled by patriotic ardor, these women writers attempted to win Western allies for China by proving that the Chinese people deserved the assistance and respect of the international community.[21]

Another writer influenced by the wartime fervor was Lao She. His critically acclaimed novel *Rickshaw Boy* (1943), a translation of the Chinese language version, is a story of two young lovers who experience a series of challenges.

In the English version's ending the hero rescues his lover from the brothel, carries her in his arms, and rushes into the woods. That dramatic ending was not the original version. In the Chinese version the hero dies in poverty, and his lover commits suicide after leading a miserable life in a brothel. According to Xiao-huang Yin, the English version's à la Hollywood dramatics were probably an attempt to imply that China—like the novel's hero—was turning the corner and entering a new era of progress after a long period of Japanese imperialism. Perhaps Lao She was making the subtle point that the Chinese were good allies of the United States.[22]

Second-Generation Autobiographers

The defensive posture also permeated the work of American-born Chinese autobiographers, including Jade Snow Wong and Pardee Lowe, who came of age in the 1940s. Like their peers, these writers felt a deep sense of alienation from their community. Their homes and community seemed far too repressive, thwarting their independence and search for self-definition. Unwilling to be drawn into the labor-intensive ethnic enclave economy in which their parents toiled, they pinned their hopes on public education to open doors of opportunity. Socialized to accept assimilationist rhetoric, these early autobiographers sought acceptance from U.S. society. To that end, they tried to distance themselves from their Chinese identity. Their writings offer a linear progression of Chinese American life from tradition to modernity, from conformity to individual freedom that accords well with the melting-pot myth. The themes they expounded on spoke to their quest for a place in U.S. life: the generation gap, the search for the American dream, interracial marriages, the tussle between Eastern and Western values, and the urgent need to demonstrate their loyalty to the republic.[23]

Pardee Lowe's *Father and Glorious Descendant* (1943), the first book-length autobiography by an American-born Chinese, appeared at a time when Chinese Americans were keen to prove their loyalty to the United States. Lowe, the son of a Chinese merchant-*cum*-community leader, used his book as a vehicle to express his faith in U.S. democracy. That faith was largely the product of a unique upbringing that foregrounded American names for his siblings and himself and a semiacculturated father who modeled American manners for his children. His public school education reinforced that developing American sensibility. Yet Lowe discovered that no matter how Americanized he was, discrimination dogged him when he tried to look for a summer job. Lowe resolved to seek accommodation; he would work harder and accept his lot. He would adapt to the racial prejudices—a strategy that stemmed in part from his alienation from the Chinese cultural tradition. Estranged from his father, who still adhered to the Chinese tradition, and repelled by the stifling Chinese family life, Lowe married a Yankee woman at a time when antimiscegenation sentiment was still strong. Yet no matter how hard Lowe tried to gain admission into U.S. society, he failed to find a job after graduating from Stanford and Harvard Universities.

Jade Snow Wong's *Fifth Chinese Daughter* (1950), like Lowe's work, also details the generational conflict and the search for acceptance into mainstream U.S. society. Like Lowe, Wong discovered that a considerable gap existed between her family's worldview and that of the mainstream society. Wong craved the chance to express her individuality; she railed against the deferential, unambitious, home-bound image her parents expected her to realize. Like Lowe, Wong's response to racism was to work harder and accept the limits imposed on her. Wong and Lowe chose passive tolerance rather than passionate anger or displeasure toward those who wronged them.

But Wong's work is also quite different from Lowe's. As a woman, Wong received far less monetary and moral support for her education from her parents. She paid for her college education with scholarships and domestic work. Although her father was also a merchant, privation marked her family's life. There is a subtle difference in the way Lowe and Wong perceived their respective journeys toward social acceptance by mainstream society: Lowe chose to distance himself from his Chinese heritage to prove his Americanness, whereas Wong sought to accomplish the same goal by highlighting the aspects of Chinese culture that conjured the Chinese as a "model minority."

Both Lowe's and Wong's works, however, are far from simple expositions of minorities who attained the American dream. In spite of the Chinatown "tours" of the supposed quaint customs and culture, which underscore the "alienness" of the Chinese, both Lowe and Wong attest to the impact of racial discrimination on Chinese Americans. Both authors, however, could find acceptance only within the white frame of reference. Lowe chose to assimilate into the dominant culture because at that time a Chinese American identity connoted inferiority to whites. Wong, less alienated from the Chinese culture, never eluded the sense of being a sojourner in a foreign land in spite of her birthright and American education. Both writers downplayed racism, attributing the generational conflicts—even failures—within the family and the community to cultural propensities rather than to limitations imposed by the larger society.

Sketches of Chinatown Life

This distorted perception of Chinese life in the United States received credence from the conformist nature of American society in the 1950s. Typically represented as an affluent age with heavy emphasis on consumption and leisure, the 1950s witnessed a reaffirmation of domesticity for women and corporatism for men. A conflict-free society supposedly prevailed. The few Chinese American sketches of Chinatown life published before the 1960s speak to that consensus. Lin Yutang's *Chinatown Family* (1948) is a maudlin story of the travails of a laundryman who has recently gone to work with his father at the latter's laundry. The characters are docile, grateful Chinese who cheerfully accept prejudice and hardship. Their eventual success in this land of plenty will come through hard work and good luck. Lin's novel simply reinforces existing Western stereotypes of the supposed model minority.[24]

Similarly, *Flower Drum Song* (1957), written by Chin Yang Lee, which was adapted into a Broadway musical and a popular motion picture, confirms the success narrative—the harbinger of the model minority myth—for Chinese Americans. The work celebrates the capacity of America's melting pot to absorb even the most alien newcomers. In the Broadway musical version, the popular theme of ethnic assimilation receives visual credence through a graduation-*cum*-naturalization party at which the partygoers do a square dance while singing the song "Chop Suey." The characters in the musical and the novel, not unlike the harmless servant image, comically and easily solve perplexing social issues—such as a shortage of female conjugal partners and the presence of job discrimination—against a Chinatown backdrop of quaint customs and exotic foods.[25]

A historical parallel may exist between these exotic guided Chinatown tours and the nineteenth-century travel books on China written by Christian missionaries and visitors. Like the earlier works, those by Wong, Lowe, Lin, and Chin offer entertaining voyeuristic insights into the adventures of the "other." Marlon K. Hom has argued that *Flower Drum Song* and other contemporaneous short stories published in the 1960s—the products of recent immigrant writers—also poke fun at American-born Chinese who are regarded as pseudo-Americans yet are not fully Chinese.

Articulations of a Chinese American Sensibility

By the time the landmark *Eat a Bowl of Tea* (1961) by Louis Chu appeared, the Chinese American community was on the threshold of change. As reflected in this novel of social realism, which had its roots in the left-wing literature of the 1930s and 1940s, the community of aging bachelors was reinvigorated in the postwar years through the reunification of families and the entry of new immigrants. Like other Chinatown bachelors, the protagonist Wah Gay is racked with guilt for abandoning his wife and family in China. To redeem himself, he arranges a marriage between his son, Ben Loy, and Chinese-born Mei Oi, the daughter of an old friend. Wah Gay decides, in a decisive move to break with the past, that Mei Oi should live in the United States and immediately start a family with Ben Loy. The plan, which allows Wah Gay to expunge his own unfulfilled responsibilities through his son, is derailed when Ben Loy turns out to be impotent. Mei Oi has an extramarital liaison and becomes pregnant. Her affair triggers a chain of revelations:

a mundane, debilitating life in Chinatown; the fallacy of patriarchal guidance; and the fragility of the sense of community. By the end of the novel the lesson is clear: the multiple self-deceptions that pervade Chinatown can be avoided if the residents move away from constricting Chinese traditions and forge ties of affection and intimacy within the family and the community.[26]

Chu's novel is a critical text in Chinese American literature because it departs from the assimilationist or Chinatown tour guide imperative found in earlier tales of Chinatown, "provides a narrative of community life at a critical historical moment, and employs 'Chinatown English' without overtones of caricature."[27] Additionally, in dramatizing the converging impact of racialized and gendered immigration laws and patriarchy on Chinese American society, as symbolically represented in Ben Loy's sexual impotence, Chu anticipated the more self-conscious articulation of such issues by Asian Americans beginning in the late 1960s.

Whereas *Eat a Bowl of Tea* shows the incipient development of a Chinese American sensibility, some later works produced during the turbulent period of the 1960s and early 1970s belie strident cultural nationalism. The Black Power and anti–Vietnam War movements gave momentum to Asian American–organized efforts to challenge racism and white cultural influence. Frank Chin's artistic contributions speak to that context. His plays *Chickencoop Chinaman* and *The Year of the Dragon*, first performed in 1972 and 1974, respectively, as well as his short stories, attempt to reclaim Chinese American manhood and provide a male-oriented Asian American heroic identity. Rejecting the stereotypes of the past, Chin offers characters who must escape the decaying, commercialized Chinatown to find a new identity. In both plays Chin explains that this identity should not be simply "American" or "Chinese." Neither is it simply a blend of both worlds; it is a distinct identity born out of racial conflicts, one with which all "Chinamen" such as himself should be proud to claim affinity. Chin's worldview, however, is limiting. The criteria used to define the Chinese American identity—native birth, English literacy, and masculine ethos—ignore the changing composition and agendas of the Chinese American community. Chin's contempt for the Chinese past borders on self-hatred. His worldview is also filled with contradictions. Even as he rejects assimilation, he invokes icons of American popular culture (such as the Lone Ranger). Chin nevertheless also taps into the heroic exploits of Chinese classics for cultural modeling. Although the identity he sought is supposed to be unique, his literary landscape features tradition-bound elders, such as those in *Flower Drum Song*, or Americanized individuals, such as those in *Fifth Chinese Daughter*. In short, the search for a Chinese American identity seems futile.[28]

Other works that share Chin's didacticism and pessimistic tone—one that is understandable given the temper of the times—include Jeffrey Paul

Chan's short stories and, to a lesser extent, Shawn Wong's *Homebase* (1979). In *Homebase*, a lyrical paean to the Chinese American heritage, Rainsford Chan, the orphaned narrator, goes on a journey to reconnect with his family of the past. For Chan, his family's origins lay in the American West, not in China. His great-grandfather's arduous labor as a railroad worker in the Sierra Nevadas allows him to lay claim to America. In modeling himself after his heroic ancestors—"the original fatherless and motherless immigrants"—Chan initiates a reconciliation among several generations that underscores the nexus between past and present and the possibility of cultural healing.[29]

Less American-centered are the works of China-born cosmopolitan writers who explore the diaspora of the *huaqiao* (overseas Chinese). These works from the 1960s and 1970s are far less concerned with defending the Chinese culture or mediating the divide between the Chinese and Western worlds. They are focused on exploring the malleable nature of identity within the parameters of diasporic social formation. Unencumbered by nation-state boundaries, the characters in these works offer a critique of Chinese and American historical and cultural hegemony. The characters, not surprisingly, suffer from a sense of personal dislocation as revealed in Chung Hua's *Crossings* (1968) and Nei Hualing's *Mulberry and Peach* (1981).[30]

Chinese Language Literature in America

The writings of Nei Hualing exemplify the increasing centrality of Chinese language literature in Chinese America. Although such literature existed before the 1950s, much of it taught Chinese traditional values and instilled in Chinese immigrants sentimental nostalgia for the ancestral land. This literature resonated for Chinese during the exclusion era; it spoke to their search for self-definition in an era of hardships and racial prejudice. In celebrating Chinese culture, these writings offered the psychological support and collective identity the melting pot refused them.[31]

Since the 1950s Chinese language literature has entered a new era. An increase in general immigration from China, as well as the upswell of Chinese students becoming immigrants, led to a resurgence in writing. The themes covered in this literature to some degree mirror those of works written in English. Hualing's *Mulberry and Peach*, originally written in Chinese, concentrates on the story of a female protagonist in America in search of the meaning of freedom and identity—a theme common in English language Chinese American writings. Similarly, the theme of generational conflict in the family has appeared in several Chinese language fictional works. So has racism of all kinds, including what is known as the "glass ceiling" (covert prejudice) professional Chinese face. Yu Lihua's *The Ordeal* (1974) revolves around the turmoil generated by a poor tenure review of Zhong Leping, a physics professor at a state university. The novel deals with the protagonist's gradual realization of the impact of racism and his efforts to challenge the unfair tenure review system.

Chinese language works that center on the Chinese experience in the United States have their own unique sensibility. Since the target readership is primarily the Chinese American community, these writings can offer controversial themes in a more honest, open way. Unencumbered by the judgments of mainstream society, writers can take a strong stand on issues such as incipient feminism among Chinese American women, class divisions within the Chinese American community, the social and mental gap between immigrants and the native born, the consequences of interracial sexual liaisons, and—most common—the daily struggle in an alien land.

From Yu Lihua's *Sons and Daughters of the Fu Family* (1976)—which explores the experience of Chinese student immigrants in the United States—to Cao Youfang's *The American Moon* (1985)—which deals with the miseries of working-class Chinese in New York City—Chinese language writers have probed the intersections of class, race, economic forces, and social environment in shaping the immigrant sensibility. Cao's novel, for example, is a poignant tale of the ups and downs of a student-turned-waiter who becomes embroiled in a work-related dispute and organizes a union. It is the gap in economic status rather than birthplace or generation that causes a rift within the Chinese American community. This gap, these writers suggest, further problematizes the efforts of poor immigrants—already mired in the daily struggle to survive—to overcome racism. Their apolitical tendencies are the result of the survival mentality they have acquired.

In Yi Li's short story "Abortion" (1979), we learn how privation and sexual harassment forced Chinese women, already relegated to the lower rungs of the labor hierarchy by a racially segmented labor market, to resort to abortion as a survival strategy. In Cao's work the class line that divides workers from employers reveals the disparities between rich and poor. The mainstream impression of Chinese as the model minority—middle class, upwardly mobile, and upstanding citizens—is exploded here. So is the notion that ethnic solidarity must prevail within the Chinese community, given its marginalized social location. Instead, what happens in the United States is not always a story of wealthy white Americans exploiting unworldly immigrants but rather sometimes involves Chinese taking advantage of other Chinese.

Writers of Chinese language literature have also explored changing gender roles as a consequence of the heavy emigration of women after World War II. As discussed previously, in America, immigrant women typically experienced a change in the balance of power in the family. With more social and economic opportunities for women than were available in the old country, they could demand more leverage at home. American values and institutions also altered women's worldview, encouraging them to assert their individuality. Yu Lihua's *Sons and Daughters of the Fu Family* tells the story of three brothers who face difficulties adjusting to their new environment, but their wives are doing well at their jobs. In *The American Moon* the couple outwardly practices conventions that seem to uphold the husband's authority at home and in business, but it is the wife who is wielding power and making decisions. Zhong Leping's wife in *The Ordeal* yearns for self-fulfillment. She chooses to find meaning in life by being the driving force behind his attempt to win tenure, as she organizes parties to court support and encourages him never to give up. Eventually, the wife leaves Zhong to pursue her own career. Chinese language literature, on the whole, has broadened and deepened readers' understanding of the socioeconomic reality Chinese newcomers confront in contemporary American life.

Feminist Voices and the Chinese American Identity

If Chinese language writings on Chinese America by recent immigrants seem less concerned with the question of identity than with other issues, the same cannot be said about English-language literature by native-born Chinese. Like their male compatriots, native-born Chinese American women who published in the post-1960s era grew up in a time when Asians in America—calling upon Yellow Power—were becoming increasingly nationalist and sensitive to the wrongs of the past. But unlike Chinese American men, the women suffered from double oppression as matters of race and gender intermeshed to limit their horizons.

Coming of age in a tumultuous era, Chinese female writers naturally probed the search for self-definition, which has resonated since the days of the *jinshan ge*. This theme reverberates in Maxine Hong Kingston's award-winning, semiautobiographical *The Woman Warrior* (1976) and the historically grounded *China Men* (1980). Of the two, *Woman Warrior* has received much more attention. Because of the foregrounding of the strong-willed mother–rebellious daughter relationship and the portrayal of the influence of sexism in Chinese American life, this book falls within the body of feminist scholarship. Kingston's "talk stories" about various "crazy women" in her extended family—such as the unmarried No-Name Aunt in China who drowns herself along with her unborn child rather than live with the shame villagers would heap upon her—present women as both victims and victors. Following the suicide the No-Name Aunt becomes a revengeful ghost who haunts those who had victimized her. By turning the common tale of a "fallen woman" committing suicide—one that appears in both classic Western and Chinese literature—into a triumph for female empowerment, Kingston suggests a resolution for the mother-daughter confrontation: the daughter becomes a woman warrior, the mythic Fa Mulan, who takes on racism in the United States.[32]

But the novel—a mingling of personal reminiscences, family events, folktales, and fantasies—is also, in an echo of Wong's *Fifth Chinese Daughter*, about the struggle to reconcile the tension between the daughter's Chinese ancestry and her American upbringing. Unlike Frank Chin, who conscientiously chose to break away from the immigrant generation, Kingston seeks a reconciliation. In the novel the immigrant's parents, who hailed from the No-Name Aunt's village, are the "necessity, the riverbank that guides [the narrator's] life," and their lack of "extravagance" speaks to their impoverished status. What ties the second generation to the first is not just the former's indebtedness to the latter for their advances in the United States but also their common marginalized existence in racist America. Like Wong, Kingston's search for self necessarily involves a definition of "home"—whether it be America, China, or somewhere else.

Woman Warrior, because of its original narrative style and exploration of gender and generational tensions, won numerous honors, culminating with the 1976 National Book Critics Circle Award for nonfiction. But Kingston's work, notwithstanding its well-deserved acclaim, was prefigured by a number of works—ranging from the Angel Island poems to the meditative prose of Shawn Wong—that also articulate protest, story telling, nostalgia, and even experimentation.[33]

Like *Woman Warrior*, *China Men* addresses the intersection of racial and national identities. *China Men*, like the works of Frank Chin and others, lays claim to America for Chinese Americans. The imposed silences, such as the angry silence of the father—which parallels that of the aunt in *Woman Warrior* who cannot tell her tale—are shattered through the narrative of talk stories. Like *Woman Warrior*, *China Man*—although a less personal journey—is about the reconciliation of present-day Chinese Americans and their immigrant forefathers, facilitated by their common roots in American soil and their shared opposition to colonialism.

Some male Asian American critics such as Jeffrey Chen, Benjamin Tong, and Frank Chin have lambasted Kingston's works. Both *Woman Warrior* and *China Men*, Chin and others have argued, uphold the racist stereotypes of Chinese American men as either weak-willed or brutish creatures. The male characters in these works, they have alleged, are also one-dimensional, oppressively patriarchal, and chauvinistic—even though both texts acknowledge the interplay of structural barriers, such as racialized and gendered immigration laws, with cultural traditions and how these in turn have established unequal gender relationships within Chinese America. Dismissing her work as that of an author who has cashed in on the "feminist fad" and thus "sold out" for economic gain, Chin also alleged that Kingston distorted Chinese traditions and language to pander to white readers' craving for Orientalism and in that sense was no better than those who tried to pass off "Chinatown tour guides" as literature.[34]

These critics have failed to note the overall vision embedded in Kingston's works, which entails the literary creation of a unique Chinese American sensibility through a process that reconstitutes history and memory. That same vision is seen in Kingston's *Tripmaster Monkey: His Fake Book* (1989), which focuses on the antics of Wittman Ah Sing, a 1960s man of letters modeled on Frank Chin. The plot centers on Wittman, who puts on a marathon show for friends and family. Along the way, Kingston manipulates Chinese literary classics and the Euro-American canon and raises the question of creating Chinese American art that will give Chinese Americans a sense of community.[35]

Following Kingston's highly publicized success, other works by women writers that deal with female-centered issues include Alice Lin's autobiographical *Grandmother Had No Name* (1988); the short stories in *Home to Stay: Asian American Women's Fiction* (1990), edited by Sylvia Watanabe and Carol Bruchac; and Fae Myenne Ng's *Bone* (1993), a novel about an immigrant family with three daughters.

Amy Tan's *The Joy Luck Club* (1989), typically seen as a thematic continuation and expansion of Kingston's *Woman Warrior*, is to date the best-known work since Kingston's by a female Chinese American writer in mainstream fiction. Tan, who like Kingston is a second-generation Chinese American, offers interlocking stories that portray the generational and cultural differences between American-born daughters and their Chinese-born mothers. Unlike Kingston's and Jade Snow Wong's works, Tan's novel deals less with the conflict between retaining old traditions and adapting to the new environment and more with the disparity between parental hopes and children's failures, with the way mothers—in the name of integration into mainstream society—push their daughters to succeed. Later made into a successful Hollywood film, *Joy Luck Club* (1993), the novel—like *Woman Warrior*—is accessible because of the apparent universality of the mother-daughter experience, particularly daughters' struggle to free themselves from controlling mothers even as they become more aware of the way their sense of self is tied inextricably to that of their mothers. Unlike *Woman Warrior*, however, Tan's novel addresses the issue of race in a nonthreatening way, sidelining historical legacy and containing the identity question within the convoluted dynamics of the mother-daughter relationship.[36]

Tan again examines the relationship between the two generations in her follow-up novel, *The Kitchen God's Wife* (1991), although here the focus is also on exposing gender inequality in China as experienced by the mother, Winnie. Those experiences as recalled through the use of irony, humor, and allegory serve as important lessons to Winnie's daughter, who at the end of the novel resolves to avoid her mother's fate and to fuse her husband's Western, rational humanism with her mother's ways of knowing and spiritualism.

Tan also wrote *The Hundred Senses* (1995), which centers on the relationship between an American-born sister and her Chinese-born stepsister and how the former learns from her stepsister to appreciate the mystical Chinese worldview.[37]

Another contemporary Chinese American female writer who deserves recognition is Eleanor Wong Telamaque. Her semiautobiographical *Its Crazy to Stay Chinese in Minnesota* (1978) takes the reader into the world of a Chinese girl who lives in a small midwestern town where she and her family are the only Chinese. Hardly a China Doll or a timid, submissive girl, she is smart, witty, outspoken, and ambitious. Yet she is uncomfortably aware of being a racial novelty in the town, even as she at times relishes the attention she garners.[38]

Poetic Visions

Chinese American poetry, like drama, has received far less critical attention than prose fiction. Yet a rich body of works reflects the increasingly diverse composition of Chinese America. They range from Shirley Geok-lin Lim's poems, which embody her Chinese-Malaysian origins, to Wing Tek Lum's writings dealing with family and love, usually within a Chinese-Hawaiian context. The themes also include the diasporic pieces of Russell Leong, a veteran of the Asian American movement, to the poetics of place of Chinese Hawaiian poet Eric Chock. Arthur Sze has meditated on the power of nature, and lesbian poets Kitty Tsui, Nellie Wong, and Merle Woo have vocalized the intersection of sexuality, community, and citizenship. The work of a number of these poets can be found in *Chinese American Poetry: An Anthology* (1991), edited by L. Ling-chi Wang and Henry Yiheng Zhao, which remains the only book-length collection of such poetry.[39]

Within this multifaceted corpus, the poems of the late 1960s and early 1970s embody the spirit of an emerging ethnic consciousness against the backdrop of the Asian American movement. Since then, the demographic changes within Chinese America have problematized efforts to shape a cohesive Chinese and Asian American identity. Poets today focus on the ways history and ideology can destabilize the sense of self.[40]

Some poets, like the prose writers, have put the "immigrant memory," the history of the trans-Pacific migration and adjustment to life in America, behind them and delved into universal themes. Alex Kuo, in his collection, *The Window Tree* (1971), reveals the influence of American romanticists in his evocation of the beauty of the New England landscape. Mei-Mei Berssenbrugge has written mostly about the relationship between nature and human beings. In his trilogy of poems, *The Intercourse* (1975), David Rafael Wang explores without inhibitions the liberating power of sex.[41]

Summary

Demographic changes have prompted writers of all genres to respond to that reality. Gish Jen's novel *Typical American* (1992) explores the bicultural transformation that occurred when Shanghai refugees of the elite class fleeing the Communist revolution came to America. Equally distant from the literary analysis of Cantonese male laborers is Ng's *Bone*, the feminist-driven, allegorical story of an immigrant family of three daughters who, like the women in *Joy Luck Club*, struggle with the legacy of history and traditions. Writers are also in step with the phenomenon of increasing interracial unions and its impact on offspring; Sigrid Nunez's *A Feather on the Breath of God* (1995) and Gus Lee's *Honor and Duty* (1994) deliberate on this issue. Perhaps a sign of the maturity of Chinese American literature is the emergence of the previously underexamined subject of heterosexual, erotic relations between adults as found in Shawn Wong's *American Knees* (1995), which marks a departure from the coming-of-age theme that had taken center stage in previous works.[42]

STAGING THE CHINESE

Unlike their strong presence in prose fiction, Chinese Americans have been less visible on the stage. At the turn of the twentieth century, Chinese representations appeared in vaudevilles, circus shows, melodramas, and as museum displays, and they functioned as exotics, comic relief, or sideshow freaks. Stereotypes of the Chinese abounded in anti-Asian plays such as *Ah Sin!* (1877) and *The Chinese Must Go* (1879). Until the 1950s' staged version of *Flower Drum Song*, most Chinese characters were played by whites.

Although the staging of Frank Chin's plays in the 1970s garnered some attention, mainstream theater remained unreceptive to Asian American artistic expression. It took David Henry Hwang's riveting play *M. Butterfly* (first performed 1988, published 1989) to shatter the barrier. Set in China, *M. Butterfly* is based on the true story of a twenty-year love affair between Song Liling, a transvestite Chinese opera singer turned spy, and a French diplomat who believed Song was a woman. The play is fairly controversial. Like *Joy Luck Club*, *M. Butterfly* has been criticized for presenting stereotypes of emasculated yet conniving "Oriental" men, particularly as represented by Liling. On the other hand, *M. Butterfly* is also an obvious subversion of Puccini's *Madame Butterfly*, an opera that articulates the white male fantasy of dominating the submissive Asian woman. Hwang's play has received accolades because of its attempt to redefine the Chinese American identity by confronting sexism, Orientalism, and imperialism. Hwang had written other well-received plays such as *FOB* (a play about the contemporary conflict between American-born and immigrant Chinese) and *The Dance and the Railroad* (which centers on the dreams and aspirations of early Chinese railroad workers), first staged in 1979 and 1981, respectively (and collected in *Broken Promises* [1983]). But it was *M. Butterfly*, with its transgression of Puccini's opera and its blend of naturalistic dialogue with expressionistic or fantastic sequences, that catapulted him into the national limelight—culminating in his receiving the Tony award for best American play in 1988.[43]

Few Chinese American playwrights other than Hwang and Chin have captured national attention. Limited by budgetary restrictions, most plays have had only minimal staging and limited engagements. The few published dramas include Laurence Yep's *Pay the Chinaman* (1990), which explores hardships in the late-nineteenth-century Sacramento Delta area, and Genny Lim's *Paper Angels* (1991), based on the experiences of Chinese detainees in the Angel Island Immigration Station.[44]

Because Chinese and other Asian American playwrights, as well as actors and technicians, have found it difficult to break into the mainstream dramatic world, nine Asian American artists—including Chinese Americans Beulah Quo and James Hong—organized East West Players in 1965 to serve as a training ground for emerging and professional artists. Recently relocated to a larger space in Little Tokyo, Los Angeles, the company has nurtured the talents of David Henry Hwang and actor B. D. Wong, among others.[45]

MEDIA ARTS

As with literature, Chinese American media arts—film and television—reflect the twin strands of a common experience of Western domination and the growing diversity of national origin, class background, gender, and dialect. Chinese American filmmaking during the activist era of the 1960s and 1970s—given its ideological role—was irreverent, subversive, and grounded in community life. Such a vision led filmmakers to prefer the documentary format (most still do) over feature films because the documentary allows an emphasis on self-definition and the subversions of official history. Gritty, antislick Chinatown documentaries that attest to that preference include Curtis Choy's portrayal of street culture in *Dupont Guy: The Schiz of Grant Avenue* (1975), the Philadelphia Chinatown community's fight against redevelopment as captured in *Save Chinatown* (1973), and *From Spikes to Spindles* (1976), which outlines the convergence of Third World political culture in New York City's Lower East Side. Perhaps the best-known movement-oriented documentary is *The Fall of the I-Hotel* (1983), which documents a powerful, collective resistance against the city's real estate interests bent on evicting the hotel's aging Asian residents.[46]

By the 1980s Asian American filmmakers were gaining access to funding and mainstream venues. Simultaneously, the movement became more institutionalized as arts centers, legal aid organizations, public health centers, and advocacy groups secured offices and professional staffs. Similarly, the disparate media arts centers (including New York Chinatown–based Asian Cinevision) that mushroomed in the 1970s to support media activity in production, exhibition, distribution, and advocacy pooled their resources in 1980 and organized the National Asian American Telecommunications Association to end stereotyped depictions of Asian Americans in the media arts and increase their visibility in public broadcasting.[47]

As Asian American cinema became more market driven and greater attention was given to art and professionalism over politics, filmmakers began branching out into documentaries for public television, low-budget feature films with limited theatrical release, and a few film school products. Of the three genres, documentaries have stood out in quality and quantity. Apparently, investors are reluctant to invest in Asian American feature films for commercial release, given their supposed lack of mass market appeal, and experimental films made by film school students vary in quality.

Innovative Documentaries

Noteworthy documentaries for the Public Broadcasting Service (PBS)—most of which address at least one of the issues of racism, identity formation, and community—have, like works of literature, typically covered turning points in Chinese American history. Outstanding documentaries include Christina Choy and Renee Tajima's *Who Killed Vincent Chin?* (1989), an exploration of the traumatic outcome of a case of mistaken identity in Detroit in 1981. Arthur Dong's colorful *Forbidden City* (1989) explodes the myth of the Chinese as "bowlegged" performers by depicting the exuberant lives of Chinatown cabaret artists who offered American-style shows for predominately white audiences in the 1930s and 1940s. Deborah Gee's provocative *Slaying the Dragon* (1990) outlines Hollywood's recycling of skewed images of Asian American women over the past sixty years, demonstrating that these images are deeply embedded within American popular consciousness. No less important is *Carved in Silence* (1988) by Felicia Lowe, which reveals the arbitrariness of the immigration clearance process on Angel Island before World War II. Earlier, Lowe made a personal diary film, *China: Land of My Father* (1979), a moving chronicle of her return to her family village in Guangdong. Like *China*, Lisa Hsia's *Made in China* (1986) also speaks to the deep, enduring ties between American-born Chinese and China.[48]

Perhaps the best-known PBS and now independent Chinese American filmmaker and producer is Loni Ding, whose *Bean Sprouts*, which began airing in 1981, was the first national children's television series to portray the lives of Chinese American children with a multicultural approach. She went on to make the critically acclaimed *Nisei Soldier: Standard Bearer for an Exiled People* (1984) and *The Color of Honor* (1987)—both of which recount the heroic deeds of Japanese American soldiers—and the stylized *Island of Secret Memories*

(1987), a program about Chinese detention on Angel Island. Ding also contributed to *With Silk Wings: Asian American Women at Work* (1990), a series of four short documentaries. Notwithstanding the title, *With Silk Wings* examines—aside from work—the immigration process, personal aspirations, and the daily challenges of these women.[49]

Feature Films and Mainstreaming

Like the documentary genre, Chinese American feature films raise questions about cultural and personal identity. Such questions, like those asked in literature, are deliberated within the conflicts that ensue when the traditions of two societies affect an individual's life. In Wayne Wang's *Dim Sum* (1985), these conflicts are placed within the context of a traditional Chinese mother who wants her American-born daughter to marry before the mother dies. Wang also made the film version of Louis Chu's novel *Eat a Bowl of Tea* in 1988. Wang, a Hong Kong–born immigrant, is probably best known for his critically acclaimed 1981 film *Chan Is Missing*. The plot centers on the efforts of a middle-aged Chinese man and his nephew to solve a mystery, but the parade of a diverse set of characters undermines the stereotype that all Chinese are alike.[50]

Perhaps the best-known Chinese American filmmaker is Taiwan-born Ang Lee. A graduate of New York University's cinema program, Lee found art house success with his film *Pushing Hands* (1992), which deals with maintaining cultural and sexual boundaries within a patriarchal family unit. His next film won critical acclaim. The comical gay-themed *The Wedding Banquet* (1993)—a touching farce about family, marriage, and commitment—won him an Academy Award nomination in the Best Foreign Film category. *The Wedding Banquet* is the second part of a trilogy, preceded by *Pushing Hands* and concluding with *Eat Drink Man Woman* (1995). The central theme of the entire trilogy is the struggle with Westernization within the Chinese diaspora of families in Taiwan and of Taiwanese Chinese immigrant families in the United States. In *The Wedding Banquet* Wai-tung, the gay son who lives in America, challenges paternal lineage and masculinity, which are at the core of Asian cultures. Immigration, however, has provoked displacement and dislocation, which play out in the realms of gender and sexuality. Yet the film, as Eileen Chia-Ching Fung has argued, ends in a reconciliation of heterosexual masculinity and patriarchal lineage when Wai-tung fathers a child with a Chinese woman who is pretending to be his wife to please his parents. The film, however, does not necessarily have a typical Hollywood happy ending; all the characters have to live with the consequences of their actions.[51]

Even as Chinese independent filmmakers receive more attention, Chinese American actors, directors, writers, and producers—like their Asian-descent counterparts—are experiencing the stirrings of mainstreaming. Joan

Chen is one of the best-known Chinese actresses in Hollywood, with major roles in blockbusters such as *The Last Emperor* (1987) and *Heaven and Earth* (1993). Jason Scott Lee has been dubbed the first Chinese American actor cast as a romantic lead with broad market appeal, with roles in *Map of the Human Heart* (1992), *Dragon: The Bruce Lee Story* (1993), and *Jungle Book* (1994). Director Wang's big break came with his involvement in the film version of *The Joy Luck Club* (1993). After the unexpected success of *The Wedding Banquet*, Ang Lee worked behind the camera on *Sense and Sensibility* (1995), based on the Jane Austen novel, and on *The Ice Storm* (1997), a dark story of a dysfunctional white family set in the 1970s. In 2002 Ang Lee directed the blockbuster success *Crouching Tiger, Hidden Dragon*, an artful take on martial arts and romance in traditional China. Action-film director John Woo, born and raised in Hong Kong, has directed three box office hits, *Broken Arrow* (1995), *Face Off* (1997), and *Mission: Impossible II (2000)*, and also in 2002 a slightly less commercially successful film, *Windtalkers*, which reclaimed the deeds of Native American soldiers during World War II.[52]

Asian American artists still have to contend with serious artistic and racial barriers. Chinese Americans involved in mainstream media arts face the risk that the culture, history, and experiences will be commodified for the consuming pleasure of mass audiences. Since the mainstream industry panders to nostalgic sentimentality and avoids controversial topics, artists often have to compromise their integrity and vision.

Artists must also contend with racist depictions of Asians and Asian Americans. Michael Camino's film *Year of the Dragon* (1984), along with *China Girl* (1987) and *Casualties of War* (1989)—all of which feature stereotypes and violence—raised objections from Asian American activist groups. *Year of the Dragon*, for example, features Hollywood actor Mickey Rourke in the role of a straight-laced lawman, Stanley White, assigned to clean up the corrupt New York Chinatown, embodied in the Chinese villain Joey Tai (John Lone). The romance subplot also misrepresents Chinese Americans; Tracy Tzu (Ariane), who plays the China Doll role, submits to White's advances. *Year of the Dragon*, as well as other "Oriental" gangster films, rejects the claim that Chinese Americans are a model minority. In the post–Vietnam War era, Chinese and other Asians are "gooks," the ubiquitous yet invisible enemy. John Lone's character in *Year of the Dragon* not only sends assassins to kill Stanley White's wife but also sends Asian thugs to rape Tracy Tzu.[53] On the other hand, the martial arts exponent Bruce Lee, in films such as the blockbuster *Enter the Dragon* (1972), is portrayed as lacking interest in sex or even a social life. Popular action thrillers like *The Shadow* (1994) and *The Phantom* (1996) have also revived Fu Manchu–like Asian characters.[54] The Asian in feature films, like the faithful servant in Western fiction, is an ambivalent sexual object: inscrutable, mysterious, unpredictable.

Television

Chinese Americans on television have fared no better than their coethnic peers in films. Like the movies, network television has portrayed Chinese Americans in a distorted manner. Until recently, Chinese American men were cast as whites' helpful domestic servants. In the series *Bachelor Father* (1957–1960), *Have Gun Will Travel* (1957–1960), *Bonanza* (1959–1973), *The Green Hornet* (1966–1967), and *Falcon Crest* (1981–1990), Chinese male actors functioned as submissive foils for heroic, overly masculine masters or employers. Another race-typed role for Chinese American men has been the loyal sidekick police detective with strong-willed white superiors—a role that revives the Charlie Chan persona. In the long-running *Hawaii-Five-O* (1968–1980), actors Kam Fong and others—without asking questions—carried out the orders of the white men in charge. Similarly, in the series *Midnight Caller* (1988–1991), actor Dennis Dun played the role of an able assistant to Jack Killian (Gary Cole), a radio talk show host who solved crimes in his spare time. Like the Chinese American male characters in literature and films, those on television are also asexual or lacking romantic inclinations. One example is Hop Sing (Victor Sen Yung) in *Bonanza*, who throughout the long run of the series seemed content to be a womanless bachelor.[55]

The female counterparts of these sexless male characters, like those in literature and films, embody sexual prowess and are attracted to white males. The theme of Asian female sexual possession by white men has appeared in a number of television Western series, including *Bonanza* and *How the West Was Won* (1978–1979), and more recently in the PBS rendition of Ruthanne Lum McCunn's semibiographical novel of the life of a woman sold into prostitution, *Thousand Pieces of Gold* (1992). The well-known actress Joan Chen has played roles akin to those of Anna May Wong; for example, in the miniseries *Tai-Pan* she is the China Doll harlot of a rugged British sea merchant. Chen was cast in a similar role in a 1989 episode of the series *Wiseguy* (1987–1990), in which she turns from a committed labor organizer into a kinky sexpot while seducing the lead character, an FBI agent. Beulah Quo is a unique exception to the common cast typing of Asian actresses. Considered a character actress, Quo has starred in a number of television series, playing a variety of multidimensional roles ranging from the Empress of Kublai Khan to a university dean. She is perhaps best known for her long-running role as Olin, the hip-talking, wise housekeeper and confidante on the daytime soap *General Hospital.*

In more recent years the general voyeuristic interest in Asian American gangs has led to a revival of the stock theme of the omnipotent role of tongs in the Chinese American community. In an episode of *Gideon Oliver* (1989), the presence of these Chinese secret societies is seen as endemic to the community. This perception has been reinforced by numerous segments on television magazine shows and specials that ignore the structural barriers—alienation, racism, parental problems, and limited job opportunities—that have led to such antisocial behavior in favor of sensationalistic, Yellow Peril coverage. In television series that have featured gang-themed episodes, such as the action-packed *MacGyver* (1985–1992), Chinatown is riddled with gratuitous violence that gangs perpetrate for the sake of profits and power. Like the nineteenth-century progenitors portrayed in literature, the contemporary Chinese American criminal exploits his countrypeople, keeps women in sexual bondage, and seeks to undermine the moral fabric of this Christian country (the United States).

Clearly, since the beginning of the television industry, the representation of Chinese Americans has been skewed to reinforce existing power relations; however, there are hopeful signs of a change for the better. The standard portrayal of the Chinese American male as a nonheroic victim or evil villain was first altered with the appearance of the program *Kung Fu* (1972–1975). Featuring the character of a Shaolin martial arts expert, the series broke new ground because Kwai Chang Caine, the lead, never ran from his attackers or allowed himself to be bullied. Unfortunately, Kwai, the offspring of an interracial union, was played by a white actor, David Carradine. *Kung Fu* was also controversial because Bruce Lee was originally considered for the lead role, but the racist perception that an Asian man could never come across as heroic on television cost him the role. No Chinese American, male or female, starred in a role until the syndicated miniseries *Vanishing Son* (1994–1995) was aired. *Vanishing Son* featured Russell Wong as Jian-Wa Chang, a fugitive from the law who is framed for two murders. Unlike Carradine's Caine, Chang is as virile and sexual as he is fearless. The show became a weekly series in 1995, but declining ratings eventually killed it.[56] Currently, B. D. Wong is the most visible Chinese American actor on television. Wong, who won a Tony for his portrayal of Song Liling in *M. Butterfly* and has starred in a number of Hollywood blockbusters such as *Father of the Bride* (1991) and *Jurassic Park* (1993), appears as a regular character in several television series.

VISUAL ARTS AND MUSIC

Chinese American contributions to the arts have included other, less visible means of expression. In the visual arts Hung Liu's 1991 San Francisco exhibit of paintings of young Chinese prostitutes from the early decades of the twentieth century is noteworthy because it documents the women's forgotten lives and interplays illusions and gazes. In her 1994 installation at San Francisco's DeYoung Museum entitled *Jiu Jin Shan* (On Gold Mountain), Liu turned her attention to the barren promise of America. The main elements of the installation are asymptotic railroad tracks covered by a mountain of fortune cookies. The lesson is clear: the early Chinese railroad laborers, like Kingston's grandfather in *China Men*, never found gold or riches as suggested by the fortune cookies, which contain no fortunes and are even not Chinese.[57]

In the visual arts—particularly in public architecture—no Chinese American has rivaled the career of Maya Lin, the daughter of educated refugees who fled Communist rule on mainland China. Lin's Vietnam Veterans Memorial in Washington, D.C., dedicated in 1982, captured the imagination of the American public but raised a firestorm of controversy. The memorial is a simple but meaningful structure: it consists of two black granite walls in the shape of a chevron, which meet at a 125-degree angle. The memorial was created to evoke "personal reflection and private reckoning" on the meaning of death and loss, to quote Lin, but some veterans, political commentators, and politicians initially believed it was antiheroic and made a mockery of the courage and sacrifice of Vietnam veterans. The passage of time, however, has proven that Lin's Asian-influenced artistic vision was accurate; the memorial has become a place of reconciliation and healing. Since designing the memorial, Lin has created other equally eloquent works of art—most notably the Civil Rights Memorial in Birmingham, Alabama, and the Peace Chapel at Juaniata College in Huntingdon, Pennsylvania.[58]

Far less well-known than Lin but no less pathbreaking is the woodcut artist Seong Moy. Born in Guangzhou in 1921, Moy immigrated to the United States at age ten. He spent his formative years in St. Paul, Minnesota, and later studied art in New York City, which brought him in contact with the modernist movement. His unique artistry shows strong ties to Chinese methods of drawing and calligraphy, as well as the influence of abstract Expressionism. His woodcuts are found in numerous permanent collections, including those at the Metropolitan Museum of Art and the Museum of Modern Art, both in New York City; the Philadelphia Museum of Art; the Victoria and Albert Museum, London; the Bibliotheque Nationale, Paris; and the Library of Congress, Washington, D.C.[59]

The participation of Chinese Americans in the arts has come of age. Perhaps no other cultural expression captures this artistic maturity as clearly as Chinese American jazz and creative music, which blend different musical styles—including African American jazz, Asian folk rhythms, Arabic modes, and reggae beats—and use Korean and Chinese as well as Western instruments. Characterized by changing meters and moods, this music, as reflected in the works of Fred Wei-han Houn (better known as Fred Ho) and Jon Jang, speaks to the rising Chinese American national consciousness—one that articulates *xungen wenzu* (searching for one's roots and ancestors) within a diasporic framework. As a young man, Ho was involved in the very end of the Asian American movement, which shaped his worldview. His music reflects pan-Asianism and its ties to the so-called Third World. In the 1980s he led two innovative music groups—the Asian American Arts Ensemble and the

Afro-Asian Music Ensemble; Jon Jang was also involved in the latter. Ho has written compositions that combine folk music elements from Asia and the Pacific Islands with a twentieth-century African American musical heritage, resulting in music that is swinging and soulful. Ho is also credited with writing the first contemporary Chinese American opera, *A Chinaman's Chance*, which premiered in 1989. The opera features a bilingual libretto (Chinese and English), as well as Chinese and Western instruments. Like Ho, Jang has written music that reflects his sociopolitical activism; his 1997 suite, *Island: The Immigrant Suite Number 1*, is based on the immigrant poetry etched on the walls of Angel Island. Like Ho, Jang has relied on Chinese and African instrumentation to convey unique sounds.[60]

Innovative, energetic, and breaking the boundaries of time, space, and culture, the arts as shaped by Chinese American writers, artists, and performers will continue to challenge both neo-assimilationism—the argument that nonwhite minorities will and must conform to the dominant American culture and institutions—and liberal pluralism—the assumption that members of diverse cultures can develop their own culture in the confines of the larger common culture. The process of forging a Chinese American sensibility in this changing republic will be ongoing, multifaceted, and even subversive.

8 Chinese American Families and Identities

"MODEL MINORITY"

Prior to the 1960s the Chinese American family faced harsh immigration laws and other structural barriers, but since that time it has undergone a transformation. No longer a fractured or split household unit, the family is now highly complex. Furthermore, because of the changing composition of new arrivals in the United States since the end of World War II and the pervasive presence of acculturative forces, the nature of Chinese American families remains fluid.

Research on Chinese American family life is still in its infancy. The literature on the Chinese American family is limited primarily because some social scientists have not considered this "model minority" as beset with social and economic problems. Also, until recently, Asian Americans were underrepresented among social scientists, so few insiders were available to conduct community-oriented research. Finally, the small number of Chinese Americans and their geographic concentration in just a few states have made them seem invisible and sociologically unimportant.[1]

Much of the existing literature to date argues that Chinese American educational and economic advancement stems from deeply held values embedded in the Chinese culture, particularly Confucianism. Strong familial ties, close control of children, traditional family values, and a focus on collective solidarity over individual interest supposedly explain why Chinese Americans have overcome racism and poverty to attain educational and income levels that exceed those of Euro-Americans. The low rates of divorce, illegitimacy, adolescent rebellion, and delinquency are also attributed to the cohesiveness of Chinese culture. Any change over time, such as the decline in female subordination, is regarded as the product of assimilation; any cultural continuity, such as economic self-sufficiency, attests to the strength of the Chinese ethos.[2]

Since the mid-1960s this overall portrait has contributed to the emergence of the model minority myth. In a reversal of negative Orientalism, Chinese (along with other Asian Americans) have received high commendation from the media and politicians for their good behavior and economic success. Such celebrations of Asian American achievements have, however, exaggerated that success and created a damaging new myth. Comparisons of incomes between Chinese and whites fail to consider that the Chinese are concentrated in states with high costs of living, which negates their higher incomes. Pundits and politicians also herald the fact that Chinese Americans enjoy a higher average family income than whites; in 1990 their incomes were $4,000 to $5,000 higher than those of white families. Such figures belie the changing context of immigration that accounts for the seemingly high household incomes. Some immigrants today start off relatively privileged; either they are part of the "brain drain" of professionals and highly skilled workers from Asia, or they are tied to the transnational capital flight to the United States. These foreign-born Chinese Americans—the majority of the Chinese American population—often earn more than their native-born counterparts. Also typically ignored is the fact that more members of Chinese American families work than is the case with white families; in 1980 white nuclear families in California had 1.6 workers per family compared with 2.0 for immigrant Chinese.[3] The 2000 census showed that as a percentage of the total population, more Chinese (18.8 percent) lived in households with five to seven or more members compared with the entire U.S. population (11.1 percent).[4]

The high percentage of large households within the Chinese population suggests the existence of a large number of extended families. Hence the higher family incomes of Chinese Americans exist because families have more workers rather than because each individual family member has a higher income than other U.S. workers. Some members of these families are self-employed; they put in long hours, enjoy few benefits, and run the risk of bankruptcy. Chinese American incomes are also distributed unevenly, with large numbers of Chinese at the top and the bottom of the income spectrum. In 1990 approximately 11 percent of all Chinese American families lived in poverty compared with 7 percent of white families—a point rarely discussed in the popular media.[5]

The model minority image is harmful to Chinese Americans in several ways. It is framed within the assimilationist paradigm, which homogenizes Chinese American families and ignores the diversity among classes and subgroups. Clearly, the myth diverts needed attention from segments of the population that are still grappling with socioeconomic barriers. This static understanding also dismisses structural forces such as immigration laws, labor market conditions, and the lack of political rights that have forced families and individuals constantly to reshape culture for survival. The myth also downplays the level of racial discrimination Chinese Americans encounter. Asian American youth face undue tension because the myth places pressure on them to succeed in school. Ironically, any academic success is probably the outcome of an effort to overcompensate for occupational barriers. Finally, the myth can fuel competition and resentment between Asian Americans and other racial minorities. In 1966 the first print media article on the Chinese American success story stated, "At a time when . . . hundreds of billions [are] be[ing] spent to uplift Negroes and other minorities, the nation's 300,000 Chinese-Americans are moving ahead on their own, with no help from anyone else."[6]

In contrasting the supposed self-sufficiency of Chinese Americans with African American demands for government support for community social services, pundits and politicians are in effect arguing that welfare and affirmative action are obsolete, since all racial minorities can emulate Asian Americans if they just work hard, stay out of politics, and assimilate into the dominant American culture. The model minority myth thus reinforces existing racial hierarchies. It can also instigate racial discrimination, even physical attacks, on Asians as retribution. The hyperbole about Asian American affluence can lead to jealousy among non–Asian Americans or to a belief that Asian American gains have come at the expense of other peoples of color. The 1992 Los Angeles riots illustrate how damaging the myth can be. Although the acquittal of white police officers charged with beating Rodney King sparked the riots, Asian Americans paid the price. Asian immigrant family-run businesses were broken into, ransacked, and looted by roving mobs, which included African American and Latino men. An estimated $1 billion in property damage and fifty-eight deaths (both Asians and non–Asian Americans) were the end results. Blacks resented the presence of Asian retail establishments in their declining neighborhoods; rumors also flew that Asian immigrants were receiving special government benefits blacks were denied. In the end, African Americans' anger fortified the model minority image of Asian Americans.[7]

CONTEXT OF FAMILY FORMATION

Changing historical and contemporary circumstances explain why Chinese American families seem cohesive and achievement oriented. Before World War II the sojourning status of most immigrants meant they were motivated to defer gratification to maximize future mobility. Then the almost complete halt of Asian immigration for several decades in the twentieth century reduced economic pressures on the Chinese American community and allowed for more social investment in the small second generation.[8]

The perceived stability of Chinese families is an illusion. Before the 1960s divorce among Chinese was rare because of the lack of alternative options outside the ghettoized family-oriented businesses. Further, the Chinese community frowned on divorce. Some women resorted to suicide. The low delinquency rate before World War II stemmed from the small number of adolescents in the population. Few Chinese turned to welfare because many immigrants were "paper sons" or "paper daughters." Their lack of knowledge about U.S. institutions and their general distrust of officials also explain why Chinese were reluctant to approach social service agencies.[9]

Legal obstacles to immigration to the United States account for the prolonged existence of extended (and pseudo-) kinship ties within the Chinese American community. Without those ties, Chinese would not have found their way to America through chain migration and fraudulent entries. Kinship-like institutions such as benevolent associations existed to ameliorate economic and political discrimination. By the same extension, family cohesiveness reflects the historical exigency of all members of the family working together as part of the adaptation to American life.[10]

The lingering legacy of anti-Asian sentiments, as reflected in the anti-immigration climate of the 1980s and 1990s; the entrenched existence of a split labor market that relegates racial minorities to low-paying, dead-end jobs; the revival of the enclave economy that embraces small-producer enterprises; and the continuing entry of new Chinese immigrants (as many as two-thirds of the Chinese in the United States in 1990 were foreign born) unattuned to U.S. culture have all perpetuated these so-called cultural dynamics. Kinship ties, benevolent associations, Chinese schools, family cohesion, and the informal transmission of Chinese heritage are still necessary for survival.

CHARACTERISTICS OF CHINESE AMERICAN FAMILIES

Since the liberalization of immigration laws in the mid-1960s, heterogeneity among Chinese American families along nativity, class, and generation lines has been a salient characteristic. Among recent immigrant families, large and extended households are fairly typical. The 1990 census showed that a greater proportion of Chinese compared with white households had three or more persons. In contrast, the majority of white households—59 percent—consisted of one or two persons.[11] Ten years later the overall pattern remained the same, as suggested in the 2000 census. The disparity between Chinese and whites can be accounted for in several ways. First, Chinese adult children tend to live at home while completing their education; even some married offspring and their families reside in their parents' homes. Furthermore, more elderly relatives live with their families than is true with white families. The size of the households has been augmented by newly arrived immigrant relatives. These circumstances explain why a smaller proportion of members of Chinese households are not relatives than is true in white households.[12]

Nuclear family units, which are more akin to Euro-American families, are found among professional suburban families. Even among these families, however, chain migration over time has increased the size of the households. As discussed previously, some recent immigrants from Taiwan and Hong Kong have set up one-person households in America, leaving their wives and children behind until they are ready to send for them through the relay immigration process.

Bureau of Census statistics for 1990 that showed that 81.6 percent of Chinese under eighteen lived in two-parent households do not necessarily indicate family stability. The low rate of divorce (2.0 percent in 1990) and the high marriage rate, which in turn produced the preponderance of two-parent household units, in fact stemmed from the rising number of reconstituted families that had been separated before the 1960s.[13] Furthermore, a number of the post–World War II conjugal unions possibly included hasty marriages in which Chinese women entered into relationships with Chinese American men to circumvent existing restrictive laws. Thus these matrimonial ties likely did not always involve strong emotional bonds and cohesive households.

Contrary to popular perception, some contemporary Chinese American families are headed by females. The 1990 Bureau of Census statistics revealed that 7.8 percent of Chinese households are headed by females, and of that figure, 28.3 percent live below the poverty line.[14] These households reflect in part the unremitting entry into the United States of displaced persons from parts of Asia experiencing economic dislocation. The figures have also been shaped by return migration of Chinese males, particularly professionals and the self-employed. These men returned to Asia to seek better fortunes, leaving their wives to shoulder the burden of child rearing and share in the responsibility of economic support.

Working-Class Immigrant Families

Most working-class immigrant parents today have had to forsake parental supervision as a result of their labor-intensive jobs in the secondary labor market or the enclave economy. Unlike those involved in family enterprises or self-employment, husbands and wives in dual-worker families experience a complete segregation of work and family life. In one study published in 1987— conducted among Chinese immigrants in New York City—82 percent of the children lived with both parents, but 32 percent did not see their fathers on a daily basis, and 21 percent reported the same about their mothers. Parents' fatigue, lack of common cultural experience, and endless separation hinder communication between them and their children. In families where parents do oversee their children's upbringing, parental authority is exercised by the mothers, who spend more time with their children than fathers do because of their domestic responsibilities.[15]

As a result of this mother-child dynamic, immigrant working-class fathers seemingly have suffered a loss of status, whereas the mothers enjoy an elevated status. As described in earlier chapters, the situation has been compounded by fathers' typical downward occupational mobility following migration to America. Mothers face different fortunes; most, who were rarely wage earners in Asia, now hold low-skilled jobs that provide some economic freedom. This reversal of gender roles has likely strained conjugal relationships at the difficult time of adjustment to life in the United States.

Some immigrant conjugal unions also experience tensions resulting from spousal incompatibility. Many new and old Chinese male immigrants still return to Asia to marry, a process that received a boost following the Chinese government's 1979 rectification of its policy toward overseas Chinese. This rectification in essence has meant that the political rights and interests of overseas Chinese and their relatives in China are once again legally protected.[16]

Encouraged by this more tolerant climate, overseas Chinese, including Chinese Americans, now return to China for a range of social and economic activities—including finding prospective conjugal partners. Consequently, the number of trans-Pacific marriages involving U.S. citizens—mostly in their mid-to late twenties—and women from China, Hong Kong, and Taiwan increased in the late 1970s and the 1980s; about 5,000 brides arrived in America in the late 1980s (figures for earlier years are not available, but the number was certainly far lower before 1979).[17] According to one study of 307 males involved in such unions, most were from working-class backgrounds with low incomes.[18]

Perhaps not surprisingly, another study found that the women these men married, like the brides of the reunited broken families, suffered from shock and a sense of betrayal when they arrived in America.[19] Led to believe their *gam saan* husbands were prosperous, they were unprepared for the harsh reality of grinding poverty and economic disempowerment. One woman interviewed remembered that "when he [her husband] was courting me, he said he was a restaurant owner and he owned a house and a car. That made me all the more excited about the marriage."[20] When she found out that the couple's apartment was tiny and poorly furnished, she complained about the deceit, and he abused her physically—apparently a common plight of the out-of-town brides.

Middle-Class Professional Families

Some middle-class, white-collar families are quite different from the Cantonese-dominated split household families of the past; families hailing from Hong Kong, Taiwan, and Southeast Asia have different linguistic and regional backgrounds. These immigrant, as well as native-born middle-class families, are often more cosmopolitan and Westernized than working-class families and seem to lead typical U.S. suburbia lifestyles. One 1982 study found that a high percentage of professional Chinese immigrants in California had been exposed to Western education and languages while still living in their country of birth, which accounts for their seemingly easy adjustment to American society.[21] Although their work and neighborhood contacts are primarily white, they may socialize with other Chinese of similar class and educational backgrounds. For example, members of the business and professional groups tend to join ethnic-oriented alumni, commercial, and political organizations, which working-class Chinese—because of their lack of time—rarely join. Both groups, according to one New York study, however, celebrate both Chinese festival days and U.S. holidays.[22]

Generally, gender roles are more equal in the professional family than they are in the working-class family. The family income is derived from the earning capacity of both husband and wife. When both are professionals, there is a sense of economic partnership and therefore some equality. One extensive study of San Francisco's Chinatown in the early 1980s reported that 51 percent of the women surveyed were "pretty satisfied" and another 21 percent were "very satisfied" with their marriages, which the researchers attribute in part to spousal relations being less patriarchally oppressive today.[23] In these relationships, women—like their working-class peers—still carried out most of the household labor, even though these families have moved toward less sex-role segregation. Unlike the situation in working-class families, professional parents, who are relatively affluent and have more time to spend with their offspring, can offer the resources for and participate actively in their children's education.[24]

It is imperative to avoid the impression that only two types of families are found in contemporary Chinese America. Aside from the working-class and professional families, there is the revived small-producer family involved in ethnic enterprises in Chinatowns or in surrounding multiracial neighborhoods. Wives and children are typically unpaid workers in these self-exploitative ventures. Women generally perform both paid work and child rearing at the same site. Finally, according to the 1990 census statistics, nearly a third of the

Chinese labor force was involved in technical occupations, which suggests the possible emergence of a type of family that has yet to be documented.[25]

The interpersonal dynamics within Chinese American families are changing and evolving as the families adapt to the challenges of life in American society. Preliminary evidence shows that as acculturation works its way into Chinese America, these families will begin to replace familial supervision—considered traditionally to be a way to show love—with more demonstrations of affection and Euro-American forms of nurturance. Instead of restrained verbal communication and discouragement of emotional expression—the by-products of a culture that emphasizes nonverbal communication, anticipation of the needs of others, and well-defined social behavior and roles—family members may become more individually assertive and less situation centered or socially dependent on each other.[26]

CHINESE AMERICAN CHILDREN

As a result of immigration reform since the mid-1960s, Chinese American children have become more diverse than in the past. The second generation no longer refers to just U.S.-born children of immigrant parentage. The new second generation encompasses foreign-born children who arrived in the United States before they attained adulthood, although they are also identified as the "one-and-a-half generation." Among Chinese American children, one study by Min Zhou based on the 1990 U.S. Census showed that the native born made up 84 percent of those up to age seventeen, although this figure includes foreign-born children up to age five. When all foreign-born children were counted, three of every ten were born outside the United States. The way changing contexts of immigration have affected children's experiences is reflected in the fact that more than three-quarters of Chinese children spoke a language other than English at home. Because immigration now involves the nuclear and sometimes the extended family, 92 percent of those surveyed lived in married-couple households. Since so many children are part of a nuclear family and a visible middle-class segment is growing, few are in families living below the poverty level.[27]

In 1990 the majority of Chinese American children were enrolled in public schools. Zhou's study also shows that the dropout rate for Chinese children can be correlated to both the length of U.S. residence and fluency in English. The longer children had been in the United States, the less likely they were to quit school. And the more fluent they were in English, the less likely they were to drop out, although bilingualism did not have a negative impact on completion of schooling. In fact, current research suggests that bilingualism—by facilitating parent-child communication and allowing children to tap into values, norms, and patterns of social relations in the ethnic community—can account for educational success in spite of immigrant status, language, and class barriers. Min Zhou's study implies that a group's distinctive cultural and social-organizational traits—ethnicity, in other words—have a role in shaping attitudes that promote academic achievement.

IDENTITY DILEMMA

The progeny of these families have to grapple with the psychological and social dilemma of the identity crisis. Many Chinese American youth feel torn between being Chinese and being American, a predicament shaped by their Chinese upbringing and American education and socialization. As a result, certain personality types have begun to emerge—ranging from the "banana," or so-called modernist who rejects or denies everything Chinese to appear completely Euro-American, to the "radical" Chinese, who adheres to the pan-ethnic Asian identity and rejects traditional Euro-American and Chinese values.[28]

The development of an Americanized identity is countered by the concomitant pull of the ethnic identity. The ethnic identity is, in turn, determined by the harsh reality of racism, which may lead one to reject or enhance his or her ethnic identity. Nativity and generational differences must also be taken into account in any analysis of ethnic identity; presumably, the progeny of the first generation, compared to their parents, would be much more assimilated into the dominant society and thus have less ethnic identification. In reality, however, the consciousness, adoption, and application of ethnic identity ebb and flow within an individual's lifetime depending on the environment encountered. A person may choose to adopt only certain aspects of ethnicity or to invoke the identity only in certain settings, such as at home but not at work or school. Furthermore, a person who lives in a predominately ethnic neighborhood will likely invoke his identity more often than one who lives in a white-dominated area.[29]

For the second generation, growing up in the United States forces them to become aware of their racialized marginality from the identity *American*. Second-generation conflicts are about differences not just of culture but also of race. Those raised in an all-white social world understand that "looking Asian" is a barrier to normalcy. Those who grew up in Chinatowns or heavily Asian neighborhoods are more cognizant of the split along nativity lines. Awareness of racial difference becomes heightened following transition into white-dominated schools. Further problematizing the identity crisis for some second-generation children is the lack of parental encouragement to identify with their Chinese background. Since they are not culturally Chinese, only physical markers set these children apart from non-Chinese. Parents and family elders who do counsel the second generation to maintain ethnic consciousness and pride as a response to racism often emphasize its primordial nature. Being Chinese is supposedly a matter of shared descent from a common ancestor. Second-generation persons, however, discover that their claim to being Chinese is tentative. Their American birth and upbringing under-cut their authenticity as "real Chinese." Low proficiency in Chinese only casts more doubt on the claim.[30]

Their parents' foregrounding of second-generation children's ethno-national identity as Chinese, however, can occur at the expense of their al-ready maligned Asian identity. The parents' counsel is understandable; the global context of successful homelands (at least before the Asian economic crisis in the late 1990s) encourages ongoing transnational ties. Yet since rac-ism in the contemporary era has involved their identity as Asians, any under-scoring of ethnonational origins implicitly belittles the significance of these young people's racial identification in mainstream society. To make matters worse, stereotypes of Asian students—hardworking, achievement oriented, yet lacking in creativity—problematize the self-definition of Chinese adoles-cents and youth. After interviewing thirty-one Chinese Americans (and thirty-three Korean Americans), Nazli Kibria concluded that the informants tended to distance themselves from such stereotypes and deflect them onto immi-grant or foreign national Asians. In sum, her informants considered being Asian American as confining, even stifling to one's individuality.

Parents, particularly foreign-born and middle-class parents, typically en-courage an accommodationist stance toward the dominant society. They urge their children to do well at school. Academic achievement will ensure success in the United States—a classic endorsement of the American dream. Regard-less of racial or skill-based barriers, anyone can "make it" in America. The appropriate response to racism was a private one, centered on individual and familial efforts. When rejected by American society, unable to deflect suspi-cions about being Chinese, and taught to ignore their Asian identity and accept racial stratification, Chinese American children can become hopelessly mired in an identity dilemma.

The conflict between assimilation and ethnicity, between mainstream American and Chinese identities, exacerbated by the shifting nature of the family, has been responsible in part for the rise in juvenile delinquency among Chinese American youths. During the exclusion era a low level of delinquency was ascribed to the small youth population and perhaps to the close integra-tion of the family. Juvenile delinquency began to surface in the 1960s. Ac-cording to a newspaper article published in New York City in 1956, of a total of 8,714 juvenile delinquents that year, only 7 were of Chinese descent. New York City police estimated in 1965 that about 3 percent of the Chinese community's teenagers were known to be juvenile delinquents, although that was the lowest rate of any racial group.[31] Against the backdrop of the decade's sociopolitical discontent, frustrated youths organized into juvenile gangs. Supposedly, such activities filled status and identity needs for those not yet incorporated into the larger society.

The continuing rise in juvenile delinquency in the 1970s and 1980s can be ascribed to several factors. Aside from the growth of the juvenile population, the increase in youth crime has resulted from several interrelated changes: the language and socializing adjustment in school; the shortage of job opportunities, especially for recent low-skilled immigrants; the lack of parental supervision; and the overall breakdown of community control as Chinatowns become less insulated and more exposed to dominant capitalism. Additionally, most of today's immigrant youngsters hail from urbanized, Westernized settings. Already influenced by the dominant youth culture, they are less willing to tolerate traditional cultural expectations.[32]

The tension engendered by the constant shifts between two worlds has resulted in attitudinal changes among both Chinese American men and women. According to one study, Asian-born Chinese American women sampled through a questionnaire were more conservative than men regarding social customs. For example, they expect special courtesies from men and consider drinking, swearing, and telling jokes to constitute bad manners. On the other hand, these same women, reflecting the impact of acculturation, gave high priority to achievements in education and intellectual areas and were not willing to be subservient in marital relationships.[33]

In the realm of sexual permissiveness, Chinese American male and female youth, notwithstanding their exposure to American life, seem more conservative than their white counterparts. According to one study of 114 Chinese male and female college students, most of the Chinese respondents—more than three-quarters of whom had grown up in non-Chinese neighborhoods—had not engaged in premarital intercourse. Most of those who had done so had delayed their first sexual experience until late adolescence or early youth. The reasons for this lower level of sexual permissiveness include (1) the need to be certain of an emotional commitment; (2) lack of social acculturation, especially among men who are saddled with the burden of attaining economic and educational success and therefore have less time for socialization; (3) the negative body image instilled in Chinese through history and popular media, which causes some to feel sexually modest; and (4) traditional Chinese culture's emphasis on modesty.[34]

Young Chinese women, compared to their male peers, encounter more pressure in their attempt to negotiate between the boundaries of family life and selfhood. Although still expected by their parents to fulfill the role of obedient daughters, enter into matrimony, and perform domestic responsibilities, these women aspire to explore new ideas and cultures. Jennifer Ng, who emigrated from Hong Kong as a child and grew up in Manhattan, recalled that during her college days her attempts to shape her selfhood were constantly thwarted by her working-class parents' insistence that she live near Chinatown while in college, suppress her ambition to be an investment consultant, and marry as soon as possible. Ng was able to board at her school rather than commute from her parents' home in Chinatown, but she had to return every weekend to work in a garment factory alongside her mother.[35] Scholars argue that Chinese American women brought up in middle-class surroundings probably have more access to education and freedom than those of working-class backgrounds. The process of staking out a self-defined identity becomes less encumbered by parental opposition as offspring come of age.

DOMESTIC VIOLENCE

The contemporary familial challenge for Chinese women also includes the issue of domestic violence. Such violence may stem from a conflict between the traditional patriarchal values of husbands and the modern gender equality sought by wives, suspicion of infidelity, unequal marital power, and an overwhelming sense of hopelessness as a result of grinding poverty and blocked economic mobility. Some husbands of battered women take advantage of their wives' immigration status before they receive permanent residency. Even though a wife can petition for permanent resident status without her spouse's signature, immigrant women are typically unaware of their rights and thus are in a vulnerable position within the marriage. The high standard of proof required to demonstrate family violence has likely deterred many female victims from seeking help.

Abused Chinese women face other barriers in resisting domestic violence. They have to grapple with widely shared assumptions that Asian cultures accept gender violence, which in turn has enabled Chinese men and the larger society to resort to "cultural defenses" of Chinese men who abuse, assault, or even murder their wives or partners. This scenario played out in the case of Dong Lu Chen, a Chinese man in New York City who killed his wife in 1987 by pounding her skull with a hammer. During the trial Chen's attorney claimed that in China, if a man believes his wife has been involved in an extramarital relationship, he will threaten to kill her; otherwise, Chinese society would consider him emasculated and morally weak. In sentencing Chen to five years' probation—the lightest sentence possible—the judge commented that Chen "was driven to violence by traditional values about adultery and loss of manhood." Violence against Chinese women was thus rationalized as the product of cultural proclivities.[36]

Chinese women who are willing to fight back in spite of this public perception run up against other roadblocks. These women in general are discouraged, perhaps even intimidated, from speaking up about domestic violence. The subject is rarely discussed within the ethnic community because it is considered a private or personal crime that happens randomly to individuals and is not a major social problem. Furthermore, women often have no idea where or to whom to turn for help. Unattuned to the U.S. social welfare system and unable to cope with their problems, women who live in Chinatowns have been reported to have a high rate of depression, and in some cases they commit suicide.[37]

GAY MEN AND LESBIANS

Like Chinese American women, Chinese American gay men and lesbians must contend with traditions while striving to define their identity within the community and in the society at large. The Chinese, as do Asian Americans generally, consider homosexuality a Western phenomenon—a myth well corroborated by the media, which rarely features or portrays gay men and lesbians of color. Chinese Americans who profess this sexual orientation are seen as having rejected the importance of Asian family and culture and having become totally assimilated into mainstream American life. Worse still, they have betrayed their ethnic group and besmirched their family's honor. Some parents of Chinese American queers[*] reject homosexuality because they associate it with gender role reversal. The men are feminine and the women look like males; gay men and lesbians, in their minds, undermine the natural boundaries of biological gender. Parents typically express disbelief, shock, and denial over their offspring's sexual orientation, as expressed in Liz Lee's recollections when she discovered her daughter's sexual identity: "I didn't accept [it] for a long time. I didn't think she would come out in the open like this. I thought she would just keep it and later on get married."[38]

Isolated from their families, Chinese American gay men and lesbians often grew up understanding little about their desires and feelings or were forced to rely on friends and acquaintances to define same-sex attraction. In Eric C. Wat's study of a group of Los Angeles Asian American men, service in the sex-segregated military in the 1950s and 1960s opened the door for sexual exploration and their eventual coming out. Other gay men and lesbians relied on gay publications for information and to help create an imagined community if a physical one was out of reach.[39]

Rejected by their ethnic community, Chinese American gays and lesbians find that their participation in the mainstream queer community is qualified. Many feel stereotyped or unacknowledged by that community. A few of the male narrators in Wat's study recalled how their service in a predominately white military heightened their racial consciousness, forcing them to confront the color line that exists in the United States. Chinese American gays and lesbians complain that white gays and lesbians consider them "exotic"

---

[*]The term *queers* is used in the positive sense and encompasses gay men, lesbians, bisexuals, and transgendered individuals.

and rarely admit the existence of racism or race-related issues in the queer community. For example, the queer community supports domestic partnership legislation that would extend employee benefits to life partners, but such legislation could create complications for Asian gays and lesbians. Until a 1990 congressional amendment, immigration laws considered "sexual deviants" as part of the undesirable list. Asian arrivals who were gay or lesbian could have been denied entry or turned down for permanent residency or naturalization on the basis of their sexual orientation. Thus Asian partners who registered their gay relationships under the requirements of domestic partnership legislation could have experienced legal complications. The mainstream queer community kept silent on the matter. More recently, the lack of vocal support for the fight against California's Proposition 187 (which passed in 1994), which denies education, health care, and social services to individuals suspected of being undocumented immigrants (which would include queers of color), has added to the impression that the mainstream queer community ignores racial difference in favor of a homogenized matrix of sexual politics.[40]

Some Asian Americans have experienced blatant racism by members of the white-dominated queer community. Commercial gay establishments have at times discouraged Asians from patronizing their businesses; in Los Angeles, for example, gay bars in the 1980s often demanded three pieces of picture identification. For Chinese immigrant queers, the blatant racism they confront in the United States is something new. Unlike their native-born coethnics who were raised experiencing racial prejudice, they grew up in racially homogeneous environments in Asia. Upon migration, they confront the politics of difference.[41]

The invisibility of Asian gays and lesbians in the queer community is compounded by the politics of tokenism and exotification. They are enlisted to participate in mainstream queer politics only to maintain balance in racial representation. Additionally, like heterosexual Chinese women and men, Chinese American gays and lesbians are often victimized by the gender and racial power relations in U.S. society. White queers consider Chinese gays and lesbians—already seen as exotic, submissive "Orientals"—to be desirable but not social equals.[42]

Because of the silence imposed by both the ethnic and queer communities, Chinese gays and lesbians—bearers of a double minority status—have had to experience the worlds of Chinese America and gay America as separate places. The "domain of the Asian American 'home' is usually kept separate from the desire of the sexual and emotional 'body,'" according to poet and editor Russell Leong.[43] Chinese and other Asian American queers take great care to keep these worlds distant from each other. For most Chinese American gays and lesbians, their self-identity is situationally determined and fluid; they may be gay in a gay leather bar but Asian when paying respects to their ancestors at the temple. To cope with this double consciousness, since the 1980s Chinese Americans have joined other Asian American queers in forming Asian American lesbian and gay organizations in major U.S. cities to spearhead political activism and provide social support. These include the Boston Gay Males and Lesbians (1979), the Asian Pacific Lesbians and Gays (Los Angeles, 1980), the Association of Lesbians and Gay Asians (San Francisco, 1981), the Asian Lesbians of the East Coast (New York, 1983), the Asian Pacifica Sisters (San Francisco, 1989), and the Gay Asian Pacific Islander Men of New York (1990).[44]

The importance of these organizations to the formation of an Asian American queer identity is best illustrated in the realm of cross-cultural desire. According to Wat, the Asian subjects in his study did not find each other desirable as sexual partners. Even though most of them were proud gay men as well as proud Asians, the two identities had not forged into a coherent gay Asian identity. This failure is historically rooted in the demasculinization of the Asian male.[45] As discussed previously, racialized and gendered immigration laws and labor conditions have forced Chinese men into womenless communities and into "female jobs." The ubiquitous occupations of the Chinese male as domestic, laundryman, and restaurant worker seem to confirm the image of the effeminate Asian man. In recent times little has changed. Media images of Asian men remain distorted, portraying them as hardworking, upstanding, yet passive "Orientals."

Already emasculated and feeling undesirable, beginning in the 1970s Chinese men confronted the cult of masculinity that promotes hypermasculine white men as the sexual icons of the gay community. The Vietnam War and its outcome shattered the image of the United States as the epitome of heterosexual masculinity. This crisis in American manhood enabled gay men to appropriate masculinity and abandon the old butch/femme (masculine/feminine) binary. When commercialized, the hypermasculine white gay male image become the sole definition of manliness, excluding Asians. It is little wonder Asian men did not find each other attractive; in fact, "the Asians all saw each other more as competitors for the attention of these white guys than as friends," recalled Terry Gock.[46] The pursuit of the white masculine ideal became central to Chinese gay men's identity, encouraging them to see white-Asian coupling as highly desirable. The archetypal white-Asian relationship functions, to quote Wat, as a "sort of fascism of desire that was predicated on a heterosexist ideology that normalizes only sexual unions between 'males' and 'females.'" Conversely, Asian-Asian relationships—given the fact that Asian men were defined as feminine—seemed unnatural, even "incestuous."[47]

The formation of pan-ethnic Asian American queer organizations was the result of a rising political consciousness forged by the intersections of race, gender, and sexuality. In Asian gay bars Chinese and other Asian men, in spite of being treated as part of the "ethnic tourism" Asian enclaves have come to represent for whites, experienced the process of community formation. Questions were raised, desires reexamined. Congregated together in the same spaces, Asian men could share common experiences. They formed informal networks that became critical for the establishment of these queer organizations. Such organizations allowed Chinese and other Asian queers to use racial analysis to structure the definition of their gay identity. With the onset of the AIDS epidemic in the early 1980s—one that continues today—some of these organizations extended their role into the areas of disease prevention and safe sex educational programs. These programs have encouraged Asian American men to question the terms and limits of their sexual relationships, including those with white partners. Through these organizations, Chinese and other Asian men have found a conduit to shape a support network, demystify white male masculinity, and resist racial imaginings.

MENTAL HEALTH

Chinese Americans, as do other racial minorities, experience certain pressures that can generate mental problems. Racism and its attending badge of inferiority can be so virulent that some Chinese Americans have internalized the negative "Oriental" image. The end result is self-hatred that has led some to reject their ethnic identification and choose to be Euro-American rather than Chinese American. In addition, some Chinese Americans experience cultural and generational conflicts when they adopt American values that clash with family customs.[48]

In spite of these problems, Chinese and other Asian Americans have consistently underutilized mental health services. In one San Francisco Chinatown study conducted in the late 1970s and early 1980s, only 5 percent of respondents sought mental health services compared with 20 percent of Americans overall who sought the same services in 1976.[49] The figure for the Chinese is disturbing because almost half of the respondents admitted to suffering from emotional tension or depression. The underutilization of services is also ironic given the fact that as early as the 1950s the suicide rate for Chinese Americans was two and a half times greater than the national rate and has remained critical, as evidenced in one 1986 study (published in 1998) that shows the suicide rate for elderly Chinese immigrants as almost three times higher than the rate for older Chinese Americans born in the United States.[50]

Chinese rarely use mental health services for several reasons. Perhaps one of the most important is the lack of knowledge about available services, particularly among new working-class immigrants. Another reason is that some Chinese ascribe to the cultural belief that mental disorders cannot be prevented. Some Chinese believe mental illness is caused by spiritual unrest, hereditary weakness, or metaphysical factors such as fate or weakness of character, which means remedies cannot be found within the realm of science or psychology. Others are reluctant to admit to psychological symptoms because of the cultural stigma attached to such admissions and to the use of mental health services. Those who seek professional counseling are regarded by coethnics as weak, immature, and lacking self-discipline. Not surprisingly, some Chinese have chosen to ignore or downplay their problems. Finally, a few who do not trust or are suspicious of Euro-American mental health professionals may choose alternative forms of treatment, ranging from herbalists to visits to the Chinese temple.[51]

Chinese Americans who do want such services find a shortage of ethnic minority and bilingual professionals in the mental health field. Existing trained professionals generally have had little or no preparation in understanding the sociocultural determinants of mental illness. Without such knowledge, such therapists rarely consider these factors when prescribing treatment: the circumstances of immigration, generation and age, degree of assimilation, educational level, socioeconomic status, occupational skills, religious beliefs, and support system.[52]

Potential Chinese patients also face ingrained myths the dominant society holds regarding the ethnic community. Some mental health professionals believe Chinese do not need mental health therapy because they are family centered and help one another. Another myth is that the Chinese culture is so strongly based on shame that Chinese are reluctant to seek help from such professionals for fear of losing face. In fact, no empirical evidence substantiates this belief. Awareness and use of mental health services will increase over time because acculturated Chinese Americans have shown a proclivity to pursue such services.[53]

RELIGIONS IN CONTEMPORARY CHINESE AMERICAN LIFE

Some Chinese Americans have relied on organized religions to overcome the emotional and mental pressures of trying to cope with life in America. The economic and social dislocations engendered by globalization of markets and labor have displaced those whose faith the People's Republic of China (PRC) considers opposed to the national ideology; PRC newcomers to America are among the most devout Chinese Christians. The flourishing of Christianity as well as Buddhism is also the product of a movement of capital, entrepreneurs, and professionals (as well as workers) to the United States who have chosen to plant roots here yet maintain ties to their countries of origin. Institutionalized religions have, in sum, competed with traditional native place and mutual aid associations for newcomers' allegiance. Research into contemporary Chinese Americans' participation in religiosity, however, has yet to reach maturity. Scholars have developed only a preliminary outline of the topic.[54]

Chinese religions today are clearly represented by many more forms of communal worship than simply "joss houses" or ancestor worship. After the U.S. immigration reforms of the mid-1960s, Chinese Buddhist organizations proliferated. A case in point is Fo Kuang Shan (Buddha's Light Mountain), which originated in Taiwan. It has expanded to the United States, and branch temples are found in Hacienda Heights, California; San Francisco; San Diego; Austin; Dallas; Denver; and New York City. The largest Fo Kuang Shan–affiliated temple is Hsi Lai Temple, otherwise known as the International Buddhist Progress Society, in Hacienda Heights. When the plan was unveiled to build this $30 million–plus structure on twenty acres of land, nearby residents—mostly whites—virulently opposed it, claiming it would create a traffic nuisance as well as introduce a "religious cult" that could demoralize area youth. The scaling back of the temple's size, however, has had little adverse impact on its transnational mission: to function as a spiritual-*cum*-cultural center, to serve as a place to teach Westerners about the Dharma, and to facilitate the exchange of cultural knowledge between East and West. Besides being a religious organization, Hsi Lai also helps Chinese immigrants adjust to life in America. It offers employment networks; organizes seminars on U.S. culture, labor market, and laws; and houses and feeds newly arrived immigrants. The temple has also functioned as a social relief center; it has donated money and books to nearby schools, engaged in environmental preservation programs, sponsored soup kitchens for the homeless, and raised relief funds for victims of disasters in the PRC and the United States. Hsi Lai Temple has also tried to foster cross-cultural understanding, introducing non-Chinese to Chinese culture through language and art classes. Chinese Americans have also become acquainted with mainstream America through Judeo-Christian–influenced celebrations and recreational courses.[55]

The other dominant Buddhist sect in the United States is the True Buddha Sect (zhenfo zong), which Taiwanese immigrant Lu Shengyan founded in the mid-1980s in Seattle, Washington. Unlike Fo Kuang Shan, which is in the Chan Buddhist tradition, the True Buddha Sect is more of a syncretic type in the Vajrayana (Tibetan Buddhist) tradition. A number of independent Chinese Buddhist temples and groups have also emerged in major U.S. cities. According to Irene Lin, the temple "provides the context for overseas Chinese to reinforce and reinvent the Chinese identity through religion, ethnicity, nationality, culture, family, and education."[56] In this postindustrial era, Buddhism—like other religions—in Chinese America has also had to accommodate the forces of fashion, to learn to appeal to its adherents' social and cultural tastes.

Christianity has a substantial Chinese American following, and it may be surpassing Buddhism in the number of adherents. Until the 1940s, Chinese churches were located within Chinatowns, reflecting the concentration of

Chinese Americans in those ethnic enclaves. Many of the churches were actually missions established for the Chinese by mainline Protestant and Catholic denominations. The geographic dispersal of Chinese to the suburbs after World War II forced churches to relocate. The number of congregations has also climbed dramatically. Within the San Francisco Bay area in the 1950s, 15 Protestant congregations existed in five counties; by the mid-1990s the number stood at 158, a tenfold increase. Nationwide in 1952 there were 66 Chinese Protestant churches: 47 were denominational, 5 were interdenominational, and 14 were independent of a denominational body. Catholic Chinese missions existed in Hawai'i, Philadelphia, Chicago, Boston, and New York City. Since then the number of Chinese Protestant churches has risen dramatically, reaching about 700 by 1994. In contrast, fewer than 150 Chinese Buddhist temples and associations remained in the mid-1990s.[57]

The overall growth of Chinese Christian churches across the United States stems from the rapid rise of the Chinese population since the mid-1960s, as well as the need for new congregations to minister to the diverse language groups (Mandarin, Taiwanese, Cantonese) and points of origin (Taiwan, the PRC, Indonesia). Part of the growth has also been rooted in the influx of college-educated professional immigrants after the 1960s who can provide leadership and financial resources to support the churches' ministry and outreach. These efforts began in the early 1960s with Chinese students studying in U.S. universities who established campus Bible study groups (BSGs). Many BSGs later became churches as more students remained in the United States. The emergence of ethnic revival movements since the 1970s has promoted general acceptance of ethnic groups and multiculturalism, including ethnic churches. Since 1989, the year the PRC government violently suppressed the student-led prodemocracy movements in China, a large number of mainland Chinese students and scholars in the United States have joined Chinese Christian churches, increasing the number of adherents in these congregations.

Most churches in the post-1960s era serve the immigrant generation but remain sensitive to the needs of the second generation. Typically, both Chinese and English services are available to accommodate language and cultural diversity. Some churches have two pastors, one born overseas who can speak Chinese and an American-educated or native-born pastor who can preach in English.

Contemporary Chinese churches exhibit both theological conservatism and organizational independence. A number of new churches established by Chinese immigrants are independent; across the United States, around half of the Chinese churches are unaffiliated with American denominations. Independent Chinese churches, however, do network selectively with non-Chinese Christian organizations and individuals. The new churches affiliated with mainline U.S. denominations prefer to associate with those that are theologically conservative and those less centrally organized; the largest group of Chinese churches affiliated with a mainline American denomination belongs to the Southern Baptist Convention, which claimed 150 Chinese churches in 1995.[58]

One sociologist who studied Chinese Christian congregations argues that Chinese Americans' draw to conservative Protestantism reveals the profound alienation that followed migration, which encourages immigrants to find order and purpose by associating with an institutionalized religion. Although Western imperialism, modernization, and nationalism in Asia have fragmented Chinese cultural traditions, many immigrants still have a high regard for traditional moral values. Chinese from Southeast Asia migrated to escape the pressures of assimilation, whereas those from mainland China or Taiwan left as a result of sociopolitical turmoil or the fear of authoritarian rule. In coming to America they hoped to make a good living but also to keep their Chinese identity. For them, conservative Christianity validates their social-ethical values. The church can assist them in retaining and reclaiming their Chinese cultural identity within American pluralism, even as it sometimes promotes the values of the Protestant ethic such as success, thrift, and delayed gratification. Through the Protestant church some Chinese Americans have been able to preserve the Chinese language, uphold Confucian moral values (the importance of family life and filial piety) and some aspects of philosophical Daoism, and celebrate the Chinese New Year and Mid-Autumn Festival as cultural celebrations stripped of religious overtones and traditional meanings. Chinese Protestants tend to reject Confucian agnosticism, the worship of Confucius, Buddhism, and religious Daoism. In contrast, a Chinese Catholic church is more likely to adopt traditional Chinese symbols and practices, such as sacrificing pig heads and fruits to venerate ancestors. The social and cultural functions of the church explain why existing theories of religious conversions related to individual psychology and personal bonds—that individuals turn to religion for emotional support and spiritual sustenance—cannot adequately explain the phenomenon of immigrant conversions. The immigrant church serves as a conversion and an assimilation agency, as well as an ethnic center for preserving selective cultural traditions. The church promotes ethnicization, or the process of becoming ethnic Americans that integrates multiple identities: Chinese, American, and Christian.[59]

INTERRACIAL MARRIAGE

Acculturated Chinese Americans have demonstrated a propensity to marry interracially. Before World War II miscegenation laws and Asian men's negative body image lowered the rate of white-Chinese unions. In the immediate postwar years, although most interracial marriages involved American servicemen stationed in Asia and their Japanese, Filipino, or Korean "war brides," about 6,000 of these marriages involved Chinese women. After the immigration laws were liberalized, the dramatic influx of new immigrants probably played a role in suppressing any increase in Chinese interracial marriage, at least for the foreign born.[60]

In the late 1970s some studies show that Chinese were engaging in out-marriage (marriage between two persons from a different race or ethnic group) at a disproportionate rate. One study, centered in Los Angeles County, found that 41.2 percent of the Chinese Americans who registered to marry in 1979 married non-Chinese (which includes other Asians and non-Asians); 30.2 percent of those surveyed entered into interracial marriages, presumably with whites.[61] These findings were confirmed by two separate studies that used the 1980 census. About 31.5 percent of Chinese marriages, according to the compiled statistics, involved non-Chinese, and 22.0 percent of Chinese marriages involved white partners.[62] An overwhelming number of the out-marriages were interracial unions. The Chinese, among Asian ethnic groups, however, have the lowest level of intermarriage; Japanese Americans have the highest rate of out-marriage.[63]

The increase in the number of out-marriages, particularly interracial ones, can be ascribed to a number of factors—some of which seem to validate an assimilationist interpretation. The civil rights movement and the attending affirmative action laws, along with declining racial prejudice, have enabled Chinese—particularly those with professional and managerial occupations—to increase their social contacts with whites, which in turn may have led to greater acceptance of Chinese as potential marriage partners. Residence and geographic mobility contribute to the opportunities conducive to intermarriage. Chinese who move out of Chinatowns and Chinese neighborhoods and into areas with low concentrations of coethnics expose themselves to more socialization with members of the dominant group and thus increase their pool of potential marriage partners. Concomitantly, this change of residence reduces the opportunity for in-group marriages as the pool of potential Chinese partners is reduced.[64]

The level of acculturation can be positively correlated with the prevalence of intermarriage. Those who have more facility with the English language and are familiar with dominant values are often more likely to consider intermarriage. Not surprisingly, interracial marriage occurs most frequently among second-generation Chinese Americans, who have the necessary skills to engage in out-group contact; further, their prolonged exposure to American values encourages them to cast aside traditional attitudes and expectations along with familial control over marital practices. Unlike members of the second generation or the native born, foreign-born immigrants—already handicapped by language and cultural barriers—are less likely to marry out of their ethnic group.[65]

Since those who intermarry seemingly must already experience frequent out-group contact and possess language and social skills, it is perhaps to be expected that most are in professional and managerial occupations rather than in manual labor or the service sector, both of which offer limited opportunities for socialization in the dominant culture. In a study published in 1987, sociologist Betty Lee Sung concluded that those who intermarried were disproportionately involved in high-status–oriented professional and technical occupations and consequently enjoyed a higher average family income than their in-group married peers.[66]

Sung also found that the non-Chinese husbands of Chinese women were highly concentrated in professional and technical occupations; very few were at the lower end of the job scale.[67] Other studies have shown that out-group married Chinese women, who are mostly concentrated in highly skilled occupations, tend to marry up. Perhaps this helps explain why Chinese women intermarry.[68] According to the hypergamy theory, individuals—males and females—sometimes choose to maximize their status in a racially stratified society through out-marriage. If this is true, highly accomplished Chinese American women can maximize their status by marrying the most advantaged individuals with the highest racial position—Caucasian men of the professional-managerial class. Chinese men can also maximize their status by marrying white women who are occupationally and educationally at a lower level but who, by virtue of the color of their skin, are in a higher racial position in society.[69]

Although Chinese women and men may enter into interracial marriages to gain upward mobility, other factors may be involved in the decision. Some marry non-Chinese because it is a personal choice; they meet a person of another race, fall in love, and get married. For both men and women, intermarriage is undoubtedly facilitated by the lowering of racial barriers and the assimilation process, but it is also tied to racial and gender power relations in today's society.[70]

Specifically, Chinese American women and men interviewed by Colleen Fong and Judy Yung cited aversion to Asian patriarchal family structure—such as overbearing or manipulative parents, strict discipline, and spousal domination or abuse—and the concomitant media promotion of white beauty and power as important variables in their decision to avoid intraethnic marriages. Nellie Tsui, who emigrated from Hong Kong, remembered that in college she found Chinese American men unattractive, whereas the Jewish colleague she married "was very feminine, very caring, and very verbal . . . he's always done the dishes no matter who cooks. . . . There's no way my father would do that. You know, it's too demeaning."[71] Chinese American women and men who intermarried considered coethnics to be too wedded to patriarchal or old-fashioned values and disinterested in or ignorant of the existing popular youth culture. Whereas they considered Chinese men and women conservative, boring, and unattractive, Caucasian men and women were extroverted and sexually appealing, and they offered racial empowerment.[72]

Since so many Chinese women and men find each other unappealing, the question of why more Chinese women than men out-marry is a salient one. In nearly all existing studies, many more Chinese American women than Chinese men intermarry. In some studies Chinese women were twice as likely as Chinese males to intermarry. Perhaps this differentiation stems from the interplay of American racial and gender hierarchy and stereotypes. Asian American women are portrayed in the media as petite, submissive, and sexually desirable, which fits the general definition of an attractive, feminine woman. This image may make Chinese women attractive to some white men. Concomitantly, white men may be drawn to Chinese women because they consider Caucasian American women too liberated, demanding, and career oriented. Meanwhile, the popular imagination regards Asian American men as desexualized, even nerdy, which goes against the image of an attractive, masculine man. Finally, Chinese American women intermarry because they want equality with their marriage partners, something they do not think they will find with Asian American men.[73]

MULTIRACIAL CHINESE AMERICANS

The phenomenon of interracial unions has led to a cohort of mixed-race people within the Chinese American population. These multiracial individuals are marginal persons in both the Chinese American community and the larger U.S. society. During the exclusion era the specter of miscegenation and general anti-Asian sentiments caused white Americans to shun not only interracial couples but also their racially mixed children. White America considered Chinese Caucasians—the products of miscegenation—physically, morally, and mentally weak. Unmixed Chinese Americans also harbored deep ambivalence toward those who were part Chinese. The biracial writer Sui Sin Far, writing at the dawn of the twentieth century, remembered that the Chinese were "a little doubtful as to whether one [a Chinese man] could be persuaded to care for me, full-blooded Chinese people having a prejudice against the half-white."[74] The sense of isolation multiracial Chinese experienced, however, ebbed to some degree following the rise of the civil rights movement, the repeal of antimiscegenation laws, the integration of neighborhoods, and the general decline in white and Chinese resistance to interracial marriages.[75]

Part-Chinese persons still face barriers. First, they are confronted with rigid racial categories that deny their existence. Until the 2000 census—which finally allowed them to claim mixed heritage—the Bureau of the Census had no separate category for mixed-race Chinese, which forced some to either choose one of the existing racial classifications or ignore the question; either way, their self-identity was compromised. Second, multiracial Chinese Americans find that they are generally treated with suspicion and are less likely than full Chinese to be included in Chinese America or the larger society. Any acceptance often comes with the condition that they renounce their non-Asian background in their interaction with the Chinese community or pass as white when interacting with the larger society. An exception to this overall pattern exists in Hawai'i, where the long history of intermarriage among this polyglot of ethnicities and the visible presence of *hapas* (people of mixed ancestry) have fostered tolerance and even acceptance of multiracial Chinese Americans. Aside from this unique case, many Chinese of mixed ancestry adopt "situational identities": they feel and act mainly white, black, or Latino when among whites or blacks or Latinos and act mainly Chinese when among Chinese.[76]

In recent decades marriage patterns among Chinese Americans have been characterized by the rising number not only of interracial marriages but also of interethnic marriages (i.e., Asian Americans marrying other Asian Americans). This new phenomenon stems from the increasing racial consciousness and unity that have been forged through the bridging of cultural and language differences by a common marginalized experience in the United States. Equally crucial in this trend is the growing homogeneity of the Asian American population in terms of socioeconomic attainment and middle-class status. If this trend persists, the development of the Asian American identity will be further encouraged.[77]

CONCLUSION

Since Chinese immigration to the United States seems set to continue unabated throughout the twenty-first century, this ethnic community will likely face challenges similar to those it is encountering today and perhaps others yet to be determined. Occupational downgrading, the glass ceiling, self-exploitation in economic life, and marginalization in mainstream politics—to name a few—may remain critical issues as long as new immigrants, who often find adjustment to U.S. society problematic, continue to enter the country. Exacerbating these problems is the persisting perception that Chinese, along with other Asian Americans, are neither white nor black. Caught in this binary understanding of race in America, Chinese Americans have either been portrayed as exemplifying the Yellow Peril or as members of the model minority. The end result of such representation has been their subordination to white domination and sometimes their placement in a circumscribed role in this racially based society.

Since the first few Chinese Americans came ashore on the eastern seaboard in the 1780s, they have demonstrated the resilience to refashion their self-identities and cultural expressions. Although divided along class, gender, generation, language, time of arrival and place of origin, and sexual orientation lines, Chinese immigrants and their native-born progeny have worked to break free from the weight of historical and societal injuctions. For most, the choice between Asia and America, between East and West, has been a false one. Rather, Chinese Americans have labored to project a fluid identity shaped by the interconnections of Asia and America. More specifically, their identity, against a backdrop of structural barriers, ultimately belies a synthesis of selective Chinese cultural values with adherence to U.S. democracy and equality. Chinese Americans, like many other racial minorities, have played a role in redefining the American national identity.

Notes

CHAPTER 1

1. Tin-Yuke Char, *The Sandalwood Mountains: Readings and Stories of the Early Chinese Immigrants in Hawaii* (Honolulu: University of Hawai'i Press, 1975), 54–57; Thomas W. Chinn, Him Mark Lai, and Philip P. Choy, eds., *A History of the Chinese in California: A Syllabus* (San Francisco: Chinese Historical Society of America, 1969), 7–8, 22.

2. Herbert Passin, quoted in Tu Wei-ming, "Cultural China: The Periphery as the Center," in *The Living Tree: The Changing Meaning of Being Chinese Today*, ed. Tu Wei-ming (Stanford: Stanford University Press, 1994), 1.

3. The information in this and the next three paragraphs is from Him Mark Lai, "The Guangdong Historical Background, With Emphasis on the Development of the Pearl River Delta Region," in *Chinese America: History and Perspectives 1991* (San Francisco: Chinese Historical Society of America, 1991), 75–81, 88.

4. L. Ling-chi Wang, "Roots and the Changing Identity of the Chinese in the United States," in *The Living Tree: The Changing Meaning of Being Chinese Today*, ed. Tu Wei-ming (Stanford: Stanford University Press, 1994), 186–187.

5. Lai, "Guangdong Historical Background," 76, 87.

6. Molly Joel Coye and Jon Livingston, *China: Yesterday and Today*, 2d ed. (New York: Bantam, 1979), 13.

7. Lai, "Guangdong Historical Background," 76–77.

8. Yu-Kuang Chu, "The Chinese Language," in *An Introduction to Chinese Civilization*, ed. John Meskill (New York: Columbia University Press, 1973), 590–591.

9. John K. Fairbank, *The United States and China*, 4th ed. (Cambridge: Harvard University Press, 1979), 43.

10. The information in this and the next three paragraphs is from Immanuel C.Y. Hsu, *The Rise of Modern China*, 4th ed. (New York: Oxford University Press, 1990), 47, 70–80; Jonathan D. Spence, *The Search for Modern China* (New York: W. W. Norton, 1990), 46.

11. On peasant life in southern China in the late Qing dynasty, see Philip C.C. Huang, *The Peasant Family and Rural Development in the Yangzi Delta, 1350–1988* (Stanford: Stanford University Press, 1990).

12. The information in this and the next three paragraphs is from Lloyd E. Eastman, *Family, Fields, and Ancestors: Constancy and Change in China's Social and Economic History, 1550–1949* (New York: Oxford University Press, 1988), 75–76, 87–88.

13. Fairbank, *United States and China*, 47–49.

14. The information in this and the next paragraph is from David Johnson, "Communication, Class, and Consciousness in Late Imperial China," in *Popular Culture in Late Imperial China*, ed. David Johnson et al. (Berkeley: University of California Press, 1985), 34–72.

15. The information in this and the next four paragraphs is from James Legge, ed., *The Chinese Classics*, 5 vols. (Oxford: Claredon, 1893–1895), 1:264–265, 309, 2:370; C. K. Yang, "The Role of Religion in Chinese Society," in *An Introduction to Chinese Civilization*, ed. John Meskill (New York: Columbia University Press, 1973), 644–645, 661–664; Eastman, *Family, Fields, and Ancestors*, 42.

16. The information in this and the next three paragraphs is from Maurice Freedman, "Ritual Aspects of Chinese Kinship and Marriage," in *Family and Kinship in Chinese Society*, ed. Maurice Freedman (Stanford: Stanford University Press, 1970), 165–179; Yang, "Role of Religion," 649–650, 664; Richard J. Smith, *China's Cultural Heritage: The Qing Dynasty, 1644–1912*, 2d ed. (Boulder: Westview, 1994), 167–168.

17. The information in this and the next two paragraphs is from John K. Fairbank, Edwin O. Reischauer, and Albert M. Craig, "Taoism and Buddhism," in *China: Yesterday and Today*, 2d ed., ed. Molly Joel Coye and Jon Livingston (New York: Bantam, 1979), 48; Kenneth Chen, *Buddhism in China* (Princeton: Princeton University Press, 1964), 436–439.

18. David Yoo, "For Those Who Have Eyes to See: Religious Sightings in Asian America," *Amerasia Journal* 22, no. 1 (1996): xvi. See also Stephan Feuchtwang, *The Imperial Metaphor: Popular Religion in China* (London: Routledge, 1992).

19. The information in this and the next two paragraphs is from Thomas W. Chinn, *Bridging the Pacific: San Francisco Chinatown and Its People* (San Francisco: Chinese Historical Society of America, 1989), 10–12.

20. Hsu, *Rise of Modern China*, 19.

21. Ibid., 47, 58.

22. See Derk Bodde and Clarence Morris, *Law in Imperial China* (Cambridge: Harvard University Press, 1967).

23. The information in this and the next paragraph is from ibid., 123–124; Spence, *Search for Modern China*, 97, 110, 114–115.

24. Eastman, *Family, Fields, and Ancestors*, 4–5.

25. Yen-p'ing Hao, *The Commercial Revolution in Ninteenth-Century China: The Rise of Sino-Western Mercantile Capitalism* (Berkeley: University of California Press, 1986), 1, 4.

CHAPTER 2

1. Ho Ping-ti, *Studies on the Population of China, 1368–1953* (Cambridge: Harvard University Press, 1959), 281–283.

2. Sucheng Chan, "European and Asian Immigration Into the United States in Comparative Perspectives, 1820s to 1920s," in *Immigration Reconsidered: History, Sociology, and Politics*, ed. Virginia Yans-McLaughlin (New York: Oxford University Press, 1990), 37–75.

3. G. William Skinner, *Chinese Society in Thailand: An Analytical History* (Ithaca: Cornell University Press, 1957), 32; Mary F. Somers Heidhues, *Southeast Asia's Chinese Minorities* (Victoria, Australia: Longman, 1974), 11–15; C. Y. Choi, *Chinese Migration and Settlement in Australia* (Sydney: Sydney University Press, 1975), 18, 28–29; Edgar Wickberg et al., eds., *From China to Canada: A History of the Chinese Communities in Canada* (Ottawa: McClelland and Stewart, 1982), 20–24; Moon-Ho Jung, "'Coolies' and Cane: Race, Labor, and Sugar Production in Louisiana, 1852–1877" (Ph.D. diss., Cornell University, Ithaca, N.Y., 2000), 129–130, 140.

4. June Mei, "Socioeconomic Origins of Emigration: Guangdong to California, 1850–1882," in *Labor Immigration Under Capitalism: Asian Workers in the United States Before World War II*, ed. Lucie Cheng and Edna Bonacich (Berkeley: University of California Press, 1984), 232; Madeline Yuan-yin Hsu, *Dreaming of Gold, Dreaming of Home: Transnationalism and Migration Between the United States and South China, 1882–1943* (Stanford: Stanford University Press, 2000), 27.

5. Chinn, Lai, and Choy, *History of the Chinese in California*, 20; "The Celestials at Home and Abroad," *Littell's Living Age* (August 14, 1852): 294.

6. The information in this and the next four paragraphs is from Yong Chen, "Internal Origins to Chinese Immigration Reconsidered," *Western Historical Quarterly* 25 (Winter 1997): 538–541; Haiming Liu, "The Social Origins of Early Chinese Immigrants: A Revisionist Perspective," in *The Chinese in America: A History From Gold Mountain to the New Millennium*, ed. Susie Lan Cassel (Walnut Creek, Calif.: Altamira, 2002), 21–36.

7. Liu, "Social Origins." The classic work on this interpretation is Oscar Handlin, *The Uprooted* (Boston: Little, Brown, 1941).

8. The information in this and the next paragraph is from Chen, "Internal Origins," 545–546; Liu, "Social Origins," 21–36.

9. On return migration, see Franklin Ng, "The Sojourner, Return Migration, and Immigration History," in *Chinese America: History and Perspectives 1987* (San Francisco: Chinese Historical Society of America, 1987), 53–71.

10. Clarence E. Glick, *Sojourners and Settlers: Chinese Migrants in Hawaii* (Honolulu: Hawai'i Chinese History Center and University Press of Hawai'i, 1980), 2–4; Ah Jook Ku, "Kauai's Chinese," in *Sailing for the Sun: The Chinese in Hawaii 1789–1989*, ed. Arlene Lum (Honolulu: University of Hawai'i Center for Chinese Studies, 1988), 47, 49, 53. For a biography of Chun Fong, see Bob Dye, *Merchant Prince of the Sandalwood Mountains: Afong and the Chinese in Hawai'i* (Honolulu: University of Hawai'i Press, 1997).

11. The information in this and the next two paragraphs is from Evelyn Nakano Glenn, *Unequal Freedom: How Race and Gender Shaped American Citizenship and Labor* (Cambridge: Harvard University Press, 2002), 193, 195–198; Ronald Takaki, *Pau Hana: Plantation Life and Labor in Hawaii* (Honolulu: University of Hawai'i Press, 1983), 32, 76–77; figures in Ronald Takaki, *Strangers From a Different Shore: A History of Asian Americans* (Boston: Penguin, 1989), 121.

12. The information in this and the next three paragraphs is from Judy Yung, *Unbound Feet: A Social History of Chinese Women in San Francisco* (Berkeley: University of California Press, 1995), 6, 19, 293; Ronald Takaki, "They Also Came: The Migration of Chinese and Japanese Women to Hawaii and the Continental United States," in *Chinese America: History and Perspectives 1990* (San Francisco: Chinese Historical Society of America, 1990), 4.

13. Lai Chun-Chuen, *Remarks of the Chinese Merchants of San Francisco, Upon Governor Bigler's Message* (San Francisco: Whitton, Towne, 1855), 3.

14. Lisa See, *On Gold Mountain: The One-Hundred-Year Odyssey of My Chinese-American Family* (New York: St. Martin's, 1995), 14–15.

15. On Chinese prostitution in America, see Benson Tong, *Unsubmissive Women: Chinese Prostitutes in Nineteenth-Century San Francisco* (Norman: University of Oklahoma Press, 1994).

16. The information in this and the next paragraph is from Takaki, "They Also Came," 4, 7–9.

17. *Littell's Living Age* (July 3, 1852): 33.

18. George Anthony Peffer, *If They Don't Bring Their Women Here: Chinese Female Immigration Before Exclusion* (Urbana: University of Illinois Press, 1999), 16–27; G. William Skinner, "Creolized Chinese Societies in Southeast Asia," in *Sojourners and Settlers: Histories of Southeast Asia and the Chinese*, ed. Anthony Reid (St. Leonard, Australia: Allen and Unwin, 1996), 51–93. On the sojourner mentality, see Wang Gungwu, *China and the Overseas Chinese* (Singapore: Times Academic, 1991), 3–21.

19. Adam McKeown, "Transnational Chinese Families and Chinese Exclusion, 1875–1943," *Journal of American Ethnic History* 18 (Winter 1999): 73–110.

20. Hsu, *Dreaming of Gold, Dreaming of Home*, 26.

21. The information in this and the next paragraph is from George Anthony Peffer, "Forbidden Families: Emigration Experiences of Chinese Women Under the Page Law, 1875–1882," *Journal of American Ethnic History* 6 (Fall 1986): 31; Karen J. Leong, "Gender, Race, and the 1875 Page Law," in *The Repeal and Its Legacy: Proceedings of the Conference on the 50th Anniversary of the Repeal of the Exclusion Acts* (San Francisco: Chinese Historical Society of America and Asian American Studies, San Francisco State University, 1994), 58–65.

22. The information in this and the next paragraph is from Robert J. Schwendinger, *Ocean of Bitter Dreams: Maritime Relations Between China and the United States, 1850–1915* (Tucson: Westernlore, 1988), 66–76, 121.

23. Marlon K. Hom, *Songs of Gold Mountain: Cantonese Rhymes From San Francisco Chinatown* (Berkeley: University of California Press, 1987), 161.

24. Huie Kin, *Reminiscences* (Peiping: San Yu, 1909), 24.

25. Him Mark Lai, Genny Lim, and Judy Yung, *Island: Poetry and History of Chinese Immigrants on Angel Island, 1910–1940* (San Francisco: Hoc Doi, 1986), 13.

26. Madeline Hsu, "Gold Mountain Dreams and Paper Son Schemes: Chinese Immigration Under Exclusion," in *Chinese America: History and Perspectives 1997* (San Francisco: Chinese Historical Society of America, 1997), 46–47, 51, 56–58; Wayne Wong, "Why Did I Live in Wichita for 65 Years?" unpublished autobiography, copy in author's possession; see, *On Gold Mountain*, 47–48.

27. Hsu, "Gold Mountain Dreams," 46–47, 51, 56–58; Tung Pok Chin with Winifred C. Chin, *Paper Son: One Man's Story* (Philadelphia: Temple University Press, 2000), 12.

28. Quoted in Sucheta Mazumdar, "In the Family," in *Linking Our Lives: Chinese American Women of Los Angeles* (Los Angeles: Chinese Historical Society of Southern California, 1984), 31.

29. Figures cited in Takaki, *Strangers From a Different Shore*, 238; Yung, *Unbound Feet*, 66.

30. Peggy Pascoe, "Race, Gender, and Intercultural Relations: The Case of Interracial Marriage," in *Writing the Range: Race, Class, and Culture in the Women's West*, ed. Elizabeth Jameson and Susan Armitage (Norman: University of Oklahoma Press, 1997), 71.

31. Peter C.Y. Leung, "When a Haircut Was a Luxury: A Chinese Farm Laborer in the Sacramento Delta," *California History* 64 (Summer 1985): 215–216.

32. Lucie Cheng and Suellen Cheng, "Chinese Women of Los Angeles: A Social Historical Survey," in *Linking Our Lives: Chinese American Women of Los Angeles* (Los Angeles: Chinese Historical Society of Southern California, 1984), 7–8.

33. The information in this and the next three paragraphs is from Huping Ling, "Family and Marriage of Late-Nineteenth- and Early-Twentieth-Century Chinese Immigrant Women," *Journal of American Ethnic History* 19 (Winter 2000): 43–63; Yung, *Unbound Feet*, 43–46.

34. John L. Fagan, "The Chinese Cannery Workers of Warrendale, Oregon, 1876–1930," in *Hidden Heritage: Historical Archaeology of the Overseas Chinese*, ed. Priscilla Wegars (Amityville, N.Y.: Baywood, 1993), 215–228; Priscilla Wegars, "Besides Polly Bemis: Historical and Artifactual Evidence for Chinese Women in the West, 1848–1930," in *Hidden Heritage*, ed. Wegars, 229–254; Roberta Greewood, "Chinatown in Ventura," in *Bridging the Centuries: History of Chinese Americans in Southern California* (Los Angeles: Chinese Historical Society of Southern California, 2001), 62–67.

35. Cheng and Cheng, "Chinese Women of Los Angeles," 8–9.

36. Benson Tong, "Asian American Girls," in *Girlhood in America: An Encyclopedia*, ed. Miriam Forman-Brunell, 2 vols. (Santa Barbara: ABC-Clio, 2001), 1:48–57; Lillian Lee Hom-Kim, "Fang H. Der, an Oral History From Baltimore, Maryland,"

in *Chinese America: History and Perspectives 1988* (San Francisco: Chinese Historical Society of America, 1988), 191.

37. Lawrence Michael Fong, "Sojourners and Settlers: The Chinese Experience in Arizona," in *Chinese on the American Frontier*, ed. Arif Dirlik (Lanham, Md.: Rowman and Littlefield, 2001), 51.

38. Ruthanne Lum McCunn, *Chinese American Portraits: Personal Histories, 1828–1988* (San Francisco: Chronicle, 1988), 79–87; Lucy M. Cohen, *Chinese in the Post–Civil War South: A People Without a History* (Baton Rouge: Louisiana State University Press, 1984), 170–171.

39. Quoted in McCunn, *Chinese American Portraits*, 83.

40. The information in this and the next paragraph is from Philip Gleason, "Americans All: World War II and the Shaping of American Identity," *Review of Politics* 43 (1981): 483–518.

41. Chinn, Lai, and Choy, *History of the Chinese in California*, 18.

42. Ku, "Kauai's Chinese," 53; Yau Sing Leong, "From Kwangtung to the Plantations, Farms, Stores, and Beyond," in *Sailing for the Sun: The Chinese in Hawaii 1789–1989*, ed. Arlene Lum (Honolulu: University of Hawai'i Center for Chinese Studies, 1988), 80–81.

43. Liping Zhu, "No Need to Rush: The Chinese, Placer Mining, and the Western Environment," *Montana: The Magazine of Western History* 49 (Autumn 1999): 42–57, figures on 45; Randall E. Rohe, "Chinese River Mining in the West," *Montana: The Magazine of Western History* 46 (Autumn 1996): 14–29.

44. Susan Lee Johnson, "'Domestic' Life in the Diggings: The Southern Mines in the California Gold Rush," in *Over the Edge: Remapping the American West*, ed. Valerie J. Matsumoto and Blake Allmendinger (Berkeley: University of California Press, 1999), 107–132; Randall E. Rohe, "After the Gold Rush: Chinese Mining in the Far West, 1850–1890," *Montana: The Magazine of Western History* 32 (Autumn 1980): 2–19; Lorraine Barker Hildebrand, *Straw Hats, Sandals, and Steel: The Chinese in Washington State* (Tacoma: Washington State American Revolution Bicentennial Commission, 1977), 14.

45. Chinn, Lai, and Choy, *History of the Chinese in California*, 36–41; Linda Bentz, "Chinese Fishing Activities in Southern California," in *Bridging the Centuries: History of Chinese Americans in Southern California* (Los Angeles: Chinese Historical Society of Southern California, 2001), 53, 55; Dolores K. Young, "The Seaweed Gatherers on the Central Coast of California," in *The Chinese in America: A History From Gold Mountain to the New Millennium*, ed. Susie Lan Cassel (Walnut Creek, Calif.: Altamira, 2002), 156–157.

46. Hildebrand, *Straw Hats*, 20; Judith Liu, "Birds of Passage: Chinese Occupations in San Diego, 1870–1900," in *Bridging the Centuries: History of Chinese Americans in Southern California* (Los Angeles: Chinese Historical Society of Southern California, 2001), 83; Sandy Lydon, *Chinese Gold: The Chinese in the Monterey Bay Region* (Capitola, Calif.: Capitola, 1985), 79–81; Edward J.M. Rhoads, "The Chinese in Texas," in *Chinese on the American Frontier*, ed. Arif Dirlik (Lanham, Md.: Rowman and Littlefield, 2001), 172.

47. The information in this and the next paragraph is from Sucheng Chan, "Introduction: The Significance of Locke in Chinese American History," in Jeff Gillenkirk

and James Motlow, *Bitter Melon: Stories From the Last Rural Chinese Town in America* (Seattle: University of Washington Press, 1987), 18–20. On Chinese contributions to California's agriculture, see Sucheng Chan, *This Bittersweet Soil: The Chinese in California Agriculture, 1860–1910* (Berkeley: University of California Press, 1986).

48. McCunn, *Chinese American Portraits*, 33–39, 89–91.

49. Lydon, *Chinese Gold*, 61–77; H. Vincent Moses and Brenda Buller Focht, "Life in Little Gom-Benn: Chinese Immigrant Society in Riverside, 1885–1930," in *Bridging the Centuries: History of Chinese Americans in Southern California* (Los Angeles: Chinese Historical Society of Southern California, 2001), 69; Jeff Gillenkirk and James Motlow, *Bitter Melon: Stories From the Last Rural Chinese Town in America* (Seattle: University of Washington Press, 1987), 16.

50. McCunn, *Chinese American Portraits*, 47–55.

51. On Chinese in the salmon-canning industry, see Chris Friday, *Organizing Asian American Labor: The Pacific Coast Canned-Salmon Industry, 1870–1942* (Philadelphia: Temple University Press, 1994); for other activities in the Pacific Northwest, see Hildebrand, *Straw Hats*, 41, 80–81; Ron Chew, *Reflections of Seattle's Chinese Americans: The First 100 Years* (Seattle: University of Washington Press and Wing Luke Asian Museum, 1994), 135–136.

52. On Chinese in the South, see Cohen, *Chinese in the Post–Civil War South*; George E. Pozzetta, "The Chinese Encounter With Florida, 1865–1920," in *Chinese America: History and Perspectives 1989* (San Francisco: Chinese Historical Society of America, 1989), 43–57.

53. Jung, "'Coolies' and Cane," 208, 540–550.

54. Frederick Rudolph, "Chinamen in Yankeedom: Anti-Unionism in Massachusetts in 1870," *American Historical Review* 53 (October 1947): 4, 8, 9; John Kuo Wei Tchen, "New York Chinese: The Nineteenth-Century Pre-Chinatown Settlement," in *Chinese America: History and Perspectives 1990* (San Francisco: Chinese Historical Society of America, 1990), 160–163, 168–173; K. Scott Wong, "'The Eagle Seeks a Helpless Quarry': Chinatown, the Police, and the Press—the 1903 Boston Chinatown Raid Revisited," *Amerasia Journal* 22, no. 3 (1996): 90.

55. Takaki, *Strangers From a Different Shore*, 87, 239; Robert S. Greenwood, *Down by the Station: Los Angeles Chinatown, 1880–1933* (Los Angeles: University of California Press, 1996), 12; Lydon, *Chinese Gold*, 181–184, 227–231, 290–295.

56. Edward Staski, "The Overseas Chinese in El Paso: Changing Goals, Changing Realities," in *Hidden Heritage: Historical Archaeology of the Overseas Chinese*, ed. Priscilla Wegars (Amityville, N.Y.: Baywood, 1993), 125–150; Sherri M. Gust, "Animal Bones From Historic Urban Chinese Sites: A Comparison of Sacramento, Woodland, Tucson, Ventura, and Lovelock," in *Hidden Heritage*, ed. Wegars, 177–214.

57. Sherri Gebert Fuller, "Mirrored Identities: The Moys of St. Paul," *Minnesota History* 57 (Winter 2000–2001): 168.

58. Paul M. Ong, "Chinese Labor in Early San Francisco: Racial Segmentation and Industrial Expansion," *Amerasia Journal* 8, no. 1 (1981): 69–92.

59. Yung, *Unbound Feet*, 295.

60. Ibid., 26; Hua Liang, "Living Between Two Worlds: Chinese American Women and Their Experiences in San Francisco and New York City, 1848–1945" (Ph.D. diss., University of Connecticut, Storrs, 1996), 163.

61. Huping Ling, *Surviving on the Gold Mountain: A History of Chinese American Women and Their Lives* (Albany: State University of New York Press, 1998), 52–61, 70–72; Hua Liang, "Living Between Two Worlds," 188, 191, 201–203; Yung, *Unbound Feet*, 83; Yen Le Espiritu, *Asian American Women and Men: Labor, Laws, and Love* (Thousand Oaks, Calif.: Sage, 1997), 34–37.

62. John Kuo Wei Tchen, *New York Before Chinatown: Orientalism and the Shaping of American Culture, 1776–1882* (Baltimore: Johns Hopkins University Press, 1999), 250–252. For a sociological study of the Chinese laundryman, see Paul C.P. Siu, *The Chinese Laundryman: A Study of Social Isolation*, ed. John Kuo Wei Tchen (New York: New York University Press, 1987).

63. Julie Courtwright, "A Slave to Yellow Peril: The 1886 Chinese Ouster Attempt in Wichita, Kansas," *Great Plains Quarterly* 22 (Winter 2002): 28, 31.

64. Gary Y. Okihiro, *Margins and Mainstreams: Asians in American History and Culture* (Seattle: University of Washington Press, 1994), xv.

65. Sucheng Chan, "A People of Exceptional Character: Ethnic Diversity, Nativism, and Racism in the California Gold Rush," *California History* 79 (Summer 2000): 77.

66. Luther W. Spoehr, "Sambo and the Heathen Chinee: Californians' Racial Stereotypes in the Late 1870s," *Pacific Historical Review* 42 (May 1973): 185–204; Quintard Taylor, *In Search of the Racial Frontier: African Americans in the American West, 1528–1990* (New York: W. W. Norton, 1998), 198; Albert S. Broussard, *Black San Francisco: The Struggle for Racial Equality in the West, 1900–1954* (Lawrence: University Press of Kansas, 1993), 15, 21.

67. The information in this and the next paragraph is from Philip S. Foner and Daniel Rosenberg, eds., *Racism, Dissent, and Asian Americans From 1850 to the Present: A Documentary History* (Westport, Conn.: Greenwood, 1993), 209–245.

68. Friday, *Organizing Asian American Labor*, 83, 85, 88–98.

69. Daniel D. Liestman, "Chinese and Indians: Interethnic Interface in the Nineteenth-Century West," in *The Repeal and Its Legacy: Proceedings of the Conference on the 50th Anniversary of the Repeal of the Exclusion Acts* (San Francisco: Chinese Historical Society of America and Asian American Studies, San Francisco State University, 1994), 160–168.

70. Taylor, *In Search of the Racial Frontier*, 227; Quintard Taylor, *The Forging of a Black Community: Seattle's Central District From 1870 Through the Civil Rights Era* (Seattle: University of Washington Press, 1994), 87, 115–116, 128.

71. Liestman, "Chinese and Indians," 160; Okihiro, *Margins and Mainstreams*, 59; Ling, "Family and Marriage," 57; Foner and Rosenberg, *Racism, Dissent, and Asian Americans*, 215–230.

72. Sucheng Chan, "The Exclusion of Chinese Women, 1870–1943," in *Entry Denied: Exclusion and the Chinese Community in America, 1882–1943*, ed. Sucheng Chan (Philadelphia: Temple University Press, 1991), 98–99.

73. Arlene Lum, "The Centenary Was Not a Time for Celebration," in *Sailing for the Sun: The Chinese in Hawaii 1789–1989* (Honolulu: University of Hawai'i Center for Chinese Studies, 1988), 119; Wickberg, *From China to Canada*, 46–51; Kay J. Anderson, *Vancouver's Chinatown: Racial Discourse in Canada, 1875–1980* (Montreal: McGill–Queen's University Press, 1991), 47–48.

74. The information in this and the next paragraph is from Lucy E. Salyer, *Laws Harsh as Tigers: Chinese Immigrants and the Shaping of Modern Immigration Law* (Chapel Hill: University of North Carolina Press, 1995), 13; Charles J. McClain and Laurence Wu McClain, "The Chinese Contribution to the Development of American Law," in *Entry Denied: Exclusion and the Chinese Community in America, 1882–1943*, ed. Sucheng Chan (Philadelphia: Temple University Press, 1991), 8–13; Greenwood, *Down by the Station*, 11.

75. McClain and McClain, "Chinese Contribution," 12.

76. Ibid.

77. Greewood, "Chinatown in Ventura," 64; Lydon, *Chinese Gold*, 187, 242, 295.

78. Quoted in Lydon, *Chinese Gold*, 135.

79. Okihiro, *Margins and Mainstreams*, 119–120, 123–124.

80. The information in this and the next two paragraphs is from Tchen, *New York Before Chinatown*, xx–xxii, 22, 40, 56–59, 97–130.

81. Ronald T. Takaki, *Iron Cages: Race and Culture in Nineteenth-Century America* (Seattle: University of Washington Press, 1979), 219–221; David Palumbo-Liu, *Asian/American: Historical Crossing of a Racial Frontier* (Stanford: Stanford University Press, 1999), 35–36.

82. Salyer, *Laws Harsh as Tigers*, 9–10.

83. Takaki, *Iron Cages*, 216–224.

84. The information in this and the next paragraph is from Victor Low, *The Unimpressible Race: A Century of Educational Struggle by the Chinese in San Francisco* (San Francisco: East/West, 1982), 10–73, 92–132, quote on 10; see also Joyce Kuo, "Excluded, Segregated, and Forgotten: A Historical View of the Discrimination Against Chinese Americans in Public Schools," in *Chinese America: History and Perspectives 2000* (San Francisco: Chinese Historical Society of America, 2000), 32–48.

85. The information in this and the next paragraph is from Alexander Saxton, *The Indispensable Enemy: Labor and the Anti-Chinese Movement in California* (Berkeley: University of California Press, 1971), 113–137, 261–265.

86. Xinyang Wang, "Economic Opportunity, Artisan Leadership, and Immigrant Workers' Labor Militancy: Italian and Chinese Workers in New York City, 1890–1970," *Labor History* 37 (Fall 1996): 486; Tchen, *New York Before Chinatown*, 179–190.

87. See Alexander Saxton, *The Rise and Fall of the White Republic: Class Politics and Mass Culture in Nineteenth-Century America* (London: Verso, 1990).

88. See Andrew Gyory, *Closing the Gate: Race, Politics, and the Chinese Exclusion Act* (Chapel Hill: University of North Carolina Press, 1998).

89. William Wei, "The Anti-Chinese Movement in Colorado: Interethnic Competition and Conflict on the Eve of Exclusion," in *Chinese America: History and Perspectives 1995* (San Francisco: Chinese Historical Society of America, 1995), 184–186.

90. Edward J.M. Rhoads, "'White Labor' vs. 'Coolie Labor': The 'Chinese Question' in Pennsylvania in the 1870s," *Journal of American Ethnic History* 21 (Winter 2002): 3–32.

91. Robert G. Lee, *Orientals: Asian Americans in Popular Culture* (Philadelphia: Temple University Press, 1999), 67–70.

92. Matthew Frye Jacobson, *Whiteness of a Different Color: European Immigrants and the Alchemy of Race* (Cambridge: Harvard University Press, 1998), quote on 74.

93. Ibid., 68–75, 161.

94. Information in this and the next two paragraphs is from Charles J. McClain, *In Search of Equality: The Chinese Struggle Against Discrimination in Nineteenth-Century America* (Berkeley: University of California Press, 1994), 18–25, quote on 22.

95. For information on Chinese in Idaho, see Liping Zhu, *A Chinaman's Chance: The Chinese on the Rocky Mountain Mining Frontier* (Niwot: University Press of Colorado, 1997), 133–140.

96. The information in this and the next two paragraphs is from McClain, *In Search of Equality*, 70–76, 104–105, 115–119.

97. Shirley Hune, "Politics of Exclusion: Legislative-Executive Conflict, 1876–1882," *Amerasia Journal* 9, no. 1 (1982): 5–27.

98. Shih-shan Henry Tsai, *China and the Overseas Chinese in the United States, 1868–1911* (Fayetteville: University of Arkansas Press, 1983), 53–59.

99. Linda Pomerantz, "The Chinese Bourgeoisie and the Anti-Chinese Movement in the United States, 1850–1905," *Amerasia Journal* 11, no. 1 (1984): 13.

100. The information in this and the next paragraph is from Salyer, *Laws Harsh as Tigers*, 16–18.

101. The information in this and the next paragraph is from Erika Lee, "At America's Gates: Chinese Immigration During the Exclusion Era, 1882–1943" (Ph.D. diss., University of California, Berkeley, 1998), 97–98, 107–108, 110, 112–113, 115–116, 136, 139–140.

102. Wickberg, *From China to Canada*, 50, 57; Lum, "Centenary," 119; Dye, *Merchant Prince*, 214, 217–218.

103. Christian G. Fritz, "Due Process, Treaty Rights, and Chinese Exclusion, 1882–1891," in *Entry Denied: Exclusion and the Chinese Community in America, 1882–1943*, ed. Sucheng Chan (Philadelphia: Temple University Press, 1991), 27, 32–40; Salyer, *Laws Harsh as Tigers*, 20.

104. Michele Shover, "Fighting Back: The Chinese Influence on Chico Law and Politics, 1880–1886," *California History* 74 (Winter 1995–1996): 409–421, 449–450; Michele Shover, "Chico Women: Nemesis of a Rural Town's Anti-Chinese Campaigns 1876–1888," *California History* 67 (December 1988): 233; Courtwright, "Slave to Yellow Peril," 25–30; Rhoads, "Chinese in Texas," 175.

105. Quoted in Hildebrand, *Straw Hats*, 51.

106. Clayton D. Laurie, "Civil Disorder and the Military in Rock Springs, Wyoming: The Army's Role in the 1885 Chinese Massacre," *Montana: The Magazine of Western History* 40 (Summer 1990): 49, 51–54.

107. Dye, *Merchant Prince*, 216; Victor Jew, "Exploring New Frontiers in Chinese American History: The Anti-Chinese Riot in Milwaukee, 1889," in *The Chinese in America: A History From Gold Mountain to the New Millennium*, ed. Susie Lan Cassel (Walnut Creek, Calif.: Altamira, 2002), 77–90.

108. Fritz, "Due Process," 46–48.

109. Salyer, *Laws Harsh as Tigers*, 24–26.

110. McClain, *In Search of Equality*, 202–203.

111. Salyer, *Laws Harsh as Tigers*, 46.

112. McClain, *In Search of Equality*, 203–213; ibid., 57–58; Yung, *Unbound Feet*, 294.

113. Bruce Edward Hall, *Tea That Burns: A Family Memoir of Chinatown* (New York: Free Press, 1998), 98–99.

114. Bentz, "Chinese Fishing Activities," 56; Lydon, *Chinese Gold*, 219.

115. The information in this and the next three paragraphs is from Salyer, *Laws Harsh as Tigers*, 57, 81, 98–99; McClain and McClain, "Chinese Contribution," 18; Fritz, "Due Process," 46, 49; Lee, "At America's Gates," 192–194.

116. John R. Wunder, "*Territory of New Mexico v. Yee Shun* (1882): A Turning Point in Chinese Legal Relationships in the Trans-Mississippi West," in *Chinese on the American Frontier*, ed. Arif Dirlik (Lanham, Md.: Rowman and Littlefield, 2001), 153–164.

117. Zhu, *Chinaman's Chance*, 143.

118. The information in this and the next paragraph is from Xiaojian Zhao, *Remaking Chinese America: Immigration, Family, and Community, 1940–1965* (New Brunswick: Rutgers University Press, 2002), 10–14; Chan, "Exclusion of Chinese Women," 114–127.

119. Mae M. Ngai, "The Architecture of Race in American Immigration Law: A Reexamination of the Immigration Act of 1924," *Journal of American History* 86 (June 1999): 69–70, 80–88, 92.

120. Zhao, *Remaking Chinese America*, 15–17.

121. Chinn, Lai, and Choy, *History of the Chinese in California*, 46; Rhoads, "Chinese in Texas," 168; Cohen, *Chinese in the Post–Civil War South*, 94.

122. Daniel D. Liestman, "Chinese Labor at the Passaic Steam Laundry in Belleville," *New Jersey History* 112 (Spring–Summer 1994): 30; Edward J.M. Rhoads, "Asian Pioneers in the Eastern United States: Chinese Cutlery Workers in Beaver Falls, Pennsylvania, in the 1880s," *Journal of Asian American Studies* 2, no. 2 (1999): 132; Chan, *Bittersweet Soil*, 332–333; Friday, *Organizing Asian American Labor*, 85–86.

123. Takaki, *Pau Hana*, 147–150.

124. Yuji Ichioka, "Japanese Immigrant Labor Contractors and the Northern Pacific and the Great Northern Railroad Companies, 1898–1907," *Labor History* 21, no. 3 (1980): 325–350; Wang, "Economic Opportunity," 485; Saxton, *Indispensable Enemy*, 217–218.

125. Yong Chen, *Chinese San Francisco, 1850–1943: A Trans-Pacific Community* (Stanford: Stanford University Press, 2000), 126.

126. The information in this and the next two paragraphs is from ibid., 127–140.

127. Yung, *Unbound Feet*, 293.

128. Ibid., 303.

CHAPTER 3

1. Salyer, *Laws Harsh as Tigers*, 111–114; Wong, " 'The Eagle Seeks a Helpless Quarry,' " 96–97.

2. The information in this and the next two paragraphs is from L. Eve Armentrout Ma, *Revolutionaries, Monarchists, and Chinatowns: Chinese Politics in the Americas and the 1911 Revolution* (Honolulu: University of Hawai'i Press, 1990), 1–40, 100–113,

139–140; "Nationalism in China: Consequences in Hawaii," in *Sailing for the Sun: The Chinese in Hawaii 1789–1989*, ed. Arlene Lum (Honolulu: University of Hawai'i Center for Chinese Studies, 1988), 103–105.

3. On China-centered nationalism in Southeast Asia, see Victor Purcell, *The Chinese in Southeast Asia*, 2d ed. (London: Oxford University Press, 1965).

4. L. Eve Armentrout Ma, "Chinatown Organizations and the Anti-Chinese Movement, 1882–1914," in *Entry Denied: Exclusion and the Chinese Community in America, 1882–1943*, ed. Sucheng Chan (Philadelphia: Temple University Press, 1991), 155–156.

5. The information in this and the next four paragraphs is from Him Mark Lai, "Historical Development of the Chinese Consolidated Benevolent Association/ *Huiguan* System," in *Chinese America: History and Perspectives 1987* (San Francisco: Chinese Historical Society of America, 1987), 16–31; Ma, "Chinatown Organizations and the Anti-Chinese Movement, 1882–1914," 148–150, 154–155; Him Mark Lai, "Retention of the Chinese Heritage: Chinese Schools in America Before World War II," in *Chinese America: History and Perspectives 2000* (San Francisco: Chinese Historical Society of America, 2000), 15; Glick, *Sojourners and Settlers*, 201–208, 212, 231–235.

6. The information in this and the next six paragraphs is from Renqui Yu, *To Save China, to Save Ourselves: The Chinese Hand Laundry Alliance of New York* (Philadelphia: Temple University Press, 1992), 12–15, 30; Shih-shan Henry Tsai, *The Chinese Experience in America* (Bloomington: Indiana University Press, 1986), 53–54; Ma, *Revolutionaries, Monarchists, and Chinatowns*, 23–24.

7. On Chinese Christians, see Welesy Woo, "Chinese Protestants in the San Francisco Bay Area," in *Entry Denied: Exclusion and the Chinese Community in America, 1882–1943*, ed. Sucheng Chan (Philadelphia: Temple University Press, 1991), 213–245; Timothy Tseng, "Chinese Protestant Nationalism in the United States, 1880–1927," *Amerasia Journal* 22, no. 1 (1996): 31–56; Timothy Tseng, "Chinese Protestant Nationalism in the United States, 1880–1927," in *New Spiritual Homes: Religion and Asian Americans*, ed. David K. Yoo (Honolulu: University of Hawai'i Press, 1999), 19–51.

8. Tseng, "Chinese Protestant Nationalism," 20; Woo, "Chinese Protestants," 238.

9. McClain, *In Search of Equality*, 237.

10. The information in this and the next two paragraphs is from Delber L. McKee, "The Chinese Boycott of 1905–1906 Reconsidered: The Role of Chinese Americans," *Pacific Historical Review* 55 (May 1986): 168–189; Tsai, *China and the Overseas Chinese*, 105, 108.

11. The information in this and the next eight paragraphs is from Sue Fawn Chung, "Fighting for Their American Rights: A History of the Chinese American Citizens Alliance," in *Claiming America: Constructing Chinese American Identities During the Exclusion Era*, ed. K. Scott Wong and Sucheng Chan (Philadelphia: Temple University Press, 1998), 98–109; Qingsong Zhang, "The Origins of the Chinese Americanization Movement: Wong Chin Foo and the Chinese Equal Rights League," in *Claiming America*, ed. Wong and Chan, 41–54; Yung, *Unbound Feet*, 157, 168; Zhao, *Remaking Chinese America*, 17–20.

12. Zhao, *Remaking Chinese America*, 21.

13. Quoted in Chung, "Fighting for Their American Rights," 115, 116.

14. McKee, "Chinese Boycott," 187; Ma, *Revolutionaries, Monarchists, and Chinatowns*, 114.

15. Ma, "Chinatown Organizations," 159–160.

16. The information in this and the next paragraph is from Shehong Chen, *Being Chinese, Becoming Chinese American* (Urbana: University of Illinois Press, 2002), 9–42.

17. Ibid., 27.

18. Hua Liang, "Fighting for a New Life: Social and Patriotic Activism of Chinese American Women in New York City, 1900–1945," *Journal of American Ethnic History* 17 (Winter 1998): 23–27.

19. The information in this and the next five paragraphs is from Chen, *Being Chinese*, 43–156.

20. The information in this and the next paragraph is from Tseng, "Chinese Protestant Nationalism," 34–36; Chen, *Being Chinese*, 157–168.

21. Philip P. Choy, "The Architecture of San Francisco's Chinatown," in *Chinese America: History and Perspectives 1990* (San Francisco: Chinese Historical Society of America, 1990), 42–49.

22. Nayan Shah, *Contagious Divides: Epidemics and Race in San Francisco's Chinatown* (Berkeley: University of California Press, 2001), 127–129; Anderson, *Vancouver's Chinatown*, 84–85.

23. Choy, "Architecture of San Francisco's Chinatown," 49.

24. Anderson, *Vancouver's Chinatown*, 86–88, 156–158.

25. Ruby Ling Louie, "Reliving China City," in *Bridging the Centuries: History of Chinese Americans in Southern California* (Los Angeles: Chinese Historical Society of Southern California, 2001), 38–43; Suellen Cheng and Munson Kwok, "The Golden Years of Los Angeles Chinatown: The Beginning," in *Bridging the Centuries: History of Chinese Americans in Southern California* (Los Angeles: Chinese Historical Society of Southern California, 2001), 32–37.

26. Arthur Bonner, *Alas! What Brought Thee Hither? The Chinese in New York, 1800–1950* (Cranbury, N.J.: Associated University Presses, 1997), 97, 102, 105, 107, 110–112; Lorraine Dong, "The Forbidden City Legacy and Its Chinese American Women," in *Chinese America: History and Perspectives 1992* (San Francisco: Chinese Historical Society of America, 1992), 125–148.

27. Ivan Light, "From Vice District to Tourist Attraction: The Moral Career of American Chinatowns, 1880–1940," *Pacific Historical Review* 43 (August 1974): 382, 387, 389–390.

28. Diane Mei Lin Mark and Ginger Chih, *A Place Called Chinese America* (San Francisco: Organization of Chinese Americans, 1982), 51; *Chinese Digest* cited in K. Scott Wong, "War Comes to Chinatown: Social Transformation and the Chinese of California," in *The Way We Really Were: The Golden State in the Second Great War,* ed. Roger W. Lotchin (Urbana: University of Illinois Press, 2000), 170.

29. See Greenwood, *Down by the Station*.

30. Takaki, *Strangers From a Different Shore*, 239.

31. Kit King Louis, "A Study of American-Born and American-Reared Chinese in Los Angeles" (Master's thesis, University of Southern California, Los Angeles, 1931), 109.

32. Betty Lee Sung, *Mountain of Gold: The Story of the Chinese in America* (New York: Macmillan, 1967), 143–144.

33. Ching Chao Wu, "Chinatowns: A Study of Symbiosis and Assimilation" (Ph.D. diss., University of Chicago, 1928), 86–93.

34. Espiritu, *Asian American Women and Men*, 29–30; Yung, *Unbound Feet*, 87–89.

35. Him Mark Lai, "Chinese Regional Solidarity: Case Study of the Hua Xian (Fah Yuen) Community in California," in *Chinese America: History and Perspectives 1994* (San Francisco: Chinese Historical Society of America, 1994), 31, 47; Chan, "Significance of Locke," 23; Lydon, *Chinese Gold*, 30.

36. Cited in Takaki, *Strangers From a Different Shore*, 252–253.

37. Peter Kwong, *Chinatown, New York: Labor and Politics, 1930–1950* (New York: Monthly Review, 1979), 61; Yu, *To Save China*, 8.

38. Sin Jang Leung, "A Laundryman Sings the Blues," trans. Marlon K. Hom, in *Chinese America: History and Perspectives 1991* (San Francisco: Chinese Historical Society of America, 1991), 13, 15.

39. The information in this and the next five paragraphs is from Kwong, *Chinatown, New York*, 62–66, 121–124; Him Mark Lai, "To Bring Forth a New China, to Build a Better America: The Chinese Marxist Left in America to the 1960s," in *Chinese America: History and Perspectives 1992* (San Francisco: Chinese Historical Society of America, 1992), 20–26.

40. Yung, *Unbound Feet*, 180–184, 188–189.

41. Him Mark Lai, "The Kuomintang in Chinese American Communities Before World War II," in *Entry Denied: Exclusion and the Chinese Community in America, 1882–1943*, ed. Sucheng Chan (Philadelphia: Temple University Press, 1991), 191, 195–196; Him Mark Lai, "China and the Chinese American Community: The Political Dimension," in *Chinese America: History and Perspectives 1999* (San Francisco: Chinese Historical Society of America, 1999), 5; Kwong, *Chinatown, New York*, 122–123.

42. Yu, *To Save China*, 56–71.

43. Glick, *Sojourners and Settlers*, 305.

44. Ibid., 305–306; Wong, "War Comes to Chinatown," 178–179.

45. Wong, "War Comes to Chinatown," 178–179; Lai, "Retention of the Chinese Heritage," 14; Zhao, *Remaking Chinese America*, 102.

46. Yung, *Unbound Feet*, 229–245; Helen Lew, "Katherine Sui Fung Cheung, Pioneer Aviatrix," in *Bridging the Centuries: History of Chinese Americans in Southern California* (Los Angeles: Chinese Historical Society of Southern California, 2001), 95–96; Hua Liang, "Living Between Two Worlds," 28–35.

47. Eiichiro Azuma, "Interethnic Conflict Under Racial Subordination: Japanese Immigrants and Their Asian Neighbors in Walnut Grove, California, 1908–1941," *Amerasia Journal* 20, no. 2 (1994): 27–56.

48. William F. Wu, *The Yellow Peril: Chinese Americans in American Fiction, 1850–1940* (Hamden, Conn.: Archon, 1982), 164–174; Julie Shuk-yee Lam, "The Chinese Digest, 1935–1940," in *Chinese America: History and Perspectives 1989* (San Francisco: Chinese Historical Society of America, 1989), 119–137; quote in *Chinese Digest* (November 15, 1935): 8.

49. *Chinese Digest* (November 15, 1935): 8.

50. William Hoy, "Reviews and Comments," *Chinese Digest* (June 26, 1936): 10.

51. Okihiro, *Margins and Mainstreams*, 143–144.

52. Gloria H. Chun, "'Go West . . . to China': Chinese American Identity in the 1930s," in *Claiming America: Constructing Chinese American Identities During the Exclusion Era*, ed. K. Scott Wong and Sucheng Chan (Philadelphia: Temple University Press, 1998), 169–170.

53. Yung, *Unbound Feet*, 226.

54. Chin, *Paper Son*, 50.

55. Sucheng Chan, "Race, Ethnic Culture, and Gender in the Construction of Identities Among Second-Generation Chinese Americans," in *Claiming America: Constructing Chinese American Identities During the Exclusion Era*, ed. K. Scott Wong and Sucheng Chan (Philadelphia: Temple University Press, 1998), 131–133, quote on 132.

56. Joel S. Frank, "Chinese Americans and American Sports, 1880–1940," in *Chinese America: History and Perspectives 1996* (San Francisco: Chinese Historical Society of America, 1996), 133, 144.

57. Chan, "Race, Ethnic Culture, and Gender," 142–144, 150.

58. "Interview with Flora Belle Jan, Daughter of Proprietor of the 'Yet Far Low' Chop Suey Restaurant, Tulare St. and China Alley, Fresno," Survey of Race Relations Collection, Hoover Institution on War, Revolution, and Peace, n.d., Stanford University.

59. McCunn, *Chinese American Portraits*, 121; see also Eleanor Wong Telamaque, *It's Crazy to Stay Chinese in Minnesota* (Nashville: Thomas Nelson, 1978).

60. Chan, "Race, Ethnic Culture, and Gender," 139–141.

61. Dong, "Forbidden City Legacy."

62. Victoria Wong, "Square and Circle Club: Women in the Public Sphere," in *Chinese America: History and Perspectives 1994* (San Francisco: Chinese Historical Society of America, 1994), 127–153; Cheng and Cheng, "Chinese Women of Los Angeles," 27–28.

63. Chan, "Race, Ethnic Culture, and Gender," 138, 144.

64. Yung, *Unbound Feet*, 129.

65. Louise Leung Larson, *Sweet Bamboo: A Memoir of a Chinese American Family* (Berkeley: University of California Press, 2001), 71.

66. Gloria Heyung Chun, *Of Orphans and Warriors: Inventing Chinese American Culture and Identity* (New Brunswick: Rutgers University Press, 2000), 19–20.

67. Henry Yu, *Thinking Orientals: Migration, Contact, and Exoticism in Modern America* (New York: Oxford University Press, 2001), 19–79.

68. Chun, "Go West," 167, 173.

69. Mark and Chih, *A Place Called Chinese America*, 88–89.

70. Chan, "Race, Ethnic Culture, and Gender," 155.

71. Wong, "War Comes to Chinatown," 170.

72. Yung, *Unbound Feet*, 133–146; Judy Chu and Susie Ling, "At Work," in *Linking Our Lives: Chinese American Women of Los Angeles* (Los Angeles: Chinese Historical Society of California, 1984), 66.

73. Chu and Ling, "At Work," 86.

74. The information in this and the next two paragraphs is from Chun, "Go West," 172, 174–176.

75. W.E.B. Dubois, *The Souls of Black Folk* (New York: Fawcett, 1961), 15.

76. The information in this and the next eight paragraphs is from Zhao, *Remaking Chinese America*, 30–46.

77. Shirley Hune, "Situating Sweet Bamboo in Chinese American History," in Lousie Leung Larson, *Sweet Bamboo: A Memoir of a Chinese American Family* (Berkeley: University of California Press, 2001), vii–xviii.

78. See Hsu, *Dreaming of Gold*, 4, 17–18, 34–40, 45–49, 124–125, 156–158.

79. Liisa Maalki, "National Geographic: The Rooting of Peoples and the Territorialization of National Identity Among Scholars and Refugees," *Cultural Anthropology* 7, no. 1 (1991): 27; quoted in ibid., 4.

80. "How to Tell Your Friends From the Japs," *Time* (December 22, 1941): 33.

81. "Growing up Chinese in Los Angeles: Eugene Moy," in *Bridging the Centuries: History of Chinese Americans in Southern California* (Los Angeles: Chinese Historical Society of California, 2001), 127.

82. Yung, *Unbound Feet*, 250.

83. William F. Strobridge, "In the Beginning . . . ," in *Duty and Honor: A Tribute to Chinese American World War II Veterans of Southern California*, ed. Marjorie Lee (Los Angeles: Chinese Historical Society of Southern California, 1998), 3.

84. Munson A. Kwok and Suellen Cheng, "Americanization of Chinese Angelenos," in *Duty and Honor: A Tribute to Chinese American World War II Veterans of Southern California*, ed. Marjorie Lee (Los Angeles: Chinese Historical Society of Southern California, 1998), 16; Hall, *Tea That Burns*, 185.

85. K. Scott Wong, "Meaning of the Military for Chinese Americans During WWII," in *Duty and Honor: A Tribute to Chinese American World War II Veterans of Southern California*, ed. Marjorie Lee (Los Angeles: Chinese Historical Society of Southern California, 1998), 8–9.

86. Wong, "War Comes to Chinatown," 174–176.

87. Chin, *Paper Son*, xviii, 45.

88. The information in this and the next paragraph is from Zhao, *Remaking Chinese America*, 66; Marjorie Lee, "Coming of Age: Chinese American Women Doing Their Part," in *Duty and Honor: A Tribute to Chinese American World War II Veterans of Southern California*, ed. Marjorie Lee (Los Angeles: Chinese Historical Society of Southern California, 1998), 54–55; Wong, "War Comes to Chinatown," 172.

89. Espiritu, *Asian American Women and Men*, 51–52; Wong, "War Comes to Chinatown," 171.

90. Victor G. Nee and Brett de Bary Nee, *Longtime Californ': A Documentary Study of an American Chinatown* (New York: Pantheon, 1973), 154.

91. Lee, "Coming of Age," 52.

92. Lani Ah Tye Farkas, *Bury My Bones in America: The Saga of a Chinese Family in California 1852–1996: From San Francisco to the Sierra Gold Mines* (Nevada City, Calif.: Carl Mautz, 1998), 118.

93. Takaki, *Strangers From a Different Shore*, 377–378.

94. L. Ling-chi Wang, "Politics of the Repeal of the Chinese Exclusion Laws," in *The Repeal and Its Legacy: Proceedings of the Conference on the 50th Anniversary of the*

Repeal of the Exclusion Acts (San Francisco: Chinese Historical Society of America and Asian American Studies, San Francisco State University, 1994), 68–69.

95. Ibid.; Helen Chen, "Chinese Immigration Into the United States: An Analysis of Changes in Immigration Policies" (Ph.D. diss., Brandeis University, Waltham, Mass., 1980), 117; Lorraine Dong, "Song Meiling in America 1943," in *The Repeal and Its Legacy: Proceedings of the Conference on the 50th Anniversary of the Repeal of the Exclusion Acts* (San Francisco: Chinese Historical Society of America and Asian American Studies, San Francisco State University, 1994), 39–46.

96. Zhao, *Remaking Chinese America*, 197; John Hayakawa Torok, " 'Interest Convergence' and the Liberalization of Discriminatory Immigration and Naturalization Laws Affecting Asians, 1943–1965," in *Chinese America: History and Perspectives 1995* (San Francisco: Chinese Historical Society of America, 1995), 8–9.

97. Torok, " 'Interest Convergence,' " 8–9.

98. Wang, "Politics of the Repeal," 70.

CHAPTER 4

1. Mely Giok-lan Tan, *The Chinese in the United States: Social Mobility and Assimilation* (Taipei: Orient Cultural Service, 1971), 40.

2. Sung, *Mountain of Gold*, 241.

3. Sucheng Chan, *Asian Americans: An Interpretive History* (Boston: Twayne, 1991), 121.

4. Ibid., 122; Judy Yung, *Chinese Women of America: A Pictorial History* (Seattle: University of Washington Press, 1986), 67; Esther Ngan-ling Chow, "Family, Economy, and the State: A Legacy of Struggle for Chinese American Women," in *Origins and Destinies: Immigration, Race, and Ethnicity in America*, ed. Silvia Pedraza and Rubén G. Rumbaut (Belmont, Calif.: Wadsworth, 1996), 119.

5. The information in this and the next paragraph is from Rose Hum Lee, *The Chinese in the United States of America* (Hong Kong: Hong Kong University Press, 1960), 65–68, 262–266.

6. Chew, *Reflections*, 147–148.

7. Lee, *Chinese in the United States*, 65–68, 262–266; Sung, *Mountain of Gold*, 144.

8. Roger Daniels, *Asian America: Chinese and Japanese in the United States Since 1850* (Seattle: University of Washington Press, 1988), 315.

9. Lee, *Chinese in the United States*, 14; Chinn, Lai, and Choy, *History of the Chinese in California*, 28; Zhao, *Remaking Chinese America*, 82.

10. The information in this and the next two paragraphs is from Zhao, *Remaking Chinese America*, 86–88, 91–92.

11. Computations based on tables in Yung, *Unbound Feet*, 293, 295–296.

12. Daniels, *Asian America*, 190–191; Chen, "Chinese Immigration," 203; Tan, *Chinese in the United States*, 43.

13. Wang Gungwu, "Upgrading the Migrant: Neither Huaqiao or Huaren," in *Chinese America: History and Perspectives 1996* (San Francisco: Chinese Historical Society of America, 1996), 1–18.

14. See Gleason, "Americans All," 483–518.

15. The information in this and the next two paragraphs is from Bill Ong Hing, *Making and Remaking Asian America Through Immigration Policy, 1850–1990* (Stanford:

Stanford University Press, 1993), 37–38; Roger Daniels, "United States Policy Towards Asian Immigrants: Contemporary Developments in Historical Perspective," in *New American Destinies: A Reader in Contemporary Asian and Latino Immigration*, ed. Darrell Y. Hamamoto and Rodolfo D. Torres (New York: Routledge, 1997), 78; Kwong, *Chinatown, New York*, 144.

16. Daniels, "United States Policy," 78; Hing, *Making and Remaking Asian America*, 37–38.

17. Hing, *Making and Remaking Asian America*, 37–38.

18. Reed Ueda, *Postwar Immigrant America: A Social History* (Boston: Bedford, 1994), 43–44.

19. Christina Lim and Sheldon Lim, "VFW Chinatown Eastbay Post #3956: A Story of the Fight for Non-quota Immigration in the Postwar Period," *Amerasia Journal* 24, no. 1 (1998): 59–83.

20. Rubén G. Rumbaut, "Origins and Destinies: Immigration to the United States Since World War II," in *New American Destinies: A Reader in Contemporary Asian and Latino Immigration*, ed. Darrell Y. Hamamoto and Rodolfo D. Torres (New York: Routledge, 1997), 20.

21. Min Zhou, *Chinatown: The Socioeconomic Potential of an Urban Enclave* (Philadelphia: Temple University Press, 1992), 64–65; Gillenkirk and Motlow, *Bitter Melon*, 43, 49.

22. The information in this and the next paragraph is from Chinn, Lai, and Choy, *History of the Chinese in California*, 29; Yung, *Unbound Feet*, 295; Daniels, "United States Policy," 79–80; Daniels, *Asian America*, 306; Tan, *Chinese in the United States*, 42–58.

23. Tan, *Chinese in the United States*, 83.

24. Ibid., 43, 46, 50–51, 83.

25. Ibid., 57–58.

26. Ibid., 83; Sung, *Mountain of Gold*, 252.

27. See Peter Kwong, *The New Chinatown*, 2d ed. (New York: Hill and Wang, 1996).

28. Ibid., 59–60.

29. Yung, *Chinese Women of America*, 82.

30. Chalsa M. Loo, *Chinatown: Most Time, Hard Time* (New York: Praeger, 1991), 49–50.

31. Lorraine Yee, "The Greatest Generation: Lorraine Yee," in *Bridging the Centuries: History of Chinese Americans in Southern California* (Los Angeles: Chinese Historical Society of America, 2001), 105; Sam Sue, "Growing up in Mississippi," in *Asian Americans: Oral Histories of First to Fourth Generation Americans From China, the Philippines, Japan, India, the Pacific Islands, Vietnam, and Cambodia*, ed. Joann Faung Jean Lee (New York: New Press, 1992), 7.

32. Loo, *Chinatown*, 61–62.

33. Kwong, *New Chinatown*, 22, 62–63.

34. Rose Hum Lee, "The Recent Immigrant Chinese Families of the San Francisco–Oakland Area," *Marriage and Family Living* 18 (February 1956): 16; J. E. Conant, "The Other Face of Chinatown," *San Francisco Examiner* (August 14, 1967): 1.

35. Loo, *Chinatown*, 69.

36. Ibid., 62; Zhou, *Chinatown*, 5, 85–86.

37. Yung, *Chinese Women of America*, 81.

38. Ibid.

39. Ibid., 80.

40. Espiritu, *Asian American Women and Men*, 57–58.

41. The information in this and the next two paragraphs is from ibid.; Lee, "Recent Chinese Immigrant Families," 20, 23; Stanford M. Lyman, *Chinese Americans* (New York: Random House, 1974), 123; Zhou, *Chinatown*, 166.

42. Lyman, *Chinese Americans*, 158–164.

43. Low, *Unimpressible Race*, 134–135.

44. The information in this and the next paragraph is from ibid., 134–135, 142–144.

45. Betty Ann Bruno, "Never Rebecca of Sunnybrook Farm," in *Asian Americans: Oral Histories of First to Fourth Generation Americans From China, the Philippines, Japan, India, the Pacific Islands, Vietnam, and Cambodia*, ed. Joann Faung Jean Lee (New York: New Press, 1992), 208–215, quote on 214.

46. Ben Fong-Torres, *The Rice Room: Growing up Chinese American—From Number Two Son to Rock 'n' Roll* (New York: Hyperion, 1994), 75.

47. Bruno, "Never Rebecca of Sunnybrook Farm," 212.

48. Fong-Torres, *Rice Room*, 6.

49. The information in this and the next four paragraphs is from Chun, *Of Orphans and Warriors*, 71–92, quote on 76.

50. The information in this and the next paragraph is from Zhao, *Remaking Chinese America*, 107–124.

51. Charles Choy Wong and Kenneth Klein, "False Papers, Lost Lives," in *Origins and Destinations: 41 Essays on Chinese America*, ed. Chinese Historical Society of Southern California and UCLA Asian American Studies Center (Los Angeles: Chinese Historical Society of Southern California and UCLA Asian American Studies Center, 1994), 355–374.

52. Mae M. Ngai, "Legacies of Exclusion: Illegal Chinese Immigration During the Cold War Years," *Journal of American Ethnic History* 18 (Fall 1998): 3–4.

53. The information in this and the next four paragraphs is from ibid., 3–35; Zhao, *Remaking Chinese America*, 162–172; Daniels, *Asian America*, 307–309; Jack Chen, *The Chinese of America* (San Francisco: Harper and Row, 1980), 215.

54. Ngai, "Legacies of Exclusion," 22.

55. Zhao, *Remaking Chinese America*, 171, 177.

56. Hing, *Making and Remaking Asian America*, 75.

57. The information in this and the next six paragraphs is from Lai, "To Bring Forth a New China," 43–52; Kwong, *Chinatown, New York*, 141–142; Chen, *Chinese of America*, 214; Chin, *Paper Son*, xvi–xvii, 74–75.

58. Lai, "Kuomintang," 197; Chen, *Chinese of America*, 214.

59. Lai, "China and the Chinese American Community," 10.

60. Yung, *Chinese Women of America*, 83.

61. The information in this and the next paragraph is from Wing Chung Ng, "Scholarship on Post–World War II Chinese Societies in North America: A The-

matic Discussion," in *Chinese America: History and Perspectives 1992* (San Francisco: Chinese Historical Society of America, 1992), 198–199.

62. Zhao, *Remaking Chinese America*, 103.

63. The information in this and the next two paragraphs is from Him Mark Lai, "Chinese Organizations in America Based on Locality or Origin and/or Dialect-Group Affiliation, 1940s–1990s," in *Chinese America: History and Perspectives 1996* (San Francisco: Chinese Historical Society of America, 1996), 25–26, 54–56.

64. Hing, *Making and Remaking Asian America*, 39–41.

65. Chen, "Chinese Immigration," 132–134.

66. Hing, *Making and Remaking Asian America*, 40.

67. Daniels, "United States Policy," 81–82.

68. Hing, *Making and Remaking Asian America*, 40–41.

69. Daniels, "United States Policy," 74, 84; Rumbaut, "Origins and Destinies," 21.

70. The information in this and the next paragraph is from Daniels, "United States Policy," 82–84.

71. Chen, "Chinese Immigration," 195–196.

72. Daniels, *Asian America*, 312–313.

CHAPTER 5

1. Hing, *Making and Remaking Asian America*, 81.

2. Larry Hajime Shinagawa, "The Impact of Immigration on the Demography of Asian Pacific Americans," in *The State of Asian Pacific America: Reframing the Immigration Debate*, ed. Bill Ong Hing and Ronald Lee (Los Angeles: LEAP Asian Pacific American Public Policy Institute and UCLA Asian American Studies Center, 1996), 66.

3. Zhou, *Chinatown*, 67; Elliott Robert Barkan, *Asian and Pacific Islander Migration to the United States: A Model of New Global Patterns* (Westport, Conn.: Greenwood, 1992), 40.

4. Zhou, *Chinatown*, 56–64.

5. Ibid., 65.

6. Ibid., 67–68.

7. Hing, *Making and Remaking Asian America*, 82; ibid., 56–57.

8. Paul Ong and John M. Liu, "U.S. Immigration Policies and Asian Migration," in *The New Asian Immigration in Los Angeles and Global Restructuring*, ed. Paul Ong, Edna Bonacich, and Lucie Cheng (Philadelphia: Temple University Press, 1994), 64.

9. Paul Ong, Edna Bonacich, and Lucie Cheng, "The Political Economy of Capitalist Restructuring and the New Asian Immigration," in *The New Asian Immigration in Los Angeles and Global Restructuring*, ed. Paul Ong, Edna Bonacich, and Lucie Cheng (Philadelphia: Temple University Press, 1994), 3–35.

10. Ong and Liu, "U.S. Immigration Policies," 65; Yen-Fen Tseng, "Suburban Ethnic Economy: Chinese Business Communities in Los Angeles" (Ph.D. diss., University of California, Los Angeles, 1994), 64.

11. Hing, *Making and Remaking Asian America*, 115–116.

12. Ueda, *Postwar Immigrant America*, 50–51.

13. Shinagawa, "Impact of Immigration," 69; Hing, *Making and Remaking Asian America*, 115.

14. Don Mar and Marlene Kim, "Historical Trends," in *The State of Asian Pacific America: Economic Diversity, Issues, and Policies*, ed. Paul Ong (Los Angeles: LEAP Asian Pacific American Public Policy Institute and UCLA Asian American Studies Center, 1994), 13–30.

15. Ibid.

16. See Jessica S. Barnes and Claudette E. Bennett, *The Asian Population: 2000, Census 2000 Brief* (Washington, D.C.: Government Printing Office, 2002); see also <http://factfinder.census.gov> for more information on the 2000 census.

17. Paul Ong and Suzanne J. Hee, "The Growth of Asian Pacific America Population: Twenty Million in 2020," in *The State of Asian Pacific America: Policy Issues to the Year 2020* (Los Angeles: LEAP Asian Pacific American Public Policy Institute and UCLA Asian American Studies Center, 1993), 13.

18. Shinagawa, "Impact of Immigration," 69, 90; Morrison G. Wong, "Chinese Americans," in *Asian Americans: Contemporary Trends and Issues*, ed. Pyong Gap Min (Thousand Oaks, Calif.: Sage, 1995), 67; Organization of Chinese Americans, "Chinese American Population Increase Reported" (May 29, 2001) <http://asianam.org/statisti.htm>.

19. The information in this and the next two paragraphs is from Timothy P. Fong, *The First Suburban Chinatown: The Remaking of Monterey Park, California* (Philadelphia: Temple University Press, 1994), 26, 29–31.

20. Loo, *Chinatown*, 69–70; Lin, *Reconstructing Chinatown*, 108–111; ibid.

21. Tseng, "Suburban Ethnic Economy," 39–40; Kwong, *New Chinatown*, 40.

22. Xinyang Wang, *Surviving the City: The Chinese Immigrant Experience in New York City, 1890–1970* (Lanham, Md.: Rowman and Littlefield, 2001), 70–80.

23. Wing-Cheung Ng, "An Evaluation of the Labor Market Status of Chinese Americans," *Amerasia Journal* 4, no. 2 (1977): 107–110; Wong, "Chinese Americans," 77.

24. The third and sixth preferences became part of a larger employment-based immigration scheme in 1990.

25. Bill Ong Hing, "Immigration Policy: Making and Remaking Asian Pacific America," in *New American Destinies: A Reader in Contemporary Asian and Latino Immigration*, ed. Darrell Y. Hamamoto and Rodolfo D. Torres (New York: Routledge, 1997), 317–318; Paul Ong and Evelyn Blumenberg, "Scientists and Engineers," in *New American Destinies*, ed. Hamamoto and Torres, 167–170; see also Wilawan Kanjanapan, "The Immigration of Asian Professionals to the United States, 1988–1990," *International Migration Review* 29 (Spring 1995): 7–32.

26. Hing, "Immigration Policy," 318.

27. Ong and Blumenberg, "Scientists and Engineers," 170.

28. Ong, Bonacich, and Cheng, "Political Economy," 26.

29. Fong, *First Suburban Chinatown*, 28–29.

30. The information in this and the next two paragraphs is from Hsiang-Shui Chen, *Chinatown No More: Taiwan Immigrants in Contemporary New York* (Ithaca: Cornell University Press, 1992), 66–68; Zhou, *Chinatown*, 72–73.

31. Zhou, *Chinatown*, 72.

32. Takaki, *Strangers From a Different Shore*, 429–430, quote on 430; see also Paul Takagi and Tony Platt, "Behind the Gilded Ghetto: An Analysis of Race, Class, and Crime in Chinatown," *Crime and Social Justice* 9 (Spring–Summer 1978): 6.

33. Don Mar, "Regional Differences in Asian American Earnings Discrimination: Japanese, Chinese, and Filipino American Earnings in California and Hawaii," *Amerasia Journal* 25, no. 2 (1999): 77, 89–90.

34. Tom Abate, "Heavy Load for Silicon Valley Workers," *San Francisco Examiner* (May 23, 1993).

35. Elisa Lee, "Silicon Valley Study Finds Asian Americans Hitting the Glass Ceiling," *Asian Week* (October 8, 1993).

36. Frank H. Wu, *Yellow: Race in America Beyond Black and White* (New York: Basic, 2002), 50.

37. Amado Cabezas et al., "Empirical Study of Barriers to Upward Mobility for Asian Americans in the San Francisco Bay Area," in *Frontiers of Asian American Studies*, ed. Gail Nomura et al. (Pullman: Washington State University Press, 1989), 87.

38. The information in this and the next two paragraphs is from U.S. Commission on Civil Rights, *Civil Rights Issues Facing Asian Americans in the 1990s* (Washington, D.C.: U.S. Government Printing Office, 1992), 135–144.

39. Paul Ong and Suzanne J. Hee, "Economic Diversity," in *The State of Asian Pacific America: Economic Diversity, Issues, and Policies*, ed. Paul Ong (Los Angeles: LEAP Asian Pacific American Public Policy Institute and UCLA Asian American Studies Center, 1994), 40–41.

40. Chow, "Family, Economy, and the State," 120.

41. Cabezas, "Barriers to Upward Mobility," 88.

42. Espiritu, *Asian American Women and Men*, 69.

43. Ong and Blumenberg, "Scientists and Engineers," 175; Timothy P. Fong, *The Contemporary Asian American Experience: Beyond the Model Minority* (Upper Saddle River, N.J.: Prentice-Hall, 1998), 111–112.

44. Bernard P. Wong, *Ethnicity and Entrepreneurship: The New Chinese Immigrants in the San Francisco Bay Area* (Boston: Allyn and Bacon, 1998), 41.

45. Ong, Bonacich, and Cheng, "Political Economy," 23–24, 27.

46. See U.S. Bureau of the Census, *1982 Survey of Minority-Owned Business Enterprises: Asian Americans, American Indians, and Other Minorities* (Washington, D.C.: Department of Commerce, 1986), 2; U.S. Bureau of the Census, *Survey of Minority-Owned Business Enterprises: Asians and Pacific Islanders, American Indians, and Alaska Natives* (Washington, D.C.: Department of Commerce, 1996), 3.

47. Kwong, *New Chinatown*, 41.

48. Wong, *Ethnicity and Entrepreneurship*, 55–58; Tseng, "Suburban Ethnic Economy," 85–86.

49. Kwong, *New Chinatown*, 26.

50. Chen, *Chinatown No More*, 65.

51. For a discussion of the enclave economy, see Don Mar, "Another Look at the Enclave Economy Thesis: Chinese Immigrants in the Ethnic Labor Market," *Amerasia Journal* 17, no. 3 (1991): 5–21.

52. Wong, *Patronage, Brokerage, Entrepreneurship, and Chinese Community of New York* (New York: AMS Press, 1988), 208–209; Ong and Hee, "Economic Diversity," 47.

53. Mar, "Another Look."

54. Keiko Yamanaka and Kent McClelland, "Earning the Model-Minority Image: Diverse Strategies of Economic Adapatation by Asian-American Women," *Ethnic and Racial Studies* 17 (January 1994): 87, 110.

55. Tseng, "Suburban Ethnic Economy," 4, 152–159.

56. Kwong, *New Chinatown*, 46–48; ibid., 61–67.

57. The information in this and the next paragraph is from Jan Lin, *Reconstructing Chinatown: Ethnic Enclave, Global Change* (Minneapolis: University of Minnesota Press, 1998), 83–87.

58. The information in this and the next paragraph is from Tseng, "Suburban Ethnic Economy," 60–67.

59. Ibid., 63–64.

60. Ibid., 60.

61. Lin, *Reconstructing Chinatown*, 100–101.

62. Wu, *Yellow*, 52.

63. Lin, *Reconstructing Chinatown*, 104.

64. Ibid., 159–161.

65. John Horton, *The Politics of Diversity: Immigration, Resistance, and Change in Monterey Park, California* (Philadelphia: Temple University Press, 1995), 20–21.

66. The information in this and the next paragraph is from Fong, *First Suburban Chinatown*, 55–117; ibid., 33, 93–99.

67. The information in this and the next paragraph is from Ong and Liu, "U.S. Immigration Policies," quote on 67; Wong, *Ethnicity and Entrepreneurship*, 74, 86–89.

68. The information in this and the next paragraph is from Miriam Ching Louie, "Immigrant Asian Women in Bay Area Garment Shops: 'After Sewing, Laundry, Cleaning and Cooking, I Have No Breath Left to Sing,'" *Amerasia Journal* 18, no. 1 (1992): 2; International Ladies' Garment Workers' Union and the New York Skirt and Sportswear Association, *The Chinatown Garment Industry Study* (New York: Abeles, Schwartz, Haeckel, and Silverblatt, 1983), 41, 59.

69. Diane Yen-Mei Wong with Dennis Hayashi, "Behind Unmarked Doors: Developments in the Garment Industry," in *Making Waves: An Anthology of Writings by and About Asian American Women*, ed. Asian Women United of California (Boston: Beacon, 1989), 161–162.

70. Evelyn Nakano Glenn, "Racial Ethnic Women's Labor: The Intersection of Race, Gender, and Class Oppression," in *Race and Ethnic Conflict: Contending Views on Prejudice, Discrimination, and Ethnoviolence*, ed. Fred L. Pincus and Howard J. Ehrlich (Boulder: Westview, 1994), 157; Yen Le Espiritu, "Race, Class, and Gender in Asian America," in *Making More Waves: New Writing by Asian American Women*, ed. Elaine H. Kim, Lilia V. Villanueva, and Asian Women United of California (Boston: Beacon, 1997), 140.

71. Chalsa Loo and Paul Ong, "Slaying Demons With a Sewing Needle: Feminist Issues for Chinatown's Women," *Berkeley Journal of Sociology* 27 (1982): 82–83.

72. Richard Kim, "A Preliminary Investigation: Asian Immigrant Women Garment Workers in Los Angeles," *Amerasia Journal* 18, no. 1 (1992): 72; Louie, "Immigrant Asian Women," 2–9.

73. Xiaolan Bao, "Holding Up More Than Half the Sky: A History of Women Garment Workers in New York's Chinatown, 1948–1991" (Ph.D. diss., New York University, 1991), 78–80.

74. Nee and Nee, *Longtime Californ'*, 285.

75. Paul Ong, "Chinatown Unemployment and the Ethnic Labor Market," *Amerasia Journal* 11, no. 1 (1984): 45.

76. Kwong, *New Chinatown*, statistics on 58; Peter Kwong, *Forbidden Workers: Illegal Chinese Immigrants and American Labor* (New York: New Press, 1997), 185, 193–198.

77. Kwong, *Forbidden Workers*, 193.

78. The information in this and the next paragraph is from Peter Kwong, "Chinese Staff and Workers' Association: A Model for Organizing in the Changing Economy?" in *New American Destinies: A Reader in Contemporary Asian and Latino Immigration*, ed. Darrell Y. Hamamoto and Rodolfo D. Torres (New York: Routledge, 1997), 183–186.

79. Bao, "Holding Up More Than Half the Sky," 148–152.

80. Kwong, "Chinese Staff," 183.

81. Lin, *Reconstructing Chinatown*, 57; Edna Bonacich, "Asians in the Los Angeles Garment Industry," in *The New Asian Immigration in Los Angeles and Global Restructuring*, ed. Paul Ong, Edna Bonacich, and Lucie Cheng (Philadelphia: Temple University Press, 1994), 151–152; Kwong, "Chinese Staff," 183, 187–188.

82. The information in this and the next paragraph is from Wang, *Surviving the City*, 100–101; Bao, "Holding Up More Than Half the Sky," 178–226.

83. Kwong, *Forbidden Workers*, 200; Lydia Lowe, "Chinese Immigrant Workers and Community-Based Labor Organizing in Boston: Paving the Way," *Amerasia Journal* 18, no. 1 (1992): 39–48.

84. Louie, "Immigrant Asian Women," 12–19.

85. Fong, *Contemporary Asian American Experience*, 135.

86. Lowe, "Chinese Immigrant Workers," 43.

87. Lin, *Reconstructing Chinatown*, 118–119.

88. Alex Hing, "Organizing Asian Pacific American Workers in the AFL-CIO: New Opportunities," *Amerasia Journal* 18, no. 1 (1992): 141–154; Kent Wong, "Building an Asian Pacific Labor Alliance: A New Chapter in Our History," in *The State of Asian America: Activism and Resistance in the 1990s*, ed. Karin Aguilar–San Juan (Boston: South End, 1994), 335–349.

89. The information in this and the next three paragraphs is from Ko-lin Chin, *Smuggled Chinese: Clandestine Immigration to the United States* (Philadelphia: Temple University Press, 1999), 11, 16–19, 49–50, 62–64, 79, 116–121.

90. Tseng, "Suburban Ethnic Economy," 33; Horton, *Politics of Diversity*, 18.

91. Elliott Robert Barkan, *And Still They Come: Immigrants and American Society, 1920s to the 1990s* (Wheeling, Ill.: Harlan Davidson, 1996), 118; Kwong, *Forbidden Workers*, 170–173.

92. Chin, *Smuggled Chinese*, 117–121.

CHAPTER 6

1. Melford S. Weiss, *Valley City: A Chinese Community in America* (Cambridge, Mass.: Schenkman, 1974), 234–235.

2. D. Y. Yuan, "Chinatown and Beyond: The Chinese Population in Metropolitan New York," *Phylon* 27, no. 4 (1966): 331.

3. Unless otherwise noted, the discussion of the Asian American movement is from William Wei, *The Asian American Movement* (Philadelphia: Temple University Press, 1993), 1–42.

4. Esther Ngan-ling Chow, "The Feminist Movement: Where Are All the Asian American Women?" in *Making Waves: An Anthology of Writings by and About Asian American Women*, ed. Asian Women United of California (Boston: Beacon, 1989), 363–364.

5. *Report of the San Francisco Chinese Community Citizens' Survey and Fact Finding Committee* (San Francisco: H. J. Carle and Sons, 1969), 55, 60–61, 91, 93, 154–155. See also Connie Young Yu, "A History of San Francisco Chinatown Housing," *Amerasia Journal* 8, no. 1 (1981): 93–109.

6. Rocky Chin, "New York Chinatown Today: Community in Crisis," *Amerasia Journal* 6, no. 1 (March 1971): 1–23.

7. Tsai, *Chinese Experience in America*, 167.

8. Lyman, *Chinese Americans*, 165–167.

9. Mike Murase, "Ethnic Studies and Higher Education for Asian Americans," in *Counterpoint: Perspectives on Asian America*, ed. Emma Gee (Los Angeles: UCLA Asian American Studies Center, 1976), 205–209; for campus strikes, see Karen Umemoto, " 'On Strike!' San Francisco State College Strike, 1968–69: The Roots of Asian American Students," *Amerasia Journal* 15, no. 1 (1989): 3–41.

10. Stanford M. Lyman, "Red Guards on Grant Avenue," in *The Asian in North America*, ed. Stanford M. Lyman (Santa Barbara: ABC-Clio, 1977), 177–199.

11. Amy Tachiki et al., eds., *Roots: Asian American Reader* (Los Angeles: UCLA Asian American Studies Center, 1971), 273–274.

12. Wei, *Asian American Movement*, 23–24.

13. The information in this and the next paragraph is from Chin, "New York Chinatown Today," 7–13; Lyman, *Chinese Americans*, 167.

14. Kwong, *New Chinatown*, 163; Tsai, *Chinese Experience in America*, 167–168.

15. Chia-ling Kuo, *Social and Political Change in New York's Chinatown: The Role of Voluntary Associations* (New York: Praeger, 1977), 107.

16. The information in this and the next two paragraphs is from Philip A. Lum, "The Creation and Demise of San Francisco Chinatown Freedom Schools: One Response to Desegregation," *Amerasia Journal* 5, no. 1 (1978): 57–73.

17. Lin, *Reconstructing Chinatown*, 130.

18. Eric Mar, "Celebrate the Chinese Progressive Association's 25th Anniversary" [electronic bulletin board] (cited February 12, 1998); available from owner—aaascommunity@listlink.berkeley.edu.

19. Tan, *Chinese in the United States*, 211–219; Kuo, *Social and Political Change*, 45.

20. Kuo, *Social and Political Change*, 183, 201.

21. The information in this and the next two paragraphs is from Wong, *Patronage, Brokerage, Entrepreneurship*, 161–162, 164, 178–182.

22. Yen Le Espiritu, *Asian American Panethnicity: Bridging Institutions and Identities* (Philadelphia: Temple University Press, 1992), 92–93.

23. "First Chinese American Woman Mayor: Lily Lee Chen," in *Bridging the Centuries: History of Chinese Americans in Southern California* (Los Angeles: Chinese Historical Society of Southern California, 2001), 147, quote on 148.

24. Quoted in Wei, *Asian American Movement*, 174.

25. Loo, *Chinatown*, 51; Kwong, *New Chinatown*, 129–130, 132–133; Susie Ling and Nancy Yee, comps., "Grassroots," in *Bridging the Centuries: History of Chinese Americans in Southern California* (Los Angeles, Chinese Historical Society of Southern California, 2001), 207.

26. The information in this and the next four paragraphs is from Kuo, *Social and Political Change*, 54–56; Kwong, *New Chinatown*, 107–108, 132–133; Loo, *Chinatown*, 75–76; Lin, *Reconstructing Chinatown*, 129.

27. Kathy Fong, "A Chinaman's Chance Revisited," *Bridge* 2 (August 1973): 19–22; Eric Mar, "San Francisco Bay Area Justice for . . ." [electronic bulletin board] (cited April 17, 1998); available from owner—aaascommunity@listlink.berkeley.edu.

28. Ling and Yee, "Grassroots," 202.

29. Tomio Geron, "APA Activism, New York Style," *Asian Week* (April 15, 1996); Richard M. Lee, "SF Anti-Asian American Violence" [electronic bulletin board] (cited April 20, 1998); available from owner—aaascommunity@listlink.berkeley.edu; Eric Mar, "SF Bay Area—Kao Week" [electronic bulletin board] (cited April 17, 1998); available from owner—aaascommunity@listlink.berkeley.edu.

30. U.S. Commission on Civil Rights, *Recent Activities Against Citizens and Residents of Asian Descent* (Washington, D.C.: Clearinghouse Publication no. 88, 1986), 56.

31. For information on anti-Asian violence in the 1970s and early 1980s and the Vincent Chin case, see Espiritu, *Asian American Panethnicity*, 137–143.

32. Ronald Takaki, "Who Really Killed Vincent Chin?" *San Francisco Examiner* (September 21, 1983).

33. Espiritu, *Asian American Panethnicity*, 143.

34. Ibid., 157–159, quote on 157–158.

35. William Wong, *Yellow Journalist: Dispatches From Asian America* (Philadelphia: Temple University Press, 2001), 117–120.

36. Lin, *Reconstructing Chinatown*, 135–137; Alexander Suh, "Yong Xin Huang Memorial" [electronic bulletin board] (cited March 2, 1998); available from owner—aaascommunity@listlink.berkeley.edu; Geron, "APA Activism."

37. Scott Kurashige, "Beyond Randoms Acts of Hatred: Analyzing Urban Patterns of Anti-Asian Violence," *Amerasia Journal* 26, no. 1 (2000): 225.

38. "Violent Hate Crimes Against Asian and Pacific Islanders Increase in 1999" (January 2, 2001) <http://www.asianam.org/hate.htm>; "Race, Ethnicity Crimes Slightly up in California, Says Report," Associated Press (August 12, 2001) <http://www.asianam.org/statisti.htm>.

39. Ling and Yee, "Grassroots," 206.

40. Espiritu, *Asian American Panethnicity*, 126; OCA (Organization of Chinese Americans), "Welfare Reform Recap" [electronic bulletin board] (cited October 15, 1997); available from owner—aaascommunity@listlink.berkeley.edu; OCA, "APA LPRs and Food Stamps Fixes" [electronic bulletin board] (cited April 14, 1998); available from owner—aaascommunity@listlink.berkeley.edu.

41. Wong, *Yellow Journalist*, 129.

42. OCA, "Restrictions to APAs Rights" [electronic bulletin board] (cited June 3, 1998); available from owner—aaascommunity@listlink.berkeley.edu; OCA, "Action Alert on Anti-Asian . . ." [electronic bulletin board] (cited June 2, 1998); available from owner—aaascommunity@listlink.berkeley.edu.

43. OCA, "OCA Convention" [electronic bulletin board] (cited June 9, 1998); available from owner—aaascommunity@listlink.berkeley.edu.

44. L. Ling-chi Wang, "Race, Class, Citizenship, and Extraterritoriality: Asian Americans and the 1996 Campaign Finance Scandal," *Amerasia Journal* 24, no. 1 (1998): 1–21; Bert Eljera, "DNC Investigates APA Contributors," *Asian Week* (January 29, 1997); quotes in "Asian Americans Charge Fund-Raising Scandal Biases Civil Rights," *Los Angeles Times* (September 12, 1997).

45. The information in this and the next paragraph is from Raul N. Ebio, "Asian Americans Charge Fund-Raising Scandals Bias Civil Rights" [electronic bulletin board] (cited September 12, 1997); available from owner—aaascommunity@listlink.berkeley.edu; Wang, "Race, Class, Citizenship, and Extraterritoriality," 6.

46. The information in this and the next paragraph is from Wang, "Race, Class, Citizenship, and Extraterritoriality," 5, 11.

47. OCA, "Bill Lee: Sign On" [electronic bulletin board] (cited November 14, 1997); available from owner—aaascommunity@listlink.berkeley.edu; OCA, "Press Release" [electronic bulletin board] (cited March 31, 1998); available from owner—aaascommunity@listlink.berkeley.edu.

48. Wong, *Yellow Journalist*, 61.

49. Fong, *Contemporary Asian American Experience*, 73.

50. Cited in Wu, *Yellow*, 44–46.

51. See Richard J. Herrnstein and Charles Murray, *The Bell Curve: Intelligence and Class Structure in American Life* (New York: Free Press, 1994).

52. An example is Sung, *Mountain of Gold*, 124–125.

53. Stanley Sue and Sumie Okazaki, "Asian-American Educational Achievements: A Phenomenon in Search of an Explanation," *American Psychologist* 46, no. 8 (1990): 913–920; statistics in Wu, *Yellow*, 52.

54. Morrison G. Wong, "Chinese Americans," in *Asian Americans: Contemporary Trends and Issues*, ed. Pyong Gap Min (Thousand Oaks, Calif.: Sage Publications, 1995), 80–81; OCA, "Bilingual Educational Program Under . . ." [electronic bulletin board] (cited June 9, 1998); available from owner—aaascommunity@listlink.berkeley.edu; Eric Mar, "Northern California Regional Meeting to . . ." [electronic bulletin board] (cited February 28, 1998); available from owner—aaascommunity@listlink.berkeley.edu.

55. L. Ling-chi Wang, "Lau v. Nichols: History of a Struggle for Equal and Quality Education," *Amerasia Journal* 2, no. 2 (1974): 16–45.

56. Wu, *Yellow*, 48; Fong, *Contemporary Asian American Experience*, 95.

57. The information in this and the next two paragraphs is from Linda Mathews, "When Being Best Isn't Good Enough: Why Yat-pang Au Won't Be Going to Berkeley," *Los Angeles Times Magazine* (July 19, 1987): 22–28, quote on 22.

58. The information in this and the next paragraph is from Jeffrey K.D. Au, "Asian American College Admissions—Legal, Empirical, and Philosophical Ques-

tions for the 1980s and Beyond," in *Reflections on Shattered Windows: Promises and Prospects for Asian American Studies*, ed. Gary Y. Okihiro et al. (Pullman: Washington State University Press, 1988), 51–56; Mitchell J. Chang, "The Educational Implications of Affirmative Action and Crossing the Color Line," *Amerasia Journal* 26, no. 3 (2000–2001): 79–80.

59. The information in this and the next paragraph is from Wong, *Yellow Journalist*, 145–147; Claire Jean Kim, "Playing the Racial Trump Card: Asian Americans in Contemporary U.S. Politics," *Amerasia Journal* 26, no. 3 (2000–2001): 50–53.

60. Lee, *Chinese in the United States*, 178.

61. Ibid., 140; Fong, *Contemporary Asian American Experience*, 249.

62. Lee, *Chinese in the United States*, 178; Fong, *Contemporary Asian American Experience*, 249.

63. Fong, *Contemporary Asian American Experience*, 250; Lin, *Reconstructing Chinatown*, 138.

64. Hing, *Making and Remaking Asian America*, 157.

65. Espiritu, *Asian American Panethnicity*, 75–77.

66. Hing, *Making and Remaking Asian America*, 157.

67. Espiritu, *Asian American Panethnicity*, 57–58. On barriers to political participation, see Paul Ong and Don Nakanishi, "Becoming Citizens, Becoming Voters: The Naturalization and Political Participation of Asian Pacific Immigrants," in *The State of Asian Pacific America: Reframing the Immigration Debate*, ed. Bill Ong Hing and Ronald Lee (Los Angeles: LEAP Asian Pacific American Policy Institute and UCLA Asian American Studies Center, 1996), 287, 289; Lin, *Reconstructing Chinatown*, 138.

68. Hing, *Making and Remaking Asian America*, 157; Grant L. Din, "A Comparison of Chinese American Voter Registration in 1983 and 1992 (With Comparative Information for Other Asian Groups)," in *The Repeal and Its Legacy: Proceedings of the Conference on the 50th Anniversary of the Repeal of the Exclusion Acts* (San Francisco: Chinese Historical Society of America and Asian American Studies, San Francisco State University, 1994), 98, 100.

69. Ong and Nakanishi, "Becoming Citizens," 285–286.

70. Stewart Kwoh and Mindy Hui, "Empowering Our Communities: Political Policy," in *The State of Asian Pacific America: Policy Issues to the Year 2020* (Los Angeles: LEAP Asian Pacific American Public Policy Institute and UCLA Asian American Studies Center, 1993), 194–195; Vitus C.W. Leung and Henry Der, "Voting Rights and Political Behavior of New Californians: A Cross-Sectional Analysis of Limited-English Proficient Chinese American Voters in San Francisco," in *The Repeal and Its Legacy: Proceedings of the Conference on the 50th Anniversary of the Repeal of the Exclusion Acts* (San Francisco: Chinese Historical Society of America and Asian American Studies, San Francisco State University, 1994), 103–104.

71. Hing, *Making and Remaking Asian America*, 159–160.

72. Din, "Comparison of Chinese American Voter Registration," 102; Lin, *Reconstructing Chinatown*, 140.

73. Hing, *Making and Remaking Asian America*, 160.

74. Ibid., 161; "GOP Finds Party a Tough Sell to Minorities," *Washington Times* (May 9, 2002) <http://www.asianam.org/APA_vote_in_presidential_election.htm>.

75. Leung and Der, "Voting Rights," 112.

76. Wong, *Yellow Journalist,* 194–198.

77. On Gary Locke, see Wong, *Yellow Journalist,* 189–194.

78. On the Chinese financial contribution to political campaigns, see Espiritu, *Asian American Panethnicity,* 61–64.

79. The information in this and the next paragraph is from Chew, *Reflections,* 148; *Bridging the Centuries,* 145–148; Espiritu, *Asian American Panethnicity,* 63–64; Wong, *Yellow Journalist,* 183–189; Wong, *Ethnicity and Entrepreneurship,* 104.

80. Lin, *Reconstructing Chinatown,* 141–144.

81. Espiritu, *Asian American Panethnicity,* 62.

82. Lin, *Reconstructing Chinatown,* 138–139.

83. Espiritu, *Asian American Panethnicity,* 75, 78.

84. On intraethnic conflict in Monterey Park, see Horton, *Politics of Diversity;* Fong, *First Suburban Chinatown.*

85. Fong, *First Suburban Chinatown,* 46, 73, 90, 109.

86. Horton, *Politics of Diversity,* 36.

87. Ibid., 50.

88. The information in this and the next paragraph is from ibid., 35–36, 75–76; Fong, *First Suburban Chinatown,* 110–119, 124.

89. The information in this and the next paragraph is from Andrew Leong, "The Struggle Over Parcel C: How Boston's Chinatown Won a Victory in the Fight Against Institutional Expansion and Environmental Racism," *Amerasia Journal* 21, no. 3 (Winter 1995–1996): 99–103.

90. The information in this and the next paragraph is from Leland T. Saito, "Asian Americans and Latinos in San Gabriel Valley, California: Ethnic Political Cooperation and Redistricting 1990–1992," *Amerasia Journal* 19, no. 2 (1993): 55–68.

91. Wang, "Roots," 207.

92. The information in this and the next paragraph is from Tsai, *Chinese Experience in America,* 172–173.

93. The information in this and the next two paragraphs is from Lai, "China and the Chinese American Community," 17–20.

94. Fenggang Yang, *Chinese Christians in America: Conversion, Assimilation, and Adhesive Identities* (University Park: Pennsylvania State University Press, 1999), 41.

95. The information in this and the next paragraph is from Wong, *Yellow Journalist,* 204–205; "Ex-UCD Scientist Acquitted of Theft," *Sacramento Bee* (August 20, 2002) <http://www.asianam.org/hottopics.htm>.

96. Wu, *Yellow,* 10–12.

97. The information in this and the next paragraph is from ibid., 10–12, 19, 21, 117–120, quote on 19.

98. Okihiro, *Margins and Mainstreams,* 33–34, 62, quote on 62.

CHAPTER 7

1. The information in this and the next three paragraphs is from Xiao-huang Yin, *Chinese American Literature Since the 1850s* (Urbana: University of Illinois Press, 2000), 16–32, 55–78, quote on 64.

2. Chun, *Of Orphans and Warriors*, 51–53.

3. Elaine H. Kim, *Asian American Literature: An Introduction to the Writings and Their Social Context* (Philadelphia: Temple University Press, 1982), 24–32.

4. Marlon K. Hom, "Chinatown High Life: A Literary Pride," in *Chinese America: History and Perspectives 1988* (San Francisco: Chinese Historical Society of America, 1988), 127.

5. Lai, Lim, and Yung, *Island*, 58.

6. June Mei and Jean Pang Yip with Russell Leong, "The Bitter Society: *Ku Shehui*. A Translation, Chapters 37–46," *Amerasia Journal* 8, no. 1 (1981): 33–67.

7. The information in this and the next four paragraphs is from Yin, *Chinese American Literature*, 85–110; Amy Ling, *Between Worlds: Women Writers of Chinese Ancestry* (New York: Pergamon, 1990), 49, 118–119, 170, 173.

8. Stuart Creighton Miller, *The Unwelcome Immigrant: The American Image of the Chinese, 1785–1882* (Berkeley: University of California Press, 1969), 201.

9. The information in this and the next three paragraphs is from Kim, *Asian American Literature*, 5, 9; Lee, *Orientals*, 114–116.

10. Wu, *Yellow Peril*, 79.

11. The information in this and the next paragraph is from Lee, *Orientals*, 88.

12. Ibid., 97–104.

13. Kim, *Asian American Literature*, 17.

14. John Haddad, "The Laundry Man's Got a Knife! China and Chinese America in Early United States Cinema," in *Chinese America: History and Perspectives 2001* (San Francisco: Chinese Historical Society of America, 2001), 31.

15. The information in this and the next two paragraphs is from ibid., 31–46.

16. The information in this and the next paragraph is from Gina Marchetti, *Romance and the "Yellow Peril": Race, Sex, and Discursive Strategies in Hollywood Fiction* (Berkeley: University of California Press, 1993), 32–45, 68–71; Eugene Franklin Wong, *On Visual Media Racism: Asians in the American Motion Pictures* (New York: Arno, 1978), 44–45.

17. Espiritu, *Asian American Women and Men*, 93–94.

18. The information in this and the next paragraph is from Renee E. Tajima, "Lotus Blossoms Don't Bleed: Images of Asian Women," in *Making Waves: An Anthology of Writings by and About Asian American Women*, ed. Asian Women United of California (Boston: Beacon, 1989), 308–317; James S. Moy, *Marginal Sights: Staging the Chinese in America* (Iowa City: University of Iowa Press, 1993), 86–91.

19. Marchetti, *Romance and the "Yellow Peril*," 113.

20. See Wenquan, "Chinatown Literature During the Last Ten Years (1939–1949)," trans. Marlon K. Hom, *Amerasia Journal* 9, no. 1 (1982): 75–100; Kim, *Asian American Literature*, 109; Sau-Ling Cynthia Wong, "Tales of Postwar Chinatown: Short Stories of *The Bud*, 1947–1948," *Amerasia Journal* 14, no. 2 (1988): 61–79.

21. Ling, *Between Worlds*, 59, 67, 71–72.

22. Yin, *Chinese American Literature*, 174–176.

23. The information in this and next four paragraphs is from Kim, *Asian American Literature*, 58–72; Ling, *Between Worlds*, 120–121; ibid., 119, 121–149; Chun, *Of Orphans and Warriors*, 42–43, 56–69.

24. Kim, *Asian American Literature*, 104–106.

25. The information in this and the next paragraph is from Lee, *Orientals*, 172–179; Marlon K. Hom, "A Case of Mutual Exclusion: Portrayals by Immigrant and American-Born Chinese of Each Other in Literature," *Amerasia Journal* 11, no. 2 (1984): 31–34.

26. Jinqi Ling, *Narrating Nationalisms: Ideology and Form in Asian American Literature* (New York: Oxford University Press, 1998), 54, 60–61, 74.

27. Sau-ling Cynthia Wong, "Chinese American Literature," in *An Interethnic Companion to Asian American Literature*, ed. King-Kok Cheung (New York: Cambridge University Press, 1997), 48.

28. Jinqi Ling, "Identity Crisis and Gender Politics: Reappropriating Asian American Masculinity," in *An Interethnic Companion to Asian American Literature*, ed. King-Kok Cheung (New York: Cambridge University Press, 1997), 319.

29. Chun, *Of Orphans and Warriors*, 120.

30. Wong, "Chinese American Literature," 49; Shirley Geok-Lin Lim, "Immigration and Diaspora," in *An Interethnic Companion to Asian American Literature*, ed. King-Kok Cheung (New York: Cambridge University Press, 1997), 289–307.

31. The information in this and the next five paragraphs is from Yin, *Chinese American Literature*, 157–177, 184–219.

32. The information in this and the next paragraph is from Suzanne Juhasz, "Maxine Hong Kingston: Narrative Technique and Female Identity," in *Contemporary American Women Writers*, ed. Catherine Rainwater and William J. Scheick (Lexington: University of Kentucky Press, 1985), 174; ibid., 231–232.

33. The information in this and the next paragraph is from Ling, *Between Worlds*, 142, 145; Ling, *Narrating Nationalisms*, 133; Sau-ling Cynthia Wong, "Autobiography as Guided Chinatown Tour? Maxine Hong Kingston's *The Woman Warrior* and the Chinese-American Autobiographical Controversy," in *Multicultural Autobiography: American Lives*, ed. James Robert Payne (Knoxville: University of Tennessee Press, 1992), 248–271.

34. Frank Chin, "This Is Not an Autobiography," *Genre* 18 (Summer 1985): 110, 130; Wong, "Autobiography as Guided Chinatown Tour?" 248–250.

35. Sau-ling Cynthia Wong, *Reading Asian American Literature: From Necessity to Extravagance* (Princeton: Princeton University Press, 1993), 206–207.

36. Leslie Bow, "Cultural Conflict/Feminist Resolution in Amy Tan's *The Joy Luck Club*," in *New Visions in Asian American Studies: Diversity, Community, Power*, ed. Franklin Ng et al. (Pullman: Washington State University Press, 1994), 245–246.

37. Phillipa Kafka, *(Un)doing the Missionary Position: Gender Asymetry in Contemporary Asian American Women's Writing* (Westport, Conn.: Greenwood, 1997), 18, 48.

38. Yin, *Chinese American Literature*, 233.

39. On Hawaiian Chinese poets, see Gayle K. Fujita Sato, "The Island Influence on Chinese American Writers: Wing Tek Lum, Darrell H.Y. Lum, and Eric Chock," *Amerasia Journal* 16, no. 2 (1990): 17–33.

40. George Uba, "Versions of Identity in Post-Activist Asian American Poetry," in *Reading the Literatures of Asian America*, ed. Shirley Geok-lin Lim and Amy Ling (Philadelphia: Temple University Press, 1992), 33–37.

41. Yin, *Chinese American Literature*, 234.

42. Kafka, *(Un)doing the Missionary Position*, 51–53, 79–80, 84.

43. Moy, *Marginal Sights*, 7–47, 115–119, 123, 126.

44. Wong, "Chinese American Literature," 52.

45. Ling and Yee, "Grassroots," 205.

46. Luis H. Francia, "Asian and Asian American Cinema: Separated by a Common Language?" in *Moving the Image: Independent Asian American Media Arts*, ed. Russell Leong (Los Angeles: UCLA Asian American Studies Center and Visual Communications, Southern California Asian American Studies Central, 1991), 103–104; Renee Tajima, "Moving the Image: Asian American Independent Filmmaking 1970–1990," in *Moving the Image: Independent Asian American Media Arts*, ed. Russell Leong (Los Angeles: UCLA Asian American Studies Center and Visual Communications, Southern California Asian American Studies Central, 1991), 17–18.

47. Stephen Gong, "A History in Progress: Asian American Media Arts Centers 1970–1990," in *Moving the Image: Independent Asian American Media Arts*, ed. Russell Leong (Los Angeles: UCLA Asian American Studies Center and Visual Communications, Southern California Asian American Studies Central, 1991), 2, 7, 8.

48. Tajima, "Moving the Image," 23.

49. Loni Ding, "Strategies of an Asian American Filmmaker," in *Moving the Image: Independent Asian American Media Arts*, ed. Russell Leong (Los Angeles: UCLA Asian American Studies Center and Visual Communications, Southern California Asian American Studies Central, 1991), 54, 59.

50. Francia, "Asian and Asian American Cinema," 104.

51. Eileen Chia-Ching Fung, "The Politics and Poetics of a Taiwanese Chinese American Identity," in *Contemporary Asian American Communities: Intersections and Divergences*, ed. Linda Trinh Võ and Rick Bonus (Philadelphia: Temple University Press, 2002), 45–59.

52. Fong, *Contemporary Asian American Experience*, 179–180.

53. Lee, *Oriental*, 190, 202.

54. See Elaine Kim, "Asian Americans and American Popular Culture," in *Dictionary of Asian American History*, ed. Kim Hyung-Chan (Chicago: Univeristy of Chicago Press, 1986), 106–107.

55. The information in this and the next two paragraphs is from Darrell Y. Hamamoto, *Monitored Peril: Asian Americans and the Politics of TV Representation* (Minneapolis: University of Minnesota Press, 1994), 7–9, 18, 33–37, 181–193; Cy Wong, "Beulah Ong," in *Bridging the Centuries: History of Chinese Americans in Southern California* (Los Angeles: Chinese Historical Society of Southern California, 2001), 117–118.

56. Jeff Yip, "A Heroic Leading Role for One Asian 'Son,'" *Los Angeles Times* (March 25, 1995).

57. Elaine H. Kim, "'Bad Women': Asian American Visual Artists Hanh Thi Pham, Hung Liu, and Yong Soon Min," in *Making More Waves: New Writing by Asian American Women*, ed. Elaine H. Kim, Lilia V. Villanueva, and Asian Women United of California (Boston: Beacon, 1997), 188–190.

58. Franklin Ng, "Maya Lin and the Vietnam Vetarans Memorial," in *Chinese America: History and Perspectives 1994* (San Francisco: Chinese Historical Society of America, 1994), 212.

59. James Watrous, *A Century of American Printmaking, 1880–1980* (Madison: University of Wisconsin Press, 1984), 181.

60. See Wei-hua Zhang, "Fred Ho and Jon Jang: Profiles of Two Chinese American Jazz Musicians," in *Chinese America: History and Perspectives 1994* (San Francisco: Chinese Historical Society of America, 1994), 175–199.

CHAPTER 8

1. Robert Staples and Alfredo Mirande, "Racial and Cultural Variations Among American Families: Racial and Cultural Variations Among Minority Families," *Journal of Marriage and the Family* 42, no. 4 (1980): 896.

2. An early example of this argument is Norman S. Haynor and Charles N. Reynolds, "Chinese American Family Life in America," *American Sociological Review* 2 (1937): 630–637; a more recent example is Tsai, *Chinese Experience in America*, 162.

3. Morrison G. Wong, "The Chinese-American Family," in *Ethnic Families in America: Patterns and Variations*, 4th ed., ed. Charles H. Mindel, Robert W. Habenstein, and Roosevelt Wright Jr. (Upper Saddle River, N.J.: Prentice-Hall, 1998), 300. For early model minority coverage, see "Success Story of One Minority Group in the U.S.," *U.S. News and World Report* (December 26, 1966): 73–78; "Asian-Americans: A Model Minority," *Newsweek* (December 6, 1982): 39–51.

4. U.S. Bureau of the Census, "Tenure, Household Size, and Age of Householder: 2000" tables, in Census 2000 Summary File 2, available at <http://factfinder.census.gov>.

5. Takaki, *Strangers From a Different Shore*, 475.

6. "Success Story of One Minority Group," 73.

7. Wu, *Yellow*, 70–73.

8. Charles Hirschman and Morrison G. Wong, "Trends in Socioeconomic Achievement Among Immigrant and Native-Born Asian Americans, 1960–1976," *Sociological Quarterly* 22 (Autumn 1981): 511.

9. Evelyn Nakano Glenn and Stacey G.H. Yap, "Chinese American Families," in *Minority Families in the United States: A Multicultural Perspective*, ed. Ronald L. Taylor (Englewood Cliffs, N.J.: Prentice-Hall, 1994), 119, 125.

10. Peter S. Li, "Fictive Kinship, Conjugal Tie and Kinship Chain Among Chinese Immigrants in the United States," *Journal of Comparative Family Studies* 8 (Spring 1977): 61.

11. Wong, "Chinese Americans," 71–72.

12. The information in this and the next paragraph is from Fong, *Contemporary Asian American Experience*, 206–207; Li, "Fictive Kinship," 57–58.

13. Fong, *Contemporary Asian American Experience*, 206.

14. Ibid., 210.

15. The information in this and the next paragraph is from Betty Lee Sung, *The Adjustment Experiences of Chinese Immigrant Children in New York City* (New York: Center for Migration Studies, 1987), 182–187.

16. Wu Xingci and Li Zhen, "*Gum San Haak* in the 1980s: A Study on Chinese Emigrants Who Return to Taishan County for Marriage," *Amerasia Journal* 14, no. 2 (1988): 23–24.

17. Ko-lin Chin, "Out-of-Town Brides: International Marriage and Wife Abuse Among Chinese Immigrants," *Journal of Comparative Family Studies* 25 (Spring 1994): 54.

18. Wu and Zhen, "*Gum San Haak*," 26.

19. Chin, "Out-of-Town Brides," 56.

20. Ibid., 60.

21. Edwin G. Clausen and Jack Bermingham, *Chinese and African Professionals in California: A Case Study of Equality and Opportunity in the United States* (Washington, D.C.: University Press of America, 1982), 81–87.

22. Chen, *Chinatown No More*, 80–81.

23. Loo, *Chinatown*, 199.

24. Glenn and Yap, "Chinese American Families," 128–129; Sung, *Adjustment Experiences*, 198.

25. Wong, "Chinese-American Family," 297.

26. Sung, *Adjustment Experiences*, 197–198; Laura Uba, *Asian Americans: Personality, Patterns, Identity, and Mental Health* (New York: Guilford, 1994), 31, 35, 40.

27. The information in this and the next paragraph is from Min Zhou, "Coming of Age: The Current Situation of Asian American Children," *Amerasia Journal* 25, no. 1 (1999): 1–27.

28. On personality types, see Stanley Sue and Derald W. Sue, "Chinese American Personality and Mental Health," in *Roots: An Asian-American Reader*, ed. Amy Tachiki et al. (Los Angeles: Continental Graphics, 1971), 72–81.

29. Uba, *Asian Americans*, 89–118.

30. The information in this and the next two paragraphs is from Nazli Kibria, *Becoming Asian American: Second-Generation Chinese and Korean American Identities* (Baltimore: Johns Hopkins University Press, 2002), 27–53, 64–65, 102–130.

31. Lucy Jen Huang, "The Chinese American Family," in *Ethnic Families in America: Patterns and Variations*, ed. Charles H. Mindel and Robert W. Habenstein (New York: Elsevier, 1976), 143–144.

32. Stanford M. Lyman, *The Asian in the West* (Reno: Desert Research Institute, 1970), 103; Glenn and Yap, "Chinese American Families," 137.

33. Jean S. Braun and Hilda M. Chao, "Attitudes Toward Women: A Comparison of Asian-Born Chinese and American Caucasians," *Psychology of Women Quarterly* 2 (Spring 1978): 200.

34. Karen Huang and Laura Uba, "Premarital Sexual Behavior Among Chinese College Students in the United States," *Archives of Sexual Behavior* 21, no. 3 (1992): 227–240.

35. "Asian-American Women Struggling to Move Past Cultural Expectations," *New York Times* (January 23, 1994).

36. Helen Zia, "Violence in Our Communities: Where Are the Asian Women?" in *Making More Waves: New Writing by Asian American Women*, ed. Elaine H. Kim, Lilia V. Villaneuva, and Asian Women United of California (Boston: Beacon, 1997), 212.

37. Ibid., 212–213; Chin, "Out-of-Town Brides," 54, 57.

38. Alice Y. Hom, "Stories From the Homefront: Perspectives of Asian American Parents With Lesbian Daughters and Gay Sons," *Amerasia Journal* 20, no. 1 (1994): 21, 23, quote on 23.

39. Eric C. Wat, *The Making of a Gay Asian Community: An Oral History of Pre-AIDS Los Angeles* (Lanham, Md.: Rowman and Littlefield, 2002), 11, 17–18.

40. Ibid., 18, 20; Connie S. Chan, "Issues of Identity Development Among Asian-American Lesbians and Gay Men," *Journal of Counseling and Development* 68 (September–October 1989): 17, 19; Ignatius Bau, "Queer Asian American Immigrants: Opening Borders and Closets," in *Q & A: Queer in Asian America*, ed. David L. Eng and Alice Y. Hom (Philadelphia: Temple University Press, 1998), 57, 60–61.

41. Wat, *Making of a Gay Asian Community*, 22, 55.

42. Ibid., 60–63.

43. Russell Leong, "Home Bodies and the Body Politic," in *Asian American Sexualities: Dimensions of the Gay and Lesbian Experience*, ed. Russell Leong (New York: Routledge, 1996), 5.

44. Dana Takagi, "Maiden Voyage: Excursion Into Sexuality and Identity Politics in Asian America," in *Asian American Sexualities: Dimensions of the Gay and Lesbian Experience*, ed. Russell Leong (New York: Routledge, 1996), 25–26.

45. Wat, *Making of a Gay Asian Community*, 64.

46. Ibid., 79–89, quote on 71.

47. The information in this and the next paragraph is from ibid., 83, 91, 102–103, 166, 173.

48. Jean Phinney, "Stages of Ethnic Identity Development in Minority Group Adolescents," *Journal of Early Adolescence* 9 (1989): 34–49.

49. Loo, *Chinatown*, 171.

50. Marshall Jung, *Chinese American Family Therapy: A New Model for Clinicians* (San Francisco: Jossey-Bass, 1998), 45–47.

51. Ibid., 45, 181–183; Uba, *Asian Americans*, 199, 215.

52. *Report of the San Francisco Chinese Community Citizens' Survey*, 116; Jung, *Chinese American Family Therapy*, 43.

53. Jung, *Chinese American Family Therapy*, 2–3.

54. Yang, *Chinese Christians in America*, 84–86; Irene Lin, "Journey to the Far West: Chinese Buddhism in America," in *New Spiritual Homes: Religion and Asian Americans*, ed. David K. Yoo (Honolulu: University of Hawai'i Press, 1999), 145–146.

55. The information in this and the next paragraph is from Lin, "Journey to the Far West," 134–168.

56. Ibid., 145.

57. The information in this and the next two paragraphs is from James Chuck, "Growth of Chinese Protestant Congregations From 1950 to mid-1996 in Five Bay Area Counties," in *Chinese America: History and Perspectives 2001* (San Francisco: Chinese Historical Society of America, 2001), 63–75; Yang, *Chinese Christians in America*, 6–7, 107–121, 128–131, 188–189.

58. Yang, *Chinese Christians in America*, 7.

59. Ibid., 140–162.

60. Morrison G. Wong, "A Look at Intermarriage Among the Chinese in the United States in 1980," *Sociological Perspectives* 32, no. 1 (1989): 88.

61. Harry L. Kitano et al., "Asian-American Interracial Marriage," *Journal of Marriage and the Family* 46 (February 1984): 179–190.

62. Wong, "A Look at Intermarriage Among the Chinese," 87–107.

63. Sharon M. Lee and Keiko Yamanaka, "Patterns of Asian American Intermarriage and Marital Assimilation," *Journal of Comparative Family Studies* 21 (Summer 1990): 287–305.

64. Wong, "A Look at Intermarriage Among the Chinese," 90.

65. Kitano et al., "Asian-American Interracial Marriage," 186; Lee and Yamanaka, "Patterns of Asian American Intermarriage," 291.

66. Betty Lee Sung, "Intermarriage Among the Chinese in New York City," in *Chinese America: History and Perspectives 1987* (San Francisco: Chinese Historical Society of America, 1987), 111–112.

67. Ibid.

68. Larry Hajime Shinagawa and Gin Yong Pang, "Marriage Patterns of Asian Americans in California, 1980," *Mellen Studies in Sociology* 3 (1990): 261–262.

69. Ibid., 261–262, 270.

70. Fong, *Contemporary Asian American Experience*, 229; see also Wen-Shing Tseng et al., *Adjustment in Intercultural Marriage* (Honolulu: Department of Psychiatry, John A. Burns School of Medicine, University of Hawai'i, 1977), 205–206.

71. Colleen Fong and Judy Yung, "In Search of the Right Spouse: Interracial Marriage Among Chinese and Japanese Americans," *Amerasia Journal* 21 (Winter 1995–1996): 85.

72. Ibid., 78, 84, 90–93.

73. Wong, "A Look at Intermarriage Among the Chinese," 95; Shinagawa and Pang, "Marriage Patterns of Asian Americans," 262; Fong and Yung, "In Search of the Right Spouse," 92–93.

74. Quoted in Paul R. Spickard, "What Must I Be? Asian Americans and the Question of Multiethnic Identity," *Amerasia Journal* 23, no. 1 (1997): 49.

75. Maria P. Root, "Multiracial Asians: Models of Ethnic Identity," *Amerasia Journal* 23, no. 1 (1997): 32.

76. Samuel R. Cacas, "New Census Category for Multiracial Persons," *Asian Week* (July 15, 1994); Spickard, "What Must I Be?" 50–54.

77. Larry Hajime Shinagawa and Gin Yong Pang, "Asian American Pan-Ethnicity and Intermarriage," *Amerasia Journal* 22, no. 2 (1996): 143.

Index